AF735549

International Trade in Indigenous Cultural Heritage

International Trade in Indigenous Cultural Heritage

Legal and Policy Issues

Edited by

Christoph B. Graber, Karolina Kuprecht and Jessica C. Lai

Members of i-call, the research centre for communication and art law, University of Lucerne, Switzerland

Edward Elgar

Cheltenham, UK • Northampton, MA, USA

© The Editors and Contributors Severally 2012

Cover illustration by Regi Widmer • Illustration & Gestaltung • Birsfelden, Switzerland

All rights reserved. No part of this publication may be reproduced, stored in a retrieval system or transmitted in any form or by any means, electronic, mechanical or photocopying, recording, or otherwise without the prior permission of the publisher.

Published by
Edward Elgar Publishing Limited
The Lypiatts
15 Lansdown Road
Cheltenham
Glos GL50 2JA
UK

Edward Elgar Publishing, Inc.
William Pratt House
9 Dewey Court
Northampton
Massachusetts 01060
USA

A catalogue record for this book
is available from the British Library

Library of Congress Control Number: 2012938068

MIX
Paper from responsible sources
FSC® C018575
FSC www.fsc.org

ISBN 978 0 85793 830 5

Typeset by Columns Design XML Ltd, Reading
Printed and bound by MPG Books Group, UK

Contents

Figures

Tables

Contributors

Christoph Antons holds a Chair in Law in the School of Law, Faculty of Business and Law, at Deakin University, Melbourne. He is Chief Investigator in the Australian Research Council Centre of Excellence for Creative Industries and Innovation (CCI) and Affiliated Research Fellow at the Max Planck Institute for Intellectual Property and Competition Law in Munich. He is the author of *Intellectual Property Law in Indonesia* (Kluwer, 2000), editor of *Law and Development in East and Southeast Asia* (RoutledgeCurzon, 2003), *Traditional Knowledge, Traditional Cultural Expressions and Intellectual Property Law in the Asia-Pacific Region* (Kluwer, 2009), *The Enforcement of Intellectual Property Rights: Comparative Perspectives from the Asia-Pacific Region* (Kluwer, 2011) and co-editor (with Michael Blakeney and Christopher Heath) of *Intellectual Property Harmonisation within ASEAN and APEC* (Kluwer, 2004) and (with Volkmar Gessner) of *Globalisation and Resistance: Law Reform in Asia Since the Crisis* (Hart, 2007). Christoph has written widely on comparative intellectual property law in Australia and Asia and on law and development, law and society and legal history in various Asian countries. Current research interests include the CCI projects 'IP in Asia' and 'Asian Creative Transformations' and the relationship between intellectual property and cultural heritage in Asia.

Francesco Bandarin is the Assistant Director-General for Culture at UNESCO. Prior to his appointment in 2010 he served as Director of the World Heritage Centre, a post he has held since 2000. Francesco Bandarin has led the development of a network of public–private partnerships for World Heritage conservation, as well as the development of a series of regional category II centres in different parts of the world. He is a specialist in architecture and urban planning, and has worked in both public and private institutions in the fields of built heritage, cultural heritage conservation, environmental heritage and cultural events, as well as architectural and urban design in developing countries. Francesco Bandarin graduated in Architecture in Venice (Italy) and in City and Regional Planning at the University of California, Berkeley. Since 1980 he has been Professor of Urban Planning at the School of Architecture of Venice. He has also worked as a consultant for bilateral and multilateral organisations on city projects and published a number of books and articles, mainly on urban conservation and the urban environment.

Catherine Bell is a Professor of Law at the University of Alberta specialising in aboriginal legal issues, dispute resolution, property law, cultural heritage law and interdisciplinary community-based legal research. She has been a visiting professor at the University of Niigata (Japan), University of Victoria, Program of Legal Studies for Native People (University of Saskatchewan) and Akitsiraq Law School for Inuit students (Nunavut). For several years she also served as a lead faculty member for the Banff Center for Management Aboriginal Leadership and Self-Government Program. She is the recipient of numerous major research grants, has been nominated for teaching awards and has recently been honoured with the Aboriginal Justice Award and a McCalla Professorship. Catherine Bell has published widely on Métis and First Nation legal and policy issues and has acted as an advisor to First Nation, Canadian government and Métis organisations. She is also the author of two books on the Métis settlements of Alberta and co-editor of, and contributing author to, *Intercultural Dispute Resolution in Aboriginal Contexts* (with Dr D. Kahane); *First Nations' Cultural Heritage and Law: Case Studies, Voices and Perspectives* (with Dr V. Napoleon); and *First Nations' Cultural Heritage and Law: Reconciliation and Reform* (with Robert K. Paterson). Current research programmes include collaborative legal research with Yukon First Nations and a legal history project on Métis constitutional rights (with Dr N. Kermoal), and an international multi-research collaborative initiative funded by the Social Sciences and Humanities Research Council of Canada on 'Intellectual Property in Cultural Heritage' with particular emphasis on indigenous peoples and the products of archaeological research.

Kathy Bowrey, Dr is Professor in the Faculty of Law and formerly an Associate Dean – Research (2008–11) at the University of New South Wales, Sydney, Australia. She was also previously an Associate Dean – Research (2006–07) at the Faculty of Law, University of Technology, Sydney. Her expertise primarily relates to intellectual property, media and information technology regulation, reflecting a broad range of interests pertaining to socio-legal history, media and cultural studies and legal theory, including research on western laws affecting indigenous cultural and intellectual property. With colleague Michael Handler, she is currently a Chief Investigator on an Australian Research Council Discovery Project (2009–11) 'Entertainment Rights in the Age of the Franchise: A Reappraisal of Personality Rights under Australian Intellectual Property Laws'. She also has a strong interest in higher education research policy and has acted as a consultant to the Council of Australian Law Deans concerning research assessment exercises. Her book publications include (co-edited with M. Handler and D. Nicol) *Emerging Challenges in IP* (Oxford University Press, 2011); (co-edited with M. Handler and D. Nicol) *Australian IP: Commentary, Law and Practice* (Oxford University Press, 2010); *Law and Internet Cultures* (Cambridge University Press, 2005).

Duane Champagne has a PhD in sociology from Harvard University (1982), where he was also a teaching fellow. Prior to his studies in sociology, he obtained a degree in mathematics from North Dakota State University (1973), from which he also holds his MA in Sociology. From 1983–84 he was Assistant Professor at the University of Wisconsin-Milwaukee. Since 1997, he has been Professor of Sociology at the University of California, Los Angeles. His main interests lie with theory, sociology of Native Americans and comparative historical analysis. His research also focuses on processes of social change and institutionalisation and variation among Native American societies and their social, economic and political responses to western influences. He has widely published on the subject of Native American societies. His publications include *The Native North American Almanac* (2nd edn, 2001) and he was a co-author with Carole Goldberg of *A Review of Explaining Race Disparities in South Dakota Sentencing and Incarceration* (2005).

Paul L.A.H. Chartrand, IPC (Canadian *Who's Who 1992–2010, The Native North American Almanac*), retired as Professor of Law in 2009 after a career during which he held teaching and other academic appointments at universities in Australia, Canada, Aotearoa/New Zealand and the United States, including a permanent appointment at the University of Saskatchewan College of Law 2002–08 and as Visiting Scholar at the National Centre for Indigenous Studies, College of Law, Australian National University, Canberra, Australia in 2007–08. He was awarded the honorary title of Indigenous Peoples' Counsel (IPC) by the Canadian Indigenous Bar Association in 2002, the Outstanding Alumni Award, QUT School of Law, Brisbane, Australia, July 2001, a USSU Teaching Excellence Award (University of Saskatchewan) in 2004, and an Eagle Feather by the Anishinabeg of Sagkeeng First Nation. Paul Chartrand's professional interests and numerous publications are mainly in the fields of law and policy pertaining to indigenous peoples. He served as a commissioner on Canada's Royal Commission on Aboriginal Peoples (1991–95) and as a commissioner on Manitoba's Aboriginal Justice Implementation Commission (1999–2001). His community activities have included assisting indigenous organisations involved in international developments at the United Nations and the Organization of American States, including participation in the development of the United Nations Declaration on the Rights of Indigenous Peoples. He has returned to live in his home community of St Laurent along Lake Manitoba and advises First Nation organisations.

Rosemary J. Coombe holds the Tier One Canada Research Chair in Law, Communication and Culture at York University in Toronto, where she teaches in the Communications and Culture Joint PhD/MA Programme, and is cross-appointed to the Osgoode Hall Law School Graduate Programme and the Graduate Programme in Social and Political Thought. Prior to being awarded one of Canada's first research chairs, she was Full Professor at the University of Toronto Faculty of Law. She did doctoral degrees in law and anthropology at Stanford University and publishes in the fields of anthropology, cultural studies and interdisciplinary legal studies. Her work addresses the cultural, political and social implications of intellectual property laws, the politics of cultural property, neoliberalism and human rights. For more detail, see her website at www.yorku.ca/rcoombe. Current research projects include participation in an international multiple collaborator research initiative on intellectual property issues in cultural heritage driven by indigenous community research, a consideration of the repatriation of intangible heritage goods, and a volume of essays on global cultural rights politics.

Susy Frankel is a Professor at the Faculty of Law, Victoria University of Wellington, New Zealand. Her main fields of research and teaching are intellectual property and international trade law. She has published a range of articles and book chapters and given numerous conference presentations on various aspects of copyright, trade marks, patents and international trade. She is Director of the New Zealand Centre of International Economic Law. Susy Frankel is the author of the treatise *Intellectual Property in New Zealand* (2nd edn, 2011). She is Chair of the New Zealand Copyright Tribunal and was previously a hearings officer for the Intellectual Property Office of New Zealand. Susy holds an appointment as a neutral arbitrator and mediator for the World Intellectual Property Organization Arbitration and Mediation Centre. She is a member of the editorial boards of the *Journal of World Intellectual Property* and the *Queen Mary Journal of*

Intellectual Property. She was consultant expert to the Waitangi Tribunal on the Wai 262 claim. Prior to becoming an academic, she practised in both New Zealand and London in the fields of intellectual property and general commercial litigation.

Martin Girsberger is Head of the Sustainable Development and International Cooperation Unit of the Swiss Federal Institute of Intellectual Property (Institute). He is responsible for the area of intellectual property (IP) – sustainable development, including the IP-related aspects of the issues of biodiversity, access and benefit-sharing, traditional knowledge, environment, food and agriculture, future scenarios of IP and the IP-related aspects of bilateral cooperation and research agreements. He is also responsible for the international cooperation activities of the Institute in the field of IP. He is head of the Swiss delegation to the Intergovernmental Committee on Intellectual Property and Genetic Resources, Traditional Knowledge and Folklore of the World Intellectual Property Organization; and a member of the Swiss delegations, among others, to the TRIPS Council of the World Trade Organization, the Convention on Biological Diversity, the Food and Agriculture Organization, the World Health Organization, the Union for the Protection of New Plant Varieties, and the United Nations Framework Convention on Climate Change. He is the author of several publications covering issues such as traditional knowledge, farmers' rights, access and benefit-sharing, plant genetic resources for food and agriculture, and intellectual property.

Carole E. Goldberg is the Jonathan D. Varat Distinguished Professor of Law, and Vice Chancellor for Academic Personnel of the University of California, Los Angeles (UCLA). In 2006, she served as the Oneida Indian Nation Visiting Professor at Harvard Law School, and in 2007 she was appointed a Justice of the Hualapai Court of Appeals. In 2010, President Barack Obama appointed her to the Indian Law and Order Commission, which is investigating and recommending ways to improve Indian country criminal justice. Carole Goldberg has written widely on the subject of federal Indian law and tribal law and is co-editor and co-author of *Cohen's Handbook of Federal Indian Law* (1982 and 2005 eds), as well as co-author of a casebook, *American Indian Law: Native Nations and the Federal System* (6th edn, 2010).

Christoph B. Graber, PhD, Professor of Law, studied law at the Universities of Bern and St Gallen, received his admission to the bar in Switzerland, obtained a PhD from the European University Institute (Florence) and received his Habilitation from the University of Bern. He was a founding member of the University of Lucerne School of Law, in 2001, where he is now Head of the research centre i-call (International Communications and Art Law Lucerne) and Director of lucernaiuris, the Institute for Research in the Fundaments of Law. He has been a Visiting Fellow/Professor at Georgetown University Law School (2000), the University of Wollongong Faculty of Law (2007) and UC Berkeley School of Law (2012). Christoph is a member of the Swiss Federal Arbitration Commission for the Exploitation of Author's Rights and Neighbouring Rights and a member of the research commission of the Swiss National Science Foundation at the University of Lucerne. He has been advisor to various branches of the Swiss Government and OECD in the fields of intellectual property, trade and culture. He has published widely (including *Intellectual Property and Traditional Cultural Expressions in a Digital Environment*, Edward Elgar,

2008). In 2010 he received, with his team, the Swiss-Academies Award for Transdisciplinary Research (the highest research prize of the Swiss Academies of Arts and Sciences).

Karolina Kuprecht studied law at the University of Zurich in Switzerland and the University of Leiden in Holland. She obtained an LLM from UCLA (University of California, Los Angeles), where she concentrated on intellectual property and trade law and carried out research on cultural property rights of Native Americans. In 2002, she was admitted to the bar in Zug, Switzerland and later as a notary public. Since then she has practised law specialising in corporate, inheritance, foundation and cultural property law with a focus on international trade and sustainability. In 2008, she joined the i-call research centre at the University of Lucerne to pursue a PhD. As the alternate project leader, she helped Christoph B. Graber to submit and pursue the International Trade in Indigenous Cultural Heritage (IT ICH) project. In 2009, she received the UNO Academia Award for her paper 'Die UN-Deklaration über die Rechte der indigenen Völker und die Restitution von Kulturgütern'. She regularly publishes and speaks about cultural property law with a focus on tangible objects and restitution claims of indigenous peoples.

Jessica C. Lai studied law and chemistry at Victoria University of Wellington, New Zealand, where she obtained an LLB Hons (First Class), MSc (First Class). For her studies, Jessica was awarded a Victoria Graduate Award, Victoria Masters Award, Curtis-Gordon Research Scholarships and a prestigious New Zealand Vice-Chancellors' Committee William Georgetti Scholarship. In Wellington, she was a Research Assistant for Susy Frankel and Meredith Kolsky-Lewis, from 2007 to 2009, at the Faculty of Law of Victoria University. She also spent some time as an editor for the Victoria University of Wellington Law Review. Jessica has focused her studies in the fields of intellectual property, particularly patent law and international trade law. She was also a research assistant and tutor for the School of Chemical and Physical Sciences, from 2005–09. Since February 2010 she has been a Research Fellow and PhD candidate for Christoph B. Graber, working on the International Trade in Indigenous Cultural Heritage (IT ICH) project, at the University of Lucerne, Switzerland, researching predominantly the protection of Māori cultural heritage, particularly with respect to intellectual property, international trade and human rights law. Jessica is the author of numerous publications in the fields of law and chemistry.

Federico Lenzerini is Professor of Public International Law, Private International Law and European Union Law at the University of Siena (Italy). He is also Professor at the LLM programme in Intercultural Human Rights on the African System of Human Rights, Miami (FL), USA, St Thomas University School of Law. He is a consultant to UNESCO (Paris). On several occasions he has been Counsel to the Italian Ministry of Foreign Affairs for international negotiations related to cultural heritage. He is the National Rapporteur (Italy) for the Mapping International Law in Europe programme of the European Society of International Law. Federico Lenzerini is a member of the Italian Society of International Law. He is the Rapporteur of the Committee on the Rights of Indigenous Peoples of the International Law Association and a member of the Committee on Cultural Heritage Law of the same association. His fields of research include human rights law, asylum and refugee law, rights of indigenous peoples, international trade law and the law of cultural heritage. Federico Lenzerini is the editor of *Reparation for Indigenous Peoples, International and Comparative Perspectives* (Oxford University Press, 2008; also published in paperback in 2009).

Fiona Macmillan is the Corporation of London Professor of Law at the Birkbeck University of London, School of Law and Visiting Professor of Law at l'Universita' degli Studi Roma Tre and the University of Technology, Sydney. She teaches in the areas of intellectual property law, cultural heritage law and international economic law. Fiona Macmillan holds degrees from the University of New South Wales and the University of London. She is admitted as a Solicitor of the Supreme Court of New South Wales. Previously, she held academic positions at the University of New South Wales, the University of Leicester and the Institute of Advanced Legal Studies, University of London. Immediately prior to her appointment in the School of Law at Birkbeck, Fiona Macmillan was Associate Professor of Law and Copyright Director of the Asia Pacific Intellectual Property Institute at Murdoch University in Western Australia. Her research is focused on intellectual property, cultural property and international economic law.

Benny Müller is a legal advisor in the Sustainable Development and International Cooperation Unit of the Swiss Federal Institute of Intellectual Property in Bern. His responsibilities include the intellectual-property-related aspects of biodiversity, access and benefit-sharing, traditional knowledge, environment, and food and agriculture. In this context, Benny Müller is a member of the Swiss delegation to the Intergovernmental Committee on Intellectual Property and Genetic Resources, Traditional Knowledge and Folklore of the World Intellectual Property Organization; the TRIPS Council of the World Trade Organization; the Convention on Biological Diversity; the Food and Agriculture Organization; the World Health Organization; the Union for the Protection of New Plant Varieties; and the United Nations Framework Convention on Climate Change. In addition to these tasks at the intersection between intellectual property and sustainable development, Dr Müller explores future scenarios of intellectual property and deals with intellectual property issues of bilateral cooperation and research agreements. During his doctoral research project in Ecuador, Benny Müller worked for a law firm in the fields of intellectual property and international legal affairs, and for a university as an associate professor in international law and international cooperation. In 2011, he published on the rights of indigenous peoples and development cooperation.

John Scott is a descendant of the Iningai people (Indigenous Australian) of central Queensland (Barcaldine area) through his father (Jack Scott) and his grandmother (Catherine Maud Evans). They are Freshwater Murris. He has a significant background in education, social policy, law, indigenous rights and traditional knowledge. He has moved through various incarnations to get where he is today, including as a leading senior high school teacher, Aboriginal Education Advisor, Chief Educational Officer for Aboriginal Programs, Senior Policy Advisor (Office of the Aboriginal Social Justice Commissioner, Australian Human Rights Commission), Deputy Director for the School of Indigenous Australian Studies at James Cook University, Manager of the Cultural Rights Unit of the National Policy Branch with the National Aboriginal and Torres Strait Islander Commission (ATSIC), Indigenous Human Rights Officer with the United Nations High Commission on Human Rights (OHCHR), and second in charge of the Secretariat of the United

Nations Permanent Forum on Indigenous Issues. He is currently the Programme Officer for Traditional Knowledge for the United Nations Convention on Biological Diversity, where he has been since 2004. He has obtained a Diploma of Secondary Teaching (Arts/Humanities), Graduate Diploma in Aboriginal Education (with Distinction) and a Master of (Indigenous) Legal Studies.

Kurt Siehr, Dr Dr hc was born in Tilsit, East Prussia (Germany). He studied Law in Hamburg and in Ann Arbor (Michigan, USA). He passed his first and second bar examinations in Hamburg and obtained a Master of Comparative Law at the University of Michigan Law School in 1963. Kurt Siehr obtained his PhD from the University of Hamburg in 1970, where he was also a research assistant and a research associate at the Hamburg Max-Planck Institute of Comparative and International Private Law from 1963–91. Kurt Siehr has a PhD from the University of Zurich Faculty of Law (Switzerland, 1980). At the University of Zurich he was a lecturer, an associate and a full professor of private law, private international law and comparative law, from 1998–2002. After his retirement in 2002, Kurt Siehr became a free research associate at the Hamburg Max-Planck Institute of Comparative and International Private Law. He is a member of several national and international associations: for example Swiss Society of International Law; German Society of International Law; German Council of Private International Law; International Law Association; International Cultural Property Society; Groupe européen de droit international privé; German Society of Comparative Law; and bilateral law associations with Israel, Italy, Turkey and the USA.

Rebecca Tsosie is a Willard H. Pedrick Distinguished Research Scholar and Professor of Law at the Sandra Day O'Connor College of Law at Arizona State University. Rebecca Tsosie, who is of Yaqui descent, joined the ASU College of Law faculty in 1994 and served as the Executive Director of the law school's Indian Legal Program from 1996–2011. She teaches in the areas of federal Indian law, constitutional law, property, cultural resources law, bioethics and critical race theory. She also holds faculty appointments in the School of Historical, Philosophical and Religious Studies and the School of Sustainability at ASU, and she is a faculty affiliate for the American Indian Studies Program. Rebecca Tsosie has published widely on doctrinal and theoretical issues related to tribal sovereignty, self-determination, environmental policy, indigenous human rights and cultural resources, and she is the co-author (with Robert Clinton, Carole Goldberg, Kevin Washburn and Elizabeth Rodke Washburn) of a leading casebook on federal Indian law. She annually speaks at many national conferences and she serves as an appellate judge for the Fort McDowell Yavapai Nation's Supreme Court and for the San Carlos Apache Tribe's Court of Appeals. She received her BA and JD degrees from the University of California, Los Angeles, and also completed a President's Postdoctoral Fellowship at the University of California. She is admitted to practice in Arizona and California.

Joseph F. Turcotte is a PhD candidate in the Communication and Culture programme at York University (Toronto, Canada) and SSHRC Doctoral Fellow. His research focuses on technological, social, cultural, political and economic changes in the early twenty-first century with a particular emphasis on intellectual property rights, international trade and Internet governance in the digital and globalised era.

Brigitte Vézina joined the World Intellectual Property Organization (WIPO) in 2006 and is currently Legal Officer in the Traditional Knowledge Division, where she works on intellectual property issues related to traditional cultural expressions. Past experience includes work in the Cultural Enterprise and Copyright Section at the United Nations Educational, Scientific and Cultural Organization (UNESCO) and with the Montreal-based intellectual property law firm Robic. Brigitte holds a Bachelor's Degree in Law (LLB) from the University of Montreal (2002) and a Masters in Law (LLM), with distinction, from Georgetown University (2005). She is a member of the Quebec Bar (2003).

Foreword

Paul L.A.H. Chartrand

In January 2011, I had the privilege of participating in a workshop on 'International Trade in Indigenous Cultural Heritage: Legal and Policy Issues' at the invitation of Christoph B. Graber, the Head of the i-call Research Centre for International Communications and Art Law at the University of Lucerne in Switzerland. The event attracted academic and legal experts from several countries, as well as representatives of some of the most relevant international institutions, such as the World Trade Organization (WTO), the World Intellectual Property Organization (WIPO) and the United Nations Educational, Scientific and Cultural Organization (UNESCO). I am honoured to have been invited by Christoph to write a foreword for the book that continues the scholarly work that was launched at that conference in a beautiful city in the Swiss mountains. In my own academic and professional career I have had to confront many of the issues that now concern the researchers, but in no sense can I profess to be an expert in the particular spheres of study that were addressed at the workshop and that are the subject of analysis in this book. The following observations are therefore offered for what they may be worth.

As the nations of the world move into the twenty-first century, there is evidence that the interests of indigenous peoples are receiving increasing attention and concern from legislators and policy-makers. The contents of this book focus upon the particular interests that are subject to international trade and market concern and regulation. An accompanying development is the emergence of international standards that aim to define minimum standards to be followed by states in their relations with indigenous peoples.

A third and critically important development has been the participation of indigenous peoples' representatives in the process of identifying their particular interests and articulating their significance to governmental and non-governmental bodies both at the state level and at the international level, a development that has contributed significantly to the first two developments.

The reconciliation of the conflicting legitimate interests at stake in these developments, that is the interests of the indigenous peoples on the one hand and the interests of other parties which are mediated by state and international institutions on the other hand, requires the design and creation of processes or institutions that have the capacity to effect a reconciliation that is just, legitimate and workable. The advantages of a transdisciplinary cooperative methodology are applied by the various authors as they address questions the answers to which promise a material contribution to historic developments that engage some of the most arcane aspects of law and international relations and some of the most humanly significant aspects of the life of indigenous peoples.

The central question being addressed by the consortium of scholars is how international law, including trade law, can contribute to allowing indigenous peoples to more actively participate in the trade of their cultural heritage. It is particularly heartening to observe the strong commitment of the participants in the project of which this book is a part, to recognise as a precondition of its work, the autonomous right of an indigenous people to retain control over all aspects of its heritage. As Christoph remarked during the workshop, '[s]uch a precondition poses many difficult questions regarding the interplay of traditional cultures and modern law. These questions are taken seriously by this project and workshop.'

There are indeed a number of challenges to be met, and I suspect that some of the challenges that have attended discussions between indigenous representatives and states' representatives in international fora, such as the drafting of the United Nations Declaration on the Rights of Indigenous Peoples (UNDRIP), will be felt in the project's work.

Indigenous peoples around the world live within the territorial boundaries of states. There they are largely governed by the laws and regulations of these states that now occupy their ancient homelands. A look at history shows that the creation of these states was accomplished by processes that at best marginalised the interests of the indigenous peoples, and at worst tried to eradicate them. This is a hard political and economic legacy to overcome. It is a challenge for states to be persuaded that the interests of indigenous peoples matter. We have many examples of state policies and practices, such as the unilateral legal taking of the lands and natural resources that illustrate a legacy where indigenous peoples themselves did not matter. The logic is that people who do not matter have no interests that matter.

This realisation leads to the next observation, which is the challenge that contemporary state institutions, such as laws and policies and political and administrative institutions, were not generally designed to accommodate and protect the interests of indigenous peoples. As a consequence it is always necessary to question the capacity of state institutions to perform any function that requires respect, recognition and protection of indigenous peoples' interests. Since indigenous peoples generally, with notable exceptions, have relatively little political influence, the task of reforming state institutions, even by parties with the best intentions, is problematic.

The main international institutions whose roles are most relevant to the subject of the book, including WIPO, WTO and UNESCO, are well-established institutions with the mandates and experience to represent the interests of the states that agreed to create them. On the other hand, the hard legacy of state–indigenous peoples' relations means that the very identification of the latter is problematic. Indigenous peoples can be readily identified in some states where they form a substantial part of the population, but how are cultural heritage interests to be respected and protected in a system of worldwide trade without first identifying the legitimate owners of the subject matter of trade? The protection of cultural heritage goes naturally to the core of a people's identity. In the UN process that led to the adoption by the General Assembly of UNDRIP, the indigenous participants would not engage in an attempt to agree on a definition. Yet the very objectives of international trade presuppose a process to identify and involve the legitimate owners of trade-related goods. There is no reason to doubt that the states must have a role in an effective system, but it is equally important to identify the indigenous parties whose participation is essential to legitimise a state-controlled trade process and system for indigenous cultural goods or services.

Another challenge that is recognised by the members of this project is the imperative, in searching for institutional recognition of indigenous peoples' interests, of reconciling distinct concepts of each side where these concepts are central to the project of protecting and promoting trade in cultural goods or services. This challenge is sometimes described as the task of reconciling 'western' ideas with the ideas of indigenous peoples. Tangentially, I may note that I find the term 'western' to be interesting in this regard, since there are indigenous peoples in western, eastern and indeed in all parts of the world where people live. However, my own limited experience has indicated that there are interesting differences and similarities between indigenous concepts and those of both western and eastern philosophies. What alerts the mind of the observer seems to be the relative importance that is given to particular ideas or values. It would, I speculate, be very difficult to demonstrate empirically that any one particular concept was entirely absent in a large part of the regional population of the world.

With regard to the reconciliation of relevant concepts within the field of study covered in this book, the concept of property has received particular attention. I am aware of at least two aspects of conceptual divergence that are the object of study: the concept of property itself and the collective nature of property in indigenous societies as compared with the common concept of individual property in 'western systems'. The following brief discussion suggests that close scrutiny may help to further a reconciliation of the minds.

If property is viewed as a social institution that regulates the relations between individual persons and tangible or intangible things, then it is apparent that the concept of property, like the Aristotelian concept of law, is a feature of all human societies. This proposition does not deny that some forms of property are held communally and not individually. What need to be reconciled, it seems, are particular contemporary applications of distinct concepts. This requirement need not be based upon the assertion that one concept is alien to the other party's accepted thought. It is often asserted that land is held communally by indigenous peoples while land is held individually in the English real property system. Yet lands were held communally in Roman law and in early English law. Other concepts related to property, such as alienability and inalienability, seem to be found in all societies as well.

There seem to be, nevertheless, some distinctions, the features of which must be carefully observed for their application to the development of international standards and institutions. The concepts of collective rights and individual rights are examples.

This has particular significance for aspects of the subject of study of this book, where existing institutions have been created for the recognition and protection of individual interests and rights and seem, at first blush, to be ill-suited to the recognition and protection of communally held property interests. The particular reference here is to the regulatory regimes that were created for the recognition and protection of intellectual property.

Western societies and legal institutions are familiar with the kinds of interests that, although they are technically held by individuals, are valuable or enjoyable only in community. Examples might include the legal structure of interests held by corporations and shareholders, and language rights, which are held by individuals but which can only be enjoyed in community.

But these issues need not detain us long. Judicial interpretation is one technique that can effectively transform one concept into another, as has been done in Latin American courts that have read original references to individual rights of ownership as including the collective interests of indigenous peoples in their lands and territories. If the objectives of respect, recognition and protection are firmly asserted by states, then their juridical institutions are capable of reconciling what might seem irreconcilable to the scholarly exegete. As stated earlier, the initial and more fundamental challenge is to get states to accept the proposition that indigenous peoples and, therefore, their collective interests do matter, as do the interests of all peoples.

Towards this fundamental objective, the international community and all states have as a guide the concept of self-determination of all peoples, which UNDRIP proclaims as a fundamental right that applies to indigenous peoples. The Declaration now stands unopposed as a fundamental human right that must guide future indigenous–state relations.

It is with a firm commitment to respect the basic right of self-determination that the participants in the i-call research project and the authors in this book pursue their professional work. They are to be commended for this collective and individual commitment to justice.

Preface

Christoph B. Graber, Karolina Kuprecht and Jessica C. Lai

The aim of this book, which is the result of a multi-year research project, is to study how international law could better contribute to promoting trade and development in indigenous cultural heritage (ICH) while, at the same time, respecting indigenous peoples' traditional values. The cover image of this book captures one of the core ideas that we want to bring across: there are acceptable uses of indigenous cultural heritage, but there is also much misappropriation and inappropriate use, as illustrated by the Cherokee car and the Russian ice skaters wearing inauthentic Aboriginal attire (image source: AP) to qualify for and compete in the 2010 Vancouver Winter Olympics, for example. The image represents the question of how it is that we could best 'rope in' the trade of these inappropriate uses.

The book emphasises a comprehensive meaning of the term ICH as frequently used by indigenous peoples themselves by incorporating tangible and intangible aspects as well as moveable and immoveable objects of indigenous peoples' cultures (including traditional cultural expressions, knowledge, practices and property). The research question inevitably poses difficult problems of legitimacy and method, as Christoph Graber's chapter demonstrates at the beginning of this book. Reflecting these difficulties, the research process leading to the present book was informed and guided by the precept of participative research, which is a typical feature of a *transdisciplinary research methodology*. The concept of participation was implemented by bringing together an eclectic group of indigenous and non-indigenous scholars and practitioners from eight different countries and selected fields of expertise. As a milestone of the research project, the group gathered for intense debates in a three-day workshop, organised by i-call, the research centre for communications and art law at the University of Lucerne, in January 2011. During the three days, participants worked intensely together in presenting and discussing the papers that – after having been worked over and reviewed in the months following the workshop – are now assembled as the chapters of this book.

Since we wanted to achieve a high degree of coherence in the output, we invested a great deal of energy into the development of the research structure that has underlain the workshop and the entire project. For this, we discussed some key questions of research – to be addressed from various perspectives of international and national law – with a core group of project partners at an early stage of project development. Later on, further academic experts in law and the social sciences, as well as non-academic stakeholders from international organisations, public administration and civil society, were invited to comment on the planned research structure. Importantly, the structuring process included experts of indigenous origin from the four countries under focus.

Methodologically, this emphasis on expert and stakeholder participation was crucial not only for assuring the transdisciplinary and interdisciplinary character of the project, but also for enhancing the practical use of the expected results. An important outcome of this preparatory work was the decision to draft a *reference paper* (outlining a procedural approach to resolve some of the pressing problems at the interface of modern law and indigenous culture) and to identify a set of questions to be addressed by the individual participants of the workshop. We felt that this was necessary for complexity reduction management, that is, to assure a coherent thread linking the various chapters of the book and to avoid transdisciplinarity and interdisciplinarity ending up in a cacophony. Luckily, the planned research structure was successful, with participants addressing the questions asked of them and commenting on thoughts contained in the reference paper, while bringing in personal insights and proposals at the same time.

After Graber's introduction on legitimacy and method, the book starts with a sociological perspective on the research topic, offered by Duane Champagne, a sociologist of Native American descent. His chapter sets the scene by identifying key aspects of indigenous social orders and worldviews that may cause fundamental difficulties when indigenous cultural heritage enters the realm of trade and commerce. The book proceeds with perspectives from the relevant fields of international law, including human and indigenous rights, international trade regulation, intellectual property, cultural property and cultural heritage law. The international focus is complemented by country reports from four countries with important indigenous populations: Australia (Aborigines and Torres Strait Islanders), Canada (First Nations), New Zealand (Māori) and the United States (American Indians). The reports allow the testing of international perspectives against national realities, to provide in-depth analyses of the relationship between international law and national law in the four countries under focus, and to compare top–down with bottom–up approaches. In the epilogue, finally, the editors summarise the insights gained from the individual chapters, identify some potential future directions of research and map out one possible way forward.

The book is unique since it is the first publication to bring together all the relevant viewpoints of international law on the topic of ICH trade and development in one volume. It contributes towards a more comprehensive protection of indigenous peoples' interests in cultural heritage trade and development, taking account of the rights of cultural self-determination and self-governance as enshrined in the United Nations Declaration on the Rights of Indigenous Peoples (UNDRIP). Thereby, the book seeks to overcome not only high legal, but also high organisational fragmentation. This is necessary because the most relevant fora of law and policy-making in the subject area, such as the World Intellectual Property Organization (WIPO), the United Nations Educational, Scientific and Cultural Organization (UNESCO), the Convention on Biological Diversity (CBD) and the World Trade Organization (WTO), generally only look at a single aspect of ICH.

For this book, choices not only had to be made in highly fragmented and complex fields of law, but also in a politically, culturally and ethically sensitive environment. The choice of Australia, Canada, New Zealand and the United States as countries of reference was important in order to enhance comparability of the country reports, to avoid additional complexity in national legal systems without Anglo-Saxon roots, and to reduce cultural diversity inherent in the concept of 'indigenous peoples' to a justifiable minimum. These countries share a similar historical background of colonisation, wholly or at least partially under the regime of the British Crown, and thus similar or at least comparable political and legal systems. The indigenous peoples on their territories form separate and distinguishable groups as compared with the immigrant society, not only with regard to culture but also with regard to their legal status within the home country. We are well aware that indigenous peoples in Australia, Canada, New Zealand and the United States are minorities. Consequently, some of the discussed political dynamics and outlined legal options may be absent in countries with an indigenous majority (for example some African or Asian countries). However, this book is not intended to provide final answers for all countries with indigenous populations. It rather serves as pioneering scientific groundwork that methodically, structurally and content-wise sets a standard for further work on ICH trade and development in other parts of the world.

Our heartfelt thanks go to the authors of the chapters, first and foremost, who invested a great deal of confidence, intellectual generosity and cooperative spirit in this project. We would also like to thank our external reviewers, Peter Drahos and Peter Yu, for their insightful comments, and our team colleagues Dorothea Endres and Angela Hefti, as well as Liz Obee, for editorial assistance and proofreading. We would like to acknowledge Regi Widmer, who designed the cover image for this book, as well as Tim Williams, Jessica Westwood, Caroline Phillips, Laura Seward and David Fairclough from Edward Elgar for great collaboration. Last but not least, this book would not have been possible without the financial support of the Swiss National Science Foundation, the Ecoscientia Foundation and the many sponsors that helped to realise the workshop leading to this volume.

PART I

Methodology and social context

1. Stimulating trade and development of indigenous cultural heritage by means of international law: issues of legitimacy and method

Christoph B. Graber*

1. INTRODUCTION

Under the effects of economic globalisation and the Internet, international trade in traditional knowledge (TK) and traditional cultural expressions (TCE) is gaining magnitude, and a debate about the law's role in protecting indigenous cultural heritage (ICH)[1] seems more necessary than ever. So far, the dominant attitude in this debate has been a defensive one. Scholars backed by prominent indigenous brokers have been arguing for some decades that the international legal order should work out efficient defences against flagrant misappropriation of ICH. The international restitution of stolen or illegally exported indigenous cultural property indeed leaves a lot to be desired and the existing intellectual property (IP) regime does not provide effective remedies against misappropriation of TK and TCE.[2] Although these concerns need to be addressed,[3] I think that the debate should not stop there. Instead, I suggest a shift from a defensive attitude to a

* The author would like to thank Christoph Antons, Peter Drahos, Karolina Kuprecht, Jessica Lai, Federico Lenzerini, Axel Tschentscher and Peter Yu for helpful comments on an earlier version of this text. The support of the Ecoscientia Foundation is gratefully acknowledged.

[1] Whereas TK, TCE (sometimes also called 'folklore'), biological and genetic resources or indigenous cultural and intellectual property (ICIP) are among the many terms that are used to describe the subject matter, indigenous peoples often prefer to speak of *indigenous cultural heritage* (ICH). Whereas most of the above-mentioned terms reflect the ways in which modern law categorises indigenous knowledge assets and thus subjects indigenous culture to a modern episteme, *indigenous cultural heritage* respects indigenous peoples' epistemological sovereignty. Accordingly, the latter term is used in this chapter.

[2] This is because the IP system leaves many modes of TK and TCE outside the scope of protection.

[3] See in particular Rebecca Tsosie, 'International Trade in Indigenous Cultural Heritage: An Argument for Indigenous Governance of Cultural Property', in this volume; Rosemary J. Coombe with Joseph F. Turcotte, 'Indigenous Cultural Heritage in Development and Trade: Perspectives from the Dynamics of Cultural Heritage Law and Policy', in this volume; Christoph Antons, 'Intellectual Property Rights in Indigenous Cultural Heritage: Basic Concepts and Continuing Controversies', in this volume; Brigitte Vézina, 'Are They In or Are They Out? Traditional Cultural Expressions and the Public Domain: Implications for Trade', in this volume; and Martin Girsberger

proactive strategy and to study whether international trade in ICH could promote social and economic development of indigenous peoples and how the law could contribute to this aim.

The concept of 'development' is understood here in line with Amartya Sen's seminal book *Development as Freedom* and '[a]ttention is thus paid particularly to the expansion of the "capabilities" of persons to lead the kind of lives they value – and have reason to value.'[4] Sen has made it clear that this philosophical concept should not be limited to the poor people in developing countries since 'the richer countries too often have deeply disadvantaged people, who lack basic opportunities'.[5] This is certainly also true for indigenous peoples who often belong to the most disadvantaged segments of society. Accordingly, there is good reason to assume in this chapter that the concept 'development as freedom' can also be extended *mutatis mutandis* to the indigenous peoples in rich countries, including the USA, Canada, Australia or New Zealand.

Adopting the view that a more active participation of indigenous peoples in the trade of their knowledge assets would promote their social and economic development raises difficult questions of legitimacy and method.

Questions of legitimacy will be posed by the potentially modernising effects of development endangering traditional ways of indigenous peoples' social organisation. For Sen, it is 'the people directly involved who must have the opportunity in deciding what should be chosen' if a traditional way of life must be given up because of modernising effects entailed by development.[6] This chapter will further elaborate on some difficult problems that must be resolved when such an approach is followed in a legal context, including conflicts between rights of the group with rights of individual members of the group.

Questions of method arise when studying how international law, including international economic law, could better contribute to furthering development interests of indigenous peoples in the trade of ICH. There will be many areas where modern[7] law and indigenous custom collide. As the indigenous sociologist Duane Champagne argued, any effort to draft better legal solutions will be challenged by unbridgeable differences between indigenous and non-indigenous worldviews.[8]

From an epistemological perspective, the difference between indigenous and non-indigenous worldviews implies that in our scientific aspirations of gaining knowledge we are ultimately always stopped at a point where a veil covers what cannot be accessed by a non-indigenous mind. What are the consequences of this insight for our research? A first

---

and Benny Müller, 'International Trade in Indigenous Cultural Heritage: An IP Practitioners' Perspective', in this volume.

4 Amartya K. Sen, *Development as Freedom,* 1st edn, New York: Anchor Books, 2000, at p. 18.

5 Ibid., at p. 15. 'Even within very rich countries, sometimes the longevity of substantial groups is no higher than that in much poorer economies of the so-called third world.'

6 Ibid., at p. 31.

7 Terms such as 'modern' (as opposed to 'traditional' or 'indigenous') or 'modernisation' are used throughout this chapter in a sociological sense to distinguish patterns of social organisation and do not entail any value judgements. Hence, I am by no means saying that a 'modern' social structure should in any way be preferred over a traditional or indigenous one.

8 See Duane Champagne, 'Indigenous Self-government, Cultural Heritage and International Trade: A Sociological Perspective', in this volume.

consequence is simply to be conscious that this difference exists and that it cannot be negotiated. From this follows the second consequence. If access to the core of the indigenous world is not possible for a non-indigenous mind, then the question is how we, as (modern) lawyers and social scientists, should methodologically deal with the impossibility of looking behind the veil.

The response that this research project has given to the problem is twofold. Following an approach of *transdisciplinary research*, we have first been very careful to include indigenous scholars and stakeholders in all steps of the research process. According to one definition, a key element of transdisciplinarity consists in participatory research, that is, the inclusion of the most relevant stakeholders in the research process.[9] In line with this exigency of transdisciplinarity, the active participation of indigenous scholars and stakeholders shall prevent the research project from falling into the traps of scientific colonialism or paternalism. However, a word of caution is necessary to avoid exaggerated expectations. As for any one group of researchers or projects, we must acknowledge that such an approach sets practical difficulties on what can be accomplished. In particular, one must bear in mind that indigenous persons designated as 'experts' for indigenous worldviews by non-indigenous systems of recognition enter a dual world which potentially distances them from indigenous peoples living traditional lives.[10] Second, we suggest relying on procedural approaches rather than on substantive solutions when dealing with indigenous issues in law and policy-making. The basic features of such a procedural approach shall be explored in this chapter.

After considering the problems related to legitimacy and method, the chapter will turn to issues related to the international law's potential in stimulating ICH trade for the sake of indigenous social and economic development. To this end it first assesses how interests of indigenous peoples in trade and development of ICH are currently institutionalised in international economic law.[11] Second, the chapter examines whether preferential trade rules for indigenous cultural goods and services would be an adequate tool to advance the interests of indigenous peoples in ICH trade and development.

2. DEVELOPMENT AS FREEDOM FOR INDIGENOUS PEOPLES

Indigenous peoples appear generally at the lower end of socioeconomic statistics and even in first world countries they belong to the most disadvantaged groups in many respects, including life expectancy, income, education, and so on.[12] From this perspective, a policy contributing to improving their social and economic development seems to be persuasive.

---

[9] Christian Pohl and Gertrude Hirsch Hadorn, *Principles for Designing Transdisciplinary Research*, Munich: oekom, 2007, at pp. 70–72.

[10] I would like to thank Peter Drahos for pointing this out.

[11] The term 'international economic law' is understood broadly to encompass also trade-related legal aspects of intellectual property, cultural property and tangible and intangible cultural heritage.

[12] For the situation in the US see the comprehensive, systematic and comparative study of social, economic and political conditions of American Indian reservations, undertaken by the Harvard Project on American Indian Economic Development over the last 20 years: Eric C. Henson et al. (eds), *The State of the Native Nations. Conditions under U.S. Policies of Self-determination*, New York: Oxford University Press, 2008.

However, critics have objected that development may have harmful effects and even destroy traditions and cultural heritage of indigenous peoples.[13] Based on Amartya Sen's concept of 'development as freedom', it is possible to respond to this objection in two stages. First, it must be recalled that, for Sen, development is viewed as an 'expansion of freedom'[14] and attention is thus given more to the end of development than to its means. Accordingly, the contributions of development to the growth of personal capabilities are more important than its contributions to economic growth. Similarly, the primary significance of the market is seen in its participatory dimension as an institution enabling freedom of interchange.[15] If the freedom aspect of the market is emphasised, the focus should not be on utilities, incomes or wealth (the 'culmination outcomes' of the market) but rather on 'the process of getting there, including the exercise of freedom'.[16] The second element of the objection relates to the potentially modernising effect of development involving the destruction of traditions and cultural heritage. Sen concedes that it would not be sufficient to dismiss this objection with the argument 'that it is better to be rich and happy than to be impoverished and traditional'.[17] Such an argument would fall short of considering that the authority and legitimacy of such a decision is problematic. As stated by Sen: 'There is an inescapable valuational problem involved in deciding what to choose if and when it turns out that some parts of tradition cannot be maintained along with economic or social changes that may be needed for other reasons.'[18]

The answer Sen offers to resolve the identified problem is *participation*. Choosing about its destiny is a decision that only a people directly involved can legitimately take. If it is up to the people involved to choose, it is necessary that they receive 'the opportunity to participate in deciding what should be chosen'.[19] From a legal perspective, one may easily agree with such a precept since allowing an (indigenous) people to decide freely on what traditions to follow is part of its collective right of self-determination and self-government as recognised by the UN Declaration on the Rights of Indigenous Peoples (UNDRIP).[20] Although UNDRIP is not a binding instrument of public international law,[21] it is relevant

---

13 For a generally defensive posture towards participation of indigenous peoples in international trade, see, for example, Champagne, supra note 8, and the discussion in Fiona Macmillan, 'Finding Space in the Margins? Recognising the Rights of Indigenous Peoples in the WTO', in this volume. See also Robert K. Paterson and Dennis S. Karjala, 'Looking Beyond Intellectual Property in Resolving Protection of the Intangible Cultural Heritage of Indigenous Peoples' (2003) *Cardozo Journal of International and Comparative Law*, 11, pp. 633–70, at p. 634.

14 Sen, supra note 4, at p. 36.

15 Ibid., at p. 6.

16 Ibid., at p. 27.

17 Ibid., at p. 31.

18 Ibid.

19 Ibid.

20 UN, Declaration on the Rights of Indigenous Peoples (UNDRIP), GA Res. 61/295 (UN Doc. A/61/L.67 and Add.1) (adopted on 13 September 2007), Articles 3 and 5, protecting the right of (collective) self-determination and the right of collective self-government, respectively.

21 On the controversy regarding the reach and impact of the right of self-determination in international law, see Daniel Thürer and Thomas Burri, 'Self-determination', in Rüdiger Wolfrum (ed.), *The Max Planck Encyclopedia of Public International Law*, available online at http://www.mpepil.com, last updated 2008 (all online sources were accessed 7 September 2011). See also Christoph B. Graber, 'Aboriginal Self-Determination vs the Propertisation of Traditional Culture:

as a political tool and will most likely influence future law and policy-making on indigenous issues at all levels.[22]

For Sen, the real philosophical quandary is the question of whether participation should also be a precept *within* a traditional people or group.[23] Ultimately, the problem is the relationship between the rights of the group and the rights of individual members of the group. This is a frequent conflict situation in indigenous contexts.[24] Here the question arises whether and, if yes, to what extent an indigenous group can internally enforce its traditional customs against dissenting individual members of the group. What should be the normative reference for deciding this question? Should it be indigenous custom or should it be modern law? Sen does not discuss this question in detail. However, the examples he provides as an illustration of his general argument clearly show that he would opt for the participatory freedom of the individual within the group and, in a case of conflict, against the customary rules of the traditional group or people. Sen argues:

> An attempt to choke off [internal] participatory freedom on grounds of traditional values (such as religious fundamentalism, or political custom, or the so-called Asian values) simply misses the issue of legitimacy and the need for the people to participate in deciding what they want and what they have reason to accept.[25]

The consequence of a normative requirement for internal participation would be that individual members of the group could *not* legitimately be required to obey with traditional custom-based decisions of the group. This is only consequent if considering Sen's general emphasis on the pre-eminence of individual freedoms.[26] However, from a legal perspective it would be necessary to introduce a distinction between indigenous and non-indigenous groups.[27] This is indispensable because the collective right of self-determination and self-government of indigenous peoples is specifically protected under

---

The Case of Sacred Wanjina Sites' (2009) *Australian Indigenous Law Review*, 13 (2), pp. 18–34, at p. 26 [hereinafter Graber, 'Aboriginal Self-Determination']; and Jessica C. Lai, 'The Protection of Māori Cultural Heritage Post-Endorsement of the UN Declaration on the Rights of Indigenous Peoples', *University of Lucerne, Switzerland*, i-call Working Paper No. 2 (2011), at pp. 8–34, available at http://www.unilu.ch/files/i-call_Working_Paper_2011_02_Lai_Maori_Cultural_Heritage__UNDRIP.pdf [hereinafter Lai, 'Māori Cultural Heritage and UNDRIP'].

22 The Declaration was adopted by the UN General Assembly on 13 September 2007. One hundred and forty-three UN Member States voted in favour, 11 abstained and four – Australia, Canada, New Zealand and the United States – voted against the instrument. Since its adoption, Australia, New Zealand, Canada and the United States have all reversed their positions and now endorse the Declaration. Colombia and Samoa have also indicated their support for the Declaration. For an account of the relevance of UNDRIP as a political tool see Lai, 'Māori Cultural Heritage and UNDRIP', supra note 21, at pp. 26–30.

23 Sen, supra note 4, at p. 32.

24 For examples of US Law see Carole Goldberg, 'A United States Perspective on the Protection of Indigenous Cultural Heritage', in this volume.

25 Sen, supra note 4, at p. 32.

26 Ibid., at pp. 146–59.

27 Sen addresses conflicts between traditional and modern worldviews in general without discussing indigenous issues in particular.

UNDRIP.[28] Affirming an unlimited and unspecified right of internal participation would thus ignore collective rights of indigenous peoples. On the other hand, an absolute rejection of modernity would risk violating human rights of individual members of the indigenous group or people. In certain cases of cultural or ritual practices of indigenous peoples (including honour killing, female circumcision or spearing and other physical punishment),[29] the primacy of indigenous customary law would indeed create conflicts with core human rights standards (*ius cogens*) and international *ordre public*. Fortunately, UNDRIP itself provides for a solution to such collisions between indigenous custom and modern law. According to Article 34 UNDRIP, indigenous peoples must respect international human rights standards when making use of the 'right to promote, develop and maintain their institutional structures and their distinctive customs, spirituality, traditions, procedures, practices'.

According to Sen, native cultures cannot escape from effects of the globalising world, even if they are harmful.[30] Because the forces of global exchange and trade are difficult to resist in a world dominated by modern information and communication technologies, the option to stop globalisation is arguably not available for local cultures.[31] In my view, however, it would be oversimplifying to see participation in a capitalist economy or the use of modern communication technologies as solely a threat to local identities. The Internet, in particular, may help indigenous communities to overcome isolation. It has indeed become extremely valuable for people living in remote areas for purposes such as schooling or telemedicine.[32] Moreover, the Internet may provide a useful tool to communicate with like-minded groups around the world and to build coalitions, particularly in international and regional policy-making. It may also offer new opportunities to communities that want to take advantage of economic globalisation, enter trade relations and gradually move towards more modern forms of social organisation.[33] If an indigenous

---

28 For the legal protection of the collective rights of self-determination and self-government of indigenous peoples under UNDRIP, see supra note 21, and accompanying text. For a philosophical defence of the argument that indigenous communities must be able to live according to their cultural practice see Chandran Kukathas, 'Are There Any Cultural Rights?', in Will Kymlicka (ed.), *Multicultural Citizenship: A Liberal Theory of Minority Rights*, Oxford: Clarendon Press, 1996, pp. 228–56. Kukathas conceives the right of the individual to leave the community to be crucial. For a discussion of this argument from a human rights perspective see Christoph B. Graber, 'Using Human Rights to Tackle Fragmentation in the Field of Traditional Cultural Expressions: An Institutional Approach', in Christoph B. Graber and Mira Burri-Nenova (eds), *Intellectual Property and Traditional Cultural Expressions in a Digital Environment*, Cheltenham, UK: Edward Elgar, 2008, pp. 96–120, at pp. 114–18.

29 On spearing as an Aboriginal form of punishment, see Heather McRae et al., *Indigenous Legal Issues, Commentary and Materials*, 3rd edn, Sydney: Thomson, 2003, at pp. 549–51.

30 Sen, supra note 4, at p. 32.

31 Ibid., at p. 240.

32 See Kyra Landzelius (ed.), *Native on the Net: Indigenous and Diasporic Peoples in the Virtual Age*, London and New York: Routledge, 2006.

33 For comprehensive analyses see Miriam Sahlfeld, 'Commercializing Cultural Heritage? Criteria for a Balanced Instrumentalization of Traditional Cultural Expressions for Development in a Globalized Digital Environment', in Christoph B. Graber and Mira Burri-Nenova (eds), *Intellectual Property and Traditional Cultural Expressions in a Digital Environment*, Cheltenham, UK: Edward Elgar, 2008, pp. 256–86, and, pointing to differences in the reception of modernity between

community incrementally shifts from tradition to modernity, it may however want to open up only certain aspects of its *lifeworld* (Husserl), while sticking to traditions with regard to spirituality and religious beliefs. Generally, indigenous groups will not be able and not want to respond to dramatic increases in demand for their products. Small really is beautiful for many indigenous groups.[34]

The differences in the social institutionalisation of creativity (and innovation) in traditional and modern societies have been elaborated elsewhere.[35] They are responsible for many shortcomings of international law in adequately protecting indigenous knowledge assets against misappropriation. Providing remedies against misappropriation or misuse is thus a prerequisite for trade in ICH being able to support indigenous development. In addition, free, prior and informed consent (FPIC) and benefit-sharing must be respected. FPIC is crucial, since indigenous peoples will be willing to produce certain artwork for commercial sale but will want to keep their sacred knowledge secret and to prevent its unauthorised disclosure and subsequent use.[36] Thus, in accordance with their traditions, they will insist that sacred and secret artefacts be kept off the art market.

A further complication is legal certainty. From the perspective of the market, a prerequisite for trade in indigenous heritage would certainly be that third-party users know what TCE and TK may or may not be (appropriately) bought or otherwise used.[37] Accordingly, definitions of TK and TCE and a determination of what subject matter can be traded seem to be necessary for the purpose of legal certainty. The question is who should provide the required definitions and determinations. Should it be international treaty law? In my view, international law should abstain from providing substantive definitions of, *inter alia*, TK and TCE (including its tradability) since this would otherwise result in a subjugation of indigenous culture under modern legal concepts. As I have emphasised elsewhere, expressions of indigenous creativity strongly depend on the geographical,

---

indigenous cultures in Australia and Southeast Asia, Christoph Antons, 'Traditional Cultural Expressions and their Significance for Development in a Digital Environment: Examples from Australia and Southeast Asia', in Christoph B. Graber and Mira Burri-Nenova (eds), *Intellectual Property and Traditional Cultural Expressions in a Digital Environment*, Cheltenham, UK: Edward Elgar, 2008, pp. 287–301.

[34] My thanks to Peter Drahos for this suggestion.

[35] For differences in the institutionalisation of creativity see Christoph B. Graber, 'Institutionalization of Creativity in Traditional Societies and in International Trade Law', in Shubha Ghosh and Robin P. Malloy (eds), *Creativity, Law and Entrepreneurship*, Cheltenham, UK and Northampton, MA: Edward Elgar, 2011, pp. 234–63 [hereinafter Graber, 'Institutionalization of Creativity']; for differences in the institutionalisation of innovation see Gunther Teubner and Andreas Fischer-Lescano, 'Cannibalizing Epistemes: Will Modern Law Protect Traditional Cultural Expressions?', in Christoph B. Graber and Mira Burri-Nenova (eds), *Intellectual Property and Traditional Cultural Expressions in a Digital Environment*, Cheltenham, UK: Edward Elgar, 2008, pp. 17–45.

[36] See Antony Taubman, 'Saving the Village: Conserving Jurisprudential Diversity in the International Protection of Traditional Knowledge', in Keith E. Maskus and Jerome H. Reichman (eds), *International Public Goods and Transfer of Technology Under a Globalized Intellectual Property Regime*, Cambridge, UK: Cambridge University Press, 2005, pp. 521–64, at p. 534.

[37] Susy Frankel, 'Trademarks, Traditional Knowledge and Cultural Intellectual Property', in Graeme B. Dinwoodie and Mark D. Janis (eds), *Trademark Law and Theory. A Handbook of Contemporary Research*, Cheltenham, UK: Edward Elgar, 2008, pp. 433–63, at p. 448 [hereinafter Frankel, 'TMs, TK and CIP'].

spiritual and social context of their production.[38] Since 'the framework requirements of the respective local culture have to be maintained',[39] it will be important to capture not only the result, but also the whole process of TK and TCE production. Consequently, international law should provide for procedural solutions rather than substantive ones. That is, rather than itself defining TCE and TK, international law should limit its jurisdiction to stating who is responsible for doing this. I will discuss problems posed by such a procedural approach in more detail in the next section.

3. INTERFACING INDIGENOUS AND MODERN WORLDVIEWS: A PROCEDURAL APPROACH

As outlined above, the 'silver bullet' for resolving problems of legitimacy in trade and development of ICH seems to be participation of indigenous holders of TK and TCE and a procedural approach to interfacing indigenous and non-indigenous worldviews. However, it needs to be clarified what participation would mean in a context of international trade and what kind of procedures would assure a fair trade-off between interests of indigenous holders of TK and TCE and interests of non-indigenous customers.

In a first step, I will clarify the concept of a 'procedural approach' in general before exploring its concrete meaning in the context of trade in ICH. The discussions on proceduralist approaches in the field of social theory generally distinguish between the concepts of procedural law and procedural justice.

3.1 Proceduralist Thinking in Social Theory

The term procedural law is used by law and society theorists to describe a form of legal rationality.[40] The point is that procedural law is characterised by a procedural form of rationality as opposed to 'substantive' legal rationality. Whereas 'substantive' law is concerned with results, procedural law – which is sometimes also referred to as 'reflexive law'[41] – is characterised by process-orientation in the design of institutional structures and in organising participation in decision-making.[42]

---

38 For Aboriginal culture in Australia the concept of the 'totemic polygon' has been introduced to describe the complex discursive relationship between the spiritual ancestors, the land, totemic custom and the traditional artist. For more information see Christoph B. Graber, 'Can Modern Law Safeguard Archaic Cultural Expressions? Observations From a Legal Sociology Perspective', in Christoph Antons (ed.), *Traditional Knowledge, Traditional Cultural Expressions and Intellectual Property Law in the Asia-Pacific Region*, The Hague: Kluwer Law International, 2009, pp. 159–76 [hereinafter Graber, 'Modern Law and CEs'].

39 Teubner and Fischer-Lescano, supra note 35, at p. 41.

40 Gralf-Peter Calliess, *Prozedurales Recht*, Baden-Baden: Nomos, 1999.

41 Gunther Teubner, 'Substantive and Reflexive Elements in Modern Law' (1983) *Law and Society Review*, 17, pp. 239–85, at pp. 266–85.

42 Ibid., at p. 257.

In contrast, the term 'procedural justice' is used to value the legitimacy[43] and/or legitimation[44] of outcomes that are arrived at through the observance of certain procedures. Procedural justice has been a concern for authors writing in the field of social psychology as well as in philosophy of the law. Within a social psychology context 'procedural justice' has been defined by Tom Tyler as the willingness of legal subjects 'to accept outcomes that are arrived at through procedures that are viewed as being fair'.[45] Whereas this definition looks at the quality of outputs from an *empirical* perspective of individual acceptance (legitimacy), legal philosophy (in the tradition of critical theory) is more interested in *normative* criteria of legitimation. Indeed, Jürgen Habermas and his school would consider legitimate outcomes to be those that have been obtained through procedures respecting a normative standard of institutional structure and participation.[46] Habermas has championed a proceduralist paradigm of law as the only available model, since both the liberal paradigm and the social-welfare paradigm have lost their persuasive power.[47] Under the proceduralist paradigm, the law is neither exclusively oriented to securing an equal distribution of rights (the liberal paradigm) nor understood as an instrument for maximising distributive justice (the social-welfare paradigm), but rather conceived as a framework guarantee for process-based rules of fair communication – as detailed in Habermas's theory of deliberative democracy.[48]

Habermas's reference to a proceduralist paradigm of law suggests that there are more commonalities than differences in the discussed approaches to phenomena of procedure, law and justice. The points of convergence of both procedural law and procedural justice writings are that they all refer to a process-based model of regulation (rather than an outcome-based model) and that *assuring the participation of stakeholders* is considered to be a key requirement.[49] As a consequence, when speaking of a procedural approach in the remainder of this chapter, I essentially refer to a process-based model of regulation where the participation of the most relevant stakeholders, including indigenous peoples, is a central element.

The social theorist's accentuation of stakeholder participation clearly resonates in more recent UN law and policy-making in the field of indigenous issues. Since the early 1970s, UN institutions have acknowledged 'that the greater the participation by indigenous

---

43 Legitimacy is the technical term used by social-psychology writers.

44 Legitimation is the technical term used by philosophy of law authors.

45 Tom R. Tyler, 'Procedural Justice, Legitimacy, and the Effective Rule of Law' (2003) *Crime and Justice*, 30, pp. 283–357, at p. 292.

46 At the level of national law such standards will be set by the constitution and will vary according to the nature of the legal or administrative procedure at issue.

47 Jürgen Habermas, *Between Facts and Norms. Contributions to a Discourse Theory of Law and Democracy*, translation by William Regh, Cambridge, MA: MIT Press, 1996, at pp. 409–10.

48 Ibid., at pp. 418–19; see also Axel Tschentscher, *Prozedurale Theorien der Gerechtigkeit. Rationales Entscheiden, Diskursethik und prozedurales Recht*, Baden-Baden: Nomos, 2000, at p. 246.

49 There is, however, an important difference in the normative assumptions of the two concepts. Whereas Habermas's concept of 'procedural justice' ultimately serves the purpose of 'democratisation', the concept of procedural law is not bound by a particular normative *a priori*. When applied to developing procedures for interfacing indigenous culture and modern law, insistence on democratic institutional structures in indigenous communities is often not an option.

peoples in an institutional process, the more legitimate are the process and its results'.[50] Whereas earlier research feared that an emphasis on procedural solutions and participation mainly served as a 'disempowering shift from substantive political goals'[51] (while calling self-determination a substantive goal), the adoption of UNDRIP made this argument groundless. Indeed, as some authors have argued more recently, the adoption of UNDRIP has underscored the importance of indigenous participation as an axiom of law and policy-making to be respected not only in relations between states but also at the domestic level.[52]

To conclude, various strands of social and legal theory view a procedural approach to be more effective than creating substantive rules.[53] This conclusion extends to resolving problems related to interfacing modern law and local traditions. Indeed, as several socio-psychological studies have demonstrated, fair procedures enhance the readiness to accept results, decisions or sentences as being just throughout different groups and cultures.[54]

3.2 A Procedural Approach to Trade in ICH

How could a procedural approach be implemented in situations where a decision must be taken about who can legitimately decide whether an asset of indigenous culture can be traded or must be treated as *res extra commercium* because of its sacred or otherwise important meaning for the community? Here, interests of traditional culture and interests of the global market will often be difficult to reconcile. Whereas an indigenous group as the holder of TK or TCE will primarily be interested in free, prior and informed consent (FPIC) when deciding about the tradability of a knowledge asset, the primary interest of the market will be legal certainty.

In practice, three types of disputes concerning control/ownership over or of TK or TCE are most likely:

---

[50] Chris Tennant, 'Indigenous Peoples, International Institutions, and the International Legal Literature from 1945–1993' (1994) *Human Rights Quarterly*, 16 (1), pp. 1–57, at pp. 49–52.

[51] Ibid., at p. 56.

[52] Claire Charters, 'A Self-Determination Approach to Justifying Indigenous Peoples' Participation in International Law and Policy Making' (2010) *International Journal on Minority and Group Rights*, 17, pp. 215–40, at pp. 230–32. See also Stephen Allen, 'The UN Declaration on the Rights of Indigenous Peoples and the Limits of the International Legal Project', in Stephen Allen and Alexandra Xanthaki (eds), *Reflections on the UN Declaration on the Rights of Indigenous Peoples,* Oxford and Portland, OR: Hart Publishing, 2011, pp. 225–56, at pp. 250–53, discussing indigenous peoples' interests in national and international law from the perspective of Habermas's work on communicative ethics.

[53] Similarly, Taubman, supra note 36, at p. 530, considers establishing alternative dispute resolution mechanisms to be more effective than creating new IP rights to assure effective protection of indigenous cultural knowledge.

[54] Günter Bierbrauer and Edgar Klinger, 'Verfahrensgerechtigkeit/Procedural Justice', in Renate Volbert and Max Steller (eds), *Handbuch der Rechtspsychologie*, Göttingen et al.: Hogrefe, 2008, pp. 507–18; and Tom R. Tyler, *Social Justice in a Diverse Society*, Oxford: WestviewPress, 1997, at pp. 75–102.

1. dispute between an indigenous community and a non-indigenous third party;
2. dispute between an indigenous community and one of its individual members;
3. dispute between two indigenous communities.

In all three cases the first and central problem requiring clarification is the definition of the indigenous community that can legitimately assert control or property rights in a knowledge asset. There exists no legally binding definition of 'indigenous peoples' at the international level.[55] The most often cited definition comes from José R. Martinez Cobo, as the Special Rapporteur of the Sub-Commission on Prevention of Discrimination and Protection of Minorities, and is contained in addendum 4 of a seminal report that he prepared in 1986–87. Paragraph 379 provides:

> Indigenous communities, peoples and nations are those which, having a historical continuity with pre-invasion and pre-colonial societies that developed on their territories, consider themselves distinct from other sectors of the societies now prevailing in those territories, or parts of them. They form at present non-dominant sectors of society and are determined to preserve, develop and transmit to future generations their ancestral territories, and their ethnic identity, as the basis of their continued existence as peoples, in accordance with their own cultural patterns, social institutions and legal systems.[56]

With regard to historical continuity, paragraph 380 requires an extended period of time reaching into the present of one or more of several factors, including occupation of ancestral lands, common ancestry with the original occupants of these lands, social organisation, language, and so on.

In line with this definition and with a view to providing practical guidance, Erica-Irene Daes, chair of the UN Working Group on Indigenous Populations from 1984 to 2001 and initial drafter of UNDRIP, suggested that four criteria should be examined in order to establish whether there is an indigenous community or group. These comprise:

1. a community's priority in time with regard to the occupation and use of a territory;
2. aspects of language and social organisation;
3. self-identification as well as self-recognition by other groups; and
4. experience of subjugation, marginalisation, dispossession, exclusion or discrimination, whether or not these conditions persist.[57]

Whereas it will be generally sufficient to rely on the self-identification of a group as indigenous, a clarification would be necessary if the control that a group derives from its indigenous identity is disputed by an indigenous or non-indigenous third party. If we start with the scenario where the third party involved is non-indigenous, the question needs to

---

[55] John Scott and Federico Lenzerini, 'International Indigenous and Human Rights Law in the Context of Trade in Indigenous Cultural Heritage', in this volume.

[56] UN, José R. Martinez Cobo, 'Study of the Problem of Discrimination Against Indigenous Populations', (UN Doc. E/CN.4/Sub.2/1986/7 and Add. 1–4, 1986).

[57] Erica-Irene Daes (Chairperson-Rapporteur of the Working Group on Indigenous Populations), 'The Concept of "Indigenous Peoples"' (1997) *Australian Indigenous Law Reporter*, 2 (1), pp. 162–74, at p. 173.

be clarified as to how indigenous laws and customs and modern law should interface. Should this collision of laws be resolved within a framework of indigenous laws and customs or within a framework of modern law?

In Australia, where such questions arise regularly in the realm of Aboriginal land claim cases, it is modern Australian law that formulates the 'interface rule'. According to Australian case law, an Aboriginal people putting forward a native title claim is required to prove:

1. the existence of a distinct community;
2. a traditional connection with or occupation of the land at issue under the laws and customs of the group; and
3. the maintenance of this connection.[58]

Aboriginal claimants bringing a native title case before a court have thus to accept that their claim will be squeezed into the doctrinal frame of native title that is provided by Australian common law. For the claimants, the unavoidable consequence of this 'choice' of modern law as the framework for resolving such a dispute is losing epistemological sovereignty since indigenous laws and customs are subjugated under the categories imposed by Australian common law.[59] To illustrate a consequence of this, it is sufficient to point to difficulties that Aborigines have been facing in the procedure of giving evidence. In earlier years, affidavits of Aboriginal witnesses were excluded by Australian judges as a means of proving links with their land arguably because they are mere 'hearsay'; statements of anthropologists, however, were recognised as evidence.[60] The situation has improved more recently in land rights disputes where Aboriginal evidence is now generally combined with anthropologists' evidence.[61] Nonetheless, observers have noted

---

58 Lisa Strelein, *Compromised Jurisprudence: Native Title Cases Since Mabo,* Canberra: Aboriginal Studies Press, 2006, at p. 13.

59 From an Aboriginal perspective, the problem of native title is its logical inconsistency. Although the source of native title is not the common law but the traditional laws and customs, the assumption that sovereignty was acquired by the Crown at the moment of British settlement is not questioned. If constructed consistently, native title would require recognition of 'a form of sovereignty' of the colonised people. In reality, however, the law of the traditional inhabitants is subjugated under the law of the colonisers and treated as an element of fact, not law. For a detailed discussion and references see Graber, 'Aboriginal Self-Determination', supra note 21, at p. 28. For an analysis of similar logical inconsistencies existing in US law, see Mark Rifkin, 'Indigenizing Agamben: Rethinking Sovereignty in Light of the "Peculiar" Status of Native Peoples' (2009) *Cultural Critique,* 72, pp. 88–124.

60 For an analysis see Christoph Antons, 'Folklore Protection in Australia: Who is Expert in Aboriginal Tradition?', in Elke Kurz-Milcke and Gerd Gigerenzer (eds), *Experts in Science and Society,* New York: Kluwer, 2004, pp. 85–103, at pp. 91–8.

61 See Christoph Antons, 'Foster v Mountford: Cultural Confidentiality in a Changing Australia', in Andrew T. Kenyon, Megan Richardson and Sam Ricketson (eds), *Landmarks in Australian Intellectual Property Law*, New York: Cambridge University Press, 2009, pp. 110–25, at p. 121. *Neowarra*, one of the biggest native title cases in Australian history, may serve as an illustration. Here, testimonials of Aboriginal witnesses were sometimes used to complement expert opinions provided by anthropologists. See, for example, *Neowarra v Western Australia* (2003) FCA 1402, at para. 25 Sundberg J. What is more, with regard to determining the significance of Wanjina

'that most of the leading native title and heritage protection judgements devote considerably more space to the evidence of anthropologists, historians and archaeologists than the evidence of Aborigines'.[62]

In contrast, the Native American Graves Protection and Repatriation Act (NAGPRA) of the United States is an example demonstrating a greater responsiveness of modern law vis-à-vis indigenous custom. The primary purpose of NAGPRA is to resolve conflicts related to the allocation of old or newly excavated human remains, funerary objects, cultural objects, and so on, of claimed indigenous ownership.[63] The law of evidence provided by the NAGPRA framework does not require an indigenous community to present sharp-edged proof meeting modern scientific standards, but accepts several soft forms of proof, including stories told by indigenous witnesses to show a *cultural affiliation* with a claimed object.[64] Although it is still modern law setting the standard for NAGPRA cases, the subordination of indigenous custom under modern law is cushioned by procedural flexibility towards indigenous social practices.

The second type of dispute, that is, disputes between an indigenous community and one of its (former) individual members, involves conflicts between traditional rights of the community and individual rights of a group member who no longer fully identifies with the values of the group. This is a type of conflict that may arise because indigenous culture cannot be immunised against modernisation and it may happen that an individual (indigenous) artist will drift from tribal to modern patterns of artistic expression, due to greater exposure to the global art system.[65] Such a 'modernised' artist may also want to commercialise his or her creations by making use of the protection afforded by modern IP law although he or she may have been 'inspired' by traditional cultural knowledge. The indigenous group, however, may claim that the individual artist in producing the artwork was making use of indigenous cultural knowledge that is controlled by the group.[66]

For a conflict rule in this case I suggest relying on UNDRIP, protecting the right of an indigenous group to live according to its cultural practices, as provided by the right of self-government. With regard to collisions between group rights and rights of individual members of the group, Article 34 UNDRIP states that, as a rule, universally respected individual human rights prevail. Consequently, a weighting of conflicting group rights and individual rights will be necessary on a case-by-case basis and considering the weight of the human rights involved. As a first step in the resolution of such a dispute, I suggest (for the reasons outlined in section 3.3, below) a procedure of *national* law providing for a

---

and Wungurr for Aboriginal culture, Justice Sundberg made extensive use of Aboriginal expertise (ibid., at paras 164–85). For detailed information on this case see Graber, 'Aboriginal Self-Determination', supra note 21.

62 Gary Edmond, 'Thick Decisions: Expertise, Advocacy and Reasonableness in the Federal Court of Australia' (2004) *Oceania*, 74, pp. 190–230, at p. 220.

63 On NAGPRA see Goldberg, supra note 24.

64 See Karolina Kuprecht, 'The Concept of "Cultural Affiliation" in NAGPRA: Its Potentials and Limits in the Global Protection of Indigenous Cultural Property Rights' (2012) *International Journal of Cultural Property*, 19, pp. 33–36, at pp. 38–41.

65 For more information see Graber, 'Modern Law and CEs', supra note 38, at pp. 168–9.

66 For examples see Peter Shand, 'Scenes from the Colonial Catwalk: Cultural Appropriation, Intellectual Property Rights, and Fashion' (2002) *Cultural Analysis,* 3, pp. 47–88.

presumption that the TK or TCE at issue is controlled by the indigenous group, according to indigenous laws and customs. Indigenous control would imply that the group would have the right to determine who is authorised to 'speak' for the group.[67] Accordingly, an individual person challenging the application of indigenous laws and customs would have to carry the burden of proof to show that modern IP law applies. Rebutting the presumption of indigenous ownership/control will be very difficult since the individual claimant would basically have to demonstrate that the knowledge assets at issue – with the approval of the indigenous community – left the 'jurisdiction' of indigenous laws and customs and entered the jurisdiction of modern law. If such a dispute cannot be resolved amicably, it should be decided by a specialised court, arbitral tribunal or other judicial authority that is in equal parts composed of indigenous and non-indigenous members.[68]

The establishment of institutions capable of assuring legal certainty is a precept for a licit market in TK and TCE to build up. Consequently, rules providing an interface between indigenous custom and modern law will be crucial. This is again a problem to be resolved primarily at the national level, and interface rules will depend on the properties of the knowledge asset traded. With regard to specific IP aspects of indigenous knowledge and culture, procedures regulating the interplay between modern law and traditional custom exist in New Zealand. These rules are designed to resolve conflicts of trade mark registration. According to the New Zealand Trade Marks Act, trade marks that are offensive to Māori must not be registered.[69] In cases of doubt as to whether a trade mark actually causes offence, the Commissioner of Trade Marks seeks advice from a specially created Māori Advisory Committee.[70] According to Susy Frankel, 'the Commissioner has not differed from the Committee's advice' to date. However, such a difference would be possible if the applicant for the trade mark 'submits contrary advice from a different group of Māori'.[71]

With regard to the third type of dispute, that is, disputes between (two or more) indigenous communities concerning control of indigenous knowledge assets, one could again learn from procedures existing under NAGPRA combining the concept of cultural affiliation with requirements of transparency and notification. The factual context of the NAGPRA procedure of interest is a request by an indigenous group for repatriation of human remains and cultural items that is addressed to a museum currently possessing the claimed objects. The request is likely to be triggered by the museum's notification of an

---

[67] Ibid., at p. 64.

[68] If the indigenous community wins, it would be up to it to decide on the basis of its laws and customs whether the TK or TCE can be traded and under what conditions ownership can be transferred to third parties. If the individual claimant wins, then he or she will be free to trade the knowledge asset according to the rules of modern IP and/or property law.

[69] See Trade Marks Act 2002 (NZ), s. 17(b)(ii).

[70] Section 177 of the Trade Marks Act requires the Commissioner of Trade Marks to appoint an advisory committee to advise the Commissioner whether the registration of a trade mark that is, or appears to be, derivative of Māori text and imagery is likely to be offensive to Māori. For more information see Susy Frankel, 'A New Zealand Perspective on the Protection of Mātauranga Māori (Traditional Knowledge)', in this volume [hereinafter Frankel, 'NZ Perspective'].

[71] Frankel, 'TMs, TK and CIP', supra note 37, at pp. 450–51.

inventory in the US Federal Register[72] or by a written summary of objects communicated to tribes that could be culturally affiliated.[73] The purpose of the inventory or summary is to provide information on the Native American human remains and cultural items in the museum's possession. Based on consultation with native representatives, cultural affiliation of the claimant will then be evaluated. If the request for repatriation is contested by another indigenous group, claiming to have a better right to the object, NAGPRA provides that the indigenous groups must resolve the dispute among themselves.[74] As long as the conflict is not resolved, the claimed object remains in the custody of the museum.[75]

3.3 Interim Conclusions

The examples of native title in Australian case law and NAGPRA in the United States show that it would not make sense to develop a one-size-fits-all solution at the international level for resolving disputes on the allocation of indigenous ownership. Indeed, UNDRIP recognises in its Preamble 'that the situation of indigenous peoples varies from region to region and from country to country and that the significance of national and regional particularities and various historical and cultural backgrounds should be taken into consideration'.[76] Accordingly, with regard to dispute settlement, the best way to take account of this plurality of indigenous cultures would probably be procedures to be agreed on at national level – possibly in a treaty concluded between the respective indigenous peoples and the state of which they are part – or in an instrument of secondary law. The concept of cultural affiliation, as applied under NAGPRA, shows that it is quite possible to work out procedures showing respect for the particularities of indigenous forms of social organisation and compensating for the difficulties indigenous claimants face when required to prove ownership, while still providing for legal certainty. What would be necessary at the level of international law would be some kind of interface rule stating who is responsible for resolving problems related to defining 'indigenous peoples', 'TK' and 'TCE'. Moreover, the codification of some guiding principles for the protection of TK and TCE would be necessary at the international level, including mutual recognition of national standards, FPIC, access and benefit-sharing and the obligation of states to protect TK and TCE against misappropriation.[77] These are all issues where human rights concerns overlap with the interests of protecting indigenous peoples' knowledge assets. It is thus an open question (going beyond the scope of this chapter) as to whether these issues should

---

[72] This requirement applies to museums and similar agencies that are federally funded; see NAGPRA of 1990, 25 U.S.C. § 3003(d).

[73] NAGPRA of 1990, 25 U.S.C. § 3004(a).

[74] NAGPRA of 1990, 25 U.S.C. § 3001(3)(C and D), see Kuprecht, supra note 64, at p. 18.

[75] For more detailed information on these NAGPRA procedures see James A.R. Nafziger et al., *Cultural Law: International, Comparative, and Indigenous*, Cambridge and New York: Cambridge University Press, 2010, at pp. 427–9.

[76] UNDRIP, supra note 20, recital 23.

[77] See Peter Drahos, 'A Networked Responsive Regulatory Approach to Protecting Traditional Knowledge', in Daniel J. Gervais (ed.), *Intellectual Property, Trade and Development. Strategies to Optimize Economic Development in a TRIPS-plus Era,* Oxford: Oxford University Press, 2007, pp. 385–415, at pp. 396–401.

be addressed in a treaty on TK and TCE or, for example, in a binding international convention on the rights of indigenous peoples.

New Zealand seems to be one of the pioneer users of procedural approaches in areas of trade in traditional knowledge. It is interesting to note that New Zealand relies on a procedural approach not only when interfacing intellectual property and traditional knowledge protection but also when reserving traditional rights of Māori in its free trade agreements.[78] The situation in New Zealand is, however, unique because the Treaty of Waitangi, concluded between the Māori and the British Crown in 1840, not only provides the Māori with strong rights to their traditional knowledge and 'treasures',[79] but generally permits Māori to negotiate on a par with the New Zealand government. To be sure, one should not idealise the situation in New Zealand, as the government is nevertheless a political body, accountable to the general population. Hence, it is liable to oppose Māori interests in seeking to balance Māori demands against the greater good for New Zealand, even if the Māori perceive that the interests are protected by the Treaty.

4. INDIGENOUS CULTURE AND DEVELOPMENT IN INTERNATIONAL ECONOMIC LAW

In the previous sections of this chapter, I found that participation of indigenous peoples is the solution to many problems of legitimacy in trade and development of ICH. Based on this insight, I proposed a procedural method to cope with differences between indigenous and modern worldviews that complicate the implementation of rules for legitimate trade in a modern legal context. In the remainder of the chapter I will study the potential of international law and policy-making to better stimulate trade and development in ICH. To this end, I will first briefly assess the current status of indigenous culture and development in international economic law and policy-making. In doing this, activities sponsored by a number of intergovernmental organisations, including the World Trade Organization (WTO), the World Intellectual Property Organization (WIPO), the United Nations Educational, Scientific and Cultural Organization (UNESCO)[80] and the Convention on Biological Diversity (CBD), stand to the fore. With the exception of UNESCO, most of these

---

[78] For more information, see Frankel, 'NZ Perspective', supra note 70.

[79] Treaty of Waitangi, Article 2. The Māori version of the Treaty uses the term 'taonga', which extends to both the tangible and intangible. See ibid; and Jessica C. Lai, 'Māori Culture in the Modern World: Its Creation, Appropriation and Trade', *University of Lucerne, Switzerland,* i-call Working Paper No. 2 (2010), at pp. 17–19, available at http://www.unilu.ch/files/icall_working_paper_2011_02_lai_maori_cultural_heritage_undrip.pdf.

[80] For the purpose of this chapter, I consider the most relevant activities of UNESCO (particularly those in the field of protecting and promoting the diversity of cultural expressions) as belonging to international economic law. As a justification it is sufficient to refer to UNESCO Convention on Cultural Diversity (CCD) recognising in its Article 1(g) (and in recital 18 of the Preamble) that cultural products have a dual nature that includes also an economic relevance as goods or services. Indeed, the CCD plays an important role in the regulation of trade and culture at the international, regional and national levels. UNESCO, Convention on the Protection and Promotion of the Diversity of Cultural Expressions, 2440 UNTS 311 (adopted on 20 October 2005, entered into force 18 March 2007). See Christoph B. Graber, 'Trade and Culture', in Rüdiger

activities are IP-centred. In section 5, I will then explore an alternative avenue for promoting trade and development in ICH that would go beyond IP-centred approaches.

4.1 WTO/TRIPS

In the WTO, development as an end of trade liberalisation is prominently anchored in the Preamble of the Marrakesh Agreement establishing the WTO[81] and in several declarations emanating from ministerial conferences. Moreover, discussions on special and differential treatment of developing countries are taking place in the Committee on Trade and Development, one of the WTO's regular bodies where all members are represented. Since the WTO is a state-centred organisation, these considerations relate to developing countries. Developmental interests of indigenous peoples, however, are not independently mentioned and there is no language in the covered agreements of the WTO directly addressing indigenous issues.[82] Whereas the interests of certain developing countries may overlap with the interests of their indigenous population to some extent, this has often not been the case for indigenous peoples of industrialised countries such as the United States, Canada, Australia and New Zealand.

While the TRIPS Agreement[83] of the WTO is without question the most important legal instrument regulating trade in creative expression and innovation, it is a matter of debate whether TK and TCE are covered by its disciplines.[84] A general feeling that numerous modes of TK and TCE remain outside the scope of IP protection led the Doha Ministerial Conference of the WTO in 2001 to explicitly instruct the TRIPS Council,[85] in paragraph 19, to examine, *inter alia*, 'the protection of traditional knowledge and folklore'.[86] In 2005, the Hong Kong Ministerial Conference reaffirmed the mandate for the TRIPS Council in paragraph 44 of its Declaration.[87] On the one hand, both Ministerial Declarations thereby formalised the TRIPS Council's work programme, which had started a few

---

Wolfrum (ed.), *The Max Planck Encyclopedia of Public International Law*, available online at www.mpepil.com, last updated 2010 [hereinafter Graber, 'Trade and Culture'].

81 WTO, Marrakesh Agreement Establishing the World Trade Organization, 1867 UNTS 154; 33 ILM 1144 (adopted on 15 April 1994, entered into force 1 January 1995).

82 See also Macmillan, supra note 13, in this volume.

83 WTO, Agreement on Trade-Related Aspects of Intellectual Property Rights, Marrakesh Agreement Establishing the World Trade Organization, Annex 1C, 1869 UNTS 299; 33 ILM 1197 (adopted on 15 April 1994, entered into force 1 January 1995).

84 Graber, 'Institutionalization of Creativity', supra note 35, at pp. 241–2.

85 The Council for Trade-Related Aspects of Intellectual Property Rights (TRIPS Council) is one of the three sectoral councils operating under the General Council. It is the body, open to all members of the WTO, responsible for the administration of the TRIPS Agreement and in particular for monitoring the operation of the Agreement.

86 WTO, 'Doha Ministerial Declaration', (WTO Doc. WT/MIN(01)/DEC/1, 2001), adopted 14 November 2001, at Doha, Qatar.

87 WTO, 'Hong Kong Ministerial Declaration', (WTO Doc. WT/MIN(05)/DEC, 2005), adopted 18 December 2005. Paragraph 44 reads as follows:

> We take note of the work undertaken by the Council for TRIPS pursuant to paragraph 19 of the Doha Ministerial Declaration and agree that this work shall continue on the basis of paragraph 19 of the Doha Ministerial Declaration and the progress made in the Council for TRIPS to date. The General Council shall report on its work in this regard to our next Session.

years before the first Declaration in the context of the review of Article 27.3(b) of the TRIPS Agreement.[88] Article 27.3(b) provides exceptions to the general rule that patents are to be available for any inventions. It relates to the issue of TK in so far as it contains the exception that allows countries to exclude certain types of inventions from patenting, that is, plants, animals and 'essentially' biological processes. On the other hand, the Ministerial Declarations did not limit the examination to questions relating to TK (and its patentability), but added to the TRIPS Council's mandate the examination of the protection of 'folklore', which tends to be examined more through the lens of copyright. Most statements made in the TRIPS Council have related to TK and relatively little has been said with respect to TCE or folklore.[89]

One of the key focuses of the discussion has been the relation of the TRIPS Agreement with the Convention on Biological Diversity (CBD;[90] see section 4.4, below).[91] Since 2003, work on this point has also been undertaken outside the work programme of the TRIPS Council as part of a consultative process carried out by the Director-General of the WTO. His report of 9 June 2008[92] was fed into the July 2008 ministerial meeting, but there was no outcome to this meeting. The fact that TK and TCE became at all an issue of WTO law is mainly a result of developing countries entering the fora where international IPRs are being discussed and negotiated.[93] According to Gervais, this has also led to a more or less direct representation of indigenous peoples' interests at an international level.[94] However, this is true only for a few countries, including Bolivia[95] and Venezuela. Beyond that, the WTO is not an organisation where indigenous interests are well represented.

---

[88] Hannu Wager, 'Biodiversity, Traditional Knowledge and Folklore: Work on Related IP Matters in the WTO' (2008) *Intercultural Human Rights Law Review*, 3, pp. 215–27, at p. 218.

[89] WTO, TRIPS Council Secretariat, 'The Protection of Traditional Knowledge and Folklore: Summary of Issues Raised and Points Made', (WTO Doc. IP/C/W/370/Rev.1, 2006), at p. 2.

[90] Rio Convention on Biological Diversity (CBD), 1760 UNTS 79; 31 ILM 818 (opened for signature 5 June 1992, entered into force 29 December 1993).

[91] Martin A. Girsberger, 'Legal Protection of Traditional Cultural Expressions: A Policy Perspective', in Christoph B. Graber and Mira Burri-Nenova (eds), *Intellectual Property and Traditional Cultural Expressions in a Digital Environment*, Cheltenham, UK: Edward Elgar, 2008, pp. 123–49, at p. 134.

[92] WTO, General Council Trade Negotiations Committee, Report by the Director-General, 'Issues Related to the Extension of the Protection of Geographical Indications Provided for in Article 23 of the TRIPS Agreement to Products other than Wines and Spirits and those Related to the Relationship Between the TRIPS Agreement and the Convention on Biological Diversity', (WTO Doc. WT/GC/W/591 – TN/C/W/50, 2008).

[93] According to Gervais '[t]he participation of these countries is essential to ensure that intellectual property norms are understood by all and updated in ways that reflect the concerns of all nations at the tables to negotiate.' Daniel J. Gervais, 'The Internationalization of Intellectual Property: New Challenges from the Very Old and the Very New' (2002) *Fordham Intellectual Property Media & Entertainment Law Journal*, 12, pp. 929–90, at p. 941.

[94] Ibid., at p. 956.

[95] Bolivia's representative stated in the TRIPS Council that Bolivia perceives TK and folklore (or TCE) as being part of one single, holistic cultural tradition, and thereby rejects the pure IP perspective realised in the TRIPS Agreement. See, for example, WTO, 'Minutes of the Meeting on 17 June 2008 of the TRIPS Council', (WTO Doc. IP/C/M/5, 2008).

4.2 WIPO

WIPO's response to the non-existent international protection of indigenous knowledge assets was the establishment of the Intergovernmental Committee on Intellectual Property and Genetic Resources, Traditional Knowledge and Folklore (IGC) in 2001. Although the discussions in the WIPO IGC on *sui generis* instruments to protect TK, TCE and genetic resources have been ongoing for more than ten years, relatively little progress has been made. After 19 sessions, the IGC has reached the stage of text-based negotiations, but no agreement is in view even with regard to the key objectives and principles of the new TCE and TK instruments, and views diverge between indigenous and non-indigenous stakeholders and often even between indigenous communities.[96] For indigenous peoples, one central question is whether the new instruments should also extend to TCE and TK of non-indigenous origin.

The idea of 'development' is strongly present in the texts drafted by the IGC.[97] With the launch of its Development Agenda 2007, WIPO generally started to look at IP from a development perspective.[98] The purpose of this broader view is to confront the vast social effects of IP law beyond creating incentives for innovation and maximising revenues. The scope of the WIPO Development Agenda includes knowledge assets of indigenous peoples in developing and developed countries.

4.3 UNESCO

Strengthening the contribution of culture to sustainable development has been a goal of UNESCO policy-making since the launch of the World Decade for Cultural

---

[96] For more information see Christoph Antons, 'Intellectual Property Rights in Indigenous Cultural Heritage: Basic Concepts and Continuing Controversies', in this volume; and Martin Girsberger and Benny Müller, 'International Trade in Indigenous Cultural Heritage: An IP Practitioners' Perspective', in this volume.

[97] In the Draft on TCE, to this end two objectives are relevant: objective (iii), which aims to 'contribute to the welfare and sustainable economic, cultural, environmental and social development of such peoples and communities'; and objective (xii), which aims to promote the development of indigenous peoples and communities and 'legitimate trading activities'. Objective (xii) promotes the use of TCE for the development of indigenous peoples and communities, where desired by them. Moreover, the objective recognises the TCE as 'an asset of the communities that identify with them, such as through the development and expansion of marketing opportunities for tradition-based creations and innovations'. WIPO, IGC, Secretariat, 'The Protection of Traditional Cultural Expressions', Nineteenth Session (WIPO Doc. WIPO/GRTKF/IC/19/4, 2011).

[98] The WIPO Development Agenda was established by the WIPO General Assembly in October 2007. It includes a set of 45 recommendations designed to enhance the development dimension of the organisation's activities. Recommendation 18 (related to norm-setting, flexibilities, public policy and public domain) urges the IGC 'to accelerate the process on the protection of genetic resources, traditional knowledge and folklore, without prejudice to any outcome, including the possible development of an international instrument or instruments.' In addition to the adoption of the Development Agenda, WIPO Member States also approved a recommendation to establish a Committee on Development and Intellectual Property. See generally the chapters in Neil W. Netanel (ed.), *The Development Agenda. Global Intellectual Property and Developing Countries*, New York: Oxford University Press, 2009.

Development (1988–98). With regard to its activities with indigenous peoples, UNESCO stresses that it is 'framed by its missions to protect and promote cultural diversity, encourage intercultural dialogue and enhance linkages between culture and development'.[99] Notwithstanding these euphonious promises, UNESCO's most relevant standard-setting instrument in this context, the Convention on Cultural Diversity (CCD),[100] does not respond sufficiently to the interests of indigenous peoples.[101] The failure to properly protect cultural interests of indigenous peoples can be explained by the drafting history of the CCD. The convention was designed by its drafters to protect national entertainment industries rather than creative expressions of indigenous peoples.[102] Indeed, a reference to TCE and indigenous peoples was introduced only at a late stage of the negotiations.[103] Although the adopted text does mention TCE and indigenous peoples a few times,[104] the relevant provisions do not address the rights of the indigenous peoples themselves but those of the states whose territory is affected.[105] Similarly, the 2003 UNESCO Convention for the Safeguarding of the Intangible Cultural Heritage[106] is not considered by indigenous peoples as adequately furthering their interests.[107]

---

[99] See http://www.unesco.org/en/cultural-diversity/action-in-favour-of-cultural-diversity/unesco-and-indigenous-peoples-partnership-for-cultural-diversity/ .

[100] Supra note 80.

[101] For a comprehensive assessment of further UNESCO instruments relevant for ICH, including the 1972 Convention Concerning the Protection of the World Cultural and Natural Heritage (1037 UNTS 151 (adopted on 16 November 1972, entered into force 17 December 1975)) and the 2003 Convention for the Safeguarding of the Intangible Cultural Heritage (2368 UNTS 1 (adopted on 17 October 2003, entered into force 20 April 2006)), see Coombe and Turcotte, supra note 3. See also Francesco Bandarin, 'International Trade in Indigenous Cultural Heritage: Comments from UNESCO in Light of its International Standard-Setting Instruments in the Field of Culture', in this volume.

[102] See Federico Lenzerini, 'Indigenous Peoples' Cultural Rights and the Controversy Over Commercial Use of Their Traditional Knowledge', in Francesco Francioni and Martin Scheinin (eds), *Cultural Human Rights*, Leiden et al.: Martinus Nijhoff Publishers, 2008, pp. 119–49, at p. 130.

[103] See Christoph B. Graber, 'Traditional Cultural Expressions in a Matrix of Copyright, Cultural Diversity and Human Rights', in Fiona Macmillan (ed.), *New Directions in Copyright Law*, vol. V, Cheltenham, UK: Edward Elgar, 2007, pp. 45–71, at pp. 54–5.

[104] Paragraph 8 of the Preamble recognises 'the importance of traditional knowledge'. Furthermore, paragraph 13 of the Preamble recognises that diversity of cultural expressions, including 'traditional cultural expressions', is an important factor that allows peoples and individuals to express and to share with others their ideas and values. Finally, paragraph 15 of the Preamble, Article 2 (principle 3) and Article 7.1(a) refer to the relevance of the CCD for persons belonging to indigenous peoples.

[105] Graber, 'Trade and Culture', supra note 80, at para. 22; Mira Burri-Nenova et al., 'The Protection and Promotion of Cultural Diversity in a Digital Networked Environment: Mapping Possible Advances to Coherence', in Thomas Cottier and Panagiotis Delimatsis (eds), *The Prospects of International Trade Regulation: From Fragmentation to Coherence*, Cambridge and New York: Cambridge University Press, 2011, pp. 359–93, at pp. 368–9.

[106] Supra note 101.

[107] As Coombe and Turcotte, supra note 3, highlight, indigenous peoples were not involved in the drafting of the UNESCO Convention for the Safeguarding of the Intangible Cultural Heritage.

4.4 CBD

Over the last few decades, the Convention on Biological Diversity (CBD)[108] has gained prominence as a forum for discussing issues of traditional knowledge. Although the CBD focuses on TK that is associated with genetic resources, discussions on disclosure or certification of origin held therein may also be relevant for other forms of TK relating to the subject matter of intellectual property applications. With regard to access to and benefit-sharing of knowledge that is held by indigenous peoples, the adoption of the Nagoya Protocol by the CBD Conference of Parties in October 2010 is most important.[109] Its Article 7 requires parties to ensure that traditional knowledge associated with genetic resources that is held by indigenous and local communities is accessed with the free, prior and informed consent (FPIC) of these communities, and that mutually agreed terms have been established.[110] It thus satisfies requirements of indigenous participation in any legal or political process involving their traditional knowledge, as outlined above (sections 2 and 3.2). Furthermore, Article 5 of the Protocol provides for the need to ensure that benefits arising from the use of traditional knowledge associated with genetic resources are shared in a fair and equitable way with indigenous peoples, in accordance with domestic regulation. Reflecting the institutionalisation of access and benefit-sharing rights of indigenous peoples in Articles 7 and 5, Scott and Lenzerini predict, in their contribution to this volume, that the Nagoya Protocol will potentially play an important role in future discussions on the regulation of trade in ICH.[111]

4.5 Summary

To summarise, it appears that the interrelationship between cultural knowledge, trade and development has entered the thinking of the most important fora of international economic law. The above assessment of activities in WTO/TRIPS, WIPO, UNESCO and CBD is confirmed in the broader context of the UN in general by the 2008 UN Creative Economy Report.[112] This report was drafted by the United Nations Conference on Trade and

---

This explains many of the identified shortcomings of this instrument and questions its legitimacy to further the interests of indigenous peoples. See also Bandarin, supra note 101.

[108] CBD, supra note 90.

[109] Nagoya Protocol on Access to Genetic Resources and the Fair and Equitable Sharing of Benefits Arising from their Utilization to the Convention on Biological Diversity (UN Doc. UNEP/CBD/COP/DEC/X/1) (adopted on 19 October 2010). For a more comprehensive assessment of the Nagoya Protocol and its relationship with the CBD, see Scott and Lenzerini, supra note 55.

[110] The Nagoya Protocol was open for signatures until 1 February 2012.

[111] Scott and Lenzerini, supra note 55.

[112] According to the United Nations Creative Economy Report 2008, 'a new development paradigm is emerging that links the economy and culture, embracing economic, cultural, technological and social aspects of development at both the macro and micro levels. Central to the new paradigm is the fact that creativity, knowledge and access to information are increasingly recognized as powerful engines driving economic growth and promoting development in a globalizing world.' (UN, UNCTAD, 'United Nations Creative Economy Report 2008 "The Challenge of Assessing the Creative Economy: Towards Informed Policy-making"', (UN Doc. UNCTAD/DITC/2008/2, 2008), at p. 3).

Development (UNCTAD) and the United Nations Development Programme (UNDP) in cooperation with UNESCO, WIPO and the International Trade Centre (ITC). It emphasised the link between the economy and culture as a 'new development paradigm' and Chapter 6.4 explicitly deals with TCE. The new trend goes hand in hand with the dynamics in the UN General Assembly, which, on 19 December 2010, adopted a resolution on culture and development as a follow-up to the 2010 UN Millennium Summit.[113] This resolution emphasises the important contribution of culture for sustainable development and for the achievement of national and international development objectives, including the Millennium Development Goals.[114] This resolution is of particular relevance, since the eight Millennium Development Goals do not mention culture explicitly.

To be sure, these noble words remain merely programmatic and not much has been undertaken to effectively improve the status of indigenous peoples and independently address their interests in the realm of culture, trade and development. Often, indigenous interests and interests of developing countries have been mentioned in the same breath. However, as recent discussions have shown, indigenous peoples have interests that are distinct from interests of developing countries.[115] International law, which is generally state-centred, does not seem to be prepared to recognise indigenous peoples' international juridical personality beyond declaratory texts. Although some international fora have intensified their efforts to facilitate indigenous participation,[116] the holders of TK and TCE face insurmountable obstacles in finding the necessary means and capacity to effectively play a part in the relevant discussions and negotiations.[117] It also seems doubtful whether any of the mentioned instruments under negotiation, could – if eventually entered into force – be successfully implemented in states where indigenous rights of self-government in cultural matters are not recognised. What is more, the ongoing discussions on creating new WIPO instruments on TCE and TK are not sufficiently coordinated with concurring debates in the TRIPS Council and/or in the CBD. The relevant activities of these fora as well as of UNESCO are determined by the respective organisation's specialisation and there is a risk that eventual outcomes will increase rather than reduce the existing fragmentation of the relevant law on ICH. These difficulties have provoked critical comments generally questioning the viability of top–down solutions to the problem.[118]

---

[113] See UNESCO, Executive Office, Sector for Culture, 'The United Nations Recognizes the Role of Culture for Development' (23 December 2010), available at http://portal.unesco.org/culture/en/ev.php-URL_ID=41466&URL_DO=DO_TOPIC&URL_SECTION=201.html

[114] See UN, United Nations Development Programme, 'What are the Millennium Development Goals?', available online at http://www.undp.org/mdg/basics.shtml.

[115] For example, see Drahos, supra note 77, at p. 394.

[116] In 2004, the Conference of Parties of the CBD established a Voluntary Trust Fund to facilitate the participation of indigenous and local communities in the work of the Convention. See UN and UNEP, 'Voluntary Fund', available at http://www.cbd.int/traditional/fund.shtml. Similarly, WIPO Members set up a Voluntary Fund in 2005 to facilitate the participation of accredited indigenous and local communities in the sessions of the IGC. See WIPO, 'Voluntary Fund', available at http://www.wipo.int/tk/en/ngoparticipation/voluntary_fund/.

[117] See Kathy Bowrey, 'International Trade in Indigenous Cultural Heritage: An Australian Perspective', in this volume; Girsberger and Müller, supra note 3; and Drahos, supra note 77, at p. 400.

[118] See Drahos, supra note 77, at pp. 414–15.

5. PROS AND CONS OF PREFERENTIAL TRADE RULES FOR INDIGENOUS PEOPLES STIMULATING A MORE ACTIVE ROLE OF INDIGENOUS PEOPLES IN GLOBAL TRADE

The analysis in the above section revealed that international economic law in its current shape does not sufficiently respond to indigenous interests in the trade and development of their cultural heritage. Whereas intellectual property aspects of international economic law have been in the foreground so far, I would now like to discuss the viability of an alternative option. The question to be studied is whether preferential trade rules for indigenous cultural goods and services would be a means for stimulating a more active role of indigenous peoples in global trade. Whereas preferential treatment in trade relations is already an important issue of international trade regulation, it has hardly been discussed whether such rules could also be drafted for indigenous peoples. The basis for the following appreciation is an earlier paper published elsewhere,[119] where I suggested studying the possibility of creating preferential rules for goods and services of indigenous origin in a WTO context and outlined a possible pathway to this end. The document was discussed as a reference paper at the expert workshop[120] from which this volume results. The following is a restatement of the original ideas and reflects what I learned from the many interesting comments expressed by a number of colleagues at that occasion.

As outlined, the WTO views the promotion of economic development as being one of the primary aims of international trade[121] and the Preamble of the WTO Agreement recognises the 'need for positive efforts designed to ensure that developing countries ... secure a share in the growth of international trade commensurate with the needs of their economic development'.[122] In this spirit, the WTO legal framework contains a number of rules providing for special and differential (S&D) treatment for developing countries, including, for example, longer transitional time periods, special rules on dispute settlement, flexibility of commitments or technical assistance.[123] Moreover, the WTO provides for a Generalised System of Preferences (GSP) exception. As GSPs are used by WTO developed-country members to increase the share of developing-country members in international trade, an exception from the most-favoured-nation (MFN) obligation of Article 1 GATT[124] is indeed necessary to avoid an inconsistency with existing multilateral obligations.

---

119 Graber, 'Institutionalization of Creativity', supra note 35.

120 The exploratory workshop on 'International Trade in Indigenous Cultural Heritage' took place in Lucerne from 17–19 January 2011. It was organised by i-call, the Research Centre for International Communications and Art Law, at the School of Law of the University of Lucerne.

121 See WTO, Doha Ministerial Declaration, supra note 86, particularly at para. 2.

122 See Marrakesh Agreement Establishing the World Trade Organization, supra note 81, Preamble, recital 2.

123 For an overview see Peter Van den Bossche, *The Law and Policy of the World Trade Organization*, 2nd edn, Cambridge: Cambridge University Press, 2008, at pp. 723–4.

124 WTO, General Agreement on Tariffs and Trade, Marrakesh Agreement Establishing the World Trade Organization, Annex 1A, 1867 UNTS 187; 33 ILM 1153 (adopted on 15 April 1994, entered into force 1 January 1995).

As Gregory Shaffer and Yvonne Apea have emphasised, it is necessary to understand the *raison d'être* and the functioning of GSPs within a historical context of colonialism. In 1947, when the GATT was signed, many signatories to the agreement still had colonies.[125] To make sure that the trade preferences granted by the colonising GATT members to their colonies would not become GATT-inconsistent, Article I:2 GATT provided for so-called 'colonial' or 'imperial' preferences. In the period of decolonisation, the former colonies sought to join forces as a group of developing countries and in 1964 UNCTAD was established as a 'counterpart to GATT that would focus on development priorities'.[126] At UNCTAD I in 1964, a report was adopted to promote the idea of trade preferences for developing countries in the form of lower tariffs.[127] Since this was inconsistent with the MFN disciplines of the GATT, a waiver for a Generalised System of Preferences favouring trade of less-developed countries was granted in 1971 for a ten-year period.[128] Shortly before the GSP waiver expired, GATT members took a decision in 1979 to permanently authorise the GSP programmes.[129] This decision, which became known as the 'Enabling Clause', was incorporated into GATT 1994.[130]

As John Jackson has pointed out, there was no legal obligation for developed countries to grant GSP programmes and 'no particularly detailed requirements as to what should be the shape and framework of GSP'.[131] As a consequence, GSP programmes were implemented by major industrialised countries at different times and with varying features.[132] Considering the rather fuzzy normative contour and multiple functionality of GSP

---

125 Gregory Shaffer and Yvonne Apea, 'GSP Programmes and Their Historical-Political-Institutional Context: Comment on Lorand Bartels', in Thomas Cottier, Joost Pauwelyn and Elisabeth Bürgi (eds), *Human Rights and International Trade*, International Economic Law Series, Oxford and New York: Oxford University Press, 2005, pp. 488–503, at p. 492.

126 Ibid., at p. 493.

127 John H. Jackson, *The World Trading System: Law and Policy of International Economic Relations*, 2nd edn, Cambridge, MA: MIT Press, 1997, at p. 322.

128 GATT Secretariat, Waiver, 'The Generalized System of Preferences' (GATT Doc. BISD 18S/24, 1971).

129 GATT, 'Differential and More Favourable Treatment, Reciprocity and Fuller Participation of Developing Countries' (GATT Doc. L/4903, 1979). Lorand Bartels, 'Conditionality in GSP Programmes: The Appellate Body Report in European Communities – Conditions for the Granting of Tariff Preferences to Developing Countries and its Implications for Conditionality in GSP Programmes', in Thomas Cottier, Joost Pauwelyn and Elisabeth Bürgi (eds), *Human Rights and International Trade*, International Economic Law Series, Oxford and New York: Oxford University Press, 2005, pp. 463–87, at p. 464.

130 For more information see Bernard Hoekman, 'More Favorable Treatment of Developing Countries: Ways Forward', in Richard Newfarmer (ed.), *Trade, Doha, and Development: Window Into the Issues*, Washington, DC: World Bank, 2006, pp. 213–21; Seung W. Chang, 'WTO for Trade and Development Post-Doha' (2007) *Journal of International Economic Law*, 10 (3), pp. 553–70; and Van den Bossche, supra note 123, at pp. 728–31.

131 Jackson, supra note 127, at p. 323.

132 According to UNCTAD, the following are currently providing GSP programmes: Australia, Belarus, Canada, the countries of the European Union, Japan, New Zealand, Norway, the Russian Federation, Switzerland, Turkey and the United States. See UNCTAD, 'Generalized System of Preferences', available at http://www.unctad.org/Templates/Page.asp?intItemID=1418&lang=1.

programmes, it seems tempting to explore whether such programmes could extend to trade preferences for cultural goods (or services) of indigenous origin.[133]

To foreclose the results of my exploration that – as mentioned above – was guided by many insightful comments from a number of colleagues, such an endeavour would be burdened by several flaws. The first flaw is related to the conditionality of GSP programmes in general. 'GSP conditionality' is a short-cut formula used to describe how GSP programmes, as a rule, provide trade preferences to developing countries under certain conditions only. The EU and the US – being the major WTO members to run a GSP programme – provide for numerous conditions to the granting of tariff preferences.[134] The open-ended scope of GSP conditionality in the EU's programme was exposed in *European Communities – Tariff Preferences*.[135] The EU GSP under scrutiny in that case provided for additional preferences that were granted to countries participating in a programme to combat drug production and trafficking. The standard of drug combat measures was apparently applied very broadly, since the European Commission found that Pakistan would meet the requirements of the scheme because of the country's 'changed position on the Taliban regime and its determination to return to democratic rule'.[136] Whereas the EU GSP provides conditions that a developing country must meet in order to be granted the additional preferences, the US follows a 'negative' approach to GSP conditionality.[137] There is a great variety of criteria that would reduce the chances of a developing country benefiting from the US GSP including, for example, communism, violation of workers' rights or child labour, or even insufficient standards of IP protection.[138]

Judgements in the academic literature regarding the pros and cons of GSP conditionality are divided. Whereas some scholars acknowledge the potential of carefully drafted conditions 'to advance the cause of human rights',[139] or to promote social goals,[140] others point to neo-colonial strands in their texture and the playing on asymmetric power relations in international trade. Philip Alston criticised the fuzzy scope of GSP programmes, which offer the US and the EC a *carte blanche* to opt for 'whatever standards they chose in a given situation'.[141] Peter Drahos and John Braithwaite denounced the US

133 See Graber, 'Institutionalization of Creativity', supra note 35, at pp. 246–8, where I have indeed suggested exploring GSP conditionality as a means to promote indigenous peoples' participation in trade with cultural heritage assets.

134 19 U.S.C. 2462. See Barnali Choudhury et al., 'A Call for a WTO Ministerial Decision on Trade and Human Rights', in Thomas Cottier and Panagiotis Delimatsis (eds), *The Prospects of International Trade Regulation: From Fragmentation to Coherence*, Cambridge and New York: Cambridge University Press, 2011, pp. 323–58, at pp. 337–8.

135 WTO, Appellate Body Report, European Communities – Conditions for the Granting of Tariff Preferences to Developing Countries, WTO Doc. WT/DS246/AB/R, adopted 20 April 2004.

136 EU Commission, 'Briefing on 12 March 2002', as quoted by Bartels, supra note 129, at p. 467.

137 Shaffer and Apea, supra note 125, at p. 494.

138 On the US GSP see Bartels, supra note 129, at p. 467; and Choudhury et al., supra note 134, at p. 337.

139 Choudhury et al., supra note 134, at p. 336.

140 For a discussion see Krista Nadakavukaren Schefer, *Social Regulation in the WTO: Trade Policy and International Legal Development*, Cheltenham, UK: Edward Elgar, 2010, at pp. 246–59.

141 Philip Alston, as quoted in Shaffer and Apea, supra note 125, at p. 497.

for having used GSP conditionality in a carrot and stick manner since the first amendment of the GSP in 1984 for the purpose of implementing higher standards of IP protection in beneficiary countries.[142] Shaffer and Apea similarly found fault with the United States' use of GSP conditionality 'as "a key lever" to press recalcitrant developing countries to agree to the inclusion of the TRIPS Agreement into the new WTO system in 1995'.[143]

The second and main flaw is the state-centralism of GSP programmes. Since indigenous peoples are not recognised as legal subjects of international law, it would be difficult to 'target' the benefits of a GSP programme at indigenous peoples. Accordingly, partners of a GSP programme would not be indigenous peoples themselves but the governments of the territories where they live. This would be problematic since the interests of indigenous peoples are often not identical to (if not in conflict with) the interests of the country where they live.[144] Would it be possible to absorb this deficiency by requiring the beneficiary country to assure participation of indigenous peoples in the drafting and administration of the GSP programme? One could consider referring to UNDRIP and obliging a beneficiary country to endorse the Declaration and respect *inter alia* the provided standards therein of indigenous self-determination and self-government or FPIC in issues related to their cultural heritage.[145] Such an approach does not seem to be excluded outright since the EU GSP provides for many references to human rights instruments.[146] According to the current EU GSP, a special incentive arrangement for sustainable development and good governance may be granted to a beneficiary country that has ratified and effectively implemented *inter alia* 16 human rights conventions.[147] In addition, the beneficiary country is obliged to accept a regulatory monitoring of the instruments' implementation as provided by the various conventions.[148]

However, in the constellation of our research involving indigenous peoples of the USA, Canada, Australia and New Zealand, this would not seem realistic. Since GSP programmes are not meant to offer preferential treatment to rich countries, it is indeed difficult to imagine a country willing to extend its GSP to the United States, for example.

To summarise, GSP programmes come at a high cost for the multilateral trading system. Although some commentators prize GSP as a means to further human rights, sceptical views prevail, criticising their fuzzy scope, and, because the allocation of benefits is frequently changed, risks of arbitrary application and a lack of legal certainty.[149] Even more important in our context is that GSP programmes are of limited benefit for indigenous peoples since preferential treatment is always granted to countries and not to groups within a country. In context, a similar objection must be raised against trade

---

[142] Peter Drahos and John Braithwaite, *Information Feudalism: Who Owns the Knowledge Economy?* New York: New Press, 2003, at pp. 86–90 and 196–7.

[143] Shaffer and Apea, supra note 125, at p. 498.

[144] According to sources quoted in Drahos, supra note 77, at p. 393, indigenous peoples are the victims rather than the partners of national governments in many parts of the world.

[145] FPIC is a requirement provided in Articles 10, 11, 19, 28, 29 and 32 of UNDRIP.

[146] Council Regulation (EC) No. 732/2008 of 22 July 2008 applying a scheme of generalised tariff preferences for the period from 1 January 2009 to 31 December 2011, OJ 2008 L211/1. See Choudhury et al., supra note 134, at p. 338.

[147] Council Regulation (EC) No 732/2008, supra note 146, Article 8(1)(a).

[148] Council Regulation (EC) No 732/2008, supra note 146, Article 8(1)(b).

[149] Shaffer and Apea, supra note 125, at p. 498.

preferences for cultural reasons as provided by the UNESCO CCD. Article 16 CCD provides that developed countries shall accord 'preferential treatment to artists and other cultural professions and practitioners, as well as cultural goods and services from developing countries'. In contrast to most other provisions of the Convention, which are of a non-binding nature, Article 16 is a clear-cut obligation.[150] However, Article 16 CCD does not recognise the specific interests of indigenous peoples in developing as well as developed countries.[151] This is due to the centrality of state sovereignty, which is a guiding principle underpinning the CCD.[152] As a consequence, all rights and obligations stemming from the CCD are attributed to states. The UNESCO example confirms that the non-existence of indigenous peoples as subjects of international law is one of the major obstacles to any adequate protection of ICH at the international level.

6. CONCLUSION

This chapter started from the insight that a non-indigenous mind cannot access the worldviews of indigenous peoples. The (non-indigenous) legal scholar's response to this epistemological relativism is to apply a procedural methodology in law and policy-making on ICH trade and development (participation of ICH holders) as well as in the process wherein these issues are scientifically reflected (participation of indigenous scholars). Opting for process-based solutions and participation would suggest preferring decentralised structures of decision-making to centralised ones. Similarly, the *principle of subsidiarity* requires that political matters should be handled at the lowest or least centralised level where an effective fulfilment of the task at issue is still possible.[153] Applying the principle of subsidiarity to deciding on the appropriate level of regulation in ICH trade and development would imply that definitions of 'indigenous peoples', 'TK' and 'TCE' should

---

150 See Christoph B. Graber, 'Substantive Rights and Obligations Under the UNESCO Convention on Cultural Diversity', in Hildegard Schneider and Peter Van den Bossche (eds), *Protection of Cultural Diversity from a European and International Perspective*, Antwerp and Portland, OR: Intersentia, 2008, pp. 141–62, at p. 151.

151 It is noteworthy that in the ongoing discussions at UNESCO on the implementation of Article 16 CCD, Switzerland – in its response to a questionnaire distributed by the Intergovernmental Committee (established under the CCD) – suggested that signatories should seek internally, that indigenous peoples benefit from preferential treatment in the trade of TK and TCE. See Swiss Confederation, 'Convention sur la protection et la promotion de la diversité des expressions culturelles, réponse de la Suisse au questionnaire sur l'art 16 – Traitement preferentiel' (2009), available online at http://www.unesco.org/culture/culturaldiversity/Suisse, at pp. 3–5.

152 Rachel Craufurd Smith, 'The UNESCO Convention on the Protection and Promotion of Cultural Expressions: Building a New World Information and Communication Order?' (2007) *International Journal of Communication*, 1, pp. 24–55, at p. 37. The sovereignty of the state parties in the cultural field is included in Article 2(2) as one of the eight guiding principles underpinning the Convention.

153 Subsidiarity is an organising principle that is well established in a number of federal constitutions around the world, in the European Union and in international law. For an overview and further references see Isabel Feichtner, 'Subsidiarity', in Rüdiger Wolfrum (ed.), *The Max Planck Encyclopedia of Public International Law*, available online at http://www.mpepil.com/, last updated 2007.

be made at the national level – considering the above highlighted plurality of indigenous cultures around the world. Rules of international law, however, would be needed to guarantee a framework of minimal standards or to provide interface and coordination rules. With regard to minimal standards, international law should provide for obligations for states to respect a number of key principles, including indigenous self-government, collective rights attribution, FPIC and access and benefit-sharing, and so on. With regard to coordination, commentators have convincingly argued for the principle of mutual recognition of national standards in preference to a national treatment requirement.[154] A question for further research would be whether minimal standards and interface rules should be established in the planned WIPO treaties on TK, TCE and genetic resources (GR) or rather in a future binding international instrument on indigenous rights.

As the second part of the chapter revealed, international law's potential for stimulating ICH trade and development is rather limited. Although the relevant fora of international economic law as well as the UN are aware of the linkage between ICH trade and development, so far few concrete effects have resulted from a remarkable production of soft and hard norms on TCE, TK and GR. I also learned that my original idea of using preferential trade rules as an instrument for furthering ICH trade and development does not withstand further examination. Besides much collateral damage to the multilateral trading order, such a scheme would not be in the interest of indigenous peoples, mostly because of international law's state-centralism. Considering the many obstacles top–down solutions of international law are faced with, it makes sense to study bottom–up alternatives more closely, including the use of private certification standards to advance ICH trade and development.[155] As the reader of this volume will note, several contributors have referred to such new approaches[156] and the final chapter enters into this discussion in more depth.[157] Exploring international law's potential to empower indigenous peoples in developing autonomous local projects of ICH commercialisation would be an important contribution to further indigenous self-determination and self-government in the contexts of culture, trade and development.

[154] See Susy Frankel, 'Attempts to Protect Indigenous Culture through Free Trade Agreements', in this volume; and Drahos, supra note 77, at p. 401.

[155] Christoph B. Graber and Jessica C. Lai, 'Indigenous Cultural Heritage and Fairtrade – Voluntary Certification Standards in the Light of WIPO and WTO Law and Policymaking' (2011) *Prometheus*, 29, pp. 287–308.

[156] See for example Coombe and Turcotte, supra note 3 .

[157] See Christoph B. Graber, Karolina Kuprecht and Jessica C. Lai, 'The Trade and Development of Indigenous Cultural Heritage: Completing the Picture and a Possible Way Forward', in this volume.

2. Indigenous self-government, cultural heritage and international trade: a sociological perspective

Duane Champagne

1. INTRODUCTION

International agencies, such as the World Trade Organization (WTO), have given more attention in recent years to formulating international laws for regulating intellectual property rights in ways more agreeable to indigenous peoples.[1] The newly focused attention, undoubtedly, is a product of indigenous peoples voicing their views against the non-consensual commodification of many aspects of indigenous culture. A primary goal of international laws regulating intellectual property is to increase and broaden the possibilities of international markets. While protecting rights to creative production and ownership, international bodies want to ensure that intellectual properties and cultural expressions are efficiently allocated within the global market. Appropriately rewarding cultural and intellectual creativity leads to greater productivity and increased value. International law and agencies want to encourage greater cultural expression, value, creativity and productivity. Can the market goals of international law on property rights be reconciled with indigenous views?

Indigenous peoples have experienced great difficulty protecting music, art, dance and medicinal remedies. Cultural expressions such as dance, ceremony, music and art are treated as folk art. Folk art is unprotected under national and international law and is therefore in the public domain.[2] Folk art is not considered the immediate creative production of contemporary indigenous peoples; it is a product of long tradition and the work often is not attributed to a particular author or artist. Many non-indigenous artists and corporations have appropriated and used indigenous art forms and medicinal knowledge.

International law has had great difficulty incorporating indigenous rights and points of view. The concepts of creativity, private ownership and market distribution are often foreign to the central norms and values still held by many, if not most, indigenous peoples around the world. For example, Tlingit families and clans own ceremonial property such as insignia, songs, dances and art, and distribute ownership through potlatches that honour

1 Because the author is a Native American scholar of sociology, the term 'indigenous peoples' in this chapter refers to those from the United States of America (US), unless otherwise indicated.

2 Brigitte Vézina, 'Are They In or Are They Out? Traditional Cultural Expressions and the Public Domain: Implications for Trade', in this volume.

clan ancestors. Granted that indigenous peoples currently are approaching the marketplace as participants, they want to do so in their own ways and negotiate the terms of participation. International law, furthermore, recognises nation states and is the law of nation-state relations. However, indigenous peoples are not recognised as political entities within the international arena, even after passage of the UN Declaration on the Rights of Indigenous Peoples (UNDRIP).[3]

The usual procedure of international law agencies is to work through nation states to manage social and property relations with indigenous peoples. This method does not make direct contact with indigenous peoples and their norms and values of ownership and possible commodification. Many indigenous peoples have entered the art and cultural expression markets, although sometimes groups within indigenous communities have hotly debated the cultural appropriateness of producing certain art for market sale. In international law, individuals own art and art expression. The market is seen as a negotiation between individual sellers and buyers. Some indigenous artists are willing to sell certain art forms or expressions. Individualised sale of art, however, bypasses the social and political framework of indigenous communities and whether there is collective permission within an indigenous nation for individual members to commodify specific parts of culture.[4]

Implementing an agreeable international trade policy in indigenous cultural heritage is impeded by several difficult issues at the intersection of international law and indigenous cultures. International trade law and regulations work through international bodies and nation states and have been concerned with indigenous issues only recently and often in ways not directly engaged with indigenous communities and points of view. Nation states have more direct contact with indigenous peoples, but in many nation states indigenous peoples and their rights tend to take low priority, if not ignored completely. Some nation states can have laws and articles in their constitutions for addressing indigenous issues, but often the laws are not enforced or supported.

Many international fora and documents do not identify or define indigenous peoples.[5] UNDRIP does not define who are indigenous peoples and the only criterion given is that indigenous peoples must self-identify.[6] Nation states are left to identify indigenous peoples and issues when they arise. Who is to receive benefits or protection as indigenous

---

3 UN, Declaration on the Rights of Indigenous Peoples (UNDRIP), GA Res. 61/295 (UN Doc. A/61/L.67 and Add.1) (adopted on 13 September 2007).

4 Nancy M. Mithlo, *'Our Indian Princess': Subverting the Stereotype*, Sante Fe, NM: School for Advanced Research Press, 2008, at pp. 95–9.

5 Anthanasios Yupsanis, 'The Concept and Categories of Cultural Rights in International Law – Their Broad Sense and the Relevant Clauses of the International Human Rights Treaties' (2010) *Syracuse Journal of International Law and Commerce*, 37 (2), pp. 207–66, at pp. 244–6.

6 Mattias Ahren, 'The Provisions on Lands, Territories and Natural Resources in the UN Declaration of the Rights of Indigenous Peoples: An Introduction', in Claire Charters and Rodolfo Stavenhagen (eds), *Making the Declaration Work: The United Nations Declaration on the Rights of Indigenous Peoples,* Copenhagen: International Work Group for Indigenous Affairs, 2009, pp. 200–216, at pp. 201–3; and Claire Charters, 'The Legitimacy of the UN Declaration on the Rights of Indigenous Peoples', in Claire Charters and Rodolfo Stavenhagen (eds), *Making the Declaration Work: The United Nations Declaration on the Rights of Indigenous Peoples,* Copenhagen: International Work Group for Indigenous Affairs, 2009, pp. 280–303, at pp. 288–9.

people, if there are no clear definitions or understanding? Granted, the great diversity of cultural and political communities of indigenous peoples the world over makes any concise definition, at least for the moment, a difficult challenge. Nevertheless, how indigenous peoples understand their rights, and their cultural and political autonomy, is deeply rooted in their own cultural norms and values, institutional relations and world-views.

The fact that indigenous communities are not extensions of, or to a large extent congruent with, present-day nation state cultural and economic relations suggests they are societies of a different order. The development of the nation states in which they reside continues to be in a direction away from the cultural and political forms that indigenous peoples uphold. Modernisation theory suggests that indigenous peoples will assimilate into nation states as citizens, but around the world many, if not most, indigenous communities have sought to maintain their own identities, cultures, territories and forms of government. The present-day world is only partially a system of nation states; there are many indigenous and other forms of government that are not entirely assimilated into nation state or international law. This statement does not reflect an ideological view, rather there are about 370 million people in the world who live in about 50,000 indigenous communities, where indigenous peoples uphold their cultures and ways of life. The present-day world includes indigenous communities that wish to continue into the future in ways that are informed by their own values and institutional orders. If so many indigenous peoples did not hold onto their communities and life ways, the issues of indigenous rights and international trade would not be before us.

To develop greater understanding about ways to improve and make more acceptable international trade in indigenous knowledge and indigenous cultural expression, the points of view and motivations of indigenous peoples need to be explored. There is much literature about indigenous peoples and many theories of their social and cultural organisation. To understand the motivation of indigenous peoples, it is helpful to try to understand their views of the world, institutional relations and values. This method involves hermeneutics, or what Max Weber called '*verstehen*'. The researcher has to put him- or herself into the cultural and institutional context of the other groups, to understand their motives and patterns of social action.[7]

Sociological theory provides tools for understanding social and cultural orders. Indigenous peoples, at least to a large extent, can be defined or characterised by their cultures, communities, polities and economies. Understanding contemporary international trade in indigenous culture will require historical analysis as well as investigation into indigenous organisation of culture, economic ethics, political order and collective normative orders. Furthermore, indigenous peoples do not live in isolation but are currently swept into

---

[7] Max Weber, *The Methodology of the Social Sciences*, New York: Free Press, 1949, at pp. 78–88, 99–105 and 150; Wilhelm Dilthey, *Introduction to the Human Sciences: An Attempt to Lay a Foundation for the Study of Society and History*, Detroit: Wayne State University Press, 1988, at pp. 301–23; Hans H. Gert and Charles Wright Mills (eds), *From Max Weber: Essays in Sociology*, New York: Oxford University Press, 1946, at pp. 55–74; Talcott Parsons, *The Structure of Social Action*, vol. II, New York: Free Press, 1949, at pp. 748–68; and Bronislaw Malinowski, *Argonauts of the Western Pacific*, Prospects Heights, IL: Waveland Press, 1984, at p. ix.

contemporary globalised cultural, political and economic relations. To understand contemporary international trade and indigenous cultural heritage issues, it will be helpful to tease out patterns of market and cultural participation in national and global markets and cultural relations. In what ways do indigenous peoples choose to participate in the marketplace? How do they react to nation state and international trade law that regulate market actions regarding indigenous cultural knowledge and artistic expression? What are the conditions that will enable indigenous communities to accept national or international regulations for protecting cultural heritage and encouraging trade in cultural knowledge and expression? By investigating the trade and cultural relations of indigenous peoples from their own cultural point of view, some insight can be gained on possible approaches to international trade and regulation of indigenous cultural heritage in ways indigenous peoples might find agreeable and useful.

Creating international laws and regulations for marketing indigenous cultural properties requires significant understanding of who indigenous peoples are and how they approach markets. International laws covering the marketing of indigenous cultural heritage should be done with consent and negotiation with indigenous peoples. Not to address the indigenous peoples in international law-making, when indigenous interests are at stake, will lead to years of conflict and renegotiation, and will not satisfy many indigenous peoples. The plan of the present chapter is to present an interpretation of indigenous social, political and cultural organisation in the language of the social sciences. Processes of social change are discussed with special reference to the social construction of markets and indigenous subsistence markets. After presenting the background information, a series of criteria are suggested for guiding negotiations on international law-making about indigenous cultural heritage or property. The process of law-making for regulating indigenous market participation should be understood within a multicultural, multinational, multi-institutional and multi-legal context. Such an understanding requires concepts and knowledge about which few legal scholars are trained. Sociology and other social science fields study multicultural interpretations of law and markets, and their insights should prove valuable for constructing workable international law regulation of trade in indigenous heritage and property. The greater knowledge that international lawmakers have about indigenous social, political and cultural organisation, as well as patterns of market participation, the greater will be the possibilities for creating agreeable, enduring and efficient regulation of markets affecting indigenous property and cultural rights. A primary goal of this chapter is to present criteria and conditions under which indigenous peoples may negotiate and accept international law and regulation of their cultural production.

2. INDIGENOUS SOCIETAL ORDERS

Sociological theory and literature is founded on the development of modernity, including contemporary nation states. Indigenous peoples are not the central focus of sociological theory or empirical work. The classical texts and theories assume indigenous societies are at the beginning of an evolutionary chain leading to contemporary societies. These evolutionary and modernist approaches assume that indigenous peoples and communities will fade away and disappear, or at best that indigenous peoples will assimilate and integrate into the new democratic nation states. Indigenous peoples and issues have been pushed to the margins in most theoretical views. Indigenous societies often were characterised as 'primitive' or 'pre-capitalist'. Indigenous peoples, however, have persisted to the present and show signs of future continuity and change. They have become part of the present-day international civil society and are engaged in negotiations with nation states on a variety of cultural, political, economic and other issues. Today, no theory of national and international social orders can be complete without understanding the place and position of indigenous peoples.

Sociologists, however, have worked to develop capabilities for analysing indigenous societies. Denying racial theories, sociologists and anthropologists have argued that differing complexes of cultural codes were responsible for understanding much of the variation in human social organisation, at least from a descriptive point of view.[8] All people were equal or similar, but social orders varied by cultural content and institutional relations.[9] In this view all humans could be brought within the cultural realm of contemporary nation states and most people would join the contemporary society and enjoy the rights of modernity. Developing a unified theory in sociology required a finite group of concepts to describe patterns of social change toward contemporary modern institutions. While some historians and anthropologists might argue that indigenous cultures are inherently unique, sociology is premised on concepts and theories that compare and mark patterns of change and difference between and among societies.

2.1 Differentiation Theory

Many writers and scholars have commented on the resemblance of holistic or organic interpretations of traditional indigenous cultural orders to systems theory.[10] The systems theories of Talcott Parsons, while evolutionary and modernist, provide concepts for classifying patterns of change and function from communities referred to as indigenous societies to contemporary nation states. While the evolutionary and modernist views of Parsons can be put to one side, he argues, among other issues, that societies have four main system requisites: culture, polity, economy and community.[11]

---

[8] Emile Durkheim, *The Elementary Forms of the Religious Life*, translation by Karen E. Fields, New York: Free Press, 1995 (first published 1912 in French), at pp. 462–88; and Jeffrey C. Alexander, *Theoretical Logic in Sociology*, vol. II, Berkeley: University of California Press, 1982, at pp. 261–96.

[9] David H. Thomas, *Skull Wars: Kennewick Man, Archaeology, and the Battle for Native American Identity*, New York: Basic Books, 2000, at pp. 70, 78, 103–5, 109 and 190–91.

[10] Nicholas C. Peroff, 'Lovelock's Gaia and Tribal Peoples: Alternative Futures' (2008) *Social Evolution & History*, 1 (7), pp. 26–39; Nicholas C. Peroff, 'Gaia, Complexity, and American Indian Tribes: Common Ground for Compatible Theories', in Paul Cilliers and Kurt Richardson (eds), *Explorations in Complex Thinking*, Boston: ISCE Publishing, 2007, pp. 25–34; and Nicholas C. Peroff, 'Indian Gaming, Tribal Sovereignty, and American Indian Tribes as Complex Adaptive Systems' (2001) *American Indian Culture and Research Journal*, 25 (3), pp. 143–59.

[11] Talcott Parsons, *Societies: Evolutionary and Comparative Perspectives*, Englewood Cliffs, NJ: Prentice-Hall, 1966, at pp. 30–50 [hereinafter Parsons, *Societies*]; Talcott Parsons, *The Evolution of Societies*, Englewood Cliffs, NJ: Prentice-Hall, 1966, at pp. 6–10 and 24–50 [hereinafter Parsons, *Evolution*].

In short, culture refers to the values and worldview of the societal group. Polity refers to the capacity or organisation of decision-making. Economy refers to organisation of production and provision of resources to the societal system. Community refers to the collection of shared rules and norms.

Very few sociological theorists characterised the range of social orders in this way and the theory provides several advantages for the understanding of indigenous peoples. The theory provides ways of understanding the organisation of the subsystems of culture, polity, economy and community. First, the theory states that all societal orders, including indigenous societies, have polities, or political functions. According to this argument, indigenous societies make political decisions, although in a very non-western and non-bureaucratic manner. Such argument is analogous to the viewpoints of many indigenous communities that insist they have rights and powers to self-government. While government or polity in indigenous societies is not the same as in nation states and often does not perform the same operations as in nation states, each indigenous society has or has had a way to make political decisions.

According to the famous definition of the state by Max Weber, the state is the institution that controls the means of legitimate force. 'Today we have to say that a state is a human community that [successfully] claims the monopoly of the legitimate use of physical force within a given territory.'[12] Among indigenous communities, political leaders often did not have concentrated political powers. Often some form of sacrilege, witchcraft or murder was reason to take action, often by lineage, village or religious leaders. Indigenous communities had processes for adjudicating cases. Whether punishment was according to clan revenge, banishment or payment of restitution, the rulings were obeyed and honoured within the political community. Such decisions were acts of legitimate authority and force and constituted features of a political state, according to Weber's definition. Indigenous polities do not resemble contemporary legal-bureaucratic governments and liberal democracies. Indigenous polities have forms of political process that are often based on consensual discussions among local and relatively autonomous political groupings.

The rules, organisation and processes of indigenous government vary and represent one of the features of wide diversity among indigenous peoples. The political salience of indigenous societies tends to be ignored by contemporary international and national fora and is often the cause of much misunderstanding about indigenous peoples. Indigenous societies have mechanisms to enforce their norms and rules against anyone who might break them.

The theory of differentiation provides a means for characterising differences between indigenous and modern societies according to differing levels of functional specialisation of systems and subsystems. Indigenous societies, or so-called primitive societies, have relatively non-differentiated systems and subsystems of polity, culture, economy and community.[13] In other words, indigenous societies are holistic and the relations of community, polity, economy and culture are tightly interrelated and overlapping. Modern

---

12 Gert and Mills, supra note 7, at pp. 78–9.

13 Parsons, *Societies*, supra note 11, at pp. 32–5; and Parsons, *Evolution*, supra note 11, at pp. 28–31; see also Jeffrey C. Alexander and Paul Colomy (eds), *Differentiation Theory and Social Change: Comparative and Historical Perspectives*, New York: Columbia University Press, 1990, at pp. 88–162.

societies have market economics, relative separation of culture, polity, economy, and complex specialisation of organisation and function within polity, culture and economy. In many indigenous societies, polity, religion, kinship, community and economic organisation are decentralised and overlapping. One of the issues for contemporary indigenous societies in developing relations with nation states and international fora is the differences in the structural organisation of functional specialisation between the two types of society.

2.2 Levels of Differentiation

It may be useful to elaborate on some of the implications of the structure of non-differentiated indigenous societies and their subsystems. There are several levels of functional differentiation – institutional, cultural and interactive.[14]

Institutional differentiation refers to the relative autonomy of the major societal systems of: polity, economy, culture and community. As already said, indigenous societies have relatively overlapping major institutions of culture, community, economy and polity. For example, Takic speaking peoples of southern California lived in patrilineal lineages where members of the lineage were political and ceremonial leaders and the lineage owned exclusive territory, occupied an independent village and had a unique sacred bundle. People gathered in a big house to discuss ceremonial, political and social issues.[15] Kinship was a powerful unifying force for political, ceremonial, economic and community organisation and issues.

Differentiation within the subsystem of culture can be characterised as the relations between: religion, ceremony, art, causality and morality.[16] The greater the relative autonomy of each component of culture, the greater possibilities each element will develop in secular and creative ways. Modern societies are characterised by relatively differentiated culture spheres where religion is comparatively autonomous from theatre, art, interpretations of cause and effect and a moral interpretation for the use of art. The efforts of Galileo to challenge the Catholic Church's interpretation of the solar system in the early 1500s are an example of the ultimate development of separation of religion and morality from causality, or science.[17]

Indigenous societies have relatively non-differentiated cultural relations, meaning that religion, causality, art, ceremony and morality are tightly interrelated. A primary example is the efficacy of a ceremony to help cure, or set in moral balance, someone who is ill. For example, Navajo healing ceremonies include sand paintings, ceremony and songs, and are associated with the belief that the ill person made some moral infraction that caused the illness. The ceremony assists the patient in restoring balanced relations with spirit beings

---

[14] Talcott Parsons, *The Social System*, New York: Free Press, 1951, at pp. 167–77.

[15] William Duncan Strong, *Aboriginal Society in Southern California*, Berkeley: University of California Press, 1929; Guide to the Alfred L. Kroeber Papers, 1869–1972, 'Excerpts From the Writings of A.L. Kroeber on Land Use and Political Organization of California Indians, with Comments by Harold E. Driver 1953', The Bancroft Library, *University of California, Berkeley*, Collection No. BANC FILM 2049 BANC MSS C-B 925, reel-frame 152:271, folder 26, at pp. 11–12 [hereinafter Driver].

[16] Parsons, *Societies*, supra note 11, at pp. 129–40.

[17] Ibid.

and thereby achieve the restoration of respectful and beneficial relations with the cosmic order. The sand paintings are destroyed after the ceremonies since they are considered as power beings that, if disrespected, would cause additional harm.[18] Art is seen as a means of curing and not as an end in itself. The very different understanding of the cosmic and non-differentiated features of culture in indigenous societies contrasts with the secular and more differentiated understanding of art in western nations.

The non-differentiation of cultural elements provides some insight into why indigenous peoples are reluctant, or forbidden, to sell some forms of art as commodities. As in the Navajo case, sand paintings are used in ceremonial and curing activities and cannot be sold. The sand paintings are a form of art, but not in the western sense where it is differentiated from moral, religious, causal and ceremonial significant or social-cultural context. Art has an entirely different meaning and sociocultural context in indigenous societies. The selling of a ceremonial sand painting will invite harm to the Navajo, the curer and patient, as the power being of the sand painting has been disrespected and its powers are no longer used for beneficial purposes. Some form of harm, such as more or continued illness or other misfortune, can be expected to haunt the patient, buyer and curer.

The forms of differentiation at the interactive level, where individuals are associating, refer largely to role differentiation. Roles in large industrial societies are many and numerous. In indigenous societies, roles are considerably fewer, but there are many roles such as political leaders, female leadership and ceremonial positions, ceremonial or healing roles, warrior roles, elder roles and numerous other assigned roles and positions. For example, among the Tlingit, all participants in the potlatch receive traditional potlatch names, or titles, that designate rank. The more successfully an individual participates, the higher the rank or title assigned to that individual in recognition of contributions to providing goods for giveaway in the potlatch.[19] The most complex differentiation occurs at the interactive level in indigenous societies which have the most designated roles for community members.

2.3 Differentiation within Culture, Polity, Economy and Community

Institutional differentiation refers to the relative autonomy of the major societal spheres or functions of polity, culture, economy and community. As already mentioned, indigenous societies have relatively little differentiation among the four main societal spheres.

Culture can be conceptualised as relations between religion, art, ceremony, morality and causality. Indigenous societies show relatively little differentiation among all five cultural

---

[18] Trudy Griffith-Pierce, *Earth is My Mother, Sky is My Father: Space, Time and Astronomy in Navajo Sandpainting*, Albuquerque: University of New Mexico Press, 1992, at pp. 174–200; and Gladys A. Reichard, *Navajo Religion: A Study of Symbolism*, Princeton: Princeton University Press, 1950, at pp. 80–122 and 694–736.

[19] Kalevero Oberg, *The Social Economy of the Tlingit Indians*, Seattle: University of Washington Press, 1973, at p. 103; Oliver Salisbury, *Quoth the Raven: A Little Journey Into the Primitive*, Seattle: Superior, 1962, at p. 215; and Arthur C. Parker, 'The Traditional Narrative of the Origin of the Confederation of the Five Nations', in William N. Fenton (ed.), *Parker on the Iroquois*, Syracuse: Syracuse University Press, 1968, pp. 5–119, at pp. 106–7.

elements. In terms of polity, indigenous polities tend to be decentralised and decision-making is often based on forming consensus among autonomous subgroups such as bands, villages, lineages or clans. Political leaders are sometimes hereditary and can make decisions, but leadership depends on continuous support from autonomous subunits. If a consensus cannot be reached among the most important social groups and leaders, no decision is made at all. In some societies, with no consensus, subgroups and individuals are free to make their own choices. When consensus is reached, however, the decision is binding on all participating subgroups. Indigenous societies may have multiple leadership roles, sometimes male and female and supporting roles, such as elders, men's and women's groups who have influence on decision-making.[20] Larger political entities were created by coalitions of autonomous and consenting subgroups.

Economy for indigenous societies is not based on markets, nor do they use an extensive division of labour. Goods and services are exchanged as gifts and through ceremonies and in trade. Families, lineages, clans or villages usually organise labour and food production. Local economic self-sufficiency often contributes to local political autonomy. Indigenous societies are redistributive. Surpluses are expected to be given away in exchange for kinship or political loyalty, or for future consideration of goods of equal value. Individuals trade, gift and exchange goods and services, but do not accumulate individual wealth or reinvest in the means of production to produce goods according to demand.[21]

Communities for indigenous societies are often composed of lineages, bands, families, villages or coalitions among the same. Often communities are formed by common language, shared agreements and mutual respect for land allocations and often share common religious teachings, ceremonies and, therefore, mutual trade and marriage ties. Political identities, however, are often tied to local groups rather than to the community of shared culture and ceremonial participation. Sharing language and common ceremonial alliances usually does not create pacts of mutual military aid, or defence, or political unity. Shared cultural and community norms and values are often more broadly dispersed than are local political identities and groupings. Communities might share similar or the same ceremonies, but mutually recognise distinct territories and local autonomous political authorities. Such arrangements are analogous to saying that all Spanish-speaking people do not share the same government or political identity.[22]

---

[20] Parker, supra note 19, at pp. 97–107; William C. Fenton, 'Cultural Stability and Change in American Indians Societies' (1953) *Journal of the Royal Anthropological Institute of Great Britain and Ireland*, 83, pp. 169–74, at p. 172; John Noon, *Law and Government of the Grand River Iroquois*, New York: Viking Fund Publications in Anthropology, 1949, at p. 28; and Rupert Ross, *Dancing With a Ghost: Exploring Indian Reality*, Markham, Ontario: Octopus Publishing, 1992, at pp. 8, 23 and 159.

[21] Duane Champagne, *Social Change and Cultural Continuity among Native Nations*, Lanham, MD: AltaMira Press, 2007, at pp. 25–49 and 260–64 [hereinafter Champagne, *Social Change*]; and Katherine M. Weist, 'Giving Away: The Ceremonial Distribution of Goods among the Northern Cheyenne of Southeastern Montana' (1973) *Plains Anthropologist*, 18 (60), pp. 97–103, at p. 97.

[22] Alfred L. Kroeber, 'The Nature of the Land-Holding Groups in Aboriginal California [1954–1962]', Guide to the Alfred L. Kroeber Papers, 1869–1972, The Bancroft Library, *University of California, Berkeley*, Collection No. BANC FILM 2049 BANC MSS C-B 925, reel-frame 152:525, folder 29, at pp. 11–12; and Driver, supra note 15, at pp. 5–35, 81–2 and 112–13.

The theory of functional differentiation suggests that societal change is an evolutionary unfolding through history of increasingly more complex forms of functional differentiation toward a pattern called complex differentiation, often called modern. Indigenous societies, however, have not followed the pattern of increased differentiation. Thousands, if not most, of present-day indigenous societies retain relatively non-differentiated institutional and cultural forms. The non-differentiated institutional and cultural arrangements of indigenous societies are often a hindrance to change. Overlapping cultural and institutional arrangements require significant cultural and institutional adjustments from societal members and therefore hinder change. For example, establishing a constitutional government within a lineage-based cultural society requires removing kinship and culture from political organisation and processes. Such change is possible, often occurring in crisis situations or with strong external influences, but is inhibited by the resistance of societal members who are unwilling to abandon long-standing arrangements of kinship, religion and political rules and process.

The continuity and survival of indigenous societies to the present day, in many ways, defies the modernist interpretation. Despite hundreds of years of colonial competition, and cultural and political globalisation, thousands of indigenous societies continue to operate within the present-day social and political context. Tremendous and often hostile forces have not been enough to destroy, transform or assimilate indigenous communities. Most indigenous communities have not moved in a pattern toward increased functional differentiation, although they have suffered cultural, political and economic marginalisation. Indigenous peoples have displayed a considerable amount of institutional and cultural conservatism. There are strong tendencies among indigenous peoples to prefer their traditional institutional and cultural orders and change reluctantly and often in the face of strong external influences. There appears not to be any internal cultural or institutional dynamic that drives indigenous peoples toward the more differentiated institutional and cultural patterns similar to those found in western or modern societies. The non-differentiated arrangements of indigenous societies as a form of institutional and cultural obstacles to change help us understand the conservatism and continuity of indigenous societies. Indigenous peoples may accept change, but they often want to change in ways that are compatible with their present social and cultural arrangements, which usually includes non-differentiated cultural, institutional and interactive relations.[23]

3. WORLDVIEW

A major characteristic of indigenous peoples is that they have creation teachings. The creator figure or force forms the world and often provides cultural rules, ceremonies, and social and political organisation for the people. Sometimes cultural rules and laws are bestowed by intermediary figures, often trickster figures. Many indigenous communities believe the creator figure or force is a benevolent gift-giver. The cosmic order is a gift from the creator and the people must be thankful through ceremonies and respectful acts and ways. Each indigenous society has a creation teaching and so there are thousands of them,

---

[23] Champagne, *Social Change*, supra note 21, at pp. 59–62, 278–80 and 306–7; and Malinowski, supra note 7, at pp. x–xiv, 49–80, 146–94 and 350–65.

sometimes sharing variations on a similar theme. For example, the Algonkian and Iroquoian peoples of the woodlands region of the United States share a similar, but not the same, Earth Diver teaching about Sky Women, who form the land, or Turtle Island, from a small amount of dirt gathered by an animal, who dives to the bottom of the ocean to secure the land.[24]

The creation teachings, however, are complex and diverse and usually specific to each indigenous culture or community. Indigenous peoples are somewhat analogous to Greek city states, where although the Greeks shared a common culture and collective festivals and games, they were often bitter warring enemies. Each city state had its own specific collection of patron gods and specific relations to the sacred. The city states saw themselves as distinct and unique political entities. In ancient times, there was no unified Greek nationality.[25] Similarly with indigenous peoples, each culture has a specific creation teaching and has specific relations to the creator and the cosmic order. The specific and unique relations to the sacred create separate, unique and autonomous identities. In part, the numerous indigenous creation traditions help explain the presence of thousands of distinct and autonomous indigenous cultures observed historically and at present.

The argument of worldview, as determined by creation teachings, complements the arguments already given about non-differentiation of cultural elements: religion, causality, ceremony, art and morality. The non-differentiation of culture argument is based on the interrelatedness of cultural elements, but worldview provides another layer of culture and meaning that is not entirely distinct from the non-differentiation argument. There are many features of culture, but here the focus is on the organisation of society, norms and laws and the possibilities for change. There are several themes that are derivative of indigenous worldviews that may have importance for understanding the use, laws and marketing of indigenous art and culture expressions. Some of these issues are: a subsistence labour ethic, cultural heritage and obligations, international or cosmological understandings and the direct relation to the sacred.

3.1 Cultural Heritage

The gifts of the creator and of intermediary gift-givers are varied. Most distinctly the creator often gives land. The land the people live on is a sacred place. The people are collective caretakers of the land and their role, in respect for the creator, is to maintain the land for future generations. The creation teachings often provide the gifts of social order,

---

[24] Oneida Nation, 'The Haudenosaunee Creation Story' (1994–2011), available at http://www.oneidaindiannation.com/history/creationstory (all online sources were accessed 9 September 2011); and Native Art in Canada, 'The Creation of Turtle Island: The Ojibway Story' (2007–2011), available at http://www.native-art-in-canada.com/turtleisland.html; see also Ake Hultkranz, *The Religions of the American Indians*, Berkeley: University of California Press, 1967, at pp. 9–56; Lowell J. Bean, *Mukat's People: The Cahuilla Indians of Southern California*, Berkeley: University of California Press, 1972, at pp. 160–89; Rodney Frey, *The World of the Crow Indians: As Driftwood Lodges*, Norman, OK: University of Oklahoma Press, 1987, at pp. 3–27 and 177–80; and Popol Vuh, *The Definitive Edition of the Mayan Book of the Dawn of Life and the Glories of Gods and Kings*, translation by Dennis Tedlock, New York: Simon & Schuster, 1985.

[25] Thucydides, *The Peloponnesian War*, New York: Modern Library, 1951, at pp. 11–13; and Michael Grant, *The Rise of the Greeks*, New York: Charles Scribner's Sons, 1987, at pp. xiii–xiv.

such as lineage, band, village, clan, moiety or regional relations. Indigenous nations are often granted sacred bundles and associate ceremonies. If there are no collective ceremonies, often the ceremonies are performed in local forms of social organisation. When lineages, bands, villages, clans, moieties or other social forms have sacred bundles and ceremonies, each social unit often has a distinct social, cultural and political identity, designated by a unique relation to the creator as signified by the unique sacred bundles and ceremonies. The songs, dances and ceremonies are the collective property of the gifted social unit. The group has possession of a sacred bundle, but it is not owned by any particular individual. For example, there is a Keeper of the Sacred Buffalo Hat among the Cheyenne people, but the Keeper is entrusted to protect and maintain the power being of the bundle. The Buffalo Hat, however, is not the private property of the Keeper or his family.[26] Many forms of cultural ceremonial expression, songs, dances and contents of the sacred bundles are the collective heritage of the group that was gifted through the creation or associated teachings.

Because the sacred bundles and associated ceremonial activities are seen as gifts from the creator, any breaking of the ceremonial rules is seen as disrespect for the creator's benevolence and, thereby, invites the loss of the creator's protection from worldly ills or misfortunes. The selling of cultural ceremonial expressions or associated sacred bundles will invite collective misfortune.

Furthermore, since in many cases the cultural, social and community institutions are given as gifts from the creator, the institutional relations of many indigenous communities are considered sacred. Again the change or abandonment of the gifts of the creation teachings suggests possible misfortune and loss of protection. Since institutional and political organisation and relations are often provided within creation stories, there is strong motivation to preserve the social and community organisation as originally given. The strong tie between the sacred and functionally non-differentiated institutional and cultural relations provides the motivation to preserve an already conservative social order from any change that might disturb relations with the sacred.[27]

3.2 Social and Cultural Autonomy

Relations between indigenous individuals and many forms of collectives and the sacred are direct. In the Americas, when a group gathers for decision-making or discussions, they often smoke a pipe. The smoke from the pipe goes to the sky and creates a link with the creator, who oversees that the discussions are true and respectful so they will have the blessings of the creator.[28] Social units, such as villages or lineages, that have specific recognition from the sacred with specific ceremonies, sacred bundles, songs and dances, also have a direct tie to the sacred. Such groups usually exercise considerable cultural and

---

26 Father Peter J. Powell, *The Cheyennes, Maheoo's People: A Critical Bibliography*, Bloomington: Indian University Press, 1980, at pp. vii–xxiv and 1–15.

27 See, for example, Duane Champagne, *Social Order and Political Change: Constitutional Governments among the Cherokee, the Choctaw, the Chickasaw and the Creek*, Stanford: Stanford University Press, 1992, at pp. 1–49 [hereinafter Champagne, *Social Order*].

28 Ed McGaa, *Mother Earth Spirituality: Native American Paths to Healing Ourselves and Our World*, New York: Harper & Row, 1990, at pp. 51–112; see also David M. Lucas, 'Our Grandmother

political autonomy. Usually there are no other political entities between the community and the sacred order. The social, political and cultural autonomy of the designated group exercises considerable autonomy. The group usually has land and relatively self-sufficient economic resources. Relations with external groups are carried on through consensual negotiations. Agreements are made through discussions and development of consensual agreement among the entire local community.

The right of autonomy also extends to individuals. Praying, participation in ceremonies, seeking visions and sweats are ways of seeking knowledge and information from the sacred.[29] In some indigenous cultures, individuals, usually boys, seek a vision quest. The purpose of the vision quest is to consult with the sacred world to be granted information about a person's role and tasks in life. Usually the vision seeker is granted signs that are explained in a vision, or elders assist in explaining a vision sequence to a young man. Certain objects symbolic of the vision quest instructions are gathered by the quester and carried in a bag or personal sacred bundle. Often the individual does not inform others, except some elder assistants, about the vision quest instructions or the meaning of the item in the personal sacred bundle. Once an individual has received life-way instructions and knowledge and has a path opened to him or her, no other person has the right to interfere with an individual's decisions and relations to the sacred, or as guided by spiritual helpers. Each individual has a part to play in the creator's plan for the universe and no human individual can guide a person in another direction. Individuals are given considerable religious and political autonomy. It is often difficult to directly command an individual, even by respected leadership or elders. The autonomy at the individual level contributes to the autonomy at the collective level and political processes include both individual and collective autonomies and hence a considerable amount of consensus for binding decisions.[30]

The claims made by indigenous peoples for rights to autonomy are an expression of cultural heritage and religious understanding. The land and political and cultural autonomy are granted by the creator. Many indigenous peoples believe they have been put on Earth to carry out sacred collective and individual tasks. Each autonomous indigenous unit, if so designated in their creation or cultural teachings, believes it has the right to make decisions under the rules and auspices of the creator. It is not the place for any human group to intervene or to change the rules. Peoples have a purpose and role to play in the plan of the universe and they fulfil their obligations in part by observing and maintaining their ceremonial commitments and relations with the animate forces of the universe.

Nation states and international bodies move directly into this space between culturally and religiously autonomous indigenous groupings and the creator. Indigenous peoples often are reluctant to assimilate culturally and politically into nation states. Submitting to

---

of the Shawnee: Messages of a Female Deity', 87th Annual Meeting of the National Communication Association (Atlanta, GA, 1–4 November 2001), at p. 14, available at http://www.native-languages.org/shawnee-legends.htm.

[29] McGaa, supra note 28, at pp. 51–60 and 75–84; and Lucas, supra note 28, at pp. 11, 14–17 and 19–20.

[30] Champagne, *Social Order*, supra note 27, at pp. 20–31; Powell, supra note 26, at pp. vii–xxiv and 1–15; Paul Radin, *Primitive Man as Philosopher*, New York: Dover Publications, 1957, at pp. 19–62; and Lucas, supra note 28, at pp. 11, 14–17 and 19–20.

international and nation state law and culture often runs directly against indigenous beliefs of their own religious and political autonomy. Indigenous demands for political and cultural autonomy are often seen as threatening the roots of nation state status. Most likely, indigenous peoples do not see it in the same way. The demands for cultural and political autonomy are congruent with indigenous beliefs of who they are in the creator's plan. They have strong institutional and religious grounds for preserving their way of life and carrying on relations given to them from within the sacred order. Refusal to cooperate with the social change programmes of nation states is not a refusal of cooperative relations with the nation state, but rather a preference, or even sacred imperative, to remain committed to the ways and identities of their own cultures. Indigenous peoples want respectful relations with nation states, and often are willing to accept full citizenship, but not as a trade for abandoning indigenous society. Rather, indigenous groups are willing to accept citizenship but want the right to participate in and uphold the autonomy of their own cultural communities.[31]

Indigenous peoples see the world as a universe of autonomous groupings, analogous to their own forms of social organisation. Each group respects the cultural, political and territorial autonomy of the others. Relations are established through consensual agreements and understandings, often treaties of friendship like in early colonial times. Currently, nation states are seen by indigenous peoples as distinct cultural and political autonomies, which indigenous peoples do not want to destroy or change, but rather prefer to have consensual and democratic relations with. In return indigenous peoples want nation states to respect their political, religious, institutional and territorial autonomy. They offer cooperation, respect and participation as citizens, as long as indigenous autonomies are respected and supported by the nation state.

The refusal of indigenous peoples to readily participate in nation-state political and cultural communities and market economies is often seen as radical and threatening. Demands from indigenous activists for return of land, self-government and alternative cultural ways of living and governing do not conform to the basic institutional and cultural assumptions of liberal democratic states. The absence of common cultural and institutional grounds is a major obstacle for negotiation and better relations. Not only is there the absence of cultural and institutional common ground, but indigenous positions and viewpoints are not well understood, or are considered too different.

A primary goal of indigenous peoples is to preserve and carry on their cultural and institutional imperatives and they have strong motivations to defend and carry on their own ways of cultural and institutional order. The indigenous movement is a very conservative movement. Indigenous peoples have the misfortune of defending cultures and political forms that are not recognised and are alien to nation states. Most nation states ignore indigenous positions, since there are no mechanisms under liberal democratic governments to recognise and support indigenous positions. In most nation states, indigenous peoples, at best, are classified as citizens, with rights of minority or ethnic groups. Such

---

[31] Duane Champagne, *Notes From the Center of Turtle Island*, Lanham, MD: AltaMira Press, 2010, at pp. 127–46; Charles Wilkinson, *Blood Struggle: The Rise of Modern Indian Nations*, New York: W.W. Norton & Company, 2005, at pp. 3–88; and Lucas, supra note 28, at pp. 2, 8–10, 12–14 and 17–18.

positions do not fully appreciate or recognise the cultural, religious, territorial and political conditions or viewpoints of indigenous peoples.

3.3 Indigenous Cosmic Order and Economy

Indigenous governments manage more than relations between group members or international relations. Many indigenous creation teachings define the relations between peoples and the animate beings of the universe. The Earth and all its animate and inanimate beings are the gift of the creator. Indigenous government is about managing relations with tribal members and other human nations, but also with the animate powers, including plants and animals. Humans are not at the centre of the cosmological order, but rather are one force among many other animate forces. In Christianity, only humans have souls and therefore are viewed as part of the sacred order within a universe of soulless beings and powers. For Christians, the real or sacred world is in heaven, while the earthly existence is full of trial, hardship, suffering and soulless material existence. The goal in Christianity is to reunite with God in heaven. Christianity is an other-worldly religion, where the present-day Earth is devalued, as raw material, in favour of salvation in the next, sacred world.[32]

In indigenous worldviews, people have animate spirits and powers, but so do plants, animals and other animate forces.[33] The universe is full of animate powers that have purpose, personality and play significant roles in the direction of the universe. In contrast to Christianity, indigenous peoples live in a this-worldly environment, where rewards and punishments will happen in the present world and the next world is less emphasised. The breaking of moral or sacred codes results in retaliation or suffering in this world. The punishments take the form of illness, death, defeat in battle, poor crops or bad luck in hunting. To develop and maintain a healthy nation, ceremonial and political leaders must maintain respectful relations with the animate forces, including human nations, in the cosmological order. Whenever someone or a group suffers from illness or misfortune, the interpretation is that those people transgressed a moral or sacred law and are, therefore, punished for disrespectful behaviour. While curers may administer medicine, a full cure requires re-establishing balances or respectful relations with animate forces that were offended. Ceremonies are designed to restore supportive relations with animate powers and, thereby, restore moral order and the health and well-being of the patient, or transgressing group. Cosmic relations are a give and take of reciprocities with animate powers.[34]

---

[32] See, for example, Max Weber, *The Sociology of Religion*, Boston: Beacon Press, 1963, at pp. 151–206.

[33] Steven T. Newcomb, *Pagans in the Promised Land: Decoding the Doctrine of Christian Discovery*, Golden, CO: Fulcrum, 2008, at pp. 135–6.

[34] Kenneth M. Morrisson, 'Native American Religious Life: Creating Through Cosmic Giving', in Duane Champagne (ed.), *The Native North American Almanac*, Detroit, MI: Gale, 2001, pp. 685–700; and John Loftin, 'Traditional Religious Practices Among Contemporary American Indians', in Duane Champagne (ed.), *The Native North American Almanac*, Detroit, MI: Gale, 2001, pp. 700–709.

Humans need to take food, clothing, medicines and other goods from the environment. Consuming food and goods often requires the death of other animate beings such as plants and animals. Creation or trickster teachings often establish covenant relations between humans and plants and animals. Animals will assist the people for their well-being and survival, as long as the people honour and respect the plants and animals. The animals and plants agree to sacrifice themselves for human consumption and survival, but the people agree not to over-exploit those plants and animals. People are allowed to take from the environment only those materials needed for their survival and well-being. The people respect the animals and plants by providing honouring ceremonies. The people thank the plants and animals for their sacrifice and beg their forgiveness. They take the lives of the plants and animals only to fulfil their needs for survival and life. In return, the souls of the animals and plants are preserved and are reborn to replenish the Earth in the future. If the people are disrespectful, the plants and animals will decline to sacrifice themselves for the people's benefit. The people will suffer drought, poor crops and have little luck at hunting. Indigenous governments are not only responsible for managing relations within the nation and between nations, but also for managing relations with the nations of plants, animals and other animate forces.

The effort to regulate international cultural heritage markets is complicated by the subsistence economic orientations of most contemporary indigenous communities. Indigenous peoples did not manage capitalist markets and most often participated in the present global market as labourers, or traders of goods and expressions of cultural heritage. Indigenous worldviews, valuing relations with the land and animate powers, do not encourage the use of land, labour and capital to produce goods and services according to the demands of the market.[35] When indigenous peoples were entirely self-sufficient, over-exploitation of resources and accumulation of personal wealth were generally disapproved of. While many people gathered resources, kinship and moral imperatives suggested that goods and often art should be redistributed within the community. Often the redistribution was designed to create ties and supportive social and political networks. Often, however, as among the Cheyenne, surplus goods were distributed to the most needy.[36] Given the subsistence labour ethic and redistributive obligations, enterprising individuals transformed their accumulated wealth into social and political influence.[37] Indigenous peoples distributed goods through kinship networks, through ceremonies and

35 Max Weber, *The Protestant Ethic and the Spirit of Capitalism*, New York: Charles Scribner's Sons, 1958, at pp. 47–78. For Latin America see Stefano Varese, *Witness to Sovereignty: Essays on the Indian Movement in Latin America*, Copenhagen: International Work Group on Indigenous Affairs, 2000, at pp. 123, 202, 249, 258–9, 264 and 270.

36 Weist, supra note 21, at pp. 97–103.

37 Weber, *The Protestant Ethic and the Spirit of Capitalism*, supra note 35, at pp. 59–62; E.E. Rich, 'Trade Habits and Economic Motivation Among the Indians of North America' (1960) *Canadian Journal of Economics and Political Science*, 26 (1), pp. 35–53, at p. 53; Arthur Ray, *Indians and the Fur Trade*, Toronto: University of Toronto Press, 1974, at p. 68; James Adair, *Adair's History of the American Indians*, Johnson City, TN: Wautaga Press, 1930, at pp. 394–6 and 444; Thomas Norton, *The Fur Trade in Colonial New York, 1886–1776*, Madison: University of Wisconsin Press, 1974, at p. 70; Raoul Narroll, 'The Causes of the Fourth Iroquois War' (1969) *Ethnohistory*, 16, pp. 51–82, at pp. 58–9; Dean H. Smith, *Modern Tribal Development: Paths to Self-Sufficiency and Cultural Integrity in Indian Country*, Walnut Creek, CA: AltaMira Press, 2000,

personal giveaways. Generally a gift given required a return gift or obligations of social and political support. Trade in songs, dances and art were prevalent and extended over long distances. However, some songs, stories, dances, sacred bundles and art associated with specific ceremonies or under the stewardship of collective groups, such as clans and lineages, could not be traded or given away.

Indigenous peoples did not behave in the market according to the expectations of Europeans. For indigenous peoples, their worldview prohibited them from taking from the environment more than they needed. However, they were fully enabled to take what they needed to support their accustomed way of life. Proper protocols of maintaining sustainable and renewable plant and animal supplies were supplemented with ceremonial and spiritual understandings that preserved the spirits of the beings taken to meet the subsistence needs of the indigenous peoples.[38] To this day, many indigenous individuals and groups do not conform to non-indigenous expectations of market behaviour. Regulation of trade in cultural objects and expression needs to take into account that indigenous peoples will want to approach participation in the market from their own point of view and with their own ways of organising economic actions.[39]

4. SOCIAL CHANGE IN INDIGENOUS SOCIETIES

Indigenous societies have strong tendencies toward conservatism and motivations for preserving their existing social and cultural orders with relatively non-differentiated cultural and institutional relations, worldviews that define and sacralise institutional relations, and a strong emphasis on autonomous individual and collective actions. Subsistence economy and economic orientations characterise indigenous societies and contribute to their conservative orientations. The persistence of so many indigenous communities and their strong orientations toward cultural continuity and preservation suggest that indigenous societies will remain part of present-day group and institutional ecology. Indigenous societies do not show strong tendencies or an internal cultural dynamic that might suggest that they will move on their own accord toward patterns of increased cultural and institutional differentiation.

Indigenous societies do change over time, but not necessarily in the same pattern as western societies, or along the patterns suggested by modernisation theory. All societies have institutional orders that are interpreted and renegotiated by their members. Indigenous communities have their own patterns of change. In North America, during the colonial period, there were many religious or revitalisation movements. Under changing economic and political conditions, some indigenous peoples accepted new cultural instructions from the creator, which legitimated change in cultural and institutional relations. Many indigenous communities with trickster figures have understandings that

---

at pp. 80–82; Paul Phillips, *The Fur Trade*, Norman, OK: University of Oklahoma Press, 1961, at p. 524; and Sherman Uhler, *Pennsylvania Indian Relations to 1754*, Allentown, PA: Donecker, 1951, at p. 61.

[38] Kat Anderson, *Tending the Wild: Native American Knowledge and the Management of California's Natural Resources*, Berkeley: University of California Press, 2006, at pp. 125–86.

[39] Champagne, *Social Change*, supra note 21, at pp. 275–80 and 300–307.

tricksters are creative and destructive manifestations of change. Nevertheless, the cultural motivations found from within indigenous societies do not lead to rapid or clear patterns of increased cultural and institutional differentiation after patterns similar to western experiences. Left to their own devices, most indigenous peoples will not gravitate toward modern or contemporary forms of social order.

Since international law and nation states want to regulate markets to maintain their competition and creative production, it is useful to investigate how indigenous peoples participate in markets and, in particular, art and knowledge markets.

4.1 Indigenous Market Participation

If a primary goal of international fora is to regulate the market for indigenous intellectual property and cultural expression for its protection, creativity and production, how do indigenous peoples approach the marketplace? As already stated, the worldviews and institutional and cultural non-differentiation of indigenous peoples support subsistence economy and ethics. Indigenous peoples will produce to support their community and individual needs. When those needs are met, there is little incentive to produce more and the worldview of indigenous peoples suggests that they stop production. Otherwise, they will risk retaliation from the power beings, who are disturbed by their overproduction. Subsistence economies and ethics can be observed among many, if not most, indigenous communities to the present day.

Like the worldviews and institutional orders that support subsistence economies, so are market economies supported in analogous ways. Markets are supported by business laws, upholding of contracts, predictable court decisions and stable legal histories, separation of political processes from courts and business management, protection of private property and an economic ethic of accumulation and reinvestment.[40] Markets are supported by institutional and cultural regulations that are very different from those found in indigenous subsistence economies. Indigenous peoples traded and produced for trade, but not for capitalist markets. Max Weber defined rational capitalism as the organisation of land, labour and capital according to the demands of the market.[41]

A key to capitalist markets is the requirement of continuous reinvestment and innovation to produce cheaper and better goods. Once the world has engaged competitive and innovative capitalist enterprises, all business groups and individuals must follow suit, otherwise they will become impoverished. This argument is called the Iron Cage.[42] It suggests that all nations and peoples must participate and compete in the market or face economic marginalisation.

Most indigenous communities, at the present time, do not have the institutional and cultural support needed for the individualist capitalist entrepreneur envisioned by Weber

---

40 Max Weber, *General Economic History*, New Brunswick, NJ: Transaction Books, 1981, at pp. 302–13; Weber, *The Protestant Ethic and the Spirit of Capitalism*, supra note 35, at pp. 302–14 and 338–70; and Emile Durkheim, *The Division of Labor in Society*, New York: Free Press, 1984, at pp. 319–21.

41 Weber, *The Protestant Ethic and the Spirit of Capitalism*, supra note 35, at pp. 47–79.

42 Ibid., at pp. 181–3.

and western markets. In many cases, indigenous peoples are not willing to participate in the marketplace according to the western or modern standards of economic entrepreneurship.

Already impoverished before relegation to reservations, Indians became dependent on government economic support. Since there were few economic opportunities, many Indians turned to selling handicrafts, art work and sometimes goods of collective cultural heritage. Railroads brought tourists and often led to interest and demand for indigenous art and the performance of dances and songs. Many famous leaders, such as Sitting Bull, joined the Bill Cody Wild West Show and other troupes and made a living demonstrating dances, songs and acting out Indian historical events for European and American audiences. The meeting and interaction of indigenous peoples from many nations, all sharing the experience of selling their cultural dances, costumes, history and songs for entertainment, began to create pan-Indian pow-wows and secular dancing such as various fancy dances for men and women. The fancy dances were crowd pleasers and developed into their own contemporary styles. Many traditional dances and songs, rife with cultural context and meaning, were too dry for broader audiences, who had little understanding of indigenous cultures and communities.

Indigenous peoples were less well off materially on reservations than they were in traditional times. Greater emphasis emerged for selling art, handicrafts, dances, songs and photographs. Some Indians moved to Chicago and Hollywood to participate in the filming of westerns. Economic need and necessity, rather than market entrepreneurship, dominated the motivations of Indian actors.[43] Few made significant amounts of money, but it was paying work. The commodification of indigenous imagery and history led to some work for indigenous people. However, indigenous peoples were neither entrepreneurs nor controllers of their images, stories or art.

4.2 Selling off Indigenous Cultural Heritage

As tourist and art markets emerged for indigenous works, many tribal communities debated about which works could be sold and which could not. There was always a trade for goods and art among indigenous peoples. Some goods were easily sold to tourists and collectors. However, collectors paid premium prices for some art works such as Navajo sand paintings, Pueblo ceramics, baskets and katchina dolls. Some tribal members took the position that none of the works that were informed by sacred and collective heritage themes should be sold. For example, katchina dolls and sand paintings were attached to specific ceremonies and were considered powerful spirit beings in their own right.

Indigenous peoples sold art out of necessity, performed dances and appeared in traditional costume. In part they had the skills to make the showings, but also reservation people needed cash income in the new market system. Sellers of culturally informed art and cultural expressions often replied to their critics that they were not selling cultural heritage, or power beings, and did not make the katchina dolls or sand paintings according to the prescribed manner. Rather, the production of art was largely according to the demands and needs of the tourists or collectors and the art had no significance within the

---

43 Deirdre Evans-Pritchard, 'The Portal Case: Authenticity, Tourism, Traditions, and the Law' (1987) *The Journal of American Folklore*, 100 (397), pp. 287–96, at p. 287.

tribal context and, therefore, did not violate sacred law or violate relations with power beings, which would retaliate.[44] These debates continue.

The formation of art markets, outside the context and meaning of indigenous worldviews, represents a functional differentiation of cultural subsystems. Art is being produced without moral, religious, causal and ceremonial significance. Not all art is produced this way, but objects for tourist and collector markets are produced as articles of secular consumption and have no negative moral or causal significance for the buyer, seller or collective indigenous community.

Many indigenous dance companies operate in similar ways. The dances are shown to non-indigenous audiences, but with no explanation of the purpose or meaning of the dance, or even the story the dance is telling. One usually gets only the name of the dance and the tribal community where the dance originated. The audience can only judge the rhythm and movements of the dancers, without understanding the meaning of the movements. Critics who write commentary can only comment on the dance movements, as if the dances were abstract contemporary movements. The dances, on a stage, are out of indigenous community context and no context is provided. Without greater understanding of the culture and worldviews of the indigenous nations from where the dances originated, it is not clear whether they break sacred rules. Perhaps the dance troupes are selecting only social dances that do not have spiritual significance and are not part of the sacred collective heritage. It is also not clear whether the dance troupes have been given permission to perform the dances.

The art and cultural expression business is largely an individual or handicraft-based industry. Some artists work at the high end of the indigenous art market, but they usually are producing art in modern or contemporary art methods. For example, many artists in the United States are graduates of the Institute of American Indian Arts (IAIA) located in Santa Fe, New Mexico. The artists are trained in modern abstract methods and produce abstract art that is informed by indigenous cultural themes. Most likely the abstract paintings and sculptors do not violate any imagery or objects of protected collective heritage of any particular indigenous nation. Any indigenous artist, however, should be conscious of the cultural heritage of his or her indigenous community. Certain objects, images and cultural actions are probably not for sale under any conditions, and indigenous artists, as well as buyers, should seek permission from the tribal community for any art or cultural expressions that might violate tribal understandings and beliefs.[45]

Many indigenous individuals engage in the art and cultural expression markets out of economic necessity and with subsistence orientations. Few indigenous persons manage or own significant industrial production of indigenous art or cultural expression. Most entrepreneurial indigenous people, especially those that participate in the high-end art market, often leave indigenous communities, since the necessary institutional and market conditions are not present. Market conditions are better defined within the national and

---

[44] Mithlo, supra note 4, at pp. 54–74; David Penney, 'Native Art', in George Horse Capture, Duane Champagne and Chandler C. Jackson (eds), *American Indian Nations: Yesterday, Today and Tomorrow*, Lanhan, MD: AltaMira Press, 2007, pp. 51–8, at pp. 52–3.

[45] Duane Champagne and Carole Goldberg, 'Changing the Subject: Individual Versus Collective Interests in Indian Country Research' (2005) *Wicazo Sa Review*, 20 (1), pp. 49–69.

international arenas. However, most indigenous communities in the world still depend largely on subsistence economies and enter national and international markets as labourers or traders.[46]

4.3 Alternative Options

Indigenous communities generally have not been supportive of individual market entrepreneurship and most have not developed the legal and political framework for individual business ownership. In the United States and Canada, tribal communities have preferred a mix of economic systems, including individual businesses, subsistence economy and collective tribal businesses. Tribally owned or operated businesses and corporations have become a preferred way for indigenous communities to approach the market system. Indigenously managed casino establishments generally follow the collective control and ownership model. In the US, tribal casino and other business profits are shared equally among members or redistributed in community building or support programmes. Casino profits are considered collective property.[47] The very successful Mississippi Choctaw enterprises are managed through the tribal government, as if the tribal government was a holding company.[48] Tribal members work for the tribe and the collective well-being, in ways that they do not work for individual entrepreneurs. In California, general councils composed of families tied to traditional villages operate governments, corporations and indigenous communities. The traditional general councils decline to write constitutions and are reluctant to grant powers to an executive, courts or administrators.[49] The general councils make all the important decisions and manage casinos with hundreds of millions of dollars in annual income. Sometimes, economic management is delegated by the general council to a tribal corporation that manages economic assets, but often business decisions are made directly by the general council.[50]

---

46 Penney, supra note 44, at pp. 53–8.

47 Steven A. Light and Kathryn R.L. Rand, *Indian Gaming and Tribal Sovereignty: The Casino Compromise*, Lawrence, KS: University Press of Kansas, 2005, at pp. 77–118.

48 Robert H. White, *Tribal Assets: The Rebirth of Native America*, New York: Henry Holt & Co, 1990, at pp. 55–114; Stephen Cornell and Joseph P. Kalt, 'Two Approaches to the Development of Native Nations; One Works, the Other Doesn't', in Miriam Jorgensen (ed.), *Rebuilding Native Nations: Strategies for Governance and Development*, Tucson, AZ: University of Arizona Press, 2007, pp. 3–33, at pp. 4 and 13; Stephen Cornell, 'Enhancing Rural Leadership and Institutions: What Can We Learn From American Indian Nations?' (2005) *International Regional Science Review*, 28, pp. 441–64; and Anne de Bruin and Peter Mataira, 'Indigenous Entrepreneurship', in Anne De Bruin and Ann Dupuis (eds), *Entrepreneurship: New Perspectives in a Global Age*, Burlington, VT: Ashgate Publishing, 2003, pp. 169–84, at p. 175.

49 Kate Spilde Contreras, 'Cultivating New Opportunities: Tribal Government Gaming on the Pechanga Reservation' (2006) *American Behavioral Scientist*, 50 (3), pp. 1–38, at pp. 10–30; Eve Darian-Smith, *New Capitalists: Law, Politics,and Identity Surrounding Casino Gaming on Native American Land*, Belmont, CA: Thomson-Wadsworth, 2004, at pp. 70–94; and Clifford E. Trafzer, *The People of San Manuel*, Patton, CA: San Manuel Band of Mission Indians, 2002, at pp. 131–41.

50 Contreras, supra note 49, at pp. 18–28; and Trafzer, supra note 49, at pp. 115–31. Some of the southern California tribes that maintain general councils as centrally powerful in the tribal government are: the San Manuel Band of Mission Indians, Pala Band of Mission Indians, Pauma Band of Mission Indians, Rincon Luiseño Band of Mission Indians, Saboba Band of Mission

Modernisation theory does not predict that indigenous communities can approach the marketplace with non-differentiated forms of kinship, government, corporation and community. Nevertheless, indigenous peoples may develop sustained economic market capabilities, while maintaining intact major aspects of their non-differentiated institutional and cultural orders.

5. INTERNATIONAL LAW AND INDIGENOUS PEOPLES

Despite the gap in shared cultural understanding and institutional orders, indigenous peoples are willing to work and live within nation states, if they can be recognised, respected and treated in democratic ways.[51] Nation states provide protection and can provide needed resources and support to indigenous communities.[52] Nevertheless, indigenous peoples want to develop through their own cultures and institutional frameworks and want to retain political and cultural autonomy. They are willing to accept limited government powers. Indigenous worldviews do not envision absolutely autonomous nations, but rather human groups intertwined with each other, ideally in respectful and consensual relations. Indigenous peoples do not see themselves as the centre of creation, but as part of creation and embedded in a web of human and cosmological forces. Such worldviews, if approached properly and under the right conditions, should enable indigenous peoples to engage nation states and international fora as partners in the development of respectful, harmonious and productive relations.

Most contemporary positive law is created by nation states and international fora. In most countries, indigenous peoples are usually not parties to the creation of laws or have little to do with implementation of the laws. Some countries have adopted international indigenous rights standards as national law, but often the laws are ignored or not given enough guidance, support or procedural pathways, often resulting in conflict. Peru, for example, incorporated international standards of indigenous human rights into the national constitution and laws. Nevertheless, a major government-supported economic development initiative did not secure indigenous informed consent. Indigenous groups did not want to stop development, but wanted development to proceed in ways that were in

---

Indians, Santa Ynez Band of Mission Indians, San Pasqual Band of Mission Indians and others. Some tribes, such as the Viejas Band of Mission Indians and Pechanga Band of Mission Indians, have general councils that are responsible primarily for land issues and elect a tribal council to manage day-to-day issues and operations. Other tribes, such as the Agua Caliente Band of Cahuilla Indians and the Morongo Band of Mission Indians, have constitutional governments that recognise the general council as the body politic of the government. See http://www.cnr.berkeley.edu/classes/espm-50/11California.pdf.

[51] Paul L.A.H. Chartrand, 'Citizenship Rights and Aboriginal Rights in Canada: From "Citizens Plus" to "Citizen Plural"', in John-Erik Fossum, Johanne Poirier and Paul Magnette (eds), *The Ties That Bind: Accommodating Diversity in Canada and the European Union*, Brussels: Peter Lang, 2009, pp. 129–54.

[52] Diaz de Jesus and Pedro de Jesus Alejandro, 'Alto Balsas, Guerrero: An Experience in the Struggle for Autonomy', in Aracely Burguete Cal y Major (ed.), *Indigenous Autonomy in Mexico*, Copenhagen: International Work Group for Indigenous Affairs, 2000, pp. 134–59, at pp. 151–6, 140–42 and 150–52.

harmony with the environment and were more beneficial to a broader range of people.[53] Adoption of constitutional laws and international laws are only a beginning step. Often indigenous communities are not empowered enough within nation states to protect their interests and rights, even with support of constitutional and international law, as well as inclusion of indigenous political parties or representatives within the government of the nation state.[54] Nation states need to ensure that indigenous and nation-state law act in concert and protect individual and collective rights.[55]

Creating and implementing new laws is a process of social change and institutionalisation. Institution-building usually works best when the involved community or communities share common cultural and institutional ground.[56] As already argued, indigenous peoples do not share common cultural or institutional ground with nation states. The processes of institution-building, therefore, will be both multicultural and involve differing patterns of institutional order. Here relatively non-differentiated cultural and institutional relations associated with indigenous communities are paired with significantly more differentiated political and economic orders associated with nation states. Values and goals associated with differing worldviews between nation states and indigenous communities will also underscore differing preferences and patterns of action. Differing institutional and cultural orders require a greater consciousness of each other's positions and a willingness to develop cooperative understanding. Institution- or nation-building among indigenous communities has gained considerable attention in recent decades. Recently, more emphasis has been given to empowering indigenous communities to enable them to make political and culturally informed decisions.

Much of the international trade literature assumes that all participants are culturally willing and able to engage in competitive market relations. Most indigenous peoples are not socially or culturally disposed to engage in markets and often prefer to maintain their own social orders, while increasingly, though not necessarily consensually, participating in market relations. The commodification of indigenous culture and intellectual property is a process that is alien to, and often incongruent with, indigenous ways of life. Current international efforts to incorporate indigenous peoples into international trade agreements too often assume that indigenous communities and social actions are already compatible

---

[53] WW4, 'Peru: President Garcia Refuses to Sign Indigenous Rights Law', World War 4 Report (25 June 2010), available at http://www.ww4report.com/node/8785.

[54] Eva Josefsen, 'The Experience of Saami', in Kathrin Wessondorf (ed.), *Indigenous Parliament? Realities and Perspectives in Russia and the Circumpolar North*, Copenhagen: International Work Group for Indigenous Affairs, 2005, pp. 178–209, at p. 193. In the Taiwanese case indigenous groups gained political party status and were able to use education as political power brokers and gain access to other resources. However, they were not able to achieve indigenous recognition or make progress on self-government or territorial issues. Kun-hui Ku, 'Rights to Recognition: Minority/Indigenous Politics in the Emerging Taiwanese Nationalism' (2005) *Social Analysis*, 49 (2), pp. 99–121.

[55] Abigail Griffith, 'The Struggle between Indigenous Folkways and National Law: Resolving the Past and Present', Council on Hemispheric Affairs (18 June 2001), available at http://www.coha.org/the-struggle-between-indigenous-folkways-and-national-law-resolving-the-past-and-the-present/.

[56] Leon H. Mayhew (ed.), *Talcott Parsons on Institutions and Social Evolution. Selected Writings*, Chicago: University of Chicago Press, 1985, at pp. 117–18.

with market culture and orientations. Consequently, the discussion of seeking market participation from indigenous communities does not fully appreciate the gulf between international market requirements and the economic and social foundations of indigenous communities. Any international trade agreement that will consensually admit indigenous trade and commerce must accept and appreciate contemporary indigenous social, political and economic relations and their significant differences from contemporary international market institutions and trade laws.

Developing agreements over international trade with indigenous nations is an exercise in accommodating thousands of different communities, cultures and economic institutions. Cross-cultural economic relations and agreements are not well understood and still less well executed. The predominance of contemporary international markets tends to marginalise indigenous economic orders. From a sociological point of view, the problem can be stated as one of developing consensually based multicultural economic institutions. The literature on cross-cultural institution-building suggests some necessary preconditions for establishing stable and workable relations.[57] The work develops at least six necessary conditions for establishing fully operational cross-cultural institutional relations with indigenous nations: fairness, indigenous control, resources, economic management, cooperative government-to-government relations and cultural compatibility.[58] The latter conditions are applied toward developing national or international laws for regulating property, ownership and trade of indigenous cultural heritage.

5.1 Fairness

A well-known condition for the regulation of markets is that courts, law and political institutions must be fair and not unnecessarily interfere with the day-to-day operations of business. Contracts must be enforceable and businesses must be able to predict legal and political outcomes that affect business transactions. Unstable legal and court decisions will discourage business and investment. Most contemporary nation states have laws that regulate the national market and courts with established business legal precedents. Indigenous communities, however, are often not market-oriented and often do not have courts, business laws or political relations that foster or develop market activity. In many cases, indigenous peoples rely on nation-state courts and law, but not necessarily with consent.

If indigenous communities do not trust nation-state courts to protect their property or ownership rights, there is a large disincentive to participate and produce for a national market. The national courts may not have knowledge or understanding of indigenous property norms, or will not take them into account in national law. Consequently, the

---

[57] Carole Goldberg and Duane Champagne, *Final Report: Law Enforcement and Criminal Justice Under Public Law 280*, Washington, DC: US Department of Justice, 2008, at pp. 473–89; and Duane Champagne, Carole Goldberg and Kevin Washburn, *A Study of the Administration of Justice in Indian Country*, Washington, DC: Department of Justice, 2010, at pp. 36–74 and 263–72; For more support for the theoretical perspective see Duane Champagne and Carole Goldberg, *Captured Justice: Native Nations and Public Law 280*, Durham, NC: Carolina Academic Press 2012, at pp. 22–50.

[58] Champagne, Goldberg and Washburn, supra note 57, at pp. 36–74.

national courts may not prove supportive to indigenous peoples who work within subsistence economies. National courts could be asked to extend their legal scope and understanding to support indigenous norms and laws of ownership, exchange and protection of cultural heritage. Such cultural requirements, however, may be burdensome to the courts. Nevertheless, indigenous peoples may not consider the court system fair unless their own norms and values of economic exchange and ownership are incorporated into the economic law and respected in practice.

Indigenous communities might prefer, or be asked, to enforce their own norms of exchange and ownership. However, such norms must be consistently applied to all members of the indigenous community in an equal manner. Indigenous governments might be asked to strengthen their institutions for regulating disputes within subsistence and market activity. Indigenous communities and governments, as they enter the web of nations, should be held to the same human rights standards as other nations.[59] Differences between nation states and indigenous peoples about philosophy, content and application of human rights and laws regulating the economy should be subjects of further discussion and consensus formation.

5.2 Indigenous Control

Indigenous governments need to define and protect their property rights to collective cultural heritage. In conflicts between indigenous individuals and collective ownership, according to indigenous norms, collective ownership should prevail. Indigenous governments should also have the power to decide among members on controversial issues regarding the sale and use of cultural items to non-indigenous members. For example, if two groups debate whether a certain form of art, say sand paintings, are in the protected sacred category and, therefore, not marketable, the indigenous authorities should have the option to decide the issue. Whenever possible, decisions of collective ownership should be made by the indigenous community's governing system according to its rules, as long as the decisions are fair and equitable according to the indigenous norms and values of the particular community.

Indigenous governments should have the option to regulate production and trade within their local communities. Indigenous governments should be recognised by national governments and international governments as partners with national and international authority over the regulation of trade and protection of cultural heritage property. Greater ability to manage and invest in the local production and economy by indigenous peoples has been positively associated with greater economic success.[60] Indigenous communities should have the option to organise and regulate subsistence production, individual businesses and businesses of collective indigenous organisation. The option to organise

---

[59] Angela R. Riley, 'Good (Native) Governance' (2007) *Columbia Law Review*, 107 (5), pp. 1050–125, at pp. 1107–25.

[60] Stephen Cornell and Joseph P. Kalt, 'Sovereignty and Nation-Building: The Development Challenge in Indian Country Today' (1998) *American Indian Culture and Research Journal*, 22 (3), pp. 187–214, at pp. 187–9; and Stephen Cornell and Joseph P. Kalt, 'Pathways From Poverty: Economic Development and Institution-Building on American Indian Reservations' (1990) *American Indian Culture and Research Journal*, 14 (1), pp. 89–125, at pp. 102–8.

corporate structures in a western style should also be open for those communities who may want to move in that direction. Indigenous governments may want to create indigenous-owned enterprises within their traditional boundaries. Individual indigenous individuals, or groups, as citizens, may decide to organise business enterprises under national law, but would be subject to indigenous, national and international laws regulating trade and protection of property and expression of cultural heritage.

Indigenous communities should also make determinations about membership and whose art may represent their cultural heritage. Contemporary artists or performers may sell art or performances that are informed by their cultural affiliation, but often are not selling collective heritage. When there is dispute about such issues, the collective community, its governments or other institutions that manage such issues, should have the power to decide. In matters of collective indigenous cultural heritage, collective indigenous institutions or governments should have powers to determine the disposition of such expressions or objects. Questions of authenticity of art and expression as a product from a specific indigenous group should be reserved as a collective right.

5.3 Resources

Indigenous, national and international governments and agencies will require enough human and material resources and commitment to regulate and support the trade and protection of items of cultural heritage. For example, indigenous and national governments and international fora need to have sufficient resources to enforce the laws for protecting and regulating trade and ownership of cultural heritage items and expressions and tradeable goods.[61]

5.4 Economic Management

Laws need to promote conditions for efficient, creative and productive trade and marketing, as well as protection of sacred items of cultural heritage. Producers need artistic skills, cultural knowledge and business management capabilities over the factors of production to compete in the market.[62] International law should be flexible enough to regulate and support subsistence, individual and collective indigenous approaches to the market.

5.5 Cooperative Government-to-Government Relations

Indigenous, national and international governments must be mutually supportive and cooperative in the design and implementation of laws and agencies for regulating and protecting the ownership and trade of indigenous cultural heritage. Indigenous peoples must have access and veto power over decisions that affect their cultural heritage and economic trade capabilities. Indigenous peoples will need more than consulting privileges

---

[61] Yupsanis, supra note 5, at pp. 250–51.

[62] Brian Calliou, 'The Culture of Leadership: North American Indigenous Leadership in a Changing Economy', in Duane Champagne, Karen J. Torjesen and Susan Steiner (eds), *Indigenous Peoples and the Modern State*, Lanham, MD: AltaMira Press, 2005, pp. 47–68, at pp. 53–9.

and should participate as government-to-government entities. Whenever possible, agreements should be made directly with indigenous governments. When not practical, pan-indigenous organisations and non-governmental organisations may present the needs and issues of indigenous governments. However, ultimately, each indigenous nation will want to protect its own specific properties of collective cultural heritage and will need access to and agreement with national governments and international fora. Indigenous communities will not be satisfied with anything less than consensus understanding and incorporation of their viewpoints and interests. Greater cooperation and greater co-governance with indigenous communities in the construction, regulation, implementation and maintenance of laws concerning protection and trade of cultural heritage properties and expression will improve participation, consensus and economic trade and creativity.[63] Indigenous governments and peoples need democratic and consensual relations with national and international law-making agencies or legislatures. Greater government-to-government cooperation and co-governance over market regulation should enhance economic efficiencies and provide better protection for sacred items of collective cultural heritage.

5.6 Cultural Compatibility

Economic relations with indigenous peoples need to be understood as multicultural, multi-institutional and multi-jurisdictional networks of relations. While subsistence economies are often integrated with market economies, the values, norms and institutional organisation of markets and subsistence economies are very different. In subsistence economies, production and trade is conducted to acquire enough goods or money to support a given standard of living, to a large extent determined by the norms and values of the indigenous community. Work and trade is aimed at satisfying acquisition of a culturally determined bundle of goods. The needs of a community or individual are culturally agreed upon. However, the basic needs of a community or individuals may change, especially with increasing access to manufactured goods and services. If a flat screen television becomes a standard economic requirement in a community, individuals and groups will strive to work or trade to acquire the new standard of material well-being. Greater market consumption requires greater amounts of work and trade to secure cash and consumer goods available on the market.

Indigenous communities have rules and moral codes regulating consumption and, therefore, work and trade. Non-indigenous market actors and international trade regulators need to be conscious of the methods and values that inform the actions of indigenous producers. Many indigenous individuals will not maximise production or adjust production according to changes in market demand. The institutions that regulate the subsistence economy may consist of local families, kinship groups, villages and other social forms. National and international laws and regulations should be conscious of indigenous subsistence trade and production patterns and have an interest in their stable and continuous operation.

---

63 John Ackerman, 'Co-Governance for Accountability: Beyond Exit and Voice' (2004) *World Development*, 32 (3), pp. 447–63, at pp. 447, 455 and 459.

Laws regulating production, trade and protection of cultural heritage, however, should not limit or preclude the formation of new economic approaches to national and international markets. Furthermore, participation in national and international markets should not be restricted to predominantly individual and corporate business forms. Indigenous peoples are often looking for sustainable economic possibilities, but want to approach the marketplace on their own terms, which preserve their values, institutions and collective organisation.

Nation states and international fora should not take the opportunity of negotiated arrangements to impose their own values and institutions of market regulation over indigenous communities.[64]

6. CONCLUDING THOUGHTS

Creating an international body of law that will enable consensual commodification of indigenous cultural and intellectual assets is, or should be, a goal for nation states, international agencies and indigenous nations. Each indigenous nation has its own views and decision-making processes for determining cultural ownership and the possibilities of sale in market or other exchanges. Since there are thousands of indigenous nations, the problem before international agencies is considerable. A global set of rules for regulating international property rights needs to have the consent of indigenous nations. The international law needs to recognise, uphold and respect the ownership norms and values of indigenous nations as specific collective political entities. Indigenous nations need a voice within the process of creating international law and they also should have veto power over international and national laws or procedures that violate indigenous values and norms. Indigenous nations and individuals may enter the secular international and national markets, but should be allowed to do so on their own cultural and political grounds.

---

64 Katy Moran, 'Benefit Sharing Under the Convention of Biological Diversity', in Mary Riley (ed.), *Indigenous Intellectual Property Rights: Legal Obstacles and Innovative Solutions*, Walnut Creek, CA: AltaMira Press, 2004, pp. 153–72, at pp. 154–8; and Mary Riley, 'The Amerindian Rights Movement in Guyana and Its Influence', in Mary Riley (ed.), *Indigenous Intellectual Property Rights: Legal Obstacles and Innovative Solutions*, Walnut Creek, CA: AltaMira Press, 2004, pp. 99–123, at pp. 99–100, 108 and 114–16.

PART II

International law perspectives

3. International indigenous and human rights law in the context of trade in indigenous cultural heritage

John Scott and Federico Lenzerini

1. INTRODUCTION

In recent decades, the matter of indigenous peoples' rights has emerged as a priority in the context of the development of international law. The growing attention for the rights and dignity of indigenous peoples has eventually translated into a number of legal instruments, which take into account the cosmologies (visions of life) of the peoples concerned, as well as the specificity of their legal structures and customary laws. This has led to the need to reconsider certain legal concepts, which were traditionally structured on the sole basis of the western point of view and firmly focused on individual rights.

Among these concepts, the legal understanding of cultural heritage is included. In fact, in the context of indigenous peoples' cosmologies, cultural heritage is the bedrock of the identity of the peoples concerned, attaining spiritual and cultural values and going much beyond its usual western-based connotation as a tradeable commodity. This reality translates into a situation where traditional legal parameters, to a large extent, are not able to grasp or take into account the significance and peculiarities of indigenous cultural heritage, especially when it comes to international trade in such heritage.

This chapter explores in detail the specificity of trade in indigenous cultural heritage, with special attention to the particular aspects not currently addressed in international law, and also suggests some possible solutions *de lege ferenda*. However, before delving into this, it is useful to provide some necessary background in order to fully understand the issues at hand through analysing some preliminary concepts, including 'working definitions' of indigenous peoples, cultural heritage, traditional cultural expressions and traditional knowledge. In addition, the status of indigenous peoples' rights in international law – in the context of the broader area of human rights – will be explored.

2. INDIGENOUS PEOPLES: A COMMON UNDERSTANDING

At the international level, the expression 'indigenous peoples' encompasses a wide variety of realities which may hardly be subsumed within a single definition. In addition, for many indigenous peoples, even the very idea of being 'classified' through a 'definition' remains highly controversial. Historically defined by others to their detriment, indigenous peoples remain wary of and resistant to definitions, not only of themselves but also of their heritage – both tangible and intangible – including traditional knowledge. This reluctance was confirmed during the many years of debate at both the Working Group on Indigenous Populations (WGIP) and the Working Group on the Draft Declaration on the Rights of Indigenous Peoples, wherein observers from indigenous organisations developed a common position and rejected the idea of a formal definition of indigenous peoples that would be drafted by states.[1] This position was eventually shared by governmental delegations, well aware that the lack of a definition of 'indigenous peoples' would grant them a wider margin of manoeuvre at the domestic level in deciding whether or not certain communities living within the national territory are to be considered as 'indigenous'. Consequently, at its fifteenth session, in 1997, the WGIP concluded that a definition of indigenous peoples at the global level was not possible at that time, and not necessary for the adoption of the Declaration on the Rights of Indigenous Peoples.[2]

On the other hand, however, for a legal instrument to be applicable and to produce its effects properly, it is indispensable to delineate precisely who are the beneficiaries of its provisions. Understanding their qualifying characteristics is essential for ensuring that indigenous peoples may benefit from the existing legal instruments and provisions, which safeguard and promote their rights. It is also a necessary prerequisite in understanding the intricate relationships between culture and the flow of products and services, in the context of the world trade system, taking into account the historical experiences and cultural identities of indigenous peoples.

2.1 Who are Indigenous Peoples?

There are approximately 370 million indigenous people in some 90 countries worldwide.[3] However, many indigenous peoples may not be recognised as such in their countries of

---

1 An example of the position of indigenous representatives is included in the 1996 report of the WGIP, stating as follows:

> We, the Indigenous Peoples present at the Indigenous Peoples Preparatory Meeting on Saturday, 27 July 1996, at the World Council of Churches, have reached a consensus on the issue of defining Indigenous Peoples and have unanimously endorsed Sub-Commission resolution 1995/32. We categorically reject any attempts that Governments define Indigenous Peoples. We further endorse the Martinez Cobo report (E/CN.4/Sub.2/1986/Add.4) in regard to the concept of "Indigenous". Also, we acknowledge the conclusions and recommendations by Chairperson-Rapporteur Madame Erica Daes in her working paper on the concept of Indigenous peoples (E/CN.4/Sub.2/AC.4/1996/2).

See UN, Economic and Social Council (ECOSOC), Commission on Human Rights, Sub-Commission on Prevention of Discrimination and Protection of Minorities, 'Discrimination Against Indigenous Peoples, Report of the Working Group on Indigenous Populations on its Fourteenth Session', (UN Doc. E/CN.4/Sub.2/1996/21, 1996), at para. 31 [hereinafter UN, ECOSOC, 'Discrimination Against Indigenous Peoples'].

2 See UN, Department of Economic and Social Affairs, Commission on Human Rights, Sub-Commission on Prevention of Discrimination and Protection of Minorities, 'Human Rights of Indigenous Peoples, Report of the Working Group on Indigenous Populations on its Fifteenth Session Geneva, 28 July–11 August 1997', (UN Doc. E/CN.4/Sub.2/1997/14), at para. 129. See also UN, ECOSOC, 'Discrimination Against Indigenous Peoples', supra note 1, at paras 153–4.

3 See UN Permanent Forum of Indigenous Issues (UNPFII), 'About UNPFII and a Brief History of Indigenous Peoples and the International System', available at http://www.un.org/esa/socdev/unpfii/en/history.html (all online resources were accessed 9 September 2011).

origin; some are referred to as ethnic minorities, tribal peoples, traditional peoples, scheduled tribes or local communities. They usually continue to live in and sustainably manage their traditional territories – which are often biological, cultural and linguistic areas of crucial significance within the territorial state – struggling to pursue their distinctive diversity and transmit it to future generations.

During the 30-year-long debate concerning indigenous issues at the United Nations (UN), as well as at the International Labour Organization (ILO), considerable discussion was devoted to the problem concerning a definition of 'indigenous peoples', but no such definition has ever been adopted in any UN final legal instrument. The most cited description of the concept of 'indigenous' was prepared by José R. Martinez Cobo, the Special Rapporteur of the Sub-Commission on Prevention of Discrimination and Protection of Minorities, in his famous Study on the Problem of Discrimination against Indigenous Populations.[4] Significant discussions on the subject have continued within the context of the drafting and negotiation of a Draft Declaration on the Rights of Indigenous Peoples and by the WGIP since 1982. An explanation of the concept of 'indigenous and tribal peoples' is contained in Article 1 of the 1989 ILO Convention No. 169 Concerning Indigenous and Tribal Peoples in Independent Countries (ILO Convention No. 169).[5]

2.1.1 Martinez Cobo's Study on the Problem of Discrimination against Indigenous Populations

The working definition of 'indigenous communities, peoples and nations' offered by the study of Martinez Cobo reads as follows:

> Indigenous communities, peoples and nations are those which, having a historical continuity with pre-invasion and pre-colonial societies that developed on their territories, consider themselves distinct from other sectors of the societies now prevailing on those territories, or parts of them. They form at present non-dominant sectors of society and are determined to preserve, develop and transmit to future generations their ancestral territories, and their ethnic identity, as the basis of their continued existence as peoples, in accordance with their own cultural patterns, social institutions and legal systems.[6]

The element of historical continuity:

> may consist of the continuation, for an extended period reaching into the present of one or more of the following factors: a) Occupation of ancestral lands, or at least of part of them; b) Common ancestry with the original occupants of these lands; c) Culture in general, or in specific manifestations (such as religion, living under a tribal system, membership of an indigenous community, dress, means of livelihood, lifestyle, etc.); d) Language (whether used as the only

---

[4] UN, ECOSOC, Commission on Human Rights, Sub-Commission on Prevention of Discrimination and Protection of Minorities Working Group on Contemporary Forms of Slavery, 'Study on the Problem of Discrimination Against Indigenous Populations', (UN Doc. E/CN.4/Sub.2/1986/7 and Add. 1–4, 1981). The study was launched in 1972 and was completed in 1986, thus making it the most voluminous study of its kind, based on 37 monographs.

[5] ILO Convention No. 169 Concerning Indigenous and Tribal Peoples in Independent Countries, 1659 UNTS 383 (adopted on 27 June 1989, entered into force 5 September 1991).

[6] UN, ECOSOC, 'Study on the Problem of Discrimination Against Indigenous Populations', ch. 5, supra note 4, at para. 379 (UN Doc. E/CN.4/Sub.2.1982/2/Add.6).

> language, as mother-tongue, as the habitual means of communication at home or in the family, or as the main, preferred, habitual, general or normal language); e) Residence on certain parts of the country, or in certain regions of the world; f) Other relevant factors.[7]

In terms of subjective parameters, the two elements to determine whether a person is indigenous are the fact of belonging to an indigenous population 'through self-identification as Indigenous (group consciousness)', as well as recognition and acceptance by the community concerned 'as one of its members (acceptance by the group)'. The latter element 'preserves for these communities the sovereign right and power to decide who belongs to them, without external interference'.[8]

It is important to stress that the study emphasises that not every criterion listed above needs to be met for a group to be considered as 'indigenous'. This shows that the Special Rapporteur had clearly perceived the need to ensure that the full diversity of the world's indigenous peoples is taken into account, in order for his working definition to be responsive to the reality and needs of those peoples.

2.1.2 ILO Convention No. 169 concerning Indigenous and Tribal Peoples in Independent Countries

Article 1(b) of ILO Convention No. 169 contains an explanation of indigenous peoples, considered as:

> peoples in independent countries who are regarded as indigenous on account of their descent from the populations which inhabited the country, or a geographical region to which the country belongs, at the time of conquest or colonization or the establishment of present state boundaries and who irrespective of their legal status, retain some or all of their own social, economic, cultural and political institutions.

Paragraph 2 of Article 1 adds that self-identification as 'indigenous' 'shall be regarded as a fundamental criterion for determining the groups to which the provisions of this Convention apply'. The Convention distinguishes between 'indigenous' and 'tribal' peoples, on account of the fact that there are ethnic communities who are not 'indigenous' in the literal sense, in the countries in which they live, but who nevertheless live in a similar situation. According to Article 1(a) 'tribal peoples' are those communities 'whose social, cultural and economic conditions distinguish them from other sections of the national community, and whose status is regulated wholly or partially by their own customs or traditions or by special laws or regulations'. Some examples may be the Afro-descended tribal peoples in Central America, or tribal peoples in Asia or Africa – such as the San or Maasai – who may not meet all the requirements established by the Convention to be considered 'fully' indigenous. Nevertheless, it is to be emphasised that such a distinction only operates within the scope of Convention No. 169, while outside of its context both concepts are encompassed by the general notion of 'indigenous peoples'. In fact, most of the peoples classified by the Convention as 'tribal' refer to themselves as 'indigenous', and within the UN no distinction is drawn between 'indigenous' and 'tribal' peoples. This better reflects the need that the full diversity of the world's indigenous peoples, in all regions of the

---

7 Ibid., at para. 380.
8 Ibid., at paras 381–2.

world, is captured, in light of their diversity and ongoing struggle as politically marginalised populations, in order to foster social justice and human rights.

2.1.3 Understanding the term 'indigenous peoples' in light of the UN Declaration on the Rights of Indigenous Peoples

The lack of any definition of 'indigenous peoples' in the UN Declaration on the Rights of Indigenous Peoples (UNDRIP),[9] adopted by the General Assembly on 13 September 2007, has reopened the debate concerning whether or not the drafting of such a definition would actually be opportune.

During the process leading to the adoption of UNDRIP, indigenous peoples argued strongly against the inclusion of a definition, for principled as well as strategic reasons. Foremost in their minds was their right to define themselves, as well as the fear that the Declaration could be applied too narrowly. Last but not least, there was the fear that the further negotiations that would have been necessary in order to obtain agreement on such a controversial issue among the wide variety of states and indigenous peoples could further prolong the process of adoption of the Declaration.

However, the main reason why the need to reconsider this position is advanced by many scholars and also by a number of indigenous experts is the fact that the lack of a definition in UNDRIP allows state governments to adopt their own characterisation of indigenous peoples and, ultimately, to circumvent the duties/obligations laid down by the Declaration. The likelihood of this approach is epitomised by the declaration of vote expressed by the representative of Indonesia on the day UNDRIP was adopted. He said that, on account of the understanding of the term 'indigenous peoples' accepted by his government, and in light of the political, social and anthropological reality of his country, 'the rights stipulated in this Declaration accorded exclusively to Indigenous peoples are not applicable in the context of Indonesia'.[10] In a similar way, the delegate from India declared that his government 'regard[s] *the entire population of India* at the time of our independence, and its successors, to be Indigenous'.[11]

The most recent authoritative discussion on the subject at issue was developed by the International Law Association's (ILA) Committee on the Rights of Indigenous Peoples in 2010.[12] In particular, the Committee suggested that a definition/understanding may be useful for two reasons: a) in order to assess the scope of application of UNDRIP, with respect to which a precise legal conceptualisation of the categories of people to whom it is addressed could be helpful to increase its effectiveness; b) and – consistent with what we have just noted – in order to prevent that certain states may claim that the Declaration is not applicable in their territory in light of the assumed absence of indigenous communities within their borders. In developing its own understanding of the term 'indigenous peoples', the ILA Committee opts for a broad description capable of addressing the rich diversity characterising the different indigenous communities in the world, including

---

[9] UN, Declaration on the Rights of Indigenous Peoples (UNDRIP), GA Res. 61/295 (UN Doc. A/61/L.67 and Add.1) (adopted on 13 September 2007).

[10] See UN, General Assembly, '108th Plenary Meeting', (UN Doc. A/61/PV.108, 2007), at p. 4.

[11] Ibid., at p. 1 (emphasis added).

[12] See ILA, 'The Hague Conference 2010 – Rights of Indigenous Peoples', at pp. 6–9, available online at http://www.ila-hq.org/en/committees/index.cfm/cid/1024.

tribal peoples of Asian and African regions. In arguing for the inclusion of tribal peoples, it was emphasised that this is consistent with the practice of the WGIP and that indigenous and tribal peoples share similar characteristics concerning their need for protection and the types of difficulties they face irrespective of the sources of their oppression or historical injustices suffered. The ILA Committee notes that, while an official 'definition' continues to be inappropriate, a number of common characteristics or understandings have been advanced, most recently, within the Permanent Forum on Indigenous Issues. The most appropriate understanding is based on the following characteristics: a) *self-identification*: self-identification as both indigenous and as a people; b) *historical continuity*: common ancestry and historical continuity with pre-colonial and/or pre-settler societies; c) *special relationship with ancestral lands*: having a strong and special link with the territories occupied by their ancestors before colonial domination and surrounding natural resources. Such a link will usually form the basis of the cultural distinctiveness of indigenous peoples; d) *distinctiveness*: having distinct social, economic or political systems; having distinct language, culture, beliefs and customary law; e) *non-dominance*: forming non-dominant groups within the current society; f) *perpetuation*: perseverance to maintain and reproduce their ancestral environments, social and legal systems and culture as distinct peoples and communities.

The African Working Group on Indigenous Populations/Communities, with respect to the application of the term at issue within the African context, has also agreed that the use of characteristics or criteria is more useful than a formal definition.[13] The Working Group noted that, while the key criterion is self-identification, the way that different factors may apply will vary according to the different situations and experiences of the communities concerned. Therefore, the aforementioned criteria should be characterised by a sufficient degree of flexibility in their application. Consistently, not in all cases do *all* the listed criteria need to be met for a community to be recognised as indigenous. A flexible approach allows the differences existing among the diverse communities to be fully considered in conceptualising indigenous peoples.[14]

---

[13] See African Commission on Human and Peoples' Rights (ACHPR) and International Work Group for Indigenous Affairs (IWGIA), 'Report of the African Commission's Working Group of Experts on Indigenous Populations/Communities, submitted in accordance with the "Resolution on the Rights of Indigenous Populations/Communities in Africa"', Banjul, 2005, at p. 88, available at http://iwgia.synkron.com/graphics/Synkron-Library/Documents/publications/Downloadpublications/Books/AfricanCommissionbookEnglish.pdf.

[14] It is interesting to note that the recently adopted Protocol on the Protection of Traditional Knowledge and Expressions of Folklore which was signed by nine states at the African Regional Intellectual Property Organization (ARIPO) Diplomatic Conference in Swakopmund, Namibia, on 13 September 2010, takes a different approach from the African Commission's Working Group of Experts on Indigenous Populations/Communities, as it diplomatically avoids to even mention the term 'indigenous peoples' with respect to the African context, by using (but not defining) the term 'local and traditional communities'. See ARIPO, 'Swakopmund Protocol on the Protection of Traditional Knowledge and Expressions of Folklore', Diplomatic Conference of ARIPO (Namibia, 2010), available at http://www.cbd.int/doc/measures/abs/msr-abs-aripo-en.pdf.

3. CULTURAL HERITAGE, TRADITIONAL CULTURAL EXPRESSIONS AND TRADITIONAL KNOWLEDGE

From an indigenous perspective, cultural heritage represents a broad concept which incorporates all tangible and intangible aspects of the culture of indigenous peoples, including bio-cultural heritage, traditional cultural expressions, knowledge, innovations and practices. This heritage is based on their continuing relationship with, and access to, their territories and resources, according to a holistic perception typical of indigenous peoples' vision of life. For this reason, the working definition of cultural heritage to be adopted, in light of the purposes of the present chapter, should be broad enough in its scope to include the specific complexity of the heritage of indigenous peoples, as a concept which coincides with the cultural identity of the peoples concerned and constantly recreates in a parallel way their social and human development.

At the international level, a definition of culture and cultural heritage corresponding to this approach is offered by the 1982 Mexico City Declaration on Cultural Policies, according to which culture is interpreted to be:

> the whole complex of distinctive spiritual, material, intellectual and emotional features that characterize a society or social group. It includes not only the arts and letters, but also modes of life, the fundamental rights of the human being, value systems, traditions and beliefs.[15]

Consistent with this notion, the Mexico City Declaration defines the cultural heritage of a people as including:

> the works of its artists, architects, musicians, writers and scientists and also the work of anonymous artists, expressions of the people's spirituality, and the body of values which give meaning to life. It includes both tangible and intangible works through which the creativity of that people finds expression: languages, rites, beliefs, historic places and monuments, literature, works of art, archives and libraries.[16]

In this respect, it goes without saying that the examples mentioned in this definition are not exclusive. In particular, with regard to indigenous peoples, other elements of their cultural heritage include lands, territories and natural resources, as both expressions of their spirituality and as 'values which give meaning to [their] life'.

With respect to 'traditional cultural expressions', this term expresses a concept which, more than by a *definition* in the proper sense of the word, is suitable to be expressed through a *description*. This is an important *caveat* as a 'description' is characterised by inherent flexibility, making it adaptable to the innumerable diverse social and environmental situations existing in the different parts of the world. This approach is reflected in Article 1 of WIPO's (World Intellectual Property Organization) Draft Articles on the Protection of Traditional Cultural Expressions/Expressions of Folklore,[17] which, after

---

[15] UNESCO, Mexico City Declaration on Cultural Policies (UNESCO Doc. CLT/MD/1) (adopted on 6 August 1982).

[16] Ibid., at para. 23.

[17] WIPO, Intergovernmental Committee on Intellectual Property and Genetic Resources, Traditional Knowledge and Folklore (IGC), Secretariat, 'Draft Articles on the Protection of

providing a very detailed explanation of the concept in point, adds that the 'specific choice of terms to denote the protected subject matter should be determined at the national, sub-regional, and regional levels'; to this sentence we would add the term 'local' after 'regional'. As for the description of 'traditional cultural expressions' offered by Article 1 of the Draft Articles, it is conceived as:

> any form, tangible or intangible, in which traditional culture [and knowledge] are embodied and have been passed on from generation to generation, including, but not limited to: (a) phonetic or verbal expressions, such as stories, epics, legends, poetry, riddles and other narratives; words, signs, names, and symbols; (b) musical or sound expressions, such as songs, rhythms, and instrumental music; (c) expressions by action, such as dances, plays, ceremonies, rituals, games, puppet performances, and other performances; (d) tangible expressions, such as material expressions of art, handicrafts, architecture and spiritual forms.

The same provision expressly adds that '[p]rotection shall extend to any traditional cultural expression or expression of folklore which is the unique product of an indigenous people or local community and belongs to that people or community as part of their cultural or social identity or heritage'.

To an equivalent extent, the concept of 'traditional knowledge' is also hardly circumscribable within the narrow borders of a definition. According to Article 3.2 of the 2011 WIPO Intergovernmental Committee on Intellectual Property and Genetic Resources, Traditional Knowledge and Folklore's (IGC's) Revised Objectives and Principles on the Protection of Traditional Knowledge, the term in point refers:

> to the content or substance of knowledge resulting from intellectual activity in a traditional context, and includes the know-how, skills, innovations, practices and learning that form part of traditional knowledge systems, and knowledge embodying traditional lifestyles of indigenous and local communities, or contained in codified knowledge systems passed between generations. It is not limited to any specific technical field, and may include agricultural, environmental and medicinal knowledge, and knowledge associated with genetic resources.[18]

Even though the provision in point makes it clear that this 'definition' is valid '[f]or the purpose of these principles only', it can be considered an adequate description of the concept in point also for the purposes of the present chapter. However, it is essential to emphasise that – to a similar extent of what we have noted with respect to the concept of 'traditional cultural expressions' – the 'definition' in point is to be understood as characterised by a wide degree of flexibility, to make it possible to be adapted to the specific peculiarities of the different communities concerned.

Traditional Cultural Expressions/Expressions of Folklore prepared at IWG 1', (WIPO Doc. WIPO/GRTKF/IC/17/9, 2010), Annex.

[18] WIPO, IGC, Secretariat, 'The Protection of Traditional Knowledge: Revised Objectives and Principles', (WIPO Doc. WIPO/GRTKF/IC/18/5, 2011), Annex. For more details on the concepts of 'traditional cultural expressions' and 'traditional knowledge' see Christoph Antons, 'Intellectual Property Rights in Indigenous Cultural Heritage: Basic Concepts and Continuing Controversies', in this volume; and Martin Girsberger and Benny Müller, 'International Trade in Indigenous Cultural Heritage: An IP Practitioners' Perspective', in this volume.

4. HUMAN RIGHTS AND INDIGENOUS PEOPLES' RIGHTS IN INTERNATIONAL LAW

4.1 The Evolution of the Promotion of Indigenous Peoples' Rights at the International Level

The action for the development of the rights of indigenous peoples at the international level can be divided into three stages. These stages are lobbying (with national and colonial governments), listening (by governments and the international community) and a deeper listening, resulting in the progressive transposition of indigenous rights into international law rules.

In colonial times various indigenous peoples lobbied their governments and monarchs in order to obtain recognition and respect of their rights, often in response to mistreatment and dispossession of their lands. For example, in the early 1900s, while their national governments were totally ignoring their rights and aspirations, Aboriginal Australians, Māori and Salish delegations visited King George of Britain in order to obtain support for their struggle. In the 1930s, a number of indigenous delegations (including some coming from the USA and New Zealand) had also visited the League of Nations in Geneva, but they were refused an official audience.[19]

After the end of the Second World War, the new world society, devastated by the terrible events of the conflict, became a florid ground for the acceleration of civil rights movements in many countries, including the United States of America and Australia. In the latter country, Aboriginal Australians were finally recognised as Australian citizens after the pivotal 1967 constitutional referendum and voted as Australian citizens for the first time in the 1969 elections.[20] In some regions, particularly Africa, strong decolonisation movements rose up and countries moved away from colonial powers towards independence. Therefore, the indigenous rights movement started to evolve in coincidence with the wider development of human rights at the international level. However, the evolution of the two processes was in no way parallel. In fact, human rights legal instruments adopted after the Second World War focused on the protection of individual rights, while group or collective rights were considered as subsumed within, or even at odds with, individual rights. As a consequence, for a long time indigenous peoples continued to be marginalised by legal rules which developed without taking into account their diversity, needs and worldviews as well as the inherently collective nature of their cultures, that is, their 'cosmologies'. In some circumstances, indigenous peoples could indirectly benefit from the application of individual human rights, but this happened on an incidental basis as no specific rules existed which addressed them as distinct peoples with peculiar needs.

In this period, indigenous peoples continued to try to advance their rights through lobbying. However, the international community was unable or unwilling to accept their

---

19 See UNPFII, supra note 3.

20 John Scott and New South Wales Board of Studies, *A Political Dreaming: Our Place, Indigenous Aspirations for Constitutional Law Reform*, Sydney: Office of the Board of Studies NSW, 1998.

calls for recognition of collective rights, as the human rights discourse remained unilaterally centred on individual rights, and firmly based on the western conception of rights.

In the 1950s, the UN started to listen to indigenous peoples. However, the attention devoted to them was characterised by an utterly paternalistic and western-oriented approach, resulting in a total incapacity to understand them and their distinctiveness. Such an approach resulted in the adoption of ILO Convention No. 107 Concerning the Protection and Integration of Indigenous and Other Tribal and Semi-Tribal Populations in Independent Countries (ILO Convention No. 107).[21] This Convention represented the first attempt to codify international obligations of states in respect of indigenous and tribal populations and was the first international convention on the subject. It was ratified by 27 countries, ten of which have subsequently denounced it after the adoption of ILO Convention No. 169. Its assimilationist approach reflected a commonly held view that indigenous and tribal peoples, over time, had no option but to lose their distinct identities and become part of the broader societies surrounding them. This approach fell into question in the late 1960s and 1970s, when the UN began to consider indigenous issues in a more sensitive manner, taking into consideration their distinctiveness as well as their calls to self-determination. A Committee of Experts convened in 1986 by the Governing Body of the ILO concluded that 'the integrationist approach of the Convention was obsolete and that its application was detrimental in the modern world'.[22] This led to the drastic revision of ILO Convention No. 107, eventually resulting in the adoption of ILO Convention No. 169. The latter Convention may be considered as the first 'modern' international legal instrument on indigenous peoples, providing for a relatively satisfactory range of rights in their favour; however – at the time of this writing – the fact that it has been ratified by only 22 states[23] makes it of limited applicability.

The third phase of the evolution of the promotion of indigenous peoples' rights at the international level is represented by the stage of deep listening and responding, consistent with the ability that indigenous Australians call 'Dadirri'[24] – deep listening and quite still awareness. This translated into the recognition of indigenous peoples' rights in the context of international law. Indigenous peoples themselves provided a huge contribution to the development of this stage, through participating in various international fora for over 30 years. During this period, significant advancements occurred in the field, starting from ILO Convention No. 169 through to UNDRIP, which at the moment of writing represents the ultimate standard-setting instrument concerning indigenous peoples' rights. It is very

---

21 ILO Convention No. 107 Concerning the Protection and Integration of Indigenous and Other Tribal and Semi-Tribal Populations in Independent Countries, 328 UNTS 24 (adopted on 26 June 1957, entered into force 2 June 1959), revised in 1989 by ILO Convention No. 169 Concerning Indigenous and Tribal Peoples in Independent Countries, 1659 UNTS 383 (adopted on 27 June 1989, entered into force 5 September 1991). Even though, since the adoption of ILO Convention No. 169, ILO Convention No. 107 is no longer open for ratification, it is still in force for 17 countries, a number of which have significant populations of indigenous peoples.

22 ILO, 'Convention No. 107', available at http://www.ilo.org/indigenous/Conventions/no107/lang–en/index.htm.

23 See the website of the International Labour Organization at http://www.ilo.org/ilolex/cgi-lex/ratifce.pl?C169.

24 'Dadirri' is a word from the Ngangikurungkurr Tribal Group from the Daly River Region in Far Northern Australia.

significant that, during the phase in point, the collective rights of indigenous peoples were finally recognised and these peoples reached a wide degree of visibility. However, these outcomes still represent 'intermediate' results. In the future they must lead towards the improvement of the *effectiveness* and actual enjoyment of indigenous peoples' rights, through the effective implementation of the relevant standards by governments at the domestic level and, eventually, to the improvement of living conditions of indigenous peoples consistent with their own expectations and needs. For this purpose, UNDRIP should be properly applied and incorporated into domestic legal systems, leading to the effective realisation of collective rights of indigenous peoples and to the establishment of a safe environment for cultural development, including in the context of trade in cultural heritage.

With respect to UNDRIP it is to be noted that, as a declaration of principles adopted by the General Assembly of the UN, it does not have a legally binding status. This notwithstanding, it reflects the collective views of the UN, and must therefore be taken into account by all UN members in good faith. Despite its non-directly-binding status, UNDRIP has a strong moral force and huge legal significance. First, in many of its parts it reflects actual state obligations under other sources of international law, particularly customary international law as well as principles previously affirmed – directly or indirectly – by human rights treaties that are legally binding and enforceable.[25] In addition, the first sentence of its Preamble – according to which the General Assembly, in adopting the Declaration, is guided 'by the purposes and principles of the Charter of the UN, and good faith in the fulfilment of the obligations assumed by states in accordance with the Charter' – shows that UNDRIP represents the direct emanation and realisation of some of the principles affirmed by the UN Charter, the binding character of which is undeniable. As a consequence – to the extent that compliance with the rules proclaimed by UNDRIP constitutes a necessary precondition for the proper realisation of the principles expressed by the UN Charter – the provisions of the Declaration with respect to which this equation applies are also to be considered as having binding force, as their violation would result in a breach of the UN Charter.[26]

An interesting example of how indigenous rights are taken into account in the development of international standards is offered by the negotiation and adoption of the 2010 Nagoya Protocol on Access to Genetic Resources and the Fair and Equitable Sharing of Benefits arising from their Utilization to the Convention on Biological Diversity (Nagoya Protocol).[27] In fact, Article 8(j) of the 1992 Convention on Biological Diversity[28] – dealing

---

[25] See ILA, supra note 12, at p. 6.

[26] See Federico Lenzerini, 'International Law, Indigenous Peoples and UN Mechanisms', in Manickam C. Raj and Jyothi Raj (eds), *World Parliament of Indigenous Peoples*, Tumkur: Ambedkar Resource Centre, 2011, pp. 152–72, at pp. 161–2.

[27] Nagoya Protocol on Access to Genetic Resources and the Fair and Equitable Sharing of Benefits Arising from their Utilization to the Convention on Biological Diversity (UN Doc. UNEP/CBD/COP/DEC/X/1) (adopted on 29 October 2010). See Convention on Biological Diversity, 'The Nagoya Protocol on Access and Benefit-sharing', available at http://www.cbd.int/abs/.

[28] Rio Convention on Biological Diversity, 1760 UNTS 79; 31 ILM 818 (opened for signature 5 June 1992, entered into force 29 December 1993).

with *in situ* conservation of innovations and practices of indigenous and local communities embodying traditional lifestyles relevant for the conservation and sustainable use of biological diversity – is considered a cross-cutting issue within the various thematic areas which make up the Convention. This provision is therefore taken into consideration in the context of any programme aimed at implementing the Convention itself. Furthermore, during the negotiations leading to the adoption of the Nagoya Protocol, a positive environment was nurtured through considering indigenous peoples and local communities as essential partners in saving life on Earth. The parties consequently affirmed that indigenous peoples and local communities are central to and play a key role in giving realisation to the purposes of the Convention, consisting in achieving its three goals of conservation, sustainable use of biodiversity and the equitable sharing of benefits arising from the utilisation of genetic resources. These peoples and communities, with their knowledge and wisdom, indeed provide a formidable contribution in solving some of the most serious problems ever faced by humanity, including the unsustainable use of resources, massive extinction of plants and animals and climate change. Therefore, in the context of the Convention, indigenous peoples are considered not as mere stakeholders, but rather as rights-holders, and their effective participation has been guaranteed with respect to all matters of interest to them.

4.2 International Human Rights Standards and Indigenous Peoples' Rights

In the UN context, the 1966 Covenants on human rights[29] represent, chronologically, the first binding international instruments making the advancement and enforcement of certain rights of indigenous peoples possible. As a whole, they specify the basic civil, political, economic, social and cultural rights of individuals and, to a limited extent, of peoples. Article 1 common to the International Covenant on Economic, Social and Cultural Rights (ICESCR) and the International Covenant on Civil and Political Rights (ICCPR) proclaims the right to self-determination of peoples, which includes the right to freely dispose of their natural wealth and resources and not to be deprived of their means of subsistence. Although at the time the two covenants were adopted the term 'peoples' used in common Article 1 was probably understood to refer to national peoples only, the subsequent evolution of international law has widely expanded the scope of the term in point, to the extent that, at present, it is unquestionable that it includes indigenous peoples, as entities who preserve an intrinsic connection with their ancestral territories as well as their own distinct societies, including their own legal systems. This is confirmed by a huge body of practice developed by both domestic[30] and international bodies,[31] and has recently

---

[29] UN, International Covenant on Economic, Social and Cultural Rights (ICESCR), 993 UNTS 3; 6 ILM 360 (adopted on 16 December 1966, entered into force 3 January 1976); UN, International Covenant on Civil and Political Rights (ICCPR), 999 UNTS 171 and 1057 UNTS 407; 6 ILM 368 (adopted on 16 December 1966, entered into force 23 March 1976).

[30] See, in particular, the renowned sentence of the Supreme Court of Canada in the case of *Re: Secession of Quebec* (1998) 2 SCR 217, 37 ILM 1340.

[31] See, *inter alia*, UN, ICCPR, Human Rights Committee, 'Concluding Observations: Canada', (UN Doc. CCPR/C/79/Add.105, 1999); 'Concluding Observations: Mexico', (UN Doc. CCPR/C/79/Add.109, 1999); 'Concluding Observations: Norway', (UN Doc. CCPR/C/79/Add.112, 1999);

found expression in Article 3 of UNDRIP.[32] The latter instrument, considered as a whole, clearly shows that the content of the right in point does not extend to include a right for indigenous peoples to secede from the territorial state where they live. On the other hand, however, it must not be considered as a *sui generis* right specially accorded to indigenous peoples. Therefore, apart from the right to secede (which only applies to colonised peoples and national peoples subject to foreign occupation, although it is debatable whether it may also apply in other specific cases on an exceptional basis),[33] the right to self-determination is applicable to indigenous peoples to the same extent as to any other people. As for the content of the right to self-determination, it is explicated by Article 4 of UNDRIP, according to which indigenous peoples, in exercising their right to self-determination, have the right to autonomy or self-government in matters relating to their internal and local affairs. Given the centrality of culture and cultural heritage to indigenous identity, the right to autonomy undoubtedly extends to their natural resources and knowledge.

In addition to the right to self-determination, indigenous peoples' rights are indirectly safeguarded by a few provisions of the two covenants which, although aimed at protecting rights of an individual nature, cover in practice some fundamental prerogatives of collective character. This happens in particular with Article 27 ICCPR, protecting the right

---

'Concluding Observations: Australia', (UN Doc. A/55/40, 2000); 'Concluding Observations: Sweden', (UN Doc. CCPR/CO/74/SWE, 2002); 'Concluding Observations: New Zealand', (UN Doc. CCPR/CO/75/NZL, 2002); 'Concluding Observations: Finland', (UN Doc. CCPR/CO/82/FIN, 2004); 'Concluding Observations: Canada', (UN Doc. CCPR/C/CAN/CO/5, 2006); 'Concluding Observations: Norway', (UN Doc. CCPR/C/NOR/CO/5, 2006); 'Concluding Observations: United States', (UN Doc. CCPR/C/USA/Q/3/CRP.4, 2006). UN, Committee on Economic, Social and Cultural Rights, 'Concluding Observations: The Philippines', (UN Doc. E/C.12/PHL/CO/4, 2008); 'Concluding Observations: Sweden', (UN Doc. E/C.12/SWE/CO/5, 2008). See also Commission of the European Communities, 'The Second Northern Dimension Action Plan 2004–2006', (COM(2003) 343 final of 10 June 2003) (affirming, at p. 20, the need for 'protecting inherited rights of self-determination, land rights and cultural rights of indigenous peoples'). African Commission on Human and People's Rights (ACHPR), *Katangese Peoples' Congress v Zaire*, Communication No. 75/92, 1995, at para. 6; ACHPR, *Centre for Minority Rights Development (Kenya) and Minority Rights Group International on behalf of Endorois Welfare Council v Kenya*, Communication No. 276/2003, 2010, at para. 162; ACHPR, 'Advisory Opinion of the African Commission on the United Nations Declaration on the Rights of Indigenous Peoples', adopted in May 2007, at para. 22, available online at http://www.achpr.org/english/Special%20Mechanisms/Indegenous/Advisory%20opinion_eng.pdf; Inter-American Commission of Human Rights (IACHR), 'Report on the Situation of Human Rights of a Segment of the Nicaraguan Population of Miskito Origin', (OEA/Ser.L/V/II.62, doc. 10 rev. 3, 1983), at para. 15; IACHR, 'Resolution No. 12/85', (Case No. 7615, Brazil, 5 March 1985), at paras 24, 31 and 33, available at http://www.cidh.oas.org/annualrep/84.85eng/brazil7615.htm; IACHR, 'The Human Rights Situation of the Indigenous People in America', (OEA/Ser.L/V/II.108, Doc. 62, 2000), at p. 125.

[32] Article 3 UNDRIP affirms that 'Indigenous peoples have the right to self-determination. By virtue of that right they freely determine their political status and freely pursue their economic, social and cultural development.'

[33] We refer, in particular, to the situation hypothesised by the Supreme Court of Canada in *Re: Secession of Quebec*, supra note 30, according to which it is possible that a minority people within the state has a right to 'external self-determination … where a definable group is denied meaningful access to government to pursue their political, economic, social and cultural development', at para. 138.

of persons belonging to ethnic, religious or linguistic minorities – *in community with the other members of their group* – to enjoy their own culture, to profess and practise their own religion, or to use their own language. This provision translates in practice into a state obligation to ensure the safeguarding of particular ways of life 'associated with the use of land resources, especially in the case of indigenous peoples', including 'such traditional activities as fishing or hunting and the right to live in reserves protected by law'.[34] These prerogatives assume a collective dimension, since, even though the rights protected under Article 27 are individual rights, 'they depend in turn on the ability of the minority group to maintain its culture, language or religion'. Therefore, it is necessary that states adopt positive measures 'to protect the identity of a minority and the rights of its members to enjoy and develop their culture and language and to practise their religion, in community with the other members of the group'.[35]

As emerges from the passages just quoted, indigenous peoples have a very special relationship with their traditional lands and waters, representing an essential element to be preserved in order to make the realisation of their collective and individual rights concretely possible. The said relationship is so intimate and spiritually driven that it is not properly correct to assert that the land belongs to indigenous peoples; rather, most indigenous peoples would say that *they belong to the land*. In this respect, the term 'land' is to be intended in its broadest meaning, as the *total environment* of the areas that indigenous peoples occupy or otherwise use,[36] therefore including not only territories as such but also waters and surface and sub-surface resources located therein. In the last few decades, international law has progressively recognised indigenous land rights – as collective prerogatives – taking into account their character of essential pre-requisite to allow indigenous peoples to preserve and develop their distinct cultural identities.[37] At present, it can be reasonably asserted that the collective right of indigenous peoples to their traditional lands is recognised by customary international law, in the form of a particular manifestation of the right to property.[38] However, the previously emphasised strict connection of indigenous land rights with their cultural identity makes such rights stronger than 'ordinary' private property rights. This is clear in Article 14 of ILO Convention No. 169 – recognising indigenous peoples' rights of ownership and possession over the lands that they traditionally occupy – as well as in Article 26 UNDRIP, proclaiming the rights to own, use, develop and control the lands, territories and resources that indigenous peoples have traditionally owned, occupied or otherwise used or acquired.

---

[34] See Human Rights Committee, 'General Comment No. 23: The Rights of Minorities (Article 27)' (UN doc. CCPR/C/21/Rev.1/Add.5, 1994), at para. 7.

[35] Ibid., at para. 6.2. See also Christoph B. Graber, 'Using Human Rights to Tackle Fragmentation in the Field of Traditional Cultural Expressions: An Institutional Approach', in Christoph B. Graber and Mira Burri-Nenova (eds), *Intellectual Property and Traditional Cultural Expressions in a Digital Environment,* Cheltenham, UK and Northampton, MA: Edward Elgar, 2008, pp. 96–120, at pp. 105–7; and Jessica C. Lai, 'The Protection of Māori Cultural Heritage: Post-Endorsement of the UN Declaration on the Rights of Indigenous Peoples', *University of Lucerne, Switzerland,* i-call Working Paper No. 2 (2011), at pp. 31–2, available at http://www.unilu.ch/files/i-call_working_paper_2011_02_lai_maori_cultural_heritage__undrip.pdf.

[36] See ILO Convention No. 169, Article 13.2.

[37] See ILA, supra note 12, at pp. 20–25; and the practice cited at pp. 43–50.

[38] Ibid., at p. 51.

In addition, Article 15 of ILO Convention No. 169 makes it clear that exploitation of resources pertaining to indigenous lands is only possible after consultation with the people concerned and through ensuring that they participate in the benefits of such exploitation and receive fair compensation for any damage sustained. Furthermore, pursuant to Article 16, relocation of indigenous peoples from their lands is only possible as an exceptional measure and with their free, prior and informed consent or through appropriate procedures established by law, with the option of return, whenever possible, as well as with full compensation for any resulting loss or injury.

In the two decades following the adoption of ILO Convention No. 169, the status of indigenous land rights in international law has been further reinforced and consolidated, as demonstrated by UNDRIP, which excludes any possibility of relocating indigenous peoples from their traditional lands except with their free, prior and informed consent and after agreement on fair and just compensation.[39] The Declaration, therefore, recognises an absolute right to veto in favour of the peoples concerned in this respect. As for the exploitation of indigenous lands and/or resources, Article 32 UNDRIP commends states to cooperate in good faith with the communities concerned in order to obtain their free, prior and informed consent, in addition to establishing effective mechanisms for just and fair redress in the event such exploitation takes place. Even though this provision is not totally clear on whether or not it establishes a right to veto in favour of indigenous peoples, its requirements to make the exploitation of indigenous lands and/or resources possible are undoubtedly stricter than those established in Article 15 of ILO Convention No. 169. The provision in point is complemented by Article 29, proclaiming the right of indigenous peoples to the conservation and protection of the environment and the productive capacity of their lands and resources.

Finally, with regard to land rights, it is notable that, pursuant to Article 28 UNDRIP, indigenous peoples have the right to 'restitution or, when this is not possible, just, fair and equitable compensation, for the lands, territories and resources which they have traditionally owned or otherwise occupied or used, and which have been ... taken ... without their free, prior and informed consent'.

Cultural rights also (and in particular) play a key function for indigenous peoples. Culture has in fact a fundamental role in the preservation and advancement of the identity and collective rights of indigenous peoples, as well as of all individual rights of their members. As clearly emerges from the preceding assessment, all main rights of indigenous peoples – including self-determination and land rights – assume a markedly cultural connotation and find their very *raison d'être* as prerogatives strictly intertwined with the cultural identity of the peoples concerned. To properly illustrate the importance of cultural rights for indigenous peoples, one could assert that culture is the cradle of all their rights, which, therefore, exist and are shaped depending on the cultural distinctiveness of the specific community concerned.

In concrete terms, cultural rights translate into an innumerable amount of prerogatives, encompassing all elements that are essential for the preservation of indigenous peoples' cultural identity. These prerogatives have therefore to be established on a case-by-case basis, depending on the elements that are perceived as fundamental by a given indigenous

---

[39] See UNDRIP, Article 10.

community for its own survival. This approach has been followed by the main international human rights bodies, as epitomised by the interpretation given to Article 27 ICCPR by the Human Rights Committee, previously explained. In addition, it has been further specified by human rights monitoring bodies operating at the regional level. In particular, in its 2005 judgment concerning the case of the *Moiwana Community of Suriname*,[40] the Inter-American Court of Human Rights (IACrtHR) found that the fact that the respondent state had forcibly deprived the said community of the possibility of honouring its deceased persons according to its own traditions amounted to inhuman treatment of its members, in light of the special significance of those traditions for the cultural identity of the group. This conclusion was reached on account of the fact that, as emphasised by the Court:

> [i]f the various death rituals are not performed according to N'djuka tradition, it is considered a moral transgression, which will not only anger the spirit of the individual who died, but may also offend other ancestors of the community. This leads to a number of 'spiritually-caused illnesses' that become manifest as actual physical maladies and can potentially affect the entire natural lineage. The N'djuka understand that such illnesses are not cured on their own, but rather must be resolved through cultural and ceremonial means; if not, the conditions will persist through generations.[41]

Similarly, in a recent case the African Commission on Human and Peoples' Rights (ACHPR) emphasised that:

> protecting human rights goes beyond the duty not to destroy or deliberately weaken minority groups, but requires respect for, and protection of, their religious and cultural heritage essential to their group identity ... [The State is obliged] to promote and protect traditional values recognised by a community. ... [C]ulture [is to be understood] to mean that complex whole which includes a spiritual and physical association with one's ancestral land, knowledge, belief, art, law, morals, customs, and any other capabilities and habits acquired by humankind as a member of society – the sum total of the material and spiritual activities and products of a given social group that distinguish it from other similar groups.[42]

The centrality of cultural rights in the life of indigenous peoples is well perceived by UNDRIP, which places them in a crucial position within the whole text. First, Article 8 expresses the general principle according to which '[i]ndigenous peoples and individuals have the right not to be subjected to forced assimilation or destruction of their culture'. Also, Article 12 provides for the right of indigenous peoples 'to manifest, practise, develop and teach their spiritual and religious traditions, customs and ceremonies; the right to maintain, protect, and have access in privacy to their religious and cultural sites; the right to the use and control of their ceremonial objects; and the right to the repatriation

---

[40] IACrtHR, *Case of the Moiwana Community v Suriname* (15 June 2005) Series C No. 124 García-Ramírez P, available online at http://www.corteidh.or.cr/docs/casos/articulos/seriec_124_ing.pdf.

[41] Ibid., at para. 86(9).

[42] See African Union, ACHPR, *Centre for Minority Rights Development (Kenya) and Minority Rights Group International on behalf of Endorois Welfare Council v Kenya*, supra note 31, at para. 241.

of their human remains'. Furthermore, according to Article 13, indigenous peoples have the right 'to revitalise, use, develop and transmit to future generations their histories, languages, oral traditions, philosophies, writing systems and literatures, and to designate and retain their own names for communities, places and persons'.

In the context of cultural rights, in view of the purposes of the present chapter, special significance is played by the right of indigenous peoples to their collective creativity. In general terms the right in point – as an individual prerogative – is generally recognised by Article 27.2 of the Universal Declaration of Human Rights (UDHR),[43] according to which '[e]veryone has the right to the protection of the moral and material interests resulting from any scientific, literary or artistic production of which he is the author'. This provision was subsequently included, nearly verbatim, in Article 15 of the ICESCR, together with the rights to take part in cultural life and to enjoy the benefits of scientific progress. Although these rights are expressed as individual prerogatives, with respect to indigenous peoples they assume a communal dimension, extending their scope to the collective creativity, traditional knowledge and traditional cultural expressions of these peoples. This implies that State Parties must take measures 'to guarantee that the exercise of the right to take part in cultural life takes due account of the values of cultural life, which may be strongly communal or which can only be expressed and enjoyed as a community by indigenous peoples'.[44] In addition, by virtue of the Article in point, indigenous peoples have the right:

> to act collectively to ensure respect for their right to maintain, control, protect and develop their cultural heritage, traditional knowledge and traditional cultural expressions, as well as the manifestations of their sciences, technologies and cultures, including human and genetic resources, seeds, medicines, knowledge of the properties of fauna and flora, oral traditions, literature, designs, sports and traditional games, and visual and performing arts. States parties should respect the principle of free, prior and informed consent of indigenous peoples in all matters covered by their specific rights.[45]

---

[43] UN, Universal Declaration of Human Rights, UN GA Res. 217A (III) (UN Doc. A/810) (adopted on 10 December 1948).

[44] See UN, Committee on Economic Social and Cultural Rights, 'General Comment No. 21, Right of Everyone to Take Part in Cultural Life, Art. 15, para. 1 (a), of the International Covenant on Economic, Social and Cultural Rights', (UN doc. E/C.12/GC/21, 2009), at para. 36. The Committee continues by stressing that

> [t]he strong communal dimension of indigenous peoples' cultural life is indispensable to their existence, well-being and full development, and includes the right to the lands, territories and resources which they have traditionally owned, occupied or otherwise used or acquired. Indigenous peoples' cultural values and rights associated with their ancestral lands and their relationship with nature should be regarded with respect and protected, in order to prevent the degradation of their particular way of life, including their means of subsistence, the loss of their natural resources and, ultimately, their cultural identity. States parties must therefore take measures to recognize and protect the rights of indigenous peoples to own, develop, control and use their communal lands, territories and resources, and, where they have been otherwise inhabited or used without their free and informed consent, take steps to return these lands and territories. (Ibid. (footnotes omitted))

See also, consistently, paras 16(e) and 49(d).

[45] Ibid., at para. 37; see also paras 50(c) and 55(e).

In proclaiming this principle, the ICESCR reproduced the provision affirmed by Article 31 UNDRIP, which adds that indigenous peoples also have the right 'to maintain, control, protect and develop their intellectual property over such cultural heritage, traditional knowledge, and traditional cultural expressions'. This Article pairs with Article 11, providing for the collective right of indigenous peoples to practise and revitalise their cultural traditions and customs, including 'the right to maintain, protect and develop the past, present and future manifestations of their cultures, such as archaeological and historical sites, artefacts, designs, ceremonies, technologies and visual and performing arts and literature'. In the event that the cultural, intellectual, religious and spiritual property of indigenous peoples is taken without their free, prior and informed consent or in violation of their laws, traditions and customs, the communities concerned have the right to obtain appropriate and effective redress. Article 12 UNDRIP is also of significance in this respect, since, as noted above, it recognises the right of indigenous peoples to the use and control of their ceremonial objects; when these objects are in possession of states, they must seek to enable their repatriation and/or access to them by the communities concerned. Finally, Article 24 UNDRIP is worth mentioning, providing for the right of indigenous peoples 'to their traditional medicines and to maintain their health practices, including the conservation of their vital medicinal plants, animals and minerals'; in fact, for the peoples concerned, traditional medicine is usually to be considered as a manifestation of traditional knowledge and traditional cultural expressions.

The strength of the provisions just mentioned is reinforced by the circumstance that the right in point represents a prerogative directly arising from the principle of self-determination of peoples. In fact, as previously noted, the latter right is explicated by common Article 1.2 of the 1966 UN Covenants as presupposing that '[a]ll peoples may, for their own ends, freely dispose of their natural wealth and resources without prejudice to any obligations arising out of international economic co-operation, based upon the principle of mutual benefit, and international law. In no case may a people be deprived of its own means of subsistence.' In consideration of their fundamental significance for the cultural identity of indigenous peoples, the concepts of 'natural wealth and resources' and 'means of subsistence' include traditional knowledge, traditional expressions and cultural heritage. Therefore, indigenous peoples should be afforded the right to freely determine the use of their traditional resources and heritage in all contexts, including trade.

With respect to the context in point, a significant role may be played by the Nagoya Protocol, representing a major accomplishment of the tenth meeting of the Conference of the Parties to the Convention on Biological Diversity, which was adopted after more than six years of intense and sometimes difficult negotiations. The Protocol aims to advance the implementation of one of the three core objectives of the Convention, that is, the fair and equitable sharing of benefits arising from the utilisation of genetic resources. However, it may potentially play a significant role in ongoing discussions concerning the regulation of international trade in indigenous cultural heritage. During the negotiations, indigenous peoples were successful – thanks to their perseverance and systematic participation in the negotiating process – in ensuring that their rights were adequately safeguarded in the final text of the Protocol, by using UNDRIP as the legal framework establishing minimum standards. UNDRIP is 'noted' in the 26th preambular paragraph. A fundamental outcome achieved by indigenous negotiators was the recognition, in Article 7, of the requirement that indigenous communities give their prior and informed consent or approval as a necessary condition for accessing their traditional knowledge associated with genetic resources. The preamble contains several paragraphs of specific significance to indigenous peoples and their traditional knowledge, including references to Article 8(j) of the Convention, the interrelationship between genetic resources and traditional knowledge and their inseparable nature, the diversity of circumstances in which traditional knowledge is owned or held (including by countries), as well as the clause according to which nothing in the Protocol shall be construed as diminishing or extinguishing the existing rights of indigenous peoples. Among the substantive provisions, in addition to Article 7, Article 5 is of particular significance. This Article provides for the need to ensure that the benefits arising from the use of traditional knowledge associated with genetic resources as well as from the use of genetic resources held by indigenous communities are shared in a fair and equitable way, in accordance with domestic legislation. The same Article also requires that sharing of benefit is based on mutually agreed terms. The Protocol represents one of the first international legal instruments of direct relevance to indigenous peoples' rights negotiated after the adoption of UNDRIP. Even though reaffirming the sovereign right of states over their natural resources (in the third preambular paragraph and in Article 6), it is regarded by the majority of indigenous peoples participating in the negotiation process as a satisfactory outcome, even better than was expected (although not perfect). This outcome further confirms that a new conscience has matured within the international community recognising that the rights of indigenous peoples are to be effectively safeguarded in all contexts that are of importance to their cultural identity, including traditional knowledge, traditional cultural expressions and trade in cultural heritage.

The rules of international law concerning restitution of cultural heritage of indigenous peoples are also of particular significance for the purposes of the present chapter. In this context, in addition to Articles 11 and 12 UNDRIP, already noted, it is opportune to focus our attention on the 1995 UNIDROIT Convention on Stolen or Illegally Exported Cultural Objects (UNIDROIT Convention).[46] This Convention is especially meaningful for the reason that it recognises the extraordinary character of indigenous cultural heritage even though it is not an instrument having the specific purpose of safeguarding indigenous peoples' rights. The acknowledgment of the special importance of the said heritage is clear from the third preambular paragraph, which expresses the deep concern of the negotiators of the Convention for the damage frequently caused by illicit trade in cultural objects 'to the cultural heritage of national, tribal, indigenous or other communities'. Among the other pertinent provisions it is also notable that, according to Article 5.3(d), a court or other competent authority of a State Party must order the return of an illegally exported cultural object if the requesting state establishes that the removal of the object from its territory significantly impairs 'the traditional or ritual use of the object by a tribal or indigenous community', the latter being a circumstance which attributes to the object in point a *significant cultural importance*.[47]

In addition to the UNIDROIT Convention, several other international legal instruments, essentially of soft-law character, advocate restitution of cultural heritage of which

---

46 UNIDROIT Convention on Stolen or Illegally Exported Cultural Objects, 34 ILM 1322 (adopted on 24 June 1995, entered into force 1 July 1998).

47 However, of the four states specifically in focus in this volume (see Country Reports), only New Zealand is a member of the UNIDROIT Convention so far.

indigenous peoples have been deprived without their consent, and/or other reparatory measures, including adequate compensation.[48]

4.3 Indigenous Peoples' Rights versus Human Rights: Conflicting or Mutually Supportive Concepts?

The general provision included in Article 46.2 of UNDRIP – according to which '[i]n the exercise of the rights enunciated in the present Declaration, human rights and fundamental freedoms of all shall be respected' – together with other Articles of UNDRIP of more specific character,[49] raise the question of whether, in the real world, conflicts may arise between the rights of indigenous peoples and internationally recognised human rights of non-indigenous persons. At the same time, it would also be possible that proper realisation of the collective rights of an indigenous community – that is, the rights of the *community as a whole* – may conflict with certain rights recognised individually for members of the same community, as human beings. To provide just one example, it could be possible that the allocation of political powers within the community based on customary law (for example when it is automatically assigned to the elders) – which represents an expression of the right to self-determination – conflicts with the right of all members of the community, as citizens of the territorial state, to take part in the conduct of public affairs directly or through freely chosen representatives, affirmed by Article 25 ICCPR. This and other similar instances may not be resolved through simply asserting that they are merely internal to the indigenous communities concerned, as the interest in the protection of human rights is universal and goes beyond the specific social contexts to which the individuals concerned belong.

In reality, indigenous peoples' rights and (other) human rights clearly appear to be mutually supportive, in relation to the ultimate purpose of rights protection, that is, the protection and realisation of the supreme value of human dignity, conceived in both its collective and individual connotations. The potential inconsistencies between the collective rights of indigenous communities and the individual rights of their members or other individuals must therefore be treated in the same way as any other situation in which a tension between different rights arises. In particular, according to a well-established principle of international law – *apart from inderogable rights* (particularly those amounting to *ius cogens*), which must be respected in any circumstance by all, including indigenous peoples – the scope of human rights can be limited whether and to the extent that it is necessary in order to protect the rights of others. Therefore, when one of the said inconsistencies arises, it will be necessary to draw a balance between the different rights at stake in order to ascertain whether and, if yes, to what extent they can be accommodated or, when this is not possible, which right prevails over the other in the instant case. When

[48] See Ana F. Vrdoljak, 'Reparations for Cultural Loss', in Federico Lenzerini (ed.), *Reparations for Indigenous Peoples. International and Comparative Perspectives*, Oxford: Oxford University Press, 2008, pp. 197–228, at pp. 211–26.

[49] See, for example, UNDRIP, Article 34, stating that '[i]ndigenous peoples have the right to promote, develop and maintain their institutional structures and their distinctive customs, spirituality, traditions, procedures, practices and, in the cases where they exist, juridical systems or customs, *in accordance with international human rights standards*' (emphasis added).

operating this balance, however, it is to be taken into account that most indigenous peoples' rights, as expressed by UNDRIP, represent a specification of those basic rights – particularly cultural rights, self-determination and land rights – which are essential to ensure the very survival of the communities concerned as well as the realisation of their fundamental expectations. In light of this, in principle it will be possible to derogate from the basic rights of indigenous peoples only in those cases when the rights of others (or of community members) are of such fundamental importance not to admit any exception for whatever reason.

The appropriateness of this approach is confirmed by Article 46.2 of UNDRIP itself, which makes it clear that '[t]he exercise of the rights set forth in this Declaration shall be subject only to such limitations as are determined by law and in accordance with international human rights obligations. Any such limitations shall be non-discriminatory and *strictly necessary* solely for the purpose of securing due recognition and respect for the rights and freedoms of others and for meeting *the just and most compelling requirements* of a democratic society' (emphasis added). Further confirmation is offered by the way in which human rights norms in international treaties are generally drafted. To go back to the example provided above, according to Article 25 ICCPR the right to take part in the conduct of public affairs must be granted without *unreasonable* restrictions. In the case of the organisation of political powers internal to an indigenous community, any such restrictions are to be considered *reasonable* (again, to the extent that they do not touch inderogable rights), as the political and social organisation of indigenous peoples according to their customary law usually represents a specification of their fundamental right to self-determination.

5. INDIGENOUS PEOPLES' RIGHTS AND TRADE IN INDIGENOUS CULTURAL HERITAGE

Whereas the linkages between the rights of indigenous peoples recognised by international law and trade in cultural heritage may not always be direct, international trade in indigenous cultural heritage can certainly exercise a positive or negative impact on the safeguarding, exercise and enjoyment of such rights. This is particularly true with regard to the essential elements of the cultural identity of indigenous peoples, which obviously include bio-cultural heritage and its sub-components, particularly genetic resources, traditional knowledge and traditional cultural expressions. It is for this reason that ignoring the specificity and rights of indigenous peoples in the context of trade in indigenous cultural heritage may result in breaches of such rights pursuant to international law.

However, while it is obvious in theoretical terms, this assumption may apparently be difficult to translate in practice. In fact, the main context in which international trade finds expression and legal regulation – that is, the World Trade Organization (WTO) – dedicates virtually no attention to human rights in general, and indigenous rights in particular, within its institutional framework, even though the recent adoption of the Nagoya Protocol may be seen as paving the way for a reconsideration of intellectual property rules – even in the WTO context – in a more responsive way to indigenous peoples' needs.[50] In any event, this lack of attention cannot be considered as justifying the breach of indigenous peoples' rights that arises from the operation of WTO rules. In fact, the WTO represents a legal regime that is placed within the broader context of international law; therefore, it must be operated in a way fully consistent with the basic principles governing the international legal system as a whole, which represents the fundamental *chapeau* covering all specialised regimes regulating any specific areas of interstate relations. Among these basic principles, it is indisputable that human rights – including indigenous peoples' rights – represent the supreme values informing the whole edifice of international law. As a consequence, WTO rules cannot be implemented in a way that gives rise to breaches of the said rights. This includes the requirement that international trade in indigenous cultural heritage is carried out consistently with the need of ensuring – in all circumstances – proper safeguarding of the rights of indigenous peoples, as recognised by both customary international law and treaty law and, with respect to the latter, according to the interpretation given to the relevant rules by human rights monitoring bodies. This translates in practice not only into a right of indigenous peoples to invoke the enforcement of human rights principles for trade-related issues before human rights bodies, but also into an obligation of WTO institutions to apply WTO rules consistently with the relevant internationally recognised standards on indigenous peoples' rights.

Technically speaking, in legal terms, this conclusion is corroborated by a number of arguments.

First, among the generally applicable rules of treaty interpretation – also covering WTO treaties – the principle of *evolutionary interpretation* emerges, provided for by both customary international law and Article 31.3(c) of the 1969 Vienna Convention on the Law of Treaties.[51] According to this principle, when interpreting a treaty provision, to be taken into account, together with the context, are 'any relevant rules of international law applicable in the relations between the parties'. The principle in point acquires special significance when such 'relevant rules' are human rights standards, on account of the fundamental character of these standards within the context of international law. This assumption is confirmed by the international practice developed particularly with respect to another field of international economic law, that is, international investment law. In this field, both cultural heritage protection[52] and indigenous peoples' rights have been recognised as values that must be taken into proper account in the operation of investment treaties, possibly to such an extent as to justify exceptions and derogations to the application of the latter. With particular respect to indigenous peoples' rights, in a very recent award an ICSID (International Centre for Settlement of Investment Disputes) Tribunal noted the 'strong international policy and standards articulated in numerous written instruments and interpretive decisions that favour state action to promote [the]

---

[50] See WTO, 'Nagoya Gives New Context to Old Views in Intellectual Property Council' (1 March 2011), available at http://www.wto.org/english/news_e/news11_e/trip_01mar11_e.htm.

[51] Vienna Convention on the Law of Treaties, 1155 UNTS 331, 1969; 8 ILM 679 (adopted on 23 May 1969, entered into force 27 January 1980).

[52] See, in this respect, Federico Lenzerini, 'Property Protection and Protection of Cultural Heritage', in Stephen W. Schill (ed.), *International Investment Law and Comparative Public Law*, Oxford: Oxford University Press, 2010, pp. 541–68.

rights and interests of Indigenous peoples'[53] – including a likely existing 'principle of customary international law requiring governmental authorities to consult Indigenous peoples on governmental policies or actions significantly affecting them'.[54] The Tribunal, therefore, advocated that these rights must be adequately weighed in the application of investment and trade agreements (in the instant case the said award related to a claim based on the North American Free Trade Agreement [NAFTA]). Needless to say, although developed in the context of international investment law, this practice is clearly applicable, by analogy, to the field of international trade law.

Second, it is a fact that trade in indigenous cultural heritage – if practised without ensuring proper safeguarding for the rights of the communities concerned – may result in the deprivation, to the prejudice of these communities, of cultural elements that are essential for their cultural identity as well as for the effectiveness of certain individual rights of their members. As noted by the IACrtHR,[55] such a situation may trigger very serious breaches of the internationally recognised human rights of the persons concerned, to an extent that may even reach the threshold of inhuman or degrading treatment. In this event, an inderogable right – belonging to the category of *ius cogens* – would be breached, producing an effect that is absolutely unacceptable and admits no justification pursuant to contemporary international law. In light of the fact that no effect arising from the operation of an international treaty is allowed which is at odds with rules of *ius cogens*,[56] WTO agreements must be interpreted and applied consistently with such rules. This, of course, also applies in the context of trade in indigenous cultural heritage.[57] As a consequence, when trade involving manifestations of indigenous cultural heritage is likely to affect such fundamental rights of the members of indigenous communities, an imperative requirement exists to ensure that the relevant commercial transactions are carried out by ensuring that all necessary conditions are met in order to prevent the said fundamental rights being prejudiced.

Third, the same WTO legal regime suggests that certain fundamental non-trade values are to be safeguarded when applying trade rules. In particular, according to Article XX of the General Agreement on Tariffs and Trade (GATT) 1994, restrictions to international trade are allowed when, *inter alia*, they are 'necessary to protect human, animal or plant life or health' (Article XX [b]) or are 'imposed for the protection of national treasures of artistic, historic or archaeological value' (Article XX [f]). While the latter clause is potentially applicable to indigenous peoples' cultural heritage only whether and to the extent that such heritage is also considered as heritage of the Member State concerned, Article XX [b] can be used in cases when trade in indigenous cultural heritage may result in situations threatening the (physical or mental) health of members of indigenous communities. This kind of situation is certainly likely to occur, as demonstrated by the

---

53 See ICSID, *Grand River Enterprises Six Nations, Ltd et al. v United States of America* (12 January 2011) Award (on file with the authors), at para. 186.

54 Ibid., at para. 210.

55 See IACrtHR, *Case of the Moiwana Community v Suriname,* supra note 40, and corresponding text.

56 See Vienna Convention, supra note 51, Articles 53 and 64.

57 See also Fiona Macmillan, 'Finding Space in the Margins? Recognising the Rights of Indigenous Peoples in the WTO', in this volume.

IACrtHR's findings in the *Moiwana* case.[58] It is however to be noted that, to be activated, Article XX GATT would necessarily require state action on behalf of indigenous peoples, as its chapeau makes explicit reference to measures adopted or enforced by 'contracting parties'. This would be a case in which assistance by governments would be decisive for indigenous peoples, in order to ensure effectiveness of their own rights.

The conclusions just reached are not affected by the fact that the international provisions concerning indigenous peoples' rights are mainly included in legal instruments scarcely ratified (ILO Convention No. 169) or technically non-binding (UNDRIP). In fact, the most important of the said rights are today covered by customary international law as well as – although in most cases indirectly – by international human rights treaties.[59]

Of course, there would be no need to proceed to such a sophisticated comparative interpretation of provisions belonging to different fields of international law if it were possible to specifically address the problems inherent to the issue of trade in indigenous cultural heritage *within* the WTO system itself. This would meet the need to ensure certainty of law and could be done through creating ad hoc substantive provisions or, for example, through following the procedural approach advocated by Christoph B. Graber.[60] The latter approach, based on the establishment of ad hoc preferential rules for indigenous peoples' cultural heritage, would basically allow indigenous communities themselves, through participating in the relevant decision-making process, to play a fundamental role in deciding which products among their own cultural heritage, traditional knowledge and traditional cultural expressions – and on which basis – could be made the object of trade. However, in the absence of specific rules regulating this particular issue within the WTO legal framework, WTO institutions must be aware of the need to properly address the specific legal implications attached to indigenous peoples' cultural heritage, and accommodate the operation of international trade rules accordingly.

Finally, a further option to address the problems arising from international trade of indigenous cultural heritage would rely on the accomplishment of government-assisted action in order to allow indigenous peoples themselves – through participation – to directly promote their rights within the context of the world trade system. At the present stage of international law, incisive participation of indigenous peoples in international fora, including the WTO, is mainly possible thanks to the intercession of national states. In fact, membership of international organisations necessarily requires *statehood*, which is not possessed by indigenous peoples, despite the fact that they are entitled to the right to self-determination. However, the latter right presupposes certain duties of national states when representing the interests of their people before international organisations. In particular, it is not unreasonable to assert that a sort of *parallelism* exists between the right of indigenous peoples that their own interests are adequately taken into account *internally* (that is, within the territorial state) and the same right when the national government acts

[58] See IACrtHR, *Case of the Moiwana Community v Suriname,* supra note 40, and corresponding text.

[59] See supra note 25, and corresponding text.

[60] See Christoph B. Graber, 'Institutionalization of Creativity in Traditional Societies and in International Trade Law', in Shubha Ghosh and Robin P. Malloy (eds), *Creativity, Law and Entrepreneurship*, Cheltenham, UK and Northampton, MA: Edward Elgar, 2011, pp. 234–63.

externally. As a consequence, state delegations accredited at international organisations should adequately represent the interests of the indigenous communities living in their territory, possibly through including indigenous persons among their members. A successful example of this kind of cooperation between state governments and indigenous peoples is offered by Norway and Sweden, which usually include representatives of the Sami Parliaments among the members of their official delegations participating at the meetings of international organisations concerning matters of interest to the Sami people.[61]

Apart from this, alternative forms of participation of indigenous peoples in international organisations have developed in the last decades, for example, in the context of the negotiations of UNDRIP or the Nagoya Protocol, as well as within the general scheme of participation of the civil society representatives at meetings of UN human rights bodies, according to the term established by Economic and Social Council (ECOSOC) Resolution 1996/31. In the WTO context, this participation finds expression, in particular, before the Dispute Settlement Body's panels and Appellate Body, to the meetings of which NGOs representing indigenous peoples may be entitled – at the discretion of the relevant bodies and, in practice, when solicited by them – to participate as *amici curiae*.[62]

6. CONCLUSIONS – VISIONS OF A PLURALISTIC LEGAL SYSTEM

The recent developments of international law that have led to the recognition and affirmation of the collective rights of indigenous peoples have been based on the adaptation of existing human rights standards to the needs and expectations of indigenous peoples, with the result that they are not essentially *sui generis* rights. Many of these rights find their origin in human rights instruments developed prior to UNDRIP, and are ultimately expressed – as *collective* prerogatives – in the latter instrument, which, although not binding as such, mirrors human rights standards recognised by both customary and treaty law and enforceable through existing human rights mechanisms.

The operation of these standards produces significant legal implications in the context of trade in indigenous cultural heritage. In fact, they translate into specific prerogatives – including the rights of indigenous peoples to retain control of their own cultural heritage, to free, prior and informed consent as a precondition to make its exploitation lawful, as well as to share the benefits arising from trade in such heritage – which are to be shaped in light of the unique nature of indigenous cultural identity and distinctiveness.

However, it is evident that the concrete application of the said standards, especially in legal contexts which are exogenous to human rights law – including international trade law – may only be the result of sophisticated hermeneutic operations which may be difficult to carry out in some cases. In fact, while certain conclusions, favourable to the recognition of indigenous peoples' rights, may be naturally reached by human rights

---

[61] See, for example, Indigenous Peoples in the Barents Euro-Arctic Regions, 'Saami Presidents to COP15' (2009), available at http://www.barentsindigenous.org/saami-presidents-to-cop15.4658458.html.

[62] See WTO, 'Participation in Dispute Settlement Proceedings' (2011), available at http://www.wto.org/english/tratop_e/dispu_e/disp_settlement_cbt_e/c9s3p1_e.htm.

monitoring bodies, different approaches may be adopted in the practice of other bodies operating within contexts in which human rights do not represent a primary concern.

Today, international law is a pluralistic legal system, in the context of which different interests need to be reconciled with each other. While in principle this is always possible through relying on the general principles governing international law as a whole, it would be much easier in practice if and to the extent that ad hoc rules for the protection of a given value existed within the specific areas of international law by which the said value is concerned.

Therefore, it is appropriate that existing human rights standards are complemented by specific mechanisms for the protection, development and promotion of indigenous cultural heritage to be developed in the proper fora, including the WTO. As advocated since 1993 by Erica-Irene Daes, Special Rapporteur of the Sub-Commission on Prevention of Discrimination and Protection of Minorities and Chairperson of the Working Group on Indigenous Populations, in her Study on the Protection of the Cultural and Intellectual Property of Indigenous Peoples,[63] and subsequently by a number of authors,[64] the most appropriate way to safeguard indigenous cultural heritage and traditional knowledge is represented by the development of *sui generis* systems specifically aimed at regulating all aspects related to the protection and use of such heritage and knowledge, including international trade. These systems would allow full account to be taken of the collective nature of the heritage and knowledge in point. At present, the development of *sui generis* systems for the protection of the heritage of indigenous peoples is being investigated by a number of international bodies, including the Convention on Biological Diversity and WIPO. These *sui generis* systems would promote the development of a culturally sound approach to trade in indigenous cultural heritage, although it is important to stress that no single overarching international, regional or national *sui generis* system, however broad in scope, is likely to embrace all the characteristics and peculiarities of indigenous cultural heritage in its original cultural context and its related customary law, as well as the cultural and legal diversity of the world's indigenous and local communities. It is therefore vital that *sui generis* protection be local in nature and based on relevant local (indigenous) customary laws, although general guidelines should be developed at the national and international level providing for a core of basic relevant standards. This should include a binding international framework convention capable of attracting the consent of states on the need to establish and give operation to the *sui generis* systems in point. It is however important to reiterate that these systems should ultimately be developed at the local level, in appropriate ways according to the peculiarities of local indigenous communities and their customary laws – which are inherently local in nature – in order to avoid homogenisation and standardisation.

---

63 See UN, ECOSOC, Commission on Human Rights, Sub-Commission on Prevention of Discrimination and Protection of Minorities, 'Discrimination Against Indigenous Peoples. Study on the Protection of the Cultural and Intellectual Property of Indigenous Peoples', (UN Doc. E/CN.4/Sub.2/1993/28, 1993).

64 See Federico Lenzerini, 'Traditional Knowledge, Biogenetic Resources, Genetic Engineering and Intellectual Property Rights', in Daniel Wüger and Thomas Cottier (eds), *Genetic Engineering and the World Trade System*, Cambridge: Cambridge University Press, 2008, pp. 118–48, at pp. 139–47, and the sources quoted therein.

The accomplishment of this step would pave the way for a new era of international law, in which indigenous rights would be realised more effectively and the world society would develop in a manner truly based on pluralism and cultural diversity. In order to give realisation to the very philosophy of 'international community', a truly participatory approach – driven by all sectors of civil society, including indigenous peoples, and therefore reflecting the legal and cultural diversity of the human race around the globe – should be developed, offering equal protection for all, based on the richness of cultural differences. This final and most sophisticated step – embracing a new participatory and pluralistic methodology – could direct the journey of humanity into the new millennium, making a deeper level of human dignity, equity and full enjoyment of human rights possible.

4. Finding space in the margins? Recognising the rights of indigenous peoples in the WTO

Fiona Macmillan

1. INTRODUCTION

This chapter argues that the international legal regime is systemically divided between public international law and international economic law, with very little in the way of legal mechanisms to bridge the gulf between the two systems. Some interests of indigenous peoples, including those that relate to the protection of traditional knowledge and traditional cultural expressions, are recognised in the public international law system. However, there is considerable difficulty in finding space for the recognition of these interests in the system of international economic law. This conclusion is particularly problematic in light of the systemic pre-eminence of WTO (World Trade Organization) law, largely as a consequence of the power of its dispute resolution system.

After considering the relationship between the two systems, and the respective places of indigenous peoples, cultural heritage protection and intellectual property protection within the two systems, the chapter analyses the WTO Appellate Body decision in *China – Measures Affecting Trading Rights and Distribution Services for Certain Publications and Audio-Visual Entertainment Products*[1] with a view to considering whether or not it is possible to find a space in the WTO system for the recognition of values generated in the public international system with respect to the protection of the cultural heritage of indigenous peoples.

2. THE SYSTEMIC DIVIDE IN INTERNATIONAL LAW

2.1 Origins of the Systemic Divide in the International Legal Order

This chapter argues that the current international legal order, which has emerged since the end of the Second World War, embraces a kind of schism between international economic

[1] WTO, Panel Report, *China – Measures Affecting Trading Rights and Distribution Services for Certain Publications and Audio-Visual Entertainment Products*, WTO Doc. WT/DS363/R, adopted 12 August 2009 [hereinafter WTO Panel Report, *China – Entertainment Products*]; and WTO, Appellate Body Report, *China – Measures Affecting Trading Rights and Distribution Services for Certain Publications and Audio-Visual Entertainment Products*, WTO Doc. WT/DS363/AB/R, adopted 19 January 2010 [hereinafter WTO, Appellate Body Report, *China – Entertainment Products*].

law and public international law.[2] The institutions of international economic law emerged from the Bretton Woods negotiations, which drew up the charters of the International Monetary Fund (IMF), the International Fund for Reconstruction and Development (which became the World Bank), and the International Trade Organization. Despite being the progeny of Franklin D. Roosevelt's 'one-worldism', the International Trade Organization never came into existence. Its death knell was the intense opposition that it engendered in the US,[3] although the political and business interests ranged against it were not confined to those emanating from the US.[4] However, it metamorphosed into the 1947 version of the General Agreement on Trade and Tariffs (GATT)[5] and was, accordingly, a precursor to the WTO. The United Nations organisations, which form the framework for public international law, arose from the Dumbarton Oaks negotiations. From the beginning, the mandates of these two systems of international law were distinct. The Bretton Woods institutions were to manage international economic relations, while the Dumbarton Oaks institutions were to manage the international political order. As part of this mandate, the Dumbarton Oaks institutions have taken charge of what have been described as 'state-making and war-making' functions.[6] In addition to this, the system of public international law that has been built up around the Dumbarton Oaks institutions has purported to establish international standards in areas such as the protection of human rights, of the environment and of cultural heritage.

While Roosevelt's vision of a US-led world government was not realised, it was nevertheless the case that the supranational agreements created at Bretton Woods and Dumbarton Oaks circumscribed national sovereignty in new ways. The irony of the massive decolonisation of the twentieth century has been that, while former colonies have become independent states, the meaning of statehood in terms of national autonomy is arguably more limited than ever before under the Westphalia system. The United Nations system seeks to control not only relations between states, but also the internal exercise of state power through the imposition of standards in areas such as human rights, cultural heritage and protection of the environment. The bureaucratic control of the world monetary system introduced by the World Bank and the IMF extend to both external and, in some cases, internal relations.[7] It seems unlikely that any of these supranational institutions would have obtained their power and influence without the muscle provided

---

2 For a more detailed version of this argument, see Fiona Macmillan, 'International Economic Law and Public International Law: Strangers in the Night' (2004) *International Trade Law and Regulation*, pp. 115–24.

3 See further Giovanni Arrighi, *The Long Twentieth Century: Money, Power and the Origins of Our Times*, London and New York: Verso, 1994, at pp. 276–7; Graham Dunkley, *The Free Trade Adventure: The WTO, the Uruguay Round & Globalism – A Critique*, London and New York: Zed Books, 2001, at pp. 26–8.

4 See Dunkley, supra note 3, at pp. 26–8.

5 WTO, General Agreement on Tariffs and Trade, Marrakesh Agreement Establishing the World Trade Organization, Annex 1A, 1867 UNTS 187; 33 ILM 1153 (adopted on 15 April 1994, entered into force 1 January 1995).

6 Arrighi, supra note 3, at p. 275.

7 For example the structural adjustment policies of the IMF are notorious for their control and influence over the domestic policy of states in which they have been applied: see, for example, Joseph Stiglitz, *Globalization and its Discontents*, London: Allen Lane, 2002.

by a powerful champion. This champion has, of course, been the United States, the pre-eminent global military power and the policeman of the post-Second World War world order.

While undoubtedly hegemonic, the power of the United States is, as those who opposed Roosevelt's one-worldism saw, far from total.[8] It is against this somewhat fragile dominance that the establishment of the WTO must be considered. Promoted by the US and the other OECD countries as a more comprehensive means than the GATT to order and control world trade, there are some signs that it is not proving to be quite the malleable device that some of its supporters may have hoped. There has been greater resistance to the extensive limitations that it imposes on national autonomy than appears to have been expected or anticipated. This resistance has come not only from countries that perceive in the WTO the institutionalisation of an unequal playing field in international trade relations, but it has also come from those countries that enthusiastically sponsored its establishment.[9] At the same time, the elevation of international trade relations into a system with its own constitution (the Agreement Establishing the WTO), laws (the 'covered' agreements),[10] parliament (the General Council),[11] court (the Dispute Settlement Body),[12] executive (the Ministerial Conference)[13] and bureaucracy (the Office of the WTO in Geneva), has endowed it with a public profile and weight that has arguably not been enjoyed by its Bretton Woods counterparts. The WTO may be evolving into a counter-institution to the United Nations and the system of public international law built up around it. In this, it is presenting a new challenge to the division between the economic and the political that characterises the international law system.

2.2 Relationship between the Bretton Woods and Dumbarton Oaks Systems

From their inception, little was provided in the way of legal linkage between the Bretton Woods and Dumbarton Oaks institutions. Nominally, the Bretton Woods institutions were established within the UN system,[14] but the IMF and World Bank have in practice always been independent from it. Interestingly, however, the proposed Charter of the International

---

8 Further, Arrighi makes a powerful argument for the proposition that American dominance, at least as 'the leading agency of capitalist accumulation', is now in terminal decline: Arrighi, supra note 3, especially ch. 4 and Epilogue.

9 For an assessment of the range of this resistance at the WTO Fifth Ministerial Conference at Cancún in 2003, see Fiona Macmillan, 'If Not This WTO, Then What?' (2004) *International Company and Commercial Law Review*, 3, pp. 75–83.

10 These are the multilateral and plurilateral trade agreements annexed to the WTO, Marrakesh Agreement Establishing the World Trade Organization, 1867 UNTS 154; 33 ILM 1144 (adopted on 15 April 1994, entered into force 1 January 1995), see Article II.

11 The WTO General Council is composed of representatives of all WTO members: Agreement Establishing the WTO, Article IV.2.

12 Established by the WTO, Understanding on Rules and Procedures Governing the Settlement of Disputes (DSU), Marrakesh Agreement Establishing the World Trade Organization, Annex 2, 1869 UNTS 401; 33 ILM 1226 (adopted on 15 April 1994, entered into force 1 January 1995), Article II.

13 The functions of which are laid down in the Agreement Establishing the WTO, Article IV.1.

14 See Dunkley, supra note 3, at pp. 26–7.

Trade Organization did allow a member aggrieved by an International Trade Organization decision to seek an advisory opinion from the International Court of Justice, the decision of which would be binding on the International Trade Organization.[15] This attempt at a legal interface between the ordering of the international economic and political systems did not survive the demise of the International Trade Organization. It has nevertheless been argued that the WTO is legally linked to the system of public international law and, indeed, 'is no more than a new branch of public international law'.[16] The evidence provided for this appears to rest primarily on two bases. First, a link is argued to exist on the basis that the WTO agreements are to be interpreted, according to Article 3.2 of the WTO Understanding on Dispute Settlement (DSU) and the WTO Appellate Body decision in the *Reformulated Gasoline* case,[17] consistently with Article 31 of the Treaty of Vienna governing the interpretation of treaties.[18] The second basis for this argument is the existence of exceptions from WTO obligations, such as the (in)famous 'exceptions' in the GATT,[19] which are variously reflected in a range of other WTO agreements.[20] It is frequently argued that a number of these exceptions import a link with standards of public international law.

The first argument in support of a systemic interface between public international law and international economic law is less than compelling.[21] To start off with, sharing a procedural rule on interpretation is not a substantive legal engagement. Further, it is not even the case that the two systems have common procedural rules. It is, for example,

---

15 Duncan Brack, 'Environmental Treaties and Trade: Multilateral Environmental Agreements and the Multilateral Trading System', in Gary P. Sampson and W. Bradnee Chambers (eds), *Trade, Environment and the Millennium,* New York: United Nations University Press, 1999, pp. 271–99, at p. 288, citing Steve Charnovitz, 'Restraining the Use of Trade Measures in Multilateral Agreements: An Outline of the Issues', *The Relationship Between the Multilateral Trading System and the Use of Trade Measures in MEAs: Synergy or Friction*, TMC Asser Instituut, Report of the Round Table Conference (The Hague, 22–23 January 1996).

16 Jiaxiang Hu, 'The Role of International Law in the Development of WTO Law' (2004) *Journal of International Economic Law*, 7 (1), pp. 143–67, at p. 144.

17 WTO, Appellate Body Report, *United States – Standards for Reformulated and Conventional Gasoline*, WTO Docs WT/DS2/R and WT/DS2/AB/R, adopted 20 May 1996, at pp. 16–17.

18 Vienna Convention on the Law of Treaties, 1155 UNTS 331; 8 ILM 679 (adopted on 23 May 1969, entered into force 27 January 1980).

19 GATT, Article XX.

20 See, for example, WTO, Agreement on Sanitary and Phytosanitary Measures (SPS Agreement), Marrakesh Agreement Establishing the World Trade Organization, Annex 1A, 1867 UNTS 493; 33 ILM 1125, 1153 (adopted on 15 April 1994, entered into force 1 January 1995), Article 2; WTO, Agreement on Technical Barriers to Trade (TBT Agreement), Marrakesh Agreement Establishing the World Trade Organization, Annex 1A, 1868 UNTS 120; 33 ILM 1125, 1145 (adopted on 15 April 1994, entered into force 1 January 1995), Article 2.2; and WTO, General Agreement on Trade in Services (GATS), Marrakesh Agreement Establishing the World Trade Organization, Annex 1B, 1869 UNTS 183; 33 ILM 1167 (adopted on 15 April 1994, entered into force 1 January 1995), Article XIV.

21 See also Susy Frankel, 'The WTO's Application of Customary Rules of Interpretation of Public International Law to Intellectual Property' (2006) *Virginia Journal of International Law*, 46, pp. 365–431.

questionable whether granting standing to the US in the *Bananas* dispute[22] on the basis of the doctrine of *actio popularis* is consistent with the rules on standing that operate in the International Court of Justice (ICJ).[23] It seems that the WTO will selectively employ the procedures of international law, not that it will substantively engage with the content of public international law. This is not to say that procedural devices cannot found substantive engagements between two legal systems. The provision in the Charter of the aborted International Trade Organization, mentioned above, was a procedural device that may have secured such an engagement. Thus, the problem is the apparent absence of the right sort of procedural devices.

The second argument in support of an active engagement between the two systems of international law relies upon the range of exceptions in WTO agreements said to reflect public international law norms. There is certainly truth in the proposition that the institutions of international economic law employ some concepts established internationally through the devices of public international law. However, like strangers in the night, these are in the nature of brief couplings between two bodies that achieve only the most superficial understanding of each other; and that never become obliged to each other. For example, the appeal of the argument that exceptions in the WTO agreements reflect the standards of public international environmental law soon wanes in the face of WTO Appellate Body decisions on the application of those exceptions. Of the exceptions, amongst the most fully considered in WTO jurisprudence are the so-called environmental exceptions in Article XX(b) and (g) of the GATT. These provisions were introduced in the 1947 version of the GATT and have established a line of cases beginning in 1991[24] and, thus, predating the existence of the WTO. As this line of cases shows, no GATT or WTO member country has ever successfully relied upon the environmental exceptions in the GATT. This alone might make the claim of a link between the GATT and public international environmental law rather empty. Certainly it is true that in the *Sea Turtles* case[25] the Appellate Body said that, in construing the exceptions in Article XX(b) and (g), it is necessary to take international environmental treaties into account.[26] However, a consideration of the Appellate Body decision shows that the role of the international treaties was to make it harder to claim the protection of the so-called environmental

---

22 WTO, Appellate Body Report, *European Communities – Regime for Importation, Sale and Distribution of Bananas*, WTO Docs WT/DS27/R and WT/DS27/AB/R, adopted 25 September 1997, at paras 132–8.

23 The European Communities made a convincing argument that it was not, citing *South West Africa Cases* (Second Phase) (1966) ICJ Reports 47; *Case Concerning the Barcelona Traction, Light and Power Company Limited* (Second Phase) (1970) ICJ Reports 32; *Mavrommatis Palestine Concessions Case* (1925) Series A, No. 2, 12 (PCIJ); *S S 'Wimbledon' Case* (1923) Series A, No. 1, 1 (PCIJ); *Case Concerning the Northern Cameroon* (1963) ICJ Reports 4: see supra note 22, Appellate Body Report, at paras 15 and 133.

24 GATT, Panel Report, *United States – Restrictions on Imports of Tuna* (1991) 30 ILM 1594.

25 WTO, Appellate Body, *United States – Import Prohibition of Certain Shrimp and Shrimp Products*, WTO Docs WT/DS58/R and WT/DS58/AB/R, adopted 6 November 1998.

26 See Fiona Macmillan, *WTO and the Environment*, London: Sweet and Maxwell, 2001, at pp. 91–6.

exceptions.[27] In all, there is not much evidence to support the contention that there is a significant legal interface between WTO law and the content of public international law.

Despite the legal separation of the two regimes, their institutions and activities have a clear, if changing, interrelationship.[28] The issue of international environmental regulation is a good example of the formal legal divide and substantive overlap that pervades the relationship between international economic law and public international law.[29] This is not just because of the potential for conflict between the WTO multilateral trade agreements and the obligations imposed on states under the various multilateral environmental agreements.[30] It is also because the issue of international environmental regulation cuts across the areas of economic and political management of international relations.[31] Similar claims might be made with respect to the protection of human rights and cultural heritage. At the international level, human rights and cultural heritage concerns have traditionally been seen as a preserve of the Dumbarton Oaks system. However, it is increasingly evident that the concerns are raised not only in the context of the international management of the political order, but also in relation to the international management of the economic order. With respect to the WTO, the relationship between its sphere of regulation and the protection of human rights is a matter of increasing concern to the relevant United Nations instrumentality, the Office of the High Commissioner for Human Rights (OHCHR).

Since the turn of the twenty-first century, the OHCHR has produced a series of reports analysing the substantive overlap between the international trade system and the protection of human rights.[32] For example, for the purposes of the Fifth WTO Ministerial Conference in Cancún, which took place in September 2003, the OHCHR produced a paper instancing a range of links between human rights and trade.[33] These included: the connection between discrimination on the ground of gender and the availability of anti-AIDs medications;[34] the right to health and the availability of

---

[27] Ibid., at pp. 94–5.

[28] See further Matthias Finger and Ludivine Tamiotti, 'New Global Regulatory Mechanisms and the Environment: The Emerging Linkage between the WTO and the ISO' (1999) *International Development Studies Bulletin*, 30, pp. 8–15, at p. 9.

[29] See Macmillan, supra note 26, especially ch. 9.

[30] For a summary of the areas of potential conflict, see Macmillan, supra note 26, ch. 2.

[31] See Macmillan, supra note 26, at pp. 267–8.

[32] High Commissioner for Human Rights, Report, 'The Impact of the TRIPs Agreement on the Enjoyment of All Human Rights', (UN Doc. E/CN.4/Sub.2/13, 2001); High Commissioner for Human Rights, Report 'Globalization and its Impact on the Full Enjoyment of Human Rights', (UN Doc. E/CN.4/54, 2002); High Commissioner for Human Rights, Report, 'Liberalization of Trade in Services and Human Rights', (UN Doc. E/CN.4/Sub.2/9, 2002); High Commissioner for Human Rights, Report, 'Human Rights, Trade and Investment', (UN Doc. E/CN.4/Sub.2/9, 2003).

[33] Office of the High Commissioner for Human Rights, 'Human Rights and Trade', Fifth WTO Ministerial Conference (Cancún, Mexico, 10–14 September 2003).

[34] Raising potential conflicts between the UN, Universal Declaration of Human Rights, UN GA Res. 217A (III) (UN Doc. A/810) (adopted on 10 December 1948), Article 2; the Convention on the Elimination of All Forms of Discrimination Against Women, Article 1; and the WTO, Agreement on Trade-Related Aspects of Intellectual Property Rights (TRIPS Agreement), Marrakesh Agreement Establishing the World Trade Organization, Annex 1C, 1869 UNTS 299; 33 ILM 1197 (adopted on

pharmaceuticals;[35] the right to adequate and sustainable food supplies and the opening up of agricultural markets;[36] the right to development and agricultural trade liberalisation;[37] progressive market liberalisation and the protection of economic, social and cultural rights in areas such as health, education and the protection of the environment;[38] the rights of indigenous people over their traditional knowledge and the granting of intellectual property rights over genetic resources;[39] and investors' rights and the whole range of political, economic, social and cultural rights.[40] As if to reinforce the hermetically sealed nature of the world in which the law and policy governing international economic relations is made, the OHCHR prefaced its paper with the comment that it was intended to be 'an illustration of the links between human rights and trade to assist policy makers who might not be familiar with the international human rights system'.[41]

Since both the institutions and the concerns of the international political system and the international economic system overlap it would seem reasonable for the law governing these systems to intersect. This is not what has happened. Instead, as Kennedy has observed, 'for all their similarities, the traditions and intellectual styles of public international law and international economic law remain estranged caught in an elaborate *pas-de-deux* of public and private, metropolitan and cosmopolitan sensibilities'.[42]

---

15 April 1994, entered into force 1 January 1995). See Office of the High Commissioner for Human Rights, supra note 33, at pp. 6–7.

[35] Raising potential conflicts between the UN, International Covenant on Economic, Social and Cultural Rights (ICESCR), 993 UNTS 3; 6 ILM 360 (adopted on 16 December 1966, entered into force 3 January 1976), Article 12; and the TRIPS Agreement: see Office of the High Commissioner for Human Rights, supra note 33, at pp. 7–9.

[36] Raising potential conflicts between the ICESCR; the WTO, Agreement on Agriculture, Marrakesh Agreement Establishing the World Trade Organization, Annex 1A, 1867 UNTS 410 (adopted on 15 April 1994, entered into force 1 January 1995); and the TRIPS Agreement: see Office of the High Commissioner for Human Rights, supra note 33, at pp. 9–10.

[37] Raising potential conflicts between the ICESCR, Article 11.2; the UN, Declaration on the Right to Development, GA Res. 41/128 (UN Doc. A/RES/41/128) (adopted on 4 December 1986), Article 3.3; and the WTO Agreement on Agriculture: see Office of the High Commissioner for Human Rights, supra note 33, at pp. 10–11.

[38] Raising potential conflicts between the ICESCR and the GATS: see Office of the High Commissioner for Human Rights, supra note 33, at pp. 11–13.

[39] Raising potential conflicts between the Universal Declaration on Human Rights, Article 2; the ICESCR, Articles 2.2 and 15.1; the UN, Declaration on the Rights of Indigenous Peoples (UNDRIP), GA Res. 61/295 (UN Doc. A/61/L.67 and Add.1) (adopted on 13 September 2007), Article 31; as well as the Rio Convention on Biological Diversity (CBD), 1760 UNTS 79; 31 ILM 818 (opened for signature 5 June 1992, entered into force 29 December 1993); the UN, Food and Agriculture Organization (FAO), International Treaty on Plant Genetic Resources for Food and Agriculture, 2400 UNTS 303 (adopted on 3 November 2001, entered into force 29 June 2004); and the TRIPS Agreement. See Office of the High Commissioner for Human Rights, supra note 33, at pp. 14–16.

[40] Raising potential conflicts between the UN Norms on the Responsibilities of Transnational Corporations and Other Business Enterprises with regard to Human Rights (UN Doc. E/CN.4/Sub.2/2003/12/Rev.2, 2002) and the proposed WTO Agreement on Investment: see Office of the High Commissioner for Human Rights, supra note 33, at pp. 16–19.

[41] Office of the High Commissioner for Human Rights, supra note 33, at p. 3.

[42] David Kennedy, 'The International Style in Postwar Law and Policy: John Jackson and the Field of International Economic Law' (1995) *American University Journal of International Law & Policy*, 10, pp. 671–716, at p. 671.

2.3 Consequences?

At its broadest, the attempt of the international system to divide the indivisible, the denial that the economic is part and parcel of the political, has proved a very effective weapon in suppressing and resisting politics. The preservation of political harmony and the management of political relationships has always been part of the mandate of the Dumbarton Oaks institutions and the WTO's location within the range of Bretton Woods institutions, albeit something of a latecomer, has clearly militated against it having any explicitly 'political' role in international affairs. On the other hand, there is a widespread perception that there are a number of issues that are part of the mandate of the Dumbarton Oaks institutions and their heirs, which also have 'economic' dimensions falling within the consideration of the institutions of international economic law. This suggests a need for some sort of rapprochement between the two systems in order to resolve the systemic division between public international law and international economic law, at least in areas of apparent overlap such as the protection of human rights, cultural heritage or the environment.[43] Importantly, rapprochement of the two systems would involve a recognition that the international economic order is part of the international political order. It is evident that this point is little appreciated. Yet, the rhetorical commitment of the WTO to a single global market has provoked a range of arguments that cannot be easily compartmentalised as only economic.[44] Not only do the arguments over the objective and pace of liberalisation range across the economic and the political, it is also clear that the WTO replicates the structural imbalance in world power between the developed and the developing world. It is difficult to deny that such an imbalance is related to the international political order.

A more specific consequence of the substantive overlap between the application of public international law and international economic law is that the two systems appear to be in a type of regulatory competition. It is often suggested that international economic law is winning this competition 'with economics replacing politics as law's sidekick and nemesis'.[45] If this is true, it may reflect upon the enforcement devices offered by the two systems. That is, in the rarefied world of international diplomacy, there may be a preference for the use of trade 'leverage' over trade 'sanctions', especially where that leverage is applied by a quasi (at least) judicial body, such as the WTO Dispute Settlement Body. There is also a preference in most quarters for trade leverage over war. The perception of the systemic pre-eminence of international economic law lies behind the current pressure for the WTO to take on board concerns about the effects of international

---

43 See generally, for example, ibid. See also Samir Amin, *Capitalism in the Age of Globalization*, London and New York: Zed Books, 1998, at p. 44, who proposes: 'Reconstructing the UN system in order to make it the locus of political and economic negotiations to organise the articulation of commercial and financial interdependence between the major regions of the world'.

44 See, for example, John Gray, *False Dawn: The Delusions of Global Capitalism*, New York: New Press, 1998, at p. 23: 'A global single market is very much a late-twentieth-century *political* project.' (Emphasis in original).

45 Kennedy, supra note 42, at p. 675. For example GATT has been used to settle more international environmental disputes than any other international instrument: see Steve Charnovitz, 'Participation of Nongovernmental Organizations in the World Trade Organization' (1996) *University of Pennsylvania Journal of International Economic Law*, 17, pp. 331–57, at p. 351.

trade on things such as the protection of human rights. The proposition that the WTO should become subject to disciplines imposed in the name of human rights, or that it should offer some recognition to principles emanating from human rights instruments, does not appear to be inherently objectionable. It does, however, raise some hard questions. First, one might wonder whether imposing human rights disciplines through the WTO multilateral agreements would achieve the desired effect. In particular, the fact that the WTO agreements, like the instruments of public international law, address themselves to states may undermine their effectiveness in dealing with some types of human rights abuses arising within the context of the international trading system. Second, given the apparent systemic pre-eminence of international economic law, there is a question about whether or not it is acceptable for the WTO to become the prime international institution for the protection of human rights. The WTO may not, for example, be best placed to decide when trade leverage to protect human rights is justifiable and when it is not.

3. INDIGENOUS PEOPLES IN INTERNATIONAL LAW

3.1 Locating Indigenous Peoples in the Bifurcated System

The next question for this chapter is, bearing in mind the systemic divide in international law, where (if anywhere) and how (if in any way) are indigenous peoples located within this bifurcated system? As the foregoing discussion emphasised, both systems concern themselves with nation states as formal actors. However, the apparently more pluralistic and broad-ranging base of the concerns to which public international law addresses itself has, in contrast with international economic law, afforded scope for the recognition of the rights and interests of indigenous peoples. This recognition has manifested itself, if not always explicitly, in the areas of human rights protection, environmental and resource rights protection, the protection of cultural heritage and, since 2007, explicitly in the United Nations Declaration on the Rights of Indigenous Peoples (UNDRIP).[46]

The general human rights protection granted to indigenous peoples under the UN Bill of Rights[47] is, perhaps, a good example of recognition at the less explicit end of the spectrum. Article 1.1 of the Covenant on Civil and Political Rights (CCPR) lays down a general right to self-determination in the following terms: 'All peoples have the right of self-determination. By virtue of that right they freely determine their political status and freely pursue their economic, social and cultural development.' However, it is far from clear that this right applies to indigenous peoples,[48] despite being conferred on 'peoples'. The CCPR leaves open the somewhat delicate question of how such entities might be identified or

---

[46] UNDRIP, supra note 39.

[47] UN, International Covenant on Civil and Political Rights, 999 UNTS 171 and 1057 UNTS 407; 6 ILM 368 (adopted on 16 December 1966, entered into force 23 March 1976); and ICESCR, supra note 35.

[48] See also, for example, Christoph B. Graber, 'Institutionalization of Creativity in Traditional Societies and in International Trade Law', in Shubha Ghosh and Robin P. Malloy (eds), *Creativity, Law and Entrepreneurship*, Cheltenham, UK and Northampton, MA: Edward Elgar, 2011, pp. 234–63, at pp. 248–9.

defined. While 'peoples' may, presumably, be constituted by the citizens and residents of a particular nation state, it is also clear from Article 1.3 that this is not the only method of constituting a 'people'.[49] On the other hand, it is sometimes argued that indigenous peoples are not necessarily 'peoples' for the purpose of Article 1.1 since Article 27 confers a range of somewhat more limited rights on 'ethnic, religious or linguistic minorities':

> In those States in which ethnic, religious or linguistic minorities exist, persons belonging to such minorities shall not be denied the right, in community with the other members of their group, to enjoy their own culture, to profess and practice their religion, or to use their own language.

Whether or not Article 27 applies to indigenous peoples, it should be noted that if Article 1.1 applies to indigenous peoples then there is widespread failure to observe its terms since many groups of indigenous peoples clearly do not enjoy full rights of self-determination.

More explicit recognition of the traditional knowledge and traditional cultural expressions of indigenous peoples has been made in conventions dealing with the environment and with cultural heritage. The 1992 United Nations Convention on Biological Diversity,[50] for example, recognised in its recitals:

> the close and traditional dependence of many indigenous and local communities embodying traditional lifestyles on biological resources, and the desirability of sharing equitably benefits arising from the use of traditional knowledge, innovations and practices relevant to the conservation of biological diversity and the sustainable use of its components.

And this is followed, in its substantive provisions, by Article 8(j), which provides as part of its provisions on *in situ* conservation that:

> Each Contracting Party shall, as far as possible and as appropriate: ...
>
> Subject to its national legislation, respect, preserve and maintain knowledge, innovations and practices of indigenous and local communities embodying traditional lifestyles relevant for the conservation and sustainable use of biological diversity and promote their wider application with the approval and involvement of the holders of such knowledge, innovations and practices and encourage the equitable sharing of the benefits arising from the utilization of such knowledge, innovations and practices.

In the context of cultural heritage the focus has been somewhat broadened, encompassing both the traditional knowledge and the traditional cultural expressions of indigenous peoples. So far as the UNESCO regime for the protection of cultural heritage is concerned, the particular position of indigenous peoples was given some recognition in the UNESCO Recommendation on the Safeguarding of Traditional Culture and Folklore of 1989.

---

49 CCPR, Article 1.3 provides: 'The States Parties to the present Covenant, including those having responsibility for the administration of Non-Self-Governing and Trust Territories, shall promote the realization of the right of self-determination, and shall respect that right, in conformity with the provisions of the Charter of the United Nations.'

50 CBD, supra note 39.

However, this recognition did not translate into convention provisions until the Convention for the Safeguarding of the Intangible Cultural Heritage of 2003,[51] which came into force on 20 April 2006.[52] This Convention is notable for the fact that it moves away from the strongly statist rhetoric of some earlier UNESCO Conventions. Instead, it focuses on 'communities'. Having made reference to the 1989 UNESCO Recommendation in its recitals, it continues a few paragraphs further on by '*Recognizing* that communities, in particular indigenous communities, groups and, in some cases, individuals, play an important role in the production, safeguarding, maintenance and recreation of the intangible cultural heritage, thus helping to enrich cultural diversity and human creativity'. The operative provisions of the Convention build on this by, for example, defining 'intangible cultural heritage' as including things such as 'oral traditions and expressions', 'social practices, rituals and festive events', 'knowledge and practices concerning nature and the universe' and 'traditional craftsmanship' (Article 2.2), and by requiring the states parties to 'endeavour to ensure the widest possible participation of communities, groups and, where appropriate, individuals that create, maintain and transmit such heritage, and to involve them actively in its management' (Article 15).[53]

The UNESCO Convention on the Protection and Promotion of the Diversity of Cultural Expressions of 2005,[54] which came into force on 18 March 2007, is to similar effect. In its recitals it cites, variously, the interests of 'communities', 'peoples', 'societies' and 'nations'. Explicit recognition in its recitals is given to the 'importance of traditional knowledge as a source of intangible and material wealth, and in particular the knowledge systems of Indigenous peoples'. The immediately following recital, dealing with the protection of cultural expressions, does not make explicit reference to indigenous peoples, however its concern with 'situations where cultural expressions might be threatened by the possibility of extinction or serious impairment' might suggest a particular concern with indigenous peoples, amongst others. It is, of course, obvious that 'others' in this context means other communities, societies, peoples or groups that are perceived to be in a weak, or potentially weak, position so far as the objectives of the Convention are concerned. This is clear from the only other explicit mention of indigenous peoples, which occurs in Article 7.1(a) of the Convention:

> Parties shall endeavour to create in their territory an environment which encourages individuals and social groups … to create, produce, disseminate, distribute and have access to their own cultural expressions, paying due attention to the special circumstances and needs of women, as well as various social groups, including persons belonging to minorities and indigenous peoples.

---

51 UNESCO, Convention for the Safeguarding of the Intangible Cultural Heritage, 2368 UNTS 1 (adopted on 17 October 2003, entered into force 20 April 2006).

52 Rosemary J. Coombe with Joseph F. Turcotte, 'Indigenous Cultural Heritage in Development and Trade: Perspectives from the Dynamics of Cultural Heritage Law and Policy', in this volume; and Francesco Bandarin, 'International Trade in Indigenous Cultural Heritage: Comments from UNESCO in Light of its International Standard-Setting Instruments in the Field of Culture', in this volume.

53 Coombe and Turcotte, supra note 52.

54 UNESCO, Convention on the Protection and Promotion of the Diversity of Cultural Expressions, 2440 UNTS 311 (adopted on 20 October 2005, entered into force 18 March 2007).

UNDRIP unites recognition of the human rights, environmental rights and cultural rights of indigenous peoples into a more coherent narrative. In the context of this chapter, the UNDRIP provision of particular importance is Article 31, which provides:

> 1. Indigenous peoples have the right to maintain, control, protect and develop their cultural heritage, traditional knowledge and traditional cultural expressions, as well as the manifestations of their sciences, technologies and cultures, including human and genetic resources, seeds, medicines, knowledge of the properties of fauna and flora, oral traditions, literatures, designs, sports and traditional games and visual and performing arts. They also have the right to maintain, control, protect and develop their intellectual property over such cultural heritage, traditional knowledge, and traditional cultural expressions.
>
> 2. In conjunction with indigenous peoples, States shall take effective measures to recognise and protect the exercise of these rights.

Despite Article 31.2 of UNDRIP, and in marked contrast to the public international law regime, the system of international economic law in general and WTO law in particular gives no noticeable recognition to the rights, interests, or indeed, existence of indigenous peoples. This is in no way to suggest that the interests of indigenous peoples are not implicated in WTO law. However, the question of the legal recognition of the rights and interests of indigenous peoples within the WTO is yet another example of a substantive overlap between the two systems that is not recognised through much in the way of formal or substantive legal mechanisms. Of course, the idea of indigenous peoples lurks in the undergrowth of WTO law and policy. This is most notably the case in the context of the Agreement on Trade-Related Aspects of Intellectual Property Rights (TRIPS). The TRIPS Council, for example, has been twice directed by Ministerial Declaration[55] to examine 'the protection of traditional knowledge and folklore', although its considerations to date have focused more on the former than on the latter.[56] In a more general sense, however, the question of the rights of indigenous people to protection of their traditional knowledge and traditional cultural expressions hangs over the TRIPS Agreement, although this is perhaps a particular consequence of the fact that these concerns have been raised in the deliberations of the United Nations World Intellectual Property Organization (WIPO). (More will be said below on the significance (or not) of the relationship between the WTO and WIPO in this context.) Overall, however, the powerful free trade rhetoric of the WTO, and its selective incorporation into WTO law, has had a negligible amount to say about the particular position of indigenous peoples.

3.2 The Regime on Return of Wrongfully Removed Cultural Property: The Infiltration of Free Trade Values?

The focus of this section is on the role of norms from public international law within the WTO system. However, one of the inevitable consequences of the intertwining, in substance if not in law, of the two systems is that norms from international economic law

---

[55] WTO, 'Doha Ministerial Declaration', (WTO Doc. WT/MIN(01)/DEC/1, 2001), at para. 19; WTO, 'Hong Kong Ministerial Declaration', (WTO Doc. WT/MIN(05)/DEC, 2005), at para. 44.

[56] See further, Graber, supra note 48, at pp. 244–5.

have also found their way into the public international law system. In particular, as the regime on return of wrongfully removed cultural property shows, the power of free trade discourse promoted by the system of international economic law has affected (or infected) the international protection of cultural heritage.

The UNESCO Convention on the Means of Prohibiting and Preventing the Illicit Import, Export and Transfer of Ownership of Cultural Property of 1970[57] was very much a child of its time. Compared with later UNESCO Conventions, such as the two twenty-first-century conventions referred to above, it has a strongly statist narrative, concerning itself with the 'nationality' of items of tangible moveable cultural property. One inevitable consequence of this approach is, of course, the collapsing of distinctions between the state and indigenous peoples living within the state. While the Convention requires its member states 'to oppose such practices [illicit import, export and transfer of ownership of cultural property] with the means at their disposal and particularly by removing their causes, putting a stop to current practices, and by helping to make the necessary reparations' (Article 2.2), the Convention is generally vague on the mechanisms for achieving this. In particular, there is little on the process of 'reparation'. In any case, the Convention cannot be taken to have any retroactive effect so would provide no basis for claims by indigenous peoples for return of their cultural artefacts that were wrongfully removed prior to the coming into force of the Convention.[58]

A more detailed regime for restitution and return of wrongfully removed cultural property arrived more than 20 years later in the form of the UNIDROIT Convention on Stolen or Illegally Exported Cultural Objects of 1995.[59] The Convention makes explicit reference to the 1970 UNESCO Convention and defines the subject matter with which it is concerned in the same terms.[60] The Convention provides for two different procedures. Its Chapter II lays down a procedure for the restitution of stolen cultural objects, while Chapter III deals with the return of illegally exported cultural objects. In a number of ways, the Convention, like the 1970 UNESCO Convention, was affected by ongoing concerns about the process of decolonisation and the primacy of so-called 'free' trade considerations. For example, fierce lobbying from former metropolitan powers and 'free trade' states resulted in an explicit provision on the non-retroactivity of the UNIDROIT Convention (Article 10). Thus, the demands of both developing countries and of indigenous peoples for the return of their cultural artefacts removed during the colonial period

---

[57] UNESCO, Convention on the Means of Prohibiting and Preventing the Illicit Import, Export and Transfer of Ownership of Cultural Property, 823 UNTS 231 (adopted on 14 November 1970, entered into force 24 April 1972).

[58] See also the contributions of Rebecca Tsosie, 'International Trade in Indigenous Cultural Heritage: An Argument for Indigenous Governance of Cultural Property', in this volume; and Karolina Kuprecht and Kurt Siehr, 'International Trade in Moveable Tangible Cultural Heritage of Indigenous Peoples: A European Perspective', in this volume.

[59] UNIDROIT Convention on Stolen or Illegally Exported Cultural Objects, 34 ILM 1322 (adopted on 24 June 1995, entered into force 1 July 1998).

[60] See UNESCO Convention on the Means of Prohibiting and Preventing the Illicit Import, Export and Transfer of Ownership of Cultural Property, Article 1; and UNIDROIT Convention on Stolen or Illegally Exported Cultural Objects, Article 2 and Annex.

continue to go unanswered.[61] Anxieties around the freedom and security of international trade, which had of course increased during the period between the two Conventions, also impacted on the UNIDROIT Convention. For example, the distinction between the Chapters II and III procedures was insisted on by Anglo-American states because an international provision requiring the enforcement of another state's export controls was said to be contrary to the free trade agenda (as embodied in the WTO).[62] So far as security of international trade is concerned, the sacrosanct concept of 'the bona fide purchaser for value without notice' is recognised by requiring such purchasers to be compensated if they are required to relinquish cultural objects pursuant to the processes laid down in the Convention. In this respect, the UNIDROIT Convention develops a theme already present in Article 7.b(ii) of the 1970 UNESCO Convention.

In the context of this chapter, the noticeable distinction between the 1970 UNESCO Convention and the UNIDROIT Convention is the latter Convention's retreat from the strongly statist language of the former. One consequence of this retreat is the Convention's recognition of the damage done to, amongst others, indigenous peoples as a consequence of the wrongful removal and export of their cultural artefacts. The Convention recitals note that the parties are:

> DEEPLY CONCERNED by the illicit trade in cultural objects and the irreparable damage frequently caused by it, both to these objects themselves and to the cultural heritage of national, tribal, indigenous or other communities, and also to the heritage of all peoples, and in particular by the pillage of archaeological sites and the resulting loss of irreplaceable archaeological, historical and scientific information.

While this deep concern did not manifest itself in any operative provisions for return of cultural property removed before July 1998 when the Convention came into force, it does impact in some ways on the Convention's procedures. For example, the Chapter II procedure on restitution of stolen cultural objects recognises claimants other than states and Article 3.8 extends the time limitation in respect of 'a claim for restitution of a sacred or communally important cultural object belonging to and used by a tribal or indigenous community in a Contracting State as part of that community's traditional or ritual use' with the result that such claims are not time-barred, except to the extent that they must be made within 'a period of three years from the time when the claimant knew the location of the cultural object and the identity of its possessor' (Article 3.4). Only states can be claimants for the purposes of the Chapter III procedure on return of illegally exported cultural objects, which is potentially problematic for groups of indigenous peoples, particularly if they have a generally combative relationship with the state or states in which they live. This problem is not (of course) addressed in the Convention, even though the Convention envisages states requiring return of cultural objects where their removal has significantly impaired 'the traditional or ritual use of the object by a tribal or indigenous community' (Article 5.3(d)). What such a state does with the object after its return is not a matter with which the Convention concerns itself. States that have a cooperative relationship in this

---

[61] See Ana Filipa Vrdoljak, *International Law, Museums and the Return of Cultural Objects*, Cambridge: Cambridge University Press, 2008, ch. 7.

[62] Ibid., at p. 273.

respect with indigenous peoples that make up part of their population are able to take advantage of the exception to the exception in Article 7.2. According to this provision, the disapplication of the Chapter III procedure where 'the export of a cultural object is no longer illegal at the time at which the return is requested' or where 'the object was exported during the lifetime of the person who created it or within a period of fifty years following the death of that person', does not have effect 'where a cultural object was made by a member or members of a tribal or indigenous community for traditional or ritual use by that community *and the object will be returned to that community*'.[63] It has to be admitted, however, that this question of the management of the relationship between states and indigenous peoples is largely academic so far as the UNIDROIT Convention is concerned. With the exception of New Zealand, most of the states where this is a pressing question are not members of the UNIDROIT Convention, which currently has 32 contracting states.

In the end, thanks to the combined effects of anxieties over the process of decolonisation and the insidious operation of international trade rhetoric, the UNIDROIT Convention offers little to indigenous peoples with respect to the protection of their cultural heritage. In any case, the sort of protection envisaged in the UNIDROIT Convention is only capable within its limited terms of addressing one aspect of the demands of indigenous peoples for the proper recognition of their cultural heritage in the international law regime. This chapter now proceeds to consider the question of this recognition more fully.

3.3 Indigenous Peoples and Cultural Heritage in International Law

The question of the modalities for recognition of the rights of indigenous peoples in their cultural heritage under international law is framed, understandably, by the particular context in which those rights are being considered. This, however, tends to obscure the fact that the requirements for protection and recognition of these rights vary greatly depending upon the type of cultural heritage in question and the circumstances in which the rights and interests of indigenous peoples are being considered. This section of the chapter discusses the, frequently conflicting, objectives of protection for the cultural heritage of indigenous peoples in international law. The aim of this discussion is to attempt an evaluation of the extent to which protection that facilitates trade in cultural heritage is central to claims for protection, and the extent to which it may conflict with other objectives of protection.

Peter Yu[64] has identified eight objectives for protection of the cultural heritage of indigenous peoples in international law: cultural privacy, authenticity, recognition, compensation, benefit-sharing, conservation, access and resistance. As Yu observes, '[t]hese objectives are neither exhaustive or mutually exclusive; they can be achieved through the use of different mechanisms, which range from exclusive rights to liability rules and from benefits sharing agreements to disclosure requirements.'[65]

---

63 Emphasis added.

64 Peter Yu, 'Cultural Relics, Intellectual Property, and Intangible Heritage' (2008) *Temple Law Review*, 81, pp. 433–506, at pp. 454–83.

65 Ibid., at p. 454.

3.3.1 Cultural privacy

The motivations for wishing to keep certain cultural heritage private vary. One obvious motivation is that the heritage in question is sacred and that keeping it private or secret is an inherent part of that sacredness. However, the desire for cultural privacy might also be motivated by a preference not to turn certain materials into commodities. Perhaps, as Yu observes, this might be a consequence of a general rejection of commercial culture and the values of globalisation,[66] or because the material carries certain responsibilities or obligations for the traditional owners that are not consistent with commodification.[67] Where the cultural heritage of indigenous peoples is affected by these considerations, western legal concepts of, for example, intellectual property protection (so often invoked as a legal device in this area), seem questionable, if not beside the point.

3.3.2 Authenticity

The question of authenticity on the other hand is specifically raised in the context of commodification – even if the commodification in question is sometimes involuntary. Indigenous peoples have experienced two problems, in particular, that hinge around the question of authenticity. One is the unauthorised application of certain motifs and designs forming part of the cultural heritage of a particular group to various commodities including 'tea-towels, pencil cases, key rings, tee-shirts ... wall hangings, carpets and posters'.[68] The other is the application of motifs and designs to such products where the style of those motifs and designs resembles, or makes reference to, the cultural heritage of a particular group. In the first case, copyright and moral rights law can offer some protection against unauthorised reproduction where the design is of relatively recent origin. In both cases, certification trade marks may offer some degree of protection.[69]

3.3.3 Recognition

An appreciation of the fact that cultural heritage in the form of traditional knowledge has often been used without authorisation in other products or processes has resulted in claims for proper recognition of this use. Not only is such recognition regarded as inherently just and desirable, it would also 'enable the communities to share in the benefits of the exploitation of such heritage'.[70] Proposals for compulsory disclosure of the use of traditional knowledge in patent applications are informed by exactly this demand. Demands for proper recognition also arise in the context of traditional cultural expressions. In this context the relationship between recognition, benefit-sharing and authenticity is particularly obvious:

---

[66] Ibid., at p. 457.

[67] Ibid., at p. 457. See also Duane Champagne, 'Indigenous Self-Government, Cultural Heritage and International Trade: A Sociological Perspective', in this volume.

[68] Michael Blakeney, 'Protecting Expressions of Australian Aboriginal Folklore Under Copyright Law' (1995) *European Intellectual Property Review*, 17, pp. 442–5, at p. 442.

[69] Christoph B. Graber and Jessica C. Lai, 'Indigenous Cultural Heritage and Fair Trade: Voluntary Certification Standards in the Light of WIPO and WTO Law and Policymaking' (2011) *Prometheus*, 29 (3), pp. 287–308.

[70] Yu, supra note 64, at p. 461.

Assuming that the circulation of indigenous art is inevitable, some indigenous artists want to be sure to participate in this celebration of indigenous culture. By gaining control over the circulation of their imagery, they want to ensure that the public gets an accurate account of indigenous culture and that the investment in that culture goes back to their communities.[71]

3.3.4 Compensation

As is evident from the foregoing, in some circumstances indigenous peoples may regard compensation as a proper response to the use of their cultural heritage without authorisation. Of course, compensation is not always an adequate response to the injury caused by this wrongful use. However, the fact that it may go some way towards redressing wrongs is recognised in proposals such as that of Reichman and Lewis for a 'compensatory liability regime', providing for three different rights: 'a right to prevent wholesale duplication, a right to compensation from value-adding improvers, and a right to make use of a second comer's value adding improvements for purposes of making further improvements'.[72] Such rules, Reichman and Lewis argue, would relocate traditional knowledge 'to a semicommons, from which it could freely be accessed and used for specified purposes, in return for the payment of compensatory royalties for a specified period of time'.[73]

3.3.5 Benefit-sharing

A concept that is closely related to compensation is that of benefit-sharing. The main difference between the two seems to lie in the degree of prior consent of the indigenous peoples in question. Whereas compensation suggests a foregoing wrongful act, benefit-sharing appears to involve a greater degree of volition in the relevant exploitation of cultural heritage. The concept of benefit-sharing makes an appearance in various international instruments including, as already noted above, Article 8(j) of the Convention on Biological Diversity. Scholars in search of a model by which to effectuate benefit-sharing have frequently turned to proprietary devices such as intellectual property rights, or rights that resemble intellectual property rights. Yu notes that:

> By creating artificial scarcity in the form of limited monopolies, similar to what is offered in the intellectual property system, the exclusive rights model would enable traditional communities to obtain a higher return on the use and exploitation of their cultural materials.[74]

---

71 Christine Haight Farley, 'Protecting Folklore of Indigenous Peoples: Is Intellectual Property the Answer?' (1997) *Connecticut Law Review*, 30, pp. 1–58, at p. 15, quoted in Yu, supra note 64, at pp. 462–3.

72 Jerome H. Reichman and Tracy Lewis, 'Using Liability Rules to Stimulate Local Innovation in Developing Countries: Application to Traditional Knowledge', in Keith E. Maskus and Jerome H. Reichman (eds), *International Public Goods and Transfer of Technology Under a Globalized Intellectual Property Regime*, Cambridge: Cambridge University Press, 2005, pp. 337–66, at p. 349.

73 Ibid., at pp. 354–5; see also Yu, supra note 64, at pp. 464–5; and Brigitte Vézina, 'Are They In or Are They Out? Traditional Cultural Expressions and the Public Domain: Implications for Trade', in this volume.

74 Yu, supra note 64, at p. 466.

Other suggested models for putting in place benefit-sharing schemes include the property-based stewardship model put forward by Carpenter, Katyal and Riley,[75] and the use of what Yu describes as 'knowledge transfer and research collaborative agreements'.[76] Essentially, all such schemes involve some degree of commodification of the cultural heritage in question. Obviously, therefore, they have little to say to situations involving claims to cultural privacy, as described above.

3.3.6 Conservation

The goal of conserving the cultural heritage of indigenous peoples sits in slightly odd juxtaposition to that of benefit-sharing. This is largely because the extent to which the need for conservation of cultural heritage conflicts with commodification and benefit-sharing depends on the type of heritage in question. A conflict between commodification and conservation seems inevitable in relation to some types of tangible cultural property, assuming that the indigenous group in question takes the view that conservation can only be effectively achieved where the items in question remain in the custody of their traditional owners.[77] If, however, the focus is shifted from commodification to commercial exploitation, it is possible to imagine peaceful co-existence with conservation objectives. This might occur in the context of, for example, tourism services. Similar observations might be made with respect to some types of intangible cultural heritage, such as the performance of rituals and ceremonies, but only where issues of cultural privacy are not involved.

3.3.7 Access

In contrast to the foregoing objectives of protection, access is not a demand of indigenous peoples but a demand of others with respect to the cultural heritage of indigenous peoples. In other words, there are some circumstances in which rights of access to the cultural heritage of indigenous peoples are asserted by outsiders, resulting in conflicting claims. The most likely contexts for these types of conflicts are with respect to scientific research or in relation to questions of conservation and preservation. So far as scientific research is concerned, examples of such conflicts might include certain uses of traditional knowledge for scientific purposes. Where there are no problems of cultural privacy, and the requirements of authenticity and recognition are met, this type of problem might be dealt with through compensation or benefit-sharing – although the number of qualifications contained in this sentence tend to suggest that these solutions will not always be readily available. This is starkly revealed if the focus is moved from the intangible to the tangible, where significant conflicts have arisen over access to human remains. Such situations not only involve conflicts between the claims of indigenous peoples and the external scientific community,[78] but also often implicate museums.[79] The claims to conserve or preserve

---

[75] Kristen A. Carpenter, Sonia Katyal and Angela Riley, 'In Defense of Property' (2009) *Yale Journal of Law*, 118, pp. 100–204.

[76] Yu, supra note 64, at p. 468.

[77] See also Coombe and Turcotte, supra note 52.

[78] Yu, supra note 64, at pp. 474–5, cites the example of the so-called 'Kennewick Man' or 'Ancient One'. On this controversy, see also Carpenter, Katyal and Riley, supra note 75.

[79] Yu, supra note 64, at p. 475, cites attempts to reclaim the remains of an Inuit man for reburial. On this controversy, see also Carpenter, Katyal and Riley, supra note 75. However, there are many

other types of artefacts outside the control of the relevant indigenous community similarly implicate museums, but might also be conceived of in broader terms. For example, pressure on indigenous groups not to engage in cultural practices that appear 'destructive' to non-members of the group may involve a similar type of conflict.[80] Cultural practices of this type tend to disturb values that inform the concept of the 'museum' in western thought, which involves, as Yu notes, 'a tendency to collect, or even hoard, cultural objects'.[81]

3.3.8 Resistance

Political resistance to widespread appropriation and destruction of their cultures is a dominant thread running through claims by indigenous peoples to control of their cultural heritage. Consequently, claims to heritage are not just about cultural identity, but also about political identity and the right to political self-determination. To some extent it may be possible to argue that all the objectives discussed above are sublimated in this overarching objective. If that is so, then in the context of this chapter it is necessary to consider how the objective of political resistance relates to the question of participation in the international trading system.

On balance, the various objectives canvassed above seem to reveal a defensive, rather than positive, posture towards questions of participation in the international trading system. Many of the objectives seem to be concerned with limiting the damage consequent upon a type of involuntary participation in the systems of trading and commodification. This may be, in part, a problem of perception caused by the widespread recourse to intellectual property rights as a solution to the demands of indigenous peoples with respect to the protection and use of at least some forms of their cultural heritage. Intellectual property rights are, of course, negative in nature. When used as part of the western process of commodification of cultural products, this makes perfect sense since they are merely one part of a larger commercial scheme. When they are divorced from a conscious commercial process and used only to remedy wrongs suffered, they appear inadequate and patchy. One response to this criticism might be to ask how they could be used as one part of a more positive system to protect the cultural heritage of indigenous peoples, which allows them to participate more effectively in the international trading system where this is considered appropriate. This, of course, begs the question of the extent to which intellectual property rights are a useful or desirable method of protecting the cultural heritage of indigenous peoples. This is a question to which this chapter now turns.

---

well-documented cases of this type. In relation to attempts by indigenous peoples in Australia to reclaim remains of their ancestors, for example, see Vrdoljak, supra note 61, at pp. 282–90.

[80] Yu, supra note 64, at pp. 476–8, cites as examples the practices of the Zuni with respect to their War Gods ('Ahayu:da') and the treatment by the Igbo of structures that they called 'mbaris'.

[81] Ibid., at p. 478.

4. THE PROBLEM OF INTELLECTUAL PROPERTY

4.1 Intellectual Property and Indigenous Peoples

The problems of protecting the cultural heritage of indigenous peoples through the legal devices provided by the occidental concept of intellectual property law have been well canvassed by commentators.[82] Some of this commentary has focused on the technical deficiencies of intellectual property law when it comes to protection of indigenous cultural heritage. So, in relation to traditional cultural expressions that might fall within the general purview of copyright law, the difficulties posed by the emphasis on individual authorship, the idea/expression dichotomy and the duration rules have been widely noted.[83] So far as the application of patent law to traditional knowledge is concerned, questions about novelty and inventive step have been raised alongside issues about recognition and benefit-sharing.[84] There has also been a marked lack of political will, both at the national and international level,[85] which one might suspect is a consequence of the linkage between this agenda and a wider agenda concerned with political, social and cultural self-determination for indigenous peoples. (The legal and political reluctance are surely related. Suffice it to say that the seemingly endless capacity for reinvention that intellectual property has displayed in, for example, the context of the digital revolution seems to have been singularly lacking in the context of traditional cultural expressions and knowledge.)[86]

However, it has also been noted that there is a more fundamental problem in using intellectual property law to protect indigenous cultural heritage: if we recognise traditional cultural property as intellectual property, do we do some damage to the preservation of that property – that is, to the preservation of culture and heritage of a particular group or community? Blakeney, for example, has argued that treating indigenous culture as intellectual property means corralling it into the shape of western intellectual property law.[87] If the item of indigenous culture is a story, music or artwork, it has to be fitted into copyright law; designs and symbols must fit into the netherworld of the relationship between copyright, designs and trade marks; knowledge about local flora and fauna must be fitted somewhere into patent law, plants breeders' rights or geographical indications. This will mean that different levels of protection will apply to different types of traditional

---

[82] See Christoph Antons, 'Intellectual Property Rights in Indigenous Cultural Heritage: Basic Concepts and Continuing Controversies', in this volume; Martin Girsberger and Benny Müller, 'International Trade in Indigenous Cultural Heritage: An IP Practitioners' Perspective', in this volume; and Vézina, supra note 73.

[83] See, for example, Michael Blakeney, 'The Protection of Traditional Knowledge Under Intellectual Property Law' (2000) *European Intellectual Property Law Review*, 22, pp. 251–61 [hereinafter Blakeney, 'The Protection of TK'].

[84] See Ibid.

[85] See Michael Blakeney, 'Protecting Traditional Cultural Expressions: The International Dimension', in Fiona Macmillan and Kathy Bowrey (eds), *New Directions in Copyright Law*, vol. III, Cheltenham, UK: Edward Elgar, 2006, pp. 3–14.

[86] See Kathy Bowrey, 'Alternative Intellectual Property? Indigenous Protocols, Copyleft and New Juridifications of Customary Practices' (2006) *Macquarie Law Journal*, 6, pp. 65–95.

[87] See Blakeney, 'The Protection of TK', supra note 83.

knowledge and culture. In short, as Fitzpatrick and Joyce argue, the end result is that occidental intellectual property law comes to constitute traditional, or non-western, culture and heritage.[88] In so doing, it changes the shape of that heritage in ways that are not necessarily the consequence of the reflexive cultural practice that in fact constitutes so-called traditional cultural expressions and knowledge.[89] This seems to be inimical to the very purpose of protecting cultural heritage.[90]

Protection of the cultural heritage of indigenous peoples through intellectual property devices may not only pose a threat to the vibrancy of such cultural heritage; it may also have repercussions for the development of intellectual property law as a whole. Bowrey and Anderson[91] have argued persuasively that a wide concept of the intellectual public domain, which has been advocated by many commentators as a way of preserving creativity in the face of concerns about the imperial claims of intellectual property rights over more and more material in intellectual space,[92] is prejudicial to the claims and interests of indigenous peoples over their own creativity and knowledge. Accepting this argument poses something of a problem. If intellectual property law can be melded into a system that protects the interests of indigenous peoples in their cultural heritage, that system would, in accordance with the arguments of Bowrey and Andersen, have to embrace a much more limited concept of the public domain. This would have an inevitable blow-back into intellectual property law in general, with the arguable result that what would improve the intellectual property system from the point of view of indigenous peoples would damage it in relation to general concerns about creative freedom. Perhaps it is possible to address this concern through a better-articulated notion of the public domain in intellectual space,[93] which embraces a concept of group and communal rights, belonging to less than the public as a whole, bounded by property on the outside, but inside

---

88 Peter Fitzpatrick and Richard Joyce, 'Copying Right: Cultural Property and the Limits of (Occidental) Law', in Fiona Macmillan (ed.), *New Directions in Copyright Law,* vol. IV, Cheltenham, UK: Edward Elgar, 2007, pp. 171–92.

89 As Fitzpatrick and Joyce, ibid., at pp. 171–3, argue, so-called 'traditional knowledge and culture' would never have survived if it had not been 'dynamically generative and relational' and 'capable of being utterly responsive, comprehensively self-transgressive'.

90 For more on arguments of this type, see also Graber, supra note 48, at pp. 234–5.

91 Kathy Bowrey and Jane Anderson, 'The Politics of Global Information Sharing: Whose Cultural Agendas are Being Advanced?' (2009) *Social and Legal Studies*, 18, pp. 479–504.

92 See, for example, James Boyle, *The Public Domain: Enclosing the Commons of the Mind,* New Haven, CT: Yale University Press, 2008; Carol M. Rose, 'Romans, Roads and Romantic Creators: Traditions of Public Property in the Information Age' (2003) *Law & Contemporary Problems,* 66, pp. 89–110; Eva Hemmungs Wirten, 'Don't Fence Me In: Travels on the Public Domain', in Fiona Macmillan (ed.), *New Directions in Copyright Law*, vol. VI, Cheltenham, UK: Edward Elgar, 2007, pp. 112–21; Fiona Macmillan, 'Public Interest and the Public Domain in an Era of Corporate Dominance', in Birgitte Andersen (ed.), *Intellectual Property Rights: Innovation, Governance and the Institutional Environment*, Cheltenham, UK: Edward Elgar, 2006, pp. 46–69; Fiona Macmillan, 'Altering the Contours of the Public Domain', in Charlotte Waelde and Hector MacQueen (eds), *Intellectual Property: The Many Faces of the Public Domain*, Cheltenham, UK: Edward Elgar, 2007, pp. 98–117.

93 Vézina, supra note 73.

promoting freedom and space for creativity, innovation, invention and cultural conservation.[94] However, while this may constitute a theoretically appealing solution, it is necessary to accept that the political economy of the intellectual property system, which creates constant pressure for the reduction of the intellectual public domain,[95] is much more likely to embrace its simple reduction than it is to concern itself with group rights within an enlarged public domain.

4.2 (Intellectual) Property and Cultural Heritage

So much (and much more) might be said about the problems of using the intellectual property system to protect the cultural heritage of indigenous peoples as they might be perceived from inside the system itself. However, there is also a larger issue about the use of the property paradigm for the protection of cultural heritage generally, and the cultural heritage of indigenous peoples specifically.[96] Consideration of this matter needs to be conducted by looking at the issue from outside the confines of the intellectual property system, which already has the tendency to constrain debate with its ready-made division of cultural heritage into traditional cultural expressions and traditional knowledge. In an interesting reflection of the systemic divide, on which the arguments in this chapter are predicated, many scholars coming from or working within the intellectual property paradigm tend to have difficulty embracing the wider reflections on the property paradigm that have been generated by scholars working on what might be described as the public international law side of the cultural heritage debate. At the same time, scholars and commentators who have concerned themselves with the modalities for protection of cultural heritage in the public international law context have not tended to deal with the particular perspective provided by the intellectual property law system.[97]

The question of the protection of cultural heritage within the system of public international law has been dogged by questions of terminology, which in turn reflect critical

---

[94] See further Macmillan, 'Altering the Contours of the Public Domain', supra note 92; and Fiona Macmillan, 'Many Analogies, Some Metaphors, Little Imagination: The Public Domain in Intellectual Space' (2010) *Pólemos*, 2, pp. 25–44.

[95] See further, for example, Ronald V. Bettig, *Copyrighting Culture: The Political Economy of Intellectual Property*, Boulder, CO: Westview Press, 1996.

[96] Christoph B. Graber, 'Aboriginal Self-Determination vs the Propertisation of Traditional Culture: The Case of Sacred Wanjina Sites' (2009) *Australian Indigenous Law Review*, 13, pp. 218–34.

[97] One admirable exception to this tendency is Rosemary Coombe: see her contribution, Rosemary J. Coombe with Joseph F. Turcotte: 'Indigenous Cultural Heritage in Development and Trade: Perspectives from the Dynamics of Cultural Heritage Law and Policy', in this volume; and, for example, Rosemary J. Coombe, *The Cultural Life of Intellectual Properties*, Durham, NC and London: Duke University Press, 1998; Rosemary J. Coombe, 'Intellectual Property, Human Rights, and Sovereignty: New Dilemmas in International Law Posed by the Recognition of Indigenous Knowledge and the Conservation of Biodiversity' (1998) *Indiana Journal of Global Legal Studies*, 6, pp. 59–115; and Rosemary J. Coombe, 'The Expanding Purview of Cultural Properties and their Politics' (2009) *Annual Review of Law and Social Sciences*, 5, pp. 393–412. Yu, supra note 64, is also an example of a similar approach.

questions about the object of protection.[98] Accordingly, concepts of cultural rights and cultural property have figured largely in the general landscape of cultural heritage protection. So far as the regime of international legal protection established under the auspices of UNESCO is concerned, the terminological differences tend to reflect the political preoccupations of the relevant time.[99] As Blake relates, the expression 'cultural property', as denoting the object of protection, enjoyed great currency in the earlier UNESCO Conventions.[100] However, in more recent times there has been a move away from the use of this expression for three principal reasons. First, as Blake notes:

> It [property] carries with it a range of ideological baggage which is difficult to shed when using the term in relation to ... cultural heritage ... where one needs to modify these associated traditional values in order to achieve the social goals desired. It is problematic to apply a legal concept involving the rights of the possessor to the protection of cultural resources which may involve a severe curtailment of such rights and the separation of access and control from ownership.[101]

Secondly, precisely because 'property' is a legal term of art it might not be sufficiently broad to encompass the full range of things falling within the category of cultural heritage.[102] Thirdly, the use of the word 'property' suggests commodification.[103] While this is problematic with respect to the question of cultural heritage, this objection to the use of the word takes us to the heart of the matter. This is because it is undeniably the case that cultural heritage can also comprise both tangible[104] and intangible property, which is bought and sold in the marketplace. The very fact of this co-existence, and the conflicts that it can pose, may constitute an argument in favour of identifying and keeping separate property rights and cultural heritage rights. This would allow the two interests to be weighed against each other in cases of conflict. In the context of intellectual property rights over indigenous cultural heritage, this would mean using intellectual property rights to protect commodified cultural heritage, but at the same time recognising certain cultural rights that may limit that commodification.

---

98 See, for example, Janet Blake, 'On Defining Cultural Heritage' (2000) *International and Comparative Law Quarterly*, 49, pp. 61–85; and Lyndel V. Prott and Patrick J. O'Keefe, '"Cultural Heritage" or "Cultural Property"?' (1992) *International Journal of Cultural Property*, 1, pp. 307–20.

99 See Vrdoljak, supra note 61.

100 See Blake, supra note 98, at p. 65, citing as examples the Convention for the Protection of Cultural Property in the Event of Armed Conflict of 1954 and the Convention on the Means of Prohibiting and Preventing the Illicit Import, Export and Transfer of Ownership of Cultural Property of 1970.

101 Blake, supra note 98, at pp. 65–6.

102 Ibid., at p. 66.

103 Ibid., at p. 66; Prott and O'Keefe, supra note 98, at pp. 309–12.

104 On the question of commodification of tangible cultural heritage items, see John H. Merryman, 'A Licit International Trade in Cultural Objects' (1995) *International Journal of Cultural Property*, 4, pp. 13–60; Clemency C. Coggins, 'A Licit International Trade in Ancient Art: Let There Be Light!' (1995) *International Journal of Cultural Property*, 4, pp. 61–80; and H. K. Wiehe, 'Licit International Traffic in Cultural Objects for Art's Sake' (1995) *International Journal of Cultural Property*, 4, pp. 81–90.

Despite the fact that it has tended to have fallen out of use in international legal instruments, some commentators have argued in favour of maintaining a notion of cultural property in order to protect cultural heritage interests.[105] Recently, Carpenter, Katyal and Riley have argued in favour of a property concept based on stewardship.[106] To some extent this might be conceptualised as an attempt to internalise the balancing or weighing of different interests, referred to above, within a property model. However, the property model used by Carpenter, Katyal and Riley is largely stripped of the usual legal baggage denoted by the term, and can hardly be considered to support arguments favouring the realisation of the cultural heritage rights of indigenous peoples through a standard property model.

4.3 Intellectual Property in the Systemic Divide

As the foregoing has attempted to suggest, the use of intellectual property rights to protect the cultural heritage of indigenous peoples generally is subject to serious limitations and problems. However, it is accepted that there is utility in using such rights to protect the commodified aspects of indigenous cultural heritage, provided they are balanced against the other cultural rights of indigenous peoples. The technical difficulty with this approach is that it runs up against the systemic divide between international economic law, of which intellectual property law must be regarded as a part since the advent of the WTO TRIPS Agreement, and public international law, in which cultural heritage rights in general and the rights of indigenous peoples in particular are recognised.

Nevertheless, while intellectual property law now seems firmly ensconced on the international economic law side of the equation, it is worth noting that it has a life that falls on both sides of the systemic divide. Once upon a time, prior to the explicit opening of the fissure in international law caused by the birth of the WTO, international law in the area of intellectual property was the exclusive preserve of the World Intellectual Property Organization (WIPO), a United Nations instrumentality. As is well known, notwithstanding the loss of influence occasioned by the advent of the WTO, WIPO has continued to work in a number of areas of intellectual property law, including, notably, on the question of the protection of indigenous cultural heritage. Does this dual life of intellectual property law on both sides of the systemic divide give it a special purchase in the fragmented system of international law that militates in favour of using it as a way to bridge the divide?

So far as the protection of indigenous cultural heritage is concerned, the initiatives under way in WIPO show the effect of norms coming from public international law. To the limited extent that there is anything concrete to show for it, the work of the Intergovernmental Committee on Intellectual Property and Genetic Resources, Traditional Knowledge and Folklore has moved away from a strictly intellectual-property-based model towards an approach that aims to take account of the particular considerations affecting the cultural heritage of indigenous peoples.[107] This is, at least, the case with respect to the draft provisions for the *sui generis* protection of traditional cultural

---

[105] See, in particular, Margaret Jane Radin, 'Property and Personhood' (1982) *Stanford Law Review*, 34, pp. 957–1015, which has been very influential in this area.

[106] Carpenter, Katyal and Riley, supra note 75.

[107] See Graber, supra note 48, at pp. 243–4.

expressions, which are based, as Graber observes, 'on the concept that TCE derive their significance from community recognition rather than from an individual's mark of creativity'.[108] On the other hand, the fact that the work in WIPO appears to embrace the distinction, drawn from occidental intellectual property law, between traditional knowledge (patents, geographical indications) and traditional cultural expressions (copyright, designs) shows the fundamental influence of intellectual property law, as now embedded in the WTO system, on the WIPO deliberations. In this sense, it might be argued that the work in WIPO is capable of bridging the divide between the two systems. However, in order to assert this with any confidence, it would seem necessary to make a case for the proposition that the work of the Intergovernmental Committee on Intellectual Property and Genetic Resources, Traditional Knowledge and Folklore has had some influence on the development of WTO law in this area. Evidence of this is a little thin on the ground, although some lip service has been paid to this issue.[109] Given the systemic primacy of the WTO system, the lack of evidence for any real influence from the public international law system, via WIPO, on the development of the WTO's approach to intellectual property protection of the cultural heritage of indigenous peoples tends to suggest that intellectual property law and policy at the international level has a limited ability to bridge the systemic divide in international law. This leaves us with the question of whether there is some other way for norms from public international law to influence the development or application of WTO law in this area.

5. UNDRIP, UNESCO AND THE WTO

One of the problems with the focus on intellectual property as a means for protecting the cultural heritage of indigenous peoples in the international trade context is that it tends to foreclose discussion about the types of cultural heritage that might be implicated in the international trade system. In other words, the focus on intellectual property tends to ignore to some extent questions about trade in tangible products and trade in services. Of course, trade in these types of products may have intellectual property dimensions as well. Interestingly, the two WTO cases, referred to below, that have addressed questions about trade in 'cultural products' have shown that trade in this area tends to raise issues that cross over between intellectual property, trade in goods and trade in services. In particular, the tangible/intangible distinction collapses in the face of national legislation that deals, at the same time, with both the content of cultural products and the physical product that carries that content.[110]

In order to support trade in the cultural heritage of indigenous peoples, which protects the values of indigenous peoples at the same time as allowing them to participate in the international trade system, national law needs to take a holistic approach that is not constrained by narrow distinctions between intellectual property and physical property, or

---

108 Ibid., at p. 243, citing, in support, the provision in draft Article 2 that identifies indigenous communities as the principal beneficiaries of protection.

109 For an account of WTO activity in this area, see ibid., at pp. 244–6.

110 As noted by the Appellate Body in *China – Entertainment Products*, supra note 1, at paras 118 and 195.

between trade in the tangible and the intangible. Such an approach also needs to be taken in the WTO system, where panels reviewing national legislation are just as likely (if not more likely) to encounter issues in relation to the GATT and the General Agreement on Trade in Services (GATS), as they are to be dealing with the TRIPS Agreement. In such circumstances there is a question about the extent to which the application of WTO law will be constrained by public international law and norms on the protection of cultural heritage and of the rights of indigenous peoples. Put more simply, the question is when – if ever – will WTO law take account of the provisions of conventions such as the Convention on Biological Diversity, the UNESCO Convention for the Safeguarding of the Intangible Cultural Heritage, the UNESCO Convention on the Protection and Promotion of the Diversity of Cultural Expressions, and the United Nations Declaration on the Rights of Indigenous Peoples?

This discussion is predicated on the suggestion that there may be circumstances in which national regimes seeking to give special protection to the trading rights of indigenous peoples pursuant to these public international law instruments may run counter to the WTO's foundational principles of national treatment and most favoured nation (MFN) treatment.[111] Taken together these two principles provide that a WTO Member State may not create a trade disadvantage vis-à-vis domestic goods and services for like goods or services coming from another WTO Member State, nor may they discriminate between like goods and services coming into their jurisdiction from more than one other Member State.[112] The WTO agreements laying down obligations pursuant to the principles of national treatment and MFN treatment are subject to a range of exceptions allowing governments to take steps that would amount to breaches of these principles in some cases involving pressing national priorities, but the exceptions are limited and narrowly drawn. So far as the protection of the trading rights of indigenous peoples in their cultural heritage is concerned, a national government may wish, for example, to provide for quotas, local content restrictions or subsidies for local cultural production.[113] All these sorts of devices run the risk of falling foul of WTO rules and would be permitted only if they fell within a WTO exception.

The mechanisms in WTO law that allow it to engage with public international law are limited to the exceptions laid down in certain WTO agreements. Apart from one extremely limited exception,[114] there are no specific exceptions relating to cultural rights or interests.

---

[111] See also Susy Frankel, 'Attempts to Protect Indigenous Culture through Free Trade Agreements', in this volume.

[112] Consistently with the WTO's somewhat inconsistent approach, WTO law and practice embrace a number of derogations from these principles: for example, the GATS permits measures that are inconsistent with MFN: see GATS, Article II; and the exceptions for customs unions in GATT, Article XXIV, and GATS, Article V, involve inconsistencies with both principles.

[113] That is, some of the types of devices envisaged by the UNESCO Convention on the Protection and Promotion of the Diversity of Cultural Expressions, Article 6.

[114] See GATT, Article XX(f), which provides:

> Subject to the requirement that such measures are not applied in a manner which would constitute a means of arbitrary or unjustifiable discrimination between countries where the same conditions prevail, or a disguised restriction on international trade, nothing in this Agreement shall be construed to prevent the adoption or enforcement by any contracting party of measures: (*f*) imposed for the protection of national treasures of artistic, historic or archaeological value; ...

The only possible relevant exceptions of any width seem to be in GATT, Article XX(a) and GATS, Article XIV(a). The GATT provision exempts measures 'necessary to protect public morals'. The GATS provision is a little broader, exempting measures 'necessary to protect public morals or to maintain public order'. Of course, the provisions would need to be read expansively in order to give protection to national legislation protecting the trading rights of indigenous peoples in cultural heritage that was otherwise in breach of the relevant WTO agreement. The WTO Appellate Body decision in *US – Measures Affecting the Cross-Border Supply of Gambling and Betting Services*,[115] which considered the meaning and application of GATS, Article XIV(a), suggests that such an expansive reading is not impossible. In its decision, the Appellate Body quoted with apparent approval the definitions given to 'public morals' and 'public order', respectively, in the Panel decision.[116] According to the Panel, the former 'denotes standards of right and wrong conduct maintained by or on behalf of a community or nation'.[117] The latter expression is qualified by footnote 5 of the GATS, which provides that '[t]he public order exception may be invoked only where a genuine and sufficiently serious threat is posed to one of the fundamental interests of society'. Taking this into account, the Panel found that '"public order" refers to the preservation of the fundamental interests of a society, as reflected in public policy and law'.[118] The Panel found, and the Appellate Body agreed, that since the various measures in question were concerned with preventing 'money laundering, organized crime, fraud, underage gambling and pathological gambling', they were concerned with protecting either or both of public morals or public order.[119] This reasonably expansive reading tends to suggest that measures arising under the general rubric of human rights protection would have a chance of falling within the exception. However, there is not much specific evidence of this in WTO dispute resolution proceedings.

In *China – Entertainment Products*, China sought to rely on the exception in Article XX(a) of GATT in relation to a range of measures for establishing a process of content review with accompanying selective bans on the importation and distribution of so-called 'cultural goods', comprising reading materials, audiovisual products and films for theatrical release. As the Appellate Body related in its Report:

> China emphasized particular characteristics of cultural goods, including the impact they can have on societal and individual morals. It is for this reason, according to China, that it has adopted a regulatory regime under which the importation of reading materials, audiovisual products, and films for theatrical release containing specific types of prohibited content is not permitted. To this end, China explained, its existing regulatory regime defines the content that China considers to have a negative impact on public morals and, in order to ensure that such

---

115 WTO, Panel Report, *Cross Border Gambling*, WTO Doc. WT/DS285/R, 10 November 2004; and WTO, Appellate Body Report, *Cross Border Gambling*, WTO Doc. WT/DS285/AB/R, adopted 20 April 2005.

116 WTO, Appellate Body Report, *Cross Border Gambling*, supra note 115, at para. 296.

117 WTO, Panel Report, *Cross Border Gambling*, supra note 115 at para. 6.465.

118 Ibid., at para. 6.467.

119 Ibid., at para. 6.486; WTO, Appellate Body Report, *Cross Border Gambling*, supra note 115, at para. 296.

> content is not imported into China, establishes a mechanism for content review of relevant products that is based upon the selection of import entities.[120]

In support of its contention that 'cultural goods' have particular characteristics that impact on societal and individual morals, China relied on Article 8 of the UNESCO Universal Declaration on Cultural Diversity[121] for the proposition that cultural goods are 'vectors of identity, values and meaning' and that they 'must not be treated as mere commodities or consumer goods'.[122] China also placed reliance in this respect on the UNESCO Convention on the Protection and Promotion of the Diversity of Cultural Expressions.[123] It seems that these references were largely perplexing to the Panel and Appellate Body, both of which effectively side-lined them in favour of an approach that relied upon their recurring preoccupation with the meaning of the word 'necessary' as it appears in the Article XX exceptions.

Under these circumstances it is difficult to know what weight or significance (if any) can be given to China's attempt to import values derived from the UNESCO Convention on the Protection and Promotion of the Diversity of Cultural Expressions into WTO law. Similarly, the question of whether or not the exceptions in GATT, Article XX(a) and GATS Article XIV(a) can be stretched far enough to embrace principles and values generated under the public international law system remains unanswered. One can, of course, imagine much stronger cases for this than *China – Entertainment Products*. In particular, this would seem to be true for cases that involve a direct conflict between WTO law and a right arising under public international law. In the current context, this seems unlikely with respect to the UNESCO Conventions since they impose very little by way of direct obligations, with the consequence that a direct conflict is unlikely.[124] More scope for direct conflict may be generated by Article 31 of UNDRIP, which confers rights on indigenous peoples and poses direct obligations on states. In the context of WTO law, the significance of the fact that this is a Declaration rather than a Convention seems unclear. Neither the Panel nor the Appellate Body in *China – Entertainment Products* seemed to be particularly concerned with the difference between the UNESCO Universal Declaration on Cultural Diversity and the UNESCO Convention on the Protection and Promotion of the Diversity

---

[120] WTO, Appellate Body Report, *China – Entertainment Products*, supra note 1, at para. 141 (footnotes omitted).

[121] UNESCO, Universal Declaration on Cultural Diversity, 41 ILM 57 (adopted on 2 November 2001).

[122] WTO, Panel Report, *China – Entertainment Products*, supra note 1, at para. 7.751; and WTO, Appellate Body Report, *China – Entertainment Products*, supra note 1, at para. 141n.

[123] WTO, Panel Report, *China – Entertainment Products*, supra note 1, at para. 4.207; and WTO, Appellate Body Report, *China – Entertainment Products*, supra note 1, at para. 141n.

[124] See further, Fiona Macmillan, 'The UNESCO Convention as a New Incentive to Protect Cultural Diversity', in Hildegard Schneider and Peter van den Bossche (eds), *Protection of Cultural Diversity from a European and International Perspective*, Mortsel: Intersentia, 2008, pp. 163–92. In any case, where a direct conflict occurs, Article 20.2 of the UNESCO Convention deals with this by providing that 'Nothing in this Convention shall be interpreted as modifying rights and obligations of the Parties under any other treaties to which they are parties.'

of Cultural Expressions. On the other hand, neither dispute resolution body was particularly concerned about either of these instruments, so it is hard to draw any meaningful conclusion from this.

In the end, so far as the recognition of cultural rights or rights in cultural heritage is concerned, there seems to be little evidence that developments in UNESCO have had much impact on the WTO. The side-lining of arguments about the significance of 'cultural products' in *China – Entertainment Products*, despite the citing of UNESCO instruments, seems somewhat reminiscent of the approach in *Canada – Certain Measures Concerning Periodicals*,[125] where the WTO dispute resolution bodies considered the GATT consistency of a Canadian tax on foreign 'split-run' periodicals and preferential treatment of Canadian magazines. Canada mounted an argument that no GATT violation occurred on the ground that the foreign (US) magazines were not like products on cultural grounds. This argument was ignored by the WTO dispute resolution bodies. While the argument in *China – Entertainment Products* focused on a different provision of the GATT, the treatment of 'cultural' claims does not seem dissimilar.

6. IS THERE A WAY FORWARD?

Any proposal to move forward in this highly contested territory needs not only to find a way of bridging the gap between public international law and international economic law, but it also needs to do it in a way that is responsive to the values and demands of indigenous peoples. Commodification of their cultural heritage in international trade will not always be acceptable to indigenous peoples. However, to the extent that it is, it may implicate a range of cultural heritage – tangible and intangible, moveable and immoveable – that cuts across traditional legal categories of property. This is one reason why the persistent recourse to intellectual property rights as means for protecting the cultural heritage of indigenous peoples needs to be re-thought. However, it is not only the focus of intellectual property on the protection of intangibles that is problematic in this context. As has been argued in this chapter, the intellectual property system is organised according to occidental knowledge systems and based on a conception of commodification that may be at odds with the demands and expectations of indigenous peoples. To the extent that property rights, especially in their classic occidental sense, are a useful device in the context of facilitating the participation of indigenous peoples in international trade, they need to be balanced against cultural heritage rights. In the context of international law, this balancing trick could be achieved by finding ways to bridge the gap between public international law and international economic law. More specifically, given the current systemic pre-eminence of the WTO system, not to mention its specific role in managing the international trade regime, there is a need to find devices that permit the recognition by the WTO of norms governing the rights of indigenous peoples in public international law.

---

[125] WTO, Panel Report, *Canada – Certain Measures Concerning Periodicals*, WTO Doc. WT/DS31/R, 14 March 1997; and WTO, Appellate Body Report, *Canada – Certain Measures Concerning Periodicals*, WTO Doc. WT/DS31/AB/R, adopted 30 July 1997.

Graber proposes the use of a procedural device within the WTO that would allow for an interface 'between global law and local traditions'.[126] Certainly, as this chapter has already suggested, the right type of procedural devices are capable of founding a substantive engagement between the two legal systems. Graber's carefully articulated model not only seems to fall within the ambit of 'the right type of procedural device'; it also deals with the persistent problem of identification of rights' holders in the indigenous context within a flexible administrative framework. In these senses it has the advantage over some other possible proposals for bridging the gap between the two systems, such as proposals for the amendment of the WTO agreements in order to introduce specific exceptions recognising the rights of indigenous peoples. To be effective, a proposal along these lines for the amendment of WTO law would also be likely to require some strengthening of the relevant public law instruments. For example, the conversion of UNDRIP from a declaration into a convention would be desirable, as would the enhancement of the rights of indigenous peoples in the UNESCO conventions. Another way in which Graber's proposal has advantages over proposals to amend existing WTO agreements is that it is capable of bypassing the particularly onerous procedure for amendment of WTO agreements laid down in Article X of the Agreement Establishing the WTO. However, even if theoretically less onerous to achieve, something that Graber's proposal for a procedural device shares with proposals to amend WTO agreements is the – at best – lack of political will (and – at worst – outright hostility) on the part of the powerful states in the WTO which such proposals are likely to engender. The division between the political and economic that is represented in the systemic division between public international law and international economic law is not an accident. It is, rather, a deliberate policy designed to facilitate the pre-eminence of the selective free trade agenda.

Perhaps, however, there is an alternative that can be invoked under existing WTO law that also employs the weapon of public opinion. As was noted above, China's attempts to rely on the norms generated by the UNESCO Convention on the Protection and Promotion of the Diversity of Cultural Expressions to inform the content of the exception in GATT, Article XX(a), with respect to the protection of public morals was not based on a particularly compelling argument. Nor were the attempts by China to impose a potentially protectionist censorship system the sort of thing that would be likely to generate much public sympathy or activism in the rest of the world. However, a convincing argument that sought to locate the protection of the rights of indigenous peoples within the scope of the public morals and public order exceptions in the GATT and GATS would be likely to generate considerable positive public opinion and activism. It would also have the merit of making explicit the disconnection of the two regimes of international law. This chapter, therefore, closes with the proposal that a way forward in this area would be for a relevant international organisation, such as UNESCO, to work with a sympathetic member of the WTO in order to promote a test case in the WTO on the question of the extent to which the WTO exceptions are capable of recognising the legitimate claims of indigenous peoples to particular and distinctive protection within the international trading system.[127]

---

[126] See Graber, supra note 48, at pp. 251–2.

[127] My thanks to Rosemary Coombe for this suggestion.

5. Attempts to protect indigenous culture through free trade agreements

Susy Frankel*

1. INTRODUCTION

The fundamental purpose of most modern free trade agreements (FTAs) is to extend the commitments, which may mean to further liberalise trade, that Members of the World Trade Organization (WTO) have made in that multilateral forum. FTAs also frequently include commitments in areas that are outside the WTO obligations. Protection of traditional knowledge and traditional cultural expressions (TCEs) are not specifically part of the WTO framework, in particular the Agreement on Trade-Related Aspects of Intellectual Property Rights (TRIPS Agreement).[1] Some FTAs expressly provide that the parties, or at least one of the parties, retain the ability to protect certain aspects of cultural heritage, including the protection of traditional knowledge. Other FTAs limit the possibilities for protecting traditional knowledge. This chapter analyses how FTAs might affect the aspirations of indigenous peoples, in particular, to protect their traditional knowledge. First, the chapter discusses the problems that have led to a call for the protection of traditional knowledge. The chapter then assesses the international agreements that provide varying protection for traditional knowledge and issues arising from the implementation of those international agreements in domestic law. Next is a discussion about the general approach that FTAs take when they include clauses about protection of cultural heritage. Some specific examples of clauses from FTAs are discussed. The chapter then assesses the purpose and legitimacy of protecting traditional knowledge through FTAs. Unlike TRIPS-plus provisions in FTAs, there is no creation, through FTAs, of norms for the protection (substantive or procedural) of traditional knowledge. The chapter concludes with a discussion of some of the consequences if such norms were developed through FTAs. In particular, the effects of national treatment and whether foreign courts can apply the laws of the country of origin of the traditional knowledge owners are discussed. The chapter concludes that countries who wish to protect traditional knowledge do not at present use

* Thanks to Anne Melkiau for research assistance. Thanks to Christoph Graber, Jessica Lai and Karolina Kuprecht for hosting the workshop from which this chapter developed and for their excellent editorial work, particularly comments on drafts.

[1] WTO, Agreement on Trade-Related Aspects of Intellectual Property Rights (TRIPS), Marrakesh Agreement Establishing the World Trade Organization, Annex 1C, 1869 UNTS 299; 33 ILM 1197 (adopted on 15 April 1994, entered into force 1 January 1995).

FTAs effectively for that purpose and that those countries ought to consider closely if FTAs can assist them in creating norms for the protection of traditional knowledge.

2. THE PROBLEMS THAT TRADITIONAL KNOWLEDGE-HOLDERS FACE

The development and continuing evolution of the international intellectual property system has invigorated, if not arguably created, a debate about the use of traditional knowledge sourced from either developing countries or indigenous peoples.[2] In short, these groups have sought to protect their knowledge and associated resources from exploitation in developed countries. The ways in which people and businesses in developed countries copy or use traditional knowledge to innovate or create are many and the literature is replete with examples.[3] The terminology used in a variety of international fora, and discourse about those fora, include traditional knowledge, folklore, traditional cultural expressions and biological and genetic resources.[4] This terminology is in part a matter of convenience, but it also reflects a categorisation analogous to that found in intellectual property law. Copyright and expressive uses of trade marks, on the one hand, might be analogous to traditional cultural expressions and, on the other hand, biological and genetic resources are associated with patents and plant variety rights. The traditional knowledge element is relevant to both. These categories, however, do not necessarily reflect the ways that communities, from which traditional knowledge comes, see the boundaries. This chapter discusses traditional knowledge that is connected to both traditional cultural expressions and biological and genetic resources.[5]

The central concern of the peoples who are the source of traditional knowledge, conveniently described as traditional knowledge-holders, is that they frequently do not

---

[2] There is an important difference between developing countries and indigenous peoples in this context. Internationally, and particularly at the World Trade Organization, the debate is focused on a general developing versus developed country paradigm. However, many indigenous peoples are minority populations in either developing or developed countries (for example New Zealand, Australia, Canada and the USA). Therefore, indigenous peoples' interests are frequently different from the interests of large developing countries, such as India and Brazil.

[3] See, for example, Yinliang Liu, 'IPR Protection for New Traditional Knowledge: With a Case Study of Traditional Chinese Medicine' (2003) *European Intellectual Property Review*, 325 (4), pp. 194–9; Naomi Roht-Arriaza, 'Of Seeds and Shamans: The Appropriation of Scientific and Technical Knowledge of Indigenous and Local Communities' (1996) *Michigan Journal of International Law*, 17, pp. 919–65; and Darryl A. Posey and Graham Dutfield, *Beyond Intellectual Property*, Ottawa, Canada: International Development Research Centre, 1996. Also Martin Girsberger and Benny Müller, 'International Trade in Indigenous Cultural Heritage: An IP Practitioners' Perspective', in this volume.

[4] See, for example, World Intellectual Property Organization (WIPO), Intergovernmental Committee on Intellectual Property and Genetic Resources, Traditional Knowledge and Folklore (IGC), 'The Protection of Traditional Knowledge: Factual Extraction', (WIPO Doc. WIPO/GRTKF/IC/12/5(b), 2008), at pp. 14–34.

[5] Traditional knowledge is also part of what is more broadly described as cultural heritage. See discussion of WIPO, IGC, 'Traditional Knowledge – Operational Terms and Definitions', (WIPO Doc. WIPO/GRTKF/IC/3/9, 2002).

benefit from others' use of their knowledge. They neither receive a share directly from the products or services that result from the use, nor are they acknowledged or compensated for the contribution that their traditional knowledge has made. This can occur where traditional knowledge relates to the uses of biological or genetic resources. Examples of unpermitted and unrewarded uses of genetic resources and traditional knowledge are central to the international debate over the protection of traditional knowledge and indigenous culture.[6]

Broadly, those who have the relevant knowledge may convey it to someone who enquires about the uses of a plant, or aspects of the knowledge may be well known or recorded in publicly available literature. Perhaps a particular plant is known for its anti-bacterial properties. Researchers, such as pharmaceutical companies, may use the knowledge to assist in selecting that plant to research or the knowledge could form part of the research process. In such situations, the pharmaceutical researchers could isolate the plant's active ingredient, then synthesise the active ingredient and potentially reproduce it for use as a consumer product. The problems that this sort of scenario can create are many. The benefits resulting from the use of the knowledge may not be shared with the knowledge-holders and there can be negative effects on sustainability of both the communities who provide the knowledge and the biological and genetic resources themselves. This sort of situation arises largely because those using the knowledge treat it as freely available for anyone to use in any way. However, even if the holders of the traditional knowledge made the knowledge publicly available, that does not necessarily mean that their intention was that it be freely available for use in any way.[7] From the holders' perspectives, the values of the community should guide uses of that knowledge. Those values include guardianship of the knowledge for the benefit of future generations. The concept of guardianship for future generations indicates why indigenous peoples may consider themselves as temporary custodians or holders, rather than owners, of traditional knowledge.[8]

---

6 Examples include the use of the neem tree and basmati rice, from India (see Michael Woods, 'Food for Thought: The Biopiracy of Jasmine and Basmati Rice' (2002) *Albany Law Journal of Science and Technology*, 13, pp. 123–44), and the enola bean (see Gillian N. Rattray, 'The Enola Bean Patent Controversy: Biopiracy, Novelty and Fish and Chips' (2002) *Duke Law and Technology Review*, 8, available online at http://www.law.duke.edu/journals/dltr/articles/2002dltr0008.html) (all online sources were accessed 18 September 2011).

7 See discussion of this point in Susy Frankel and Megan Richardson, 'Cultural Property and the "Public domain": Case Studies from New Zealand and Australia', in Christoph Antons (ed.), *Traditional Knowledge, Traditional Cultural Expressions and Intellectual Property Law in the Asia-Pacific Region,* Alphen aan den Rijn, Netherlands: Kluwer Law International, 2009, pp. 275–92. See also Christoph B. Graber, 'Institutionalization of Creativity in Traditional Societies in International Trade Law', in Shubha Ghosh and Robin P. Malloy (eds), *Creativity, Law and Entrepreneurship*, Cheltenham, UK and Northampton, MA: Edward Elgar, 2001, pp. 234–63, at p. 234.

8 See, for example, the discussion of the role of Māori as kaitiaki (guardians) of their matauranga Māori in Waitangi Tribunal, *Ko Aotearoa Tēnei: A Report into Claims Concerning New Zealand Law and Policy Affecting Māori Culture and Identity* (2011) Wai 262, at ch. 1 and 2, available online at http://www.waitangi-tribunal.govt.nz/news/media/wai262.asp [hereinafter *Ko Aotearoa Tēnei*]. Translated, *Ko Aotearoa Tēnei* means 'This is Aotearoa/New Zealand'. Aotearoa is the Māori name for New Zealand.

Another related problem is that the production of a synthetic active compound may be cheaper and more efficient than either extracting the compound from plants found in the region from where the traditional knowledge comes or growing enough of the plant to extract a commercially usable volume of any active ingredient.[9] Thus, if the knowledge-holders already had a market for their natural plants, that market may be undercut or future development of it curtailed. A further problem might be that indigenous peoples stop using their traditional knowledge, if they have access to synthetic and potentially cheaper products as substitutes for the traditional forms. Some may see this as integrating into the modern world and that therefore all have benefited, but it is not so simple. Where the traditional knowledge is related to plants, this, some claim, may have a negative effect on biodiversity[10] and, where those plants are used in medicinal practices, there might be negative effects on cultural diversity and indigenous peoples' cultural identity and even their health.[11]

I do not intend this chapter to be a summary of the problems that global trade brings to traditional knowledge-holders, but the above shows how the problem has emerged where biological and genetic resources are connected to traditional knowledge. Intellectual property law comes face to face with traditional knowledge because uses of biological and genetic resources, associated with traditional knowledge, can end up as patents or plant variety rights. The traditional knowledge associated with biological and genetic resources is, however, frequently about much more than the properties of a plant. It can be, for example, about the history and genealogy of people and their connection with the plant and the land on which it is found. The same or related knowledge might be shown in traditional cultural expressions.[12] Thus, while intellectual property would distinguish the patentable from the knowledge and culture, the holders of traditional knowledge do not make such a distinction.

Indigenous communities often produce works of art or craft that reflect traditional knowledge and are representations of their culture. The art of the weaver, for example, is not just the skill of the woven product, but the woven product is an expression of culture and knowledge. The products used to create the weaving (perhaps a biological resource such as flax) may also have special cultural significance.[13] A problem arises if someone then uses that woven creation in a way that ignores or, worse, is offensive to that culture.

---

[9] This issue has arisen in relation to neem, see Oliver Krackhardt, 'Beyond the Neem Tree Conflict: Questions of Corporate Behaviour in a Globalised World' (2005) *New Zealand University Law Review*, 21, pp. 347–84.

[10] See, for example, Vandana Shiva, *Protect or Plunder?: Understanding Intellectual Property Rights,* London and New York: Zed Books, 2001, at pp. 40–48.

[11] See, for example, the discussion of the prevention of the use of *rongoā Māori* (traditional Māori medicinal practices) in New Zealand and associated effects on Māori health in the *Ko Aotearoa Tēnei*, supra note 8, at ch. 7.

[12] Traditional cultural expression is used by WIPO to distinguish traditional knowledge used in arts and literature from traditional knowledge used in relation to genetic resources, see WIPO, 'The Protection of Traditional Knowledge: Revised Objectives and Principles' (WIPO Doc. WIPO/GRTKF/IC/18/5, 2011), Annex 18.

[13] See, for example, the discussion about flax in Murdoch Riley, *Māori Healing and Herbal: New Zealand Ethnobotanical Sourcebook*, Paraparaumu: Viking Sevenseas NZ Ltd, 1997, at p. 126.

Intellectual property law does a very poor job of addressing the concerns of traditional knowledge-holders. Indeed, the designers of international intellectual property law standards never had as a broad goal to protect cultural integrity or to recognise guardianship interests that holders of traditional knowledge seek to protect.[14] Intellectual property is not divorced from cultural concerns – far from it.[15] Intellectual property is a strong legal tool that protects many products of culture. However, the law is structured in a way that values the use of culture through certain property style rights. The law gives exclusive rights to owners over a certain set of uses. Intellectual property law was not and is not designed to directly protect the relationship of peoples with their culture.

3. THE INTERNATIONAL DIMENSION AND NATIONAL IMPLEMENTATION

Member States of various multilateral fora have made the link between intellectual property and traditional knowledge.[16] Two of the most significant instruments for the protection of indigenous culture, which are not primarily about intellectual property rights, are the United Nations Declaration on the Rights of Indigenous Peoples (UNDRIP)[17]

---

[14] This is true of both national intellectual property regimes and international intellectual property regimes. See, for example, Robert Merges, *Justifying Intellectual Property,* Cambridge, MA and London: Harvard University Press, 2011, who refers to first order principles of intellectual property, which he describes as (1) Lockean appropriation, (2) Kantian (liberal) individualism and (3) Rawlsian attention to distributive effects of property. See also Graber, supra note 7, at pp. 239–40.

[15] Just as culture varies, so do the discussions of the relationship between intellectual property and culture. See, for example, Rosemary J. Coombe, *The Cultural Life of Intellectual Properties: Authorship, Appropriation, and the Law,* Durham, NC: Duke University Press, 1998 and Olufunmilayo Arewa, 'Culture as Property: Intellectual Property, Local Norms and Global Rights', *University of California, Irvine School of Law,* Northwestern Public Law Research Paper No. 07–1 (2007), available at http://ssrn.com/abstract=981423. See also discussion in Susy Frankel, 'Digital Copyright and Culture' (2010) *The Journal of Arts Management Law and Society*, 40 (2), pp. 140–56, at p. 147.

[16] In addition to those discussed in this chapter, other fora include the Food and Agriculture Organization, the International Union for the Protection of New Varieties of Plants and the United Nations Educational Scientific and Cultural Organization. For a general discussion about the relevant work in these institutions, see Christoph Antons, 'The International Debate about Traditional Knowledge, Traditional Cultural Expressions and Intellectual Property', in Christoph Antons (ed.), *Traditional Knowledge, Traditional Cultural Expressions and Intellectual Property Law in the Asia-Pacific Region*, Alphen aan den Rijn, Netherlands: Kluwer Law International, 2009, pp. 39–48.

[17] UN, Declaration on the Rights of Indigenous Peoples, GA Res. 61/295 (UN Doc. A/61/L.67 and Add.1) (adopted on 13 September 2007), Article 31 provides:

> 1. Indigenous peoples have the right to maintain, control, protect and develop their cultural heritage, traditional knowledge and traditional cultural expressions, as well as the manifestations of their sciences, technologies and cultures, including human and genetic resources, seeds, medicines, knowledge of the properties of fauna and flora, oral traditions, literatures, designs, sports and traditional games and visual and performing arts. They also have the right to maintain, control, protect and develop their intellectual property over such cultural heritage, traditional

and the Convention on Biological Diversity (CBD).[18] UNDRIP includes in its scope the rights of indigenous peoples to control, protect and develop their cultural heritage, including their traditional knowledge. The CBD's prime objective is protecting biological diversity. It provides for prior informed consent and benefit-sharing in relation to uses of biological and genetic resources. The Nagoya Protocol[19] takes the CBD a step further and recognises rights of indigenous peoples to genetic resources, but only where those rights are recognised in the law of the Member States.[20] The Protocol also gives rights in relation to traditional knowledge associated with genetic resources.[21] In each case the rights are that – before a third party makes use of the genetic resource or traditional knowledge associated with the genetic resource – there be prior informed consent for the use and that benefits that flow from the use are shared.

Domestic implementation of UNDRIP, CBD and Nagoya Protocol provisions is complex. Providing rights over traditional knowledge, primarily in the form of prior informed consent for access and use, and benefit-sharing, creates a system independent of intellectual property to protect traditional knowledge. In part, such independence is necessary because the nature of the rights is different from the core intellectual property rights such as copyright and patent. Therefore, any domestic law enacted to protect traditional knowledge in the ways envisaged in UNDRIP, the CBD and the Nagoya Protocol is likely to be separate from intellectual property, and is thus *sui generis*.[22]

Even if implemented at national level, such laws are unlikely to effectively protect traditional knowledge unless the measures made pursuant to them interface with the

---

knowledge, and traditional cultural expressions. 2. In conjunction with indigenous peoples, States shall take effective measures to recognize and protect the exercise of these rights.

18 Rio Convention on Biological Diversity (CBD), 1760 UNTS 79; (1992) 31 ILM 818 (opened for signature 5 June 1992, entered into force 29 December 1993), Article 8(j) provides:

Each contracting Party shall, as far as possible and as appropriate:

Subject to national legislation, respect, preserve and maintain knowledge, innovations and practices of indigenous and local communities embodying traditional lifestyles relevant for the conservation and sustainable use of biological diversity and promote their wider application with the approval and involvement of the holders of such knowledge, innovations and practices and encourage the equitable sharing of the benefits arising from the utilization of such knowledge innovations and practices.

19 The Nagoya Protocol is a supplementary agreement to the CBD; Nagoya Protocol on Access to Genetic Resources and the Fair and Equitable Sharing of Benefits Arising from their Utilization to the Convention on Biological Diversity (UN Doc. UNEP/CBD/COP/DEC/X/1) (adopted on 29 October 2010). It will enter into force 90 days after the 50th instrument of ratification. According to the CBD website, '[i]ts objective is the fair and equitable sharing of benefits arising from the utilization of genetic resources, thereby contributing to the conservation and sustainable use of biodiversity.'

20 Nagoya Protocol, Articles 5 and 6.

21 Nagoya Protocol, Article 7.

22 For a discussion of what is *sui generis* about traditional knowledge, see Antony Taubman, 'Saving the Village: Conserving Jurisprudential Diversity in the International Protection of Traditional Knowledge', in Keith E. Maskus and Jerome H. Reichman (eds), *International Public Goods and Transfer of Technology Under a Globalized Intellectual Property Regime*, New York: Cambridge University Press, 2005, pp. 535–41.

national intellectual property law.[23] Some kind of interface, to enable the two systems to work together, is necessary to resolve conflicts between intellectual property and traditional knowledge rights. Without a method for resolution it is probable that where there is a conflict, the intellectual property regime will be unaffected by other rights. If, for example, an isolated and synthesised active compound is patented, in most countries the patent right will not be affected even if the CBD was not complied with. The only way to affect the patent right is to have some direct interface with the patent system, such as an obligation on patent owners to disclose the origin of any genetic resources used in the applicant's invention.[24] Disclosure as an interface is only likely to be effective if there are consequences for a patent applicant's failure to disclose.[25] Having consequences, such as a requirement for re-examination or invalidity, flowing from a failure to disclose should incentivise compliance with access and benefit-sharing laws.[26] However, there is no international agreement on any kind of disclosure obligation in the patent system.

Traditional knowledge has become a tradeable commodity. Some traditional knowledge-creators and knowledge-holders have taken up a fight against the exploitation and sometimes commodification of their knowledge. Others, because perhaps that fight is in part lost, seek benefits from the exploitation of their knowledge. Consequently, the WTO TRIPS Council had on its agenda a discussion about the relationship between the CBD and the TRIPS Agreement.[27] The focus of the discussion has been about the interface described above and whether the WTO should amend the TRIPS Agreement to include a disclosure requirement.[28] At the time of writing, this discussion has ceased and looks like

---

[23] To use only the intellectual property system to protect traditional knowledge is not only impossible, but some describe this as a purely defensive strategy. See Graber, supra note 7, at p. 344.

[24] For a discussion outlining types of disclosure obligations and consequences, see WIPO, 'Technical Study on Disclosure Requirements Concerning Genetic Resources and Traditional Knowledge', WIPO Publication No. 786 (WIPO Doc. WIPO/GRTKF/IWG/3/14, 2011).

[25] If a failure to disclose the origin of genetic resources meant that the patent was revoked or invalidated in some way, it is likely that parties would comply with access benefit-sharing laws so that there would not be opposition to the patents.

[26] See discussion in the *Ko Aotearoa Tēnei*, supra note 8, at ch. 2.

[27] See generally WTO, Council of Trade-Related Aspects of Intellectual Property Rights (TRIPS Council), 'The TRIPS Agreement and Convention on Biological Diversity', (WTO Doc. IP/C/W/368/Rev.1, revised 8 February 2006, WIPO Doc. IP/C/W/368/Rev.1/Corr.1, 9 March 2006), available online at www.wto.org/english/tratop_e/trips_e/ipcw368r1c1.doc; WTO, TRIPS Council, 'Review of Article 27.3(b)', (WTO Doc. IP/C/W/369/Rev.1, revised 9 March 2006), available online at www.wto.org/english/tratop_e/trips_e/ipcw369r1.doc; and WTO, TRIPS Council, 'The Protection of Traditional Knowledge and Folklore', (WITO Doc. IP/C/W/370/Rev.1, revised 9 March 2006), available online at http://www.wto.org/english/tratop_e/trips_e/art27_3b_e.htm.

[28] For a summary on the different proposals from Member States, see WTO, 'TRIPS: Reviews, Article 27.3(b) and Related Issues. Background and the Current Situation', available at http://www.wto.org/english/tratop_e/trips_e/art27_3b_background_e.htm; and Alison Hoare and Richard Tarasofsky, *Chatham House Report, Disclosure of Origin in IPR Applications: Options and Perspectives of Users and Providers of Genetic Resources,* London: Royal Institute of International Affairs, 2006.

it will not progress any further within the Doha Round negotiations of the WTO.[29] In 2010 the TRIPS Council limited its agenda to negotiations relating to a multilateral register for geographical indications, but not the traditional knowledge negotiations.[30] It is beyond the scope of this chapter to discuss fully the debate over which topics the TRIPS Council should negotiate, but any protection of traditional knowledge in the WTO through the TRIPS Agreement seems unlikely at present.

The other major international body dealing with traditional knowledge and its relationship with intellectual property issues is the World Intellectual Property Organization (WIPO). The WIPO Intergovernmental Committee on Intellectual Property and Genetic Resources, Traditional Knowledge and Folklore (WIPO-IGC) has a mandate to draft a treaty on the protection of traditional knowledge and traditional cultural expressions.[31] At the time of writing, it seems unlikely that such a treaty will, in the near future, become an extensive international agreement.

As neither WIPO nor the WTO seem likely to conclude any agreement that protects traditional knowledge, those nations who seek to protect traditional knowledge, in one form or another, have resorted to using fora such as UNDRIP and the CBD outlined above. Those fora are considerably weaker than the WTO with its dispute settlement mechanism.[32] In addition to these other fora, some nations have also included references to traditional knowledge in FTAs.[33]

4. THE FTA APPROACH

Since the TRIPS Agreement came into force, there has been a steady rise of FTAs. Intellectual property chapters in FTAs vary in their scope and depth. Such chapters may contain a variety of terms that are consistent with the TRIPS Agreement, provide a greater

---

29 See generally, WTO, Geographical Indications, available at http://www.wto.org/english/tratop_e/trips_e/gi_e.htm.

30 Many members of the TRIPS Council take the position that the Council only has a mandate to discuss the multilateral register. See the statement of Ambassador Darlington Mwape (Chair of the Special Session of the TRIPS Council), 'Multilateral System of Notification and Registration of Geographical Indications for Wines and Spirits', (WTO Doc. TN/IP/20, 22, 2010), at p. 4.

31 WIPO, General Assembly, 'Matters Concerning the Intergovernmental Committee on Intellectual Property and Genetic Resources, Traditional Knowledge and Folklore. Agenda Item 28. Decision', Thirty-eighth (19th Ordinary) Session (22 September – 1 October 2009).

32 WIPO, which, although it does not have a dispute settlement mechanism, has a much closer relationship with the WTO than the other fora. There is an agreement of cooperation between the two ('Agreement Between the World Intellectual Property Organization and the World Trade Organization' (22 December 1995), available online at http://www.wto.org/english/tratop_e/trips_e/wtowip_e.htm); and a WTO dispute settlement panel consulted WIPO on copyright (WTO, Panel Report, *United States – Section 110 (5) Copyright Act of the United States*, WTO Doc. WT/DS160/R, adopted 27 July 2000, available online at http://www.wto.org/english/news_e/news00_e/1234da.pdf). WIPO is also predominantly an intellectual property organisation and has very similar membership to the WTO.

33 In this chapter, I use free trade agreements as a term covering agreements by that name and also so-called economic partnership agreements (a term used in EU agreements), regional trade agreements (RTAs) and preferential trade agreements (PTAs).

level of protection than the minimum standards of the TRIPS Agreement (frequently known as TRIPS-plus), or include terms that are not even contemplated by the TRIPS Agreement.[34] Terms that the TRIPS Agreement does not contemplate are not TRIPS-plus, as such, but rather fall outside the scope of the TRIPS Agreement. Protection of traditional knowledge, where that protection is *sui generis*, is often likely to be outside the scope of the Agreement. Whereas protection of aspects of traditional knowledge, by means of intellectual property rights, which fall within the coverage of the TRIPS Agreement[35] are likely to be TRIPS-plus. A requirement that a patent applicant disclose use of genetic resources or traditional knowledge used in the inventive process, for example, arguably is a requirement in addition to the disclosure requirements that exist under the TRIPS Agreement[36] and is thus TRIPS-plus.[37] This is not a mere matter of labelling, but it is important because it has implications for whether any protection at domestic law is available to WTO Members on a national treatment basis.[38] Section 6 below discusses national-treatment-related issues.

The TRIPS Agreement does not address traditional knowledge of indigenous peoples directly and, as discussed below, this arguably means that such protection falls outside of the TRIPS Agreement rather than being TRIPS-plus.[39]

---

[34] For a discussion of these types of FTAs, see Susy Frankel, 'The Legitimacy and Purpose of Intellectual Property Chapters in FTAs', in Ross Buckley, Vai I. Lo and Laurence Boulle (eds), *Challenges to Multilateral Trade: The Impact of Bilateral, Preferential and Regional Agreements,* The Netherlands: Wolters Kluwer, 2008, pp. 185–99.

[35] Article 1.2 of the TRIPS Agreement, states: 'For the purposes of this Agreement, the term "intellectual property" refers to all categories of intellectual property that are the subject of Sections 1 through 7 of Part II.' The categories by heading in Part II are: Copyright and Related Rights, Trademarks, Geographical Indications, Industrial Designs, Patents, Layout-Designs (Topographies) of Integrated Circuits, Protection of Undisclosed Information and Control of Anti-Competitive Practices in Contractual Licences.

[36] TRIPS Agreement, Article 29.1 provides that

> Members shall require that an applicant for a patent shall disclose the invention in a manner sufficiently clear and complete for the invention to be carried out by a person skilled in the art and may require the applicant to indicate the best mode for carrying out the invention known to the inventor at the filing date or, where priority is claimed, at the priority date of the application.

[37] Depending on the nature of the disclosure requirement it could also be regarded as an exception to patentability and consequently justified under the *ordre public* exception, Article 27.2 of TRIPS.

[38] See discussion below, sections 7.1.1 and 7.1.2

[39] WIPO, Berne Convention for the Protection of Literary and Artistic Works, 1161 UNTS 30 (adopted on 9 September 1886), as revised at Paris (24 July 1971), Article 15(4), which is incorporated into the TRIPS Agreement via Article 9.1, provides:

> (a) In the case of unpublished works where the identity of the author is unknown, but where there is every ground to presume that he is a national of a country of the Union, it shall be a matter for legislation in that country to designate the competent authority which shall represent the author and shall be entitled to protect and enforce his rights in the countries of the Union.
> (b) Countries of the Union which make such designation under the terms of this provision shall notify the Director General by means of a written declaration giving full information concerning the authority thus designated. The Director General shall at once communicate this declaration to all other countries of the Union.

FTAs that address traditional knowledge do not, for the most part, include norms to protect traditional knowledge, such as the objectives and principles found in the discussion documents of WIPO.[40] Rather, the agreements purport to reserve the right of the parties to protect traditional knowledge or they have mere aspirational statements about the parties agreeing to discuss the protection of traditional knowledge. Alternatively, they entrench negotiation positions of the more powerful members of the FTA that are not particularly supportive of traditional knowledge protection. Section 5 of this chapter discusses examples of traditional-knowledge-related provisions in FTAs.

Many commentators argue that TRIPS-plus is imbalanced and favours large developed countries at the expense of the interests of developing countries.[41] Those seeking increased intellectual property protections use FTAs when the multilateral process is not progressing or when the more powerful party in the FTA cannot achieve its goals through the multilateral process. These are two key reasons why FTAs are an undesirable way to achieve intellectual property norms outside of the multilateral system. Indeed, this may be so of many parts of FTAs.[42] However, the protection of traditional knowledge through FTAs may not be so undesirable.[43] The traditional knowledge FTA provisions do not create the same kinds of obligations as some other intellectual-property-related FTA provisions. This is because such protection is not a result of the developed world imposing its standards on the developing world. Rather, traditional knowledge protections, in FTAs, are a method of gaining or preserving some kind of international protection in the face of

---

This was incorporated into the Berne Convention primarily to protect so-called folklore, which might not otherwise be protected under Berne because of the requirements of identified authors. See discussion of this provision in Sam Ricketson and Jane C. Ginsburg, *International Copyright and Neighbouring Rights: The Berne Convention and Beyond,* 2nd edn, Oxford: Oxford University Press, at paras 8.117–8.118. It could, therefore, appear that the Berne Convention and the TRIPS Agreement do address traditional knowledge. However, Article 15(4) of the Berne Convention only provides a mechanism for the protection of folklore as copyright works. This is not the protection that indigenous peoples seek for their traditional knowledge.

[40] See WIPO, IGC, Secretariat, 'The Protection of Traditional Knowledge: Revised Objectives and Principles', Eighteenth Session (WIPO Doc. WIPO/GRTKF/IC/18/5, 2011); WIPO, IGC, Secretariat, 'The Protection of Traditional Cultural Expressions: Draft Articles', Eighteenth Session (WIPO Doc. WIPO/GRTKF/IC/18/4 REV, 2011); and WIPO, IGC, Secretariat, 'Draft Objectives and Principles Relating to Intellectual Property and Genetic Resources Prepared at IWG 3', (WIPO Doc. WIPO/GRTKF/IC/18/9, 2011).

[41] See generally Carlos M. Correa, *Intellectual Property Rights, the WTO and Developing Countries: The TRIPS Agreement and Policy Options*, Cheltenham, UK: Zed Books, 2010.

[42] Jagdish Bhagwati has commented that 'Acting Like Termites, [F]TAs are eating away at the multilateral trading system relentlessly and progressively'; see Jagdish Bhagwati, *Termites in the Trading System: How Preferential Agreements Undermine Free Trade,* New York, USA: Oxford University Press, 2008, at Preface and generally.

[43] FTAs are often undesirable because the power imbalance is extreme. Although there is a power imbalance in some multilateral fora, small or less powerful countries can group together to negotiate for common interests. This is exactly why multilateral processes are frequently slower or unsuccessful. For a discussion of FTAs, see Susy Frankel, 'Challenging TRIPS-Plus Agreements: The Potential Utility of Non-Violation Disputes' (2009) *Journal of International Economic Law*, 12 (4), pp. 1023–65 [hereinafter Frankel, 'Challenging TRIPS-Plus Agreements'].

the refusal of powerful countries, primarily the United States, to entertain the traditional knowledge discussion at the WTO.

5. EXAMPLES OF FTAs THAT INCLUDE PROVISIONS RELATING TO TRADITIONAL KNOWLEDGE

As discussed above, the TRIPS Council began a discussion about the relationship between the CBD and the TRIPS Agreement. Some countries that proposed substantial changes to the TRIPS Agreement, in the course of that discussion, have included articles relating to traditional knowledge in their FTAs. Peru is an example. However, Peru's FTAs do not include provisions that reflect the position it has taken in the TRIPS Council. In the TRIPS Council, Peru has advocated for a requirement to disclose the origin of any biological or genetic resources with consequences for non-disclosure that would make the patent invalid.[44] In Peru's FTA with the USA, the position on traditional knowledge reflects the US position taken in the TRIPS Council that any connection between traditional knowledge and intellectual property can be resolved through contracts, rather than traditional knowledge requiring any recognition in international agreements.[45] The United States is not a member of the CBD, so unsurprisingly it does not agree to comply with the CBD. An annex to the US-Peru Trade Promotion Agreement provides:

> The Governments of the United States of America and the Republic of Peru have reached the following understandings concerning biodiversity and traditional knowledge in connection with the United States – Peru Trade Promotion Agreement signed this day:
>
> The Parties recognize the importance of traditional knowledge and biodiversity, as well as the potential contribution of traditional knowledge and biodiversity to cultural, economic, and social development.
>
> The Parties recognize the importance of the following: (1) obtaining informed consent from the appropriate authority prior to accessing genetic resources under the control of such authority; (2) equitably sharing the benefits arising from the use of traditional knowledge and genetic resources; and (3) promoting quality patent examination to ensure the conditions of patentability are satisfied.
>
> The Parties recognize that access to genetic resources or traditional knowledge, as well as the equitable sharing of benefits that may result from use of those resources or that knowledge, can be adequately addressed through contracts that reflect mutually agreed terms between users and providers.
>
> Each Party shall endeavor to seek ways to share information that may have a bearing on the patentability of inventions based on traditional knowledge or genetic resources by providing:
>
> (a) publicly accessible databases that contain relevant information; and

---

[44] See WTO, 'TRIPS Issues: Art 27.3(b), Traditional Knowledge, Biodiversity', available at http://www.wto.org/english/tratop_e/trips_e/art27_3b_e.htm [hereinafter WTO, 'TRIPS Issues'].

[45] For a summary on the different proposals available: WTO, 'WTO Doha Development Agenda the July 2008 Package – Briefing Notes – Intellectual Property: Geographical Indications and Biodiversity' (2008), available at http://www.wto.org.

(b) an opportunity to cite, in writing, to the appropriate examining authority prior art that may have a bearing on patentability.[46]

Both Peru and China provide certain protections for traditional knowledge in their respective domestic laws.[47] Yet the FTA between them does not reflect this. Rather, the FTA provides that the parties 'establish a mutually supportive relationship between the TRIPS Agreement and the Convention on Biological Diversity, regarding genetic resources and the protection of traditional knowledge and folklore'.[48] The Peru-China Agreement also allows the parties to 'place appropriate measures to protect traditional knowledge, folklore and genetic resources in accordance with international and national legislations'.[49] The FTA also provides that, subject to any future national developments, the parties will 'discuss disclosure of origin or source of genetic resources and/or prior informed consent obligation in patent applications'.[50] One wonders why these parties did not take the opportunity to create an agreement that gives greater protection to each other's traditional knowledge. It seems likely that because standards for the protection of traditional knowledge are evolving and there is no international norm for such protection, the FTA parties wanted to avoid being too prescriptive. Even so, the fact that both China and Peru protect traditional knowledge means that there are some common norms between the countries' laws and, therefore, they could have embedded some of those norms in an agreement. They could have, for example, agreed to a general norm not to allow for the unfair use or misappropriation of traditional knowledge.[51]

Also, both countries support the development of the WIPO principles. If the concern is to preserve differences in their laws, then retaining those differences is possible. A broad norm preventing the misappropriation of traditional knowledge in accordance with the WIPO principles is possible because the WIPO principles are not completely prescriptive; rather they are minimum standards for protection that countries can implement in a variety of ways. The WIPO principles do not prescribe detailed national laws and if they become a

---

46 United States-Peru Trade Promotion Agreement, 'Understanding Regarding Biodiversity and Traditional Knowledge' (signed on 12 April 2006), available online at http://www.ustr.gov/sites/default/files/uploads/agreements/fta/peru/asset_upload_file719_9535.pdf.

47 See Peru Domestic Laws: Law No. 29316 amends, incorporates and regulates miscellaneous provisions on the implementation of the Trade Promotion Agreement signed between Peru and United States; Law No. 27811 of 24 July 2002 introducing a Protection Regime for the Collective Knowledge of Indigenous Peoples Derived from Biological Resources; Law No. 28216 on the Protection of Access to Peruvian Biological Diversity and the Collective Knowledge of Indigenous Peoples, available online at http://www.wipo.int/wipolex/en/profile.jsp?code=PE; and China Domestic Laws: Regulations on Protection of Traditional Arts and Crafts; Regulation of the People's Republic of China on Traditional Chinese Medicines; Intangible Cultural Heritage Law, available online at http://www.wipo.int/wipolex/en/profile.jsp?code=CN.

48 Peru-China FTA (signed on 18 April 2009), ch. 11 ('Intellectual Property'), Article 145 ('Genetic Resources, Traditional Knowledge and Folklore'), available online at http://fta.mofcom.gov.cn/bilu/annex/bilu_xdwb_en.pdf.

49 Ibid., Article 145.3.

50 Ibid., Article 145.4.

51 A general international norm along these lines has been discussed in the WIPO-IGC. See WIPO, 'Consolidated Analysis of the Legal Protection of Traditional Cultural Expressions', (WIPO Doc. WIPO/GRTKF/IC/5/3, 2003), at p. 58.

binding treaty, in anything like their current form, they will provide considerable scope for national autonomy over implementation.[52]

Apart from the Peru-China Agreement, discussed above, China's FTAs generally have a conspicuous lack of traditional knowledge protection. That is probably because China's FTAs for the most part do not include intellectual property chapters.[53] One exception is the China-New Zealand FTA, which provides, 'Subject to each Party's international obligations, the Parties may establish appropriate measures to protect genetic resources, traditional knowledge and folklore'.[54]

More recently, and perhaps marking the beginning of a new trend, the China-Costa Rica FTA includes provisions for the protection of genetic resources, traditional knowledge and folklore. The parties broadly note the contribution of genetic resources, traditional knowledge and folklore to scientific, cultural and economic development.[55] The parties also provide:

> (2) [They] acknowledge, reaffirm and encourage the effort to establish a mutually supportive relationship between the TRIPS Agreement and the Convention on Biological Diversity regarding genetic resources and the protection of traditional knowledge and folklore.
>
> (3) Subject to the parties international and domestic laws the parties are able to adopt or maintain measures to promote and share the benefits which arise from the use of traditional knowledge, innovations and practices relevant to the conservation of biological diversity.[56]

Finally, the parties agree to discuss disclosure of origin of the source of genetic resources and prior informed consent subject to developments in domestic law and the international multilateral fora.[57]

New Zealand does not have protections for traditional knowledge in a way that is directly comparable to the laws of Peru or China.[58] Under New Zealand's trade mark law the Commissioner of Trade Marks must not register a sign that is contrary to Māori

---

[52] This is related to the way national treatment functions, see discussion in section 7 of this chapter below.

[53] See China-ASEAN FTA (signed on November 2002, entered into force July 2005), available online at http://fta.mofcom.gov.cn/topic/chinaasean.shtml; China-Pakistan FTA (signed on 24 November 2006, entered into force July 2007), available online at http://fta.mofcom.gov.cn/topic/enpakistan.shtml; and China-Chile FTA (signed on 18 November 2005, entered into force October 2006), available online at http://fta.mofcom.gov.cn/topic/enchile.shtml. China-Singapore FTA (signed on 23 October 2008), available online at http://fta.mofcom.gov.cn/topic/ensingapore.shtml.

[54] NZ-China FTA, (signed on 7 April 2008), ch. 12 ('Intellectual Property'), Article 165 ('Genetic Resources, Traditional Knowledge, Folklore'), available online at http://www.chinafta.govt.nz/1-The-agreement/2-Text-of-the-agreement/0-downloads/NZ-ChinaFTA-Agreement-text.pdf.

[55] China-Costa Rica FTA (signed on 8 April 2010), ch. 10 ('Intellectual Property'), Article 111.1 ('Genetic Resources, Traditional Knowledge and Folklore').

[56] Ibid.

[57] Ibid., Article 111.4.

[58] For a discussion of the Wai 262 claim in New Zealand, see Susy Frankel, 'A New Zealand Perspective on the Protection of Mātauranga Māori (Traditional Knowledge)', in this volume [hereinafter Frankel, 'A NZ Perspective'].

values.[59] However, this is a law that creates an interface between intellectual property law and traditional knowledge protection. It is not a protection of traditional knowledge *per se*.[60] It remains to be seen whether New Zealand will enact laws to protect traditional knowledge. However, within most of New Zealand's FTAs there are provisions relating to traditional knowledge, folklore and genetic resources.[61] Other FTAs only refer to traditional knowledge.[62] An example is the Trans-Pacific Strategic Economic Partnership Agreement, which provides, 'Subject to each Party's international obligations the Parties affirm that they may … establish appropriate measures to protect traditional knowledge'.[63] All of New Zealand's FTAs qualify these apparently permissive provisions with reference to such measures only being permissible if they are consistent with the TRIPS Agreement.

In addition to provisions relating directly to traditional knowledge, New Zealand's FTAs somewhat uniquely include provisions that refer to the Treaty of Waitangi. The Treaty of Waitangi is the Treaty that was entered into between Māori, New Zealand's indigenous people, and the British Crown when New Zealand was colonised.[64] These FTA provisions state that New Zealand may adopt measures that are necessary for it to honour its obligations under the Treaty of Waitangi.[65] An example of this sort of provision appears in the New Zealand-China FTA, which provides:

---

[59] Trade Marks Act 2002 (NZ), s. 17, see also Susy Frankel, 'Third Party Trade Marks as a Violation of Indigenous Cultural Property: A New Statutory Safeguard' (2005) *Journal of World Intellectual Property*, 8, pp. 83–98.

[60] See also Frankel, 'A NZ Perspective', supra note 58.

[61] See NZ-Thailand Closer Economic Partnership (signed on 19 April 2005 and entered into force 1 July 2005), ch. 12 ('Intellectual Property'), Article 12.5(1)(d), available online at http://www.mfat.govt.nz/downloads/trade-agreement/thailand/thainzcep-december2004.pdf; NZ-Malaysia FTA (signed on 26 October 2009), ch. 11 ('Intellectual Property'), Article 11.6 ('Traditional Knowledge') and Article 11.4(2)(e) ('Cooperation on Notification and Exchange of Information'), available online at http://www.mfat.govt.nz/downloads/trade-agreement/malaysia/mnzfta-text-of-agreement.pdf; Trans-Pacific Strategic Economic Partnership NZ (Brunei, Chile, New Zealand and Singapore) (signed on 3 June 2005, entered into force 28 May 2006), ch. 10 ('Intellectual Property'), Article 10.3(3)(d) ('General Provisions'), available online at http://mfat.govt.nz/Trade-and-Economic-Relations/2-Trade-Relationships-and-Agreements/Trans-Pacific/index.php; NZ-China FTA, supra note 54, ch. 12 ('Intellectual Property'), Article 165 ('Genetic Resources, Traditional Knowledge, Folklore'); ASEAN-Australia/NZ FTA, (signed on 27 February 2009), ch. 13 ('Intellectual Property), Article 8 ('Genetic Resources, Traditional Knowledge, Folklore'), available online at http://www.asean.fta.govt.nz/assets/Agreement-Establishing-the-ASEAN-Australia-New-Zealand-Free-Trade-Area.pdf.

[62] NZ-Malaysia FTA, supra note 61, ch. 11 ('Intellectual Property'), Article 11.6 ('Traditional Knowledge') only refers to the protection of traditional knowledge. It does not make any reference to protection of folklore or genetic resources; Article 11.4(2)(e) ('Cooperation on Notification and Exchange of Information') article only refers to promoting cooperation between parties so as to promote any measures necessary to protect traditional knowledge. Trans-Pacific Strategic Economic Partnership NZ, supra note 61, ch. 10 ('Intellectual Property'), Article 10.3(3)(a) – enables the protection of TK generally subject to the international obligations of both parties.

[63] Trans-Pacific Strategic Economic Partnership Agreement, supra note 61, Article 10.3.

[64] See generally Claudia Orange, *The Treaty of Waitangi,* Wellington: Bridget Williams Books, 1987.

[65] NZ-Thailand Closer Economic Partnership, supra note 61, ch. 15 ('General Exceptions'), Article 15.8; NZ-Malaysia FTA, supra note 61, ch. 17 ('General Exceptions'), Article 17.6;

> 1. Provided that such measures are not used as a means of arbitrary or unjustified discrimination against persons of the other Party or as a disguised restriction on trade in goods and services, nothing in this Agreement shall preclude the adoption by New Zealand of measures it deems necessary to accord more favourable treatment to Maori in respect of matters covered by this Agreement including in fulfilment of its obligations under the Treaty of Waitangi.
>
> 2. The Parties agree that the interpretation of the Treaty of Waitangi, including as to the nature of the rights and obligations arising under it, shall not be subject to the dispute settlement provisions of this Agreement. Chapter 16 (Dispute Settlement) shall otherwise apply to this Article. An arbitral tribunal established under Article 188 may be requested by China to determine only whether any measure referred to in paragraph 1 is inconsistent with their rights under this Agreement.[66]

Another kind of an example of traditional knowledge protection is found in the European Union Agreement with the Caribbean, known as the CARIFORUM states. In this Agreement, references are found to the CBD because all members of the Agreement belong to the CBD. The Agreement provides:

> 1. Subject to their domestic legislation the [parties] … respect, preserve and maintain knowledge, innovations and practices of indigenous and local communities embodying traditional lifestyles relevant for the conservation and sustainable use of biological diversity and promote their wider application with the involvement and approval of the holders of such knowledge, innovations and practices and encourage the equitable sharing of the benefits arising from the utilization of such knowledge, innovations and practices.
>
> 2. The [parties] … recognise the importance of taking appropriate measures, subject to national legislation, to preserve traditional knowledge and agree to continue working towards the development of internationally agreed sui generis models for the legal protection of traditional knowledge.
>
> 3. The [parties] … agree that the patent provisions of this sub-section and the Convention on Biological Diversity shall be implemented in a mutually supportive way.
>
> 4. The [parties] … may require as part of the administrative requirements for a patent application concerning an invention which uses biological material as a necessary aspect of the invention, that the applicant identifies the sources of the biological material used by the applicant and described as part of the invention.[67]

The parties also agree to exchange views and information on the multilateral discussions and to review their agreement in light of developments at WIPO and at the WTO.[68]

Trans-Pacific Strategic Economic Partnership NZ, supra note 61, ch. 19 ('General Exceptions'), Article 19.5; NZ-China FTA, supra note 54, ch. 17 ('General Exceptions'), Article 205; ASEAN-Australia/NZ FTA, supra note 61, ch. 15 ('General Provisions and Exceptions'), Article 5; NZ-Singapore FTA (signed on 18 July 2005), available online at http://www.worldtradelaw.net/fta/agreements/nzsingfta.pdf, Part 11 ('General Provisions'), Article 74.

[66] NZ-China FTA, supra note 54, Article 205.

[67] Economic Partnership Agreement between the CARIFORUM States and The European Community and its Member States (signed on 15 October 2008), Article 1 ('Genetic Resources, Traditional Knowledge and Folklore'), available at http://ec.europa.eu/world/agreements/downloadFile.do?fullText=yes&treatyTransId=12969.

[68] Ibid., Article 1 ('Genetic Resources, Traditional Knowledge and Folklore'), at paras 5 and 6.

There is no uniformity in the way that the above sorts of FTA provisions are included in FTAs. In one sense that is not surprising in view of the lack of international agreement on traditional knowledge issues, but in another way this makes little sense when viewed from the perspective of why countries enter into FTAs. The reasons for this are many, but broadly countries enter into FTAs to obtain a better position than that which is currently available at a multilateral level. It could be said that the Peru-US FTA puts the US in a better position than at the multilateral level, as its view that contract law should be relied on has not been adopted internationally. However, Peru in making this concession is not in a better position. It is in a worse position having conceded in a bilateral forum its international negotiating position. The Peru-China FTA also illustrates a failure to seize an opportunity to adopt the WIPO-IGC traditional-knowledge-related objectives and principles, which both parties broadly support.[69] The EU-CARIFORUM Agreement contains a voluntary approach to disclosure of biological and genetic resources in patent applications. This reflects the voluntary approach to this in Europe. The EU-CARIFORUM Agreement simply agrees to follow international developments. New Zealand's FTAs appear to be statements preserving national autonomy over traditional knowledge protection. Whether such clauses are necessary is debatable, but they perhaps clarify the position.

None of the above examples of traditional knowledge in FTAs are substantive obligations to protect traditional knowledge and, as such, their effectiveness is questionable. However, their effectiveness depends, in part, on the FTA provisions' relationship with the TRIPS Agreement and how that relationship is, or might be, interpreted. The next part discusses the relationship between traditional knowledge and the TRIPS Agreement.

6. THE TRIPS AGREEMENT AND TRADITIONAL KNOWLEDGE

The TRIPS Agreement is silent on the protection of traditional knowledge, traditional cultural expressions and cultural heritage.[70] It does not directly address the protection or non-protection of these things. However, the TRIPS Agreement is not without impact on the protection of traditional knowledge and matters relating to cultural heritage. The relationship between intellectual property protection and traditional knowledge is such that the subject matters overlap. A TCE, for example, can be analogous to a copyright work or a trade mark, although the legal protections, if any, may be very different. The TRIPS Agreement provides for worldwide minimum standards of intellectual property and those standards do not protect traditional knowledge, but rather protect copyright works, trade marks and patented inventions[71] that in some instances exploit that traditional knowledge. It is not accurate, therefore, to suggest that the TRIPS Agreement has no impact on the protection of traditional knowledge, but it certainly does not provide any minimum standards for the protection of traditional knowledge.

---

[69] See generally WTO, 'TRIPS Issues', supra note 44.

[70] See discussion in supra note 39.

[71] See supra note 35.

6.1 TRIPS-plus or Outside of TRIPS

Article 1.1 of the TRIPS Agreement allows parties to provide more extensive protection than that provided for in the Agreement, if additional protection does not conflict with the TRIPS Agreement.[72] One example of where many countries have provided protection that is more extensive is the copyright term. The TRIPS Agreement minimum is that copyright shall last for the life of the author plus 50 years, or 50 years where the calculation of the term of protection is not dependent on the author's life.[73] Many countries provide copyright protection for the more extensive period of life plus 70 years.[74] The more extensive term is undoubtedly TRIPS-plus.

The TRIPS Agreement requirements of protections relating to trade marks and geographical indications provide another example. The Agreement does not provide any minimum protection with regard to Internet domain names. Such protection may sometimes be related to trade marks, but there is no requirement to protect Internet domain names. In the Australia-United States FTA (known as AUSFTA), the parties agreed to certain protection for domain names.[75] This is a wholly new area of protection that the TRIPS Agreement does not directly address and, therefore, it could be more accurately described as outside of TRIPS, that is, a *sui generis* regime, rather than TRIPS-plus. Drawing a line between what is within or outside of TRIPS is sometimes difficult and is controversial. The controversy arises broadly for two reasons. First, if the protection is within the subject matter coverage of the TRIPS Agreement, it must not conflict with other parts of the TRIPS Agreement. If it does conflict with part of the Agreement it may require an exception that is TRIPS-compatible.[76] Secondly, if a matter is outside of the scope of TRIPS and outside of any international intellectual property agreement, then, in domestic law, additional protection does not have to be available on a national treatment[77] basis. A controversial example of whether something is within or outside of the scope of the TRIPS Agreement is the European database unfair extraction right. The European Union treats this as outside the ambit of the TRIPS Agreement, and consequently not subject to national treatment, because the Agreement does not require the protection of data.[78] The alternative

---

[72] I have argued elsewhere that there must be a limit to this more extensive protection in the TRIPS Agreement to fulfil its object and purpose, see Frankel, 'Challenging TRIPS-Plus Agreements', supra note 43.

[73] This applies to copyright works such as films and sound recordings.

[74] The longer term is found, for example, in the European Union, the USA and Australia.

[75] United States-Australia Free Trade Agreement (AUSFTA) (2004) 43 ILM 1248 (signed on 18 May 2004, entered into force 1 January 2005).

[76] TRIPS-compatible exceptions are ones that comply with the three-step tests found in Articles 13, 17 and 30 of the TRIPS Agreement, relating to copyright trade marks and patents respectively.

[77] The principle of national treatment requires that countries provide the same intellectual property protection to foreigners as that available to its own nationals. See TRIPS Agreement, Article 3.

[78] Article 10.2 TRIPS Agreement requires protection of databases that are intellectual creations. The provision does not require the protection of the data. Rather it requires the protection of the whole database and what in some jurisdictions is described as its selection and arrangement. In accordance with Article 9.2 TRIPS Agreement, copyright 'extends to expressions and not to ideas, procedures, methods of operation or mathematical concepts as such'. Although the words 'data' or

argument is that the EU database right ought to be subject to national treatment because protecting data from unfair extraction is a greater level of database protection than the TRIPS Agreement requires. The TRIPS Agreement requires that the selection and arrangement of databases that are intellectual creations are protected.[79] This issue becomes particularly difficult when countries protect data not as a *sui generis* unfair extraction right, but as part of copyright.[80]

Another example that illustrates the difficulty of defining the TRIPS Agreement subject matter boundaries is the requirements of trade mark protection. The TRIPS Agreement requires protection of trade marks that are 'words including personal names, letters, numerals, figurative elements and combinations of colours'.[81] Many countries have sound and smell marks and some FTAs require protection of these sorts of trade marks.[82] The TRIPS Agreement does not require protection of smell and sound marks because it states that 'members may require, as a condition of registration, that signs be visually perceptible' and such marks are not visually perceptible. In that sense one could say that sound and smell marks are outside the scope of the TRIPS Agreement, but that is arguably not correct. Such marks are within the same category as those that the TRIPS Agreement requires are protected.[83]

A *sui generis* type of protection for traditional knowledge (that is, a regime that provides a form of protection outside of the scope of intellectual property law) is arguably outside of the scope of the TRIPS Agreement and not subject to national treatment, unless the country with such a law chooses to apply it on a national treatment basis. However, as discussed above, within the TRIPS Council and at WIPO there is ongoing discussion

---

'information' are not expressed in that Article, it embodies the principles that copyright does not protect information or facts, but protects the mode of their expression. Some commentators have argued that the EU database protection is nevertheless intellectual property as defined in the TRIPS Agreement and ought to be subject to the national treatment obligations of the Paris Convention; WIPO, Paris Convention for the Protection of Industrial Property, 828 UNTS 303 (adopted on 20 March 1883, entered into force 16 April 1970), as revised at Stockholm (14 July 1967). See P. Bernt Hugenholtz, 'Implementing the European Database Directive', available at www.ivir.nl/publications/hugenholtz/PBH-HCJ-LIB.doc, citing Herman C. Jehoram, 'Ontwerp EG-richtlijn databanken' (1992) *IER*, 4, pp. 129–33, at p. 133. See also Jerome H. Reichman and Pamela Samuelson, 'Intellectual Property Rights in Data?' (1997) *Vanderbilt Law Review*, 50, pp. 51–166.

[79] See TRIPS Agreement, Article 10.2.

[80] In *Desktop Marketing Systems v Telstra Corporation Limited* (2002) 119 FCR 491, the High Court of Australia (its highest court) held that industrious collection of telephone directory data in electronic form was sufficiently original to amount to originality for copyright purposes. Subsequently in *IceTV Pty Limited v Nine Network Australia Pty Limited* (2009) HCA 14, the High Court of Australia held that certain listings of TV programmes might not be original. See also a discussion of the scope of minimum rights and national treatment in Ricketson and Ginsburg, supra note 39, at para. 6.97.

[81] TRIPS Agreement, Article 15.1.

[82] For a discussion of trade mark provisions in FTAs, see Burton Ong, 'The Trademark Law Provisions of Bilateral Free Trade Agreements', in Graeme B. Dinwoodie and Mark D. Janis (eds), *Trademark Law and Theory: A Handbook of Contemporary Research,* Cheltenham, UK: Edward Elgar, 2008, pp. 229–61, at p. 229.

[83] TRIPS Agreement, Article 1.2.

about the link between intellectual property law and the protection of traditional knowledge. Accordingly, some aspects of traditional knowledge protection may be TRIPS-plus or they may be legitimate exceptions to TRIPS protection as provided for in the Agreement.[84]

6.2 The Interface of TRIPS Agreement Protection and Traditional Knowledge Protections

The discussion at the WTO about the relationship between the CBD and the TRIPS Agreement, although now stalled, had largely centred on whether the TRIPS Agreement should include a requirement that a patent applicant should disclose the origin of any biological or genetic resources involved in the development of an invention. There are many complexities to this discussion, including what the disclosure obligation should be and what, if any, consequences there should be for a failure to disclose.[85] The negotiations about any sort of disclosure requirement do not look likely to succeed in the WTO, but there have been developments in the CBD context.[86] Failing any multilateral agreement, the question arises as to whether countries that enact a disclosure requirement in their domestic law, in any event, are compliant with the TRIPS Agreement. The disclosure requirement is relevant here because it is an example of a method of protection of traditional knowledge that is arguably within the scope of the TRIPS Agreement. It is arguably TRIPS-plus because it is more extensive protection than the required minimums of the TRIPS Agreement.[87] Additionally, a disclosure requirement that resulted in a patent being invalid or revoked in some way could be characterised as a legitimate exception under the TRIPS Agreement.[88]

Where countries seek to address protection of traditional knowledge through the intellectual property regime, questions of TRIPS Agreement compliance are relevant. *Sui generis* regimes that do not directly utilise intellectual property rights, covered by the TRIPS Agreement, do not trigger issues of TRIPS Agreement compliance. Against this background, this chapter now assesses the effects of traditional knowledge protections in FTAs.

7. THE EFFECTS OF TRADITIONAL KNOWLEDGE PROTECTIONS IN FTAs

As discussed above, the main reason that any party enters into a FTA is to achieve something different from that which is achievable in the multilateral process. Broadly, in relation to traditional knowledge, this might be any recognition that traditional knowledge might be protectable at all. However, the nature and variety of traditional-knowledge-related provisions in FTAs may not have any significant effect. In order to consider this

84 TRIPS Agreement, Articles 27 and 30.
85 See supra note 25.
86 See discussion in section 3 above, about the Nagoya Protocol.
87 TRIPS Agreement, Article 1 provides that parties may provide more extensive protection.
88 TRIPS Agreement, Article 27(2) and (3) would be relevant.

further it is first useful to explain the role of non-discrimination provisions in the WTO agreements and how that relates to why the WTO allows FTAs at all and, in particular, the legitimacy of intellectual property chapters in FTAs.

7.1 Intellectual Property in FTAs

7.1.1 National treatment

National treatment requires that foreign nationals must be treated the same as domestic nationals under domestic intellectual property law.[89] National treatment does not work alone and is coupled with minimum standards. The TRIPS Agreement requires that minimum standards are enacted into national laws. A country must apply those minimum standards on a national treatment basis. International intellectual property agreements are framed around a combination of minimum standards and national treatment.

FTA parties might agree to enact domestic laws of a higher standard than the TRIPS Agreement. In most domestic intellectual property laws, there will be one law and national treatment will operate, for the most part, to ensure one law applies to all. National treatment, therefore, provides the means through which most possible sorts of intellectual property discrimination are avoided.[90] In addition to national treatment, the TRIPS Agreement was the first multilateral intellectual property agreement to introduce the most-favoured-nation principle (MFN). MFN ensures that a country cannot give better protection to some foreigners than others.[91]

7.1.2 Most favoured nation

Intellectual property chapters in FTAs are one aspect of a bigger picture that relates to FTAs between WTO Members more generally. The GATT[92] and GATS[93] provide certain MFN exemptions that are part of the economic incentives for FTAs. In essence, the MFN exceptions allow FTAs to apply only to the parties to those FTAs. That is, concessions do not have to apply to non-parties. The equivalent MFN exception does not exist in the

---

[89] TRIPS Agreement, Article 3 contains the national treatment provision.

[90] For the most part, MFN is not necessary for the domestic law to apply to foreigners. The only exception would be where a foreigner has a better intellectual property right than domestic nationals. Such instances are rare. However, in those instances, MFN operates to make sure there is equal treatment between foreigners. For further discussion of this, see Susy Frankel, 'The WTO's Application of "the Customary Rules of Interpretation of Public International Law" to Intellectual Property' (2006) *Virginia Journal of International Law*, 46, pp. 365–431, at p. 382.

[91] Although MFN allows for FTAs to increase intellectual property standards, the possibility of increases through bilateralism existed before the TRIPS Agreement. Indeed, out-of-control bilateralism is often credited as being the cause of the Berne and Paris Conventions. See Ricketson and Ginsburg, supra note 39, at ch. 1.

[92] WTO, General Agreement on Tariffs and Trade, Marrakesh Agreement Establishing the World Trade Organization, Annex 1A, 1867 UNTS 187; 33 ILM 1153 (adopted on 15 April 1994, entered into force 1 January 1995).

[93] WTO, General Agreement on Trade in Services, Marrakesh Agreement Establishing the World Trade Organization, Annex 1B, 1869 UNTS 183; 33 ILM 1167 (adopted on 15 April 1994, entered into force 1 January 1995).

TRIPS Agreement.[94] The most discussed consequence of this is that the USA and the EU, in particular, use FTAs to increase intellectual property standards.[95] The consequences of TRIPS-plus standards have been far-reaching and, therefore, the reasons for the absence of an MFN exception in the TRIPS Agreement merit scrutiny.

In the goods context, MFN functions as a tool to drive tariffs and other barriers down, but the TRIPS Agreement is not an agreement that has tariffs or other market access barriers.[96] In essence all intellectual property is a kind of trade barrier and the TRIPS Agreement is a recognition that a certain level of intellectual property protection has been agreed to in the trade context.[97] In that context MFN has functioned as a tool to increase protection. There is no express indication in the TRIPS Agreement that the purpose of the MFN provision is to increase protection. The drafting history of the TRIPS Agreement suggests that primarily the inclusion of MFN in the TRIPS context was justified in order to apply 'GATT discipline' to intellectual property.[98]

The Brussels draft and Chairman's draft, of 1990, included in the MFN provision something which was close to an MFN exemption.[99] The relevant draft exemption from the application of MFN stated:

> Exempted from [the MFN] obligation are any advantage, favour or privilege accorded by a Party …
>
> exceeding the requirements of this Agreement and provided in an international agreement to which the party belongs, provided that such agreement is open for accession by all parties to this Agreement, or provided that such Party shall be ready to extend such advantage, favour, privilege or immunity, on terms equal to those under the agreements, to the nationals of any other party so requesting and to enter into good faith negotiations to this end.

This provision was not included in the Uruguay Round 'Dunkel draft' of 1991.[100] There were likely to have been differing views as to inclusion or not of an MFN exemption. Drafting history aside, the role of MFN in GATT- and GATS-related aspects of FTAs does not transfer easily to intellectual property. MFN was not a tool of multilateral intellectual property agreements before the TRIPS Agreement. Neither of the main intellectual

---

[94] TRIPS Agreement, Article 4 contains the relevant MFN provision.

[95] See, for example, Peter Drahos, 'Expanding Intellectual Property's Empire: The Role of FTAs' (November 2003), available at http://ictsd.net/downloads/2008/08/drahos-fta-2003-en.pdf, where he coins the phrase 'the global ratchet for intellectual property'.

[96] In the GATS context there seems to be a growing body of FTAs that detract from GATS obligations, see Rudolf Adlung and Peter Morrison, 'Less than the GATS: "Negative Preferences" in Regional Services Agreements' (2010) *Journal of International Trade Law,* 13 (4), pp. 1103–43.

[97] See generally Frankel, 'Challenging TRIPS-Plus Agreements', supra note 43.

[98] The Preamble of the TRIPS Agreement provides, '*Recognising* … the applicability of the basic principles of GATT 1994'.

[99] For an explanation of the drafting history of TRIPS and the significance of each of these drafts, see Daniel Gervais, *The TRIPS Agreement: Drafting History and Analysis*, 3rd edn, London: Sweet and Maxwell, 2008, at pp. 10–26.

[100] Draft Agreement on Trade-Related Aspects of Intellectual Property Rights, including trade in counterfeit goods contained in the 'Dunkel Draft', (GATT Doc. mtn.tnc/w/fa, 1991); see ibid., at pp. 186–7.

property treaties incorporated into the TRIPS Agreement (the Berne Convention[101] and the Paris Convention[102]) include MFN clauses.

The main effect of the TRIPS Agreement MFN, combined with national treatment and minimum standards, is that intellectual property standards only increase; they cannot come down. This creates a spill-over effect from TRIPS-plus FTAs to create new international norms outside of the multilateral process. Because of the absence of the MFN exception, this spill-over effect is greater than in either of the GATT or GATS contexts. Whether or not this MFN effect is appropriate is questionable because it transforms the universally understood role of MFN into a tool to increase intellectual property norms without multilateral negotiations.

In the context of traditional knowledge, the FTA provisions do not have this increasing-standards and norm-pushing effect. This is because there is no uniformity between the provisions and, as outlined above, the provisions are not substantive obligations, but are primarily aspirational. Many of the traditional-knowledge-related provisions from FTAs are an agreement to discuss the issues in the future or declare a kind of national autonomy over the space to make traditional knowledge laws in the future. If the traditional knowledge articles in FTAs amounted to substantive obligations, as discussed in the next section, several interesting issues would arise in relation to which international regulatory model, national treatment or something else is appropriate.

7.2 National Treatment and Other International Regulatory Regimes

The applicability of national treatment to traditional knowledge protection raises some interesting issues. If FTA parties agree to protect each other's traditional knowledge, this protection would effectively be for domestic law. The entire point behind protecting traditional knowledge is to 'recognize a vast array of different customs and practices that exist amongst the indigenous peoples of the world'.[103] National treatment does not readily lend itself to recognising traditional knowledge differences because national treatment is premised on applying a common set of minimum legal standards.

An example illustrates the potential difficulties of applying national treatment to traditional knowledge protection in domestic law. If Peru agreed to protect traditional knowledge, including traditional knowledge that is connected to China, how would such an agreement work? Does Peru provide protection based on Peruvian traditional knowledge or based on Chinese traditional knowledge protection? Somehow, a Peruvian court or other relevant authority would need to ensure that protection of Chinese traditional knowledge is based on Chinese law.[104] This is because traditional knowledge protection at

---

[101] Berne Convention, supra note 39.

[102] Paris Convention, supra note 78.

[103] Peter Drahos, 'Towards an International Framework for the Protection of Traditional Group Knowledge and Practice', *Elements of National Sui Generis Systems for the Preservation, Protection and Promotion of Traditional Knowledge: Innovations and Practices and Options for an International Framework*, UN Conference on Trade and Development (Geneva, Switzerland, 4–6 February 2004), at pp. 27–8.

[104] This is not straightforward. It seems less than likely that there would be sufficient judges or even expert counsel in Peru to have the necessary skills to apply Chinese law and vice versa.

national law, where it exists, is often based on rules that relate to communities and their customs and norms, which might even derive from customary law. Therefore, protection should be based on those norms rather than foreign norms. Say, for example, the reason one country (A) protects its peoples' traditional knowledge is because of the relationship between indigenous people and that knowledge and some kind of proof of that relationship is required;[105] however, the reason for protection of traditional knowledge in another country (B) is proof of habitation in a particular area. In such a situation it makes no sense to apply country A's requirements to protect traditional knowledge that comes from country B. The reason for the protection should be the reason that the traditional knowledge is protected in country B. This might require country A to recognise a foreign standard as to why something is protectable traditional knowledge.

The international regulatory mechanism that is often used to recognise foreign standards is not national treatment, but mutual recognition.[106] The essence of mutual recognition is that two countries recognise each other's standards, where those standards are not necessarily the same. One possible defect of mutual recognition is that countries may be required to recognise very different standards from their own. However, countries do not tend to enter into mutual recognition arrangements unless they have at least some commonality of norms. Mutual recognition can become a stepping stone to increase the amount of common norms to a level of detail that may eventually lead to greater commonality of standards or even harmonisation of laws. Mutual recognition is, however, applicable to the existence of the standard that grants the right. So, for example, if there is a register of traditional knowledge-holders and associated traditional knowledge, mutual recognition might allow recognition of what is on the register.[107]

Apart from national treatment or mutual recognition, there is reciprocity. Reciprocity is where protection only has to be given in country A to a claimant from country B if country B provides the same protection in its domestic law. For example, under the Berne Convention a copyright term of protection beyond the minimum of life plus 50 years or the *droit de suite* can be made available on a reciprocal rather than national treatment basis.[108] Reciprocity differs from mutual recognition where one country recognises another's standards. A reciprocal arrangement does not necessarily require the recognition of a foreign national standard in domestic law. Reciprocity, however, may be the least desirable

---

105 See *Ko Aotearoa Tēnei*, supra note 8, at ch. 2, and discussion in Frankel, 'A NZ Perspective', supra note 58.

106 Mutual recognition is often thought to be an effective way to achieve greater harmonisation in trade agreements relating to goods. This is the model used between Australia and New Zealand. See Australian Productivity Commission, 'Bilateral and Regional Trade Agreements Research Report' (13 December 2010), available at http://www.pc.gov.au/projects/study/trade-agreements.

107 The WIPO-IGC principles also suggest the creation of registers 'in the interests of transparency, certainty and the conservation of traditional knowledge'. See WIPO, IGC, Secretariat, 'The Protection of Traditional Knowledge: Revised Objectives and Principles', Eighteenth Session (WIPO Doc. WIPO/GRTKF/IC/18/5, 2011), Annex, at p. 77 (Article 8) and at p. 107 (Article 11).

108 Berne Convention, Articles 7(8) and 14ter respectively.

model because it provides less incentive and, in the traditional knowledge context, less likelihood of any international norms developing.[109]

National treatment and mutual recognition represent the ways in which international agreements are structured to achieve a level of norms. Mutual recognition allows for the recognition of foreign standards or laws in ways that national treatment usually does not because national treatment requires that the same standards are applied to domestic and foreign nationals.

There is, however, another way to achieve recognition of foreign standards in domestic law and to retain the broad principle of national treatment. That involves having local laws that are based on international norms, applied on a national treatment basis, but including in those laws something along the lines that for the purposes of laws protecting traditional knowledge the law of the people whose knowledge is used will apply. This has the effect of recognising diversity at the enforcement, rather than the standard-setting, part of the law. Courts can then, consistent with principles of territoriality, apply local laws to infringement, but that local law can effectively be the foreign law for certain purposes.

The Peru and China example above can illustrate how this might work. A misappropriation in Peru of Chinese traditional knowledge, for example, would be a matter that the Chinese complainant could bring before the Peruvian courts and the court could apply the relevant Chinese traditional knowledge law because that is what Peruvian law requires it to do.

Another approach, which relates more to jurisdiction than choice of law, would be for the Chinese courts to hear a dispute relating to an alleged violation of Chinese traditional knowledge, where that violation took place in Peru. In other words, the Chinese court could hear a foreign infringement claim. The hearing of foreign infringements is controversial under the private international law of intellectual property.[110] There is also the difficulty of whether the defendant has any connection to the foreign forum and, if that connection is absent, whether the court can take jurisdiction.

One advantage of a choice of law approach is that it is consistent with the principle of territoriality.[111] Territoriality is particularly strong in patent law, where there is a clear rule that any determinations of validity of patents must be undertaken by the country where the

---

[109] Peter Drahos discusses how reciprocity worked to internationalise semi-conductor chip protection but it is not likely to work in relation to traditional knowledge. See supra note 103, at pp. 28–9.

[110] For an explanation of the private international law issues in intellectual property see François Dessemontet, Rochelle Dreyfuss and Jane Ginsburg (reporters), *Intellectual Property Principles Governing Jurisdiction, Choice of Law, and Judgments in Transnational Disputes*, USA: American Law Institute (ALI), 2008 (electronic version), available online at http://www.wipo.int/wipolex/en/details.jsp?id=7687. For an explanation of the genesis of the ALI Report see Rochelle Dreyfuss, 'The ALI Principles of Transnational Intellectual Property Disputes: Why Invite Conflicts?' (2005) *Brooklyn Journal of International Law*, 30 (3), pp. 819–48, at p. 819.

[111] For a discussion of some of these and related issues see Graeme B. Dinwoodie, 'Towards an International Framework for the Protection of Traditional Knowledge', *Elements of National Sui Generis Systems for the Preservation, Protection and Promotion of Traditional Knowledge: Innovations and Practices and Options for an International Framework,* UN Conference on Trade and Development, (Geneva, Switzerland, 4–6 February 2004), available at http://www.unctad.org/trade_env/test1/meetings/tk2/UCNTAD%20Paper(0129).pdf.

patent was granted.[112] This approach has its roots in the belief that to do otherwise would be an unjustified encroachment on a country's sovereignty.[113] The approach of the law providing for application of foreign law would not require the country in which the litigation took place to accept any determinations of a foreign institution, such as a patent office, such that the misappropriation of traditional knowledge invalidates a patent. This is particularly relevant to traditional knowledge issues because of the proposals to protect traditional knowledge through the requirement of disclosure of the origin of genetic resources in the patent system.[114]

These details and procedural aspects will be important.[115] At present, however, the international norms for the protection of traditional knowledge are a long way from being agreed and both the WTO and WIPO-IGC environments are set against a backdrop of national treatment being the most usual model.[116]

8. CONCLUSION

Countries that are serious about protecting traditional knowledge have not been able to gain agreement over norms in the trade forum of the WTO. Outside of the multilateral system there is an opportunity to agree to norms through FTAs. FTAs are imperfect instruments and have been shown to do some harm to aspects of international intellectual property law, particularly where parties to the FTA are not in reality equal negotiators. Nevertheless, FTAs could provide an opportunity to start the spread of some norms for the protection of traditional knowledge, particularly when the multilateral venues are not making progress. Parties to FTAs have not taken this opportunity most probably because they have not generally favoured FTAs as norm-setting instruments, but have strived to use multilateral fora.

In some FTAs, the negotiating parties may have resisted creation of norms for the protection of traditional knowledge, such as illustrated by the USA-Peru Agreement. Advocates of traditional knowledge do not only enter into FTAs with countries who will not agree to protect traditional knowledge and seek TRIPS-plus; they enter into FTAs with like-minded parties. It is difficult to see why like-minded parties such as Peru and China, or even Chile or Brazil, do not seize the opportunity to start agreeing to certain norms. There may be difficulties with turning this into an international norm-development story in the same way that TRIPS-plus has created norms of increased protection. However, an opportunity seems to have been, and continues to be, missed. In any event, such countries

---

112 See *GAT v LuK* (2006) C-4/03; and *Roche v Primus* (2006) C-539/03.

113 See, for example, *Potter v The Broken Hill Proprietary Company Ltd* (1906) 3 CLR 479. This approach of the Australian courts was followed for a long time in New Zealand and in the United Kingdom also.

114 See discussion in Dinwoodie, supra note 111.

115 For a discussion of 'procedural' in this context, see Christoph B. Graber, 'Stimulating Trade and Development of Indigenous Cultural Heritage by Means of International Law: Issues of Legitimacy and Method', in this volume.

116 This issue has been generally raised in the WIPO-IGC. See WIPO, IGC, 'Practical Means of Giving Effect to the International Dimension of the Committee's Work', Eighth Session (WIPO Doc. WIPO/GRTKF/IC/13/9, 2005).

should not agree to conditions that undermine the protection for traditional knowledge protection in the future and will no doubt continue to progress the debate over the protection of traditional knowledge in multilateral fora other than the WTO, such as WIPO.

6. Intellectual property rights in indigenous cultural heritage: basic concepts and continuing controversies

Christoph Antons*

1. INTRODUCTION: TRADITIONAL CULTURAL EXPRESSIONS AND DECOLONISATION

The developments at international level in the debate on what intellectual property (IP) lawyers refer to as traditional cultural expressions (TCEs) have to be seen in the context of the decolonisation movements after the Second World War. Post-war developments saw the formation of the United Nations (UN) and the emphasis on human rights in the UN Charter.[1] With this emphasis came development programmes for indigenous peoples and the recognition of indigenous rights in ILO Convention No. 107 of 1957 Concerning the Protection and Integration of Indigenous and Other Tribal and Semi-Tribal Populations in Independent Countries.[2] The decolonisation movements also initiated or renewed a parallel debate about the repatriation of items of cultural heritage. There was a remarkable shift in this discussion from 'cultural heritage of mankind' to cultural particularism and an emphasis on 'cultural property', as John Henry Merryman has pointed out with reference to the Preambles of the 1954 Hague Convention for the Protection of Cultural Property in the Event of Armed Conflict,[3] on the one hand, and the UNESCO Convention on the Means of Prohibiting and Preventing the Illicit Import, Export and Transfer of Ownership of Cultural Property of 1970,[4] on the other hand.[5]

* The author would like to thank the workshop participants and editors, in particular Jessica Lai, for their helpful comments on earlier drafts.

1 UN, Charter of the United Nations, 1 UNTS XVI (adopted on 26 June 1945, entered into force 24 October 1945).

2 ILO Convention No. 107 Concerning the Protection and Integration of Indigenous and Other Tribal and Semi-Tribal Populations in Independent Countries, 328 UNTS 24 (adopted on 26 June 1957, entered into force 2 June 1959).

3 UNESCO, Convention for the Protection of Cultural Property in the Event of Armed Conflict, 249 UNTS 240 (adopted on 14 May 1954, entered into force 7 August 1956).

4 UNESCO, Convention on the Means of Prohibiting and Preventing the Illicit Import, Export and Transfer of Ownership of Cultural Property, 823 UNTS 231 (adopted on 14 November 1970, entered into force 24 April 1972).

5 John H. Merryman, 'Two Ways of Thinking about Cultural Property' (1986) *The American Journal of International Law*, 80 (4), at pp. 831–53, as quoted in Derek Gillman, *The Idea of Cultural Heritage*, Cambridge: Cambridge University Press, 2010, at pp. 41–62.

This chapter aims at adding an IP perspective to the debate on international trade in indigenous cultural heritage. It will examine the international discussion about the options for legal protection of TCEs and expressions of folklore (EoF) and pay particular attention to the position of developing countries in international negotiations. In accordance with the author's current research, examples will be drawn in particular from Asian developing countries. Because of the crucial role of emerging economies such as China, India or Brazil in international trade talks and their interest in traditional knowledge (TK) protection, it is submitted that the role of developing countries provides an important consideration in addition to the position taken by the countries studied in this volume.[6]

The initial focus in this debate after decolonisation was on what was then still termed 'folklore', artistic expressions at the local level. Such artistic expressions of indigenous and local people often had an 'exotic' appeal in the industrialised world and they became important in the cultural encounter between the colonising West and the colonised peoples of Asia, Africa and Latin America. While such expressions had previously often been regarded as primitive and unskilled, artistic movements of the early twentieth century such as expressionism discovered and valued the archaic symbolism and power of such artistic expressions and they began to incorporate it into their art.[7]

At a time when the imperial powers were ruling much of the world, the people producing the objects of fascination in the colonies were not asked what they thought about the inspiration their artistic expressions provided to European art movements. While the symbolism of non-western crafts was appreciated, literal copying was not common and the appreciation was still confined to an avant-garde circle. Decolonisation and the arrival of new media able to spread cultural expressions around the world were soon to change this state of affairs. With the arrival of radio and phonogram came the creation of a global music industry able to bring American jazz or Italian opera to even the most remote corners of the world. The new industry had an appetite for new thrills and musicians were eager to engage with musicians from elsewhere. While it had been common for European composers of the nineteenth century to use their respective own folk traditions and to borrow from neighbours on occasion, American jazz and pop music went far beyond local shores. Itself a blend of African and European influences, it began to incorporate Latin American music from the 1940s and Asian music from the 1960s onwards.[8] Conveniently

---

6 See Christoph B. Graber, 'Institutionalization of Creativity in Traditional Societies and in International Trade Law', in Shubha Ghosh and Robin P. Malloy (eds), *Creativity, Law and Entrepreneurship*, Cheltenham, UK and Northampton, MA: Edward Elgar, 2011, pp. 234–63 [hereinafter Graber, 'Institutionalization of Creativity in Traditional Societies']; Christoph Antons, 'IP Law Reform in Developing Countries after the Global Financial Crisis' (2009) *International Review of Industrial Property and Copyright Law*, 40 (8), pp. 881–2.

7 Derek Gillman, supra note 5, at pp. 53–62; and Dietmar Elger, *Expressionismus: Eine deutsche Kunstrevolution*, Cologne: Benedikt Taschen Verlag, 1988, at pp. 79–80, 93–4 and 119–20. For a fascinating comparison of the work of the artist collective 'The Blue Rider' and ethnographic objects in the Munich Museum of Ethnography that inspired it, see the various contributions in Staatliches Museum für Völkerkunde München, *Der Blaue Reiter und das Münchner Völkerkundemuseum*, Kunstkabinett, vol. III, Munich: Hirmer, 2009.

8 Christoph Antons, 'Traditional Cultural Expressions and their Significance for Development in a Digital Environment: Examples from Australia and Southeast Asia', in Christoph B. Graber and

for music producers, under copyright principles 'traditional' folk music in the public domain could be easily adapted and turned into new copyrighted works.

Worldwide hit records based on songs from Africa or Latin America in the 1960s and 1970s belatedly led to several copyright disputes in recent years.[9] The disputes achieved wider significance, however, in a debate about the recognition of IP rights (IPRs) as part of cultural heritage and as cultural property. As such, they were increasingly taken up by national governments, in particular those of developing countries.[10]

2. FROM THE BERNE CONVENTION TO THE WIPO/UNESCO TUNIS MODEL LAW AND THE MODEL PROVISIONS

Coinciding with such high-profile cases was a widespread attempt during the 1960s and 1970s to incorporate some form of folklore protection into the new national copyright laws of newly independent nations. As a consequence, folklore protection was included in the discussions concerning the revision of the Berne Convention at the Diplomatic Conference in Stockholm in 1967.[11] The result was Article 15.4 Berne Convention, which leaves it to relevant national legislation of Member States to designate a 'competent authority' to represent, protect and enforce rights to 'unpublished works where the identity of the author is unknown, but where there is every ground to presume that he is a national of a country of the Union'. Countries that designate such an authority must notify the Director General of the World Intellectual Property Organization (WIPO) and provide full information (Article 15.4.b).

During the 1960s and 1970s, a number of developing countries in Latin America and Africa included folklore protection in their new copyright acts.[12] The usual approach was to regard folklore as part of the cultural heritage of the nation and to use the 'authors of unknown identity' formula of Article 15.4 Berne Convention. Some laws differed from the

---

Mira Burri-Nenova (eds), *Intellectual Property and Traditional Cultural Expressions in a Digital Environment*, Cheltenham, UK: Edward Elgar, 2008, pp. 287–301, at p. 297 [hereinafter Antons, 'TCEs and their Significance for Development'].

[9] Rian Malan, 'Where Does the Lion Sleep Tonight?', *Rolling Stone* (25 May 2000), available online at http://www.3rdearmusic/com/forum/mbube2.html (all online sources were accessed 25 August 2011); Simon Robinson, 'It's a Lawsuit, a Mighty Lawsuit', *Time Magazine* (25 October 2004); Owen Dean, 'The Return of the Lion' (2006) *WIPO Magazine*, 2, pp. 8–10; and Pedro Escribano, '"El condor pasa" patrimonio cultural de la nación', *La República* (13 April 2004).

[10] Michael Halewood, 'Indigenous and Local Knowledge in International Law: A Preface to Sui Generis Intellectual Property Protection' (1999) *McGill Law Journal*, 44, pp. 953–98.

[11] WIPO, Berne Convention for the Protection of Literary and Artistic Works, 828 UNTS 222 (adopted on 9 September 1886), as revised at Stockholm (14 July 1967). See Graber, 'Institutionalization of Creativity in Traditional Societies', supra note 6, at pp. 240–42.

[12] The WIPO/UNESCO model provisions of 1985 mention the following countries and respective years of their copyright acts: Tunisia, 1967; Bolivia, 1968; Chile, 1970; Morocco, 1970; Algeria, 1973; Senegal, 1973; Kenya, 1975; Mali, 1977; Burundi, 1978; Ivory Coast, 1978; and Guinea, 1980: see UNESCO/WIPO, *Model Provisions for National Laws on the Protection of Expressions of Folklore Against Illicit Exploitation and Other Prejudicial Actions*, Paris and Geneva: UNESCO/WIPO, 1985, at para. 5.

Berne Convention, however, in protecting published as well as unpublished works.[13] The Convention concerning the African Intellectual Property Organization (OAPI Convention) of 1977 became the first regional treaty to make reference to folklore protection. In 1973, the government of Bolivia sent a memorandum to the Director General of UNESCO, in which it requested that UNESCO look into the possibility of an international instrument on the protection of folklore, which was to be attached as a protocol to the Universal Copyright Convention.[14] The resulting Model Provisions for National Laws on the Protection of Expressions of Folklore Against Illicit Exploitation and other Prejudicial Actions [the 'Model Provisions'] drafted by a joint Working Group of UNESCO and WIPO experts were finally adopted in 1982 and published in 1985. A few years earlier, in 1976, both UNESCO and WIPO had assisted a Committee of Governmental Experts convened by the Tunisian government to draft and adopt the Tunis Model Law on Copyright ['Model Law'] for developing countries, which made extensive reference to folklore.[15]

The main provision on folklore in the Tunis Model Law is section 6, dealing with 'works of national folklore'. It foresees the exercise of the rights to folklore by a 'competent authority' without limitation in time. In the commentary to the provision, it is suggested that the competent authority could be the body responsible for the administration of authors' rights in a country. An exception can be made for use for non-commercial purposes by a public entity. The provision further prohibits the importation of copies of such folkloristic material made abroad without the authorisation of the competent authority. Section 2 of the Model Law on derivative works states that works derived from national folklore are also protected as original works. The list of protected works in section 1 mentions folkloristic expressions such as tapestry and handicraft, but it refers to section 6 for any work that constitutes national folklore. As an optional provision, section 5bis exempts folklore from the fixation requirement preferred in some copyright systems. Folklore is defined in the definition section 18 as 'all literary, artistic and scientific works created on national territory by authors presumed to be nationals of such countries or by ethnic communities, passed from generation to generation and constituting one of the basic elements of the traditional cultural heritage'.

The Tunis Model Law constitutes an attempt at the national regulation of folklore by using copyright principles. The commentary speaks of its potential for economic expansion as well as of the intimate link to the individual character of each people. It sees the national authority as empowered to represent the people that create the material. Apart from the suggestion referring to collecting societies, the Model Law leaves it to the various governments to develop solutions in forming representative competent authorities and how precisely their empowerment by the originators of the material can be achieved. The

---

13 Ibid., at paras 6–7.

14 Ibid., at para. 15. WIPO, Universal Copyright Convention, 943 UNTS 169 (adopted on 6 September 1952, entered into force 16 September 1955), as revised at Paris (24 July 1971).

15 International Bureau of WIPO, 'The Protection of Expressions of Folklore: The Attempts at International Level' (1998) *Intellectual Property in Asia and the Pacific*, 56/57, available online at http://itt.nissat.tripod.com/itt9903/folklore.htm; and Janice Weiner, 'Protection of Folklore: A Political and Legal Challenge' (1987) *International Review of Industrial Property and Copyright Law*, 18 (1), pp. 56–92.

Tunis Model Law thus appears as a document drafted in the spirit of a time when economic development was regarded to a large extent as a state-led and state-planned process. Reference to the individuals and communities generating the material is made in the definitions in section 18 and in the commentary to section 6, but their role remains very limited. Although many copyright acts of developing countries at the time used elements of the Tunis Model Law as the departure point,[16] the joint expert committee of UNESCO and WIPO commented almost a decade later on the occasion of the release of the Model Provisions in 1985 that 'at least so far, legal protection of folklore by copyright laws and treaties does not appear to have been particularly effective or expedient'.[17] The committee noted in particular that until the drafting of the Model Provisions, no notification designating a national authority under Article 15.4 of the Berne Convention had been deposited with the Director General of WIPO.[18] It noted further that 'one has the impression that copyright law is, after all, not the right kind of law for protecting expressions of folklore'.[19] Mentioned as problematic in this context are, in particular, such features of copyright as individual originality and the limited duration of copyright protection.

The experiences of countries that have used the approach of the Tunis Model Law certainly confirm this analysis. Indonesia, for example, adopted the Tunis Model Law approach in Article 10 of the Indonesian Copyright Act of 1982. The Indonesian provision mixes principles drawn from heritage protection and cultural property with the 'national folklore' concept drawn from the Tunis Model Law.[20] This generated a nationalist discourse on IP and national heritage and a few conflicts with neighbouring Malaysia about what currently should be regarded as primarily cultural heritage rather than IP.[21] In spite of such cross-border disputes, the relevant provision in Indonesia has actually never been implemented and the institutional framework for implementation has yet to be created. The implementation of the copyright approach to 'national folklore', therefore, has not generated any tangible results. However, in spite of such not very successful examples, the copyright approach to folklore has remained popular. According to the

---

16 For the example of Indonesia's Copyright Act of 1982, see Christoph Antons, *Intellectual Property Law in Indonesia*, London: Kluwer Law International, 2000, at pp. 84–90; and Christoph Antons, 'What is "Traditional Cultural Expression"? International Definitions and Their Application in Developing Asia' (2009) *The WIPO Journal*, 1, pp. 103–16 [hereinafter Antons, 'Traditional Cultural Expression'].

17 UNESCO/WIPO, supra note 12, at para. 10.

18 The WIPO, IGC, 'Final Report on National Experiences with the Legal Protection of Expressions of Folklore', (WIPO Doc. WIPO/GRTKF/IC/3/10, 2002), at p. 9 [hereinafter WIPO, IGC, 'Final Report on National Experiences'], reports one designation under Article 15.4 by India.

19 UNESCO/WIPO, supra note 12, at para. 10.

20 Antons, *Intellectual Property Law in Indonesia*, supra note 16; Antons, 'Traditional Cultural Expression', supra note 16; and Christoph Antons, 'Asian Borderlands and the Legal Protection of Traditional Knowledge and Traditional Cultural Expressions', *Modern Asian Studies (in print)* [hereinafter Antons, 'Asian Borderlands'].

21 Antons, 'Traditional Cultural Expression', supra note 16; Antons, 'Asian Borderlands', supra note 20; Stephen Fitzpatrick, 'Malaysia "Steals" Bali Dance', *The Australian* (26 August 2009); 'Malaysia Urges Indonesia to Drop Plans to Sue over Folk Song', *Jakarta Post* (8 October 2007); and 'Indonesian Outrage over a Dance', *Asia Sentinel* (25 August 2009).

current WIPO website, collecting legislative texts on the protection of TCEs (expressions of folklore) no less than 27 countries in Africa, Asia, Latin America and the Pacific have provisions referring to folklore as part of their copyright acts.[22]

Some of the lessons from the discussion generated by the 'national folklore' approach of the Tunis Model Law are visible in the 1982 UNESCO/WIPO Model Provisions, published in 1985. Firstly, different from the Tunis Model Law, the Model Provisions offer a *sui generis* approach to folklore protection against illicit exploitation and other prejudicial action. As a consequence, the document uses the term 'expressions of folklore' rather than 'works'. Secondly, in contrast to the Tunis Model Law, the Model Provisions move away from the rather narrow focus on 'national folklore' and acknowledge the communities and individuals producing the material. It is recognised that 'the artistic heritage of communities is a more restricted body of traditional values than the entire traditional artistic heritage of the nation'.[23] 'Traditional artistic heritage developed and maintained by a community' is understood as representing a special part of the 'cultural heritage of the nation'.[24] The greater role granted to local communities becomes especially visible from those parts of the Model Provisions that deal with the process of authorisation and with the question as to who should authorise permitted forms of utilisation. Here, the Model Provisions decide on a system of preliminary authorisation rather than subsequent checks of permitted use. The commentary points out that preliminary authorisation and previous clearance combined with sanctions was preferred, because it would provide certainty for users of the system and allow the entities supervising the system to prevent harm at the outset rather than being confined to damage control.[25]

The Model Provisions leave sensitive areas to the discretion of national legislators by offering various bracketed options for regulation. As for the authorising entity, the Model Provisions realise that countries have very different policies with regard to recognising traditional rights of communities. As a consequence, the authorising entity can be either a 'competent authority' as in the Tunis Model Law, where EoF are regarded as 'property of the nation', or the authorisation can be left to the relevant community itself, where 'aboriginal or other traditional communities are recognized as owners fully entitled to dispose of their folklore' and 'sufficiently organized to administer the utilization of the expressions of their folklore'.[26] The commentary suggests as options for the 'competent authority' the Ministry of Culture or of Arts, any public institution for matters related to folklore, an authors' society or similar institution or a representative body of the community concerned.[27] If the legislators choose a 'competent authority', the provisions offer the possibility for an additional supervisory authority, in particular for matters related to the fixation and allocation of fees. In such cases, decisions can be appealed by both applicants and concerned communities. Alternatively, if authorisation is granted directly by the community, such mechanisms are not necessary. The commentary suggests,

22 See WIPO, 'Legislative Texts on the Protection of Traditional Cultural Expressions (Expressions of Folklore) (TCEs)', available at http://www.wipo.int/tk/en/laws/folklore.html.

23 UNESCO/WIPO, supra note 12, at para. 33.

24 Ibid.

25 Ibid., at para. 48.

26 Ibid., at para. 49.

27 Ibid., at para. 76.

however, that if authorisation were granted by designated representatives rather than the 'community as such', the representatives would qualify as a competent authority.[28] While this seems obvious, it is rather difficult to imagine how the 'community as such' could grant authorisation on a regular basis without involving designated representatives. In the end, the expert committee recommended that an important role be given to the representatives of various folklore communities of a country and that representatives of cultural and ethnological institutions, including museums, should be associated with the work of the competent authority.[29]

The *sui generis* Model Provisions represent a clear step forward in recognising the nature of folklore, its origin and administration in comparison with the previous approach focused on copyright and 'national folklore'. Nevertheless, they also raise a number of concerns. Firstly, they provide for copyright-style exceptions to protection in section 4 in the interests of education, utilisation by way of illustration in the work of an author or authors and borrowing of EoF for creating an original work. A further exception is 'incidental utilization', for which section 4(2) provides the examples of current events reporting or inclusion of folkloristic expressions in a photograph, film or television broadcast. The concern here is that many expressions regarded as folkloristic can have secret and sacred meanings and they may play a role in religious rituals of communities.[30] Where such religious connotations are involved, it seems not entirely appropriate and probably unrealistic to expect communities to consent to their use in the interests of education, artistic development or news reporting. In particular, in cases where communities struggle for a greater degree of self-determination within nation states, they may advocate a tighter control of their cultural expressions and not be content with educational or other uses that benefit mainstream society rather than their own.

Similar objections can be raised, secondly and more generally, against the requirement that utilisations subject to authorisation must be made 'with gainful intent and outside their traditional or customary context'. This leaves outside the scope of protection utilisations by national and public bodies that are not of a commercial nature. Again, where religious and secret/sacred expressions are involved, such non-commercial use may still be offensive and inappropriate. Further, where the community seeks to restrict the use of the material for commercial or non-commercial reasons, public use by institutions of mainstream society may compete with such purposes. Finally, it would not permit the use of folkloristic expressions by community members with gainful intent, although they may in fact be entitled to such use under their customary law. In such a situation, a national law that interferes in community affairs could create conflicting entitlements and lead to disputes.

Thirdly, in view of the cross-border nature of at least some of the material and the difficulties in establishing its origin with certainty, some of the criminal penalties for offences could be of concern, at least where offences are due to negligence rather than wilful intent. Fourthly and finally, while the Model Provisions give communities an important role in the authorisation process, they are ambiguous with regard to the

---

28 Ibid., at para. 77.

29 Ibid., at para. 79.

30 Graber, 'Institutionalization of Creativity in Traditional Societies', supra note 6, at pp. 237–8.

distribution of collected fees. The commentary is clear in stating that the community should decide how to use such fees, if they authorise the utilisation and that the state in such case should ensure its share 'if at all' only via taxes or other appropriate measures.[31] Section 10 of the provisions, however, allows for the conclusion that all fees collected, independently from the collecting entity, must be used for the purpose of promoting or safeguarding national culture or folklore. Where a competent authority is involved, the provisions recommend to pay a percentage of the fees to the community and to allow the authority to retain a percentage for administrative purposes. Most benefit-sharing models that are currently being practised seem to have followed this latter approach, with differences in the percentage that is being retained by representative agencies, on the one hand, and that is being transferred to communities, on the other hand.[32]

Subsequent to the drafting of the Model Provisions, the joint expert committee of UNESCO and WIPO in 1984 also developed a Draft Treaty for the Protection of Expressions of Folklore against Illicit Exploitation and Other Prejudicial Actions.[33] Adoption of such a treaty, however, was ultimately found to be premature mainly for two reasons: the lack of appropriate sources for the identification of EoF considered for protection; and the lack of workable mechanisms for settling the questions of folkloristic expressions that can be found in several countries of a region simultaneously. As we shall see later, these questions continue to pose problems.

---

[31] UNESCO/WIPO, supra note 12, at p. 26.

[32] For examples from Bangladesh, Pakistan and India, see Surinder K. Verma, 'Protection of Traditional Knowledge in the SAARC Region and India's Efforts', in Christoph Antons (ed.), *Traditional Knowledge, Traditional Cultural Expressions and Intellectual Property Law in the Asia-Pacific Region*, Alphen aan den Rijn, Netherlands: Kluwer Law International, 2009, pp. 315–39, at pp. 325–38. For Sri Lanka, see Indunil Abeyesekere, 'The Protection of Expressions of Folklore in Sri Lanka', in Christoph Antons (ed.), *Traditional Knowledge, Traditional Cultural Expressions and Intellectual Property Law in the Asia-Pacific Region*, Alphen aan den Rijn, Netherlands: Kluwer Law International, 2009, pp. 341–62, 343–4 and 346–7. For examples from Indonesia, the Philippines and India, see Christoph Antons, 'The International Debate about Traditional Knowledge and Approaches in the Asia-Pacific Region', in Christoph Antons (ed.), *Traditional Knowledge, Traditional Cultural Expressions and Intellectual Property Law in the Asia-Pacific Region*, Alphen aan den Rijn, Netherlands: Kluwer Law International, 2009, pp. 39–65, at pp. 53–64 [hereinafter Antons, 'The International Debate about Traditional Knowledge']. For Peru, see Carlos Correa, 'Access to Knowledge: The Case of Indigenous and Traditional Knowledge', in Gaëlle Krikorian and Amy Kapczynski (eds), *Access to Knowledge in the Age of Intellectual Property*, New York: Zone Books, 2010, pp. 237–52, at pp. 242–3 [hereinafter Correa, 'Access to Knowledge']. For a critical view of such models see Michael R. Dove, 'Use of Global Legal Mechanisms to Conserve Local Biogenetic Resources: Problems and Prospects', in Michael R. Dove, Percy E. Sajise and Amity A. Doolittle (eds), *Conserving Nature in Culture: Case Studies from Southeast Asia*, New Haven, CT: Yale University Southeast Asian Studies, 2005, pp. 279–305, at p. 298.

[33] A copy of the treaty is attached as Annex IV to the WIPO, IGC, 'Final Report on National Experiences', supra note 18.

3. FROM 'EXPRESSIONS OF FOLKLORE' TO 'TRADITIONAL CULTURAL EXPRESSIONS' AND 'TRADITIONAL KNOWLEDGE'

In cultural policies, a significant broadening of the concept of 'culture' from its previous high art definition to one that includes modes of life, value systems, traditions and beliefs occurred after the Mexico City Declaration on Cultural Policies of 1982.[34] From the late 1980s onwards, the debate about the international protection of EoF became increasingly linked with a new debate related to heritage and culture based on such a broadened understanding of the concepts. It concerned genetic resources (GRs) and forms of traditional knowledge relevant for the new biotechnology industry, for medicines and the conservation of biodiversity. This new debate was initially conducted in different international fora than the one on EoF. The first one of these was the UN Food and Agriculture Organization (FAO). With strong developing country membership, FAO had traditionally been critical of IPRs in agriculture. As for plant GRs important for agricultural innovation, FAO had sponsored the International Undertaking on Plant Genetic Resources for Food and Agriculture of 1984, which regarded plant GRs as 'heritage of mankind' and as freely accessible and exchangeable.[35] The concept of 'farmers' rights' emerged during discussions in the FAO Commission on Genetic Resources for Food and Agriculture, in which developed countries favoured the harmonisation of the International Undertaking with the International Union for the Protection of New Plant Varieties (UPOV) and the exemption of plant breeders' rights protected varieties from the common heritage principle. As a counterweight against the expansion of IPRs in food and agriculture, the notion of 'farmers' rights' was introduced.[36] It was given a more concrete meaning in FAO resolution 5/89 of 1989, which became an annex to the 1983 International Undertaking. Accordingly, 'farmers' rights' were defined as:

> Rights arising from the past, present and future contribution of farmers in conserving, improving and making available Plant Genetic Resources, particularly those in the centres of origin/diversity. These rights are vested in the International Community, as trustees for present and

---

[34] UNESCO, Mexico City Declaration on Cultural Policies (UNESCO Doc. CLT/MD/1) (adopted on 6 August 1982). See William Logan, Michele Langfield and Máiréad N. Craith, 'Intersecting Concepts and Practices', in Michele Langfield, William Logan and Máiréad Nic Craith (eds), *Cultural Diversity, Heritage and Human Rights: Intersections in Theory and Practice*, London and New York: Routledge, 2010, pp. 3–20, at p. 6; and John Scott and Federico Lenzerini, 'International Indigenous and Human Rights Law in the Context of Trade in Indigenous Cultural Heritage', in this volume.

[35] Michael Blakeney, 'Intellectual Property Aspects of Traditional Agricultural Knowledge', in Peter Drahos and Michael Blakeney (eds), *IP in Biodiversity and Agriculture: Regulating the Biosphere*, London: Sweet & Maxwell, 2001, pp. 29–52, at p. 44; and Carlos Correa, 'Access to Plant Genetic Resources and Intellectual Property Rights', in Peter Drahos and Michael Blakeney (eds), *IP in Biodiversity and Agriculture: Regulating the Biosphere*, London: Sweet & Maxwell, 2001, pp. 101–32, at pp. 103–7.

[36] Halewood, supra note 10, at p. 970.

> future generations of farmers, for the purpose of ensuring full benefits of farmers and supporting the continuation of their contributions, ...[37]

While the concept of farmers' rights represents a first recognition of traditional knowledge for the more limited field of food and agriculture, the subsequent Convention on Biological Diversity (CBD), concluded at the Rio Biodiversity Summit of 1992, firmly established the wider concept of 'traditional knowledge' in the minds of policy-makers. In Article 8(j) parties of the CBD were required, subject to national legislation, to

> respect, preserve and maintain knowledge, innovations and practices of indigenous and local communities embodying traditional lifestyles relevant for the conservation and sustainable use of biological diversity and promote their wider application with the approval and involvement of the holders of such knowledge, innovations and practices and encourage the equitable sharing of the benefits arising from the utilization of such knowledge, innovations and practices ... [38]

Apart from Article 8(j), 'traditional cultural practices' are mentioned in Article 10(c) of the CBD, which requires parties 'as far as possible and as appropriate' to protect and encourage 'customary use of biological resources in accordance with traditional cultural practices that are compatible with conservation or sustainable use requirements'.

The traditional knowledge provisions of the CBD have to be seen against the background of a fundamental shift in the understanding of GRs from heritage of mankind to the sovereign rights of nation states to grant access to and exploit such resources, as stated in Article 3 of the CBD[39] and now reaffirmed in the Nagoya Protocol on Access to Genetic Resources and the Fair and Equitable Sharing of Benefits Arising from their Utilization to the Convention on Biological Diversity.[40] They have further to be seen in the context of a shift from 'top–down' to 'bottom–up' strategies in environment protection and development policies and a greater role for neo-liberal ideas and private property concepts that accompanied these developments.[41] A final influence is what has been called the 'new

---

[37] FAO, 'Farmer's Rights', Twenty-Fifth Session of the FAO Conference (FAO Res. 5/89, 1989).

[38] Rio Convention on Biological Diversity (CBD),1760 UNTS 79; 31 ILM 818 (opened for signature 5 June 1992, entered into force 29 December 1993).

[39] Christoph Antons, '*Sui Generis* Protection for Plant Varieties and Traditional Knowledge in Biodiversity and Agriculture: The International Framework and National Approaches in the Philippines and India' (2010) *The Indian Journal of Law and Technology*, 6, pp. 89–139 [hereinafter Antons, '*Sui Generis* Protection for Plant Varieties']; and Christoph Antons, 'The Role of Traditional Knowledge and Access to Genetic Resources in Biodiversity Conservation in Southeast Asia' (2010) *Biodiversity and Conservation*, 19, pp. 1189–1204.

[40] Nagoya Protocol on Access to Genetic Resources and the Fair and Equitable Sharing of Benefits Arising from their Utilization to the Convention on Biological Diversity (UN Doc. UNEP/CBD/COP/DEC/X/1) (adopted on 29 October 2010).

[41] Stephen B. Brush, 'Protecting Traditional Agricultural Knowledge' (2005) *Washington University Journal of Law and Policy*, 17, pp. 77–8; Tania Murray Li, *The Will to Improve: Governmentality, Development and the Practice of Politics*, Durham, NC and London: Duke University Press, 2007; and Peter Newell, 'The Marketization of Global Environmental Governance: Manifestations and Implications', in Jacob Park, Ken Conca and Matthias Finger (eds), *The Crisis of Global Environmental Governance: Towards a New Political Economy of Sustainability*, Oxford and New York: Routledge, 2008, at pp. 77–95.

indigenism'[42] referring to the international collaboration of various national and regional movements of indigenous peoples to shape their rights discourses and develop common strategies in their bargaining with national governments.[43] EoF now became integrated into these new paradigms and linked with the much broader concept of traditional knowledge advanced by indigenous groups, environmentalists and human rights lawyers and activists, often under the even broader term of 'cultural heritage'.[44]

While the question of physical access to GRs and associated traditional knowledge became the task of the Ad Hoc Open-Ended Working Group on Access and Benefit-Sharing of the CBD, WIPO became responsible for the IP side of the debate.[45] Between May 1998 and November 1999, WIPO embarked on fact-finding missions to 28 countries to find out about the IP-related needs and expectations of traditional knowledge-holders.[46] Interestingly, WIPO chose for these missions a very wide definition of traditional knowledge, which included EoF as a subset.[47] In its final report on the outcome of these missions, WIPO's working definition of traditional knowledge included 'tradition based literary, artistic and scientific works, performances, inventions, scientific discoveries, designs, marks, names and symbols, undisclosed information and all other tradition-based innovations and creations resulting from intellectual activity in the industrial, scientific, literary or artistic field'.[48] The concept was illustrated by a picture of overlapping circles, whereby heritage as the widest concept included traditional knowledge, which in turn included overlapping circles of EoF and indigenous knowledge. The working definition crossed the entire range of IPRs, although it distinguished IP-related forms of traditional knowledge from even wider forms of 'indigenous cultural and intellectual property' advocated by human rights advocates and representatives of indigenous groups. The holistic understanding of 'indigenous cultural and intellectual property' was supported by cultural heritage experts advocating a widening of the term 'cultural property' to 'cultural heritage' and a recognition of the parallels to environmental law.[49] At the international

---

42 Ronald Niezen, *The Origins of Indigenism: Human Rights and the Politics of Identity*, Berkeley, Los Angeles and London: University of California Press, 2003 [hereinafter Niezen, *The Origins of Indigenism*]; and Ronald Niezen, *A World Beyond Difference: Cultural Identity in the Age of Globalization*, Malden, MA, Oxford and Carlton, Vic.: Blackwell Publishing, 2004, at pp. 66–74.

43 Antons, 'The International Debate about Traditional Knowledge', supra note 32, at pp. 40–41; and Christoph Antons, 'Traditional Knowledge in Asia: Global Agendas, Local Subjects', in John Gillespie and Randall Peerenboom (eds), *Regulation in Asia: Pushing Back on Globalization*, London and New York: Routledge, 2009, at pp. 68–72 [hereinafter Antons, 'Traditional Knowledge in Asia: Global Agendas, Local Subjects'].

44 Lyndel V. Prott, 'Problems of Private International Law for the Protection of the Cultural Heritage' (1989) *Recueil de Cours de l'Académie de la Haye*, 217, pp. 215–317, at p. 310; and Rosemary J. Coombe, 'The Expanding Purview of Cultural Properties and Their Politics' (2009) *Annual Review of Law and Social Science*, 5, pp. 393–412, at p. 398.

45 Halewood, supra note 10, at pp. 985–7.

46 WIPO, IGC, 'Final Report on National Experiences', supra note 18, at pp. 12–16.

47 Ibid., at p. 13.

48 WIPO, *Intellectual Property Needs and Expectations of Traditional Knowledge Holders – WIPO Report on Fact-finding Missions on Intellectual Property and Traditional Knowledge*, Geneva: WIPO, 2001, at p. 25.

49 Prott, supra note 44, at p. 310. See also Gillman, supra note 5, at p. 48.

level this wider understanding of cultural heritage was adopted by Erica-Irene Daes, the Special Rapporteur of the UN Sub-Commission on Prevention of Discrimination and Protection of Minorities.[50] It was embraced by Terri Janke in her report 'Our Culture: Our Future' written in 1998 for the Australian Aboriginal and Torres Straits Islander Commission (ATSIC). Her definition of the material for protection included also indigenous ancestral remains, sacred indigenous sites, 'cultural environment resources' such as minerals and species and even languages,[51] as far as they concern 'the recording of cultural customs and expressions, the particular language which may be intrinsic to cultural identity, knowledge, the skill and teaching of culture'.[52]

The different definitions started a discussion about the conceptualisation of the subject matter. Mainly three positions can be identified in the relevant literature: the first position uses a very wide holistic definition of 'cultural and intellectual property' that departs from a broad understanding of 'cultural heritage' in which IP is a mere subset. As such, it goes far beyond IP-related material and it includes principles of IP within the 'cultural property' concepts of conventions such as the 1970 UNESCO Convention. The second position is in accordance with the original WIPO working definition of traditional knowledge. It concentrates on IP aspects of cultural expressions, but maintains that it is somewhat unrealistic and against the nature of the material to be protected to distinguish clearly between scientifically relevant TK and the more artistically oriented EoF. The third position is the current position developed during the WIPO negotiations. It acknowledges the crucial link between TK and EoF, but argues that it is more convenient and in the interest of achieving tangible outcomes to treat the material separately and to draft separate sets of policies for both fields. Reasons mentioned are that the advanced stage of the work on EoF merits distinct consideration of this subject matter and that the sheer breadth and diversity of what may be included in traditional knowledge suggests that a more limited focus may be desirable and more productive. Finally, and perhaps most important from an IP perspective, the rights that would be relevant in respect of artistic/cultural material are different from those relevant to technical/scientific materials.[53]

---

50 WIPO, IGC, 'Final Report on National Experiences', supra note 18.

51 Terri Janke, *Our Culture: Our Future – Report on Australian Indigenous Cultural and Intellectual Property Rights*, Sydney: Michael Frankel and Company, 1998, at pp. 11–12.

52 Ibid., at p. 48.

53 WIPO, IGC, 'Final Report on National Experiences', supra note 18, at pp. 31–2; Christoph Antons, 'Traditional Knowledge and Intellectual Property Rights in Australia and Southeast Asia', in Christopher Heath and Anselm Kamperman Sanders (eds), *New Frontiers of Intellectual Property Law: IP and Cultural Heritage, Geographical Indications, Enforcement and Overprotection*, Oxford and Portland, OR: Hart Publishing, 2005, pp. 37–51 [hereinafter Antons, 'TK and IPRs in Australia and Southeast Asia']; and Antons, 'TCEs and their Significance for Development', supra note 8, at p. 288.

4. TOWARDS A TREATY? THE WIPO INTERGOVERNMENTAL COMMITTEE ON INTELLECTUAL PROPERTY AND GENETIC RESOURCES, TRADITIONAL KNOWLEDGE AND FOLKLORE AND ITS REVISED OBJECTIVES AND PRINCIPLES

The WIPO Intergovernmental Committee on Intellectual Property and Genetic Resources, Traditional Knowledge and Folklore (IGC) convened for the first time in 2001. As far as EoF were concerned, the initial sessions dealt with the details of the mandate to look into an update of the Model Provisions in light of the experience countries had made, improve the protection of handicrafts and establish an international *sui generis* system.[54] During further sessions, the IGC established a voluntary fund to allow for greater participation of representatives of indigenous and local groups, it drafted separate sets of principles, objectives and policy options for the three interrelated issues of its mandate and, specifically, for EoF or TCEs as they were now increasingly called, a gap analysis document. The WIPO General Assembly renewed its mandate during its session in September/October 2009. The renewal came with the obligation to undertake text-based negotiations with the objective of reaching agreement on a text of an international legal instrument (or instruments) which will ensure the effective protection of GRs, TK and TCEs. The new mandate foresaw regular sessions of the IGC as well as three intersessional working groups (IWGs) during the 2010–11 biennium.[55] During the WIPO General Assembly Session in September/October 2011, the mandate was again renewed for the 2012–13 biennium.[56]

The first IWG in July 2010 focused on TCEs, regarded as 'the most mature' of the three subject areas.[57] The streamlined text resulting from the IWG meeting was tabled at the 17th Session of the IGC, together with the latest version of the Revised Objectives and Principles. The Draft Articles were then again tabled at the 18th and 19th Sessions of the IGC,[58] and an informal open-ended drafting group was established to work further on the text.[59] Meanwhile, two further IWG meetings have produced Draft Articles on the Protection of Traditional Knowledge, and Options on Intellectual Property and Genetic Resources.[60]

---

54 WIPO, IGC, 'Final Report on National Experiences', supra note 18, at pp. 16–17.

55 WIPO, General Assembly, 'Report of the Thirty-Eighth (19th Ordinary) Session, Geneva, 22 September – 1 October 2009', (WIPO Doc. WO/GA/38/20, 2009), at para. 217.

56 WIPO, Assemblies of Member States of WIPO, 'Matters Concerning the Intergovernmental Committee on Intellectual Property and Genetic Resources, Traditional Knowledge and Folklore. Agenda Item 31. Decision', Fortieth (20th Ordinary) Session (26 September – 5 October 2011), available at http://www.wipo.int/export/sites/www/tk/en/documents/pdf/decision_assemblies_2011.pdf.

57 WIPO, 'Experts Break New Ground in Traditional Cultural Expressions Talks', *WIPO News & Events* (23 July 2010).

58 WIPO, IGC, Secretariat, 'The Protection of Traditional Cultural Expressions: Draft Articles', (WIPO Doc. WIPO/GRTKF/IC/19/4, 2011) [hereinafter WIPO, IGC, 'TCE Draft Articles. 2011'].

59 WIPO, IGC, Secretariat, 'Report', (WIPO Doc. WIPO/GRTKF/IC/18/11, 2011), p. 10.

60 Respectively: WIPO, IGC Secretariat, 'Draft Articles on the Protection of Traditional Knowledge Prepared at IWG2', (WIPO Doc. WIPO/GRTKF/IC/18/7, 2011); and WIPO, IGC,

If one examines the draft texts and the underlining, slashes and square brackets that signal controversial issues in the Draft Articles and in the Revised Objectives and Principles, it soon becomes clear that the difficulties in finding agreement continue to lie in particular in three areas: firstly, the definition of the subject matter of protection and its relationship to other forms of IPRs; secondly, the question of how to delineate the circle of beneficiaries and the related question as to how rights should be managed; and, thirdly, the scope of protection and the role of exceptions. To understand the reasons for the continuing controversies, it is useful to get an appreciation of the various political and economic interests driving the debate. Firstly, in the general TK/TCE/GR debate, the different interests of developed and developing countries are often mentioned. Scope of protection is of great concern here. On the one hand, as the discussions at the end of the previous biennium showed, most developing countries hope for a binding international agreement with a strong scope of protection. Developed countries, on the other hand, prefer a relative informality and stress the importance of exceptions and of a viable public domain as well as the difficulties in harmonising any new laws with currently existing IPRs. Clearly, however, the main economic concern of the industrialised countries is related to the TK debate and to the link between GRs and IPRs.[61] In comparison to the value of TK and with the exception of settler colonies with substantial indigenous minorities and an interest in providing economic incentives in this field, the economic interest of most developed countries in TCE protection seems rather negligible. TCEs are of concern to much of the developed world in particular because of their link to the other areas of this complex negotiating process. Comparatively speaking, therefore, it may be much easier to reach international agreement on TCEs than on any of the other agenda items of the IGC mandate. The most recent discussions of the IWG confirm this assessment. In particular the discussion about the relationship of IP and GRs has not yet generated a draft text, but only a statement of options.[62]

Secondly, there is the sub-national level of the debate. This concerns the important question of the exact mechanisms of distribution of royalties and other benefits between national governments and the 'traditional' and 'local' communities that produce the EoF, but it concerns also the definition of the subject matter. Although the secret/sacred nature of material is not exclusive to indigenous cultures, indigenous peoples are more likely to have cultural expressions that are regarded as secret and/or sacred. Because of their vulnerable position vis-à-vis the majority and their aspirations to achieve greater self-determination, they tend towards more restrictive positions on cultural expressions.[63] At

Secretariat, 'Options on Intellectual Property and Genetic Resources: Summary of Discussions at IWG 3', (WIPO Doc. WIPO/GRTKF/IC/18/10, 2011) [hereinafter WIPO, IGC, Secretariat, 'Options on Intellectual Property and Genetic Resources'].

[61] See also Graber, 'Institutionalization of Creativity in Traditional Societies', supra note 6, at pp. 244–5, who mentions that most statements in parallel discussions in the WTO TRIPS Council have related to TK and that relatively little has been said with respect to TCE or folklore.

[62] WIPO, IGC, Secretariat, 'Options on Intellectual Property and Genetic Resources', supra note 60.

[63] For the variety of approaches enforcing secrecy, including via religious and customary taboos, see Christoph Antons, 'Legal Culture and History of Law in Asia', in Christopher Heath (ed.), *Intellectual Property Law in Asia*, London: Kluwer Law International, 2003, at p. 21; Antons, 'TK and IPRs in Australia and Southeast Asia', supra note 53, at p. 42.

the same time, their culture is usually a way of life that remains strong at the margins of mainstream society.[64] Indigenous representatives, therefore, tend to be less agreeable to the dividing up of their culture in a manner that suits the need of a field such as IP law. The recent controversy regarding the representation of indigenous groups during the formulation of the draft articles on the protection of TK at the 18th Session of the IGC in May 2011 confirms that the interests of national governments and indigenous communities are not always identical.[65]

4.1 The Subject Matter of Protection

As was indicated earlier, the subject matter of protection can be approached from a holistic perspective, from a perspective of a broad meaning of 'traditional knowledge' that includes 'traditional cultural expressions' or from an IP perspective that distinguishes between TK and TCE. The first perspective in particular finds support in much of the anthropology and social science literature on the topic, but it also finds support among human rights and environmental lawyers, among indigenous commentators and occasionally in the IP literature.[66] In general, however, IP relates to the protection of commercialised and industrialised forms of knowledge and IP experts often find the local variety and changing nature of traditional knowledge systems difficult to accommodate.[67] The WIPO negotiations after all are aiming at the creation of international rules and principles that apply to as many cases as possible. To a certain extent, this requires the levelling out of local differences and peculiarities.

This legal categorising and the different understandings of traditional knowledge if viewed from a legal or anthropology perspective become perhaps clearer if the concepts of 'local' or 'indigenous' knowledge as used by anthropologists and those of 'traditional knowledge' and 'traditional cultural expressions' used by lawyers are more closely

---

[64] Vivien Johnson, *Dreamings of the Desert: Aboriginal Dot Paintings of the Western Desert*, Adelaide: Art Gallery of South Australia, at p. 16.

[65] William New, 'New Texts in Play in WIPO Traditional Knowledge, Genetic Resources Talks', *Intellectual Property Watch* (12 May 2011), available at http://www.ip-watch.org/weblog/2011/05/12/new-texts-in-play-in-wipo-traditional-knowledge-genetic-resources-talks; and William New, 'Indigenous Peoples Won't Be "Wished Away" in Traditional Knowledge Talks', *Intellectual Property Watch* (14 May 2011), available at http://www.ip-watch.org/weblog/2011/05/14/indigenous-peoples-won%E2%80%99t-be-%E2%80%9Cwished-away%E2%80%9D-in-traditional-knowledge-treaty-talks/.

[66] See for example Janke, supra note 51; Coombe, supra note 44; Brendan Tobin, 'The Role of Customary Law and Practice in the Protection of Traditional Knowledge Related to Biological Diversity', in Christoph Antons (ed.), *Traditional Knowledge, Traditional Cultural Expressions and Intellectual Property Law in the Asia-Pacific Region*, Alphen aan den Rijn, Netherlands: Kluwer Law International, 2009, pp. 127–56, at p. 128; and Michael Blakeney, 'Protection of Traditional Knowledge by Geographical Indications', in Christoph Antons (ed.), *Traditional Knowledge, Traditional Cultural Expressions and Intellectual Property Law in the Asia-Pacific Region*, Alphen aan den Rijn, Netherlands: Kluwer Law International, 2009, pp. 87–108, at pp. 105–7 [hereinafter Blakeney, 'Protection of Traditional Knowledge'].

[67] For such difficulties in the relationship of property lawyers to cultural heritage more generally see Lyndel V. Prott and Patrick J. O'Keefe, '"Cultural Heritage" or "Cultural Property"?' (1992) *International Journal of Cultural Property*, 1 (2), pp. 307–20, at p. 314.

examined. Anthropologists, such as Ellen and Harris, regard such concepts as fluid. They have identified for the field of environmental knowledge a large number of different terms with partly overlapping meanings. Instead of a definition, they offer a list of loosely worded characteristics. The more important ones on this list are that: (1) indigenous knowledge is local, rooted to a particular place and set of experiences and generated by people living in those places; (2) it is orally transmitted, or transmitted through imitation and demonstration; (3) it is empirical rather than theoretical; (4) it is constantly changing, although often represented as static; (5) its distribution is socially differentiated, for example by gender and age; and (6) it is holistic and situated within broader cultural traditions, so that separating the technical from the non-technical is problematic.[68]

Apart from the problem of how far knowledge is 'rooted' to particular places, exactly such a separation of the technical from the non-technical is, however, important for IP law experts and WIPO's Intergovernmental Committee in the search for a definition of the subject matter. IP experts prefer to speak of 'traditional knowledge' and 'traditional cultural expressions'. Accordingly, 'traditional knowledge' *stricto sensu*[69] is defined in the WIPO working definition for the committee as 'knowledge resulting from intellectual activity in a traditional context', including various parts of traditional knowledge systems, 'knowledge embodying traditional lifestyles of indigenous and local communities' and 'contained in codified knowledge systems passed between generations'. The working definition is not 'limited to any specific technical field' and gives as examples agricultural, environmental and medicinal knowledge and knowledge associated with GRs.[70]

While it is generally fairly wide, the working definition is nevertheless restricted to 'technical fields'. In contrast to the characteristics listed by the anthropologists, it distinguishes between the technical and the non-technical. In line with that distinction, the WIPO working definition treats TK of a technical nature separately from TCEs, which includes all the material that relates to traditional arts, crafts and ritual.

This bifurcation of the knowledge for the purposes of the IP discussion has sometimes been criticised as distorting the holistic way in which it is conceptualised and transmitted.[71] Nevertheless, the various working definitions have been reasonably well accepted by now for the purposes of the WIPO discussions by the participating parties as well as by observers from indigenous organisations. The reason for the acceptance of the terminology is presumably that everyone is interested in a positive outcome of the IGC deliberations. From the viewpoint of indigenous organisations, an international agreement that protects their knowledge and cultural expressions in different parts is still better than no agreement. In this regard, at least, the interests of indigenous organisations seem to be in accordance with those of the governments of developing countries. When it comes to

---

68 Roy Ellen and Holly Harris, 'Introduction', in Roy Ellen, Peter Parkes and Alan Bicker (eds), *Indigenous Environmental Knowledge and its Transformations*, London and New York: Routledge, 2000, pp. 1–33, at pp. 2–5.

69 As opposed to traditional knowledge *lato sensu*, which includes traditional cultural expressions, see WIPO, IGC, Secretariat, 'Glossary of Key Terms Related to Intellectual Property and Traditional Cultural Expressions', (WIPO Doc. WIPO/GRTKF/IC/19/INF/7, 2011), at pp. 26–7 [hereinafter WIPO, 'TCE Glossary'].

70 Ibid.

71 See Blakeney, 'Protection of Traditional Knowledge', supra note 66, at p. 105.

implementation of the concepts, however, the approach is different. It is interesting to note that some governments of developing countries have adopted rules for the promotion and protection of traditional knowledge that have not necessarily respected the distinction between technical knowledge and artistic expressions, but often merged them in domestic legislation.[72] In the most recent WIPO deliberations the issue occasionally resurfaces, for example when experts from Guatemala and the Indian Council of South America (CISA) support the inclusion of 'sacred places' in the list of protected subject matter, while others preferred to speak of 'spiritual forms'.[73] The most recent Draft Article 1.1 developed by the IWG refers to the overlap by speaking of '"Traditional cultural expressions" … in which traditional culture and knowledge are embodied and have been passed on'.[74]

The legal working definitions are, however, also different from the anthropological and holistic definitions in two further aspects: first, they are not confined to orally transmitted knowledge only, but clearly include also knowledge transmitted in writing. Therefore, the traditional knowledge concept of WIPO is clearly much wider than the more locally confined and predominantly orally transmitted indigenous knowledge.[75] In accordance with the arguments presented by India and other Asian developing countries, it includes mainstream traditions that are widely used at the national level, such as Ayurvedic medicine or Yoga in India,[76] traditional Chinese medicine in China[77] or *jamu*

---

72 For examples of legislation merging traditional knowledge and traditional cultural expressions from the Philippines, India and Indonesia, see Christoph Antons, 'Traditional Knowledge, Biological Resources and Intellectual Property Rights in Asia: The Example of the Philippines' (2007) *Forum of International Development Studies*, 34, pp. 1–18; Prashant Reddy, 'The National Biodiversity Authority Invites Comments on Draft Amendments', *Spicy IP* (2 February 2010), available at http:spicyipindia.blogspot.com/2010/02/national-biodiversity-authority-invites.html; Antons, '*Sui Generis* Protection for Plant Varieties', supra note 39, at pp. 134–5; and Antons, 'Asian Borderlands', supra note 20.

73 See the comments of the Rapporteur Justin Hughes in WIPO, IGC, 'Draft Articles on the Protection of Traditional Cultural Expressions/Expressions of Folklore Prepared at IWG 1', (WIPO Doc. WIPO/GRTKF/IC/17/9, 2010), at pp. 2–3 [hereinafter WIPO, IGC, 'TCE Draft Articles. IWG 1']; for the latest version see WIPO, IGC, Secretariat, 'TCE Draft Articles. 2011', supra note 58, at p. 3.

74 See also the critical remarks made by the Delegation of Belgium fearing confusion with TK; WIPO, IGC, 'Draft Report', Seventeenth Session (WIPO Doc. WIPO/GRTKF/IC/17/12 Prov. 2, 2011), at p. 13 [hereinafter WIPO, IGC, 'Draft Report. Seventeenth Session'].

75 See the definition of 'indigenous knowledge' in WIPO, IGC, Secretariat, 'Glossary of Key Terms Related to Intellectual Property and Traditional Knowledge', Nineteenth Session (WIPO Doc. WIPO/GRTKF/IC/19/INF/8, 2011), Annex, at pp. 8–9.

76 Verma, supra note 32, at pp. 336–8.

77 Bryan Bachner, 'Back to the Future: Intellectual Property Rights and the Modernisation of Traditional Chinese Medicine', in Christopher Heath and Anselm Kamperman Sanders (eds), *New Frontiers of Intellectual Property Law: IP and Cultural Heritage, Geographical Indications, Enforcement and Overprotection*, Oxford and Portland, OR: Hart Publishing, 2005, pp. 1–36.

in Indonesia.[78] However, such written knowledge especially is often widely spread across borders and claims to it may lead to disputes.[79]

Secondly, the WIPO working definition identifies 'indigenous and local communities' as knowledge-holders, so these knowledge-holders do not necessarily have to be communities that have been identified as 'indigenous' in the sense of Canadian First Nations or Australian Aborigines. What it requires is that they live to some extent traditional lifestyles and that they pass on their knowledge from generation to generation. 'Local communities' are defined in the current glossary prepared for the negotiations in reference to the CBD as 'the human population in a distinct ecological area who depend directly on its biodiversity and ecosystem goods and services for all or part of their livelihood and who have developed or acquired traditional knowledge as a result of this dependence, including farmers, fisherfolk, pastoralists, forest dwellers and others'.[80] The knowledge (and the associated cultural expressions) is, therefore, no longer exclusive to marginalised indigenous communities, but moved towards the centre where it becomes the knowledge of mainstream communities and is represented and defended by the nation state. The definition of the knowledge-holders as the beneficiaries of international TK/TCE protection has been one of the most controversial issues during the WIPO negotiations and a more detailed discussion of it will follow in the subsequent section of this chapter. However, it appears that the wider concept of local communities derived from the context of the CBD works to the disadvantage of indigenous communities and their more specific claims regarding cultural expressions.

Another controversial issue regarding the subject matter of TCE protection is in how far the material must be 'authentic', 'genuine' or (the current wording of the Draft Principles) 'characteristic of a community's cultural and social identity and cultural heritage'. This discussion also re-appears under the eligibility criteria for beneficiaries of Article 2. While the 'characteristic' requirement had been criticised earlier as too burdensome, anthropologists and social scientists have also been critical of authenticity requirements more generally, because they too can become onerous for communities that have to fulfil the expectations of lawyers and administrators with regard to 'tradition' and 'traditional lifestyles'.[81] They have also pointed to the 'strategic essentialism' that can develop, when activists from or working on behalf of indigenous communities attempt to present a

---

[78] Christoph Antons and Rosy Antons-Sutanto, 'Traditional Medicine and Intellectual Property Rights: A Case Study of the Indonesian *jamu* Industry', in Christoph Antons (ed.), *Traditional Knowledge, Traditional Cultural Expressions and Intellectual Property Law in the Asia-Pacific Region*, Alphen aan den Rijn, Netherlands: Kluwer Law International, 2009, pp. 363–84.

[79] Antons, 'Asian Borderlands', supra note 20.

[80] WIPO, 'TCE Glossary', supra note 69, at pp. 16–17. For examples of wider definitions in national legislation that include families and farmers, see Antons, 'Asian Borderlands', supra note 20.

[81] For a critical perspective, see Sonia Smallacombe, 'On Display for its Aesthetic Beauty: How Western Institutions Fabricate Knowledge about Aboriginal Cultural Heritage', in Duncan Ivison, Paul Patton and Will Sanders (eds), *Political Theory and the Rights of Indigenous Peoples*, Cambridge: Cambridge University Press, 2000, pp. 152–62; Peter Sutton, *Native Title in Australia: An Ethnographic Perspective*, Cambridge: Cambridge University Press, 2003, at p. 22; and Jeffrey Sissons, *First Peoples: Indigenous Cultures and Their Futures*, London: Reaktion Books, 2005, at pp. 37–59.

unanimous picture of cultural identity to make it fit into categories of national or international law. This may lead to a representation of culture 'as a pre-existing given ... rather than as something creatively reworked during struggles to actualize rights'.[82] Representatives at the WIPO IGC have further asked questions as to who would determine what was characteristic and at which stage that would be done (see, for example, the comments by the French representative and the representative of the Saami Council).[83]

The IWG has tried to avoid the discussion about 'characteristic' or 'authentic/genuine' and initially proposed the following: 'Protection shall extend to any traditional cultural expression or expression of folklore which is the unique product of an Indigenous people or local community and belongs to that people or community as part of their cultural identity or heritage.' The proposal has been rightly criticised because of the difficulties it could create where TCEs are shared by several local communities.[84] For many forms of TCEs it is not only quite common, but even the norm that they are shared by several neighbouring communities that have influenced each other over centuries.[85] Comments on the Draft Principles in fact correctly acknowledge that TCEs do not have to be unique but are rather 'the products of cross-cultural exchange and influence and intra-cultural exchange, within one and the same people whose name or designation may vary on one side or another of a frontier'.[86] Perhaps in recognition of these difficulties the current draft Article 1.3 provides that the specific choice of terms should be determined at the national, sub-regional and regional levels. The term 'unique' further seems to be too close to the copyright concept of originality. This is not helpful, because the relative lack of originality of many TCEs is precisely the reason for the discussion of *sui generis* TCE laws. Similar objections can be raised against the requirement that the TCE 'belongs' to a people or community. In the latest version tabled at the 19th Session of the IGC, both terms have been bracketed and the more general terms 'indicative/characteristic product of a people or community' and 'used and developed by that people or community' have been introduced.[87]

---

82 Jane K. Cowan, Marie B. Dembour and Richard A. Wilson, 'Introduction', in Jane K. Cowan, Marie B. Dembour and Richard A. Wilson (eds), *Culture and Rights: Anthropological Perspectives*, Cambridge: Cambridge University Press, 2001, pp. 1–26, at pp. 10–11 and 19.

83 WIPO, IGC, Secretariat, 'Report', Fifteenth Session (WIPO Doc. WIPO/GRTKF/IC/15/7, 2010), at p. 34.

84 See the comments by Silke von Lewinski in WIPO, IGC, 'TCE Draft Articles. IWG 1', supra note 73, at p. 3.

85 For cross-cultural and cross-border influences due to trade, colonisation and warfare in Southeast Asia, see Anne Richter, *Arts and Crafts in Indonesia*, San Francisco: Chronicle Books, 1994; Rens Heringa and Harmen C. Veldhuisen, *Fabric of Enchantment: Batik from the North Coast of Java*, Los Angeles: Los Angeles County Museum of Art, 1996; and James C. Scott, *The Art of Not Being Governed: An Anarchist History of Upland Southeast Asia*, New Haven, MA and London: Yale University Press, 2009. See also the comments by the representative of the Tulalip Tribes in WIPO, IGC, 'Draft Report. Seventeenth Session', supra note 74, at p. 18.

86 WIPO, IGC, Secretariat, 'The Protection of Traditional Cultural Expressions/Expressions of Folklore: Revised Objectives and Principles', (WIPO Doc. WIPO/GRTKF/IC/17/4, 2010), Annex, at p. 9 [hereinafter WIPO, IGC, 'TCE Revised Objectives and Principles'].

87 WIPO, IGC, 'TCE Draft Articles. 2011', supra note 58, at p. 4. These changes were proposed by India during the 17th Session of the IGC, see WIPO, IGC, 'Draft Report. Seventeenth Session', supra note 74, at p. 14. See, however, on the same page, also the criticism of the US.

There is further still some confusion with regard to the role of individuals in TCE protection and the relationship of TCE protection to copyright and other conventional IPRs. Protected in Draft Article 1 of the Revised Objectives and Principles are 'the products of creative intellectual activity, including individual and communal activity'. In Article 1 of the IWG Draft, the reference to individuals has been deleted, but they are mentioned in Article 2 as potential beneficiaries and Article 1 refers to Article 2 for that matter. Many statements at the 17th Session of the IGC stressed the collective nature of the expressions.[88] In this view, individuals can benefit, therefore, only indirectly as members of their respective communities. The commentary on Draft Article 1 of the Revised Principles focuses on the control of the material by the community. It explains that the individual plays a central role in the development and recreation of TCEs, but to recognise a TCE it is not relevant whether it was made collectively or by an individual. The commentary continues to explain that:

> even a contemporary expression made by an individual ... can be protected as TCE/EoF, provided it is characteristic of a community's cultural and social identity and heritage and was made by the individual having the right or responsibility to do so in accordance with the customary law and practices of that community.[89]

This understanding of the individual's role throws up several urgent questions: what will happen to cultural expressions at the intersection of TCE and modern art, for example the cultural expressions of 'urban Aborigines' or of artists and artisans in Diaspora? The Delegation of the United States correctly pointed out that TCEs were only alive when carried in people.[90] The commentary provided by the IGC allows the conclusion that in practice only traditionally produced material would be covered, where production and motives are still strongly governed by customary laws. That may be realistic for some Aboriginal communities, where customary laws are still strong. However, it is a less realistic notion for many local communities in modernising developing countries, where customary laws coexist with many other modernising influences. 'Tribal arts' here often coexist with the 'court arts' of a feudal past and of the most powerful ethnic groups in the country and it is often this 'court art' that becomes symbolically prominent in the creation of a new national culture.[91] Cultural expressions that are of interest for the creation of 'national culture' are, therefore, equally if not more threatened, but perhaps no longer

---

88 See, for example, the statements made by the delegations of Egypt, Trinidad and Tobago and the representative of the Indian Council of South America (CISA); WIPO, IGC, 'Draft Report. Seventeenth Session', supra note 74, at pp. 12–13, 14 and 17. Different, however, the delegation of Canada, at p. 20 of the Draft Report.

89 WIPO, IGC, 'TCE Revised Objectives and Principles', supra note 86, at p. 14.

90 Ibid., at p. 16. See also Antons, 'TK and IPRs in Australia and Southeast Asia', supra note 53, at p. 49. On individual versus collective rights in heritage protection more generally, see also Gillman, supra note 5, at pp. 28–30. On ownership and possession with regard to indigenous artefacts, see Prott and O'Keefe, supra note 67, at pp. 314–15.

91 Erik Cohen, *The Commercialized Crafts of Thailand: Hill Tribes and Lowland Villages*, Honolulu: University of Hawai'i Press, 2000; Robyn J. Maxwell, *Textiles of Southeast Asia: Tradition, Trade and Transformation*, Hong Kong: Periplus Editions, 2003; and Antons, 'TCEs and their Significance for Development', supra note 8, at p. 294.

'traditional' enough to be protected as TCE. For Aboriginal societies, the current draft means that 'tribal' culture is favoured over urban minority cultures.[92] However, in cases of mixed urban and traditional styles, when exactly is a cultural expression traditional enough to qualify as TCE and who will decide this issue?

Further, if the focus on TCEs under customary law is retained, there is the possibility of overlap with copyright law in particular in countries with relatively low requirements regarding the standard of originality. The delegations of the Republic of Korea and of Norway raised this issue in commenting on Draft Article 1 of the Revised Objectives and Principles.[93] This overlap possibility with copyright exists in particular because Draft Article 3 mentions also adaptations as protected by a future TCE law. The delegations of Australia and Japan also raised the potential impact of such a broad control via *sui generis* TCE legislation on the public domain. To some extent, a currently bracketed Article 5.4(b) on exceptions and limitations proposes a solution. It attempts to secure a general exception for 'the creation of an original work of authorship by the beneficiaries or in association with them inspired/borrowed by traditional cultural expressions'.

4.2 The Beneficiaries of Protection and Their Role in the Management of Rights

It seems that the discussion about the beneficiaries proceeds somewhat differently in settler societies with large aboriginal minorities such as the USA, Canada, Australia and New Zealand, on the one hand, and in young post-colonial nation states in the developing world, on the other hand. Although there is much debate about the details, settler societies with a relatively young history of colonisation and with relatively distinct aboriginal cultures have felt a strong need to initiate a process of reconciliation, for which there is broad support in mainstream society. Aboriginal groups in such societies push for greater recognition of their rights and for a certain degree of self-determination. As pointed out by Christoph B. Graber,[94] the discussion in international human rights law on the status of Article 1 of the UN Convention on Civil and Political Rights,[95] and the distinction between 'peoples' in Article 1 and 'minorities' in Article 27 is of extreme importance here. Until recently, such debates were regarded as inappropriate in many developing countries in Asia, Africa and the Caribbean. With a few exceptions, the view here is usually that the entire population of the country is indigenous or that there are no identifiable indigenous people and that it would not be appropriate and not practical to differentiate among the population in accordance with time of arrival in a particular territory. The traditional communities producing TCEs are regarded as local (if relatively close to mainstream society) or as tribal (if living relatively isolated). This leads to a tendency to think of folkloristic expressions as 'national folklore' and as 'property of the nation'. The disregard of community interests is justified with the reasoning that local communities are so close

---

92 Smallacombe, supra note 81, at p. 155.

93 WIPO, IGC, 'TCE Revised Objectives and Principles', supra note 86, at p. 17.

94 Graber, 'Institutionalization of Creativity in Traditional Societies', supra note 6, at pp. 248–9. On the importance of this distinction more generally, see Robert Paine, 'Aboriginality, Multiculturalism and Liberal Rights Philosophy' (1999) *Ethnos,* 64 (3), pp. 325–49.

95 UN, International Covenant on Civil and Political Rights, 999 UNTS 171 and 1057 UNTS 407; 6 ILM 368 (adopted on 16 December 1966, entered into force 23 March 1976).

to mainstream society that they become integrated in the greater national context, whereas tribal communities are regarded as backward and in need of assimilation to mainstream society. In both cases, the rights of such communities are seen as not deserving any special protection.[96]

An international movement of indigenous peoples has recently started to change this state of affairs. In addition to formal international conventions, this international movement has also aimed at informal cooperation between groups and communities with similar problems. 'Indigenism', as this development has been termed,[97] goes back to the 1960s when indigenous Sami from Scandinavia began to stress similarities with North American Indians.[98] Cooperation intensified in the early 1970s, international conferences were organised and the World Council of Indigenous Peoples was established in 1975.[99] In 1982, the UN Working Group on Indigenous Populations within the UN Economic and Social Council was formed. The UN framework considerably extended the indigenous movement and widened the debate from the issue of indigenous people in settler states to self-determination and recognition of marginalised minorities more generally. The founders of the international movement of indigenous people were joined by ethnic communities from Asia and Africa.[100] Many of the groups that began to attend Working Group meetings came from countries in which 'indigenous peoples' were not officially recognised. The anthropologist Jeffrey Sissons criticised the fact that this led to the 'possibility for almost any people with a subsistence based culture to claim membership in international indigenous forums'.[101]

---

[96] For relevant government policies in Southeast Asia see the contributions in Christopher R. Duncan, *Civilizing the Margins: Southeast Asian Government Policies for the Development of Minorities*, Ithaca, NY and London: Cornell University Press, 2004; Prasit Leepreecha, Don McCaskill and Kwanchewan Buadaeng, *Challenging the Limits: Indigenous Peoples of the Mekong Region*, Chiang Mai: Mekong Press, 2008; and Geoffrey Benjamin, 'On Being Tribal in the Malay World', in Geoffrey Benjamin and Cynthia Chou (eds), *Tribal Communities in the Malay World: Historical, Cultural and Social Perspectives*, Singapore and Leiden: Institute of Southeast Asian Studies-International Institute for Asian Studies, 2003, pp. 7–76. See also the statements of the delegations of China, Egypt and Morocco in WIPO, IGC, 'Draft Report. Seventeenth Session', supra note 74, at pp. 22–3.

[97] Niezen, *The Origins of Indigenism*, supra note 42.

[98] Henry Minde, 'The Challenge of Indigenism: The Struggle for Sami Land Rights and Self-Government in Norway 1960–1990', in Svein Jentoft, Henry Minde and Ragnar Nilsen (eds), *Indigenous Peoples: Resource Management and Global Rights*, Delft: Eburon Academic Publishers, 2003, pp. 75–107, at p. 79; and Anna Lowenhaupt Tsing, 'Adat/Indigenous: Indigeneity in Motion', in Carol Gluck and Anna Lowenhaupt Tsing (eds), *Words in Motion: Toward a Global Lexicon,* Durham, NC and London: Duke University Press, 2009, pp. 40–66, at pp. 54–8.

[99] Sissons, supra note 81, at pp. 21–3; and Ken S. Coates, *A Global History of Indigenous Peoples*, Houndmills, Basingstoke and New York: Palgrave Macmillan, 2004, at pp. 1–15.

[100] See, for example, the conference on *Reclaiming Balance: Indigenous Peoples, Conflict Resolution and Sustainable Development*, held in Manila in 2000 with representatives from Africa, Asia, Latin and Central America, the Middle East, North America and the Pacific, in Victoria Tauli-Corpuz and Joji Cariño (eds), *Reclaiming Balance: Indigenous Peoples, Conflict Resolution & Sustainable Development*, Baguio City: Tebtebba Foundation, 2004.

[101] Sissons, supra note 81, at p. 17.

For many people, the adoption by the UN General Assembly of the Declaration on the Rights of Indigenous Peoples (UNDRIP) in September 2007 seemed to herald a new era.[102] However, if one reads the declarations made and statements given by various national representatives in explanation of their votes, it soon becomes clear that the old attitudes have not really changed. Bangladesh criticised the lack of a clear definition of 'indigenous people' and abstained from voting.[103] India voted in favour of UNDRIP, but provided its own definition, drawn from the earlier ILO conventions. Accordingly,

> indigenous rights pertained to peoples in independent countries who were regarded as indigenous on account of their descent from the populations which inhabited the country ... at the time of conquest or colonization or the establishment of present State boundaries and who ... retained some or all of their socio-economic, cultural, and political institutions.

Thus, this interpretation means again that the entire population of India with roots going back to pre-colonial times is indigenous. 'Indigenous' is, therefore, 'Indigenous Indian' as opposed to foreign elements introduced during colonial rule. The representative of Indonesia explained that 'given the fact that Indonesia's entire population at the time of colonization remained unchanged, the rights in the Declaration accorded exclusively to indigenous people and did not apply in the context of Indonesia'.[104]

In spite of the non-binding nature of UNDRIP, some analysts believe that there is reason for optimism and that some governments such as that of Indonesia are slowly changing their position.[105] The emergence of new representative organisations such as Indonesia's AMAN (Alliance of Indonesian Adat Communities)[106] seems to confirm this view. Once established, such organisations seek to confirm territory occupied by indigenous peoples under customary law but not recognised by the state via participatory mapping projects.[107] Arguments about cultural recognition and customary law thus may swiftly turn into debates about territory and land. This has the potential to come into conflict with the prerogatives of state planning for economic development and with government ministries responsible, for example, for forestry. Under the circumstances, it remains to be seen how far governments such as Indonesia are prepared to go in recognising rights and a degree of self-determination.

The attitude of governments towards questions of national unity, multiculturalism, aboriginality and the recognition of minority and/or indigenous rights is, therefore, a

---

102 UN, Declaration on the Rights of Indigenous Peoples (UNDRIP), GA Res. 61/295 (UN Doc. A/61/L.67 and Add.1) (adopted on 13 September 2007).

103 UN, Sixty-first General Assembly of the United Nations, 'General Assembly Adopts Declaration on Rights of Indigenous Peoples: "Major Step Forward" Towards Human Rights for All, Says President', 107th and 108th Meetings (UN Doc. GA/10612, 2007), at p. 11, available online at http://www.un.org/News/Press/docs/2007/ga10612.doc.htm.

104 Ibid., at pp. 12–13.

105 Gerard A. Persoon, '"Being Indigenous" in Indonesia and the Philippines', in Christoph Antons (ed.), *Traditional Knowledge, Traditional Cultural Expressions and Intellectual Property Law in the Asia-Pacific Region*, Alphen aan den Rijn, Netherlands: Kluwer Law International, 2009, pp. 195–216.

106 'Adat' is the commonly used term for customary law in Indonesia. For a detailed discussion see Lowenhaupt Tsing, supra note 98, at pp. 40–64.

107 Evi Mariani, 'Mapping Home and Hoping for Recognition', *Jakarta Post* (17 July 2010).

crucial factor in the discussion about potential beneficiaries of any form of TCE protection. Differences about national policy priorities in this regard can be expected between national governments concerned about national unity and a unified administration of rights and representatives of indigenous and local communities in favour of greater decentralisation and local powers for decision-making and resource allocation. These differences become clear if one examines the amendments suggested to the latest version of the Revised Objectives and Principles.[108] Article 2 of the draft defines the beneficiaries. While the original draft of the Article spoke simply of 'TCEs/EoF', the delegation of Morocco proposed to add the word 'national'. It reminded the IGC during the 16th Session of the term 'national' folklore and thought that there should also be 'national' TCEs.[109] Similar proposals focusing on cultural harmony and the nation came from Egypt and from Caribbean nations such as Barbados and Jamaica.[110] The 'national folklore' that played such a prominent part in the Tunis Model Copyright Law is, therefore, back on the agenda. Similarly, while the draft principles spoke of 'indigenous peoples and traditional and other cultural communities' as beneficiaries, Iran and Morocco proposed to add 'individual groups, families, tribes, nations' and 'the nation' respectively.[111] Indonesia in its comments also stressed the role of the government as facilitator of TCE/EoF protection and as beneficiary if TCE owners could not be identified.[112]

Discussions continue also regarding the eligibility criteria of the second part of Article 2 that beneficiaries must be entrusted with the custody, care and safeguarding of TCEs in accordance with their customary law and practices[113] and that TCEs/EoFs must be characteristic of the beneficiaries' cultural and social identity and cultural heritage.

The different views on the role of national authorities versus self-determination[114] are also visible from the streamlined and shortened version of the article that the IWG has drafted. In its first draft,[115] it provided two options: Option 1 listed 'indigenous peoples, local communities and cultural communities' as beneficiaries, whereas Option 2 was seeking to benefit generally 'peoples and communities' followed by the examples of 'indigenous peoples, local communities, cultural communities and/or nations'. There were also two options with regard to the laws and practices that are to govern the TCEs. Under Option 1, TCEs were entrusted or held simply in accordance with 'the relevant law and/or practices'. Under Option 2, the TCEs were held under 'their law and/or practices',

---

108 WIPO, IGC, 'TCE Revised Objectives and Principles', supra note 86, at p. 20.

109 WIPO, IGC, Secretariat, 'Draft Report', Sixteenth Session (WIPO Doc. WIPO/GRTKF/IC/16/8 Prov. 2, 2010), at pp. 36–7 [hereinafter WIPO, 'Draft Report. Sixteenth Session'].

110 Ibid., at p. 46; WIPO, IGC, 'Draft Report. Seventeenth Session', supra note 74, at pp. 13 and 17.

111 WIPO, IGC, 'TCE Revised Objectives and Principles', supra note 86, at p. 20.

112 Ibid., at p. 22.

113 WIPO, IGC, 'Draft Report. Seventeenth Session', supra note 74, at p. 19; WIPO, IGC, 'TCE Revised Objectives and Principles', supra note 86, at p. 23. On the difficulties of reviving customary laws, see Martin Chanock, 'Branding Identity and Copyrighting Culture: Orientation towards the Customary in Traditional Knowledge Discourse', in Christoph Antons (ed.), *Traditional Knowledge, Traditional Cultural Expressions and Intellectual Property Law in the Asia-Pacific Region*, Alphen aan den Rijn, Netherlands: Kluwer Law International, 2009, pp. 177–94.

114 Graber, 'Institutionalization of Creativity in Traditional Societies', supra note 6, at p. 239.

115 WIPO, IGC, 'TCE Draft Articles. IWG 1', supra note 73, at p. 5.

which would be a reference to forms of customary/local laws, in particular if the first option of beneficiaries (that does not mention 'nations') was chosen.

In a similar process as with the Draft Principles, this Draft Article 2 has meanwhile been amended during the 17th IGC session,[116] so that the first option in the first part now also includes 'nations' and (in brackets) 'individuals of those communities', whereas the second option has been enlarged by reference to 'individual groups and families and minorities'. The two alternatives in the second part have also been amended, so that it is now clear that 'law and/or practices' in the first option are 'the relevant national/domestic laws and/or practices'. In the second option, 'their laws and/or practices' is now wider and 'including customary law and community protocols', so the importance of customary law has been reduced. As in the discussion of the Draft Principles, the widening of the concept to include 'nations', 'families' and 'minorities' and 'national laws' was advocated by delegations from countries such as Indonesia, Iran, China, Egypt and Morocco.[117]

The same issues returned in Article 4 of the Revised Provisions on Management of Rights. Prior authorisation to use (which Australia would like to replace with 'to do acts within the rights of indigenous peoples') in the previous version was meant to come directly from the community concerned where the community so wishes or from an agency acting at the request, and on behalf of the community. Here, the delegation of Mexico proposed to replace the term 'community' with 'indigenous peoples and communities and each of the groups, families, tribes, nations, traditional and other communities or countries' and with 'indigenous people and community or the traditional and other cultural communities or the nations' respectively.[118] The streamlined IWG Draft Articles would here simply refer back to the definition of beneficiaries in Article 2.[119] However, it triggered further discussions in the 17th Session of the IGC with regard to the establishment of a national/competent authority responsible for the collection and distribution of benefits. Here again, delegations from countries such as Iran and Algeria were favouring national approaches, while representatives of indigenous organisations supported by some national delegations were in favour of decentralised approaches focusing on communities. The delegation of the EU and its Member States suggested supervision of the competent authority by WIPO, whereas the representative of Knowledge Ecology International (supported by the delegations of South Africa and the USA) proposed a more general obligation of transparency in the management of financial benefits.[120]

The issue is likely to remain controversial. Representatives of indigenous organisations have complained that they have no immediate input in the drafting process. They only participate as observers. While they are allowed to make contributions and proposals, they need to find the support of national delegations for their proposals, which otherwise will be dropped.[121] It is correct that some countries (such as Bolivia) have a strong representation of the indigenous population among the political elite.[122] Such countries, however, are

116 WIPO, IGC, 'Draft Report. Seventeenth Session', supra note 74, Annex II, at p. 5.
117 Ibid., at pp. 19–23.
118 WIPO, IGC, 'TCE Revised Objectives and Principles', supra note 86, at p. 35.
119 WIPO, 'Draft Report, Seventeenth Session', supra note 74, Annex II, at p. 10.
120 Ibid., at pp. 28–30.
121 See the clarification of the Chair, ibid., at p. 12.
122 Graber, 'Institutionalization of Creativity in Traditional Societies', supra note 6, at p. 245.

the exception. If the wider version of the terminology, including nations, families and so on, prevails, the discussion will continue at the national level, in particular in young post-colonial nation states that provide only very limited recognition for indigenous or local community rights. If the gap between national and local interests is too wide, there is a chance that the protection remains unimplemented or that indigenous and/or local communities disengage, because they find that there is too little to gain from the system.[123]

Similarly as with the notion of 'unique' TCEs 'belonging' to communities, it is equally important for the identification of beneficiaries to recall the relatively permissive boundaries of ethnic communities and their territories in particular in many developing countries. Communities here frequently live on both sides of borders that were drawn by colonial powers or post-colonial nation states without their involvement.[124] Thus, the 'relevant laws and/or practices' of the WIPO IWG may well be the laws of several countries or provinces. As a result, there have recently been a number of cross-border disputes about cultural heritage and IP across the borders of Southeast Asian countries such as Indonesia and Malaysia.[125] The concept of cultural property that is now frequently used by communities and by nation states for claims based on tradition and identity has its origin in UNESCO conventions, such as the UNESCO Convention on the Means of Prohibiting and Preventing the Illicit Import, Export and Transfer of Ownership of Cultural Property. However, since the drafting of this Convention in 1970, the concept has expanded from the repatriation of tangible cultural objects to include intangible subject matter, as is evidenced by the UNESCO Convention for the Safeguarding of the Intangible Cultural Heritage of 2003.[126] It has further been expanded from a concept relevant for State Parties of the Convention to include first nations and indigenous communities.[127]

---

123 See Christoph B. Graber, 'Stimulating Trade and Development of Indigenous Cultural Heritage by Means of International Law: Issues of Legitimacy and Method', in this volume; and Correa, 'Access to Knowledge', supra note 32, at p. 243. See also Lorraine V. Aragon and James Leach, 'Arts and Owners: Intellectual Property Law and the Politics of Scale in Indonesian Arts' (2008) *American Ethnologist*, 35 (4), pp. 607–31, at p. 617, who found during research in Indonesia that with regard to draft laws for the protection of TK/TCEs '[f]ew arts practitioners from the archipelago's over 350 ethnolinguistic groups have heard about the new laws. Even fewer expressed desires for increased state regulation.'

124 Thongchai Winichakul, *Siam Mapped – A History of the Geo-Body of a Nation*, Honolulu: University of Hawai'i Press, 1994; Grant Evans, *A Short History of Laos: The Land In Between*, Chiang Mai: Silkworm Books, 2002; and Søren Ivarsson, *Creating Laos: The Making of a Lao Space Between Indochina and Siam, 1860–1945*, Copenhagen: NIAS Press, 2008.

125 Fitzpatrick, supra note 21; 'Malaysia Urges Indonesia to Drop Plans to Sue over Folk Song', supra note 21; Antons, 'Traditional Cultural Expression', supra note 16, at p. 54; Antons, 'The International Debate about Traditional Knowledge', supra note 32, at pp. 113–14; Antons, 'Traditional Knowledge in Asia: Global Agendas, Local Subjects', supra note 43, at p. 74; and Antons and Antons-Sutanto, supra note 78, at pp. 382–3.

126 UNESCO, Convention for the Safeguarding of the Intangible Cultural Heritage, 2368 UNTS 1 (adopted on 17 October 2003, entered into force 20 April 2006). See Logan et al., supra note 34, at p. 6; and Rosemary J. Coombe with Joseph F. Turcotte, 'Indigenous Cultural Heritage in Development and Trade: Perspectives from the Dynamics of Cultural Heritage Law and Policy', in this volume.

127 Ana Filipa Vrdoljak, *International Law, Museums and the Return of Cultural Objects*, Cambridge: Cambridge University Press, 2008, at pp. 206–11.

This increases the likelihood of conflicts between communities and across borders, because different from the tangible national treasures of previous heritage protection, the current intangible cultural heritage including knowledge and skills can be held simultaneously by many people in different places and on different sides of borders. Governments that have mixed intellectual and cultural property introduce the state focus of the previous heritage concept into IP laws such as copyright and they put the national government in charge of such rights.[128] With cultural/IP then subject to national regulation, it has the potential to generate disputes between neighbouring nation states and communities with identical claims to culture.

As a way forward, Graber has suggested that in cases of such disputes a World Trade Organization (WTO) Commission should verify and formally adopt decisions about TCEs made at community level.[129] Easier to establish may be an agency at regional level, for example in the context of ASEAN, SAARC, Mercosur, ARIPO or OAPI. At least, this will ensure that regional cross-border issues about similar forms of heritage and cultural property are addressed first, before the discussion moves to the international level. Success at this level might be greater, although indigenous groups will have to ensure representation in such a regional model.

4.3 The Scope of Protection and Exceptions/Limitations

Yet another still contentious area is the scope of protection and the extent to which exceptions and limitations should apply. The scope of protection is regulated in Draft Article 3 of the Revised Principles and Objectives in a layered manner.[130] It gives holders of registered TCEs 'of particular value or significance' the right to prevent forms of use that may affect their economic and moral rights, to prevent the use of signs, names and symbols for commercial purposes and as a kind of trade mark and to prevent the illegitimate fixation, representation, publication, communication or use of TCEs. For non-registered TCEs, it seeks to guarantee moral rights such as attribution and prevention of passing off and some form of remuneration or benefit-sharing, where the use is for 'gainful intent'. Finally, for secret TCEs, Draft Article 3 seeks to guarantee prevention of disclosure.

The representatives of indigenous organisations such as the Sami Council have criticised that Draft Article 3 is worded in the negative instead of spelling out clearly the property rights of indigenous peoples as right holders. They are also concerned about the registration/notification requirements that may well be impossible to observe for spiritual or cultural reasons and also because of concerns about unauthorised use.[131] Finally, they take the view that benefit-sharing should not only apply where there was 'gainful

---

[128] Antons, 'Asian Borderlands', supra note 20; and Antons, 'Traditional Cultural Expression', supra note 16.

[129] Graber, 'Institutionalization of Creativity in Traditional Societies', supra note 6, at pp. 251–2.

[130] WIPO, IGC, 'TCE Revised Objectives and Principles', supra note 86, at pp. 24–8.

[131] WIPO, 'Draft Report. Sixteenth Session', supra note 109, at p. 35. See also Graber, 'Institutionalization of Creativity in Traditional Societies', supra note 6, at p. 239.

intent'.[132] The delegation of New Zealand agreed and proposed to consider alternatives to registration or registration systems that minimise risks. The delegation of Australia, on the other hand, expressed concern about the prohibition on the acquisition of IPRs over TCEs, which should actually still remain an option for individual indigenous creators. It asked whether only the acquisition in unfair circumstances would be covered. It also stressed the need to examine the impact on both indigenous communities and the public domain of state claims to non-attributed TCEs. The USA was concerned about coverage of derivative works/adaptations and its impact on the public domain and freedom of expression of both people within indigenous/local communities and others. The Delegation of India thought that there was a need to clearly recognise collective ownership and not just rights to prohibit and that mere equitable remuneration was inappropriate in view of the exclusive rights of the community, which should also have the right to assign a TCE rather than merely to give free, prior and informed consent.[133]

The current streamlined version of Draft Article 3 by the IWG no longer mentions registration. It provides three alternatives. In the first alternative, secret TCEs are relatively uncontroversial and should receive the strongest protection against unauthorised fixation, disclosure, use or other exploitation. Nevertheless, in the course of the 17th Session of the IGC, this article again generated lengthy discussions about the beneficiaries. Some delegations requested again that 'nation' be added to indigenous, local and cultural communities, whereas others wondered how nations could possibly hold secret TCEs or the moral rights foreseen in Article C of the provision.[134] The article now has a bracketed paragraph that beneficiaries shall obtain only equitable remuneration or benefit-sharing where a good faith/proven effort was made to locate them. Lack of acknowledgment of traditional sources in the view of some delegations should be excused where omission is dictated by the manner of use. The remaining two alternatives are streamlined versions of these principles.

The current Draft Article 5 on exceptions and limitations provides a copyright-style list of exceptions, which has in fact become longer in comparison with the Model Provisions. Apart from a relatively uncontroversial subsection 1 that is meant to ensure that communities themselves are not restricted in using their material, there was discussion at the 17th Session of the IGC about a proposal by the USA, which made the exceptions subject to national law and introduced the three-step test for them.[135] The proposal was opposed as too broad by some national delegations and representatives of indigenous organisations. It received qualified support from EU Member States, who also asked for a link between national/domestic legislation, on the one hand, and the Berne Convention and WIPO Copyright Treaty,[136] on the other hand, in the parallel subsection 2. The delegation of New Zealand referred to difficulties experienced with the implementation of the three-step test in this context and proposed an alternative subsection 2 that focused on exceptions and

132 WIPO, 'Draft Report. Sixteenth Session', supra note 109, at p. 42.
133 Ibid., at pp. 38–42.
134 WIPO, IGC, 'Draft Report. Seventeenth Session', supra note 74, at pp. 23–8.
135 Ibid., at pp. 30–33.
136 WIPO Copyright Treaty, 36 ILM 65 (adopted on 20 December 1996, entered into force 6 March 2002).

limitations being compatible with fair practice and not being offensive and providing acknowledgment of indigenous/local communities where possible.

5. CONCLUSIONS

The protection of TCEs/EoF via the principles of IP law has been on the negotiation agenda of international organisations such as UNESCO and WIPO for 35 years. Much progress has been made in understanding the nature of the material, the interests of the beneficiaries and the difficulties involved in protecting it. In the early days of the debate, governments in the developing world tended to see 'national folklore' as yet another potential element of the national development plans popular at the time. The various communities maintaining the cultural heritage were rarely mentioned. The potential differences between indigenous/local individual creators and their communities were not paid attention to, because a paternalistic state was taking care of it all anyway. Copyright held or exercised by the national government or its agencies was the preferred mode of protection. In some countries, the national approach to copyright in folklore was further mixed with the cultural property principles drawn from the UNESCO Convention on the Means of Prohibiting and Preventing the Illicit Import, Export and Transfer of Ownership of Cultural Property, concluded in 1970. Mostly, the copyright approach to folklore seems not to have worked and provisions have often remained unimplemented or were not used by relevant communities.

The 1982 UNESCO/WIPO Model Provisions were a step forward, because they considered a *sui generis* approach and they acknowledged the role of individuals and communities producing the material. For the first time, they also foresaw the potential for communities to decide about appropriate forms of use by themselves rather than leave the decision to a 'competent authority' of the nation state. By the early 1990s, however, it was clear that none of these previous models had been particularly successful and that the Model Provisions had failed to gain the support of national governments.[137] In this situation, the TCE debate was revived, however, in the broader context of the debate about TK related to biodiversity, medicine and agriculture, which had its roots in the Convention on Biological Diversity. Because of this context, the focus on indigenous and local communities became now more widely accepted and it coincided with an increasingly strong international indigenous movement. The new context also brought the concept of 'traditional knowledge' as part of a much broader understanding of cultural heritage, of which TCEs are merely a sub-part. This holistic view of the subject matter is often advocated by human rights, environmental and cultural heritage lawyers, social scientists and indigenous representatives, but also by some governments.[138]

The WIPO IGC started with such a wide definition of the subject matter, but soon moved back to a more IP-inspired approach that distinguished again between TK and TCEs and the separate subset of GRs. After much preparatory work and collection of information, the IGC has now entered 'text-based negotiations' supported by IWGs. TCEs are regarded

137 Halewood, supra note 10, at p. 968.

138 Graber, 'Institutionalization of Creativity in Traditional Societies', supra note 6, at p. 20, footnote 95.

as the 'most mature' subject matter. Since the economic interests and controversies about TCEs are comparatively limited, it may indeed be the best hope for the conclusion of a treaty. Obstacles remain, however. Many developed countries are still opposed to the conclusion of a binding treaty and they want further clarification of the concepts. This concerns, for example, the definition of the subject matter. While parties seem to have largely settled the debate about the TK/TCE divide, discussion continues about the question of how to define 'authenticity' and the role of individual creators vis-à-vis their communities.

Perhaps the most difficult issue is the division of roles between communities and state agencies with regard to the management of rights. Many governments in the developing world have difficulties in recognising the concept of 'indigenous peoples', which they regard as divisive. Questions about the recognition of local or indigenous communities are difficult political questions about decentralisation, self-determination, national unity and control over resources. Although many countries have signed UNDRIP, they have done this with many reservations. In view of the 'national folklore' proposals that some delegations have made during the IGC deliberations, it is unlikely that a treaty with a community-focused definition of beneficiaries only will be concluded. Presumably, it will leave the choice to individual countries and many will opt for a centralised administration of TCEs. This could lead to conflicts at the regional and international level between states that claim the rights to TCEs of communities that live in fact on both sides of borders. The fusion of cultural property concepts and IP laws leads to exaggerated claims in some developing countries that import the 'cultural patrimony' approach of cultural heritage laws into IP. It remains important to bear in mind the relatively recent mapping of national territories in much of the developing world and that the strict enforcement of national and territorial borders is a recent phenomenon that is often not in accordance with cultural boundaries. Proposals for a supervisory role of the WTO or other international organisations may be difficult to implement, because of the entrenched interests of national governments, on the one hand, and indigenous and local communities, on the other hand. TCEs are only a relatively minor part of the negotiation package of TK/TCE/GR and this diminishes the prospect of achieving solutions that strongly differ from those advocated for TK and GR. Some form of oversight at the regional level may have better prospects to succeed here.

Finally, the lessons from the introduction of IP laws in the developing world over the past few decades must also be observed. Registration requirements, as useful as they may be in identifying beneficiaries, create city-centred bureaucracies that may no longer be alien for local businesses, but that are far removed from the sphere of local and rural communities. Geographical indications and certification marks face similar problems but rural communities may overcome these in a collective manner, in which case such 'branding' of their TCEs can prove a very useful and simple manner of using the IP system. Equally, registration systems by regional organisations may be able to provide greater reliability than national systems and help to mitigate regional and international disputes over TCEs.

In summary, the thinking about IP of TCEs has come a long way since the beginning of the debate in the 1960s. Whatever the outcome of the current negotiations, the perhaps biggest achievement at this stage is the enhanced respect and sensitivity for this material and its cultural context that in practical terms is slowly changing the attitudes of buyers and users of TCEs. The indigenous struggle to gain greater recognition in nation-based solutions to the TCE issue from an economic perspective, however, is likely to continue for the foreseeable future. From the viewpoint of the governments of many developing countries, where traditions are still very much alive, it is appropriate that the international debate has been extended to include TK/TCEs used at the national level and by mainstream communities. From the point of view of many indigenous representatives, however, this wider understanding of the subject matter and the beneficiaries works to the disadvantage of their specific concerns with regard to securing the survival of their TCEs and the benefits from their use.

7. International trade in indigenous cultural heritage: an IP practitioners' perspective

Martin Girsberger and Benny Müller

1. INTRODUCTION

Indigenous cultural heritage (ICH) – which includes moveable and immoveable cultural property, traditional knowledge (TK) and traditional cultural expressions (TCEs) – has been an important topic at the international level for a number of years. ICH and its sub-elements have been discussed in different international fora, each with its own focus and addressing different aspects of ICH. These fora include the United Nations Educational, Scientific and Cultural Organization (UNESCO), the World Trade Organization (WTO), the World Intellectual Property Organization (WIPO), the Convention on Biological Diversity (CBD), the Food and Agriculture Organization (FAO), and various human rights bodies. Participating in these discussions are stakeholders with greatly diverging views and interests, namely developed and developing countries, indigenous peoples, scientists, artists, private industry, non-governmental organisations (NGOs) and the public at large.

Resolving the issues related to ICH at the international, national and sub-national levels requires answers to numerous and complex legal, social, economic and scientific questions. Furthermore, these issues may be highly controversial from a political point of view, as they relate, among other things, to the North–South relationship and the treatment of minorities by the dominant power within a state. While many issues remain unresolved, these discussions resulted in different forms of international instruments, including legally binding agreements, United Nations (UN) resolutions and conference declarations.

When looking at 'the bigger picture', one can find numerous issues that are at the base of the discussions on ICH. These include:

- the destruction of the environment in general and the habitat of indigenous peoples in particular, and the continued loss of biological diversity;
- the loss of TK and TCEs and the apparent need for their improved safeguarding, conservation and protection. In this regard, it is crucial to mention the right of indigenous peoples 'to maintain, control, protect and develop their cultural heritage, traditional knowledge and traditional cultural expressions, as well as the manifestations of their sciences, technologies and cultures, including human and

genetic resources, seeds, medicines, knowledge of the properties of fauna and flora, oral traditions, literatures, designs, sports and traditional games and visual and performing arts',[1] and 'the right to maintain, control, protect and develop their intellectual property over such cultural heritage, traditional knowledge, and traditional cultural expressions';[2]

- the call for an increased recognition and protection of the rights of indigenous peoples more generally, including the right to self-determination;
- the globalisation of all facets of life; and
- issues related to trade, intellectual property rights (IPRs), and the public domain.

The international debate addresses the interlinkage between trade in ICH and IPRs under the clusters TK and TCEs. Therefore, this chapter focuses on the international efforts to protect TK and TCEs by existing or currently discussed measures in the IP system. Of primary importance in this regard are the negotiations in the Intergovernmental Committee on Intellectual Property and Genetic Resources, Traditional Knowledge and Folklore (IGC) of WIPO regarding one or more international legal instruments on the protection of TK and TCEs, and, to a lesser extent, the negotiations in the WTO on paragraph 19 of the Doha Declaration. The chapter also describes the funding of the participation of indigenous representatives in the negotiations of the IGC through the WIPO Voluntary Fund. Moreover, the chapter will comment on the 'procedural approach to interfacing global law and local traditions'[3] from an international intellectual property perspective.

2. TERMINOLOGY

2.1 Indigenous Cultural Heritage, Traditional Knowledge and Traditional Cultural Expressions

2.1.1 General

In the context of the topic of this chapter, different terms and concepts are used. Besides ICH, these include traditional, elders' and indigenous knowledge; and traditional cultural expressions, folklore and cultural property.

When comparing the terminology employed, it becomes apparent that the concepts and definitions are not used uniformly. For example, this holds true for the term ICH:

---

[1] UN, Declaration on the Rights of Indigenous Peoples (UNDRIP), GA Res. 61/295 (UN Doc. A/61/L.67 and Add.1) (adopted on 13 September 2007), Article 31.1.

[2] Ibid.

[3] As suggested in Christoph B. Graber, 'Institutionalization of Creativity in Traditional Societies and in International Trade Law', in Shubha Ghosh and Robin P. Malloy (eds), *Creativity, Law and Entrepreneurship*, Cheltenham, UK and Northampton, MA: Edward Elgar, 2010, pp. 234–63.

Article 31.1 of the United Nations Declaration on the Rights of Indigenous Peoples (UNDRIP)[4] seems to view 'ICH', 'TK' and 'TCEs' as three separate values, whereas Article 2.1 of the UNESCO Convention for the Safeguarding of the Intangible Cultural Heritage (CSICH)[5] and the definition of ICH advanced by Erica-Irene Daes[6] seem to view TK and TCEs as two components of ICH. It becomes easily apparent that the lack of uniform terminology does not aid the discussions on ICH.

For the purposes of this chapter, the three key terms – ICH, TK and TCEs – are used as follows.[7]

2.1.2 Indigenous cultural heritage (ICH)

With regard to the term ICH, we adopt the following broad definition:

> The heritage of indigenous peoples is comprised of all objects, sites and knowledge the nature or use of which has been transmitted from generation to generation, and which is regarded as pertaining to a particular people or its territory. The heritage of an indigenous people also includes objects, knowledge and literary or artistic works which may be created in the future based upon its heritage.
>
> The heritage of indigenous peoples includes all moveable cultural property as defined by the relevant conventions of UNESCO; all kinds of literary and artistic works such as music, dance, song, ceremonies, symbols and designs, narratives and poetry; all kinds of scientific, agricultural, technical and ecological knowledge, including cultigens, medicines and the rational use of flora and fauna; human remains; immoveable cultural property such as sacred sites, sites of historical significance, and burials; and documentation of indigenous peoples' heritage on film, photographs, videotape, or audiotape.
>
> Every element of an indigenous peoples' heritage has traditional owners, which may be the whole people, a particular family or clan, an association or society, or individuals who have been

---

4 UNDRIP, Article 31.1 refers to 'cultural heritage, traditional knowledge and traditional cultural expressions'.

5 UNESCO, Convention for the Safeguarding of the Intangible Cultural Heritage, 2368 UNTS 1 (adopted on 17 October 2003, entered into force 20 April 2006), Article 2.1 defines 'intangible cultural heritage' as

> 'the practices, representations, expressions, knowledge, skills – as well as the instruments, objects, artefacts and cultural spaces associated therewith – that communities, groups and, in some cases, individuals recognize as part of their cultural heritage. This intangible cultural heritage, transmitted from generation to generation, is constantly recreated by communities and groups in response to their environment, their interaction with nature and their history, and provides them with a sense of identity and continuity, thus promoting respect for cultural diversity and human creativity. For the purposes of this Convention, consideration will be given solely to such intangible cultural heritage as is compatible with existing international human rights instruments, as well as with the requirements of mutual respect among communities, groups and individuals, and of sustainable development.'

6 Below, at section 2.1.2.

7 For further discussion on the meaning of the terms, see Christoph Antons, 'Intellectual Property Rights in Indigenous Cultural Heritage: Basic Concepts and Continuing Controversies', in this volume.

> specially taught or initiated to be its custodians. The traditional owners of heritage must be determined in accordance with indigenous peoples' own customs, laws and practices.[8]

With this broad understanding, ICH covers TK and TCEs.

2.1.3 Traditional knowledge (TK)

There is no internationally agreed definition of the term TK. Article 1 of the current WIPO IGC draft substantive provisions on the protection of TK contains two options.[9]

Besides the lack of an internationally agreed definition of 'TK', the issue of terminology is further complicated by the following factors: in some cases, a distinction is made between almost identical or at least closely related forms of TK. It is, thus, rather a difference in terminology than substance, that is, different terms are used to designate the same or at least similar forms of TK. In other cases, terms used to designate differing forms of TK are at the same time used interchangeably to designate one and the same form of TK. This confusion in the use of terminology applies to terms such as 'indigenous knowledge', 'traditional indigenous knowledge', 'elders' knowledge', 'local knowledge' and 'traditional ecological knowledge'. To worsen matters, folklore, also termed TCEs, is in some cases also considered to be a form of TK.

---

[8] Erica-Irene Daes (Special Rapporteur of the UN Sub-Commission on Prevention of Discrimination and Protection of Minorities and Chairperson of the Working Group on Indigenous Populations), 'Discrimination Against Indigenous Peoples, Protection of the Heritage of Indigenous People', (UN Doc. E/CN.4/Sub.2/1995/26, 1995), at p. 10, paras 11–13; in conformity with the Sub-Commission on Prevention of Discrimination and Protection of Minorities, 'Cultural and Intellectual Property of Indigenous Peoples', Res. 1993/44, 35th Meeting (1993); reported in its Report of the 45th Session (UN Doc. E/CN.4/Sub.2/1993/45, 1993); and UN Commission on Human Rights, 'Cultural and Intellectual Property of Indigenous Peoples', Decision 1994/105 (UN Doc. E/CN.4/DEC/1994/105, 1994).

[9] 'Draft Articles on Traditional Knowledge as Prepared at IGC 19', in WIPO, General Assembly (GA), 'Matters Concerning the Intergovernmental Committee on Intellectual Property and Genetic Resources, Traditional Knowledge and Folklore (IGC)', Fortieth (20th Ordinary) Session (WIPO Doc. WO/GA/40/7, 2011), Annex B, at p. 6 [hereinafter WIPO, 'TK Draft Articles']. Option 1: 'For the purposes of this instrument, the term "traditional knowledge" refers to the know-how, skills, innovations, practices, teachings and learning, resulting from intellectual activity and developed within a traditional context.'

> Option 2: 'Traditional knowledge is knowledge that is dynamic and evolving, resulting from intellectual activities which is passed on from generation to generation and includes but is not limited to know-how, skills, innovations, practices, processes and learning and teaching, that subsist in codified, oral or other forms of knowledge systems. Traditional knowledge also includes knowledge that is associated with biodiversity, traditional lifestyles and natural resources.'

It should be noted that, according to Article 1.2 of the current TK draft provisions, not all TK would enjoy protection under this WIPO instrument; it has to fulfil additional 'criteria for eligibility'.

2.1.4 Traditional cultural expressions (TCEs)

Parallel to TK, there exists no internationally agreed definition of the term TCEs and the WIPO IGC is currently considering two different options.[10]

It may be of interest to point out that, at the outset of its work, the IGC referred to 'folklore', which was later changed to 'traditional cultural expressions'/'expressions of folklore'. This change in terminology was made because the term 'folklore' has been criticised by some as having the negative connotation of 'being associated with the creations of lower or superseded civilizations'.[11] However, no change in subject matter or content was intended. Therefore, the terms 'traditional cultural expressions' and 'expressions of folklore' are to be understood as synonymous in the IGC context.

2.2 Indigenous Peoples

2.2.1 General concept

There is no international agreement on the term 'indigenous peoples', or even on the need for a clear-cut definition. Generally, indigenous communities, peoples and nations are understood as:

> those which having a historical continuity with pre-invasion and pre-colonial societies that developed on their territories, consider themselves distinct from other sectors of societies now prevailing in those territories, or parts of them. They form at present non-dominant sectors of society and are determined to preserve, develop, and transmit to future generations their ancestral territories, and their ethnic identity, as the basis of their continued existence as peoples, in accordance with their own cultural patterns, social institutions and legal systems.[12]

---

[10] 'Draft Articles on Traditional Cultural Expressions as Prepared at IGC 19', in WIPO, GA, 'Matters Concerning the Intergovernmental Committee on Intellectual Property and Genetic Resources, Traditional Knowledge and Folklore (IGC)', Fortieth (20th Ordinary) Session (WIPO Doc. WO/GA/40/7, 2011), Annex A, at p. 4 [hereinafter WIPO, 'TCE Draft Articles']. Option 1: 'Traditional cultural expressions are any form of artistic expression, tangible or intangible, in which traditional culture [and knowledge] are embodied including, but not limited to: (a) phonetic or verbal expressions; (b) musical or sound expressions; (c) expressions by action; and (d) tangible expressions of art.' Option 2: 'Traditional cultural expressions are any form of expressions, tangible or intangible, or a combination thereof, which are indicative of traditional culture and knowledge and have been passed on from generation to generation, including, but not limited to: (a) phonetic or verbal expressions, such as stories, epics, legends, poetry, riddles and other narratives; words, signs, names, and symbols; (b) musical or sound expressions, such as songs, rhythms, and instrumental music, the sounds which are the expression of rituals; (c) expressions by action, such as dances, plays, ceremonies, rituals, rituals in sacred places and peregrinations, traditional sports and games, puppet performances, and other performances, whether fixed or unfixed; and (d) tangible expressions, such as material expressions of art, handicrafts, works of mas, architecture, and tangible spiritual forms, and sacred places.' Following common practice of international negotiations, text between square brackets means that the language is only proposed and has not been agreed. According to Article 1.2 of the current TCEs draft provisions, protection under this WIPO instrument only extends to TCEs that meet additional eligibility criteria.

[11] Michael Blakeney, 'The Protection of Traditional Knowledge Under Intellectual Property Law' (2000) *European Intellectual Property Review*, 22, pp. 251–61, at p. 251.

[12] José R. Martinez Cobo (Special Rapporteur of the Sub-Commission on Prevention of Discrimination and Protection of Minorities), 'Study of the Problem of Discrimination Against

A broader, but at the same time more precise, working definition establishes four criteria:

(a) Priority in time, with respect to the occupation and use of a specific territory;

(b) The voluntary perpetuation of cultural distinctiveness, which may include the aspects of language, social organization, religion and spiritual values, modes of production, laws and institutions;

(c) Self-identification, as well as recognition by other groups, or by State authorities, as a distinct collectivity; and

(d) An experience of subjugation, marginalization, dispossession, exclusion or discrimination, whether or not these conditions persist.[13]

2.2.2 Terminology in intellectual property instruments

No international instrument on intellectual property contains a definition of 'indigenous peoples' or a related/similar term. This notwithstanding, the terms and definitions mentioned in the following instruments are of interest to the issue of this chapter:

- In the current WIPO IGC draft substantive provisions, both Article 2 on the protection of TK and Article 2 on the protection of TCEs contain different options with regard to 'beneficiaries of protection'. In the ongoing negotiations, a large number of states and indigenous observers argue that only 'indigenous peoples and local communities' or 'indigenous and local communities' should benefit from the protection of TK/TCEs, while others want to include additional beneficiaries such as 'traditional communities', 'cultural communities', 'nations', 'families' or 'individuals'.[14]
- Article 2(a) of the WIPO Performances and Phonograms Treaty (WPPT)[15] defines the term 'performers' as meaning 'actors, singers, musicians, dancers, and other persons who act, sing, deliver, declaim, play in, interpret, or otherwise perform literary or artistic works or expressions of folklore'.

Indigenous Populations. Conclusions, Proposals and Recommendations', (UN Doc. E/CN.4/Sub.2/1986/7/Add.4, 1987), at para. 379.

[13] Erica-Irene A. Daes (Chairperson-Rapporteur of the UN Economic and Social Council, Commission on Human Rights, Sub-Commission on Prevention of Discrimination and Protection of Minorities, Working Group on Indigenous Populations), 'Standard-Setting Activities: Evolution of Standards Concerning the Rights of Indigenous People. Working Paper on the Concept of "Indigenous People"', Fourteenth Session (UN Doc. E/CN.4/Sub.2/AC.4/1996/2, 1996), at para. 69.

[14] WIPO, 'TCE Draft Articles', supra note 10, at p. 7; and WIPO, 'TK Draft Articles', supra note 9, at p. 9.

[15] WIPO Performances and Phonograms Treaty (WPPT), 2186 UNTS 203; 36 ILM 76 (adopted on 20 December 1996, entered into force 20 May 2002).

3. TO WHAT EXTENT CAN IP LAW PROTECT INDIGENOUS TCEs, TK AND/OR CULTURAL PROPERTY?

3.1 General

There are different meanings attached to the relationship between the protection of ICH and the intellectual property system. Using the example of handicrafts, the question can be if there is or if there should be an intellectual property protection for a traditional indigenous motif as such; or if an individual creator of a contemporary adaptation of a traditional motif is or should be entitled to intellectual property protection; or if it is or should be possible to oppose the granting of intellectual property rights to an individual creator on the grounds that the work has been inspired by an ICH.

Frequently, a differentiation is made between defensive and positive protection. The former refers to legal measures to prevent the acquisition of intellectual property rights over ICH or adaptations – at least the acquisition by parties other than the traditional holders. The latter means legal measures to ensure that traditional holders may protect their ICH by (conventional or *sui generis*) intellectual property rights.

Different legal measures are available to protect TK and TCEs. As intellectual property rights protect intellectual assets, they are frequently mentioned as a measure when analysing the positive protection of TK and TCEs. This can take the form of existing intellectual property rights such as patents, geographical indications, trade marks and designs, or newly established *sui generis* intellectual property rights, that is, new forms of intellectual property rights specifically designed to protect TK and TCEs.

3.2 Arguments in Favour of Protecting TK and TCEs by Intellectual Property Rights

The following arguments speak in favour of protecting TK and TCEs by intellectual property rights:

The intellectual property rights system has been a well-functioning system for the protection of intangible assets for decades – even if the degree and the extent of afforded protection are sometimes subject to criticism. Thus, considerable experience and expertise exist regarding the application and enforcement of these rights. Most states have established at least a minimal system of intellectual property at the national level and put the necessary rules, procedures and authorities in place. This also holds true for the regional and international level, where numerous fora and conventions on intellectual property exist. The large majority of states – 184 – are Members of WIPO,[16] a specialised agency of the United Nations, which administers 24 treaties concerning the protection of intellectual property, the global protection system and classification,[17] and 153 states are also Members of the WTO and its Agreement on Trade-Related Aspects of Intellectual

[16] The list of the Member States of WIPO is available online at http://www.wipo.int/members/en (all online sources were accessed 18 November 2011).

[17] For a list of the WIPO-administered treaties, see http://www.wipo.int/treaties/en.

Property Rights (TRIPS).[18] This agreement sets minimal standards for the protection of intellectual property, and requires its Members without adequate protection of intellectual property to introduce such protection within specified periods of time.[19] Thus, all Members of the WTO will have introduced legal systems protecting intellectual property when the relevant transitional periods have expired.

The holders of TK and TCEs have not – or have only to a very limited extent – been able to participate in international trade. Because intellectual property rights are increasingly becoming important assets in international trade, intellectual property rights protecting TK and TCEs could function as a link between western society and the holders of TK and TCEs, including in particular indigenous peoples, enabling them to better participate in international trade.

To a certain extent, existing forms of intellectual property rights do offer protection for ICH. For example:

- trade marks, geographical indications and unfair competition law may serve to protect the authenticity of traditional goods and services;
- copyright law can protect contemporary adaptations of TCEs and, in some cases, TCEs per se;
- patents may be used to protect new innovations that are based on TK;
- secret TK and TCEs may be protected as confidential information;
- the Berne Convention[20] provides for the protection of 'unpublished works of unknown authors', the Rome Convention[21] covers sound recordings of TCEs, and the WPPT[22] protects performances of TCEs.

In addition to the existing forms of intellectual property rights, TK and TCEs could also be protected by new forms of intellectual property rights specifically designed to protect TK and TCEs, that is, newly established *sui generis* intellectual property rights. These new rights could be designed so as to meet the particular policy objectives of the protection of TK and TCEs, and the specific needs of the holders of TK and TCEs. The IGC of WIPO is currently discussing specific provisions concerning such *sui generis* rights.

3.3 Arguments in Favour of Protecting TK and TCEs by Other Legal Measures

The following arguments speak in favour of protecting TK and TCEs by legal measures other than intellectual property rights:

---

[18] WTO, Agreement on Trade-Related Aspects of Intellectual Property Rights (TRIPS), Marrakesh Agreement Establishing the World Trade Organization, Annex 1C, 1869 UNTS 299; 33 ILM 1197 (adopted on 15 April 1994, entered into force 1 January 1995). The list of the Member States is available online at http://www.wto.org/english/thewto_e/whatis_e/tif_e/org6_e.htm.

[19] The transitional arrangements of the TRIPS Agreement are included in Articles 65 and 66.

[20] WIPO, Berne Convention for the Protection of Literary and Artistic Works (adopted on 9 September 1886), as revised at Paris (24 July 1971) and as amended on 28 September 1979.

[21] WIPO, Rome Convention for the Protection of Performers, Producers of Phonograms and Broadcasting Organisations, 496 UNTS 43 (adopted on 26 October 1961, entered into force 18 May 1964).

[22] WPPT, supra note 15.

Market forces determine the monetary/economic value of intellectual property rights; accordingly, great demand for subject matter protected by an intellectual property right creates a high monetary value, whereas small demand creates small monetary/economic value. The market for most TK and TCEs will likely be limited on a global scale (even if their socioeconomic and, above all, spiritual value may be of particular importance to the holders); thus, due to the small demand for these subject matters, the monetary/economic value for the IPRs protecting them will also be small. If, however, the protection of TK and TCEs is intended as an incentive for their conservation or further use and improvement, rights protecting them should have adequate monetary/economic value. Otherwise, their function as incentives for these activities concerning TK and TCEs will be minimal. The general lack of economic value, thus, speaks against protecting TK and TCEs through existing intellectual property rights.

Present intellectual property rights are awarded for specific innovations or creations achieved by specific or specifiable innovators. Holders of intellectual property rights are, thus, individual natural or legal persons. However, it may be difficult, if not impossible, to distinguish specific innovators or creators of TK and TCEs. This distinction, however, is necessary if TK and TCEs are to be protected by existing intellectual property rights.

To be of value, intellectual property rights must be enforceable, which in turn depends on several factors, including the following: first, holders of intellectual property rights must have access to functioning and fair administrative and judicial systems. Second, to be able to provide these systems, states must have the necessary financial means. Third, states must have the political will to enforce intellectual property rights. Potential holders of IPRs protecting TK and TCEs, however, are often ethnic, political or economic minorities. According to Stephen Brush,

> [g]roups that control the greatest wealth of indigenous knowledge and biological resources may be the most marginalized by nation-states – for example, the Kurds of Iraq or the Mayan peasants of Guatemala. Few states accept the rights of indigenous groups per se, and even fewer can be expected to lend their political and legal apparatus to promote intellectual property rights of indigenous groups.
>
> ... The history of prejudice and discrimination against indigenous peoples and ethnic minorities around the world suggests that the benefits from intellectual property protection for biological resources and indigenous knowledge will not reach indigenous people.[23]

Questionable enforcement of intellectual property rights protecting TK and TCEs, thus, speaks in favour of alternative legal forms. Acquisition and enforcement of intellectual property rights also requires access to financial, legal and scientific means. Indigenous peoples as potential holders of such rights, however, generally lack these. Unless other sources provide these means, indigenous peoples are unlikely to be able to acquire and enforce existing intellectual property rights. Moreover, the protection of TK and TCEs by existing intellectual property rights causes substantial expenses. These expenses can occur due to necessary administrative bodies and procedures, litigation and scientific investigations. These expenses, however, will consume a large part of, or even surpass, the benefits

[23] Stephen B. Brush, 'Indigenous Knowledge of Biological Resources and Intellectual Property Rights: The Role of Anthropology' (1993) *American Anthropologist*, 95, pp. 653–70, at pp. 664–5.

potentially arising from intellectual property rights, which, at least from a purely monetary point of view, would render these rights useless and without value.

Furthermore, non-western societies, including many indigenous peoples, reject the notion of private property for religious beliefs, their worldview or other reasons. Instead, they consider gods, ancestors, communities or other entities to be the holders of TK and TCEs. Protecting TK and TCEs through existing intellectual property rights – a form of private property – would, thus, either force indigenous peoples rejecting private property to accept such rights against their beliefs, or prevent them from being able to benefit from this form of protection.

Finally, TK and TCEs arise from ancient (although dynamic), often secret and sacred traditions and practices, while the idea behind the intellectual property system is to incentivise creativity and innovation as well as to maintain a rich public domain.

3.4 Prospects and Limits of a Procedural Approach from an IP Perspective

Christoph B. Graber has previously suggested a procedural approach to interface global law and local traditions.[24] Acknowledging the importance of distinguishing between tradeable and non-tradeable TCEs, Graber proposed that a WTO Member wishing to benefit from preferential treatment has to involve indigenous communities in the decision-making process to identify tradeable TCEs. A special WTO commission should then formally adopt the decision.

Certainly, it is vital that rights-holders and other interested stakeholders can fully participate in a decision-making process. The indigenous community that owns a particular TK or TCE needs to be identified and their prior informed consent obtained when its ICH is to be traded. In addition, due regard has to be given to the customary law that regulates the internal procedures of the community.

The WTO has a powerful role in regulating international trade, also with regard to IP. Despite that, or actually because of it, changes to the system are slow and hard to achieve, as the example of the stalled Doha Round negotiations clearly shows. This may be one reason why, at least in the IP context, negotiations to ensure the protection of TK and TCEs and discussions about an enhanced participation of indigenous communities have taken place much more in WIPO than in the WTO so far. Therefore, this chapter focuses primarily on the developments at the WIPO IGC.

As described below, the critical importance of indigenous participation is generally recognised in the IGC – not only in the draft provisions on the administration of rights within the emerging legal instruments on TK and TCEs, but also with regard to the norm-setting activities of the forum itself, where indigenous representatives can actively participate. On the other hand, the fact that the IGC is currently elaborating such new instruments seems to indicate that, in the opinion of the WIPO Member States, a better procedural involvement of indigenous communities may be necessary but not sufficient to guarantee the effective protection of TK and TCEs. At the same time, a register with legally constitutive effect (comparable to the confirmation on the ownership granted by a

---

24 Graber, supra note 3.

specialised WTO commission in the approach of Graber) is not provided for in the current IGC draft instruments.

3.5 Conclusions

Based on the preceding discussion, the authors conclude the following: realising the protection of TK and TCEs through intellectual property rights appears to be an obvious and viable solution. Existing forms of intellectual property rights have been used to protect various forms of intangibles for a long time. Thus, considerable experience and expertise exist regarding the application and enforcement of these rights. Furthermore, existing institutional structures such as patent offices could be used.

Despite these advantages, the protection of TK and TCEs through existing intellectual property rights has a number of disadvantages. It is therefore necessary to consider in greater detail how new, specifically designed *sui generis* forms of intellectual property rights could be established in order to take into account the shortcomings that existing forms of intellectual property rights may have for the protection of TK and TCEs. However, to a certain extent, existing forms of intellectual property rights such as patents, geographical indications, trade secrets or plant breeders' rights could serve as models when designing such new rights.

Where such *sui generis* forms of intellectual property rights are deemed to be unsuitable as well – for example because potential beneficiaries oppose the notion of intellectual property rights per se – solutions have to be sought elsewhere.

One crucial point has to be kept in mind: the effective and efficient protection of TK and TCEs will not be possible with just a single measure; a 'one-size-fits-all' approach will, thus, not be feasible. Instead, a multitude of approaches have to be taken, including existing intellectual property rights and new *sui generis* intellectual property rights, as well as other measures, such as databases, an international electronic gateway linking those databases, and the disclosure of the source of TK in patent applications.

4. RECENT DEVELOPMENTS AT THE INTERNATIONAL LEVEL

4.1 World Intellectual Property Organization (WIPO)

4.1.1 Past efforts – Model Provisions (1982) and fact-finding missions (1998–99)

WIPO has been active in the area of TCEs (or folklore) for several decades. Resulting from these efforts were the 'Model Provisions for National Laws on the Protection of Expressions of Folklore Against Illicit Exploitation and Other Prejudicial Actions' (Model Provisions) of 1982.[25] This *sui generis* model for the intellectual-property-type protection of TCEs was elaborated by WIPO together with UNESCO.

---

[25] Model Provisions for National Laws on the Protection of Expressions of Folklore Against Illicit Exploitation and Other Prejudicial Actions (1982, last amendment 1985), available online at www.wipo.int/tk/en/documents/pdf/1982-folklore-model-provisions.pdf.

Over 1998–99, WIPO carried out numerous fact-finding missions, which involved a wide range of stakeholders, including indigenous and local communities, NGOs, governments, researchers and private industry. The WIPO fact-finding consultations resulted in the report 'Intellectual Property Needs and Expectations of TK Holders'.[26] This report distilled the central needs and expectations expressed during the consultations in the form of 21 key recommendations.

4.1.2 Intergovernmental Committee (IGC) of WIPO

A. General The IGC of WIPO was established by the WIPO General Assembly in 2000.[27] Up until now, the IGC has met for 19 sessions, usually lasting one week.

The IGC is mandated to address three substantive issues, namely the intellectual-property-related aspects of genetic resources, traditional knowledge and folklore (or, according to current terminology, TCEs).

Progress on the three substantive issues of the IGC – genetic resources, TK and TCEs – has not been even. At this point in time, work on TCEs seems to be the most progressed and specific, closely followed by TK, whereas progress on genetic resources has been made at a much slower pace.

B. Mandates The mandate of the IGC has been prolonged by the WIPO General Assembly several times since the creation of the IGC in 2000. Each renewed mandate asked the IGC to focus on another aspect of the issues arising.

The mandate for the biennium 2012–13[28] requests the IGC to continue its text-based negotiations with the objective of reaching agreement on texts of one or several international legal instruments[29] for the protection of genetic resources, TK and TCEs. Under the just-renewed mandate, at least four more sessions are foreseen to take place in 2012–13; IGC-20 to IGC-22 are exclusively dedicated to genetic resources, TK and TCEs, respectively. In the previous biennium 2010–11, four sessions of the IGC (IGC-16 to IGC-19) and three Intersessional Working Groups (IWGs) took place. These IWGs were expert groups, each dedicated to one of the substantive issues.

---

26 WIPO, 'Intellectual Property Needs and Expectations of TK Holders. Report on Fact-finding Missions on Intellectual Property and Traditional Knowledge (1998–1999)' (April 2001), available online at http://www.wipo.int/tk/en/tk/ffm/report/index.html.

27 WIPO, GA, Secretariat, 'Report of the 26th Session of the WIPO General Assembly, 25 September – 3 October 2000', (WIPO Doc. WO/GA/26/10, 2000), at paras 27–71, particularly at para. 71.

28 WIPO, GA, 'Matters Concerning the Intergovernmental Committee on Intellectual Property and Genetic Resources, Traditional Knowledge and Folklore. Agenda Item 31. Decision', Fortieth (20th Ordinary) Session (26 September – 5 October 2011), available online at http://www.wipo.int/tk/en/documents/pdf/decision_assemblies_2011.pdf.

29 The legal nature of the future instruments continues to be an open issue. The term 'international legal instruments' in the IGC mandate was chosen because the WIPO Member States are still divided about whether the instruments under negotiation shall be legally binding or non-binding.

C. Terminology Due to the existence of three legally binding international agreements on access and benefit-sharing containing definitions of the term 'genetic resources',[30] it seems appropriate that the IGC refers to these definitions in its work on genetic resources. In contrast, since there are no internationally agreed definitions of the terms 'TK' and 'TCEs', the IGC will have to establish its own definitions. Accordingly, the draft substantive provisions on the protection of TK and of TCEs contain draft definitions of the two terms in the respective Articles 1 (as outlined above). However, up until the present, the IGC has not been able to find consensus on this matter.

D. Traditional knowledge As mandated by the General Assembly, the IGC has, in its work on TK, focused its efforts in the previous 2010–11 biennium on text-based negotiations for drafting one or more international legal instruments for the effective protection of TK.

The existing draft text for TK consists of three parts, namely policy objectives, guiding principles and substantive provisions. In addition, the relevant document contains commentaries on particularly contentious draft Articles prepared by the facilitator of the IGC's negotiations on TK, which help to better understand some of the draft wording. However, the considerable overall length of the document as well as the numerous square brackets in the draft substantive provisions indicating the lack of consensus, make it difficult to assess the draft provisions.[31] Controversial points include the scope and term of protection and the relation between the protection of TK and the existing system of intellectual property rights.

Besides this, the IGC discussed and adopted in past sessions several concrete measures with regard to TK, including the development of inventories of online databases and periodicals, as well as a toolkit on TK.[32]

E. Traditional cultural expressions Parallel to TK, the IGC focused its efforts in the 2010–11 biennium on text-based negotiations for drafting one or more international legal instruments for the effective protection of TCEs.[33] Compared with the other two substantive issues, more progress has been made on TCEs.

---

[30] These are the Rio Convention on Biological Diversity (CBD), 1760 UNTS 79; 31 ILM 818 (opened for signature 5 June 1992, entered into force 29 December 1993); Nagoya Protocol on Access to Genetic Resources and the Fair and Equitable Sharing of Benefits Arising from their Utilization to the Convention on Biological Diversity (2010) (UN Doc. UNEP/CBD/COP/DEC/X/1) (adopted on 29 October 2010); and the UN Food and Agriculture Organization (FAO), International Treaty on Plant Genetic Resources for Food and Agriculture, 2400 UNTS 303 (adopted on 3 November 2001, entered into force 29 June 2004).

[31] WIPO, 'TK Draft Articles', supra note 9.

[32] See generally WIPO, IGC, Secretariat, 'Inventory of Traditional Knowledge-Related Periodicals', (WIPO Doc. WIPO/GRTKF/IC/3/5, 2002); WIPO, IGC, Secretariat, 'Inventory of Existing Online Databases Containing Traditional Knowledge Documentation Data', (WIPO Doc. WIPO/GRTKF/IC/3/6, 2002); and WIPO, IGC, Secretariat, 'Report on the Toolkit for Managing Intellectual Property When Documenting Traditional Knowledge and Genetic Resources', (WIPO Doc. WIPO/GRTKF/IC/5/5, 2003).

[33] WIPO, 'TCE Draft Articles', supra note 10.

Some participants in the negotiations on an international legal instrument for the protection of TCEs view these negotiations as being less complex, while others view them as 'more mature' than the discussions on TK and genetic resources, and thus call for 'an early harvest' with regard to TCEs. Still, many – also fundamental – issues remain unresolved with regard to the protection of TCEs. This holds true particularly for the scope of protection and the relationship with other intellectual property rights, especially copyright.

F. Genetic resources Progress in the IGC on genetic resources has been the slowest so far. This is due to the fact that some delegations preferred to deal with genetic resources in other international fora, namely the CBD and the WTO. Up until the present, as regards genetic resources, the IGC has only discussed draft objectives and principles[34] along with options for further or continued work;[35] thus, in contrast to TK and TCEs, the IGC has not discussed specific text of substantive provisions on genetic resources to date. However, numerous specific proposals have been submitted by WIPO Member States in this regard.[36]

G. Lessons learned – the way forward The IGC is mandated to draft one or several international legal instruments to be submitted to the WIPO General Assembly 2012, which will take stock of and consider the text(s), progress made and decide on convening a Diplomatic Conference, and will consider the need for additional meetings. At this point in time, the IGC has established two drafts of substantive provisions on TK and TCEs, the latter being more advanced than the former; furthermore, with regard to genetic resources, the work of the IGC has not yet moved beyond draft objectives and principles, a document listing options for further work, and proposals from certain Member States.

Some consider the results achieved so far by the IGC as meagre,[37] while others refer to the complex issues arising with regard to the intellectual-property-related aspects of genetic resources, TK and TCEs, and the difficulties posed by the controversial negotiation process on these complex problems.

When assessing the progress made during the past 19 IGC sessions and analysing the reasons for the rather limited specific results achieved so far, a number of factors weigh in.

The protection of genetic resources, TK and TCEs raises many complex technical and legal issues. It is, thus, only natural that finding an international solution takes time. The issues arising are not only complex technically and legally, but they are also 'new' issues requiring 'unique', 'tailor made' and 'creative' solutions and concepts. TK and TCEs are very specific types of intellectual assets and do not quite fit the existing intellectual property system of patents, trade marks, and so on. Hence it is a challenging task to adequately capture the essence of TK and TCEs and to protect them by adapting the corresponding intellectual property tools or by elaborating *sui generis* norms. When

---

34 WIPO, IGC, Secretariat, 'Draft Objectives and Principles Relating to Intellectual Property and Genetic Resources', (WIPO Doc. WIPO/GRTKF/IGC/20/4, 2011).

35 WIPO, IGC, Secretariat, 'Options for Future Work on Intellectual Property and Genetic Resources', (WIPO Doc. WIPO/GRTKF/IGC/20/5, 2011).

36 See the documents for IGC-20 at http://www.wipo.int/meetings/en/details.jsp?meeting_id=25008.

37 See Antons, supra note 7.

turning to academia for help, negotiators can find some proposed solutions; but most of them are just emerging, and for some issues there appear to be no – or at least no practical or politically feasible – solutions at hand, yet.

The protection of genetic resources, TK and TCEs also raises complex political issues. These relate to the North–South relationship, globalisation in trade and other aspects of life, intellectual property rights, and the treatment of indigenous peoples as minorities by the dominant power within a state. This makes evident that finding agreement on the protection of genetic resources, TK and TCEs is a challenging endeavour, as the views will not only differ between the different Member States of WIPO, but also between states and non-state actors – the latter participating in the IGC as observers.

Many other comparable international processes also took time to be concluded. The negotiations on the International Treaty on Plant Genetic Resources for Food and Agriculture (International Treaty)[38] of FAO took about seven years to be concluded, and the negotiations on the Nagoya Protocol on Access and Benefit-Sharing took about five years. Considering that the CBD already contains basic provisions on TK (Article 8(j)) and on access and benefit-sharing (Article 15), and that the resulting international agreement is merely a protocol to the CBD, this is also a considerable period of time.

The text-based negotiations in the IGC on one or several international legal instruments are in a controversial and – for some – conflicting relationship with other international processes. This holds true in particular for the negotiations in the ongoing Doha Round of the WTO on the relationship between the TRIPS Agreement and the CBD and the issue of disclosure requirements, and the just-concluded negotiations on the Nagoya Protocol on Access and Benefit-Sharing. At issue was the question of which international forum should be competent to address the issues at hand. Should the CBD, for example, be competent to regulate disclosure requirements in the patent system? Or should this be left to WIPO and the WTO? And which international forum should regulate TK? Should this be all three of the mentioned fora or primarily or exclusively the IGC of WIPO? This relationship between the relevant international fora remains at least partly unresolved, further complicating the negotiations in the IGC.

Against the background of the technical and legal complexity, some participants in the negotiations of the IGC lack the necessary expertise or may only have expertise in one area, but not in all areas under discussion. This may particularly hold true for small delegations with just one expert being present, or for delegations represented only by their diplomatic mission personnel, which generally lack in-depth technical expertise and follow not only the negotiations in the IGC, but also in other WIPO committees and other international fora present in Geneva, thus limiting the possibilities to dedicate the required attention to the IGC negotiations.

The IGC spent considerable time on resolving procedural issues at past sessions. For example, it took the IGC almost two full sessions (IGC-15 and IGC-16) to find an agreement on the modalities for the IWGs, leaving only very limited time to discuss the substantive issues at these sessions. Looking back at all 19 sessions of the IGC, one has to conclude that procedural issues – as important as it may be to clarify them – took away

---

38 UN FAO, supra note 30.

considerable time that the IGC could have spent on substantive issues, allowing it to make more rapid progress than it actually has.

As in many other international negotiations, considerable time could have been saved with better time management. This includes avoiding lengthy and/or purely political statements, repetitious opening statements as well as statements on other points than those under discussion. Furthermore, time could have been saved by other simple measures such as starting the sessions more on time and omitting coffee breaks. The time saved this way would again have provided the IGC with additional opportunities to discuss substance.

A considerable limiting factor was the fact that the IGC did not follow a systematic approach in its discussions on the three substantive issues. Such an approach would have required the IGC, at the outset of its efforts, to agree on the policy objectives of its work and to clarify relevant terminology by establishing at least working definitions of relevant key terms. The IGC, however, did not discuss these fundamental issues in detail and, thus, there is still a lack of consensus on policy objectives and on relevant terminology.

The negotiations on the Nagoya Protocol for Access and Benefit-Sharing concluded in 2010 allow several lessons to be learned of relevance to the efforts of the IGC. One of them is that the negotiations on the Protocol lacked until the very end a common understanding and agreement on the basic elements and the policy objectives of the future protocol. This caused the negotiations to sometimes turn in circles. A more structured approach would have been helpful to achieve faster and sounder progress. The same holds true for the ongoing negotiations in the IGC. Based on the lessons learned from the CBD process, it would be most helpful for the IGC to apply a well-structured approach and clarify the basic issues at the outset of its negotiations and not leave them unresolved until the end. This notwithstanding, it is obvious that negotiations on complex and politically sensitive issues – whether in the CBD, WIPO, WTO or any other international forum – are always a most challenging undertaking. Still, a clear and well-structured approach can only be conducive to the successful conclusion of any negotiations. On the positive side, the negotiations on the Protocol also showed that international consensus can be reached on very complex issues, if there is adequate political will of those involved in the negotiations to find such consensus.

4.2 World Trade Organization (WTO)

4.2.1 General

The TRIPS Agreement, one of the main pillars of the WTO, entered into force 1 January 1995. Currently, 153 states are Members of the WTO[39] and, thus, bound by the TRIPS Agreement.

The TRIPS Agreement does not contain specific provisions on ICH or its components such as TK or TCEs. This notwithstanding, its provisions in Part II on 'Standards Concerning the Availability, Scope and Use of Intellectual Property Rights' basically also apply to TK or TCEs, namely the provisions on copyright and related rights (Articles

[39] See WTO, Marrakesh Agreement Establishing the World Trade Organization, 1867 UNTS 154; 33 ILM 1144 (adopted on 15 April 1994, entered into force 1 January 1995).

9–14), trade marks (Articles 15–21), geographical indications (Articles 23–24), patents (Articles 27–34), and trade secrets (Article 39).

4.2.2 Review of Article 27.3(b) TRIPS Agreement

Even though the TRIPS Agreement lacks specific provisions on TK and TCEs, they are at issue in the discussions of the TRIPS Council on the review of Article 27.3(b) of the TRIPS Agreement, which started in 1999. Several delegations submitted communications, including, for example, Switzerland in 2001.[40] The focus of these communications was on TK and other issues, whereas TCEs (or folklore according to the terminology employed in paragraph 19 of the Doha Declaration) were not specifically addressed. However, a few delegations, in the context of the protection of TK, also referred to 'cultural expressions'. For example, a group of developing countries, in a communication of 1999, included 'cultural expressions' in the definition of 'TK',[41] and Australia, in a communication of 2001, referred to 'indigenous cultural expression' and the protection of designs, music and other art forms generated by indigenous communities.[42] It has to be noted that both of these communications predate the Ministerial Conference of Doha of 2001 and were, thus, not submitted in the context of the discussions of the TRIPS Council on paragraph 19 of the Doha Ministerial Declaration.

4.2.3 Paragraph 19 of the Doha Ministerial Declaration (2001)

The issues of TK and folklore were explicitly included in the agenda of the TRIPS Council at the 4th Ministerial Conference of the WTO (Doha, Qatar, November 2001). In paragraph 19 of the Doha Ministerial Declaration, the Ministers:

> instruct the Council for TRIPS, in pursuing its work programme including under the review of Article 27.3(b), the review of the implementation of the TRIPS Agreement under Article 71.1 and the work foreseen pursuant to paragraph 12 of this declaration, to examine, inter alia, the relationship between the TRIPS Agreement and the Convention on Biological Diversity, the protection of traditional knowledge and folklore, and other relevant new developments raised by members pursuant to Article 71.1. In undertaking this work, the TRIPS Council shall be guided by the objectives and principles set out in Articles 7 and 8 of the TRIPS Agreement and shall take fully into account the development dimension.[43]

Up until now, however, the discussions of the TRIPS Council on paragraph 19 have focused on the relationship between the TRIPS Agreement and the CBD; this holds particularly true for the last few years, where discussions were largely limited to the issue

---

[40] WTO, Council for Trade-Related Aspects of Intellectual Property Rights (TRIPS Council) – Communication from Switzerland, 'Review of Article 27.3(b): The View of Switzerland', (WTO Doc. IP/C/W/284, 15 June 2001), at paras 13–19.

[41] WTO, TRIPS Council, Communication from Bolivia, Colombia, Ecuador, Nicaragua and Peru, 'Review of the Provisions of Article 27.3(b). Proposal on Protection of the Intellectual Property Rights Relating to the Traditional Knowledge of Local and Indigenous Communities', (WTO Doc. IP/C/W/165, 1999), at para. 5.

[42] WTO, TRIPS Council, Communication from Australia, 'Review of Article 27.3(b)', (WTO Doc. IP/C/W/310, 2001), at para. 28.

[43] WTO, Ministerial Conference, 'Ministerial Declaration', Fourth Session (WTO Doc. WT/MIN(01)/DEC/1, 2001), at para. 19.

of disclosure requirements in patent applications. In contrast, other issues of TK, and even more so of folklore, were hardly addressed.[44]

5. PARTICIPATION OF INDIGENOUS PEOPLES IN THE WIPO IGC

5.1 General

One of the main stakeholders in the discussions of the IGC are local and indigenous communities as the holders of TK and TCEs. To facilitate the participation of their representatives in the work of the IGC, three measures were put in place: (1) indigenous and local communities can apply for ad hoc observer status to attend the IGC sessions; (2) at the beginning of each IGC session, a half-day panel with indigenous speakers is held; and (3) the WIPO Voluntary Fund finances the participation of indigenous representatives in the IGC sessions.

5.2 Ad hoc Observer Status for Indigenous Representatives in IGC

Participation in the IGC sessions is not limited to the 184 WIPO Member States. Intergovernmental organisations may also participate, as well as international and regional non-governmental organisations (NGOs), including representatives from indigenous peoples, which are permanent observers to WIPO or which are specifically accredited ad hoc status to the IGC.[45] As one of the formal decisions at the beginning of each session, the IGC grants ad hoc observer status to those observers which applied for accreditation.[46] At present, there are more than 100 observers accredited to attend the IGC sessions.[47]

The accredited observers may take the floor in the plenary sessions of the IGC, normally after the representatives of governments and intergovernmental organisations have done so. The accredited observers, however, generally may not participate in informal proceedings such as informal consultations among government representatives. With regard to the text-based negotiations, observers are allowed to introduce proposals during the IGC sessions and during the written commenting periods sometimes established between IGC sessions. Such proposals are kept in the draft text if there is support from at least one Member State.

---

44 WTO, TRIPS Council, Secretariat, 'The Protection of Traditional Knowledge and Folklore. Summary of Issues Raised and Points Made', (WTO Doc. IP/C/W/370/Rev.1, 2006), at para. 6.

45 WIPO, IGC, 'Report Adopted by the Committee', (WIPO Doc. WIPO/GRTKF/IC/1/13, 2001), at para. 18. See also, generally, WIPO, 'Intergovernmental Committee: Accreditation Process', available at http://www.wipo.int/tk/en/igc/accreditation.html; and WIPO, 'NGO Participation', available at http://www.wipo.int/tk/en/ngoparticipation/.

46 See, for example, WIPO, IGC, Secretariat, 'Accreditation of Certain Organizations', (WIPO Doc. WIPO/GRTKF/IC/17/2, 2010), the annex of which contains a list of those observers having applied for accreditation by IGC-17.

47 A list of all accredited observers is available online at http://www.wipo.int/tk/en/igc/ngo/accreditedlist.pdf.

Observers may also participate in the IWGs. As regards participation rights, there was in the view of the authors hardly any difference between experts from Member States and (indigenous and non-indigenous) experts from accredited observers in the drafting groups of the IWGs.

In 2011, the WIPO General Assembly invited the IGC to review its procedures with a view to 'enhancing the positive contribution of observers' to the IGC process. It also requested the Secretariat of WIPO to prepare a study on the participation of observers in the work of the IGC outlining 'current practices and potential options' in this regard.[48]

5.3 IGC Panel of Indigenous and Local Communities

Since 2005, each session of the IGC is preceded by a half-day of presentations at the 'Panel of Indigenous and Local Communities'. Speakers at this panel usually come from local or indigenous communities, and the panel is chaired by one of their representatives. The panel addresses various topics of immediate relevance to the discussions of the IGC. Topics covered so far include 'Making *Sui Generis* Protection Work: Best Practices in Community-Led Strategies for the Protection of Traditional Knowledge and Traditional Cultural Expressions'[49] (IGC-19, July 2011); 'Indigenous Peoples' Collective Rights and Intellectual Property'[50] (IGC-18, May 2011); and 'What role does the "public domain", or a similar concept to it, play in your indigenous, traditional or local community?'[51] (IGC-17, December 2010).

These panels have proven useful to the deliberations of the IGC, as they allow the indigenous representatives to address the government representatives directly and in greater detail than would be possible in a statement during the plenary of the IGC. The usefulness and impact of these panels quite obviously depend on the topic chosen and also on the quality of the presentations made by the indigenous representatives. It is regrettable that the number of government representatives attending the indigenous panels is usually considerably smaller than in the plenary sessions of the IGC.

5.4 WIPO Voluntary Fund

The WIPO General Assembly established the Voluntary Fund for Accredited Indigenous and Local Communities[52] in 2005. This fund provides financial support to representatives

---

[48] For this purpose, the WIPO Secretariat prepared a 'Note on Existing Mechanisms for Participation of Observers in the Work of the WIPO Intergovernmental Committee on Intellectual Property and Genetic Resources, Traditional Knowledge and Folklore' (10 October 2011), available online at http://www.wipo.int/export/sites/www/tk/en/documents/pdf/note_igc_participation.pdf.

[49] WIPO, IGC, Secretariat, 'Information Note for the Panel of Indigenous and Local Communities', (WIPO Doc. WIPO/GRTKF/IC/19/INF/5, 2011), at para. 2.

[50] Ibid., at para. 2.

[51] Ibid., at para. 3.

[52] See WIPO, 'Voluntary Fund', available at http://www.wipo.int/tk/en/ngoparticipation/voluntary_fund/index.html. See generally WIPO, *A Stronger Voice for Indigenous and Local Communities in WIPO's Work on Traditional Knowledge, Traditional Cultural Expressions and Genetic Resources: The WIPO Voluntary Fund*, Geneva and New York: WIPO (WIPO Publication No. 936(E)).

of indigenous and local communities accredited by the IGC in order to facilitate their participation in the sessions of the IGC and the three IWGs foreseen in the biennium 2010–11.

The objective criteria for support and operation of the fund have been laid down by the WIPO General Assembly.[53] The funded representatives are selected at the IGC session preceding the session for which funding is requested. The selection is made by an Advisory Board, which consists of nine members, namely the Chair or one of the Vice-Chairs of the IGC as well as five government and three indigenous representatives. The Fund has chosen between about 5 and 16 representatives to be funded for each IGC or IWG session, with the number of funded representatives decreasing lately due to the fact that the fund did not receive any donations between February 2008 and March 2011 and the consequently rapidly decreasing financial resources available for funding.

Up until July 2011, the Voluntary Fund had received approximately CHF0.5 million. Donations were made by the Swedish International Biodiversity Program, the Governments of France and Norway, the Christensen Fund, the Ministry of Science and Technology of South Africa, an anonymous contributor and the Swiss Federal Institute of Intellectual Property, which donated CHF250,000, or about half of the total funds available.[54] In addition, in September 2011 Australia also announced a significant contribution to the Voluntary Fund.

5.5 Transplantation of Procedures Into International Trade Context

The question arises whether this broad and facilitated participation of indigenous representatives could be 'transplanted' into the WTO context. This question likely has to be answered in the negative, mainly for two reasons: first, taking into account the fact that observership in the WTO is much more limited compared with, for example, WIPO, it seems quite unlikely that the WIPO Voluntary Fund may serve as a model for the WTO. Second, as the extent and depth of the discussions in the WTO on TK and folklore up to now have been very limited, the WTO's discussion may be of less direct interest to indigenous peoples than discussions in other fora, such as WIPO.

6. CONCLUSIONS

This chapter discusses the issue of international trade in indigenous cultural heritage from an IP perspective. Many of the complex issues arising in this regard remain unresolved at this point in time. This includes not only basic issues such as terminology and policy objectives of protection measures, but also more specific topics such as the detailed design

---

[53] These rules are available in WIPO, 'Establishment of the WIPO Voluntary Fund for Accredited Indigenous and Local Communities', annexed to: WIPO, GA, Secretariat, 'Participation of Indigenous and Local Communities: Establishment of a Voluntary Fund: Recommendation of the Intergovernmental Committee on Intellectual Property and Genetic Resources, Traditional Knowledge and Folklore', Thirty-Second (17th Ordinary) Session (WIPO Doc. WO/GA/32/6, 2005).

[54] WIPO, IGC, Secretariat, 'Voluntary Fund for Accredited Indigenous and Local Communities: Information Note on Contributions and Applications for Support', (WIPO Doc. WIPO/GRTKF/IC/19/INF/4, 2011), at para. 3.

and legal nature of such measures. From the perspective of IP practitioners, WIPO and in particular its IGC have been the most active in this regard. Considerable progress has been made lately on the way to reaching agreement on texts of one or several international legal instruments for the protection of TCEs, TK and genetic resources. This progress notwithstanding, much work lies ahead when trying to find a consensus on these issues.

8. Are they in or are they out? Traditional cultural expressions and the public domain: implications for trade

Brigitte Vézina*

1. INTRODUCTION

1.1 An Example: A Bitter-Sweet Lullaby[1]

In June 2009, the 'Archives internationales de musique populaire' (AIMP), an ethnomusical archive within the Geneva Museum of Ethnography, faced an unusual problem. In an email, TLS Music Services, a music production company based in California, USA, was asking permission to use a sample of a lullaby recorded on a CD released by AIMP in 1991, directed by Italian ethnomusicologist Serena Facci and entitled 'Zaire: between Lakes and Forests; Music of the Nande' (our translation). The requested sample was intended to be used as a loop in the introduction of 'Need to find', a song by rising star of Jamaican dub music, Terry Lynn. In fact, as explained in the email, the use of the Congolese lullaby was meant to support the Afro-Jamaican identity of Terry Lynn. According to TLS Music's website, the song 'Need to find' was part of the 'Red Stripe Website Project', a marketing operation launched by Jamaican beer brand Red Stripe, with the aim of celebrating *the global influence, importance and appeal of the rhythms and*

---

* This chapter was composed by drawing on materials prepared by the WIPO Secretariat and WIPO staff. With permission, it draws significantly on WIPO, Intergovernmental Committee on Intellectual Property and Genetic Resources, Traditional Knowledge and Folklore (IGC), Secretariat, 'Note on the Meaning of the Term "Public Domain" in the Intellectual Property System with Special Reference to the Protection of Traditional Knowledge and Traditional Cultural Expressions/Expressions of Folklore', (WIPO Doc. WIPO/GRTKF/IC/17/INF/8, 2010), of which the author here was one of the principal drafters. This chapter also brings the information presented to the IGC into a renewed focus for the benefit of a wider audience. The author is grateful to Wend Wendland for his thorough review and valuable advice. The views expressed in this chapter are not necessarily those of WIPO or any of its Member States. Any mistakes or errors are the author's own responsibility. For more on WIPO's work concerning TCEs, please visit http://www.wipo.int/tk/en/folklore/ (all online sources were accessed 5 September 2011).

[1] The author is grateful to Laurent Aubert, curator of the Ethnomusicology Department, Geneva Museum of Ethnography, for having kindly supplied this example, which has been translated and simplified for the purposes of the present chapter. A fuller and more detailed account may be found in Aubert's article, in Laurent Aubert, 'Woodstock en Amazonie et la superstar du ghetto de Kingston' (2010) *Gradhiva*, 12, pp. 140–57.

beats of Jamaican music. Deeming the case rather suspicious, AIMP decided at first to formally oppose any free use of the lullaby. It was then reassured that the song would 'not be distributed commercially' but would be released – at least on the Internet – in 50,000 units, in exchange for which AIMP would receive an advance of US$3,000.

AIMP was baffled. Was this 'Deep Forest'[2] all over again? Or, on the contrary, was TLS Music earnestly willing to share the royalties? Unwilling to make any decision on its own, AIMP contacted Facci, the ethnomusicologist who had made the recordings, to get her point of view. 'As you know,' she answered, 'the territory of the Banande is at war. … I'll try to see if it would be possible to give money to the maternity clinic in Lukanga or some other charity in the region.' In a subsequent letter, Facci informed AIMP that Margaret, the woman who had interpreted the recorded lullabies, had passed away. Believing that the amount proposed 'could be used in memory of Margaret, who was really a wonderful old woman', Facci asked AIMP to forward the following message to TLS Music: 'The Congolese lullaby in *Need to find* was sung in 1988 by Margaret, a Munandi woman, in a village near Butembo (Democratic Republic of the Congo).'

Upon reflection, AIMP decided to accept TLS Music's proposal, given that its approach had been relatively honest and transparent and, thus, worthy of consideration. In addition, AIMP was convinced that the song would anyway pop up on the market – the master had been ready for several weeks and the song was already being disseminated on the Internet. A lawsuit was risky and could go on forever, while its outcome was far from certain. Besides, the proposed amount was significant enough to have an impact on the financial situation of the maternity clinic in Lukanga. 'Need to find' was uploaded on 8 July 2009, and although agreements were signed, AIMP is still awaiting the first payment.

1.2 The Issue: TCEs as Objects of International Trade and Elements of the Public Domain?

As the above example illustrates, traditional cultural expressions, such as the Nande lullabies, are precious tokens of a community's identity, cultural continuity and living

[2] The case of 'Deep Forest' is a much-publicised example of the use of an ethnographic sound recording that raised IP issues, particularly regarding proper attribution and benefit-sharing. In 1969 or 1970, Swiss-French ethnomusicologist Hugo Zemp made a recording in Malaita, Solomon Islands, of a lullaby chant called 'Rorogwela' performed by a woman named Afunakwa. As the maker of the sound recording, Zemp owned the copyright therein. He deposited his recording with a UNESCO ethnomusicology archive. The recording was copied from the UNESCO catalogue without permission from Zemp, and the chant then re-mixed, fused with 'techno-house' dance rhythms and produced as the successful song 'Sweet Lullaby' on the 1992 CD 'Deep Forest'. Large profits were made from sales of the record, with no returns to the Malaita community and wrong attribution (the track was described by its publisher as 'a rare and unusual mix of ambient modern music and the songs of the Pygmies of the Central African Rain Forest.' See Steven Feld, 'A Sweet Lullaby for World Music' (2000) *Public Culture*, 12 (1), pp. 145–71; Felicia Sandler, 'Music of the Village in the Global Marketplace – Self-Expression, Inspiration, Appropriation, or Exploitation?', *University of Michigan*, PhD Dissertation (2001), at pp. 58–9; Sherylle Mills, 'Indigenous Music and the Law: An Analysis of National and International Legislation' (1996) *Yearbook for Traditional Music*, 28, pp. 57–85; and Dionysia Tabureguci, 'The Pacific's Stolen Identity', *Island Sun* (25 September 2008), p. 6.

heritage.[3] The fact that a Jamaican singer wished to use them to reconnect with her African roots is perhaps telling in that respect. What this example also shows is that TCEs have a commercial potential and may be traded across borders, across oceans and, certainly, beyond their cultural context. Nowadays, more often than not, trade in TCEs does not, indirectly, let alone directly, involve the holder(s) of the TCE, but rather third parties who have a – sometimes purely – commercial interest in their trade. Quite positively, this example nonetheless demonstrates a certain degree of awareness of the ethical and legal issues involved in the use of TCEs. What remains problematic is enforcement in the absence of a clear legal right.

This case is not an isolated one. The TCE literature[4] is replete with accounts of such intercultural, international uses, and most of them probably go unreported, unnoticed. Nevertheless, records of such uses, which could be qualified as 'misuses' or 'misappropriations', have been brought to the attention of the international community for decades, and ensuing calls for their protection have found an echo in the work of the World Intellectual Property Organization (WIPO).[5] Notably, WIPO established, in 2000, the WIPO Intergovernmental Committee on Intellectual Property and Genetic Resources, Traditional Knowledge and Folklore (IGC) – a forum where negotiations take place over an intellectual-property-based protection system for these elements of the world's cultures.

What may explain – or, at least, shed some light on – this widespread phenomenon of trade and exchanges, is that cultural heritage (and elements thereof, such as TCEs) has, generally and for some time, been considered as part of the universal common heritage of mankind.[6] It was indeed held that cultural heritage belonged to all mankind and that,

---

[3] In the WIPO context, TCEs are any form, whether tangible or intangible, in which traditional culture and knowledge are expressed. They are maintained, used or developed by a community and are characteristic of the latter's cultural heritage. A working description may be found in WIPO, IGC, 'The Protection of Traditional Cultural Expressions: Draft Articles', Twenty-Second Session (WIPO Doc. WIPO/GRTKF/IC/22/4, 2012), Article 1 [hereinafter WIPO, 'TCE Draft Articles'].

[4] See, for example, WIPO, IGC, Secretariat, 'Consolidated Analysis of the Legal Protection of Traditional Cultural Expressions', Fifth Session (WIPO Doc. WIPO/GRTKF/IC/5/3, 2003), especially Part V ('Examples of Appropriation and Misappropriation', pp. 30–34) [hereinafter WIPO, 'Consolidated Analysis']; and WIPO, *Minding Culture: Case-Studies on Intellectual Property and Traditional Cultural Expressions*, Geneva: WIPO, 2003.

[5] In 1996, the WIPO Committee of Experts on a Possible Protocol to the Berne Convention and the Committee of Experts on a Possible Instrument for the Protection of the Rights of Performers and Producers of Phonograms recommended that 'provision should be made for the organization of an international forum in order to explore issues concerning the preservation and protection of expressions of folklore, IP aspects of folklore, and the harmonization of the different regional interests.' See WIPO, Committee of Experts on a Possible Protocol to the Berne Convention; and Committee of Experts on a Possible Instrument for the Protection of the Rights of Performers and Producers of Phonograms, 'Report Adopted by the Committees', (WIPO Doc. BCP/CE/VI/16-INR/CE/V/14, 1996), at para. 269. WIPO, Berne Convention for the Protection of Literary and Artistic Works (adopted on 9 September 1886), as revised at Paris (24 July 1971) and as amended on 28 September 1979.

[6] See the preamble to the UNESCO Hague Convention for the Protection of Cultural Property in the Event of Armed Conflict, 249 UNTS 240 (adopted on 14 May 1954, entered into force 7 August 1956): 'Being convinced that damage to cultural property belonging to any people

therefore, cultural heritage could not be privately owned, and was, thus, freely appropriable, marketable, and tradeable by anyone.[7] What that meant, from an IP point of view, was that cultural heritage, including TCEs, was in the public domain.[8]

In more recent times, some (but by no means all) communities and countries have become increasingly aware of the commercial value of their own TCEs and have claimed IP protection over them, potentially with a view to exploiting them commercially for economic development. It is indeed a basic tenet of IP law that creators may 'reap' what they have 'sown'.[9] Likewise, it has been claimed that very fundamental grounds for the demand to protect cultural heritage may be seen in 'natural justness'[10] and a sense that legitimate holders should be the ones enjoying the benefits accruing from the use and trade of their TCEs.

1.3 Outline of the Chapter

The chapter first gives an overview of recent developments at WIPO, especially of the state of negotiations. It then briskly reflects on the IP protection currently available for TCEs – for reasons exposed below, it focuses on performers' rights in expressions of folklore. The chapter then flips the coin and seeks to pin down the rather elusive meaning of the 'public domain'. Following this bipolar reflection, it tries to answer the difficult question: are TCEs in or are they out of the public domain? Based on the proposed answer, the chapter examines the two possible ways of dealing with that state of fact: (1) the establishment of an international *sui generis* system, which would actually *fish* the TCEs *out* of the public

---

whatsoever means damage to the *cultural heritage of all mankind*, since each people makes its contribution to the culture of the world' (emphasis added). See also Article 1(3) of the UNESCO Declaration of the Principles of International Cultural Cooperation, Fourteenth Session of the General Conference (adopted on 4 November 1966): 'all cultures form part of the common heritage belonging to all mankind.' See also the Preamble of UNESCO, Convention Concerning the Protection of the World Cultural and Natural Heritage, 1037 UNTS 151 (adopted on 16 November 1972, entered into force 17 December 1975): 'Considering that parts of the cultural or natural heritage are of outstanding interest and therefore need to be preserved as part of the *world heritage of mankind* as a whole' (emphasis added).

7 See, for example, UNESCO, 'Intellectual Works of Universal Value that Have Fallen into the Public Domain and are Regarded as Forming Part of the Common Heritage of Humanity', General Conference, Thirtieth Session (UNESCO Doc. 30 C/56, 1999), and its annex 'Castellón Declaration on New Prospects for the Common Heritage of Humanity'.

8 See William van Caenegem, 'The Public Domain: Scientia Nullius?' (2002) *European Intellectual Property Review*, 24 (6), pp. 324–30.

9 See *Millar v Taylor* (1769) 98 ER 201, at p. 218 ('it is not agreeable to natural justice, that a person should reap the beneficial pecuniary produce of another man's work'), as quoted in Patricia Loughlan, 'Pirates, Parasites, Reapers, Sowers, Fruits, Foxes … The Metaphors of Intellectual Property' (2006) *Sydney Law Review*, 28 (2), pp. 211–26, at p. 220. See also Sumathi Subbiah, 'Reaping What They Sow: The Basmati Rice Controversy and Strategies for Protecting Traditional Knowledge' (2004) *Boston College International and Comparative Law Review*, 27 (2), pp. 529–59.

10 Reto M. Hilty, 'Legal Protection of Cultural Heritage in a World of Intellectual Property Rights', in Wolrad Prinz zu Waldeck und Pyrmont et al. (eds), *Patents and Technological Progress in a Globalized World*, Berlin and Heidelberg: Springer, 2009, pp. 763–79, at p. 768.

domain by granting TCE holders economic and/or moral rights over their TCEs; or (2) the protection of public domain TCEs, either through the extension of moral rights protection or through the establishment of a paying public domain, which would not grant holders any rights or decision power, but would allow a fair payment or sharing of benefits in cases of use by third parties. Lastly, the chapter looks at the implications, consequences or impact of these possibilities for the tradability of TCEs. The chapter does not offer any conclusion, but sets the scene for discussion.

2. RECENT DEVELOPMENTS IN THE WIPO IGC

At WIPO, negotiations on the protection of TCEs (as well as traditional knowledge and on the interface between IP and access and benefit-sharing in genetic resources, neither covered in this chapter) are taking place in the IGC, a negotiation body created in 2000 that brings together WIPO Member States, intergovernmental organisations and accredited non-governmental organisations. Through the latter, participation of indigenous and local communities is made possible, thanks notably to a Voluntary Fund for Accredited Indigenous and Local Communities.[11]

In September 2011, WIPO Member States renewed the mandate of the IGC, adopting a clearly defined work programme, based on sound working methods, to guide its work over the 2012–13 biennium. On TCEs, the text currently under negotiation consists of draft articles.[12] Under a *sui generis* approach, the draft articles seek to respond to several issues, notably the determination of what exactly TCEs are, the delimitation of the acts of misuse or misappropriation that are forbidden, and the characterisation of who could benefit from protection.

In addition to biannual sessions of the IGC, working groups (IWGs) have met between sessions to accelerate the negotiations. IWG 1 took place in July 2010 and dealt chiefly with TCEs. During that meeting, experts, participating in their personal capacities, took part in the drafting of revised articles. At its 17th, 18th and 19th sessions – respectively in December 2010, May and July 2011 – the IGC further examined and streamlined those articles. Moreover, the WIPO Secretariat prepared a glossary of key terms to facilitate the negotiations.[13]

According to its mandate, the IGC 'will, during the next budgetary biennium (2012/2013), and without prejudice to the work pursued in other fora, expedite its work on text-based negotiations with the objective of reaching agreement on a text(s) of an international legal instrument(s) which will ensure the effective protection of GRs, TK and TCEs.'[14] The IGC is requested to submit the text(s) to the 2012 General Assembly, which

---

[11] Information on the IGC may be found online at http://www.wipo.int/tk/en/igc/.

[12] They are currently available in WIPO, 'TCE Draft Articles', supra note 3.

[13] WIPO, IGC, Secretariat, 'Glossary of Key Terms Related to Intellectual Property and Traditional Cultural Expressions', Twenty-Second Session (WIPO Doc. WIPO/GRTKF/IC/22/INF/8, 2011).

[14] WIPO, General Assembly, 'Matters Concerning the Intergovernmental Committee on Intellectual Property and Genetic Resources, Traditional Knowledge and Folklore – Agenda Item 31. Decision', Fortieth (20th Ordinary) Session (26 September – 5 October 2011).

will take stock of and consider the text(s) and progress made, and will decide on convening a Diplomatic Conference.

Three thematic IGC sessions were held before the September 2012 General Assembly, the first of which took place in February, dealing with GRs, the second one in April on TK, and the third one in July, addressing TCEs.

Lastly, a new publication entitled 'Intellectual Property and the Safeguarding of Traditional Cultures: Legal Issues and Practical Options for Museums, Libraries and Archives' was recently issued.[15] This publication offers IP information for cultural institutions whose collections comprise TCEs and presents examples of best practices from around the world, drawn from various institutional and community experiences.

3. EXISTING IP LAW TO PROTECT TCEs: A NEIGHBOURING RIGHT FOR PERFORMERS

It has been contended that the classical IP system currently operates to exclude most TCEs from IP protection, thereby relegating them to the public domain. But in fact, the existing IP system can play a part in protecting TCEs, depending on which elements are to be protected and why precisely they are to be protected. This type of protection is however limited; one may speak of *indirect* protection, for TCEs cannot be directly protected by the current system, which fails to match their distinct character.

Existing laws on IP can (with some exceptions) offer protection to creations *based on* TCEs (copyright and related rights), to collections or databases of TCEs (including compilations), or to secret elements of TCEs (confidential information). Moreover, trade marks, unfair competition law and geographical indications (GIs) can be helpful in protecting the reputation associated with TCEs. On GIs, in the words of one scholar:

> the local control on a territorial connection explains why at IGC 5, the point was made that TCEs that can be qualified as goods, such as handicraft items, can also be protected by GIs. In this instance, a GI can be affixed to a product that is made from natural resources or through knowledge held by an indigenous group. Furthermore, some TCEs consisting of names, signs, or other indications can themselves serve as GIs.[16]

One advantage is that these rights can be enforced internationally and are applicable to tradeable goods.

This chapter does not examine in full detail the many ways in which the current IP system may provide indirect protection to TCEs. Issues of criteria for protection and scope

---

[15] Molly Torsen and Jane Anderson (for WIPO), 'Intellectual Property and the Safeguarding of Traditional Cultures: Legal Issues and Practical Options for Museums, Libraries and Archives', WIPO Publication No. 1023, available online at http://www.wipo.int/export/sites/www/tk/en/publications/1023.pdf.

[16] Anselm Kamperman Sanders, 'Incentives for and Protection of Cultural Expressions: Art, Trade and Geographical Indications' (2010) *Journal of World Intellectual Property*, 13 (2), pp. 81–93.

of protection have been extensively analysed elsewhere. It rather focuses on the only[17] international specifically recognised system of protection of TCEs, or expressions of folklore: the 1996 WIPO Performances and Phonograms Treaty (WPPT).[18] The WPPT provides that the definition of 'performer' expressly includes the performer of an expression of folklore.[19] The term 'folklore' itself is, however, not defined in the treaty. Performers enjoy, on the basis of a neighbouring right, moral rights (Article 5), various exclusive rights of fixation, reproduction, public communication, distribution or rental established in Articles 6 to 10, and a right to remuneration in the case where the performance is recorded on a phonogram that is published for commercial purposes (Article 15). For instance, a performer of a traditional song, chant, folk tale, poem or instrumental music has the right to set the conditions for the recording (the fixation) of the performance and for the way in which the recording is distributed and commercialised, even if the expression of folklore is not itself eligible for copyright protection.

However, this form of protection is subject to certain limits, which makes it less advantageous from the perspective of indigenous peoples and traditional communities. Three of these limits are examined here.[20] First, protection only concerns *intangible* expressions of folklore that can be performed, that is, played, sung, recited, declaimed, and so on. Traditional songs, tales and dances may, thus, be protected, but as far as *tangible* expressions of folklore embodied on a support are concerned, neighbouring rights do not

---

[17] Of course, other types of IP protection are available at the international level, notably trade marks and GIs, but these are not specifically identified in any international instrument as pertaining precisely to TCEs. Besides, arguably, Article 15.4 of the Berne Convention also deals with the protection of TCEs at the international level, but its use has been very limited.

[18] WIPO Performances and Phonograms Treaty (WPPT), 2186 UNTS 203; 36 ILM 76 (adopted on 20 December 1996, entered into force 20 May 2002). According to the WPPT, performers of expressions of folklore in contracting states can expect to receive protection in other contracting states. For countries that have not ratified the WPPT, though, and depending on national laws, a performance of a TCE may not be protected if the relevant national law does not require the protection of performances of expressions of folklore other than those defined as literary and artistic works in the copyright sense. As at 30 March 2011, 87 States had ratified the WPPT.

[19] Article 2(a) WPPT: 'performers are actors, singers, musicians, dancers and other persons who act, sing, deliver, declaim, play in or otherwise perform literary and artistic works or expressions of folklore.' By contrast, the International Convention for the Protection of Performers, the Producers of Phonograms and Broadcasting Organizations, 1961 (Rome Convention) – and the Agreement on Trade-Related Aspects of Intellectual Property (TRIPS Agreement) – require the protection of performances of literary and artistic works, whether protected by copyright or not. It is almost universally accepted that, as expressions of folklore do not correspond to the concept of literary and artistic works proper, the definition of performers in the Rome Convention does not extend to performers who perform expressions of folklore. See WIPO, Rome Convention, 496 UNTS 43 (adopted on 26 October 1961, entered into force 18 May 1964); and WTO, TRIPS Agreement, Marrakesh Agreement Establishing the World Trade Organization, Annex 1C, 1869 UNTS 299; 33 ILM 1197 (adopted on 15 April 1994, entered into force 1 January 1995).

[20] The analysis is taken in part from: WIPO, 'Consolidated Analysis', supra note 4; and WIPO, IGC, Secretariat, 'The Protection of Traditional Cultural Expressions: Draft Gap Analysis', Thirteenth Session (WIPO Doc. WIPO/GRTKF/IC/13/4(b) Rev, 2008). See also Agnès Lucas-Schloetter, 'Folklore', in Silke von Lewinski (ed.), *Indigenous Heritage and Intellectual Property: Genetic Resources, Traditional Knowledge and Folklore*, The Hague, London and New York: Kluwer Law International, 2004, pp. 259–367, at pp. 270–71.

apply. Second, protection does not operate in the audiovisual sector, for the WPPT does not extend to the visual part of performances; only the *aural* aspects are protected, that is, those that may be perceived by the human ear.[21] Third, protection does not extend to the use of folklore as such, but to its performer; hence holders cannot avoid an independent performance of their folklore.[22] Consequently, protection may not directly *benefit* the *community* that is the origin of the folklore (the *holder* of the expression) if the performer is not a member of that community.

The layer of protection currently afforded to TCEs may seem rather flimsy. Would that mean that, in an IP system, TCEs that cannot benefit from IP protection would be considered as being in the public domain and, thus, freely usable and tradeable by anyone? In the IGC, the Delegation of the Russian Federation has argued that, in the Russian Federation, expressions of folklore were not protected by copyright, in accordance with national legislation, which further provided that works that had never enjoyed protection on the territory of the Russian Federation should be deemed to be in the public domain.[23]

Before trying to answer this very difficult question, should we not first try to determine what exactly the public domain is? The multiplicity of views in the debate on the protection of TCEs actually warrants an analysis of the role, contours and boundaries of the public domain.[24] Yet, any such analysis is fraught with interpretation risks, and this chapter ventures only to scope the meanings of the public domain, generally and in specific reference to TCEs.

4. TRADITIONAL CULTURAL EXPRESSIONS AND THE PUBLIC DOMAIN

Throughout the course of the IGC's deliberations, the issue of the public domain has been referred to time and again. At its 16th session, the IGC commissioned the WIPO Secretariat to prepare an information document on the meanings of the public domain, which was issued at the 17th session under the title 'Note on the Meanings of the Term

---

21 It should be noted that work continues on the development of an instrument for the protection of audiovisual performances in WIPO. The Standing Committee on Copyright and Related Rights recommended at its 22nd session, held in June 2011, that the General Assembly resume the suspended 2000 Diplomatic Conference which would consider an international instrument on the Protection of Audiovisual Performances. A Preparatory Committee of the Diplomatic Conference took place on 30 November and 1 December 2011, while the Diplomatic Conference is taking place in June 2012. See WIPO, Preparatory Committee of the Diplomatic Conference on the Protection of Audiovisual Performances, Director General, 'Agenda, Dates, Venue and Other Organizational Questions for the Diplomatic Conference', (WIPO Doc. AVP/PM/5, 2011).

22 Hilty, supra note 10, at p. 777.

23 WIPO, IGC, 'Report', Second Session (WIPO Doc. WIPO/GRTKF/IC/2/16, 2001), at para. 24 [hereinafter WIPO IGC, 'Report. Second Session'].

24 See WIPO, 'Consolidated Analysis', supra note 4, at para. 15.

Public Domain in the Intellectual Property System with Special Reference to the Protection of Traditional Knowledge and Traditional Cultural Expressions/Expressions of Folklore'.[25]

4.1 Definitions of the Public Domain: Generally

Generally, in IP law,[26] the public domain consists of materials that are not subject to exclusive IP rights and which are, therefore, freely available to be used or exploited by any person. Most definitions of the public domain contain three main components: (1) the legal status of material; (2) freedoms to use material; and (3) accessibility of material. For example, *Black's Law Dictionary* defines the public domain as:

> The universe of inventions and creative works that are *not protected* by intellectual property rights and are therefore *available for anyone to use without charge*. When copyright, trademark, patent, or trade-secret rights are lost or expire, the intellectual property they had protected becomes part of the public domain and can be appropriated by anyone without liability for infringement.[27]

The *first* component relates to the legal status of the material. The public domain consists of information resources free from IP rights,[28] or IP-free resources,[29] or 'information artefacts unencumbered by IP rights',[30] that is, every intellectual product that was never or no longer is under IP protection.[31] Put differently, it is made up of: (i) material that was ineligible for protection in the first place,[32] for example material of insufficient originality

---

[25] WIPO, IGC, 'Note on the Meaning of the Term "Public Domain" in the Intellectual Property System with Special Reference to the Protection of Traditional Knowledge and Traditional Cultural Expressions/Expressions of Folklore', (WIPO Doc. WIPO/GRTKF/IC/17/INF/8, 2010).

[26] The public domain is an important concept in other areas of law as well. See Edward Lee, 'The Public's Domain: The Evolution of Legal Restraints on the Government's Power to Control Public Access through Secrecy or Intellectual Property' (2003) *Hastings Law Journal*, 55 (91), pp. 94 –209, at p. 97.

[27] Brian E. Garner (ed.), *Black's Law Dictionary*, 8th edn, St Paul, MN: Thompson West, 2005, at p. 1027 (emphasis added).

[28] Pamela Samuelson, 'Mapping the Digital Public Domain: Threats and Opportunities' (2003) *Law and Contemporary Problems,* 66 (1–2), pp. 147–71.

[29] Uma Suthersanen, 'A2K and the WIPO Development Agenda: Time to List the "Public Domain"' *UNCTAD-ICTSD Project on IPRs and Sustainable Development*, Policy Brief No. 1 (2008).

[30] James Boyle, 'The Second Enclosure Movement and the Construction of the Public Domain' (2003) *Law and Contemporary Problems*, 66, pp. 33–74, at pp. 59–60 and 68; and James Boyle, 'Foreword: The Opposite of Property?' (2003) *Law and Contemporary Problems,* 66, pp. 1–32, at pp. 29–30.

[31] Suthersanen, supra note 29.

[32] The public domain may include 'abstract subject matter, such as ideas or discoveries … ', information, concepts, principles, laws of nature, and so on. See ibid. Some, however, do not see such material as being part of the public domain. See, for example, Mark Rose, 'Nine-Tenths of the Law: The English Copyright Debates and the Rhetoric of the Public Domain' (2003) *Law and Contemporary Problems,* 66, pp. 75–87, at p. 80; see also Wendy Gordon, 'On Owning Information: Intellectual Property and the Restitutionary Impulse' (1992) *Virginia Law Review*, 78,

to qualify for copyright protection; (ii) material 'freed' by invalidation or expiry of the IP right; and (iii) material that was eligible for protection but in respect of which protection was waived.

As far as the copyright system is concerned, the public domain is said to be a foundational principle.[33] The Berne Convention for the Protection of Literary and Artistic Works applies to all works which, at the moment of the Convention's coming into force, 'have not yet fallen into the public domain in the country of origin through the expiry of the term of protection' (Article 18(1)).[34] Under the Convention, the public domain is:

> the scope of those works and objects of related rights that can be used and exploited by everyone without authorization, and without the obligation to pay remuneration to the owners of copyright and related rights concerned – as a rule because of the expiry of their term of protection, or due to the absence of an international treaty ensuring protection for them in the given country.[35]

At this first component's core is an emphasis on the *absence* of IP rights. Therefore, the public domain is defined in relation to what is protected under IP laws, such that it is 'simply whatever is left over after various tests of legal protection have been applied … , the "negative" of whatever may be protected'[36] or 'the opposite of the scope of copyright protection.'[37] But although it may be common to conceive of material as either being in an IP-free public domain or encumbered by IP rights, the public domain literature reveals a continuum of states in between those endpoints.[38] Hence, the public domain is not necessarily the opposite of property, or simply the residue of what is not protected by IP.[39] For example, as copyright protection is territorial, a work may be protected in one country but in the public domain in another. Further, while the economic rights of copyright

---

pp. 149–281, at p. 163. The public domain may also include material that was created before any copyright law existed and portions or aspects of otherwise copyrighted works that copyright does not protect. See Julie Cohen et al., *Copyright in a Global Information Economy*, New York: Aspen Law and Business, 2002. Some prefer a stricter definition, which focuses only on works the copyright of which has ended. See WIPO, Committee on Development and Intellectual Property (CDIP) (prepared by Séverine Dusollier), 'Scoping Study on Copyright and Related Rights and the Public Domain', Seventh Session (WIPO Doc. CDIP/7/INF/2, 2011) [hereinafter WIPO Scoping Study].

33 Jessica Litman, 'The Public Domain' (1990) *Emory Law Journal*, 39, pp. 965–1023.

34 Supra note 5.

35 Mihály Ficsor (for WIPO), *Guide to the Copyright and Related Rights Treaties by WIPO and Glossary of Copyright and Related Rights Terms*, WIPO, 2003, at p. 305.

36 Edward Samuels, 'The Public Domain in Copyright Law' (1993) *Journal of the Copyright Society of the USA*, 41, pp. 137–82, quoted in Pamela Samuelson, 'Enriching Discourse on Public Domain' (2006) *Duke Law Journal,* 55, pp. 101–69 , at p. 105.

37 WIPO Scoping Study, supra note 32, at p. 6

38 Samuelson, supra note 36, at p. 151.

39 See Sara Boettiger and Cecilia Chi-ham, 'Defensive Publishing and the Public Domain', in Anatole Krattiger et al. (eds), *Intellectual Property Management in Health and Agricultural Innovation: A Handbook of Best Practices*, vol. I, Oxford, UK: MIHR, 2007; and Davis, CA: PIPRA, 2007, pp. 879–95.

eventually expire, moral rights may subsist longer, and sometimes in perpetuity.[40] We will come back to this issue in section 5.2.1.

The *second* component of most definitions of the public domain revolves around the distinction between material that is freely usable and material on which an owner can exercise exclusive rights.[41] Public domain material is said to be free or available for any member of the public to use[42] for any purpose without having to obtain the consent or permission of a right-owner and without charge. Moreover, the term is used to refer to intellectual material or elements in which no one can establish or maintain proprietary interests, that is, which are ineligible for private ownership. Material in the public domain is not the private property of any individual; it is instead common and open to the public for use without restriction.[43]

Some definitions of the public domain focus on freedoms to use material even when works embodying this material are protected by IP rights.[44] That is, the public domain includes not only unprotected subject matter but also unprotected uses of copyrighted works, including copyright exceptions or fair use.[45] The public domain may, thus, be said to include 'unregulated, implicitly licensed, unambiguously fair, and otherwise privileged uses of IP-protected information resources',[46] yet contested uses are generally excluded.[47] Also included might be uses of works still protected by copyright, but legitimised through the operation of a licence, even if implicit.[48] For instance, material made available under Creative Commons licences may, subject to how the licences are structured, be considered in the public domain.[49] Lastly, orphan works and out-of-print works also occupy a grey area which may be said to be part of the public domain.[50]

---

[40] The Berne Convention does not impose any duration of the moral right. In many countries, the duration of moral rights follows that of the economic rights; in others, it differs: it can be longer or shorter, and cease upon the death of the author.

[41] Yochai Benkler, 'Free as the Air to Common Use: First Amendment Constraints on Enclosure of the Public Domain' (1999) *New York University Law Review,* 74, pp. 354–446, at pp. 361–2; as quoted in Samuelson, supra note 36, at p. 121.

[42] See, for example, Copyright and Fair Use, Stanford University Libraries, 'Welcome to the Public Domain', available at http://fairuse.stanford.edu/Copyright_and_Fair_Use_Overview/chapter8/8-a.html ('The public owns these works, not an individual author or artist. Anyone can use [them] without obtaining permission, but no one can ever own [them].')

[43] R. Anthony Reese, 'The New Unpublished Public Domain 2' (August 2005) (unpublished manuscript), at p. 48, as quoted in Samuelson, supra note 36, at p. 135.

[44] Samuelson, supra note 36, at p. 146.

[45] WIPO Scoping Study, supra note 32, at pp. 9 and 11.

[46] Benkler, supra note 41, at pp. 361–2. See also Robert Merges, 'A New Dynamism in the Public Domain' (2004) *University of Chicago Law Review*, 71, pp. 183–203, at p. 184; as quoted in Samuelson, supra note 36, at p. 121.

[47] Samuelson, supra note 36, at p. 146.

[48] WIPO Scoping Study, supra note 32, at pp. 9 and 11. See also David Nimmer et al., 'The Metamorphosis of Contract Into Expand' (1999) *California Law Review*, 87, pp. 17–77, at p. 23; as quoted in Samuelson, supra note 36, at p. 151. See also Samuelson, supra note 36, at p. 121.

[49] Samuelson, supra note 36, at pp. 123 and 152. See also Creative Commons, 'Choosing a License', available at http://creativecommons.org/about/licenses/.

[50] WIPO Scoping Study, supra note 32, pp. 9 and 11.

The *third* and last component of most definitions of the public domain deals with availability and accessibility of material. It is argued that 'a domain must be public in the sense of being publicly *accessible* to be a public domain'.[51] This contention calls for two remarks. First, and contrary to some perceptions, not all material that is publicly available or accessible through a free and open source is in the public domain. It should moreover be noted that accessibility is a relative concept; there are various degrees of 'accessibility'.[52] For example, paintings hung on the walls of public museums may be freely accessible and reproduction by means of photography may be permitted, but it does not mean that the paintings are in the public domain. Likewise, being able to view a reproduction of a work, or, in fact, a TCE, on the Internet does not mean that it is in the public domain.[53]

Second, perhaps in contradiction with the above contention, the fact that something is in the public domain through lack of IP protection does not necessarily guarantee that it is freely accessible and available.[54] Indeed, public domain material is not always free from any cost or encumbrance, such as laws that protect classified information. Moreover, a considerable amount of information is publicly accessible (for example court records) if one is willing to take time and effort to discover it, but is, practically speaking, not accessible.[55] Technical protection measures may further restrict uses and be backed up by legislated anti-circumvention rules, thereby affecting the accessibility of public domain materials.

Similarly, some definitions of the public domain include unpublished or undisclosed works, which, although 'IP-free', are in fact inaccessible due to their protection through personal property rights to physically control their access and use.[56]

4.2 The Public Domain in the Context of the IGC's Discussions on TCEs

In the course of the IGC's discussions, several points of view have been voiced concerning the public domain concept and its relation with the protection of TCEs through IP laws, rules or principles. They are presented here under two main headings, according to the more or less favourable light in which the concept is cast.

---

51 Samuelson, supra note 36, at p. 166 (emphasis added). See also Reese, supra note 43, at p. 48.

52 Samuelson, supra note 36, at p. 153. Some information may be maintained as a closely guarded secret. Secrets may be licensed or otherwise distributed to one or more persons subject to implicit or explicit confidentiality restrictions. (See, for example, James Pooley, *Trade Secrets*, New York: Law Journal Press, 1997, at § 9.04[2].) Licences vary in restrictiveness regarding who may access and use the information and for what purposes.

53 It has been argued that digital recording and documentation of cultural heritage may contribute to their easy access for inappropriate use and exploitation by third parties, as the content may be considered part of the public domain when displayed. This issue is dealt with in the WIPO Publication No. 1023, supra note 15.

54 See WIPO Scoping Study, supra note 32, at p. 7. See also Statement by the Delegation of Nigeria in WIPO, IGC, 'Report', Fifth Session (WIPO Doc. WIPO/GRTKF/IC/5/15, 2003), at para. 37 [hereinafter WIPO IGC, 'Report. Fifth Session'].

55 Samuelson, supra note 36, at p. 154.

56 Reese, supra note 43, at pp. 24–5.

4.2.1 Importance of the public domain for the protection of TCEs

It is a fairly common assertion in the copyright discourse that the public domain is a valuable resource and that maintaining it as rich and robust is an important public policy goal.[57] It is also contended that creativity depends on the ability to access and draw upon a corpus of existing public domain material. Authors do not conjure up new works from nothing[58] and almost every cultural creation has antecedents in the public domain.[59] Accordingly, the public domain acts as the:

> laws' primary safeguard of the raw material that makes authorship possible… [it] should be understood not as the realm of material that is undeserving of protection, but as a device that permits the rest of the system to work by leaving the raw material of authorship available for authors to use.[60]

In other words, the public domain has a 'central importance in promoting the enterprise of authorship'.[61] It is not a place separate and apart from the realm of IP-protected content,[62] or 'what is left after the contours of copyright have been drawn, but … a repository of resources of its own'.[63] It 'foster[s] the development of artistic culture', being part of the 'cultural landscape'.[64] Pleas for a vibrant public domain emphasise its positive functions for society: as a building block for the creation of new knowledge, as an enabler of competitive imitation,[65] follow-on creation,[66] free or low-cost access to information,[67] public access to cultural heritage,[68] in short, as 'a fertile foundation on which creators can build new works, as well as a rich source of content for education'.[69]

---

57 See Boettiger and Chi-ham, supra note 39.

58 Litman, supra note 33, at p. 965.

59 See Graham Dutfield and Uma Suthersanen, 'Innovation and Development', in Uma Suthersanen, Graham Dutfield and Kit Boey Chow (eds), *Innovation Without Patents. Harnessing the Creative Spirit in a Diverse World*, Cheltenham, UK: Edward Elgar, 2007, pp. 3–12.

60 Litman, supra note 33, at pp. 967–8.

61 Ibid.

62 Julie Cohen, 'Copyright, Commodification and Culture: Locating the Public Domain', in Lucie Guibault and P. Berndt Hugenholtz (eds), *The Public Domain of Information: Identifying the Commons in Information Law,* The Netherlands: Kluwer, 2006, pp. 121–66; as quoted in Samuelson, supra note 36.

63 WIPO Scoping Study, supra note 32, at p. 6.

64 Cohen et al., supra note 32.

65 See, for example, Tyler T. Ochoa, 'Origins and Meanings of the Public Domain' (2002) *University of Dayton Law Review*, 28, pp. 215–67, at p. 215; as quoted in Samuelson, supra note 36.

66 See, for example, Litman, supra note 33, at p. 966.

67 See, for example, Molly S. Van Houweling, 'Distributive Values in Copyright Law' (2005) *Texas Law Review*, 83, pp. 1535–79, at p. 1575; as quoted in Samuelson, supra note 36.

68 See, for example, Ochoa, supra note 65, at p. 215. ('We take it for granted that the plays of Shakespeare and the symphonies of Beethoven are in the public domain and may be freely copied, adapted, and performed by anyone.')

69 Joint Statement by IFLA (International Federation of Library Associations), EIFL (Electronic Information for Libraries) and EBLIDA (European Bureau of Library Information and Documentation Associations), 'Committee on Copyright and other Legal Matters (CLM)', Provisional Committee on Proposals Related to a WIPO Development Agenda, Second Session, Geneva, 26–30 June 2006, available at http://www.ifla.org/III/clm/p1/A2K-7.htm.

Likewise, in the context of TCEs, it has been advocated that the public domain character of cultural heritage is valuable, as a source of further creativity and innovation. It is through sharing and contemporary adaptation and arrangement that cultural heritage is kept alive, regenerated, revitalised and transmitted to future generations. This allows for the ongoing protection of TCEs and serves several of the objectives associated with their safeguarding and preservation. This corresponds to a robust and dynamic public domain as a source of cultural exchange and creativity, thereby contributing to economic development. These arguments are based on the premise of the IP system as it has developed over the past hundreds of years in the western world. The Delegation of the European Union and its Member States have stated in the IGC that European folklore was considered to be part of the public domain, but that other countries and cultures might have different concerns and interpretations.[70] This would seem to corroborate the 'western' perspective in the debate: the concept of the public domain is important for TCEs to act as a counter to IP norms and principles and the creation of *sui generis* rights based thereon. To be sure, that Delegation also contended that 'the fact that folklore for the most part is in the public domain does not hamper its development – to the contrary, it allows for new creations derived from or inspired by it at the hands of contemporary artists.'[71] There exists, the argument goes, a balance of interests according to which members of TCE-holding communities as well as others are free to create on the basis of TCEs, and acquire and benefit from any IP that may subsist in the creations.[72] This balance was chiselled into international customary law as the principle of 'common heritage of humankind' and has allowed TCEs to develop, evolve and flourish. The idea of maintaining this balance, and the dangers of skewing it, has been put forth in the following terms:

> Those who advocate IP protection for their own expressions of folklore would create monopolies of exploitation and would naturally then be faced with monopoly claims from other regions. Exchange or interaction could thus be made more difficult, if not impossible. Indeed, IP protection should only be used where appropriate and beneficial to society in that it stimulates creativity and investment while respecting the interests of others and of society at large.[73]

Following this line of thought, the (over-)protection of TCEs by IP would not be warranted, as it would run counter to the current balance characterising the IP system; the public domain would shrink, leaving less material to build on. Moreover, legal certainty would be diluted.[74] If strict private property rights were to be established over cultural heritage, neither members of the relevant communities nor the cultural industries would be able to create based on it.[75] Another formulation of the argument focuses on the dynamic

---

[70] WIPO IGC, 'Report. Second Session', supra note 23, at para. 169.

[71] See European Community comments on WIPO, IGC, 'Preliminary Systematic Analysis of National Experiences with the Legal Protection of Expressions of Folklore', Fourth Session (WIPO Doc. WIPO/GRTKF/IC/4/3, 2002); and WIPO, 'Consolidated Analysis', supra note 4, at para. 27.

[72] WIPO, 'Consolidated Analysis', supra note 4, at para. 19.

[73] Expressions of Folklore: Document submitted by the European Community and its Member States, WIPO, IGC, 'Expressions of Folklore', Third Session (WIPO Doc. WIPO/GRTKF/IC/3/11, 2002).

[74] Ibid.

[75] Ibid.

nature of TCEs: full IP protection could cast TCEs in concrete, thereby risking their very existence, *freezing* the culture in a historic moment and denying their holders a contemporary voice.[76]

4.2.2 Inadequacy of the public domain concept for the protection of TCEs

TCEs' relation with the public domain is contested, if not criticised, notably by indigenous peoples and traditional communities.[77] An oft-cited argument goes as follows: since TCEs were never protected by IP, how can they be part of a public domain? It is true that the notion being a construct of the IP system, is embedded in the IP episteme[78] and can seem to members of indigenous cultures like a tool of western imperialism.[79] For those traditional cultures that do not make property distinctions, the concept of the public domain is an alien one, for which there often is no comparative idea.[80] It has been argued that the IP framework, including the public domain, overlooks and is at odds with the different norms, rules and regulations established by customary laws and indigenous laws and legal systems, which regulate communication, sharing, use and applications of TCEs.[81] 'TCEs are not in the *public domain* because indigenous peoples have failed to

---

[76] Ibid. See also Christine H. Farley, 'Protecting Folklore of Indigenous Peoples: Is Intellectual Property the Answer?' (1997) *Connecticut Law Review*, 30 (1), pp. 1–57; and WIPO, 'Consolidated Analysis', supra note 4.

[77] See, for example, Commission on Human Rights, Sub-Commission on the Promotion and Protection of Human Rights Working Group on Indigenous Populations, 'Review of Developments Pertaining to the Promotion and Protection of the Rights of Indigenous Peoples, Including their Human Rights and Fundamental Freedoms: Principal Theme: Indigenous Peoples and the International and Domestic Protection of Traditional Knowledge. Joint Statement from the Indigenous World Association and Indigenous Media Network', Twenty-third Session (UN Doc. E/CN.4/Sub.2/AC.4/2005/CRP.3, 2005).

> ('We … strongly reject the application of the public domain concept to any aspect related to our cultures and identities … We equally reject the application of IPR regimes to assert patents, copyrights, or trade mark monopolies for products, data, or processes derived or originating from our … cultural expressions, when conducted without due authorization by our peoples. … We request that the elaboration of an international instrument should, inter alia, take into account alternatives to the application of the public domain concept … ')

See also Anupam Chander and Madhavi Sunder, 'The Romance of the Public Domain' (2004) *California Law Review*, 92, pp. 1331–73, at p. 1335.

[78] 'The history of the concept [of the public domain] and its relation to the development of IP rights show that the two have developed hand in hand, as an outcome of Western intellectual movements during the late Enlightenment and the Age of Reason.' Statement by the representative of the Tulalip Tribes of Washington in WIPO IGC, 'Report. Fifth Session', supra note 54, at para. 56.

[79] See Chander and Sunder, supra note 77, at p. 1335.

[80] Statement by the representative of the Tulalip Tribes, supra note 78, at para. 56.

[81] See Statement by the representative of the Saami Council in WIPO IGC, 'Report. Fifth Session', supra note 54, at para. 53. See also Brad Sherman and Leanne Wiseman, 'Toward an Indigenous Public Domain?', in Lucie Guibault and P. Bernt Hugenholtz (eds), *The Future of the Public Domain,* 1st edn, The Netherlands: Kluwer Law International, 2006, pp. 259–79, as quoted in Samuelson, supra note 36, at p. 140 ('… it is necessary to create and recognize the domains established under customary or indigenous law as new spaces within the legal landscape, rather than merely applying spatial configurations developed in other contexts to Indigenous creations.').

take the steps necessary to protect the knowledge in the western IP system, but from a failure of governments and citizens to recognize and respect the customary law regulating its use.'[82] These often include social restrictions on who, if anyone, can use or create expressions and under what circumstances. Under such customary laws, the balance against the 'western IP' public domain seems irrelevant.

5. TWO COURSES OF ACTION: *SUI GENERIS* PROTECTION OR A 'PROTECTED' PUBLIC DOMAIN

Although the debate still rages on, in light of the above brief analysis of the meaning of the term 'public domain', from a strictly classical IP focus and within the boundaries of IP as a closed system, TCEs *as such*[83] are currently considered to be in the public domain. Does this mean that they could never benefit from any kind of protection? Some see the public domain as something immutable: 'what goes into [the public domain] must stay there.'[84] However, recent legal history shows that some material in the public domain may be privatised and it is widely attested that the public domain's barriers can be porous, with the help of legislative intervention. After all, as we have seen above, in 1996, international IP protection (through the WPPT) was extended to the performances of certain TCEs formerly generally considered in the public domain.

We may think of two main courses of action to address TCEs in the public domain: either by creating a right, thereby *fishing* TCEs *out* of the public domain,[85] or by maintaining them in the public domain, but subjecting their use to moral rights protection or to a payment or form of benefit-sharing.

5.1 *Sui Generis* Protection of TCEs

It is a trite contention that IP can be used as a tool to help commercialise the products to which it is attached and to exclude free-riding competitors. Many have indeed noted the

---

82 Statement by the representative of the Tulalip Tribes of Washington, supra note 78.

83 TCEs 'as such' or 'pre-existing' or 'underlying' TCEs are distinguished from TCE-based or TCE-inspired contemporary creations. The latter, according to existing copyright law, would potentially benefit from copyright protection, whereas the former would be considered part of the public domain. In other words, a distinction is made 'between (i) pre-existing, underlying cultural heritage and traditional culture, which may be referred to as traditional culture or folklore *stricto sensu* and (ii) contemporary literary and artistic productions created by current generations of society and based upon or derived from pre-existing cultural heritage and traditional culture'; WIPO, 'Consolidated Analysis', supra note 4, para. 12.

84 Diane L. Zimmerman, 'Is There a Right to Have Something to Say? One View of the Public Domain' (2004) *Fordham Law Review*, 73, pp. 297–375, at pp. 300, 312, 336–42 and 371.

85 It has been stated that it is critically important for any *sui generis* systems of protection to include some form of protection for TCEs in the public domain. Statement by the Delegation of New Zealand, in WIPO, IGC, 'Report', Sixth Session (WIPO Doc. WIPO/GRTKF/IC/6/14, 2004), at para. 41.

'commoditising effect' of IP,[86] which has been used as an argument in favour of affording IP rights to TCEs *as such*, for IP could contribute to stimulating sustainable economic development of their owners' community. But while many argue for a form of IP protection of TCEs, a paramount objective of a *sui generis* protection system is to maintain a balance between the various goals that IP, as a tool, could reach. Protection would need to strike a balance between positive protection against abuses of TCEs and the encouragement of their further development and dissemination, as well as individual creativity inspired by TCEs. Indeed, some contend that failing to account for the need for balance by overprotecting TCEs could result in hindering the sustainable development of their bearers.[87] Balance would also have to be reached between preservation and the free exchange of cultural experiences. Much of these arguments relates to the importance of maintaining the public domain.

As previously mentioned, the IGC is currently negotiating a form of *sui generis* protection of TCEs.[88] Draft Article 3, entitled 'Scope of Protection', is currently made up of several alternative wordings. It is not our purpose to analyse the contents of the proposed article, especially since it is in a state of constant flux, but suffice it to make some general observations. Common to all alternatives is a provision on secret TCEs, which would prevent any unauthorised fixation, disclosure, use or other exploitation. As for other TCEs (non-secret), a bundle of rights are listed in the article, endowing it with a distinct copyright flavour. These rights range from the rights of fixation, disclosure, reproduction, public performance, translation or adaptation, making available or communicating to the public, distribution, use or other exploitation. The article also includes trade-mark-like protection and prevents use for commercial purposes, sale of articles that are not genuine or not authentic, and disparaging or offending uses, for example. The article provides a caveat for use in good faith. One alternative also foresees equitable remuneration. The article finally provides for moral rights protection, notably attribution, reputation and integrity. How the article might further evolve through the mechanics of international negotiation is a fascinating question very much worth following. Quite clearly, the provision would virtually *fish out* some TCEs from the public domain and would alter the porous boundaries of this intangible realm. Whether the evolving text will achieve the preservation of the system's intrinsic balance is a matter for WIPO Member States, as participants in the IGC, to determine.

5.2 Protecting the Public Domain

Depending on the more or less strict reading that one makes of the definition of the public domain, material therein may receive some form of protection, even if it is not *fished out* of

---

86 See, for example, Christoph B. Graber, 'Institutionalization of Creativity in Traditional Societies and in International Trade Law', in Shubha Ghosh and Robin P. Malloy (eds), *Creativity, Law and Entrepreneurship*, Cheltenham, UK and Northampton, MA: Edward Elgar, 2011, pp. 234–63.

87 See Michael Brown, *Who Owns Native Culture?*, Cambridge, MA and London: Harvard University Press, 2003, at pp. 142 and 252; and Hilty, supra note 10, at p. 776.

88 See also Christoph Antons, 'Intellectual Property Rights in Indigenous Cultural Heritage: Basic Concepts and Continuing Controversies', in this volume.

it. This may either be by endowing it with perpetual moral rights protection or by subjecting its use to a form of payment, retribution or benefit-sharing mechanism.

5.2.1 Moral rights protection for public domain material

Because copyright works do fall into the public domain after a certain time, some countries use so-called public domain legislation to prevent or sanction use that would prejudice the integrity, authenticity, identity, essence, cultural value or reputation of such works.[89] Some also provide for the right of paternity or attribution.[90] Such legislation is basically designed to provide moral rights in perpetuity.[91]

Defending the integrity of works that are considered as national cultural heritage of the state is often the public policy purpose of such legislation.[92] The public authorities or representatives of authors act as 'watchdogs' for the integrity of cultural monuments and as defenders of the collective interests. For example, the African Intellectual Property Organization (OAPI) suggests that, after the expiry of protection of the economic rights, the national collective rights administration body is entitled to ensure compliance with moral rights for the benefit of the authors.[93]

Some countries, for example Algeria, Kenya and Rwanda, to name a few, include in their copyright regime specific protection for TCEs that generally aligns, where it exists, with the protection of public domain works.[94] This scheme would appear to provide the appropriate safeguard to indigenous peoples and traditional communities' cultural interests, especially sacred TCEs. However, the way the legislation is drafted, protection extends only to works whose copyright protection has expired and to those that would have qualified for such protection had the legislation existed at the time that they were created. For these reasons, TCEs have the same difficulties that they have with copyright. Furthermore, it is the state that has the authority to exercise the moral right to control and defend the integrity of public domain material. This may, in some cases, be problematic, especially where the state is not representative of the communities. The search for a solution, thus, still goes on.

---

[89] 'Study of Comparative Copyright Law: Protection of Works in the Public Domain' (1981) *Copyright Bulletin*, 15(2), pp. 30–35, at p. 33, as quoted in Michael Blakeney (for the WIPO, Roundtable on Intellectual Property and Traditional Knowledge), 'What is Traditional Knowledge? Why Should it be Protected? Who Should Protect It? For Whom?: Understanding the Value Chain', (WIPO Doc. WIPO/IPTK/RT/99/3, 1999).

[90] WIPO Scoping Study, supra note 32, at p. 36.

[91] This exists in Algeria, Brazil, Costa Rica, Denmark and Italy. In most countries, this competence has never been exercised. See also UNESCO's 'Draft Recommendation to Member States on the Safeguarding of Works in the Public Domain, Item 7.5 of the Provisional Agenda', (UN Doc. 25 C/32, 1989); and WIPO Scoping Study, supra note 32, at p. 36.

[92] See Marie-Alice Chardeaux, *Les choses communes*, Paris: LGDJ, 2006, at para. 211. See also Adolf Dietz, *Le droit d'auteur dans la Communauté européenne*, Study for the European Commission, 1976, at para. 165; and Blanche d'Ormesson-Kersaint, 'The Protection of Works in the Public Domain' (1983) *Revue Internationale du Droit d'Auteur*, 116, pp. 72–150, at p. 125.

[93] Annex VII of the Bangui Agreement of the OAPI provides that the moral rights shall be without limit in time (see Article 22(2)). See also WIPO Scoping Study, supra note 32, at p. 39.

[94] See WIPO Scoping Study, supra note 32, at p. 13.

5.2.2 A paying public domain

The idea of a paying public domain, or *domaine public payant*, can be traced back to French author Victor Hugo[95] – who proposed that remuneration be provided for the benefit and encouragement of new generations of creators – and has been adopted in a few jurisdictions.[96] Under such a system, a fee is imposed for the use of works in the public domain. Generally, the system works like a compulsory licence: the use is conditional upon payment of the prescribed fee but not upon securing prior authorisation. In some countries, only the commercial or for-profit exploitation of public domain material is subject to payment.

It has been argued that the operation of such a system may constitute an impediment to the free use of public domain material. The extent of such interference depends, at least in part, on the amount of the fees, which varies considerably. The uses to which the royalties are put also greatly vary: from welfare and cultural purposes, such as the funding of young creators, to the social benefits of creators in difficulty and the promotion of creative works. Sometimes, as in Algeria, the remuneration is dedicated not to the assistance of individual living creators, but to the preservation of the public domain itself. In such cases, the collected fees can be viewed as ways to fund the protection of the public domain, by sharing the burden of financing the public availability of public domain material with its commercial exploiters.[97]

The public domain to which such a regime applies is usually only composed of works of which copyright has expired, but some countries apply it to TCEs. The system has been proposed as a model to protect TCEs,[98] directed at indigenous arts councils,[99] or for the nurturing of traditional works[100] by providing monetary compensation for indigenous communities. The idea was investigated in the early 1980s by UNESCO and WIPO.[101]

---

95 Victor Hugo, opening speech of the Congrès Littéraire International of 1878.

96 Italy was often cited as an example of a western country applying such a system, which it abrogated in 1996. Nowadays, regimes exist in Algeria, Kenya, Rwanda, Senegal, Republic of the Congo, Côte d'Ivoire, Tunisia and Paraguay. The pre-eminence of African countries can be explained by the Bangui Agreement, which provides for such a regime for the exploitation of expressions of folklore and works or productions that have fallen into the public domain (section 59, (as amended in 1999) Annex VII, title I).

97 WIPO Scoping Study, supra note 32, p. 38

98 Antony Taubman and Matthias Leistner, 'Traditional Knowledge', in Silke von Lewinski (ed.), *Indigenous Heritage and Intellectual Property: Genetic Resources, Traditional Knowledge and Folklore*, 2nd edn, The Hague, London and New York: Kluwer Law International, 2008, pp. 59–179, at p. 84. See also Section 17 of the Tunis Model Law on Copyright of 1976, which encourages the use of *domaine public payant* to assist developing countries to 'protect and disseminate national folklore'; Edwin R. Harvey, 'The *domaine public payant* in Comparative Law with Special Reference to Argentina' (1994) *Copyright Bulletin*, XXVIII (4), pp. 29–39.

99 See Farley, supra note 76.

100 Michael Blakeney, 'The Protection of Traditional Cultural Expressions', available at http://www.ecap-project.org/fileadmin/ecapII/pdf/en/activities/regional/aun_sept_07/traditional_cultural_expressions_word.pdf.

101 See the work of the UNESCO Committee of Non-Governmental Experts on the 'Domaine Public Payant' (1982) *Copyright Bulletin,* XVI (3), pp. 46–54, at p. 49. See also Adolf Dietz, 'A Modern Concept for the Right of the Community of Authors (Domaine Public Payant)' (1990) *Copyright Bulletin,* XXIV (4), pp. 13–28.

Notably, a proposal for a Public Domain Commission was made in the IGC at its 9th session. The representative of Music in Common, speaking on behalf of renowned American folk musician Peter Seeger, made the following statement:

> Old songs, worldwide, now in the public domain are often 'adapted and arranged' and the new song copyrighted. We propose that a share, .01% or 99.99%, of the ... royalties go to the place and people where the song originated. Every country should have a Public Domain Commission to help decide what money goes where. ... The public domain ... [does] not mean that monies generated by sale somewhere not be returned to their source of inspiration, namely the peoples or countries whence they [have] arisen. Indeed, it would be one function of the Public Domain Commission to ensure that two apparently contradictory purposes [are] served: to ensure preservation and development of a natural resource for the benefit of all and, at the same time, to limit use by those seeking to profit from it and to ensure that a reasonable portion of those profits [are] returned to the source to sustain it.[102]

However, the effectiveness of such a system has not really been assessed and the extent to which it can protect TCEs has been questioned, in at least two respects.[103] First, the administration and collection of fees can be a great burden for collective societies, particularly in developing countries. Second, it has been contended that it would not be a satisfactory solution for communities whose priority is control over their TCEs rather than remuneration.[104] What is more, the model has not been widely accepted in the world and its international effect on trade would be non-existent. Nonetheless, the concept, focusing on TK, has been implemented in Peru.[105]

The shortcomings of every explored possibility for the IP protection of TCEs have prompted continuing negotiations. But how do these questions affect, if at all, the tradability of TCEs?

6. TRADE IMPLICATIONS FOR TCEs

6.1 Benefits of Trade for TCE holders

It has been abundantly argued that trade in TCEs can have many benefits for their holders and the many cultures of the world. Notably, it can contribute to enhancing cultural

[102] Statement by the Representative of Music in Common, document in WIPO, IGC, 'Draft Report (Second Draft)', Ninth Session (WIPO Doc. WIPO/GRTKF/IC/9/14/Prov. 2, 2006), at para. 120. The author here believes that the amounts stipulated, being nearly nothing or nearly everything, are to show that the amount does not really matter; it is the principle that counts.

[103] See Marie Niedzielska, 'The Intellectual Property Aspects of Folklore Protection' (1980) *Copyright: Monthly Review World Intellectual Property Organisation*, 16, pp. 339–46, at p. 344.

[104] This is further reported on in a report on national and regional experiences with the protection of TCEs; WIPO, IGC, 'Final Report on National Experiences with the Legal Protection of Expressions of Folklore', Third Session (WIPO Doc. WIPO/GRTKF/IC/3/10, 2002).

[105] See Taubman and Leistner, supra note 98, at p. 147.

exchanges, promoting cultural diversity and even to the preservation of traditions.[106] It may also foster the economic development of TCE-holding communities, for TCEs can be of considerable economic value.[107] It is not surprising that 'some forms of folklore, like arts and crafts, have become an important source of income in developing countries and for local and indigenous communities.'[108] The sale of cultural objects and the holding of a cultural event, be it to develop cultural awareness or for monetary gain, have significantly risen.[109]

6.2 Trade of TCEs by Third Parties

Unfortunately, it has been equally widely reported that substantial commercial and individual interests, especially multinational companies from developed countries, are using, exploiting and commercialising TCEs for profit-making purposes.[110] Plainly, these third-party entrepreneurs often have greater capacity to commodify the elements of indigenous and traditional cultures. As a result, 'developing countries – those countries who usually dispose of the cultural heritage in question – are confronted with a foreign exploitation of their own resources beyond their control.'[111] What is more, trade in TCEs by outsiders carries a host of risks: goods are often of lesser quality, the association with the source community is skewed, and the original holders get no retribution for the use of their TCEs, such as through participation in the profits.[112]

What may certainly explain, at least in part, the significant level of appropriation, without remuneration or attribution, is the 'public domain' character of most TCEs. If they are perceived to be part of a free, unregulated common domain, why would anyone need to ask permission for their use and offer remuneration for their exploitation in trade?

---

[106] Martin Kretschmer, 'The Economics of Geographical Indications', Queen Mary and Fordham University, NY Joint Seminar Series (Barbican, London, November 2003); as quoted in Kamperman Sanders, supra note 16.

[107] See Lucas-Schloetter, 'Folklore', in von Lewinski (ed.), supra note 20, pp. 339–505, at p. 340–41.

[108] Daniel Wüger, 'Prevention of Misappropriation of Intangible Cultural Heritage', in Joseph M. Finger and Philip Schuler (eds), *Poor People's Knowledge – Promoting Intellectual Property In Developing Countries*, Washington DC: The World Bank, 2004, pp. 183–206, at pp. 183 and 185. See also Kamperman and Sanders, supra note 16.

[109] Kristen A. Carpenter, Sonia K. Katyal and Angela R. Riley, 'Clarifying Cultural Property: A Response' (2010) *International Journal of Cultural Property*, 17, pp. 581–898, at p. 590.

[110] See, for example, Statement by the representative of the Saami Council in WIPO IGC, 'Report. Fifth Session', supra note 54, at para. 53. See also Wend Wendland, 'Intellectual Property, Traditional Knowledge and Folklore: WIPO's Exploratory Program' (2002) *IIC International Review of Intellectual Property and Competition Law*, 33 (4), p. 499; and Graham Dutfield, *Intellectual Property Biogenetic Resources and Traditional Knowledge*, London: Earthscan Publication, 2004, at p. 18.

[111] Dutfield, supra note 110, at p. 18.

[112] Carpenter, Katyal and Riley, supra note 109.

6.3 Effects of IP Protection of TCEs on Trade

To counter the fact that trade in TCEs is and remains the *de facto* privilege of third parties, a natural reaction would consist in ensuring that TCE-holding communities have the power to decide whether they wish to trade in their TCEs or not, and on which terms. If they do wish to trade, efforts should be made to stimulate, encourage and support them in converting TCEs into marketable products.

One way to confer control over decision-making on the trade of TCEs entails their propertisation, the bestowing upon them of (intellectual) property rights. Practically speaking, the grant of IP rights over TCEs confers a monopoly to rights holders over, *inter alia*, the trade of their TCEs. Legal protection could then constitute an incentive 'for developing countries and their ethnic groups or cultural communities to achieve an advancement of their position in the global economy'.[113] This may be done through existing IP laws, such as GIs, which can help create a differentiated market for TCEs with localised characteristics.[114]

The effect will likely be the commodification of TCEs, because 'it is quite difficult to pursue the goals of propertization without some form of commodification'.[115] Put differently, 'underneath property concepts there always lurks the spectre of commodification – that is, an inexorable tendency to treat property as fungible and alienable'.[116] In fact, several indigenous and traditional communities have already propertised and commodified their cultures, or aspects thereof.[117]

However, some have deemed it unwise for the global economy to confer a monopoly on the trade of TCEs on their holders. Indeed, too extensive or rigid a right can risk freezing cultural exchanges and fencing up the public domain, defeating its purpose as a dynamic pool of inspiration for further creation. It has also been contended that 'in the long run, the interests of the countries concerned would be harmed as well'.[118] The best way to protect TCEs would then be 'to maximize their use and engagement with few or no legal restrictions'.[119]

---

[113] Hilty, supra note 10.

[114] Kamperman Sanders, supra note 16.

[115] Carpenter, Katyal and Riley, supra note 109, at p. 589.

[116] Margaret Jane Radin, *Reinterpreting Property*, Chicago: Chicago University Press, 1993, at pp. 191–202; quoted in Michael F. Brown, 'Culture, Property and Peoplehood: A Comment on Carpenter, Katyal and Riley's "In Defence of Property"' (2010) *International Journal of Cultural Property*, 17, pp. 569–79, at p. 576.

[117] Ibid., at p. 575, quoting John Comaroff and Jean Comaroff, *Ethnicity, Inc.*, Chicago: University of Chicago Press, 2009, at p. 29. See also Carpenter, Katyal and Riley, supra note 109, at p. 590.

[118] Hilty, supra note 10, at p. 779.

[119] Jon M. Garon, 'Localism as a Production Imperative: An Alternative Framework to Promoting Intangible Cultural Heritage and Expressions of Folklore', *Bits Without Borders. Law, Communications and Transnational Culture Flow in the Digital Age*, Michigan State University College of Law Intellectual Property & Communications Law Program Conference (East Lansing, Michigan, 24–25 September 2010), at p. 9 (footnotes omitted), available at http://www.law.msu.edu/bits/papers/GaronLocalism.pdf.

Be that as it may, conferring IP rights over TCEs might not increase, at least in the short term, their trade volume, *ceteris paribus*. For one, not all TCE-holding communities are interested in or willing to offer their TCEs commercially and to make them available for trade. Second, more often than not, they do not have the same business capacity as third-party entrepreneurs in developed countries to trade in their own cultural assets.

Yet the status quo is hardly a satisfying situation, not least for the TCE holders themselves. The quest for a way out thus goes on.

6.4 Still Searching for a Compromise

For their holders, TCEs sometimes represent a confidential, deeply personal and spiritual resource, one that may never be subject to exploitation or use, or be available for any purpose.[120] For these secret and sacred or otherwise culturally significant TCEs, the issue is clear-cut: 'holistic notions of knowledge and indigenous expressions often sit uneasy with the liberties that modern business takes with what indigenous peoples perceive to be sacred.'[121] A holder's refusal to commercialise cult objects used for their own spiritual, religious or whatever purposes should therefore be respected.[122]

In view of the particularly sensitive character of some TCEs, an essential measure would be to confer protection on these undoubtedly inalienable and *untradeable* TCEs and to ensure that they are not to be traded by anyone, except according to the wishes of their holders and based on their customary rules and practices, if applicable.

At least as far as tangible TCEs are concerned, this first essential step could be taken on the basis of the protection available to non-tradeable property (dubbed *res extra commercium* or *choses hors commerce*); for example, the Quebec Civil Code excludes certain sacred properties (*res sacrae*) from being treated as objects of trade.[123] Resorting to IP protection would in that specific case not even be necessary and even though the public

---

120 Danielle M. Conway-Jones, 'Safeguarding Hawaiian Traditional Knowledge and Cultural Heritage: Supporting the Right to Self-determination and Preventing the Commodification of Culture' (2005) *Howard Law Journal*, 48, pp. 737–62; as quoted in Kamperman Sanders, supra note 16. See also Statement by the representative of Tupaj Amaru, in WIPO IGC, 'Report. Fifth Session', supra note 54, at para. 80; and 'Implementing a Traditional Knowledge Commons. Opportunities and Challenges', Developments following the Traditional Knowledge Commons Workshop (Cape Town South Africa, December 2009), at p. 40, available online at http://www.naturaljustice.org/images/naturaljustice/implementing%20tkc.pdf.

121 Christoph Antons, 'Traditional Knowledge and Intellectual Property Rights in Australia and Southeast Asia', in Christopher Heath and Anselm Kamperman Sanders (eds), *New Frontiers of Intellectual Property Law: IP and Cultural Heritage, Geographical Indications, Overprotection, Enforcement*, London: Hart Publishing, 2005, pp. 37–51; as quoted in Kamperman Sanders, supra note 16.

122 Hilty, supra note 10, at p. 777.

123 *Res sacrae* is a sub-category of Roman law under *res nullius* (property belonging to no one). See Peter Stein (ed.), *William W. Buckland, A Text-Book on Roman Law from Augustus to Justinian*, 3rd edn, New York: Cambridge University Press, 1963. For a thorough analysis, see Robert K. Paterson and Dennis S. Karjala, 'Looking Beyond Intellectual Property in Resolving Protection of the Intangible Cultural Heritage of Indigenous Peoples' (2003) *Cardozo Journal of International and Comparative Law*, 11, pp. 633–70, at pp. 659–60.

domain character of the TCEs would remain unchanged, their use beyond the traditional and customary context would not be permitted.

For other, non-secret or non-sacred TCEs, especially those of potentially high commercial value, one possible way forward could be to reinforce and practically support the business capacity and hone the business skills of TCE holders. This strategy would focus on the market advantage that TCE holders could rest upon in order to compete locally and globally. Of course, such an avenue could only be explored if it reflected the identity, desires and aspirations of the community as well as if it respected cultural sensitivities.

Increasing their capacity to trade, through awareness-raising and training programmes, could perhaps constitute a pragmatic line of action, while negotiations for their substantial legal protection continue at the international level. Technically, this implies the adaptation of the traditional skills and of the products to meet the requirements of the market (local, but also global) and the improvement in market access and supply.[124] Moreover, in parallel, use of the current IP system, such as trade marks and GIs, could be encouraged in order to sustain a traditional skill base.[125] In that respect, promotion of a balanced use of IP tools within indigenous peoples and traditional communities could form an integral part of a comprehensive approach to the protection of TCEs. This could also permit the use of licensing mechanisms to ensure that whenever TCEs are being used in trade, benefits accruing from such exploitation are shared with their holders.

It should be emphasised that, even though IP is designed to provide incentives to create and trade, it is not a mechanism to compensate the holders who preserved and developed TCEs.[126] Their safeguarding and preservation, therefore, would not necessarily be assured through IP protection, and complementary measures would be needed to ensure 'careful curatorial protection'.[127]

7. CONCLUSION

As forewarned in this chapter's introduction, it is not the author's aim to advance any conclusions. But a few points may be mentioned in closing. As we have seen, existing IP provides only indirect protection to TCEs; it can directly protect contemporary tradition-based cultural expressions, but fails to protect pre-existing cultural heritage, which it relegates to the public domain. An important assessment is that the definition of the public domain is likely to respond to a number of different worldviews and take into account the current work undertaken at WIPO to protect TCEs by a *sui generis* form of IP. Notably, the public domain should be careful not to overlook the common property regimes of other

---

124 Maureen Liebl and Tirthankar Roy, 'Handmade in India: Traditional Craft Skills in a Changing World', in Finger and Schuler (eds), supra note 108, pp. 53–73, at p. 67.

125 The use of certification trade marks has been discussed by Christoph B. Graber and Jessica C. Lai, 'Indigenous Cultural Heritage and Fairtrade – Voluntary Certification Standards in the Light of WIPO and WTO Law and Policymaking' (2011) *Prometheus*, 29 (3), pp. 287–308.

126 See Consolidated Analysis, supra note 4, at para. 25.

127 Garon, supra note 119, at p. 9 (footnotes omitted).

cultures.[128] There is, it is contended, not one public domain but a number of different, overlapping public domains.[129]

At the heart of the debate lies the question of whether the public domain status of TCEs – free and unregulated, and therefore subject to inappropriate uses – curtails efforts to protect the interests of indigenous peoples and traditional communities, by failing to offer the greatest opportunities for creation, development, cultural exchange and trade. Resistance to providing IP protection to TCEs relies on the necessity to keep them available as a source of further creation. In that vein, if one views the public domain as a kind of 'zero sum game', every expansion of IP concomitantly shrinks the public domain.[130] But if one views ideas and information as public domain resources, then artistic and cultural creation can concomitantly expand the public domain, for the ideas and information in these works will be dedicated to an IP-free public domain upon publication, and protected material will eventually[131] fall into the public domain, becoming available to further nurture creativity.

---

[128] WIPO Scoping Study, supra note 32, at p. 12.

[129] Margaret Raven, 'Rethinking the Public Domain: A Challenge for Knowledge-Sharing Societies in the Information Age' (2005) *Work In Progress*, 17 (2), at p. 23.

[130] See David Lange, 'Recognizing the Public Domain' (1981) *Law and Contemporary Problems*, 44, pp. 147–78, at p. 171.

[131] The question of the term of protection is not discussed in this chapter. It is assumed that protection of TCEs would be limited in time, at least as far as the economic aspects are concerned.

9. International trade in indigenous cultural heritage: an argument for indigenous governance of cultural property

Rebecca Tsosie*

1. INTRODUCTION

This chapter examines the possibilities, advantages and limits of adjusting international trade law to protect indigenous cultural heritage, focusing on the international law dimensions of tangible forms of indigenous cultural property, as a distinctive category of cultural heritage.[1] Specifically, I address how indigenous peoples are defined within international cultural property law and how that body of law handles questions of indigenous culture, including definitions of traditional knowledge and traditional cultural expressions. Finally, I explore how indigenous peoples are represented, procedurally or otherwise, within international organisations and institutions.

The overriding issue, of course, is whether it is possible to adjust international trade law to protect indigenous cultural heritage. Specifically, what rules might promote fair trade in indigenous cultural heritage? Many scholars have written important work highlighting the unique nature of cultural expression within indigenous societies and the challenges of reconciling indigenous cultural systems with international trade law.[2] The implicit premise of many scholars is that international trade is the engine for globalisation and our

---

* The author would like to thank Christoph B. Graber, Karolina Kuprecht and Jessica Lai for organising the fascinating workshop on International Trade in Indigenous Cultural Heritage that led to this volume, and extend a special note of thanks to Karolina Kuprecht for her patient and meticulous attention to the editorial process. I am grateful for the support of my colleagues at ASU, including the staff of the Indian Legal Program, my research librarians at the Ross-Blakely Law Library, Alison Ewing, David Gay and Tara Mospan, and my research assistants, Timothy Koch (class of 2012) and Mykil Bachoian (class of 2011).

[1] Although I reference intangible cultural heritage and assert the relevant linkages between intangible and tangible forms of cultural heritage, primary discussions of that topic in this book are found within Christoph Antons, 'Intellectual Property Rights in Indigenous Cultural Heritage: Basic Concepts and Continuing Controversies'; Martin Girsberger and Benny Müller, 'International Trade in Indigenous Cultural Heritage: An IP Practitioners' Perspective'; and Rosemary J. Coombe with Joseph F. Turcotte, 'Indigenous Cultural Heritage in Development and Trade: Perspectives from the Dynamics of Cultural Heritage Law and Policy', in this book.

[2] See, for example, Christoph B. Graber, 'Institutionalization of Creativity in Traditional Societies and in International Trade Law', in Shubha Ghosh and Robin P. Malloy (eds), *Creativity, Law and Entrepreneurship*, Cheltenham, UK and Northampton, MA: Edward Elgar,

existing rules are set up to favour the attendant norms, which are pervasive and all-encompassing. Our global economy requires free trade of goods and an open marketplace in which competitors flourish. The market system depends upon conceptions of private property and also upon a global commons, the creative domain, in which competitors freely innovate new goods and services for consumption. The nation states structure the system, often to favour their particular interests. Though legal rights may be articulated through multilateral conventions, they are often dependent for their implementation upon effective domestic laws. Indigenous peoples are viewed as distinctive populations, for purposes of international law, but their actual legal rights are dependent upon the willingness of the nation states to acknowledge their interests. Because indigenous peoples lack the status of states within the international structure, they lack any ability to negotiate conventions as equal political actors. This set of circumstances supports the pervasive view that we must fit indigenous peoples into the larger normative structure in a way that honours their interests, while still allowing the dominant economic structure to flourish.

The challenges for indigenous peoples under this approach are enormous. To the extent that indigenous peoples seek to vindicate their rights to their cultural heritage, they must identify alternative norms perhaps stemming from conceptions of distributional justice or human rights law that are sufficient to persuade the nation states to guard against the exploitation of indigenous peoples. Based on the discussions to date, this is an uphill battle and one that depends upon the ability to: (1) define who is an indigenous people; (2) define indigenous cultural heritage; (3) differentiate a series of complex categories of cultural heritage, including cultural property, intellectual property, traditional cultural expressions and traditional knowledge; and, finally, (4) decide whether any of those categories merit legal protection, primarily because the category is the functional equivalent of some European-derived category that merits legal protection, for example property or intellectual property.

Not surprisingly, each prong of this approach represents a challenge for indigenous people. First, there is no universal understanding of which groups fall within the rubric of 'indigenous peoples' and that is a deeply divisive question in many regions of the world, given their disparate histories and settlement patterns.[3] Even in settler societies such as the United States, which have a fairly clear understanding of the distinctions between Native American groups and the dominant society, the issue becomes controversial in relation to the distinction between 'federally recognised' American Indian and Alaskan Native groups and 'non-recognised' groups, including many tribes in California and Native Hawaiians. Secondly, international conventions and declarations have multiple definitions of 'cultural heritage' and these are not always consistent with categories of indigenous cultural heritage, defined under international human rights law or domestic law. And

---

2011, pp. 234–63; Christoph B. Graber and Mira Burri-Nenova (eds), *Intellectual Property and Traditional Cultural Expressions in a Digital Environment*, Cheltenham, UK and Northampton, MA: Edward Elgar, 2008; and Christoph Antons (ed.), *Traditional Knowledge, Traditional Cultural Expressions and Intellectual Property Law in the Asia-Pacific Region*, Alphen aan den Rhijn, Netherlands: Kluwer Law International, 2009.

[3] See S. James Anaya, *International Human Rights and Indigenous Peoples*, Austin, TX: Wolters Kluwer Law & Business, 2009, at pp. 27–30.

finally, there are hotly contested debates about whether aspects of indigenous cultural heritage in fact constitute 'property' or 'intellectual property' and whether they should be protected under standard legal doctrines, constitute the subject of '*sui generis*' rights or remain unprotected.

Consequently, the 'compare and contrast' approach is really quite fruitless for indigenous peoples and it also evokes the doctrine of discovery within international law. As we know, the doctrine of discovery was a tool for European colonisation of lands occupied by indigenous peoples. The doctrine held that the first Christian European nation to 'discover' and 'settle' such lands could appropriate them, through 'purchase or conquest', because indigenous peoples did not maintain 'property' rights in their lands on the same basis as civilised European peoples.[4] The asserted justification was that indigenous peoples lacked laws that entitled them to the same treatment as civilised European nations (whose citizens would have their property rights protected under the law of conquest while the transition in political governance took place) and that they did not possess the same 'moral right' to their lands because they were seen as nomadic hunters and gatherers, rather than settled agriculturalists.[5] In the eighteenth and nineteenth centuries, the normative differences between indigenous peoples and Europeans were used to deny them equal rights to land.[6] Today, they are used to deny indigenous peoples protection for their cultural heritage under a variety of analogous rationales.

In this chapter, I will advocate that we recognise the rights of indigenous peoples to their cultural heritage, including the right to govern their cultural property and engage in trade with respect to aspects of their cultural heritage that they deem capable of alienation. In undertaking this argument, my starting place is the norm of indigenous self-determination and the necessity for modern nation states to qualify their domestic laws and international agreements accordingly. I am cautiously optimistic that we can develop a workable structure for the regulation of indigenous cultural heritage within domestic and international law, and this chapter is directed toward that end, although I also intend to acknowledge some of the potential pitfalls of such an approach. Section 2 of this chapter offers a foundational account of the norm of indigenous self-determination and the importance of recognising rights to cultural heritage in the service of this norm. Section 3 of the chapter engages the substantive basis for recognising indigenous rights to cultural heritage as an aspect of international law, with an emphasis on the category of 'cultural property'. Section 4 of the chapter examines the premise of indigenous governance of cultural property for purposes of domestic US and tribal law. Section 5 of the chapter examines some of the arguments for and against legal recognition of rights to indigenous cultural heritage and offers recommendations for the future.

---

4 See *Johnson v McIntosh* (1823) 21 US 543 Marshall J.

5 See ibid.

6 See Robert A. Williams Jr, *The American Indian in Western Legal Thought: The Discourses of Conquest*, New York: Oxford University Press, 1990.

2. SELF-DETERMINATION: THE FOUNDATION OF INDIGENOUS GOVERNANCE OF CULTURAL HERITAGE

The UN General Assembly adopted the Declaration on the Rights of Indigenous Peoples[7] (UNDRIP) by an overwhelming majority vote in 2007. Although the United States originally dissented, as did Canada, New Zealand and Australia, President Obama recently reversed that position, as have the governments of the other settler states.[8] Thus, UNDRIP, while purely prescriptive, represents a universal charter of rights, outlining the minimum standards that ought to guide nation states in their relationship with indigenous peoples to ensure that indigenous peoples thrive under conditions of justice and that their human rights are respected. In this sense, UNDRIP is useful in opening a discussion about the rights of indigenous peoples. I will draw upon UNDRIP's provisions to show that the United States has an obligation to respect the rights of indigenous peoples within its borders, including their rights to cultural heritage, and to implement these rights through domestic law. Other countries have a similar set of duties to the indigenous peoples within their borders, although they may choose to negotiate their own modes of accommodation.

My central argument in this chapter is that indigenous self-determination is best served through an intercultural legal framework that acknowledges the autonomy rights of native peoples. With respect to indigenous rights to cultural heritage, this requires an examination of the interactive framework established by tribal law, domestic federal law and international law. For the sake of clarity, I will limit my discussion to the indigenous groups within the United States, although I believe that the general approach can be extended to indigenous peoples within other nation states.

2.1 The Right to Self-Determination and US Federal Indian Law

The central premise of UNDRIP is that indigenous peoples have a right to self-determination as 'peoples', and that many distinctive rights, for example, to land, resources and culture, flow from that right. UNDRIP takes the position that indigenous peoples ought to have access to all the rights that stem from national citizenship (that is, access to public institutions and services), and that the nation state should also recognise their distinctive status as 'peoples' with a right to 'self-determination'. At first glance, these requirements seem to be present within US law. Since the 1924 Indian Citizenship Act, native peoples in the United States have been entitled to full national citizenship. Furthermore, there are many court cases from the 1960s and 1970s explicitly recognising rights of equal state citizenship, including voting rights and access to public education. In addition, the United States has formally acknowledged the separate political status of federally recognised native nations under federal law and articulated a domestic policy

---

7 See UN, Declaration on the Rights of Indigenous Peoples (UNDRIP), GA Res. 61/295 (UN Doc. A/61/L.67 and Add.1) (adopted on 13 September 2007).

8 See President Obama, 'Remarks by the President at the White House Tribal Nations Conference' (16 December 2010), available at http://www.whitehouse.gov/the-press-office/2010/12/16/remarks-president-white-house-tribal-nations-conference (all online sources were accessed 6 September 2011).

favouring native self-determination. The only residual question is whether the domestic concept of 'self-determination' is compatible with the right described by UNDRIP.

In addressing that question, it is first necessary to examine how the right to 'self-determination' is defined by UNDRIP. Article 3 states that '[i]ndigenous peoples have the right to self-determination. By virtue of that right, they freely determine their political status and freely pursue their economic, social, and cultural development.' This language tracks that of Article 1 of the Covenant on Civil and Political Rights, which identifies the right of self-determination as belonging to all 'peoples'. Article 4 further explains that 'in exercising their right to self-determination', indigenous peoples 'have the right to autonomy or self-government in matters relating to their internal and local affairs, as well as ways and means for financing their autonomous functions'. Article 46 clarifies that nothing within UNDRIP authorises or supports 'any action which would dismember or impair, totally or in part, the territorial integrity or political unity of sovereign and independent states', indicating that the extraordinary remedy of secession is not available in the service of indigenous self-determination.

The language in Articles 3 and 4 appears to be compatible with US federal Indian law, which recognises the inherent sovereignty of federally recognised Indian tribes and their distinctive status as 'domestic dependent nations' which maintain a 'trust relationship' with the federal government. US federal Indian law recognises that tribal governments have inherent sovereignty over their members and their territory, although there are many jurisdictional limitations on the ability of tribal governments to exercise authority over non-members. In the United States, tribal governments are autonomous under their own legislative, judicial and executive bodies, and they also have the capacity to exercise authority under delegations of federal power.[9] Thus, the concept of tribal sovereignty under US federal Indian law provides one context to understand how the right of self-determination is expressed under current law. UNDRIP posits that nation states can negotiate different political models, depending upon their respective circumstances. It is clear that the United States has negotiated a model for self-determination with the federally recognised tribal governments within its borders. Building on that foundation, the United States must engage the interests of indigenous peoples in governing their cultural heritage.

2.2 Indigenous Rights to Cultural Heritage as an Aspect of Self-Determination

As S. James Anaya has explained, there are several composite norms embedded within the concept of indigenous self-determination.[10] One of the primary norms is that of cultural integrity.[11] This norm 'upholds the right of Indigenous groups to maintain and freely develop their cultural identities in coexistence with other sectors of humanity'.[12] The norm of cultural integrity is addressed throughout UNDRIP. For example, Article 11 states that

[9] See in more detail Carole Goldberg, 'A United States Perspective on the Protection of Indigenous Cultural Heritage', in this volume.

[10] S. James Anaya, *Indigenous Peoples in International Law*, 2nd edn, Oxford: Oxford University Press, 2004, at p. 129.

[11] Ibid., at pp. 131–41.

[12] Ibid., at p. 131.

'[i]ndigenous peoples have the right to practise and revitalise their cultural traditions and customs', which includes the right to 'maintain, protect and develop the past, present and future manifestations of their cultures', such as 'historical sites, artefacts, designs, ceremonies, [and] technologies'. Nation states have the obligation to 'provide redress through effective mechanisms', including restitution, for any 'cultural, intellectual, religious [or] spiritual property' taken without the 'free, prior, informed consent' of indigenous peoples, or in violation of their 'laws, traditions and customs'.

Article 12 of UNDRIP recognises that indigenous peoples have 'the right to manifest, practise, develop and teach their spiritual and religious traditions, customs and ceremonies', which includes the rights to protect sacred sites, control their ceremonial objects, and repatriate their human remains. States have the duty to enable these rights of access and repatriation. Article 13 of UNDRIP specifically protects the rights of indigenous peoples to 'revitalize, use, develop and transmit to future generations' their histories, languages, oral traditions, philosophies, literatures and place-names. Nation states have the obligation to protect these rights within the dominant society's 'political, legal and administrative proceedings'.

These are only representative examples of the many aspects of indigenous cultural heritage that are protected by UNDRIP. 'Cultural heritage' is expressed through tangible and intangible aspects of culture and, as demonstrated above, there are many articles within UNDRIP relevant to the definition of indigenous cultural heritage. UNDRIP recognises that, historically, indigenous peoples have not been adequately protected by the basic 'civil rights' that are guaranteed to all citizens (such as the right of an individual to religious freedom) and, therefore, nation states must take actions to specifically protect indigenous peoples' rights. The cultural differences responsible for the historic failure of nation states to protect indigenous rights become a positive source of rights under UNDRIP's approach. UNDRIP accurately describes the spiritual context of many indigenous cultures, the unique relationship between indigenous lands and lifeways, and the intergenerational nature of indigenous rights, which depend upon the ability of the group to transmit the relevant knowledge to each successive generation. All of these features provide a context for the expression of indigenous rights to cultural heritage.

Article 31 of UNDRIP is *explicitly* directed toward the right of indigenous peoples to protect their cultural heritage, traditional knowledge and traditional cultural expressions. This Article represents the broadest statement of cultural rights within UNDRIP and therefore provides the best platform for understanding indigenous rights to cultural heritage.[13] This Article should also be read in connection with Article 8(j) of the Convention on Biological Diversity (CBD),[14] an existing multilateral treaty that overtly links indigenous rights to cultural heritage.

This chapter will now turn to a discussion of indigenous 'cultural heritage' as it is expressed by these provisions and other instruments of international law.

---

[13] See Jessica C. Lai, 'The Protection of Māori Cultural Heritage: Post-Endorsement of the UN Declaration on the Rights of Indigenous Peoples', *University of Lucerne, Switzerland*, i-call Working Paper No. 2 (2011), at pp. 33–36, available at http://www.unilu.ch/files/i-call_working_paper_2011_02_lai_maori_cultural_heritage__undrip.pdf.

[14] Rio Convention on Biological Diversity (CBD), 1760 UNTS 79; 31 ILM 818 (opened for signature 5 June 1992, entered into force 29 December 1993).

3. AN ANALYSIS OF INDIGENOUS CULTURAL HERITAGE UNDER INTERNATIONAL LAW

The forces of globalisation have accentuated the need for nation states to consider the rights of native peoples to their lands and natural and cultural resources as they negotiate multilateral treaties on international trade, climate change and the management of shared resources, including water and fish. Article 37 of UNDRIP specifically requires states to 'honour and respect' the 'treaties, agreements, and other constructive arrangements' that they have articulated with indigenous peoples, providing formal validation of an intercultural approach to indigenous rights. Thus, international law explicitly recognises the importance of articulating indigenous rights under domestic law, including treaty law, and with attention to the customary laws of indigenous groups. That is the structure of indigenous self-determination, which provides the starting place for the inquiry about indigenous rights to cultural heritage.

There are a variety of international conventions and declarations on cultural heritage that address rights to cultural property, traditional knowledge and traditional cultural expressions. These instruments are primarily directed to serve the interests of nation states, but they do affect the interests of indigenous peoples. In accordance with my argument in favour of indigenous governance, I will first discuss the instruments that are particular to indigenous cultural heritage, and then address the broader context of international cultural heritage law.

3.1 International Law Focused on Indigenous Cultural Heritage

Article 31 of UNDRIP and Article 8(j) of the CBD are the two provisions most useful for articulating a foundation to protect indigenous rights to cultural heritage.

3.1.1 Article 31 of the UN Declaration on the Rights of Indigenous Peoples

Article 31 of UNDRIP provides that:

> Indigenous peoples have the right to maintain, control, protect and develop their cultural heritage, traditional knowledge and traditional cultural expressions, as well as the manifestations of their sciences, technologies and cultures, including human and genetic resources, seeds, medicine, knowledge of the properties of fauna and flora, oral traditions, literatures, designs, sports and traditional games and visual and performing arts. They also have the right to maintain, control, protect and develop their intellectual property over such cultural heritage, traditional knowledge, and traditional cultural expressions.
>
> In conjunction with indigenous peoples, States shall take effective measures to recognize and protect the exercise of these rights.

Article 31 accurately recognises that most indigenous peoples do not separate the tangible and intangible components of their cultural heritage. For example, a medicine bundle is a tangible object, but it may be the songs and knowledge that go with the bundle that enable its effective use in the cultural life of a native community.[15] Therefore, it may not be appropriate to abstract the nature of a medicine bundle as 'cultural property' from the traditional knowledge and traditional cultural expressions that are integrated with it. Similarly, native people may consider photographs of human remains or cultural objects to have a similar significance to the tangible objects.[16] The representation and meaning of these objects is of fundamental importance, necessitating limitations on who can see or touch the remains and also on who can see pictures of the remains. Article 31 demonstrates the multiple categories of indigenous cultural heritage and recognises rights in objects and expressions, as well as the ability for indigenous peoples to assert 'intellectual property' rights to aspects of their traditional knowledge which they seek to use or protect from misuse.

This integrated and broad construction of indigenous rights to cultural heritage may be of concern to proponents of free access and trade, as well as a broad 'public domain' or 'creative commons'. In fact, there has been a concerted effort among scholars and policy-makers to separately define and distinguish 'cultural property' and 'intellectual property' from 'traditional knowledge' and 'traditional cultural expressions', recognising only the former two categories as worthy of legal protection. For example, Stephen Munzer and Kal Raustiala acknowledge the need to give limited protection to certain interests associated with indigenous 'traditional knowledge' (for example, where 'unjust enrichment' would result from pirating indigenous knowledge for commercial benefit), but argue that most of the interests within the category of 'traditional knowledge' do not support legal protection under property theories or any other theory, and would in fact jeopardise the integrity of the public domain.[17] UNDRIP counsels a different approach. According to UNDRIP, it is unjust to refuse to recognise indigenous norms purely because they might conflict with the interests of the dominant society. UNDRIP takes the position that it is necessary to engage in dialogue with indigenous peoples about their rights and interests, and following that dialogue, nation states are asked to 'take effective measures' to protect the rights of indigenous peoples. This mode of accommodation places a sense of responsibility upon indigenous groups to articulate their interests, which suggests the primacy of tribal law in structuring a further accommodation of rights. At that point, the nation state has an obligation to effectively protect the rights of indigenous peoples within its domestic law, and ensure that those rights are respected within international accords.

---

15 See William E. Farr, 'Troubled Bundles, Troubled Blackfeet: The Travail of Cultural and Religious Renewal', *Montana The Magazine of Western History* (Autumn 1993), at pp. 3–17 (discussing the dispute over a set of Blackfeet medicine bundles entrusted by their native owners to a non-Indian trader, who, without authorisation, published pictures of the bundles and their contents in an art book and then sold the collection to a Canadian museum, asserting that the bundles were no longer 'alive' in the cultural life of the community, because the knowledge of the songs and stories had been 'lost').

16 See, for example, Kathryn Milun, 'Keeping While Giving Back: Computer Imaging and Native American Repatriation' (2001) *Political and Legal Anthropology Review*, 24 (2), pp. 39–57, at p. 39 (presenting the dispute over ownership of digital depictions of a set of Native American human skeletal remains between the Northern Paiute people and the anthropologist who took the pictures and claimed them as her 'intellectual property').

17 See Stephen R. Munzer and Kal Raustiala, 'The Uneasy Case for Intellectual Property Rights in Traditional Knowledge' (2009–10) *Cardozo Arts & Entertainment Law Journal*, 27, pp. 37–97.

The CBD exemplifies the procedural approach recommended by UNDRIP, in the context of indigenous rights to biodiversity. In that sense, both documents support the general claim of Christoph B. Graber that international legal instruments are most effective when they support procedural approaches to protection of indigenous rights, rather than substantive approaches that would require comprehensive and universal solutions.[18]

3.1.2 Article 8(j) of the Convention on Biological Diversity

The Convention on Biological Diversity represents a collective effort among nation states to articulate the global importance of managing biological diversity in the service of preservation and also benefit-sharing. Article 8 of the CBD describes the primary set of Convention obligations to conserve biological diversity and recognises the *in situ* approach as being the best mechanism to achieve this. Under Article 8, each contracting party has the obligation to establish protected areas where special measures must be taken to preserve biological diversity, and then develop guidelines for the selection, establishment and management of protected areas.

Article 8(j) explicitly recognises the rights of indigenous peoples to their traditional knowledge and provides that 'subject to its national legislation', each contracting party ought to:

> respect, preserve and maintain knowledge, innovations, and practices of indigenous and local communities embodying traditional lifestyles relevant for the conservation and use of biological diversity and promote their wider application with the approval and involvement of the holders of such knowledge, innovations and practices and encourage the equitable sharing of the benefits arising from the utilization of such knowledge, innovations, and practices.

This provision is important because it acknowledges that natural resources can also be cultural resources, that intangible knowledge exists in relationship to tangible aspects of the environment. It also recognises that indigenous peoples and other land-based communities are part of the ecosystems that the Convention seeks to protect and that they possess knowledge and expertise that can be of utility to the nation states. This provision not only recognises that indigenous communities possess 'traditional knowledge' about their environments and resources, but also conditions benefit-sharing upon the 'approval and involvement' of indigenous peoples. Thus, the norm of indigenous governance is to some extent represented within the CBD, even though it is a document intended for adoption only by the nation states.[19]

UNDRIP also speaks to these issues, agreeing that indigenous peoples have the right to 'maintain, control, protect and develop' their traditional knowledge (Article 31) and that the 'states shall consult and cooperate in good faith' with indigenous peoples 'in order to

---

[18] See in more detail Christoph B. Graber, 'Stimulating Trade and Development of Indigenous Cultural Heritage by Means of International Law: Issues of Legitimacy and Method', in this volume.

[19] For the representation of indigenous governance in the Nagoya Protocol on Access to Genetic Resources and the Fair and Equitable Sharing of Benefits Arising from their Utilization to the Convention on Biological Diversity (UN Doc. UNEP/CBD/COP/DEC/X/1) (adopted on 29 October 2010), see John Scott and Federico Lenzerini, 'International Indigenous and Human Rights Law in the Context of Trade in Indigenous Cultural Heritage', in this volume.

obtain their free, prior and informed consent before adopting and implementing legislative or administrative measures that may affect them' (Article 19).

In conclusion, UNDRIP and the CBD work together to promote a sense of responsibility among nation states to consider the unique rights of indigenous peoples to their lands and natural and cultural resources as they govern these resources through domestic law and through international agreements with other nation states. The United States ought to focus on its responsibility towards native peoples – which is articulated as a 'trust responsibility' under US federal Indian law – rather than viewing these international instruments as a 'limitation' upon its power to promote national policies, even if these policies may harm important tribal interests. The premise of international human rights laws is that nation states should strive to ensure that their laws and policies do not harm vulnerable groups, including indigenous peoples, who lack adequate political power to ensure that their interests are respected.

3.2 International Cultural Heritage Law

International cultural heritage law is diffuse and the enforceable provisions are directed primarily toward the protection of tangible cultural property, while those provisions engaging intangible cultural heritage are largely prescriptive. Although conventions are international treaties and may become binding upon nation states upon their acceptance and ratification, their enforceability is generally premised upon the nation state's agreement to enter an optional protocol submitting itself to an international forum for cases of alleged breach.[20] In the United States, Congress must ratify all treaties and must also enact domestic legislation in order to implement the provisions of a treaty. Consequently, very few international instruments relevant to cultural heritage are enforced as a matter of US domestic law.

Having acknowledged the limitations of international cultural heritage laws in the United States, it is useful to examine them to see how cultural heritage is defined and protected domestically. The concepts of 'cultural resources' and 'cultural preservation' are fairly recent innovations within European and American law (dating in most cases to the nineteenth and twentieth centuries), although the notion that cultural objects should be given special treatment during time of war dates back to the Roman Empire.[21] Cicero distinguished between 'ordinary war booty' and the illegal removal of art and architectural decoration from public monuments. Similarly, Emeric de Vattel distinguished 'cultural property' from the types of moveable property that could constitute legitimate war booty.[22] These views were incorporated into international treaties. For example, the Treaty of Vienna in 1815 required France to return art works that had been taken from throughout Europe during the Napoleonic wars or to make restitution if the artwork had already been

---

[20] One example of an Optional Protocol is found in the UN, International Covenant on Civil and Political Rights, 999 UNTS 171 and 1057 UNTS 407; 6 ILM 368 (adopted on 16 December 1966, entered into force 23 March 1976).

[21] See Patty Gerstenblith, *Art, Cultural Heritage and the Law*, Durham, NC: Carolina Academic Press, 2004, at p. 469.

[22] Emeric de Vattel, *The Law of Nations or the Principles of Natural Law*, translated and edited by Joseph Chitty, 1844 (first published 1758, in French), at book 3, chs 13–14.

sold to other nations.[23] No similar requirement existed for the looting of indigenous cultural property from the lands colonised in the Americas, Australia or New Zealand. 'Primitive art' was distinguished from 'fine art' until quite recently, justifying the wholesale plunder of indigenous cultural objects and human remains from their rightful communities of origin. The lack of effective protection for indigenous cultural property remains an ongoing issue within international human rights law. Millions of cultural objects and human remains exist in museums and in the hands of private collectors throughout the world. International repatriations to indigenous groups have taken place in a limited number of cases, as a matter of grace and moral persuasion, not because there is any law requiring this to occur.

In the modern era, the nation states have articulated their interests in cultural heritage within a variety of conventions. The 1954 Hague Convention for the Protection of Cultural Property in the Event of Armed Conflict defines 'cultural property' as 'moveable or immovable property of great importance to the cultural heritage of every people' and emphasises the importance of preserving cultural heritage during times of armed conflict, stating that any harm to national cultural property is a 'harm to the cultural heritage of all mankind'.[24] Significantly, nations are asked to identify their cultural property through the use of distinctive emblems.[25] Similarly, the 1972 UNESCO Convention Concerning the Protection of the World Cultural and Natural Heritage (World Heritage Convention)[26] pertains to natural sites and historic sites within the territorial boundaries of nation states and calls for states to protect these sites from damage. Nation states are asked to nominate sites for inclusion in a register, and all parties to the Convention are then required to refrain from taking any deliberate measures that might damage the site. This Convention may indirectly assist the interests of indigenous peoples. For example, to the extent that a nation state acts to nominate an indigenous sacred site to the register, it would have the obligation to protect the site under its national laws and all state parties would be required to refrain from taking actions that would harm the site (for example, through mining operations or dam projects).[27]

The 1970 UNESCO Convention on the Means of Prohibiting and Preventing the Illicit Import, Export and Transfer of Ownership of Cultural Property (1970 Convention)[28] is

---

[23] See Gerstenblith, supra note 21, at pp. 470–71.

[24] The Hague Convention for the Protection of Cultural Property in the Event of Armed Conflict, 249 UNTS 240 (adopted on 14 May 1954, entered into force 7 August 1956), Article I.

[25] Ibid., Article VI.

[26] UNESCO, Convention Concerning the Protection of the World Cultural and Natural Heritage, 1037 UNTS 151 (adopted on 16 November 1972, entered into force 17 December 1975).

[27] The United States, for example, currently has 21 sites listed on the World Heritage list, available online at http://whc.unesco.org/en/list. This list includes eight cultural sites, 12 natural sites and one mixed site. There are indigenous sites on the list, including Cahokia Mounds, Chaco Canyon, Mesa Verde National Park and the Pueblo of Taos. There is also a site in Hawaii, Papahanaumokuakea, which is of cultural significance to the Native Hawaiian people, and is listed as a mixed cultural and natural site. See on the World Heritage Convention also Coombe and Turcotte, supra note 1.

[28] UNESCO, Convention on the Means of Prohibiting and Preventing the Illicit Import, Export and Transfer of Ownership of Cultural Property, 823 UNTS 231 (adopted on 14 November 1970, entered into force 24 April 1972).

directed toward the protection of national cultural property from illicit transfer within international trade. Prior to 1970, the problem of looting had been the subject of several treaties, for example those between the United States and Mexico protecting the rights of the Mexican government to its pre-Columbian artefacts, and was to some extent covered by domestic US laws, such as the National Stolen Property Act[29] criminalising the interstate or foreign transfer of 'stolen property'. The 1970 Convention defines 'cultural property' as property which, on religious or secular grounds, is specifically designated by each state as being of importance for archaeology, prehistory, history, literature, art or science. The Convention follows the 'common heritage of mankind' rationale for protecting national interests in cultural property, and requires all state parties to respect the cultural heritage within the territories for which they are responsible, taking all appropriate measures to prohibit and prevent the illicit transfer of cultural property. Thus, as of 1970, all items of cultural property must be exported and imported in accordance with the source country's laws. The United States became a party to the Convention in 1983 and Congress enacted the Cultural Property Implementation Act of 1983 (CPIA) to enforce the provisions of the Convention.[30]

The CPIA implements the Convention primarily through two mechanisms. First, the statute prohibits importing into the United States cultural material (including cultural property, archaeological resources at least 250 years old and ethnographic material) that is identified as stolen from an institution in another State Party, and requires the United States to assist in its recovery if it is imported. Secondly, the CPIA applies specific import or other controls at the request of another State Party to archaeological and ethnological materials (produced by a 'tribal or nonindustrial society') when those materials are specifically identified as comprising a state's cultural patrimony and in danger of being pillaged. Thus, the 1970 Convention addresses indigenous cultural property as an aspect of national cultural patrimony and its effective implementation is dependent upon the enactment of domestic laws within the source nation. The 1995 UNIDROIT Convention on Stolen or Illegally Exported Cultural Objects[31] is complementary to the 1970 Convention and is intended to deal with the issues of limitation (repose) and good faith acquisition in the private marketplace. So far, only 29 states have signed onto this Convention. These issues are dealt with under US law by the CPIA.

All of the above Conventions are directed toward the protection of tangible cultural property. They all reflect the 'cultural heritage of all mankind' rationale for protecting tangible cultural property, typically espoused by nation states. To the extent that indigenous cultural heritage is considered to be an aspect of a nation state's protected cultural property, it may become eligible for protection under the standards of the Conventions at issue, as well as under the domestic laws (such as the CPIA) that implement these protections. International law protecting intangible cultural heritage is still emergent and is, for the most part, not effective to protect the interests of indigenous peoples. As Rosemary Coombe and Joseph Turcotte observe, the term intangible cultural heritage only recently emerged in the context of the 2003 UNESCO Convention for the Safeguarding of

---

29 National Stolen Property Act, 18 U.S.C. §§ 2314–2315 (2006).

30 Cultural Property Implementation Act of 1983, 19 U.S.C. §§ 2601–2613 (2011).

31 UNIDROIT Convention on Stolen or Illegally Exported Cultural Objects, 34 ILM 1322 (adopted on 24 June 1995, entered into force 1 July 1998).

the Intangible Cultural Heritage (2003 Convention),[32] although earlier initiatives sought to affirm the importance of creative diversity and promote the actions of nation states to protect specific forms of creative expression, for example folklore.[33] The obstacles to development of a coherent legal framework to protect intangible cultural heritage are daunting. Perhaps most importantly, there is lack of clear agreement on the definition of intangible cultural heritage. Legal protection for intangibles is generally confined to categories of intellectual property law (such as copyright, patent and trade mark). These categories contain clear definitions within domestic law and are suitable subjects for international conventions. As Coombe and Turcotte note, there is a perceived overlap between intangible cultural heritage and intellectual property, which emphasises proprietary models for protection. Not only is this understanding antithetical to many of the cultural interests that indigenous peoples have, but it inspires resistance on the part of nation states to adopt enforceable protections for intangible cultural heritage. The nation states are unwilling to impair the dominant economic model for intellectual property protection. As a result, the nation states have treated indigenous peoples' interests as a form of moral claim, which can be protected by soft law in the form of recommendations for the conservation and protection of diverse forms of cultural expression.

The international conventions on intangible cultural heritage that are currently in place largely operate as prescriptive suggestions to the nation states. For example, the 2003 UNESCO Convention serves its stated objective by counselling respect for local communities, the need to raise awareness about the importance of intangible cultural heritage and the need to provide for international cooperation and assistance.[34] The 2003 Convention tracks the approach of the World Heritage Convention, attempting to foster global recognition that some societies live their cultural traditions and that is where protection is needed, rather than focusing attention on artefacts. In this respect, the 2003 Convention provides that each State Party should prepare one or more inventories of the intangible cultural heritage present in its territory, as part of a consultative process with relevant communities, groups and non-governmental organisations, and transmit this report to the Intergovernmental Committee set up to promote the Convention's purposes.[35] Although the Convention has a special process to identify intangible cultural heritage in need of urgent safeguarding, there are no enforcement provisions attached to this Convention that would deter state actors from destroying such resources, and the obligation of nation states to contribute funding to assist in protecting intangible cultural heritage is purely optional.[36]

Similarly, the 2005 UNESCO Convention on the Protection and Promotion of the Diversity of Cultural Expressions (2005 Convention) serves its stated objective by encouraging dialogue among cultures to foster intercultural respect and build bridges

---

[32] UNESCO, Convention for Safeguarding of the Intangible Cultural Heritage, 2368 UNTS 1 (adopted on 17 October 2003, entered into force 20 April 2006) [hereinafter 2003 Convention].

[33] See Coombe and Turcotte, supra note 1.

[34] 2003 Convention, Article 1.

[35] See ibid., at Articles 5–7 (organisation and functions of Committee); Article 11 (role of State Parties); Article 12 (inventories).

[36] See ibid., at Articles 16–18.

among peoples.[37] The Convention seeks to articulate the link between culture and development for all countries, and it encourages countries to work cooperatively with one another in a spirit of partnership. Importantly, the Convention affirms the sovereignty of the nation states to implement measures that they deem necessary to foster diversity of cultural expressions within their territorial boundaries.[38]

The 2005 Convention supports the predominant economic values of the existing international trade structure, while encouraging the nation states to be sensitive to particular cultural values and forms of expression. In particular, the Convention counsels nation states to pay attention to the special circumstances and needs of women as well as various social groups, including persons belonging to minorities and indigenous peoples.[39] In this respect, indigenous peoples are treated as vulnerable social groups in need of the fostering care of the national governments. Similarly, where a particular circumstance arises that places cultural expressions at risk of extinction, under serious threat or in need of urgent safeguarding, the Convention identifies a process to report this exigency to the Intergovernmental Committee set up to administer the Convention and obtain the Committee's recommendations.[40] The 2005 Convention provides suggestions to nation states on how to promote cultural diversity and a procedural mechanism to encourage nation states to take protective measures on behalf of vulnerable populations, particularly when certain forms of cultural expression may be in imminent danger of destruction. However, the Convention does not establish legal rights for cultural groups, nor does it provide a tangible enforcement structure to ensure that the stated purposes are met.

Both the 2003 and 2005 Conventions contain broad and ambiguous definitions of intangible cultural heritage and cultural expressions. In fact, Lyndel Prott attributes the lack of effectiveness of the 2003 Convention to its vague definition of intangible cultural heritage.[41] The 2003 Convention maintains that:

> The 'intangible *cultural* heritage' means the practices, representations, expressions, knowledge, skills – as well as the instruments, objects, artefacts and cultural spaces associated therewith – that communities, groups and, in some cases, individuals recognize as part of their *cultural* heritage. This intangible cultural heritage, transmitted from generation to generation, is constantly recreated by communities and groups in response to their environment, their interaction with nature and their history, and provides them with a sense of identity and continuity, thus promoting respect for cultural diversity and human creativity.[42]

---

[37] UNESCO, Convention on the Protection and Promotion of the Diversity of Cultural Expressions, 2440 UNTS 311 (adopted on 20 October 2005, entered into force 18 March 2007), Article 1 [hereinafter 2005 Convention].

[38] Ibid.

[39] Ibid., at Article 7(1)(a).

[40] Ibid., at Article 8.

[41] See generally Lyndel Prott, 'UNESCO International Framework for the Protection of the Cultural Heritage', in James A.R. Nafziger and Ann M. Nicgorski (eds), *Cultural Heritage Issues: The Legacy of Conquest, Colonization and Commerce*, Leiden: Martinus Nijhoff, 2009, pp. 257–85.

[42] Ibid., at p. 273.

Despite the vague language of its definition, the 2003 Convention at least prescribes an inventory process to identify intangible cultural heritage in need of protection. The 2005 Convention, however, defines cultural expressions as those expressions that result from the creativity of individuals, groups and societies, and that have cultural content, a description that is so broad that it is legally meaningless.[43] Other scholars have noted a similar ambiguity within the many definitions of traditional knowledge and traditional cultural expressions generated within the committees of the World Intellectual Property Organization (WIPO), which makes it difficult to associate these concepts with standard categories of intellectual property law, which do create legally enforceable rights.[44]

An additional complication, as Prott observes, is that the major market nations do not agree on the relevance of culture to international trade. Prott asserts, for example, that France and Canada favour the protection of cultural interests within the global marketplace, while the United States is committed to a truly open market that fosters competition.[45] According to Prott, the primary value of the cultural heritage conventions is to foster a policy of mutual supportiveness among the nation states by establishing intergovernmental bodies to facilitate collaboration on the objectives of each treaty. The committees provide a forum for the discussion of best management practices and have an important educational function. The governance role resides with the nation states who choose to become parties to the convention. Within each convention, the national sovereignty of the states is emphasised and parties adhere to their obligations within an environment that supports the mutual and multiple functions of the national governments, including interests of national security, sustainable development and economic stability.

Indigenous peoples are affected by these international conventions and agreements, but they do not have the governance role. The definitions generated by committees within UNESCO and WIPO attempt to characterise the importance of 'intangible cultural heritage' to traditional indigenous communities, but the attempt results in a vague and potentially unlimited set of cultural attributes which do not resemble anything that the law recognises as capable of 'ownership'. This massive 'top–down' effort by international policy-makers has little resonance with tribal governance structures. Building on the effort to articulate an effective foundation for indigenous self-determination, I will argue that indigenous governance of cultural heritage primarily exists as an aspect of domestic US and tribal law. Tribal governments can grapple with the issues of what aspects of their cultural heritage ought to be protected and how this can occur. They can then engage with the US government about what modifications ought to be made to domestic law to enable the enforcement of tribal law. Because the primary responsibility for discussing US law regulating indigenous cultural heritage resides with Carole Goldberg in this volume, I will

---

43 2005 Convention, Article 4(3). See Christoph B. Graber, 'Substantive Rights and Obligations under the UNESCO Convention on Cultural Diversity', in Hildegard Schneider and Peter van den Bossche (eds), *Protection of Cultural Diversity from an International and European Perspective*, Antwerp: Intersentia, 2008, pp. 141–62.

44 See, for example, Christoph Antons, 'Introduction' to *Traditional Knowledge, Traditional Cultural Expressions and Intellectual Property Law in the Asia-Pacific Region*, supra note 2, at pp. 1–5.

45 Prott, supra note 41, at p. 272.

keep the following discussion very brief and focused on the argument that I am making here with respect to indigenous governance of cultural property.

4. INDIGENOUS GOVERNANCE OF CULTURAL PROPERTY AS AN ASPECT OF DOMESTIC AND TRIBAL LAW

In my view, indigenous self-determination is best served through an intercultural framework that acknowledges the autonomy rights of native peoples. With respect to indigenous rights to cultural heritage, this requires an inquiry into the interactive framework established by tribal law and domestic federal law. With respect to the sub-category of indigenous cultural heritage described as 'cultural property', I will point out some of the conceptual challenges to broad recognition of indigenous rights to cultural property, and then discuss how US domestic law has dealt with some of those challenges.

4.1 Conceptual Challenges to the Legal Protection of Indigenous Cultural Heritage

In other work, I have discussed several of the conceptual challenges to the legal protection of indigenous cultural heritage.[46] In particular, the following conceptual challenges relate to the argument I am developing. First, there is a pervasive inability among scholars and policy-makers addressing indigenous cultural heritage to distinguish 'objects of art' from 'cultural objects'. As a result, discussions about indigenous rights to cultural heritage get stymied by a discussion about the merits of an open marketplace and a robust public domain.[47] This might be useful to a discussion of 'art' and the marketplace, but it seems misguided in relation to the concept of 'cultural property' used by national governments to protect their own cultural patrimony from free trade in the open market. Secondly, there is a similar disconnect between scholars and policy-makers addressing indigenous rights to cultural heritage that stems from competing viewpoints about the significance of 'culture' to notions of 'ownership' (for example, within property law) and 'access' (for example, in the service of benefit-sharing). There is a pervasive tendency to associate the rights of indigenous peoples with those of nation states that encompass them, rather than recognising their rights to their cultural property as equal to the rights of the nation states. Nation states have the right to claim cultural property and protect it under international agreements. Indigenous peoples are dependent upon the nation states to recognise indigenous cultural property as part of the nation state's cultural patrimony for purposes of international protection, which leads to the assumption that the rights of the nation state in some sense are representative of the rights of the indigenous peoples within its borders. So, for example, the United States might claim aspects of Native American cultural identity as constituent parts of 'American' identity. In that sense, the distinctive claims of

---

[46] See Rebecca Tsosie, 'Who Controls Native Cultural Heritage? "Art", "Artifacts", and the Right to Cultural Survival', in James A.R. Nafziger and Ann M. Nicgorski (eds), *Cultural Heritage Issues: The Legacy of Conquest, Colonization, and Commerce*, Leiden: Martinus Nijhoff Publishers, 2009, pp. 3–36. [hereinafter Tsosie, 'Who Controls Native Heritage?'].

[47] See Munzer and Raustiala, supra note 17.

indigenous peoples to their cultural heritage either become subsumed within the protection afforded to the nation state or go unprotected.

4.1.1 The difference between native 'art' and native 'artefacts'

Many of the current difficulties with the legal protection of Native American art and culture relate to the conceptual gaps between the respective cultural understandings of native people and Anglo-American people about the difference between 'art' and 'artefacts'.[48] Following on the history of plunder that was attached to European colonisation of native peoples and their lands, Euro-Americans tend to see all Native American cultural objects as 'art'. The carved poles of Northwest Coast Indians, such as the Haida and Tlingit, are highly sought as objects of art, as are Hopi kat'sinas and the Zuni war gods. There is a huge black market in the American Southwest for Anasazi pottery looted from ancient sites, and in many cases, the actual mummified and skeletal human remains of these native peoples are traded as well. In contemporary times, artefact hunters have claimed to be ignorant of the difference between 'pre-historic artefacts' and contemporary sacred objects, such as medicine bundles and ceremonial masks, which are also sought by collectors.[49] To complicate the issue, some collectors will assert that native people are active players in the marketplace for Native American art, placing jewellery, rugs and other items for sale, allegedly along with cultural and ceremonial artefacts. The result appears to be a profound confusion about what aspects of native cultural heritage are permissibly placed into commerce as 'art', and which, if any, ought to be protected from sale or trade as 'cultural property'.

I believe that it is necessary to make a fundamental distinction between '*cultural property*', meaning items that are part of the cultural heritage of a tribal government or native people and which are significant to the native nation's survival as a distinctive people and culture, and '*commercial products*', which are items intentionally manufactured and created by native artists for the purpose of economic development. I believe that native nations should have the same ability as nation states to define what constitutes their cultural property and they should not be forced to accept the 'common heritage of mankind' theory for cultural preservation because native cultural property is used to promote *cultural survival*. Harm to indigenous cultural property threatens the core survival of a living people and is not merely a harm to the 'cultural heritage of all mankind'. I believe that native people are entitled to govern their own cultural heritage and that this is one very important feature of the right of self-determination. I also believe that native people have the right to profit from their cultural expressions, if they choose to do so. The Hopi people, for example, claim the kat'sinas as a central aspect of their culture and there are very sacred figurines which may not be alienated from the tribe and which certainly constitute tribal cultural property. On the other hand, the Hopi people have developed a secular art form derived from cultural symbols, and Hopi artists are authorised

---

[48] See Tsosie, 'Who Controls Native Heritage?', supra note 46, at pp. 5–7.

[49] See, for example, *United States v Diaz* (1974) 499 F 2d 113 Merrill J (9th Cir) (upholding defendant's argument that the Antiquities Act of 1906, 16 U.S.C. § 433 (2011) was unconstitutionally void for vagueness as applied to the charge of stealing a ceremonial mask from the San Carlos Apache reservation because the mask was created within recent years and could not constitute 'an object of antiquity').

to create kat'sinas for the marketplace. The Hopi people have claimed a form of cultural copyright to these commercial products, asserting that non-Hopis (even if they are Native American) have no right to produce or market these figurines. It is and should be the domain of the Hopi people to differentiate symbols and items as 'cultural property' or as 'commercial products'.

4.1.2 Culture, ownership and access

Another central problem with the existing framework for cultural resources protection is that it does not correspond to native understandings of cultural heritage. Rights to 'ownership' and 'access' within native and western cultures are developed in accordance with disparate cultural norms. So, for example, American cultural resources law is premised on the notion that heritage resources belong to the 'collective past' of the American people as a 'melting pot' of different cultures. Similarly, American cultural resources law distinguishes between 'history' and 'prehistory', and there is a pervasive belief that no one can own aspects of 'prehistory'. That is why there is a significant controversy in the United States over who should have the right to control ancient human remains and whether they are sufficiently related to modern groups to be designated as 'Native American' human remains.[50]

In comparison, most native peoples, such as the Navajo, do not even have a word for 'prehistory'. Rather, their histories begin at the creation of life and of this world. Not surprisingly, tribal cultural heritage laws tend to adopt a very comprehensive definition of cultural heritage. For example, the Code of the Confederated Tribes of the Warm Springs Reservation in Oregon defines tribal cultural heritage protection as a 'trust' on behalf of all tribal members, which includes 'the management of ancient and contemporary cultural use sites and materials which are fundamental in the recognition of the traditional lifeways, values and histories' of those tribes. The Code is inclusive of traditional foods, medicines, sacred sites and associated aspects of tribal culture, whether these are found on or off the reservation and regardless of the current 'ownership' of the lands. Similarly, the Code of the Eastern Band of Cherokee Indians specifically protects all ancestral human remains regardless of where they are found, and the Code provides that the graves and remains of the Cherokee people and their ancestors are sacred and must not be disturbed. If they are inadvertently disinterred, the Code provides that the remains and associated funerary objects should be immediately reburied and must not be subjected to destructive skeletal analysis. There are, of course, jurisdictional challenges to the full implementation of these tribal laws. However, they comprise a core structure for the legal articulation of native rights to cultural heritage, including cultural property.

Another challenge to refining notions of ownership and access is that native cultures do not commonly differentiate between the tangible and intangible aspects of their cultural heritage. Under Euro-American law, tangible items may be protected under 'property law' and intangibles are selectively protected as 'intellectual property'. This property rights framework, which dominates both national and international law, posits that property can be 'owned' by individuals or by groups that possess a corporate identity. 'Cultures' do not 'own' property under this view. Rather, individuals own real and personal property and

---

[50] See *Bonnichsen v United States* (2004) 367 F 3d 864 Gould J (9th Cir).

nation states own cultural property that is emblematic of their national identity, as well as public lands and resources. Churches and other religious organisations can own religious property on behalf of their members, but the larger 'cultural group' associated with a religion (for example, the 'Jewish culture') is not perceived to have analogous rights of ownership. So, for example, the state of Israel may own property, as may a specific Jewish synagogue, or an individual Jewish person. However, it would be considered nonsensical to try to define a property right of all 'Jewish' people to their 'culture'.

In fact, the pervasive view is that 'culture' is not static, but is a dynamic, constantly shifting collection of symbols, values and norms, that is shared and transformed through a multitude of processes. Property, on the other hand, is a 'specific bundle of rights' that is protected by the state in accordance with theories supporting the private ownership of resources and the transfer of such rights in the marketplace to their highest and best use. Culture cannot and should not be 'commodified', under this view, although to the extent that native people have true 'property' interests, these might be protected under standard legal doctrines. These views are carefully analysed by Kristen Carpenter, Sonia Katyal and Angela Riley in their comprehensive work, 'In Defense of Property', which endorses the importance of indigenous cultural property as an aspect of 'personhood' and in the furtherance of 'tribal sovereignty, self-determination and cultural survival'.[51] I will not replicate their excellent analysis, but agree with their central premise that the dominant views on 'property' and 'culture' consistently work against recognition of indigenous peoples' rights to 'cultural property'.

Therefore, the autonomy rights associated with native self-determination are quite important to generating an effective theory of indigenous governance of cultural property. Native peoples as governments are appropriate holders of cultural property. Tribal law must explicate what is 'cultural property' and may not be alienated from the tribe, as compared with 'commercial products', which derive from tribal culture but are appropriately placed in commerce. This effort is emergent within US domestic law and I will highlight some of the features of this system of Native American cultural resource laws.

4.2 The Existing Framework for Protection of Indigenous Cultural Property in the US

To date, indigenous cultural heritage in the United States has been protected to some extent through the combined effect of federal and tribal law (and to a lesser extent, state law), as it pertains to particular categories of cultural heritage. The Native American Graves Protection and Repatriation Act (NAGPRA),[52] for example, protects native rights to human remains, funerary objects, sacred objects and objects of cultural patrimony, if the objects meet the statutory definitions of these terms and if the objects are either held by federal agencies or federally funded institutions as of the effective date of the statute or are thereafter excavated from federal or tribal lands, or if the objects are commercially 'trafficked' within interstate commerce. Under NAGPRA, tribal law is used to delineate the nature of an object as a 'sacred object' or 'object of cultural patrimony', and both sets

---

[51] Kristen A. Carpenter, Sonia K. Katyal, Angela R. Riley, 'In Defense of Property' (2009) *Yale Law Journal*, 118, pp. 1022–32, at p. 1024.

[52] 25 U.S.C. §§ 3001–3012, 18 U.S.C. § 1170.

of objects can be accurately designated as tribal cultural property. Under NAGPRA, 'sacred objects' are defined as 'specific ceremonial objects which are needed by traditional Native American religious leaders for the practice of traditional Native American religions by their present day adherents'. This definition requires an active and ongoing use for the object in the cultural and religious life of native practitioners. 'Cultural patrimony', on the other hand, includes objects 'having ongoing historical, traditional, or cultural importance central to the Native American group or culture itself, rather than property owned by an individual Native American, and which, therefore, cannot be alienated, appropriated, or conveyed by any individual Native American'. Such objects must have been considered inalienable by the Native American group at the time the object was separated by the group.

To date, there have been several federal court cases protecting medicine bundles, ceremonial masks and other regalia as tribal 'cultural patrimony'.[53] Federal law criminalises the interstate transfer of Native American human remains or cultural objects in commerce and also carefully regulates the excavation of these items from federal lands, in order to protect the interests of native nations. If the remains or objects are in the custody of a federal agency or federally funded museum, NAGPRA requires that the items be repatriated to the community of origin upon the request of the native nation. Many states, such as Arizona, have adopted statutes prescribing similar protections for Native American human remains, funerary objects (and in some cases, cultural objects), excavated on state or private land.[54]

The protections for Native American cultural heritage are limited and largely restricted to tangible objects. There are other statutes that impact tangible cultural heritage, such as the National Historic Preservation Act,[55] which covers historical sites and also protects eligible 'Traditional Cultural Properties', including some Native American sacred sites. The Archaeological Resources Protection Act[56] protects archaeological resources on public lands, including human remains and cultural objects. However, these respective statutory protections are largely confined to cultural resources on federal public lands or those impacted by federally funded projects.[57] American property law governs many other cases, allowing private owners to maintain an 'ownership' interest in Native American cultural objects that are located on private land or where 'title' was conveyed prior to the effective date of any protective law, allowing the holder to assert a valid 'right of possession'. In sum, the fundamental precepts of American property law, which construct a 'private property' interest that is protected against undue governmental interference by the Fifth Amendment, have constrained a broader application of federal or state law that would require the reversion of land or personal property to the original Native American owners in order to serve broader cultural interests.

It is even more difficult for native people to protect the 'intangible' aspects of their cultural heritage, such as their songs, ceremonies, stories and traditional knowledge. The reason for this is that US domestic law supports a broad construction of 'intangible'

---

53 See, for example, *United States v Corrow* (1997) 119 F 3d 796 Porfilio J (10th Cir).

54 Arizona Revised Statutes Annotated §§ 41–844 to 41–846 (2004).

55 National Historic Preservation Act of 1966, 16 U.S.C. §§ 470a-470w-6.

56 The Archaeological Resources Protection Act, 16 U.S.C. §§ 470aa-470mm.

57 For more details, see Goldberg, supra note 9.

cultural heritage as a 'commons' that is widely accessible to all ('the public domain') and limits the right of any individual to 'exclude' others from the 'cultural commons'.[58] Federal law confers only limited protection to authors, artists and inventors, allowing an exclusive property right to emerge primarily where the creator/inventor has generated value through his or her own labour and initiative, thus earning an 'intellectual property right' that falls within one of the constitutionally protected categories of rights: copyrights, patents and trade marks. To a lesser extent, the law of trade secrets or misappropriation can be used to protect certain creations or inventions that do not fit squarely within the logic of the standard doctrines of intellectual property law. This has a positive construction because it indicates that the constitutional framework does not preclude recognition of other rights to intangible resources, when this is necessary to serve the interests of justice. However, because Native American claims are often a poor fit for both the standard categories of intellectual property rights, as well as the limited doctrinal expansions that have been recognised through collateral laws, their interests are often entirely disregarded.

One important exception is the Indian Arts and Crafts Act (IACA),[59] originally enacted in 1935 to promote a market for Indian arts and crafts and to prevent goods falsely marketed as 'Indian art' from impairing this market. The statute was substantially amended in 1990 and 2000 to provide enhanced civil and criminal penalties for the fraudulent sale and misrepresentation of goods as 'Indian made'. The statute is patterned after US trade mark law, giving eligible tribes and their members the exclusive right to market goods as 'Indian made'. The IACA serves the economic interests of Indian nations in creating a vibrant market for their commercial products. It does not protect the interests of native peoples in protecting the intangible aspects of their cultural heritage from other harms, including the harm of cultural appropriation. Non-Indians are free to copy Native American designs, symbols, songs and other cultural forms so long as they do not fraudulently misrepresent the origin of their products. This 'free cultural exchange' is considered beneficial and, in fact, many aspects of tribal cultures are considered to be part of the 'public domain'.

In sum, US domestic law provides limited protection for indigenous rights to tangible cultural property, primarily in the context of 'sacred objects' and 'objects of cultural patrimony'. US domestic law also protects the economic interests of Indian tribes in marketing their commercial products as 'Indian art'. Thus, to some extent, US domestic law responds to the notion that indigenous 'cultural property' should be protected from illicit trade, while also recognising the right of native peoples to actively participate in the marketplace by developing a commercial product premised upon indigenous art forms. There is still much work to be done, primarily to elaborate the aspects of intangible cultural heritage that must be protected from appropriation and misuse.

---

[58] See on this topic Brigitte Vézina, 'Are They In or Are They Out? Traditional Cultural Expressions and the Public Domain: Implications for Trade', in this volume.

[59] 25 U.S.C. § 305. For details, see Goldberg, supra note 9.

5. RECOMMENDATIONS FOR THE FUTURE

This chapter has described a framework for understanding the significance of indigenous cultural heritage and generated an argument in favour of indigenous governance of cultural property. I am aware of the challenges to this approach, many of which are raised by Michael F. Brown in his book, *Who Owns Native Culture?* and in his response to Carpenter, Katyal and Riley's article, 'In Defense of Property'.[60] I will distil those objections into the following points. Brown raises a concern that indigenous peoples are attempting to claim an unlimited and exclusive 'property right' in all aspects of their cultures, and, in so doing, are mimicking the worst behaviour of private corporate actors, while truly underestimating the value of the public domain to them. He asserts that appeals to 'sovereignty' are merely a 'slogan', and do not constitute a supportable justification for group control over cultural heritage. According to Brown, 'even the most resilient political sovereignty cannot insulate a community from outside influence'.[61] Brown is troubled by the 'vaguely defined and expansive' notion of cultural property endorsed by Carpenter, Katyal and Riley and other proponents of indigenous cultural rights. He sees no limitations to the asserted claims of indigenous peoples to their cultural productions, knowledge and biological inheritance, and thus fears that this expansive set of claims will intrude upon the legitimate interests of others within a pluralistic society. Brown maintains that cultural production is served by a robust 'commons' and cases of explicit injustice can be resolved through an appeal to more limited remedies, such as the denial of intellectual property rights to non-native actors seeking to profit from the appropriation of indigenous knowledge.

Although Brown raises some valuable concerns, his argument is beset by the same conceptual mistakes outlined earlier in this chapter. Brown adopts the same 'compare and contrast' approach that is typically used to deny indigenous peoples recognition of their distinctive interests in their cultural heritage, and he conflates appeals to tribal political sovereignty with the right of indigenous peoples to self-determination. Brown also presents the standard 'slippery slope' argument that is used to discredit novel claims (meaning those that are not a good fit for standard categories of rights), along with a general appeal to the paramount value of cultural pluralism.

UNDRIP affirms that indigenous peoples have the *right to self-determination*, meaning autonomy over their 'internal and local affairs'. Within domestic federal Indian law, the principle of inherent sovereignty is used to denote a similar constellation of autonomy rights. Importantly, the *political* sovereignty of native nations under US law, which is qualified by their status as 'domestic dependent nations' under federal law, is distinct from their *cultural* sovereignty, which is the unqualified right of tribal governments to articulate their own norms and values in structuring their collective futures.[62] Tribal cultural heritage

---

[60] Michael F. Brown, *Who Owns Native Culture?*, Cambridge, MA: Harvard University Press, 2003; and 'Culture, Property, and Peoplehood: A Comment on Carpenter, Katyal, and Riley's "In Defense of Property"' (2010) *International Journal of Cultural Property*, 17, pp. 569–79, at p. 569.

[61] Brown, 'Culture, Property, and Peoplehood', supra note 60, at p. 571.

[62] See Wallace Coffey and Rebecca Tsosie, 'Rethinking the Tribal Sovereignty Doctrine: Cultural Sovereignty and the Collective Future of Indian Nations' (2001) *Stanford Law & Policy Review*, 12 (2), pp. 191–221, at p. 196.

in many ways constitutes the core of inherent sovereignty and cultural integrity is a fundamental part of indigenous self-determination. The cultural sovereignty of native nations is not limited by the same jurisdictional framework that limits their political sovereignty (that is, through limitations on tribal jurisdiction over non-members).[63] Native peoples have always been the owners of their cultural property, traditional knowledge and traditional cultural expressions. For purposes of rights to cultural heritage, there should be no analogy to the 'doctrine of discovery' which separated the Indians' 'right of occupancy' in their aboriginal lands from the remainder of the bundle of rights that constitutes 'title' under Anglo-American property law.

It is abundantly clear that tribes have full authority to regulate their tangible and intangible cultural heritage under tribal law. This falls within their inherent sovereign authority and has never been affirmatively taken away by Congress. It is up to tribal governments to structure the positive content of their rights to cultural heritage, both tangible and intangible. This is the realm of tribal cultural sovereignty and the responsibility rests with native nations. Tribal political sovereignty *will* become an issue with respect to determining who is bound by tribal law. Tribal governments have the right to regulate the conduct of their members with respect to the rights that are attached to tribal cultural heritage.[64] Tribal governments also have the capacity to enact ordinances that preclude removal of tangible cultural patrimony that is collectively owned by the tribe, and such restrictions are binding upon both members and non-members.[65] This right is also recognised by NAGPRA, which effectuates the tribe's right to repatriate objects of cultural patrimony that were designated under tribal law as 'inalienable' at the time they were taken from the tribe and criminalises 'trafficking' in protected cultural objects.

The only difficulty will be in deciding how existing jurisdictional limitations constrain tribal power to protect aspects of their cultural heritage that have fallen into the hands of non-members and are being misappropriated for commercial gain or other uses. The challenges of protecting intangible cultural heritage are of particular concern. So, for example, can a non-Indian appropriate a traditional tribal song and then gain a 'copyright' to his or her 'original expression' of that song in a different medium (for example, rap

---

63 Ibid., at pp. 194–5.

64 Tribal governments enjoy full civil and criminal jurisdiction over tribal members on their reservations, subject to the specific protections of the Indian Civil Rights Act (ICRA) of 1968, 25 U.S.C. §§ 1301–1303. ICRA claims are adjudicated in tribal court, using tribal law. See Matthew Fletcher's analysis of free speech: Matthew L.M. Fletcher, 'Theoretical Restrictions on the Sharing of Indigenous Biological Knowledge: Implications for Freedom of Speech in Tribal Law' (2005) *Kansas Journal of Law and Public Policy*, 14 (3), pp. 525–60. Thus, tribes are free to employ a different set of norms to adjudicate whether the expressive conduct is indeed authorised under tribal law. For example, it is clear that many expressive acts (such as the ability to take photographs) can be sharply limited to protect tribal interests in maintaining the sanctity of ceremonial activities.

65 See, for example, *Chilkat Indian Village v Johnson* (1993) 20 Indian Law Report 6127 (Chilkat Tr Ct) (applying tribal ordinance forbidding sale or removal of 'artifacts, clan crests' and other art forms collectively owned by members of the Chilkat Indian Village to a non-Indian art collector who removed important cultural objects from the Village, with the assistance of certain tribal members, and ordering the return of the objects). For more details, see Goldberg, supra note 9.

music)?[66] This is an area that ought to be protected under federal law. An analogy can be made to the IACA. Although individual Indians can apply for a trade mark under US law if they meet the requirements, very few have the economic means and commercial presence to do so. The IACA recognised that non-Indians were appropriating the traditional art forms of Native Americans and then falsely marketing these items as 'Indian made', which harmed the economic interests of the tribal governments and tribal members, and also resulted in a harm to the market because consumers would have no way of knowing what was 'authentic' Indian art. So, that statute effectively gives Indians (as defined by the statute) the right to exclude non-Indians from producing 'Indian art', and thereby gives a 'trade mark' to Indians to protect the integrity of the market. If the IACA was not 'pre-empted' by US trade mark law, then, by analogy, other injustices that are currently not covered by the technical requirements of patent and copyright law might also be addressed by innovative applications of federal law. There is some support for this in Australia, where the Federal Court in the *Bulun Bulun v R & T Textiles* case recognised an indigenous group's communal interest in the visual depiction of a sacred site, describing the group as the equitable owner of the copyright, while the individual Aboriginal artist was the legal owner, acting as a 'fiduciary' for the group in defending it against infringement by a non-native company that appropriated the design for use on t-shirts.[67] The notion of an 'equitable' ownership may be constructive in preventing the type of cultural harm that accompanies many cases of explicit cultural appropriation of sacred symbols, songs and ceremonies.

Similarly, to the extent that a tribe maintains traditional knowledge about the medicinal use of a plant, this is most often not protected by patent law, although pharmaceutical companies can manufacture a product from the active compound of the plant which can be protected by patent law. This is the type of traditional knowledge which may be of broad public benefit, but is also of great importance to tribal governments. Traditional knowledge is a valuable cultural resource which ought to be protected against misuse, misappropriation and exploitation. If the general US laws do not protect this resource, the United States has a responsibility to protect the unique rights of indigenous peoples through alternative laws. An equitable extension of US patent law might be useful toward this end, and it would be perfectly supportable under principles of US federal Indian law which describe the United States as a 'trustee' for its native peoples and authorise Congress to enact laws for the benefit of native peoples. It would also be consistent with the provisions of UNDRIP and Article 8(j) of the CBD.[68]

The ultimate point is to acknowledge that tribal customary law systems maintain a basic concept of 'property', meaning a bundle of rights with respect to resources. There are clearly cultural differences which mean that principles such as 'equitable group ownership' may more accurately describe the way rights must be protected. In addition, with respect to traditional knowledge, there may be conditions upon the transfer of the knowledge, even within the group. It should not be assumed that all members of a group

---

66 See Angela Riley, 'Straight Stealing' (2005), *Washington Law Review*, 80, pp. 69–164 (giving an account of such a controversy).

67 *Bulun Bulun v R & T Textiles Pty Ltd* (1998) 157 ALR 193. On this case see Kathy Bowrey, 'International Trade in Indigenous Cultural Heritage: An Australian Perspective', in this volume.

68 See Scott and Lenzerini, supra note 19.

are entitled to equal access to traditional knowledge. Nor should it be assumed that groups are willing to create databases for the knowledge, in order to prevent the attempts of corporations to patent products based on traditional knowledge. The disclosure or recording of cultural knowledge may constitute a separate harm. Indeed, the concept of 'cultural harm' underlies many tribal objections to the use of genetic data and samples, as well as DNA testing of human remains.[69] The fact that there are differences in cultural understandings about property is not a reason to deny rights to the resources. Rather, it is a point of reference to open dialogue about the rights of specific native nations to their cultural property and other aspects of their cultural heritage.

6. CONCLUSION

I return full circle to the question that inspired this chapter: 'Can we adjust international trade law to protect indigenous cultural heritage?' This is a complex and fascinating question that requires careful thought. I have taken the position that the nation states have a duty to engage in a dialogue with indigenous peoples about their respective rights and interests in their cultural heritage. In the United States, this means (at a minimum) a consultation between the US government and the federally recognised American Indian and Alaskan Native tribes, and an effort to develop effective modifications within US domestic law to protect the central interests of native nations in governing their cultural property. The United States should also engage multilateral treaties on cultural heritage in a way that respects domestic treaties and laws protecting native peoples. Native peoples have a responsibility to engage in a tribal process to articulate the positive content of tribal inherent sovereignty as cultural sovereignty, and they must generate effective laws regulating aspects of their cultural heritage which they hope to protect from harm. Without this initial step to protect tribal cultural heritage from within, it will be quite difficult to persuade the United States or other nation states to step in and protect what they think of as 'cultural heritage'. Through this combined effort by nation states and native governments, we have the capacity to generate new categories of law that can overcome the mythology of discovery and effectively protect the rights of indigenous peoples.

---

69 See, for example, Rebecca Tsosie, 'Cultural Challenges to Biotechnology: Native American Genetic Resources and the Concept of Cultural Harm' (2007) *Journal of Law, Medicine & Ethics*, 35 (3), pp. 396–411.

10. International trade in moveable tangible cultural heritage of indigenous peoples: a European perspective

Karolina Kuprecht and Kurt Siehr

1. INTRODUCTION

Indigenous cultural heritage in the form of moveable, tangible objects has been travelling to Europe since the discovery of indigenous peoples' territories. Treated as curiosities in early times, the objects today form an important part of ethnographic collections kept in European museums, scientific institutions and private collections. They also nourish a flourishing international market in tribal art. Sotheby's auction sales in tribal art of May 2011 exceeded US$21.8 million and went way beyond prior expectations.[1] At the third 'Parcours des mondes' in Paris of 2011, 40 tribal art dealers exhibited and the number of visitors tripled.[2]

In the law, indigenous objects qualify as 'cultural property'[3] if they are of importance for archaeology, prehistory, history, art or science and thus fall under the broad definition of cultural property according to the UNESCO Convention on the Means of Prohibiting and Preventing the Illicit Import, Export and Transfer of Ownership of Cultural Property (UNESCO Convention 1970).[4] As such they are protected by national and international cultural property regulations which not only prohibit the damaging and taking of cultural

[1] AMA Art Media Agencies, 'Results of Tribal Art Sale at Sotheby's New York' (16 May 2011), available at http://www.artmediaagency.com/en/15893/results-of-tribal-art-sale-at-sothebys-new-york/ (all online sources were accessed 8 November 2011).

[2] Claude Pommereau, 'Xe Salon International des art premiers. Paris, capital du monde' (2011) *Beaux Arts Magazine*, 327, p. 122, who interpreted the success of the Parcours as a manifestation of Paris as the world capital of tribal arts.

[3] This chapter uses the term 'cultural property' for moveable, tangible forms of cultural heritage. Thereby, one should recall that using the term 'property' in the context of cultural heritage is generally problematic, as it triggers the understanding of a right which authorises exploiting, alienating and excluding others from access. These elements not only contradict the collective function of cultural heritage as stressed by indigenous peoples, but may also be restricted in modern cultural heritage law. See for example Lyndel V. Prott, 'The International Movement of Cultural Objects' (2005) *International Journal of Cultural Property*, 12, pp. 225–48, at p. 226.

[4] UNESCO, Convention on the Means of Prohibiting and Preventing the Illicit Import, Export and Transfer of Ownership of Cultural Property, 823 UNTS 231 (adopted on 14 November 1970, entered into force 24 April 1972), Article 1, [hereinafter UNESCO Convention 1970].

property in times of war, but also punish theft and clandestine excavation in times of peace. They also restrict international trade in cultural property when considered illicit.[5]

Such existing cultural property law in many ways neither captures nor truly resolves the issues arising with regard to indigenous cultural property. The law forgoes reflecting the particular interests of the indigenous peoples[6] which often substantially differ from those of other interest groups such as collectors, dealers, auctioneers, museum professionals, art historians, archaeologists, ethnographers or cultural officials of the state. Only slowly, the international community and some legal remedies of human rights have started to reflect indigenous cultural property claims in particular with regard to the human remains of their ancestors,[7] lost sacred,[8] ritual[9] or ceremonial objects[10] and objects of cultural patrimony[11] or communal importance.[12]

This chapter explores this new international awareness of indigenous cultural property in the context of trade and evaluates how the law deals with the existing international human rights standards. It thereby looks from a European point of view at international and European cultural property law, which is, however, still far from implementing indigenous cultural property human rights standards in a satisfactory encompassing way. The chapter explores the basic legal limits which work as major obstacles against legislative solutions for indigenous people's cultural property claims and looks into alternative ways of resolution. It thereby starts with the voluntary activities going on in Europe for dealing with indigenous cultural property claims and then pursues Christoph Graber's proposal for a procedural approach.[13] It explores whether the procedures of alternative dispute resolution or cultural diplomacy could work as a complementary or

---

[5] For an in-depth outline and discussion of such regulations see Kurt Siehr, 'International Art Trade and the Law' (1993), *Recueil des cours/Académie de Droit International; Collected Courses of the Hague Academy of International Law*, 243 (VI), pp. 9–292 [hereinafter Siehr, 'International Art Trade and the Law']; and Kerstin Odendahl, *Kulturgüterschutz: Entwicklung, Stuuktur and Dogmatik eines ebenübergreifenden Normensystems*, Tübingen: Mohr Siebeck, 2005.

[6] The question about who 'indigenous peoples' are and whether the term should be legally defined is outlined, *inter alia*, by Christoph B. Graber, 'Stimulating Trade and Development of Indigenous Cultural Heritage by Means of International Law: Issues of Legitimacy and Method', in this volume [hereinafter Graber, 'Stimulating Trade and Development']; and John Scott and Federico Lenzerini, 'International Indigenous and Human Rights Law in the Context of Trade in Indigenous Cultural Heritage', in this volume.

[7] United States Native American Graves Protection and Repatriation Act of 1990, 25 U.S.C. §§ 3001–3013, 18 U.S.C. § 1170, § 3001(3) [hereinafter NAGPRA]; UN, Declaration on the Rights of Indigenous Peoples (UNDRIP), GA Res. 61/295 (UN Doc. A/61/L.67 and Add.1) (adopted on 13 September 2007), Article 12.1 [hereinafter UNDRIP].

[8] NAGPRA, § 3001(3)(C); UNIDROIT Convention on Stolen or Illegally Exported Cultural Objects, 34 ILM 1322 (adopted on 24 June 1995, entered into force 1 July 1998), Article 3(8) [hereinafter UNIDROIT Convention 1995].

[9] UNIDROIT Convention 1995, Articles 5(3) and 7(2).

[10] UNDRIP, Article 12.

[11] NAGPRA, § 3001(3)(D).

[12] UNIDROIT Convention 1995, Article 3(8).

[13] Graber, 'Stimulating Trade and Development', supra note 6. See also Christoph B. Graber, 'Institutionalization of Creativity in Traditional Societies and in International Trade Law', in Shubha Ghosh and Robin P. Malloy (eds), *Creativity, Law and Entrepreneurship*, Cheltenham, UK

alternative solution to substantive law in implementing the international human rights standards for indigenous cultural property. Throughout the chapter, Rebecca Tsosie's strong argument for indigenous governance of cultural property, as presented in this volume,[14] serves as a constant point of reference.

2. CULTURAL PROPERTY TRADE AND REFLECTION OF INDIGENOUS INTERESTS IN THE LAW

2.1 Trade in Cultural Property and the Law

In the field of international cultural property law, there is a fervent discussion going on about the balance between free trade of cultural property and the adequate protection of cultural property. The legal framework of the World Trade Organization (WTO) exempts cultural property from trade liberalisation, if the objects are considered 'national treasures'. Article XX(f) of the General Agreement on Tariffs and Trade (GATT)[15] explicitly allows contracting parties to take reasonable measures 'for the protection of national treasures of artistic, historic or archaeological value'. However, the provision leaves a great scope for action and many details open for discussion.

2.1.1 Trade-restrictive perspective

Lyndel V. Prott, for example, a distinguished academic and former director of UNESCO's Division of Cultural Heritage, defends trade-restrictive cultural property protection measures. She stresses the fact that regulation of cultural property exchange is needed since trade in cultural property has been, and still is, a one-way flow into the direction of wealthy societies and countries, and thus equals exploitation rather than exchange.[16] In addition, she notes that cultural property law and regulations should not just be about works of art, antiquities and ethnographic objects as 'the sort of things that dealers deal in, collectors collect, and museums acquire and display'.[17] There are also many groups 'not comfortable with having their cultural objects considered as commodities for the market'.[18]

2.1.2 Trade-friendly perspective

On the other hand, the scholar John H. Merryman, a pioneer in academic studies on cultural property law, strongly emphasises the importance of trade liberalisation for cultural property. He appraises the idea of free trade in cultural property as an important counterforce to national over-retention and notes that cultural exchange is also the primary

---

and Northampton, MA: Edward Elgar, 2011, pp. 234–63, at pp. 251–2 [hereinafter Graber, 'Institutionalization of Creativity in Traditional Societies and in International Trade Law'].

14 Rebecca Tsosie, 'International Trade in Indigenous Cultural Heritage: An Argument for Indigenous Governance of Cultural Property', in this volume.

15 WTO, General Agreement on Tariffs and Trade, Marrakesh Agreement Establishing the World Trade Organization, Annex 1A, 1867 UNTS 187; 33 ILM 1153 (adopted on 15 April 1994, entered into force 1 January 1995).

16 Prott, supra note 3, at p. 228. See also Tsosie, supra note 14.

17 Prott, supra note 3, at p. 236.

18 Ibid., at p. 228.

underlying goal of the UNESCO Convention 1970.[19] The Preamble of the Convention stresses the importance of an interchange of cultural property among nations for scientific, cultural and educational purposes which 'increases the knowledge of the civilization of Man, enriches the cultural life of all peoples and inspires mutual respect and appreciation among nations'.

2.1.3 A converging consensus with regard to indigenous cultural property

These opposed opinions converge with regard to trade in indigenous cultural property. Prott uses tribal and indigenous communities' interests as one reason for international cultural property trade restrictions. She emphasises that such communities belong to groups which do not generally regard creators of their cultural property as artists of tradeable objects, but rather as bearers of a communal tradition.[20] Merryman leaves his trade-friendly line of argument for indigenous cultural property and pleads for an exception in cultural property law by stating: 'It seems right that objects of ritual/religious importance to living cultures remain with or be returned to the representatives of those cultures.'[21] Both authors thus agree that trade in indigenous cultural objects requires specific consideration.

2.2 Reflection of Indigenous Cultural Property Interests in the Law

2.2.1 Human rights standards

The trade-sceptical consensus with regard to indigenous cultural property of Merryman and Prott is supported by an important and interesting national law. In 1990, the United States enacted the Native American Graves Protection and Repatriation Act (NAGPRA).[22] This Act requires federal agencies and museums to inventory their Native American holdings, make the inventories public and, at the request of tribes, prioritise the return of sacred objects, cultural patrimony and human remains, as Carole Goldberg describes in more detail in her chapter to this volume.[23] The more than 20 years of experience with the Act have shown that legal coercion to acknowledge the role and participation of Native American tribes in the ultimate disposition and control of their cultural property is capable of having very positive effects on trade in indigenous cultural property in a broad sense. It stimulated a lively knowledge exchange between cultural institutions and Native Americans, it increased the interest in Native American cultures and effected the opening of many new museums under tribal control. At the same time, the activities under NAGPRA have

---

[19] John H. Merryman, 'Cultural Property Internationalism' (2005) *International Journal of Cultural Property*, 12, pp. 11–39, at p. 31 [hereinafter Merryman, 'Cultural Property Internationalism'].

[20] Prott, supra note 3, at p. 236.

[21] Merryman, 'Cultural Property Internationalism', supra note 19, at p. 13.

[22] See supra note 7.

[23] Carole Goldberg, 'A United States Perspective on the Protection of Indigenous Cultural Heritage', in this volume.

supported an important cultural revitalisation of Native American communities and helped to reconcile some profoundly different value systems existing in the United States.[24]

Other legal activities trying to reflect indigenous peoples' interests in their cultural property have taken place on an international level. Human rights standards for indigenous cultural property claims were established with the effect that newer international cultural property agreements started to reflect indigenous interests in their cultural property.[25] In the most recent Declaration on the Rights of Indigenous Peoples of 2007 (UNDRIP),[26] the core provisions on indigenous cultural property are Articles 11 and 12. Article 11 stipulates a right of indigenous peoples to practise and revitalise their cultural traditions and customs, including 'the right to maintain, protect and develop the past, present and future manifestations of their cultures, such as archaeological and historical sites, artifacts, designs, ceremonies, technologies and visual and performing arts and literature'. In paragraph 2, this article requires states to provide effective mechanisms for redress, 'which may include restitution, developed in conjunction with indigenous peoples'. Article 12 affirms the rights of indigenous peoples 'to the use and control of their ceremonial objects' as well as 'to the repatriation of their human remains'. In paragraph 2 it requires that '[s]tates shall seek to enable the access and/or repatriation of ceremonial objects and human remains in their possession through fair, transparent and effective mechanisms developed in conjunction with indigenous peoples concerned'.

UNDRIP is a non-binding instrument of international law. However, the Committee on the Rights of Indigenous Peoples of the International Law Association (ILA) performed important legal research that came to the conclusion that parts of UNDRIP qualify as binding international customary law, such as the right of indigenous peoples to reparation and redress for the wrongs suffered.[27] In their contribution to this volume, John Scott and Federico Lenzerini describe binding cultural property human rights which led to that conclusion, such as provisions of the 1966 Covenants on human rights,[28] the 1989 ILO Convention No. 169[29] and case law of international human rights courts.[30]

---

[24] The Harvard Project on American Indian Economic Development, *The State of the Native Nations: Conditions under U.S. Policies of Self-determination,* New York: Oxford University Press, 2008, at pp. 289–90. Karolina Kuprecht, 'The Concept of "Cultural Affiliation" in NAGPRA: Its Potential and Limits in the Global Protection of Indigenous Cultural Property Rights' (2012), *International Journal of Cultural Property*, 19, pp. 33–63.

[25] See Francesco Bandarin, 'International Trade in Indigenous Cultural Heritage: Comments from UNESCO in Light of its International Standard-Setting Instruments in the Field of Culture', in this volume.

[26] See supra note 7.

[27] International Law Association (ILA), Committee: Rights of Indigenous Peoples, 'The Hague Conference 2010 – Rights of Indigenous Peoples – Interim Report', at pp. 51–52, available online at http://www.ila-hq.org/en/committees/index.cfm/cid/1024.

[28] UN, International Covenant on Economic, Social and Cultural Rights, 993 UNTS 3; 6 ILM 360 (adopted on 16 December 1966, entered into force 3 January 1976); and UN, International Covenant on Civil and Political Rights, 999 UNTS 171 and 1057 UNTS 407; 6 ILM 368 (adopted on 16 December 1966, entered into force 23 March 1976).

[29] ILO Convention No. 169 Concerning Indigenous and Tribal Peoples in Independent Countries, 1659 UNTS 383 (adopted on 27 June 1989, entered into force 5 September 1991).

[30] Scott and Lenzerini, supra note 6. See also Karolina Kuprecht, 'Human Rights Aspects of Indigenous Cultural Property Repatriation', in Kerstin Odendahl and Peter J. Weber (eds),

2.2.2 UNESCO Convention 1970

These human rights developments came too late to specifically influence the most important international cultural property convention, the UNESCO Convention 1970 with more than 120 Member States. The Convention neither mentions nor specifically addresses indigenous cultural property. If an indigenous object falls under the broad definition of cultural property in Article 1 of the Convention, it benefits as any other cultural property from the acknowledgement of potential national export restrictions as requested by the Convention.[31] An indigenous object equally enjoys a potentially enhanced chance for repatriation if illegally exported or stolen and if the state takes the necessary steps.[32] However, any legal implementation of such trade restrictions as well as the decision about repatriation claims lies in the sole competence and responsibility of the states. As a non-self-executing Convention, its legal effect and impact depends on the Member States translating the provisions of the Convention into their national law.[33] Every Member State thus decides whether new cultural property laws are necessary to comply with the Convention. Thereby, as the Convention does not address indigenous peoples' interests, states have unlimited discretion in deciding whether they implement measures specifically requiring indigenous peoples' governance or at least involvement with regard to their cultural property.

2.2.3 UNIDROIT Convention 1995

The self-executing UNIDROIT Convention on Stolen or Illegally Exported Cultural Objects (UNIDROIT Convention 1995), with 32 contracting Member States,[34] in its Preamble explicitly mentions tribal and indigenous cultural property as of concern. It furthermore provides for a restitution claim of states, if such return of an object is justified by the traditional or ritual use by a tribal or indigenous community.[35] Finally, as an exception, it allows restitution claims for objects exported during the lifetime of the creating person or within 50 years following the death of that person, if the object was made by a member or members of a tribal or indigenous community for traditional or ritual use.[36] Thus, in contrast to the UNESCO Convention 1970, indigenous peoples' interests found their way into international cultural property law 25 years later. The

---

Kulturgüterschutz – Kunstrecht – Kulturrecht: Festschrift für Kurt Siehr zum 75. Geburtstag aus dem Kreise des Doktoranden- und Habilitandenseminars 'Kunst und Recht', Baden-Baden etc.: Nomos et al., 2010, pp. 191–226.

31 UNESCO Convention 1970, Articles 3, 5(a), 6 and 7.

32 UNESCO Convention 1970, Articles 7(b)(ii), 13(b) and 15.

33 UNESCO Convention 1970, Preamble. Patrick J. O'Keefe, *Commentary on the UNESCO 1970 Convention on the Means of Prohibiting and Preventing the Illicit Import, Export and Transfer of Ownership of Cultural Property*, 2nd edn, Leicester: Institute of Art and Law, 2007, at pp. 98–146.

34 See supra note 8. On 28 June 2011, Sweden ratified the UNIDROIT Convention 1995 as the last country at the time of writing.

35 UNIDROIT Convention 1995, Article 5(3)(d). See further to this problem Kerstin Asmuss, *Ansprüche indigener Völker auf Rückführung rechtswidrig ausgeführten Kulturgutes. Eine Untersuchung für Ansprüche aus Art. 5 UNIDROIT-Konvention 1995 und aus allgemeinem Völkerrecht*, Baden-Baden: Nomos, 2011.

36 UNIDROIT Convention 1995, Article 7(1)(b).

UNIDROIT Convention 1995 not only mentions indigenous peoples; it even slightly enhances the possible scope for legal action for indigenous peoples living on a Member State territory vis-à-vis other Member States and their inhabitants. Yet, possibilities are still limited to 'stolen' or 'illegally exported' cultural property and remain, for stolen objects, within the Convention's harmonised property law system. For illegally exported objects, indigenous peoples rely on the discretion of the nation state to act on their behalf.

2.2.4 State laws

Despite the international consensus and the clear tendency of international law to acknowledge the specific interests of indigenous peoples in their cultural property, European states provide little national law to respond. This becomes obvious when looking at the legal situation in the three countries with the biggest art markets in Europe.

A. The United Kingdom In the United Kingdom, the question of how to balance trade interests in cultural property with the need to protect them against illicit trade on the other hand was hotly discussed and temporarily resolved in 2002, when the state accepted membership to the UNESCO Convention 1970. An important milestone in the preceding debate leading to this step was the report on the return and illicit trade of cultural property by the Select Committee on Culture, Media and Sport of 18 July 2000 (UK Report I).[37] This Report underlines the indigenous peoples' interests as an important element that needs to be taken into account when talking about the liberalisation of cultural property trade. It stated:

> In examining the case for liberalisation of the trade in classical antiquities and of the export laws of some European States, it is possible to lose sight of the worldwide impact of the illicit trade in cultural property. … It is important to bear in mind the view that many indigenous communities have a prior claim to their own cultural property whatever the wishes of western collectors.[38]

The Report furthermore establishes that most repatriation claims against museums in the United Kingdom are associated with artefacts taken during the colonial era. It thereby acknowledges that many objects were removed from their communities under questionable circumstances. An analysis of such claims revealed two common elements that would be typical for such claims. First, they often go beyond wrongful taking (such as theft) and need not imply recognition of the illegitimacy of past transfers of ownership. Second, the objects reclaimed have special significance to an originating community or their successors. The Report furthermore considered the growing recognition of the concept of the cultural patrimony of indigenous peoples as having influenced Australian and North American museum policies on the return of cultural property.[39] Ultimately, however, the

---

[37] House of Commons, Select Committee on Culture, Media and Sport, Seventh Report, 'Cultural Property: Return and Illicit Trade', HC 371-I, II and III (18 July 2000), available at www.publications.parliament.uk/pa/cm199900/cmselect/cmcumeds/371/37102.htm [hereinafter UK Report I].

[38] Ibid., at para. 69.

[39] Ibid., at paras 125–6.

Report filtered human remains as the only category of indigenous cultural property that deserved specific treatment.[40]

A second report, this time specifically on human remains, followed in November 2003 (UK Report II).[41] The outcome of this Report was a single new section in the revised Human Tissue Act 2004 (section 47).[42] It is devoted to de-accessioning[43] rights and policies of British museums and empowers nine governing museum bodies (including The Trustees of the British Museum) to 'transfer from their collection any human remains which they reasonably believe to be remains of a person who died less than one thousand years before the day on which this section comes into force if it appears to them to be appropriate to do so for any reason, whether or not relating to their other functions'.[44]

Thus, despite the thoughts which the UK Reports I and II devoted to indigenous interests, only one single legislative measure concerning human remains followed. For any other (indigenous) cultural property, the UK Report I considered new legislation inappropriate and recommended instead a case-by-case solution. It required specific parliamentary sanction through new primary legislation, if a special case can be made for return of an object in circumstances affecting national museums and galleries.[45] The Report's recommendation that the United Kingdom become a member to the UNIDROIT Convention 1995[46] has been neglected so far.

B. France France had to deal with indigenous peoples' interests in their cultural property only recently, when a restitution claim that had smouldered for more than 20 years came to the surface.[47] At the request of New Zealand, acting through the Te Papa Museum of Wellington, the city of Rouen agreed to give back mokomokai, tattooed preserved Māori heads, stored in the Rouen city Museum for Natural History, Ethnography and Prehistory.[48] The Prefect of the region, however, stopped the undertaking. He alleged, supported by a decision of the administrative court of Rouen and affirmed by the appellate court of Douai, that the Rouen city Museum was a museum of France and the

---

[40] Ibid., at para. 153.

[41] Department for Culture, Media and Sport, Cultural Property Unit, Normon Palmer and James Dowling, 'The Report of the Working Group on Human Remains' (November 2003, updated February 2007), available at http://webarchive.nationalarchives.gov.uk/+/http://www.culture.gov.uk/images/publications/wghr-_reportfeb07.pdf.

[42] Human Tissue Act 2004 (UK). The Act replaced the Human Tissue Act 1961, the Anatomy Act 1984 and the Human Organ Transplants Act 1989.

[43] 'De-accessioning' is the technical term for the official removal of an item from a library, museum or art gallery.

[44] Human Tissue Act 2004 (UK), s. 47(2).

[45] UK Report I, supra note 37, at para. 199(xi).

[46] Ibid., at para. 199(vi).

[47] Thibault de Ravel d'Esclapon, 'Têtes maories: proposition pour un retour en Nouvelle-Zélande', *Le Blog Dalloz* (9 July 2009), available at http://blog.dalloz.fr/2009/07/tetes-maories-proposition-pour-un-retour-en-nouvelle-zelande/.

[48] 'Muséum d'histoire naturelle, d'ethnographie et de préhistoire de la ville de Rouen.'

mokomokai would form part of a public collection.[49] According to the French Heritage Code, such public collections would be principally inalienable,[50] even more so if objects were received by donation or legacy, or acquired with public means.[51] The counter-argument of the city of Rouen, that mokomokai were human remains and as such excluded from property rights according to the French Civil Code,[52] was dismissed. The dispute went up to the national government of France, which ultimately resolved the case in May 2010 by legislation. The parliament of France enacted a statute explicitly stating that mokomokai preserved in museums of France did not form part of their museum collections anymore and may be returned to New Zealand.[53]

The claim ended thus in a legislative, but one-case solution. The government missed the occasion to think about a more encompassing solution for indigenous peoples' claims for their cultural property, whether represented by their nation state or not. Christine Albanel, then Minister of Culture in France, in her speech at a symposium held in February 2008 at the Musée du Quai Branly, addressed the issue. In her introduction she declared that cultural minority rights seem even more important as they stem from communities victimised in the expansion of European colonisation and are still today sometimes marginalised in their countries.[54] Her conclusion from this statement, however, is in line with the solution found in the mokomokai case. She declared that dialogue and a case-by-case analysis is necessary for every repatriation demand.[55]

The statutory act on the mokomokai amended the Heritage Code with an obligation of the scientific commission to issue recommendations and opinions on the process of declassification of objects from the status of public collection.[56] When an object is declassified, the museum or institution holding such object has a wider scope of action. Whether this procedural improvement will be able to avoid single cases being ultimately resolved by the French parliament, is questionable. Not only the mokomokai case, but also the request for the human remains of a Hottentote woman ('Vénus hottentote') needed a

---

49 *Préfet Seine-Maritime* (2007) 5 JCP Adm 2021, 28 January 2008, Commentary by O. Amiel (TA Rouen); *Cne Rouen v Préfet de la région Haute-Normandie* (2008) 44 JCP II 10181, 29 October 2008, Commentary by C. Saujot (CAA Douai, plén.).

50 Heritage Code ('Code du patrimoine'), Act No. 2002–5 of 4 January 2002 as amended by Act No. 2010–501 of 18 May 2010 aiming at authorising the restitution of Māori heads from France to New Zealand and on the management of collections [hereinafter Mokomokai Restitution Act 2010–501], Article L451–5(1). See court decisions, supra note 49.

51 Heritage Code, Article L451–7.

52 Article 16–1 of the French Civil Code reads: '… les corps humain, ses éléments et ses produit ne peuvent faire l'objet d'un droit patrimonial' (human remains, elements and products thereof may not be the object of property rights).

53 Mokomokai Restitution Act 2010–501, supra note 50.

54 Report to the Commission of Cultural Affairs by Philippe Richert, 'Proposition de loi visant à autoriser la restitution par la France des têtes maories', Report No. 482 (2008–2009), 23 June 2009, at p. 31, available online at http://www.senat.fr/rap/l08–482/l08–482.html.

55 'Ces constats soulignent l'importance du dialogue et la nécessité d'un examen au cas par cas de chaque demande [de restitution].' Ibid., at p. 32.

56 Heritage Code, Article L115–1.

national legislative act. In 2002, the French parliament specifically enacted a law concerning the restitution of the mortal remains of Saartjie Baartman from France to South Africa.[57]

France ratified the UNESCO Convention 1970, but did not specifically implement it into national law. France also signed the UNIDROIT Convention 1995, but has not (yet) ratified it.

C. Switzerland Switzerland signed and ratified the UNESCO Convention 1970 in 2003. In contrast to the United Kingdom and France, it specifically implemented the Convention by the Federal Act on the International Transfer of Cultural Property (CPTA).[58] The CPTA does not address indigenous peoples' interests in their cultural property. However, it principally opened the possibility that Switzerland will deal with indigenous rights and the protection of their cultural property on a bilateral level. It empowered the Federal Council to conclude international treaties on the import and repatriation of cultural property.[59] As we learn from Susy Frankel in this volume, there exist bilateral trade agreements (free trade agreements) that explicitly address indigenous cultural heritage issues.[60] Based on the CPTA, Switzerland has up to now concluded bilateral cultural property agreements with two countries with significant indigenous populations (Columbia and Peru). The agreements contain no specific reference to indigenous peoples' interests in the main document.[61] The annex to the Agreement with Peru, however, which lists the protected cultural property, mentions several indigenous communities which still have cities or provinces named after them (for example Chancay, Nazca and Huari).[62] The list includes textiles, figures, masks, jewellery and other metal

---

57 Act No. 2002–323, 6 March 2002, concerning the restitution of the mortal remains of Saartjie Baartman from France to South Africa.

58 Federal Act on the International Transfer of Cultural Property ('Bundesgesetz über den internationalen Kulturgütertransfer'), 20 June 2003 (SR 44.1) [hereinafter CPTA]. English translation in Andreas F.G. Raschèr et al. (eds), *Cultural Property Transfer = Transfert des biens culturels = Trasferimento dei beni culturali = Kulturgütertransfer*, Zurich etc.: Schulthess et al., 2005, at pp. 336–420.

59 CPTA, Article 7. The concept in which national cultural property law refers to bilateral (or multilateral) agreements for regulating importation and repatriation of archaeological or ethnological material may also be found in § 2602(2) of the American Act implementing the UNESCO Convention 1970: the Cultural Property Implementation Act of 1983 [hereinafter CPIA], U.S.C. §§ 2601–2613, Public Law 97–446 (H.R. 4566), 96 Stat. 2329, approved 12 January 1983; (as amended by Public Law 100–204 [H.R. 1777], 101 Stat. 1331, approved 22 December 1987).

60 Susy Frankel, 'Attempts to Protect Indigenous Culture through Free Trade Agreements', in this volume.

61 For the actually existing bilateral cultural property agreements between Switzerland and five other states, see Eidgenössisches Departement des Innern, Bundesamt für Kultur, 'Bilateral Agreements', available at www.bak.admin.ch/themen/kulturguetertransfer/01985/index.html?lang=en.

62 The system of adding lists with specifically protected objects to cultural property law is well known from the bi- and multilateral cultural property agreements between the United States and other states according to the CPIA, see supra note 59. For a list of the actual 14 CPIA agreements see United States Department of State, Bureau of Educational and Cultural Affairs, 'Import Restrictions List & Chart', available at http://exchanges.state.gov/heritage/culprop/listactions.html.

objects, ceramics, minerals, transitory relics and even ceremonial objects such as catapults as well as human remains.[63] However, the Agreement only applies to pre-Columbian, thus very old, cultural property. In addition, according to Article III(1) of the Agreement, only the Peruvian state may reclaim the listed objects. Peruvian indigenous cultures desiring an object lost to Switzerland would thus first have to convince the Peruvian government to file a claim. Furthermore, any claim requires proof that the relevant object has been illegally imported into Switzerland after the entering into force of the Agreement.[64] Jurisdiction remains with Swiss courts, and Swiss law applies for any disputed case about objects located in Switzerland.[65] Ultimately, no reference is made to the involvement of indigenous peoples concerned or possible indigenous customary rules applicable to lost objects.

A step for Switzerland to improve acknowledgment of indigenous peoples' cultural property interests to a minimal extent would be to consider them explicitly in their bilateral agreements and to ratify the UNIDROIT Convention 1995.

3. LIMITS OF THE LAW TO REFLECT INDIGENOUS INTERESTS IN THEIR TANGIBLE CULTURAL PROPERTY

The examples of how European nation states reflect indigenous peoples' claims to govern their cultural property show a lack of state internal readiness to implement the relevant human rights standards. This might be due to insufficient international political pressure which would trigger European states to take substantial steps. More important are the limits in national and international law that impede the reflection of indigenous peoples' interests in governing their cultural property.

3.1 Dependence on and Representation through States

Indigenous peoples enjoy a special status in international human rights law, but are – as tribes or communities – neither recognised as independent states nor subjects of international law in a technical sense.[66] They are nationally bound by their governmental structures and laws and depend internationally on their host state to represent their interests.

---

[63] Agreement between the Swiss Federal Council and the Government of the Republic of Peru about the Collaboration in Preventing Illicit Trade in Archaeological Objects ('Vereinbarung zwischen dem Schweizerischen Bundesrat und der Regierung der Republik Peru über die Zusammenarbeit zur Verhütung des rechtswidrigen Handels mit archäologischen Gütern'), (adopted on 28 December 2006, not yet entered into force).

[64] Ibid., Article IV(1)(b).

[65] Ibid., Article III(2) and (3).

[66] Gudmundur Alfredsson, 'Indigenous Populations, Protection', in *Encyclopedia of Public International Law*, vol. II, Amsterdam etc.: Elsevier, 1995, at pp. 946–51. Gudmundur Alfredsson, 'Indigenous Populations, Treaties with', in ibid., at pp. 951–3. Karolina Kuprecht, 'Die UN-Deklaration über die Rechte der indigenen Völker und die Restitution von Kulturgütern', *Academic Platform Switzerland, UN Award 2009*, at pp. 3–5, available at http://www.apsun.ch/webdav/site/unoacademia/shared/Karolina_Kuprecht.pdf. In general Lillian Aponte Miranda,

3.1.1 Tribal sovereignty, recognition and self-governance of Indian tribes

The legal dependence of indigenous peoples on their state can be exemplified by some aspects of American Indian tribes' status in the United States.

American Indian tribes may have acted as independent nations with sovereign powers inside their nation and for foreign affairs in the early period of colonisation of the North American continent. Treaties were concluded between the tribes and foreign governments.[67] However, the American state courts declared that these treaties differ considerably from treaties with foreign nations, as concluded under Article 3(2) of the United States Constitution,[68] and never recognised Indian tribes as sovereign nations. In the early case of *Cherokee Nation v State of Georgia*, Chief Justice John Marshall expressed the famous opinion that Indian tribes are to be denominated 'domestic dependent nations'[69] and do not qualify as 'foreign states, in the sense of the Constitution, and cannot maintain an action in the courts of the United States'.[70]

In 1871, the uncertainty about the status of Indian tribes ended with the Indian Appropriation Act of 3 March 1871. Treaties with Indian tribes were prohibited for the future and federal legislation replaced such treaties.[71] Since then, American lawyers of constitutional law have agreed that Indian tribes are part of the United States and Indian affairs are interior and not foreign affairs. Indian tribes are subject to United States law and their status depends on their recognition by federal law. In this sense, the Indian Civil Rights Act of 1968 defines 'Indian tribes' to mean 'any tribe, band, or other group of Indians subject to the jurisdiction of the United States and recognized as possessing powers of self-government'.[72] The process of federal recognition as an Indian tribe, administered by the Office of Federal Acknowledgement within the Department of the Interior, is outlined by Goldberg in her chapter in this volume.[73]

The original sovereignty of Indian tribes that remains is a state-internal power of self-governance. According to the Indian Civil Rights Act of 1968, such self-governance means and includes 'all governmental powers possessed by an Indian tribe, executive, legislative and judicial and all offices, bodies and tribunals by and through which they are executed, including courts of Indian offences; and means of inherent power of Indian

---

'Indigenous Peoples as International Lawmakers' (2010) *University of Pennsylvania Journal of International Law,* 32, pp. 203–63.

[67] See in detail Goldberg, supra note 23.

[68] 'The judicial power shall extend … to controversies … between a state, or the citizens thereof, and foreign states, citizens, or subjects.'

[69] *Cherokee Nation v State of Georgia* (1831) 5 Peters 178, at p. 161 Marshall J.

[70] Ibid., at p. 183.

[71] Today see 25 U.S.C. § 71.

[72] Indian Civil Rights Act of 1968, 25 U.S.C. §§ 1301–1303, at § 1301 (1) [hereinafter Indian Civil Rights Act]. The definition of 'Indian tribe' by the Indian Civil Rights Act is only one definition specifically applying to this Act. Other statutes have their own definition for their proper purposes. See Carole E. Goldberg et al., *American Indian Law: Native Nations and the Federal System Cases and Materials,* 6th edn, New Providence, NJ and San Francisco, CA: LexisNexis Matthew Bender, 2010, at pp. 124–33.

[73] Goldberg, supra note 23.

tribes, hereby recognized and affirmed, to exercise criminal jurisdiction over all Indians'.[74] Within this power, tribes are considered 'sovereign' within their territory or reservation and can handle tribal affairs.[75]

3.1.2 Representation of indigenous peoples' interests on an international level

Due to the lack of recognition and power of indigenous peoples, they have to rely on their state government for implementing and representing their collective interests in their cultural property, nationally and internationally. Examples such as the case of the Hottentote woman show how much international cultural property endeavours of indigenous peoples depend on the official involvement of their home state. Only when the South African Ambassador officially requested repatriation from France was a decision taken.[76] There are states that are willing and successful in engaging in cultural property claims on behalf of their indigenous peoples, such as New Zealand.[77] Most other countries, however, show little activity in representing specific indigenous interests in cultural property. From the United States, for example, despite their exemplary state-internal solution with NAGPRA,[78] the authors do not know of a single case in which the government would have represented an Indian tribe in an international cultural property request.

The question is whether indigenous peoples have to bow down to the political unwillingness of their home state. Again looking at the United States, there not only exists a certain 'trust responsibility' of the federal government vis-à-vis Indian tribes in intergovernmental relations.[79] One could also consider the powers of the federal Department of the Interior to manage Indian affairs and all matters arising out of Indian relations[80] and the provision that obliges the United States to represent Indians in suits at law and in equity[81] as possible legal grounds for requesting state representation. It is thus worth exploring legal possibilities to enforce international representation.

Solely representing indigenous peoples in their repatriation claims would, however, not suffice as full implementation of the existing international human rights standards on indigenous cultural property. Comprehensive protection requires states to additionally install export controls with a focus on indigenous peoples' cultural property in the sense of

---

74 Indian Civil Rights Act, 25 U.S.C. § 1301 (2).

75 On the right to self-determination of Indian tribes, see for example Tsosie, supra note 14.

76 See Marie Cornu and Marc-André Renold, 'New Developments in the Restitution of Cultural Property: Alternative Means of Dispute Resolution' (2010) *International Journal of Cultural Property*, 17, pp. 1–31, at p. 10, also mentioning the request for the return of human remains from an ethnic group of Uruguay which was not returned because the Uruguayan Government did not make an official request to France.

77 For New Zealand's request for repatriation of mokomokai from France, see supra section 2.2.4.B. For the state's activities in relation to the United Kingdom see The British Museum, 'Human Remains. Request for Repatriation of Human Remains to New Zealand', *Minutes of the Meeting of the Trustees* (April 2008), available at http://www.britishmuseum.org/the_museum/news_and_press/statements/human_remains/repatriation_to_new_zealand.aspx.

78 See supra section 2.2.1.

79 See Goldberg, supra note 23.

80 25 U.S.C. §§ 1 and 2.

81 25 U.S.C. § 175.

the UNESCO Convention 1970. Indigenous peoples' interests also need to be included in bilateral cultural property agreements on import controls and restitutions with the listing of indigenous peoples' objects in the annex to such agreements.[82] In Switzerland, the requirement of clearly mentioning interests and objects in a bilateral agreement was confirmed by the Federal Court when it rejected a claim to restitute golden coins to India which were not covered by a bilateral agreement with India.[83]

The most radical – but rather unrealistic – solution for better representing international interests of indigenous peoples in their cultural property would of course be to peel back the veil of nation states' sovereignty and to attribute to indigenous peoples international standing and full recognition as subjects of international law in the field of cultural property.

3.2 Territoriality

Another important limit on indigenous peoples' interests in governing their cultural property abroad is the territoriality of the law. Even if a state is willing to implement international human rights standards, such as the repatriation of human remains, national law in principle does not bind other states. Therefore, effective regulations on cultural property would require that local provisions are applied internationally. In order to achieve this, two different strategies may be chosen: an international one or a national one.

3.2.1 International strategy

An international strategy is to conclude international agreements providing that the contracting states have to respect foreign rules on, for example, non-exportability of cultural objects, on their repatriation in defined cases or on import regulations. Examples of such agreements are the UNESCO Convention 1970, the UNIDROIT Convention 1995 and the bilateral agreements already discussed.

3.2.2 National strategy

Whereas an international strategy depends on the willingness of other states to cooperate, national statutes of international private law allow to some extent consideration of extra-territorial interests without an international agreement. In a cultural property context, a small step in this direction has been realised in Belgium. The Belgian Code of International Private Law (CDIP) of 2004 provides in Article 90:

> Law applicable to cultural property
>
> If an item, which a State considers as being included in its cultural heritage, has left the territory of that State in a way, which is considered to be illegitimate at the time of the exportation by the law of that State, the revindication [restitution] by the State is governed by the law of that State, as it is applicable at that time, or at the choice of the latter, by the law of the State on the territory of which the item is located at the time of revindication [restitution].

---

[82] See supra section 2.2.4.C.

[83] *India v Credit Agricole Indosuez (Switzerland) SA* (8 April 2005) BGE 131 III 418 (Swiss Federal Court).

> Nevertheless, if the law of the State that considers the item part of its cultural heritage does not grant any protection to the possessor in good faith, the latter may invoke the protection, that is attributed to him by the law of the State on the territory of which the item is located at the time of revindication [restitution].[84]

This provision deserves explanation. International cases of cultural property become cases of private international law when the applicable law has to be determined. Private international law or conflict of law regulations are (if not unified, as it is in discussion for the European Union) national laws, such as the Swiss Private International Law Act of 1987 (SPIL).[85] This statute determines the law most closely connected to the case as the law to be applied. The law most closely connected in moveable tangible property cases is the *lex rei sitae*, that is, the law at the place where the object is located at the time of any transaction.[86] What the Belgian CDIP provides is that normally the *lex rei sitae* applies to moveable property.[87] As an exception to this rule, Article 90 allows the application of the laws of that foreign state from which a cultural property was exported in violation of its export rules. The CDIP, therefore, deliberately applies foreign export prohibitions in local courts if a party asking for restitution can prove that a foreign state indeed prohibited the export of the cultural property in question. However, since the United States, for example, does not prohibit the export of indigenous cultural property, a tribe of American Indians could not reclaim objects exported to Belgium despite Article 90 CDIP.

The Belgian CDIP bases its exceptional provision on a proposal by the Institute of International Law (Institut de Droit International).[88] Up until now, it has been the only European country to take the proposal into account. In Switzerland, foreign export prohibitions may be taken into consideration under the conditions set forth in Article 19 SPIL. This Article reads in English translation:

> Taking into consideration mandatory provisions of foreign law
>
> (1) When interests that are legitimate and clearly preponderant according to the Swiss conception of law so require, a mandatory provision of another law than the one referred to in this Act may be taken into consideration, provided that the situation dealt with has a close connection with such other law.

---

84 International Private Law Code ('Code de droit international privé'), 16 July 2004 [hereinafter CDIP], English translation by Caroline Clijmans and Paul Torremans, in (2004) *Yearbook of Private International Law*, vol. VI, 2004, pp. 319–76, at p. 354.

85 Federal Private International Law Act ('Bundesgesetz über das Internationale Privatrecht'), 18 December 1987 (SR 291) [hereinafter SPIL].

86 See for example Article 100 SPIL.

87 CDIP, Article 87(1).

88 The Institute of International Law, 'The International Sale of Works of Art from the Angle of the Protection of the Cultural Heritage' (3 September 1991), available online at http://www.idi-iil.org/idiE/resolutionsE/1991_bal_04_en.pdf. The Institute of International Law is an association of renowned international lawyers developing international law independent of any governmental influence. It adopts resolutions of a normative character which are brought to the attention of governmental authorities, international organisations as well as the scientific community. See http://www.idi-iil.org/index.html.

(2) In deciding whether such a provision is to be taken into consideration, one shall consider its aim and the consequences of its application, in order to reach a decision that is appropriate having regard to the Swiss conception of law.[89]

The difference between Article 90 CDIP and Article 19 SPIL is that under the Belgian Code, Belgian courts are bound to apply foreign law, whereas under the Swiss Act, foreign law may 'be taken into consideration'. Swiss courts thereby consider the circumstances of the single case and the consequences of the application of foreign law. What this means has been decided by the Federal Court in the case of Indian coins. It declined to apply Indian law since Switzerland provides the possibility to conclude bilateral agreements and no such agreement exists with India.[90]

Whereas territoriality creates important limits to public cultural property law including export and import regulations, stolen objects can be recovered by the owner under national private property laws unless third parties have acquired good title in the object reclaimed, as will be discussed later, in section 3.5.

3.3 The Principle of Non-Retroactivity

Most indigenous cultural property kept and stored in Europe is old and was collected years ago. Even if legislators would be willing to reinstall indigenous governance over indigenous peoples' cultural property on their state territories, the principle of non-retroactivity is an important limitation. National legislators may enact law at any time. Courts decide cases on application of such law to situations unknown to the legislator at the time of legislation. However, in states operating under the rule of law, retroactively working legislation at the expense of the citizens is only justified in limited circumstances. If such laws are to be passed, they must provide equitable compensation to those citizens who, at the time of a transaction, relied on the present situation and acted legally.

There is a Swiss example of how the principle of non-retroactivity in the field of cultural property limits the scope of restitution activities. After the Second World War, cultural property looted by the German army or members of the Nazi party was discovered in Switzerland. Such objects were sold during the war either at auctions or individually from art dealers. Under pressure from the Allies, who referred to the London Declaration of 1943,[91] Switzerland after the war passed the Decree of the Federal Council of 10 December 1945 on Claims for Return of Objects Taken in Territories Occupied in Times of

---

[89] Andreas Bucher and Pierre-Yves Tschanz (eds), *Private International Law and Arbitration, Switzerland, Basic Documents*, Basel and Frankfurt am Main: Helbing Lichtenhahn, 1996, at p. 4.

[90] *India v Credit Agricole Indosuez (Switzerland) SA*, supra note 83.

[91] Inter-Allied Declaration against Acts of Dispossession Committed in the Territories under Enemy Occupation or Control of 5 January 1943, reprinted in Norman Palmer, *Museums and the Holocaust. Law, Principles and Practice*, London: Institute of Art and Law, 2000, at pp. 303–5 [hereinafter Palmer, *Museums and the Holocaust*]. On this Declaration, see Wilfred Fiedler, 'Die Alliierte (Londoner) Erklärung vom 5.1.1943: Inhalt, Auslegung und Rechtsnatur in der Diskussion der Nachkriegsjahre', in Jürgen Basedow et al. (eds), *Private Law in the International Arena: From National Conflict Rules towards Harmonization and Unification. Liber Amicorum Kurt Siehr*, The Hague: T.M.C. Asser Press, 2000, at pp. 197–218.

War.[92] According to this Decree owners of objects (mainly cultural property) looted during the Second World War had to return such objects to their former owners. If acquired *bona fide*, they could sue the seller of such objects for compensation. If also the seller was *bona fide* and could not get compensation from his/her seller, the Swiss Federal Government paid reasonable compensation. Such claims had to be decided exclusively by the Federal Court in Lausanne, which instituted for these trials a special Chamber called the 'Raubgutkammer' (chamber for looted objects). Claims could be filed until 31 December 1947. Thereafter the Chamber was dissolved and parties were referred again to those remedies generally available for everybody who had lost an object and rediscovered it in Switzerland. Switzerland returned to the normal system of law and stopped further compensation payments which were necessary to legitimise the retroactive obligation of owners to return validly acquired cultural property.[93]

3.4 Non-Interference with Other Rights

A most important limit to indigenous peoples' requests for governance over their cultural property is the right to property of others. This right is not only a strong, absolute right of private law, but also the most frequently codified constitutional right[94] and an important universal human rights standard.[95]

All European states have installed private property law systems, generally rooted in Roman law, which regulate and protect ownership in *res* (the material things). In the context of trade, such ownership is founded by the valid transfer of property. This either

---

92 Decree of the Federal Council of 10 December 1945 on Claims for Return of Objects Taken in Territories Occupied in Times of War ('Bundesratsbeschluss vom 10. Dezember 1945 betreffend die Klagen auf Rückgabe in kriegsbesetzten Gebieten weggenommener Vermögenswerte') (1945) AS 61, at pp. 1052–6. A second Decree of the Federal Council passed on 22 February 1946, see Benno Widmer, 'Die Richtlinien der Washingtoner Konferenz in Bezug auf Kunstwerke, die von den Nazis konfisziert wurden: Anwendung in der Schweizerischen Eidgenossenschaft' (2009) *KUR: Journal für Kunstrecht, Urheberrecht und Kulturpolitik,* 11 (3/4), pp. 86–91, at p. 86.

93 See in detail Kurt Siehr, 'Rechtsfragen zum Handel mit geraubten Kulturgütern in den Jahren 1935–1950', in Unabhängige Expertenkommission Schweiz – Zweiter Weltkrieg (UEK) (ed.), *Die Schweiz, der Nationalsozialismus und das Recht. Band 19 11: Privatrecht* Zurich: UEK Publications, 2001, pp. 125–209 at pp. 127–205.

94 This was the outcome of a compilation of the relevant provisions in national constitutions used by the Economic and Social Council to draft the UN, Universal Declaration of Human Rights, UN GA Res. 217A (III) (UN Doc. A/810) (adopted on 10 December 1948) [hereinafter Universal Declaration of Human Rights]. See Theo R.G. van Banning, *The Human Right to Property*, Antwerp: Intersentia, 2002, at p. 137.

95 Universal Declaration of Human Rights, Article 17; American Convention on Human Rights, OAS Treaty Series No. 36; 1144 UNTS 123, reprinted in Basic Documents Pertaining to Human Rights in the Inter-American System, OEA/Ser.L.V/II.82 doc.6 rev.1 at 25 (1992) (adopted 22 November 1969, entered into force 18 July 1978), Article 21; African Charter on Human Rights and Peoples' Rights, OAU Doc. CAB/LEG/67/3 rev. 5; 21 ILM 58 (1982) (adopted 27 June 1981, entered into force 21 October 1986), Article 14; and European Convention on Human Rights (adopted 4 November 1950, entered into force 3 September 1953), CETS No. 005 in Article 1 of Protocol 1 (adopted 20 March 1952, entered into force 18 May 1954), CETS No. 009. See for details van Banning, supra note 94, at pp. 57–79.

happens (1) by valid contract, for example France, Great Britain and Italy, (2) by valid contract and taking possession, for example Switzerland, or (3) by consent to transfer property and taking possession, for example Germany and Greece.[96] In trade-friendly regulations, this system of ownership transfer even includes stolen objects if the purchaser was *bona fide*, for example Italy. Other systems, which rather emphasise the protection of ownership, follow the principle *nemo plus iuris transferre potest quam ipse habet* (nobody can transfer more rights than he/she actually has), for example Germany and England. A compromise between the two solutions is that *bona fide* purchasers of stolen goods are protected after the expiration of a certain deadline and/or by a refund of the purchase price to the *bona fide* purchaser, if the stolen object has to be returned, for example France, Switzerland and Spain.[97] In some countries, specific private property regulations for cultural property exist. This is the case in Switzerland, where the Swiss Civil Code provides a *bona fide* acquisition and prescription period of 30 years for cultural property instead of the five-year period applicable to any other moveable property.[98]

In summary, all systems bar at some point the reclaiming of property either since it is lost to a *bona fide* purchaser or possessor or by expiration of time. Thus, all indigenous cultural property transferred or traded into Europe at some point principally faces private property rights of new possessors and owners. A preferred treatment of indigenous peoples' cultural property claims would require European states to abandon their old, basic private property principles, which is unlikely to happen.

The UNIDROIT Convention 1995 brings a certain international amendment to private property systems for the whole category of cultural property. However, none of the European cultural property market countries have ratified the Convention. In addition, the Convention does not work retroactively, upholds time limits and stipulates compensation for *bona fide* possessors.

4. ALTERNATIVE WAYS TO COMPLY WITH INTERNATIONAL HUMAN RIGHTS STANDARDS

4.1 Voluntary Activities

The lack of comprehensive legislative activity and the considerable legal hurdles in European countries prevent a thriving cultural (property) exchange with indigenous peoples, similar to the one triggered by NAGPRA in the United States. Despite the new legal human rights standards, activities in Europe mostly take place on a voluntary, case-by-case basis. Some examples may be mentioned.

---

96 Siehr, 'International Art Trade and the Law', supra note 5, at p. 56.

97 Ibid., at pp. 57–60. Astrid Müller-Katzenburg, *Internationale Standards im Kulturgüterverkehr und ihre Bedeutung für das Sach- und Kollisionsrecht*, Berlin: Duncker & Humblot, 1996, at pp. 165–6.

98 Swiss Civil Code, 10 December 1907 (SR 210), Articles 728(1ter) and 934(1bis).

4.1.1 Afo-A-Kom of the Kom people of Cameroon in the United States

There is an indigenous tribe in north-western Cameroon called Kom. About 100,000 people are members of the tribe and live in 43 villages spread over about 300 square miles. A King (the Fon) is the head of the tribe. In 1966, a sacred totem of 5 foot 2½ inches, the image of a king called Afo-A-Kom (literally, the Kom thing), vanished in Laikom, which is the capital of the Kom people. This loss caused great disturbance with the Kom. Only about seven years later, the Afo-A-Kom showed up again in Hanover, New Hampshire, in the exhibition 'Royal Art of Cameroon' at Dartmouth College. Aaron Furman, a respected Manhattan art dealer in indigenous art, gave the Afo-A-Kom to the exhibition on loan. Furman had acquired the Afo-A-Kom as a *bona fide* purchaser from a French art dealer in 1966. The discovery of the Afo-A-Kom by Evan Schneider, a long-time Kom scholar, caused a flurry of diplomatic exchanges and created uproar from New York to Laikom. Finally, the Afo-A-Kom was given back to Cameroon, a multilingual state of about 200 ethnic groups, and is now placed in the Bamenda Museum in North West Province of Cameroon.[99]

4.1.2 Tabot from Ethiopia in Scotland

In 1868, after the battle of Maqdala/Ethiopia, several tabots (symbols of the lost Ark of the Covenant) were looted by the British army under the command of lieutenant-general Robert Napier (1810–90) in the expedition to Abyssinia.[100] While most of the tabots are held at the British Museum in London, one of them was found in 2002, hidden in a dusty Victorian box in St John's Episcopal Church in Edinburgh. After this discovery, the Ethiopian Orthodox Church was informed and the tabot was given back to Ethiopia, where it is now being preserved in Addis Ababa Trinity Cathedral.[101]

4.1.3 Indian leather paintings from New Mexico in Switzerland

In 1758, the Swiss missionary Philipp Anton Segesser (1689–1762) of Lucerne sent home from Mexico two Indian leather paintings depicting fights between Pueblo Indians under Spanish military guidance against other Indian tribes and the French army. The leather paintings were kept with the family Segesser von Brunegg until 1986, when they were sold and returned to Santa Fé, New Mexico, where they are now exhibited in the Palace of the Governors.[102] The return triggered a juridical dispute in Switzerland which ended with the decision of the government of the Canton Lucerne in 1988. The government denied a

---

99 As to this affair see John H. Merryman, Albert E. Elsen and Stephen K. Urice, *Law: Ethics and the Visual Arts*, 5th edn, Alphen aan den Rijn, Netherlands: Kluwer Law International, 2007, at pp. 363–5.

100 Alan Moorehead, *The Blue Nile*, London: Penguin Books, 1983, at p. 275; and Volker Matthies, *Unternehmen Magdala. Strafexpedition in Äthiopien*, Berlin: Links, 2010, at pp. 131–5.

101 Matthies, supra note 100, at p. 135.

102 Jörg Sprecher, 'Rückkehr der Segesserschen Ledermalereien nach New Mexiko', in Peter J. Weber et al. (eds), *Liber discipulorum et amicorum. Festschrift für Prof. Dr. Kurt Siehr zum 65. Geburtstag*, Zurich: Schulthess, 2001, pp. 207–14.

sufficiently close connection of the leather paintings to the history of Lucerne, which would have prohibited their exportation.[103]

4.1.4 Common features

The cases share some features in common: (1) all but the first case (Afo-A-Kom) are objects which were transferred from their original holders a long time ago; (2) all clearly qualify as cultural property of indigenous peoples; (3) all objects are located abroad, that is, outside the territory of the (indigenous) party that initiated a claim for governance of the object; and (4) in all cases, there seemed to be no legal remedy which could be taken by the (indigenous) claimant in the country of location of the claimed objects. Nevertheless, in all cases the objects were given back either (a) by compensation paid to a private owner (Afo-A-Kom), (b) by donation of the present holder (tabot of Ethiopia) or (c) by sale by private owners (leather paintings of Lucerne).

This shows that in single cases, for reasons of politics, ethics or morals, indigenous cultural objects may be successfully claimed by or on behalf of indigenous peoples, even if the objects are located abroad, lost for a very long time and without enforceable, legal obligations.

4.2 Alternative Dispute Resolution

In view of the huge amount of indigenous cultural property collected and stored in Europe and the potential claims they trigger, voluntary activities are a mere drop in the ocean. The negotiations often last for years and decades and bind resources that could otherwise be invested into forward-looking cooperation and exchange with the indigenous peoples concerned. In addition, voluntary activities involve external experts, public or private organisations and institutions or the government randomly, as the cases above show. The question is whether more standardised procedural solutions could facilitate and support voluntary endeavours and help a higher amount of cases to be resolved in reasonable time.

Graber in his chapter to this volume concluded that a procedural approach would be the most effective way to interface indigenous and non-indigenous worldviews.[104] In this sense, Marie Cornu and Marc-André Renold advocate procedures of alternative dispute resolution (ADR) for cultural property cases, specifically for indigenous peoples.[105]

---

[103] Regierungsrat des Kantons Luzern 31 May 1988, Protocol No. 1328, *Luzerner Gerichts- und Verwaltungsentscheide* 1988 III No. 16.

[104] Graber, 'Stimulating Trade and Development', supra note 6. See also Graber, 'Institutionalization of Creativity in Traditional Societies and in International Trade Law', supra note 13, at pp. 251–2.

[105] Cornu and Renold, supra note 76, at pp. 4–7 and 12–13. At the moment Renold is pursuing an extensive research as to whether ADR may be used for art dispute settlements. See on ADR in art and cultural heritage Sarah Theurich, 'Alternative Dispute Resolution in Art and Cultural Heritage: Explored in the Context of the World Intellectual Property Organization's Work', in Kerstin Odendahl and Peter J. Weber, supra note 30, pp. 569–94; and Quentin Byrne-Sutton, 'Introduction: Alternative Paths to Explore', in Quentin Byrne-Sutton and Fabienne Geisinger-Mariéthoz (eds), *Resolution Methods for Art-related Disputes: Proceedings of a Symposium Organised on 17 October 1997 by the Centre du Droit de l'Art*, Studies in Art Law, vol. XI, Zurich: Schulthess, 1999, pp. 3–13.

Similarly, international organisations, agencies, national legislators and individuals have started to evaluate ADR for cultural property.[106] In consequence, the World Intellectual Property Organization (WIPO) Arbitration and Mediation Center, for example, recently set up a specific ADR Service for Art and Cultural Heritage.[107] In Australia, the submission of disputes including claims in the field of cultural property of the Aborigines to ADR proceedings is being discussed.[108] The same is happening in Canada.[109] ADR may resemble the traditional dispute resolution mechanisms of indigenous peoples more than the adversarial litigation process.[110] Does ADR thus provide the required solution for indigenous peoples' cultural property requests? To approach this question, we will look at some ADR mechanisms and briefly comment.

4.2.1 Arbitration

Parties to a dispute may agree to submit their dispute to an arbitral tribunal. The UNIDROIT Convention 1995 explicitly mentions arbitration as a possibility for resolving restitution disputes over cultural property.[111] Several national and international organisations and institutions offer institutionalised arbitration procedures at the disposal of the parties' choice. In 1998, for example, the Venice Court of National and International Arbitration was established and also offers its services for disputes concerning art

---

[106] For an overview see Irini A. Stamatoudi, *Cultural Property Law and Restitution. A Commentary to International Conventions and European Union Law*, Cheltenham, UK and Northampton, MA: Edward Elgar, 2011, at pp. 193–208; and Sarah Theurich, 'The Role of International Institutional Dispute Resolution in Art and Cultural Heritage Matters: The World Intellectual Property Organization (WIPO) and its Arbitration and Mediation Center', *International Symposium of Litigation in Cultural Property: Judicial and Alternative Means of International Dispute Resolution* (University of Geneva, 11 November 2011) (on file with the authors).

[107] For further information see WIPO Arbitration and Mediation Center, 'WIPO Alternative Dispute Resolution (ADR) for Art and Cultural Heritage', available at http://www.wipo.int/amc/en/center/specific-sectors/art/.

[108] Isabella Alexander, 'White Law, Black Art' (2001) *International Journal of Cultural Property,* 10, pp. 185–216, at pp. 208–9.

[109] Sabine von Schorlemer, 'UNESCO Dispute Settlement', in Abdulqawi A. Yusuf (ed.), *Standard-Setting in UNESCO. Normative Action in Education, Science and Culture: Essays in Commemoration of the Sixtieth Anniversary of UNESCO*, vol. I, Paris, Leiden and Boston: UNESCO, 2007, pp. 73–103.

[110] See for example Carey N. Vincenti, 'The Reemergence of Tribal Society and Traditional Justice Systems' (1995–1995) *Judicature*, 79, pp. 134–41; Ada P. Melton, 'Indigenous Justice Systems and Tribal Society' (1995–1996) *Judicature*, 79, pp. 126–33; Robert D. Cooter and Wolfgang Fikentscher, 'Indian Common Law: The Role of Custom in American Indian Tribal Courts (part I of II)' (1998) *American Journal of Comparative Law*, 46, pp. 287–338; Robert Yazzie, 'Navajo Peacemaking and Intercultural Dispute Resolution', in Catherine Bell and David J. Kahane (eds), *Intercultural Dispute Resolution in Aboriginal Contexts*, Vancouver and Toronto: UBC Press, 2004, pp. 107–15; and Larissa Behrendt, 'Cultural Conflict in Colonial Legal Systems: An Australian Perspective', in Catherine Bell and David J. Kahane (eds), *Intercultural Dispute Resolution in Aboriginal Contexts*, Vancouver and Toronto: UBC Press, 2004, pp. 116–27.

[111] UNIDROIT Convention 1995, Article 8(2). See on this Article, Lawrence M. Kaye, 'Disputes Relating to the Ownership and Status of Cultural Property', in Byrne-Sutton and Geisinger-Mariéthoz, supra note 105, pp. 35–53, at pp. 51–3.

objects.[112] The WIPO Arbitration and Mediation Center recently started to emphasise its know-how in art- and cultural-heritage-related dispute resolution and its specialised Panel, including arbitrators with expertise in art and cultural heritage.[113]

Well-known cases of cultural property arbitration evolved around disputes on looted art taken from Jewish collectors during Nazi times.[114] Italy and the Metropolitan Museum of Art stipulated in their agreement of 21 February 2006 on the return of illegally exported cultural objects (for example the krater of Euphronios) that any dispute under the agreement should be decided by an arbitral tribunal on the basis of the Rules of Arbitration and Conciliation of the International Chamber of Commerce.[115]

In matters of indigenous cultural property, there is little experience with arbitration.[116] This might be due to several important disadvantages. Arbitral tribunals, for example, unless empowered by the parties to decide *ex aequo et bono*,[117] are bound by the national laws. An arbitral tribunal may thus basically not respond to indigenous peoples' requests for the application of their customary laws and traditions. Furthermore, arbitration remains an adversarial litigation system often involving burdensome disclosure procedures and high costs, even if less regulated and formal than ordinary litigation.

4.2.2 Mediation

When parties agree on a mediation procedure, they may avoid litigation and jurisdiction. A procedure qualifies as a mediation procedure if it stands on a completely voluntary basis and if the parties, with the support of a mediator, search for a mutual solution by settlement. In contrast to litigation or arbitration, mediators neither apply national and international law, nor do they primarily search for the correct application of the law. It is the procedure most independent from the law and thus predestined for the better consideration of history, ethical and moral principles, as well as traditions and customs of indigenous peoples. It also allows the development of unconventional remedies and solutions beyond the jurisdictional scope of a judge. Both these factors are especially

---

112 Kurt Siehr, 'Resolution of Disputes in International Trade, Third Annual Conference of the Venice Court of National and International Arbitration' (2001) *International Journal of Cultural Property*, 10, pp. 122–6. In 2004, the Venice Court of National and International Arbitration and the Venice Chamber of Arbitration merged into one organisation under the name 'Venice Chamber of National and International Arbitration', see Juris International Arbitration and Mediation Centres, 'International Arbitration – Venice Chamber of National and International Arbitration' (2006) available at http://www.jurisint.org/en/ctr/160.html. Other institutions that offer arbitration are, for example, the Swiss Chambers' Court of Arbitration and Mediation, the World Intellectual Property Organization (WIPO) and the International Chamber of Commerce (ICC).

113 See WIPO Arbitration and Mediation Center, supra note 107.

114 See for example *Altmann v Republic of Austria* (Award of 15 January 2006), available online at http://www.adele.at/Schiedsspruch/Schiedsspruch.pdf

115 'The Metropolitan Museum of Art – Republic of Italy Agreement of February 21, 2006' (2006) *International Journal of Cultural Property*, 13, pp. 427–34, at p. 434.

116 See Kurt Siehr, 'Internationale Schiedsgerichtsbarkeit über Kulturgut-Streitigkeiten', in Peter Hay et al. (eds), *Resolving International Conflicts. Liber Amicorum Tibor Várady*, Budapest and New York: Central European University Press, 2009, pp. 255–66.

117 See for example Norman E. Palmer, 'Extra-curial Resolution of Contract Issues Involving Art and Antiquities: The English Experience', in Byrne-Sutton and Geisinger-Mariéthoz, supra note 105, pp. 55–81, at pp. 70–74.

advantageous for cases concerning indigenous peoples' cultural property. This potential of mediation in cultural property cases has stimulated the International Council of Museums (ICOM) to create together with WIPO the ICOM-WIPO Mediation Rules and Procedures.[118]

Whether mediation will be successful in more comprehensively resolving international indigenous cultural property claims is difficult to assess. Mediation agreements are rarely published, since confidentiality is an important feature of the procedure. There is one single, famous case on the repatriation of indigenous human remains which could ultimately be resolved by mediation. Since the 1980s, the Tasmanian Aboriginal Centre (TAC) had tried to make the London Natural History Museum (NHM) repatriate 17 human remains. When the dispute was taken to the London High Court, the judge suggested that the parties proceed with mediation. In May 2007, after a three-day-mediation session, the TAC and the NHM found an agreement which provided for the dismissal of the legal proceedings and for the repatriation of the remains to Tasmania. Repatriation took place immediately afterwards.[119]

However, mediation will similarly face many of the difficulties of other procedures with indigenous peoples' cultural property claims. Such difficulties include the deeply rooted differences in worldviews and ideas about indigenous cultural property's uses and functions, the often involved public and political interests in cultural property and the legal barriers that restrict museums' or cultural institutions' freedom of action. Nevertheless, the authors consider mediation an attractive procedure for international indigenous peoples' cultural property disputes, as it supports dialogue and speeds up solutions in a structured, but not overly regulated, environment.

4.2.3 Commissions and committees

Some countries have set up independent or governmental commissions or committees for the evaluation of cultural property restitution claims. In contrast to arbitration and mediation, commissions and committees are permanent bodies. They issue recommendations and opinions rather than decisions.[120]

In Europe, such commissions and committees generally focus on claims by holocaust victims or their heirs. Germany instituted the Advisory Commission for the Return of Cultural Property Illegally Taken by the Nazis, especially from Jewish owners.[121] It stands

---

118 International Council of Museums, 'ICOM-WIPO Art and Cultural Heritage Mediation', available at http://icom.museum/what-we-do/programmes/art-and-cultural-heritage-mediation/icom-wipo-art-and-cultural-heritage-mediation.html.

119 Cornu and Renold, supra note 76, at p. 13; and Anne L. Bandle, Alessandro Chechi and Marc-André Renold, 'Case 17 Tasmanian Humain Remains – Tasmanian Aboriginal Centre and Natural History Museum London' (2011) Platform ArThemis, Art-Law Centre University of Geneva, Case Note, available at https://plone2.unige.ch/art-adr/Affaires/case-tac-v.-natural-history-museum-london/Case%20Note%20-%20%TAC%20v.%20Natural%20History%20Museum%20London.docx/view.

120 See also Stamatoudi, supra note 106, at p. 207.

121 'Beratende Kommission im Zusammenhang mit der Rückgabe NS-verfolgungsbedingt entzogener Kulturgüter, insbesondere aus jüdischem Besitz'. See Lost Art Koordinierungsstelle Magdeburg, 'Beratende Koordinierungsstelle' (1994) available at http://www.lostart.de/Webs/DE/Kommission/Index.html.

at the disposal of both parties asking for advice as to whether a certain cultural object located in a museum should be returned to the heirs of the former Jewish owner. The advice of this Commission, of which the former President of Germany and the former President of the Federal Constitutional Court are members, is non-binding. The parties may accept this advice or start court proceedings, as happened in the Sachs case.[122] The Netherlands and the United Kingdom have also established committees for cultural property restitution claims arising from the Second World War. The Dutch Restitution Commission, in contrast to the German Committee, may issue binding opinions, after parties have agreed to submit their dispute to the Committee.[123] The Spoliation Advisory Panel in England again works with recommendations, but in a broader field of application. It not only serves in particular disputes, but also responds to governmental consultation requests.[124]

On the international level, the most prominent Committee is the UNESCO Intergovernmental Committee for Promoting the Return of Cultural Property to its Countries of Origin or its Restitution in case of Illicit Appropriation. This Committee is mandated to facilitate negotiations about cultural property restitutions, to promote bi- or multilateral cooperation on restitutions to countries of origin and to encourage research on information.[125] In October 2010, the procedure was complemented by rules on mediation and conciliation. The Committee may now propose to the parties in dispute to submit their case to this mediation procedure.[126]

No similar commissions, committees or procedures exist in Europe for indigenous peoples' cultural property disputes. Also, the UNESCO Committee and its procedures do not specifically refer to indigenous peoples' interests. However, the idea of setting up a commission or committee on indigenous peoples' issues in the realm of the United Nations, for example, would merit exploration.

---

[122] In the Sachs case, the claimant asked for the return of two posters, which the Nazi ministry for propaganda in Germany allegedly took from the claimant's father in 1938. The Kammergericht Berlin declined the claim and thereby followed the Advisory Commission that recommended not to return the posters, on 25 January 2007. See on the decision of the Kammergericht of 28 January 2010, 8 U 56/09, 'Herausgabeanspruch bei NS-verfolgungsbedingt abhanden gekommenen Sachen' (2010) *KUR: Journal für Kunstrecht, Urheberrecht und Kulturpolitik,* 12 (1), pp. 17–21.

[123] For more information see Advisory Committee on the Assessment of Restitution Applications for Items of Cultural Value and the Second World War, 'Restitution Committee', available at http://www.restitutiecommissie.nl/en.

[124] Stamatoudi, supra note 107, at pp. 205–6. The Department for Culture, Media and Sport, 'Spoliation Advisory Panel', available at http://www.culture.gov.uk/what_we_do/cultural_property/3296.aspx. See in depth Palmer, *Museums and the Holocaust*, supra note 90.

[125] UNESCO, Statutes of the Intergovernmental Committee for Promoting the Return of Cultural Property to its Countries of Origin or its Restitution in case of Illicit Appropriation, 20 C/Resolution 4/7.6/5 of the 20th session of the General Conference of UNESCO Paris (adopted 24 October – 28 November 1978), (CLT/CH/INS-2005/21, October/2005), Article 4.

[126] UNESCO, Rules of Procedure for Mediation and Conciliation in Accordance with Article 4, Paragraph 1, of the Statutes of the Intergovernmental Committee for Promoting the Return of Cultural Property to its Countries of Origin or its Restitution in Case of Illicit Appropriation, (UNESCO Doc. CLT-2010/CONF.203/COM.16/7, 2010).

4.2.4 Intermediate conclusion

ADR procedures may offer suitable structures for international indigenous cultural property disputes. They provide for venues where indigenous peoples may bring their claims outside the judicial limitations of ordinary courts and beyond states' fears of precedents in the field of cultural objects removed in the past. Up to now, mediation has seemed to be the most suitable. However, there is hardly any experience with cases involving indigenous peoples in all of the ADR procedures. Only the future will show whether the procedures will be able to overcome the limits of substantive law, which remain strong in every case involving European law.

4.3 Cultural Diplomacy

Another way of dealing with indigenous cultural property is what is called 'cultural diplomacy'. Today, the term is broadly used to describe 'the exchange of ideas, information, art and other aspects of culture among nations and their peoples to foster mutual understanding'.[127] Non-governmental institutions such as the Institute for Cultural Diplomacy have started to engage in cultural diplomacy by going beyond diplomatic, interstate relations. They promote cultural understanding by conferences, meetings and visits.[128]

In a cultural property context, Irini Stamatoudi argues that cultural diplomacy should also include exhibitions of cultural property, loans, exchange of know-how and expertise, co-organised and cooperative excavations, combined research, and coordination of cultural politics and policies. In her view, '[t]hese exchanges can be used as a bargaining tool to put pressure on the resolution of cultural property claims or as a basis for the creation of a positive friendly spirit within which such claims can be solved.'[129]

In this sense, cultural diplomacy may work as an important paving of the way for indigenous peoples' claims for governance of their cultural property. It softens allegedly immoveable positions and raises understanding. The question remains to what extent it will be able to compensate the lack of enforceability.

5. CONCLUSION

On an international level, a broad consensus and international human rights standards require special treatment of indigenous cultural property. The existing international cultural property conventions, specifically the UNESCO Convention 1970 and the

---

[127] Cynthia P. Schneider, 'Diplomacy that Works: "Best practices" in Cultural Diplomacy', *Center for Arts and Culture,* Research Paper (2003), at p. 1, citing Milton C. Cummings, 'Cultural Diplomacy and the United States Government: A Survey', *Center for Arts and Culture* (2003). See also Institute for Cultural Diplomacy, 'What is Cultural Diplomacy?', available at http://www.culturaldiplomacy.org/index.php?en_culturaldiplomacy. The Institute for Cultural Diplomacy is a non-profit, non-governmental organisation founded in 1999 with headquarters in the United States, Bulgaria, Croatia, Ecuador, Slovenia, Romania and Germany. Institute for Cultural Diplomacy, 'About the Institute for Cultural Diplomacy', available at http://www.culturaldiplomacy.org/index.php?en_abouticd.

[128] See Institute for Cultural Diplomacy, supra note 107.

[129] Stamatoudi, supra note 106, at p. 208.

UNIDROIT Convention 1995, contain little legal reference to indigenous peoples' interests and do not comply with newer international human rights standards.

On a national level, European countries remain even further away from implementing the standards into substantive national laws. Indigenous peoples' claims have triggered some European legislation on the repatriation of human remains. However, the laws neither provide encompassing solutions for human remains nor specifically consider any other category of indigenous cultural property. Europe widely upholds keeping the leverage inherent in case-by-case decisions. Most disputes about indigenous cultural property thus still rely on ethics and morality and voluntary acts.

More promising activities in the field of indigenous peoples' cultural property claims are taking place in international and non-governmental organisations that have started to engage in procedural solutions. Especially standardised mediation procedures and cultural diplomacy seem to provide suitable resolution mechanisms that allow the resolving of indigenous cultural property cases in the sense of the existing human rights standards. Both mechanisms go beyond ad hoc solutions and have the potential to support an extended and respectful exchange and cooperation with indigenous peoples. However, the crucial question remains as to whether the procedures alone will bring the issue forward. Will they be able to help to accurately respond to indigenous peoples' claims for governance of their cultural property? Will they help to subordinate the use, exchange and trade in indigenous peoples' objects to other understandings and worldviews? Will they provide sufficient participation of indigenous peoples in exchange, trade and equal cultural profit-sharing?

11. Indigenous cultural heritage in development and trade: perspectives from the dynamics of cultural heritage law and policy

Rosemary J. Coombe with Joseph F. Turcotte

1. INTRODUCTION

The protection of cultural heritage has become a matter of great concern in the past two decades and the subject of intense policy negotiations. An emerging awareness of the complexity of issues pertaining to indigenous cultural heritage (ICH) has been one consequence of this process and has arguably shaped it, enabling scholars, activists and international policymakers to more clearly understand cultural heritage as both a source of identity and a resource for sustainable development. In these global processes of deliberation, conventional international cultural policy principles that privilege the interests and agency of long-established European nation states and their definitions of cultural heritage are increasingly challenged.[1] New states and states assuming greater international prominence have put new issues on the cultural policy table, as have historically colonised peoples, minority groups and globally organised indigenous peoples' movements and their advocates. The latter, in particular, have contested the propriety of state dominance in protecting, maintaining and safeguarding heritage properties, while insisting upon the distinctive role that cultural heritage plays in the constitution of their identities and their futures as distinct peoples.[2] Linking issues of cultural heritage to the human rights principle of self-determination makes the issue of indigenous political participation in heritage management a central one. Any approach to issues of trade involving ICH must take this political context as its starting point.

Considering the obligations with respect to the trade of ICH goods under international laws and policy frameworks pertaining to cultural heritage is a far more difficult task than it first appears, for reasons which relate precisely to the ways in which indigenous peoples and their cultural traditions have been historically marginalised, subjugated, appropriated and targeted for erasure and assimilation by the modern state. As a consequence of this history of dispossession, ICH is internationally governed by a variety of distinctive legal instruments, none of which has superior jurisdiction in all contexts. The very nature of the

[1] See Laurajane Smith, *Archaeological Theory and the Politics of Cultural Heritage*, London: Routledge, 2004.

[2] See Rosemary J. Coombe, 'The Expanding Purview of Cultural Properties and their Politics' (2009) *Annual Review of Law and Social Sciences*, 5, pp. 393–412.

'goods' that concern us – those cultural forms and their material manifestations that express meaning and significance constitutive of indigenous identity – advises us to adopt legal pluralism as a starting point for governance inquiries.

Indigenous cultural forms and their manifestations have histories that pre-exist those of modern nation states and their legal hegemony and indeed – at least in those instances where the settler state was founded upon treaty relationships with indigenous nations – underwrite those states' legitimacy.[3] Consequentially, we must acknowledge indigenous customary law as a legitimate source of relevant and authoritative juridical norms for governing heritage of such significance that it implicates the identities of indigenous collectives and polities. Although international cultural heritage law continues to privilege the nation state as holding and managing all heritage goods within its borders as part of its jurisdiction, this privilege may be politically challenged as a denial of basic human rights that undermines indigenous self-determination. Moreover, to the extent that it leaves indigenous peoples dependent upon states to recognise them as deserving 'communities' who bear the appropriate form of 'culture' deserving protection, state-centred and state-dominated regimes of governance for trade in ICH are unlikely to command respect or legitimacy amongst indigenous peoples.

We have approached our topic as far as possible so that we do not overlap with the work of other contributors to the volume. Thus, for example, we deal only with intangible heritage, assuming issues specific to tangible heritage to be capably covered by Rebecca Tsosie's consideration of cultural property,[4] and we deal with TCEs and TK only incidentally, as these are categories more properly within the remit of Christoph Antons',[5] as well as Martin Girsberger and Benny Müller's coverage of the World Intellectual Property Organization's (WIPO) activities,[6] and Brigitte Vézina's chapter on the public domain.[7] Finally, we deal with the area of intangible cultural heritage primarily as it has evolved historically through UNESCO Conventions, recognising that UNESCO is part of the UN system and fundamentally committed to human rights norms as these are expressed internationally. While there may be some dispute as to whether indigenous rights are human rights or distinctive rights (even amongst indigenous peoples),[8] we will follow the UNESCO practice, which we read as deferential to indigenous rights as part of recognised international human rights norms and practice, which is part of international

---

[3] See for example the able legal argument elegantly expressed by James Sákéj Henderson, 'Sui Generis and Treaty Citizenship' (2002) *Citizenship Studies,* 6 (4), pp. 415–40.

[4] Rebecca Tsosie, 'International Trade in Indigenous Cultural Heritage: An Argument for Indigenous Governance of Cultural Property', in this volume. See also Karolina Kuprecht and Kurt Siehr, 'International Trade in Moveable Tangible Cultural Heritage of Indigenous Peoples: A European Perspective', in this volume.

[5] Christoph Antons, 'Intellectual Property Rights in Indigenous Cultural Heritage: Basic Concepts and Continuing Controversies', in this volume.

[6] Martin Girsberger and Benny Müller, 'International Trade in Indigenous Cultural Heritage: An IP Practitioners' Perspective', in this volume.

[7] Brigitte Vézina, 'Are They In or Are They Out? Traditional Cultural Expressions and the Public Domain: Implications for Trade', in this volume.

[8] This is discussed in John Scott and Federico Lenzerini, 'International Indigenous and Human Rights Law in the Context of Trade in Indigenous Cultural Heritage', in this volume.

customary – if not yet positive – law in most jurisdictions.[9] We have found it necessary to move beyond the positive doctrinal field encompassed by the international law of cultural heritage as conventionally understood, to explore cultural heritage as a field of evolving postcolonial politics in which new understandings of culture are emergent and contested. Considering the issues potentially posed by trade in indigenous intangible cultural heritage, we encountered many gaps and aporias that remain unaddressed in both the law and secondary scholarship, requiring both speculation and further questions on our part.

We begin, then, by sizing the terrain within which questions of intangible cultural heritage law and policy have emerged as international issues through a succession of UNESCO Conventions and their implementation. We explore the development of these instruments and their interpretation and operation over time to consider the growing international acknowledgement of the significance of intangible cultural heritage as fundamental to human rights and to sustainable development based on the development of human capacities. We consider the specificity of indigenous concerns in this process, before addressing the difficulties of reconciling practices of international trade with those of safeguarding and revitalising intangible cultural heritage. Finally, we consider the trade-based implications of this history, making some modest proposals for the creative deployment of certain intellectual property vehicles that might encompass and advance indigenous development and self-determination in trade contexts.

2. SIZING THE POLITICAL TERRAIN: INTERNATIONAL CULTURAL HERITAGE PROTECTION AND POLICY AS IT IMPLICATES INDIGENOUS PEOPLES

Before moving into the history of UNESCO instruments that frame the international law addressing the protection of intangible cultural heritage, we need to understand the history of the concept of cultural heritage and the objectives that underlie its protection. The term 'cultural heritage' has no single definition internationally and definitions have substantially shifted and evolved even during the latter part of the twentieth century.[10] From the 1954 Hague Definition of 'the world's inheritance of works of art and monuments of history and science'[11] through 'manifestations of human life which represent a particular view of life and witness the history and validity of that view'[12] and, more recently, 'culture and landscape that are cared for by the community and passed on to the future to serve

[9] For the argument that indigenous rights are part of international customary law, see S. James Anaya, *Indigenous Peoples in International Law*, 2nd edn, Oxford: Oxford University Press, 2004.

[10] There are five, or arguably six, UNESCO Conventions on cultural heritage that span almost 50 years, beginning with the 1956 Hague Convention, and culminating with the Convention on Cultural Diversity in 2005. Because of the ad hoc approach of the Conventions, each of which was devised to deal with an emerging issue or recognised problem, no single definition captures the meaning of the term 'cultural heritage' for all purposes.

[11] Laurajane Smith, *Uses of Heritage*, New York: Routledge, 2006, at p. 74.

[12] Lyndell Prott and Patrick J. O'Keefe, 'Cultural Heritage or Cultural Property?' (1992) *International Journal of Cultural Property*, 1 (2), pp. 307–20, at p. 201.

people's needs for a sense of identity and belonging',[13] the concept has transformed to meet changing needs and interests. The value of cultural heritage lies in its significance to human communities and these values fundamentally relate to the kinds of significance it has. Since cultural heritage may be embodied in intangible forms as well as tangible ones, we are always dealing with terrains of cultural meaning and thus of potential social contestation. The notion of heritage presupposes a focus on inherited forms that may be passed on to future generations in the reproduction of social identities.

The protection of cultural heritage may involve a number of different activities depending upon the values the heritage in question is recognised to possess. When we wish to protect cultural heritage as heritage, we seek to protect not the object or the expression or particular expressive practice per se, but the significance that the object, expression or practice has to those for whom it is cultural heritage, according to legal scholar Craig Forrest in his superb overview of the field.[14] While intangible cultural heritage may be embodied in any number of expressive forms, it is not the expression itself that laws of intangible cultural heritage regimes seek to protect (unlike intellectual property regimes that do precisely that, so as to protect an author's moral or material interests). Rather, it is the significance of the expression in the social life of a community that is, or should be, the policy focus of heritage protection, according to contemporary wisdom. Moreover, just as processes of attributing value are dynamic and evolving, so too must relevant forms of legal protection be capable of evolution and change.

Nonetheless, certain values have assumed dominance in UNESCO regimes in particular time periods, dictating the form that protection has historically assumed. Cultural heritage may have expressive value that is aesthetic, religious or moral in nature, it may have historical and scientific value, and it may have economic value, to consider three forms of value that have received particular emphasis.[15] Groups, communities, national 'publics', nation states and, in some instances, humankind as a whole may be interested in appropriate forms of valuation. The term 'culture' as a qualifier to the concept of heritage acknowledges a social collective to whom the forms have significance. The relative political power of a given community may determine whether and how heritage goods are valued. Minority groups and indigenous peoples with little formal authority in an international system dominated by nation states as sole sources of legitimate political authority have limited capacities to define the scope of their relevant heritage or to object to heritage claims made by others. Social collectives have restricted capacities to act in national and international political arenas, although minorities, indigenous peoples and local communities increasingly challenge these restrictions on human rights grounds.[16] Group rights, although evolving, have yet to gain full normative recognition in international law, but these are increasingly recognised as an important dimension of sustainable development and environmental protection. The right of communities, minorities and indigenous peoples to participate in the process of determining how cultural heritage of

---

[13] Toulani Loulanski, 'Revising the Concept of Cultural Heritage: The Argument for a Functional Approach' (2006) *International Journal of Cultural Property*, 13 (2), pp. 207–33, at p. 209.

[14] Craig Forrest, *International Law and the Protection of Cultural Heritage*, London and New York: Routledge, 2010, at pp. 3–4.

[15] Ibid., at pp. 3–5.

[16] Ibid., at pp. 8–9.

significance to them will be protected is arguably the most important issue of cultural heritage law and policy today.[17]

European state governments historically valued cultural heritage as patrimony to be used in nation-building exercises; all cultural forms located or created within state territory were considered public goods or public domain material. Still, nationalist sentiments have long co-existed with 'universalist' perspectives in which the state is considered primarily a steward or guardian for the 'common heritage of humankind'. The latter term, however, also has a long history of ideological deployment to legitimate diverse forms of plunder.[18] If cultural heritage is a public good – and the relevant 'public' may be contentious – it may still be ascribed economic value and subject to market exchange. Various combinations of public and private ventures may be deemed appropriate to realise economic value provided that cultural heritage significance is maintained. Intangible cultural heritage, for instance, is often the basis for tourism industries, which may include commodified performances, experiences of landscapes, handicraft sales and types of hospitality offered as new heritage products. It may also be the basis for new industries such as traditional medicine, ecological tourism, sustainable agriculture and environmental impact assessment.

According to a universalist position, cultural heritage is best appreciated and protected when it is visible and accessible to the largest numbers of persons.[19] Arguably, however, this privileges culturally specific presuppositions about meanings and values that may not accord with those of the group for whom such heritage is significant, whose own values must be given priority if it is to be protected *as* cultural heritage. Amongst developing countries, retaining cultural heritage has become an important means of protection because the economic benefits of tourism and the licensing of intellectual property rights promise more sustainable forms of development than the sale and export of cultural goods characteristic of their colonial past.[20] Heritage forms have scholarly value and convey information about human history and cultural development, but the conditions under which they do so are evolving to serve a broader range of interests than their historical capture as relics and antiquities to grace metropolitan museums. Those means of protection which serve general educational and scholarly needs, for example, no longer take precedence over activities that enable host communities to realise economic benefits from local patrimony. These objectives should not be presumed to be antithetical, however, as community-based archaeological research on ICH increasingly illustrates.[21]

---

17 For a process-based model of regulation where the participation of the most relevant stakeholders, including indigenous peoples, is a central element, see Christoph B. Graber, 'Stimulating Trade and Development of Indigenous Cultural Heritage by Means of International Law: Issues of Legitimacy and Method', in this volume.

18 Forrest, supra note 14, at p. 12. See also Ugo Mattei and Laura Nadar, *Plunder: When the Rule of Law is Illegal,* San Francisco, CA: Wiley Publishers, 2008.

19 Forrest, supra note 14, at p. 14.

20 Ibid., at p. 17.

21 See, for examples, the essays collected in Thomas Killian (ed.), *Opening Archaeology: Repatriation's Impact on Contemporary Research and Practice*, Santa Fe: School of American Research, 2008, at pp. 79–90; George Nicholas and Kelly Bannister, 'Copyrighting the Past? Emerging Intellectual Property Rights Issues in Archaeology' (2004) *Current Anthropology,* 45 (3), pp. 327–50; and more recently, Shelly Greer, 'Heritage and Empowerment: Community-based

With respect to intangible cultural heritage, states have recently obliged themselves to 'safeguard' heritage values, a term that legal expert Janet Blake argues is broader than the concept of protection and requires states to engage in positive actions to promote intangible cultural heritage by creating environments conducive to its flourishing and future production.[22] This requires parties to take a participatory approach in relation to 'measures aimed at ensuring the viability of the intangible cultural heritage, including ... [its] identification, documentation, research, preservation, protection, promotion, enhancement, transmission ... revitalization'.[23] Finally, legal recognition itself provides a means of 'protecting' cultural heritage by reinforcing and legitimating heritage values.[24]

The term cultural heritage has special relevance for indigenous peoples in international law precisely because one of its earliest uses as a category emerges from the realisation that international legal recognition of world heritage and cultural property had historically ill-served them. In her influential report *Protection of the Heritage of Indigenous Peoples* (1995)[25] – hereinafter the Daes Report – Erica-Irene Daes, as Special Rapporteur, stressed that in the UNESCO Declaration of the Principles of International Cultural Cooperation (1966), the free exchange of cultural knowledge was expressly linked with 'respect' and 'reciprocity' among cultures. Her study documented the extent to which respect and reciprocity have been lacking in the widespread practice of appropriation of indigenous peoples' cultural heritage by other societies. She expressed reservations about the term cultural property in international law, and suggested that the apparent division between tangible and intangible cultural heritage in international law was inappropriate as it pertained to indigenous peoples. The term cultural heritage, Daes suggested, more precisely signified the interrelationship between the tangible and intangible qualities of goods in a matrix of relationships that imply responsibilities by members of a collective that are more characteristic of indigenous values.[26] Since both cultural properties and intangible cultural goods are alienable as commodities – the latter through intellectual property laws – cultural heritage was proffered as a better concept for appreciating the

---

Indigenous Cultural Heritage in Northern Australia' (2010) *International Journal of Heritage Management*, 16 (1–2), pp. 45–58; and Jonathan Pragnall, Anne Ross and Brian Coghill, 'Power Relations and Community Involvement in Landscape-Based Cultural Heritage Management Practice: An Australian Case Study' (2010) *International Journal of Heritage Studies,* 16 (1), pp. 140–55.

[22] Janet E. Blake, *Commentary on the UNESCO 2003 Safeguarding of the Intangible Cultural Heritage*, Leicester: Institute of Art and Law, 2006, at p. 23.

[23] Janet E. Blake, 'UNESCO's 2003 Convention on Intangible Cultural Heritage: The Implications of Community Involvement in "Safeguarding"', in Laurajane Smith and Natsuko Akagawa (eds), *Intangible Heritage,* New York and London: Routledge, 2009, pp. 45–73, at p. 50 [hereinafter Blake, 'UNESCO's 2003 Convention'].

[24] Forrest, supra note 14, at p. 19.

[25] Erica-Irene Daes (Special Rapporteur of the UN Sub-Commission on Prevention of Discrimination and Protection of Minorities and Chairperson of the Working Group on Indigenous Populations), 'Protection of the Heritage of Indigenous Peoples' (UN Doc. E/CN.4/Sub.2/1995/26, 1995).

[26] See discussion in Mohsen al Attar, Nicole Aylwin and Rosemary J. Coombe, 'Indigenous Cultural Rights in International Human Rights Law', in Catherine Bell and Robert K. Paterson (eds), *Protection of First Nations Cultural Heritage: Laws, Policy and Reform,* Vancouver, BC: UBC Press, 2009, pp. 311–42, at p. 319.

complex forms of inalienability through which tangible and intangible goods together sustain indigenous collectivities. The concept of cultural heritage reflects the fact that goods of cultural significance, unlike properties per se, are not separate from the social processes that sustain their values. Understanding cultural heritage as a dynamic, expressive and productive practice of dialogue, rather than a passive appreciation for a field of static cultural works, is consonant with an international movement to revalue cultural diversity and reconceptualise heritage values that clearly situates such cultural activities in the normative field of human rights.

The human rights orientation of cultural heritage protection is found in the very first Article of the Constitution of UNESCO, which establishes that its purpose is to:

> contribute to peace and security by promoting collaboration among the nations through education, science, and culture in order to further universal respect for justice, for the rule of law, and for the human rights and fundamental freedoms which are affirmed for the peoples of the world. … by the Charter of the United Nations.[27]

Human rights principles expressly frame and limit intangible cultural heritage protections[28] and claims are politically articulated as human rights issues, especially when they involve indigenous peoples. This emphasis upon human rights as the overarching normative framework for interpreting cultural heritage law is especially important for indigenous peoples because intangible cultural heritage claims are central means by which the political, economic and social project of achieving self-determination[29] is facilitated.[30]

Principles for the protection of ICH emerged internationally in a human rights context, framed by the concerns of the Sub-Commission on the Human Rights and made their way into the United Nations Declaration on the Rights of Indigenous Peoples (UNDRIP),[31] in which heritage rights clearly relate to territorial rights from which they are deemed inseparable and indivisible.[32] Indeed, international recognition of indigenous land rights is tied to its cultural value to indigenous peoples. It is suggested that 'the protection of Indigenous peoples' land rights fits more into the category of cultural rights rather than the right to property, and human rights law has provided indigenous peoples with legal avenues for the recognition of their specific cultural attachment to their traditional

---

27 UNESCO, 'Constitution of the United Nations Educational, Scientific and Cultural Organization' (adopted 16 November 1945, amended at 31st session), Article 1.

28 The Convention on Intangible Cultural Heritage's extensive Preamble includes a prominent citation of the 1948 Universal Declaration on Human Rights and the two 1966 human rights Covenants in its second recital. Article 2(1) provides that consideration shall only be given to such intangible cultural heritage as is compatible with existing international rights instruments.

29 Forrest, supra note 14, at p. 363.

30 Val Napoleon, 'Looking beyond the Law: Questions about Indigenous Peoples' Tangible and Intangible Property', in Catherine Bell and Robert K. Paterson (eds), *Protection of First Nations Cultural Heritage: Laws, Policy and Reform*, Vancouver, BC: UBC Press, 2009, pp. 370–93, at p. 371.

31 UN, Declaration on the Rights of Indigenous Peoples, GA Res. 61/295 (UN Doc. A/61/L.67 and Add.1) (adopted on 13 September 2007).

32 Al Attar, Aylwin and Coombe, supra note 26, at p. 317, note 28.

territories.'[33] Indigenous communities' representatives and the non-governmental organisations that support them have been successful in compelling the international community to address issues of cultural protection, recognition and valuation of traditional knowledge and the integral relation of these to aboriginal territories.[34] Moreover, ICH protection is often linked to a broader project of decolonisation that stresses the inextricable link between cultural heritage and the maintenance, strengthening, transmission and renewal of indigenous peoples' identity, knowledge, laws and practices.[35]

UNDRIP has also provided a strong normative vocabulary with which to make these claims, providing as it does:

> an authoritative common understanding, at the global level, of the minimum content of the rights of indigenous peoples, upon a foundation of various sources of international human rights law ... The principles and rights affirmed in the Declaration constitute or add to the normative frameworks for the activities of United Nations human rights institutions, mechanisms and specialized agencies as they relate to indigenous peoples.[36]

Thus, human rights standards seem to be fundamental in framing most if not all principles of international ICH protection. With co-authors, Coombe has canvassed the field of international human rights law pertaining to ICH elsewhere to conclude that the rights of indigenous peoples to a measure of control over the use of their cultural heritage is widely recognised and arguably constitutes a principle of international customary law.[37]

UNESCO is the primary UN body responsible for preparing and interpreting international normative principles and instruments with regard to cultural rights as a special category of human rights in international law. International human rights norms generally demand a special sensitivity to the rights of the disadvantaged. Minorities and indigenous peoples are precisely those whose cultural rights have historically been violated, often through state-sanctioned initiatives to forcibly assimilate them, prohibit their cultural practices, penalise the use of their languages and the practice of their spiritual life, seize their cultural goods and relegate their culture to a form of historical information.[38] Over

---

[33] Jeremie Gilbert, 'Custodians of the Land: Indigenous Peoples, Human Rights and Cultural Integrity', in Michele Langfield, William Logan and Mairead Nic Craith (eds), *Cultural Diversity, Heritage and Human Rights,* Abingdon: Routledge, 2010, pp. 31–44, at p. 35.

[34] Al Attar, Aylwin and Coombe, supra note 26, at p. 323.

[35] George Nicholas et al., 'Intellectual Property Issues in Heritage Management Part 2: Legal Dimension, Ethical Considerations, and Collaborative Research Practices' (2010) *Heritage Management*, 3 (1), pp. 117–47, at p. 121.

[36] S. James Anaya (Special Rapporteur on the Situation of Human Rights and Fundamental Freedoms of Indigenous People), 'Promotion and Protection of all Human Rights, Civil, Political, Economic, Social and Cultural Rights, Including the Right to Development', UN, General Assembly, Human Rights Council, Ninth Session (UN Doc. A/HRC/9/9/Add-1, 2008).

[37] Al Attar, Aylwin and Coombe, supra note 25.

[38] George Nicholas, 'Indigenous Cultural Heritage in the Age of Technological Reproducibility: Towards a Postcolonial Ethic of the Public Domain', in Rosemary J. Coombe, Darren Wershler and Martin Zeilinger (eds), *Dynamic Fair Dealing: Creating Canadian Culture Online,* Toronto: University of Toronto Press (in press). See also, Elizabeth Coleman and Rosemary J. Coombe, 'A Broken Record: Subjecting "Music" to Cultural Rights', in James C. Young and Conrad Brunck (eds), *Ethics of Cultural Appropriation*, London: Blackwell, 2008, pp. 179–210.

the last two decades international policy has recognised that ICH is not a residual remainder of a lost past, but an evolving repertoire of knowledge, practices, innovations and expressions that are significant for maintaining the interlinked goods of cultural and biological diversity while providing the basis for sustainable development.[39] A number of international and national legal instruments promoting the ethnic, cultural, linguistic and religious identities of national minorities affirm community rights to participate in decisions that involve the use of their cultural heritage and recognise cultural diversity as grounds for sustainable development.

Our focus, therefore, is primarily upon the protection, preservation, safeguarding and development of ICH as a cultural right, rather than as an economic right, which is more properly the purview of WIPO. Nonetheless, to the extent that UNESCO is committed to maintaining both cultural identity and furthering sustainable development, it becomes necessary to consider the extent to which economic rights may need to be shaped or limited to serve these objectives.

International instruments addressing the rights of indigenous peoples, it might be argued, have fundamentally altered the international consensus on the scope and meaning of cultural rights.[40] Prior to the negotiation of UNDRIP (a 20-year process), international law largely objectified culture. Cultural rights protected heritage practices and cultural identifications with heritage goods primarily as static monuments, icons, and symbols subject to state cultural recognition,[41] not as material domains with respect to which communities other than nations might have legitimate authority and a political voice.[42] Regarded as an activity and as a resource, however, the political and economic dimensions of culture have come to the fore, putting new emphasis on community security, economic stability and sustainable development; cultural rights claims have increasingly enabled groups to achieve control over significant material resources[43] and heightened their stakes in fields of cultural representation.

Within the wider field of cultural rights (which includes the moral and material interests of authors more properly covered by a discussion of intellectual property) we focus on obligations to protect, safeguard, maintain and develop intangible cultural heritage of particular concern to indigenous peoples.[44] Although the term 'intangible cultural heritage' formally emerges only with the 2003 Convention on the Intangible

---

[39] Rosemary J. Coombe and Nicole Aylwin, 'Repositioning Cultural Heritage Ethics Using Human Rights Norms', in Rosemary J. Coombe, Darren Wershler and Martin Zeilinger (eds), *Dynamic Fair Dealing: Creating Canadian Culture Online*, Toronto: University of Toronto Press (in press).

[40] Cindy Holder, 'Culture as an Activity and Human Right: An Important Advance for Indigenous Peoples and International Law' (2008) *Alternatives,* 33, pp. 7–28.

[41] Ibid., at p. 17.

[42] Ibid., at p. 12.

[43] Bruce Robbins and Elsa Stamatapolou, 'Reflections on Culture and Cultural Rights' (2004) *South Atlantic Quarterly*, 103 (2/3), pp. 419–34.

[44] Reference will be made to other UNESCO Conventions and Instruments, as well as WIPO activities, only when these help to clarify issues that remain obscure when focusing primarily upon the major Conventions.

Cultural Heritage,[45] it would be a mistake to consider this the only UNESCO Convention concerned with the intangible dimensions of cultural heritage. Properties are only of interest to UNESCO to the extent that a property has the kind of value embraced by the term cultural heritage. Historically, the term 'cultural property' served as an expedient referent; nonetheless, 'it is essentially the value attributed to the objects that is to be protected'[46] and thus the intangible aspects that warranted policy attention. Nonetheless, critics point to the dominant meanings that property has as a concept in common law, particularly to commercial significations that privilege exclusive private rights of exclusion, alienation, exploitation, and even absolute rights of destruction that do not denote protective considerations. Although the term cultural heritage emerges in the 1972 World Heritage Convention (WHC)[47] as the target of protection, the Convention's limited application to immoveables, such as monuments, archaeological sites, relics and landscapes, is perceived to have detracted attention from the values themselves.

In some cases, state and international focus upon the fixed property unfortunately damaged the cultural values that the form was designated as heritage to protect. For example, the physical protection of world heritage sites like Angkor (and their development for more widespread appreciation) is widely acknowledged to have damaged the cultural connection between the Cambodian people and this manifestation of their heritage. By 1995 experts recognised that the concept of cultural heritage, having become too based on architectural and archaeological heritage, unduly focuses on the physical side, 'completely ignoring the question of the function in contemporary society'.[48]

Other forms of cultural heritage that lacked tangible manifestation, such as ritual, behaviour, oral histories, knowledge, skills and practices, were also slighted by this emphasis upon materiality. These intangible forms had not historically received protection, arguably because they were possessed by less powerful peoples with denigrated cultural value systems[49] whose cultural forms were often deemed primitive and backward – destined to disappear under policies of modernity, assimilation and development. To the extent that these were legally recognised, it was as folklore that was properly part of the public domain.[50] Ultimately, then, cultural heritage as a concept had become so associated with its tangible manifestations rather than the values therein embodied that policymakers deemed it necessary to add the qualifier 'intangible' to the primary term cultural heritage. This provided a clear means of referring to aspects of cultural heritage with no material fixity capable of rendering these properties (or authorship attributes capable of rendering them intellectual properties).

---

45 UNESCO, Convention for the Safeguarding of the Intangible Cultural Heritage, 2368 UNTS 1 (adopted on 17 October 2003, entered into force 20 April 2006).

46 Forrest, supra note 14, at p. 23.

47 UNESCO, Convention Concerning the Protection of the World Cultural and Natural Heritage, 1037 UNTS 151 (adopted on 16 November 1972, entered into force 17 December 1975).

48 As cited in Forrest, supra note 14, at p. 28.

49 Jessica Myers Moran, 'Legal Means for Protecting the Intangible Cultural Heritage of Indigenous Peoples in a Post-Colonial World' (2008) *Holy Cross Journal of Law and Public Policy*, 12 (71), at p. 71.

50 Coombe and Aylwin, supra note 39. See also Vézina, supra note 7.

During the 1980s, debates about the meaning and value of cultural heritage took place in relationship to larger international deliberations about the relationship between culture and development. In 1987, the UN launched its World Decade for Cultural Development (1987–97), in which a more anthropological view of culture as a way of life and form of social organisation was adopted. This served to reinforce the idea that cultural heritage could not be restricted to historical sites and monuments but needed to include oral tradition and a wider field of expressive culture.[51] In 1995, at the UNESCO General Conference, the World Commission on Culture and Development solidified this new perspective in its report, *Our Creative Diversity*, by highlighting that heritage is made up of more than monuments and historical sites, and that both tangible and intangible cultural heritage are key to 'ensuring the flourishing of human existence'.[52]

In the collective struggles of many marginalised people, culture is a concept used reflexively to engage with state and non-governmental institutions for purposes of asserting identity, demanding greater inclusion in political life, local autonomy and control over resources, while seeking new forms of engagement with global markets (as well as resistances thereto).[53] Cultural distinction has gained new international purchase as a valuable social, political and economic resource.[54] Cultural rights have become legal vehicles through which political claims are pursued; cultural rights claims now figure in struggles for political autonomy, legal entitlements to territory and other resources and designs for alternative forms of development.[55] Issues of safeguarding, managing and developing ICH are integrally embedded in this larger field of politics.

---

51 Blake, 'UNESCO's 2003 Convention', supra note 23, at p. 48.

52 Lourdes Arizpe, 'The Cultural Politics of Intangible Cultural Heritage', in Janet E. Blake (ed.), *Safeguarding Intangible Cultural Heritage: Challenges and Approaches*, Builth Wells, UK: Institute of Art and Law, 2007, pp. 25–41, at p. 32.

53 See Rosemary J. Coombe, 'First Nations Intangible Cultural Heritage Concerns: Prospects for Protection of Traditional Knowledge and Traditional Cultural Expressions in International Law', in Catherine Bell and Robert K. Paterson (eds), *Protection of First Nations Cultural Heritage: Laws, Policy and Reform,* Vancouver, BC: UBC Press, 2009, pp. 247–77.

54 As elaborated in John Comaroff and Jean Comaroff, *Ethnicity, Inc.,* Chicago: University of Chicago Press, 2009. See also, Rosemary J. Coombe, 'Legal Claims to Culture In and Against the Market: Neoliberalism and the Global Proliferation of Meaningful Difference' (2005) *Law, Culture and Humanities*, 1 (1), pp. 32–55; George Yudice, *The Expediency of Culture*, Durham: Duke University Press, 2003; and Vijayendra Rao and Michael Walton (eds), *Culture and Public Action,* Palo Alto, CA: Stanford University Press, 2004.

55 See Rosemary J. Coombe, '"Possessing Culture": Political Economies of Community Subjects and their Properties', in Mark Busse and Veronica Strang (eds), *Ownership and Appropriation,* London: Berg Publishers, 2011, pp. 105–27 [hereinafter Coombe, 'Possessing Culture']; Rosemary J. Coombe, 'Cultural Agencies: "Constructing" Community Subjects and their Rights', in Mario Biagioli, Peter Jaszi and Martha Woodmansee (eds), *Making and Unmaking Intellectual Property,* Chicago: University of Chicago Press, 2011, pp. 79–98 [hereinafter Coombe, 'Cultural Agencies']; Henrietta Marrie, 'The UNESCO Convention for the Safeguarding of the Intangible Cultural Heritage and the Protection and Maintenance of the Intangible Cultural Heritage of Indigenous Peoples', in Laurajane Smith and Natsuko Akagawa (eds), *Intangible Heritage,* New York and London: Routledge, 2009, pp. 169–92; and Bruce Robbins and Elsa Stamatapolou, 'Reflections on Culture and Cultural Rights' (2004) *South Atlantic Quarterly,* 103 (2/3), pp. 419–34.

3. THE DEVELOPMENT OF INTANGIBLE CULTURAL HERITAGE LAW AND POLICY

To explore the development of intangible cultural heritage law and policy within the international framework, we examine the UNESCO instruments most likely to impact upon indigenous intangible cultural heritage, avoiding those that pertain primarily to material cultural property except when these include sites of cultural significance to indigenous peoples from which significant forms of intangible cultural heritage might arise and require protection, preservation or development. As the following summary description of the main features of the relevant legal instruments illustrates, UNESCO's interest in and commitment to the protection of intangible ICH has become stronger as institutional concerns have focused increasingly upon maintaining cultural identities and cultural diversity.

3.1 World Heritage Convention (WHC) 1972

The WHC reflects the convergence of three international initiatives, one for protecting monuments and sites of universal value, another for conservation of natural heritage, and a declaration on the value of human environments. Coming into force in 1975, it had been adopted by virtually all states by 2009. The Convention was based upon the universalist premise that heritage is the world heritage of global humankind and to qualify for the regime's inscription and protection, it must be of 'outstanding universal value'. This concept has been amended through Operational Guidelines that have had six distinct variations since 1977, reflecting a shift from iconic and historic sites to those more representative of the world's diversity and living traditions. Contemporary Guidelines evaluate a site's integrity and authenticity within the cultural context in which the site has significance.[56] Ultimately, however, it is the state party that must identify and nominate potential sites and pledge to conserve these. State sovereignty over heritage within its territory is fundamental to the regime but state duties have little discernible positive content. While states are encouraged to adopt policies that give the cultural and natural heritage a function in the life of the community, set up services for protection, work out operating methods to counteract dangers to the heritage, and establish training centres for heritage protection, they are only asked to endeavour to do so. States are required to maintain inventories of sites suitable for inclusion in a tentative list of possible nominations and for many years have been encouraged to prepare these lists 'with the participation of a wide variety of stakeholders, including site managers, local and regional governments, local communities, NGOs, and other interested parties and partners'.[57]

The International Council on Monuments and Sites (ICOMOS) was established in 1965 and played an important role in the conceptualisation of cultural heritage. Its mandate was restricted to monuments (real property) and sites (a group of elements, whether natural or

[56] This first becomes apparent in 2005 (see UNESCO, 'World Heritage Committee Operational Guidelines for the Implementation of the World Heritage Convention', (UNESCO Doc. WHC. 05/02, 2005), at paras 87–95, available online at http://whc.unesco.org/archive/opguide05-en.pdf) (all online sources were accessed 30 November 2011).

[57] Forrest, supra note 14, at p. 251.

man-made or combinations of the two, which it is in the public interest to preserve) but did not extend to moveable property.[58] This reflected a growing interest in environmental and anthropological aspects of historical preservation[59] and an acknowledgment that the setting for archaeological works may be significant to their cultural value.[60] Sites may have heritage value because of their association with events, living traditions, ideas, beliefs or artistic and literary works of outstanding universal significance, for instance.

Still, the WHC definition of monuments 'which are of outstanding universal value from the point of view of history, art, or science' clearly privileges some kinds of intangible values over others. Similarly the definition of sites as 'works of man or combined works of man and nature' undervalues the cultural values that many indigenous communities hold with respect to natural sites.[61] Laurajane Smith provides an extensive critical discussion of how the politics of cultural resource management with respect to ICH in Australia has worked to empower archaeologists at the political expense of indigenous peoples themselves, devaluing their knowledge, denying their authority, defining their identity and in some cases even denying their contemporary existence as aboriginal peoples.[62] Despite the establishment of codes of ethics requiring archaeologists to consult with indigenous communities, some indigenous people have experienced these consultation processes as disrespectful, patronising and tokenistic – in short, monologic rather than dialogic. Significantly, Smith illustrates that many professional experts in this field remain ignorant of the political consequences of their work for indigenous peoples and the ways in which their historical pronouncements may impact upon aboriginal rights to land, resources and livelihoods. Her work helps to explain the distrust with which indigenous peoples may still greet legal processes of protecting cultural heritage and associated activities of state-initiated cultural resource management.[63]

3.2 Instrument on Cultural Landscapes 1992

The recognition of cultural landscapes as an explicit category of heritage in 1992 was one response to allegations that the World Heritage Committee's selection criteria were unbalanced and Eurocentric and failed to appreciate the significance of ICH in many parts of the world. At about the same period, following the Rio Earth Summit, global policy-makers were considering issues of biological diversity, which posited indigenous knowledge and its vulnerability as significant issues to be addressed. The WHC's definition of heritage provided an innovative and powerful opportunity for the protection of cultural

---

58 International Charter for the Conservation and Restoration of Monuments and Sites (The Venice Charter 1964) available online at http://www.international.icomos.org/charters/venice_e.htm.
59 Forrest, supra note 14, at p. 226.
60 Ibid., at p. 230.
61 Smith, supra note 11, at p. 96.
62 Ibid.
63 See also Jane Lydon, 'Contested Landscapes: Rights to History, Rights to Place: Who Controls Archaeological Places?', in Bruno David and Julian Thomas (eds), *Handbook of Landscape Archaeology*, Walnut Creek, CA: Left Coast Press, 2008, pp. 654–9.

landscapes as 'combined works of nature and man'.[64] In 1992, the World Heritage Committee adopted three categories of cultural landscapes as qualifying for listing.[65] The most easily identifiable was the clearly defined landscape designed and created intentionally by man, which embraces garden and parkland landscapes constructed for aesthetic reasons that may be associated with religious or other monumental buildings. The second category is the organically evolved landscape that 'results from an initial social, economic, administrative, and/or religious imperative and has developed its present form by association with and in response to its natural environment' falling into two sub-categories, the first pertaining to relic landscapes that are no longer evolving, and the second, a continuing landscape which retains an active social role in contemporary society.[66] The final category of 'associative cultural landscapes' was deemed 'justifiable by virtue of the powerful religious, artistic or cultural associations of the natural element rather than material cultural evidence'. Thus the 'associated intangible values' of natural places of cultural significance could provide the basis for inscription on the World Heritage List.[67]

According to UNESCO insiders, the category of cultural landscape has been crucial for legitimating the heritage of local communities and indigenous people:

> The primary difference was the acceptance of communities and their relationship with the environment. There are many places with associative cultural values, or sacred sites, which may be physical entities or mental images embedded in a people's spirituality, cultural tradition, and practice. The category of sacred sites has an immense potential, as many protected areas have been basically protected because they are sacred places. Well before the categorization of protected areas into national parks, nature reserves, and landscapes, indigenous peoples have protected their sacred sites and groves. Through these mechanisms they have contributed to preserving unique sites, biological diversity and cultural spaces transmitted to future generations.[68]

It was only in 1998, however, that the Operational Guidelines were changed to allow for the inclusion of a traditionally managed natural site – East Rennell (Solomon Islands) – to

---

64 UNESCO, Convention Concerning the Protection of the World Cultural and Natural Heritage, 1037 UNTS 151 (adopted on 16 November 1972, entered into force 17 December 1975), Article 1 [hereinafter 'Heritage Convention'].

65 UNESCO, 'World Heritage Committee Operational Guidelines for the Implementation of the World Heritage Convention', (UNESCO Doc. WHC. 2, 1992), at para. 23, available online at http://whc.unesco.org/archive/opguide92-en.pdf.

66 'Guidelines on the Inscription of Certain Types of Properties on the World Heritage List', Annex 3 to UNESCO, 'World Heritage Committee Operational Guidelines for the Implementation of the World Heritage Convention', (UNESCO Doc. WHC. 08/01, 2008), at para. 10(ii), available online at http://whc.unesco.org/archive/opguide08-en.pdf.

67 See discussion in Jean-Louis Luxen, 'The Intangible Dimension of Monuments and Sites', *ICOMOS Newsletter* (March–July 2000), available at http://www.international.icomos.org/ga2002.htm; and in Harriet J. Deacon and O. Beazley, 'The Safeguarding of Intangible Heritage Values under the World Heritage Convention: Auschwitz, Hiroshima and Robben Island', in Janet E. Blake (ed.), *Safeguarding Intangible Cultural Heritage: Challenges and Approaches,* Builth Wells, UK: Institute of Art and Law, 2007, pp. 93–107.

68 Mechtild Rössler, 'World Heritage Cultural Landscapes: A UNESCO Flagship Programme' (2006) *Landscape Research*, 31 (4), pp. 333–53, at p. 336.

be inscribed on the World Heritage List.[69] Consequentially, the involvement of local people in nomination processes was considered desirable; in 2005 the Operational Guidelines formally encouraged community involvement. Ideally, the Convention will evolve to recognise traditional management systems, customary law and traditional environmental knowledge as legitimate forms of protection and thereby 'contribute to sustainable local and regional development'.[70] New governance structures might combine community-managed systems and traditional national park management in a vision of shared responsibilities amongst stakeholders where local capacity-building and employment for community members are linked to national institutional support and indigenous peoples are considered primary beneficiaries.[71]

As Janet Blake notes, this type of landscape is exemplified by Uluru Kata Tjuta National Park in Australia and Tongariro National Park in New Zealand, where indigenous peoples assume management roles.[72] Inscribed on the World Heritage List in 1994 as a cultural landscape manifesting the interaction of humanity and its natural environment as both a 'continuing' and 'associative' cultural landscape, the management of indigenous intangible cultural heritage has been structured so as to provide economic benefits for indigenous communities that may well be relevant for considerations of trade.

In Uluru Kata Tjuta National Park, Anangu Aboriginal peoples' cosmologies are central to the site's perceived significance and are reflected in traditional management practices that provide a code of behaviour governing both interpersonal relationships and environmental management. These include ceremonies performed according to *Tjukurpa*, an indigenous philosophy often referred to in English as the Dreaming – a term that Anangu reject because it implies that the relationships between humans, animals, plants and their descendants are in some sense unreal or imaginary.[73] This philosophy is arguably local customary law in the region and is sometimes translated as 'time of the law'.[74] Moreover:

> … the material forms of Uluru and Kata Tjuta incorporate the actions, artefacts and bodies of the ancestral beings celebrated in Anangu religion and culture through narratives, elaborate song cycles, visual arts and dance. The numerous paintings in the rock shelters at the foot of Uluru express the ideas (*kulini*, or physical thinking) of *Tjukurpa*. They were made as a teaching tool … one of the park's Anangu rangers, describes the painted shelters as an 'Anangu blackboard'. It is incumbent on modern Anangu to follow *Tjukurpa*, both in their management of the environment and in their social relationships.[75]

---

69 UNESCO, 'World Heritage Committee Operational Guidelines for the Implementation of the World Heritage Convention', (UNESCO Doc. WHC. 99/02, 1999), at para. 24(ii), available online at http://whc.unesco.org/archive/opguide99-en.pdf.

70 Rössler, supra note 68, at p. 334.

71 Ibid., at p. 348.

72 Blake, 'UNESCO's 2003 Convention', supra note 23, at p. 51. See also Julia Simmonds, 'UNESCO World Heritage Convention' (1997) *Art, Antiquity and Law,* 2 (3), pp. 251–81.

73 Graeme Calma and Lynette Liddle, 'Uluru-Kata Tjuta National Park: Sustainable Management and Development', in UNESCO, *Cultural Landscapes: The Challenges of Conservation, World Heritage Papers No. 7,* Paris: World Heritage Centre, 2003, pp. 104–19, at p. 105.

74 Robert Layton, 'Relating to the Country in the Western Desert', in Eric Hirsch and Michael O'Hanlon (eds), *The Anthropology of Landscape: Perspectives on Space and Place*, Oxford: Clarendon Press, 1997, pp. 210–31.

75 Calma and Liddle, supra note 73, at p. 105.

It is precisely these spiritual 'associations' with 'country' that are protected through the Uluru Kata Tjuta National Park Board of Management, the Central Land Council and the Office for Joint Management. The landscape is actively managed by Aboriginal communities 'using traditional practices and knowledge … and management techniques to conserve biodiversity such as the use of fire and the creation and maintenance of water sources such as wells and rock waterholes'[76] as well as through maintenance of traditional ceremonial activities within Anangu communities. Management of the park, access to the sites, and the information conveyed to visitors all embody respect for Anangu ritual values and incorporate activities Anangu deem necessary for the maintenance of *Tjukurpa*, including transmission of traditional knowledge to youth to enable them to find water, food and bush medicine, ritualised visiting of sacred sites, keeping visitors safe by respecting traditional forms of power vested in sites, caretaking through rockhole cleaning and traditional burning, and keeping the country alive through ceremony and song.[77] Anangu peoples are employed in all natural resource management activities and Anangu traditional ecological knowledge of flora, fauna, habitat, seasons, places and their history is valued in park management.[78]

Protecting *Nguraritja* 'intellectual and cultural property rights' is necessary to protect traditional knowledge and Anangu cultural work. *Nguraritja* refers to traditional custodians of sites, who acquire responsibilities through birth and ancestral connections. Although all Anangu peoples are recognised as having rights to control their cultural heritage, Anangu management plans vest such rights of control as responsibilities to be exercised by *Nguraritja*.[79] The park features a cultural centre, opened ten years after the park was returned to its traditional Anangu owners; the documentation and storage of traditional knowledge as well as the transmission of *Tjurkurpa* values to future generations and to the public is one of its central missions.[80] New media such as film, video and digital sound recording store and transmit oral histories while recording relationships between songs and landscape features in the presentation of 'soundscapes' enables visitors to virtually explore the cultural landscape. Paintings on the rock faces reflect aspects of religion and ceremony and serve pedagogical purposes for both community members and visitors; Anangu use the same symbols today in sand drawings, body painting and acrylic paintings.

Indigenous participation in the management of cultural landscapes is not restricted to World Heritage sites, however. UNESCO values may be translated into the domestic policies of state parties even where sites are not nominated for inscription. For example, Canada began to recognise cultural landscapes in the 1990s and added aboriginal cultural

---

[76] Ibid., at p. 107.

[77] Ibid., at p. 109.

[78] Ibid., at p. 108.

[79] Australian House of Representatives, Standing Committee on Environment, Recreation and the Arts, 'Managing Australia's World Heritage', *Committee Report* (4 November 1996), available online at http://www.aph.gov.au/house/committee/environ/whainq/whirpt/contents.htm, last updated 7 February 2011.

[80] Calma and Liddle, supra note 73, at p. 108.

landscapes to its national parks system in 1999,[81] incorporating principles of community involvement and management that have put emphasis upon the significance of such sites to aboriginal peoples and privilege their management.[82] Certainly the evolution of world heritage to include cultural landscapes seems to better accord with indigenous values. Nonetheless, there is a long legacy of managing heritage sites in a way that privileges aesthetic values and displaces indigenous values with respect to natural sites that will need to be overcome.

Social geographer Jennifer Carter provides an extensive case study from Fraser Island in Australia that demonstrates the continuing tendency of professional experts to rhetorically 'depopulate' significant heritage sites, while misunderstanding the complex connections between nature and culture characteristic of indigenous values.[83] Despite official federal acknowledgment of the hybridity of nature and culture in heritage discourse, state planning and site management continues to maintain 'separate environmental impact and cultural heritage assessments, relying on documented evidence within a structured inventory and a material-centred approach to the categorising of "natural" or "cultural" values',[84] ignoring the indigenous imprint upon the landscape and the landscape's significance to aboriginal identity. Nonetheless, she acknowledges that the contemporary recognition of cultural landscapes 'might allow Indigenous people to more fully receive the benefits they desire through tourism, park management, fishing, education, planning, and the provision of roads and local services, and so forth. Whether or not re-nomination occurs, world heritage inscription needs to be realised as people's connection with place.'[85]

3.3 Convention for the Safeguarding of the Intangible Cultural Heritage 2003

If 'intangible cultural heritage is not an object, not a performance, not a site; ... may be embodied or given material form in any of these, but basically ... it is an enactment of meanings embodied in collective memory',[86] it is not surprising that attempts to safeguard such an amorphous corpus for regulation have involved decades of struggle. Many societies value intangible heritage passed down over generations more than the physical

---

[81] Meryl Olivier, 'Cultural Landscape Conservation Experiences in Canada', in UNESCO, *Cultural Landscapes: The Challenges of Conservation, World Heritage Papers No. 7*, Paris: World Heritage Centre, 2003, pp. 101–3.

[82] Susan Buggey and Nora Mitchell, 'Cultural Landscape Management Challenges and Promising New Directions in the United States and Canada', in UNESCO, *Cultural Landscapes: The Challenges of Conservation, World Heritage Papers No. 7,* Paris: World Heritage Centre, 2003, pp. 92–100, at p. 92.

[83] Jennifer Carter, 'Displacing Indigenous Cultural Landscapes: The Naturalistic Gaze at Fraser Island World Heritage Area' (2010) *Geographical Research*, 48 (4), pp. 398–410.

[84] Ibid., at p. 399, citing Germán I. Andrade, 'The Non-Material Values of the Machu Picchu World Heritage Site from Acknowledgement to Action' (2000) *Parks*, 10, pp. 49–62; and Sue Jackson, 'Compartmentalising Culture: The Articulation and Consideration of Values in Water Resource Management' (2006) *Australian Geographer*, 37, pp. 19–31.

[85] Carter, supra note 83, at p. 408 (footnotes omitted).

[86] Lourdes Arizpe, 'The Cultural Politics of Intangible Cultural Heritage' (2007) *Art, Antiquity and Law*, 12 (4), pp. 361–88, at p. 362.

manifestations of this heritage and view such manifestations as meaningless outside of the social context of their transmission, yet these values were effectively marginalised in global policy circles for decades. International attention was focused upon intangible cultural heritage by a remarkable confluence of concerns and energies that conjoined multiple international agencies.

The negotiation of the Convention for the Safeguarding of the Intangible Cultural Heritage (ICHC)[87] at the end of the twentieth century was influenced by a widely held concern that the dominance of commercial cultural forces had the potential to undermine the diversity of the world's cultural heritage and that the decline of languages, traditional practices and traditional knowledges posed grave consequences for the preservation of biological diversity and for sustainable development.[88] The preservation of intangible cultural heritage had thus become a matter of concern to international organisations that would not normally focus their energies on cultural matters per se. These include the United Nations Environment Programme, the Food and Agricultural Organisation (FAO), the International Labour Organization (ILO), the World Bank and the World Trade Organization, which has ensured that intangible cultural heritage is now addressed by multiple and overlapping regimes.

The intangible dimensions of culture have been long recognised by UNESCO, but no normative regime of protection emerged, despite years of attempts to facilitate law-making in this area, beginning in the early 1970s when UNESCO collaborated with WIPO to include folklore in model laws for copyright protection. It was not until 1989, however, that UNESCO adopted the Recommendation of the Safeguarding of Traditional Culture and Folklore,[89] which sought to encourage international cooperation between states and national measures for identification, conservation, protection and dissemination. Whether due to a lack of incentives and support, or to ideological opposition, few states gave effect to these proposed 'soft law' measures. The perceived overlap between intangible cultural heritage and intellectual property protections has continued to characterise international efforts, which indigenous peoples have regarded as putting too much emphasis upon proprietary models for protection.[90] Indeed, although it is beyond the scope of this chapter to argue, indigenous rejection of proprietary models arguably helped to shape the norms and values reflected in the ICHC and its Operational Guidelines. Adopted in 2003 and entered into force in 2006, the ICHC had over 100 state parties by 2008.

The full impact of the Convention is yet to be realised because guidelines for implementation have only recently been established.[91] The prehistory of its adoption is, however, of special significance to indigenous peoples. The ICHC is the product of negotiations

---

87 Supra note 45.

88 Toshiyuki Kono, 'UNESCO and Intangible Cultural Heritage from the Viewpoint of Sustainable Development', in Abdulqawi A. Yusef (ed.), *Standard Setting in UNESCO: Normative Action in Education, Science and Culture,* Leiden: Martinus Nijhoff and UNESCO Publishing, 2007, pp. 237–65, at p. 237.

89 'Recommendation on Safeguarding Traditional Culture and Folklore', in UNESCO, 'Records of the General Conference. Twenty-fifth Session. Resolutions', 1989, Annex I.B, available online at http://unesdoc.unesco.org/images/0008/000846/084696e.pdf#page=242.

90 Marrie, supra note 55, at p. 181.

91 Nonetheless, because it is relatively recent and because the scholars and activists involved in its negotiation are still with us and deliberately documented its negotiation and are actively studying

marked by considerable political tension both between state parties and between states and those advocating for more local interests. Impetus for early developments such as the 'Living Human Treasures' programme to celebrate 'exponents of traditional culture' came from Japan and Korea, who felt that criteria for recognition in the WHC disregarded the qualities of their cultural traditions. Moreover, frustration in the Global South with the criteria used to populate the World Heritage List and a perceived lack of global interest in the living form of cultural heritage in practical activities are amongst the reasons UNESCO was urged to amend the WHC to incorporate intangible cultural heritage.[92]

The failure of global efforts to protect folklore, the marginalisation of community interests in heritage, and the incorporation of folklore under WIPO's intellectual property mandate and its perceived tendencies to commercialisation were also factors in building the political will to develop an independent normative regime.[93] The Masterpieces of Oral and Intangible Heritage of Humanity programme in 1997 was thus launched as an awareness-raising and educational tool to alert states to the importance of safeguarding oral heritage in danger of disappearing. Critics, however, assert that the programme privileges 'colourful and exotic examples of intangible heritage, that represent nationally valued cultural events or performances, and which coincide with romanticised Western perceptions, while Indigenous works remain under-represented'.[94] Moreover, historical records suggest that the programme perturbed states with large indigenous populations.[95] Nonetheless, the ensuing debates about the propriety of the term 'masterpiece', the notion of 'universal value' and the importance of involving practitioner communities worked to clear the political ground for the ICHC.

The scope of UNESCO's interest in ICH is quite limited. Avoiding overlap with other UN agencies such as WIPO, ILO, World Health Organization (WHO), Convention on Biological Diversity (CBD) and United Nations Conference on Trade and Development (UNCTAD), it seeks primarily to further its priority policies in the field of culture, which at this point in time were the promotion of cultural diversity and cultural identity – hence the emphasis on the processes *within communities* that generate such diversity and identity.[96] Influenced, if only negatively, by prior collaborations between UNESCO and WIPO, many deliberators rejected the term folklore as being too oriented to products, rather than symbols, values and processes; they saw it as neglecting the practitioners and

---

its implementation, we have a remarkable body of scholarship exploring its key concepts, against which its implementation can be assessed.

[92] Noriko Aikawa-Faure, 'From the Proclamation of Masterpieces to the Convention for the Safeguarding of Intangible Cultural Heritage', in Laurajane Smith and Natsuko Akagawa (eds), *Intangible Heritage,* New York and London: Routledge, 2009, pp. 13–44, at p. 15.

[93] Harriet J. Deacon et al., *The Subtle Power of Intangible Heritage: Legal and Financial Instruments for Safeguarding Intangible Heritage,* Cape Town: HSRC Press, 2004, at p. 17.

[94] Laurajane Smith and Natsuko Akagawa, 'Introduction', in Laurajane Smith and Natsuko Akagawa (eds), *Intangible Heritage,* New York and London: Routledge, 2009, pp. 1–12, at p. 4, citing Richard Kurin, 'Comments' (2002) *Current Anthropology*, 43 (1), pp. 144–5; Richard Kurin, 'Safeguarding Intangible Cultural Heritage in the 2003 UNESCO Convention: A Critical Appraisal' (2004) *Museum International*, 56 (1–2), pp. 66–76; and Barbara Kirshenblatt-Gimblett, 'Intangible Heritage as Metacultural Production' (2004) *Museum International*, 56 (1–2), pp. 52–64.

[95] Smith and Akagawa, supra note 94, at p. 3.

[96] Ibid.

communities whose stake in creating, performing, enacting, preserving and disseminating traditional cultural forms was primary.[97] They favoured more holistic anthropological understandings of culture that put indigenous and traditional knowledge into an ecological context that emphasised ways of life or livelihood. Indeed, some participants felt that the Daes Report definition of intangible cultural heritage more clearly captured the spirit and meaning of the range of forms that a new instrument or Convention should attempt to protect.[98] The eventual definition of intangible cultural heritage adopted in the Convention is widely acknowledged to be vague but perhaps this is a strength given the unpredictability of those forms it may be asked to protect. Article 2.1 defines the intangible cultural heritage as:

> … the practices, representations, expressions, knowledge, skills – as well as the instruments, objects, artefacts and cultural spaces associated therewith – that communities, groups and, in some cases, individuals recognize as part of their cultural heritage. This intangible cultural heritage, transmitted from generation to generation, is constantly recreated by communities and groups in response to their environment, their interaction with nature and their history, and provides them with a sense of identity and continuity, thus promoting respect for cultural diversity and human creativity.

Noriko Aikawa-Faure, responsible for the programme of intangible cultural heritage in UNESCO Headquarters from 1993 and witness to numerous and various deliberations leading to the Convention, shows how criticisms of the earlier folklore deliberations triggered the creation of the ICHC and that perceptions of indigenous peoples' interests informed many of the expert reports relied upon to define intangible cultural heritage while shaping the principle of safeguarding that evolved to replace the concept of protection.[99] Nonetheless, according to indigenous critics, 'the general tone of this Convention and its provisions fall way below that of the two benchmark instruments by which it can be evaluated, namely, the UNDRIP and ILO Convention (No. 169) Concerning Indigenous and Tribal Peoples in Independent Countries (ILO Convention 169).'[100] Critical scholars have pointed to the divergence between the Convention Preamble, which provides the only mention of indigenous peoples (recognised for their important role in

---

[97] Aikawa-Faure, supra note 92, at p. 21. During the Convention's negotiation, experts routinely reaffirmed that UNESCO 'should not duplicate the activities of other organisations, particularly in the field of economic rights for which specialised agencies such as WIPO and World Trade Organization (WTO) have specific expertise' and that its emphasis should be upon 'the cultural dimension of ICH covering the domains not yet covered by other organizations' (ibid., at p. 34). Francesco Francioni, in particular, emphasised the limits of the intellectual property rights approach, especially its failure to respect, acknowledge or ensure the viability of the societal structures and processes through which cultural products are derived, or recognise innovations that are the collective expressions of social necessities transmitted from generation to generation, as discussed in Federico Lenzerini, 'Indigenous Peoples' Cultural Rights and the Controversy Over the Commercial Use of Their Traditional Knowledge', in Francesco Francioni and Martin Scheinin (eds), *Cultural Human Rights*, Leiden and Boston: Martinus Nijhoff Publishers, 2008, pp. 119–50, at p. 144.

[98] Blake, 'UNESCO's 2003 Convention', supra note 23, at pp. 49–51.

[99] Aikawa-Faure, supra note 91.

[100] Marrie, supra note 55, at p. 174.

producing and safeguarding ICH), and the substantive provisions of the Convention, which require that state parties engage in activities with respect to intangible cultural heritage that may not be welcomed by indigenous communities themselves.[101] For example, the global demand that states create inventories and attempt to publicise intangible cultural heritage may be met with great distrust by indigenous peoples, who are only too familiar with state attempts to locate, catalogue and 'salvage' their cultural goods and traditions. Long subject to state surveillance activities on cultural grounds, they are unlikely to welcome such initiatives.

The Convention does, however, require that states respect 'customary practices governing access', thereby acknowledging that indigenous peoples may have traditional strictures against the recording and transmission of some cultural forms, but this does not necessarily empower indigenous peoples with agency because indigenous peoples are historically quite familiar with having their 'customs' determined by state powers for ends that are not their own. There is very little in the Convention itself, save for exhortations to involve communities, that would seem to provide independent *political* agency to those indigenous peoples whose heritage is endangered. The most ready explanation for the limits of the Convention 'is that Indigenous peoples were not included in the negotiation processes, either by having direct representation (for example, through the Working Group on Indigenous Populations or the UN Permanent Forum on Indigenous Issues), or by having Indigenous representation in the national delegations sent to negotiate the Convention'.[102]

It is worth noting that not only did many western countries not see any necessity for the Convention, those countries with significant indigenous populations expressed the most grave reservations[103] indicating that international political support for indigenous community control over intangible cultural heritage remains limited. While there were no votes against the Convention, a number of countries, notably Australia, Canada, the UK, Switzerland and the USA, abstained.[104] This might suggest that these states are unlikely to use the Convention on behalf of indigenous peoples' interests. There is certainly no guarantee that inventories established and maintained by states will reflect the perils of cultural survival facing indigenous peoples as they themselves perceive these.

The capacities of the Convention to meet indigenous peoples' needs for the safeguarding, maintenance and development of their ICH lie in implementing and giving effect to the principles of community involvement that are unique to it, and arguably unprecedented in international law. The specific character of ICH itself is necessarily dependent upon its continuing enactment by its practitioners; only by securing their involvement and participation in the maintenance and development of their heritage will it be safeguarded.[105] In this sense, the safeguarding of ICH is an exercise of cultural rights. If, as a matter of international law, states have primary agencies and duties, the Convention is structured so as to encourage state safeguarding activities to raise awareness of ICH in communities and to actively encourage community involvement in implementation. Recognising that global

---

101 See, for example, Moran, supra note 49.
102 Marrie, supra note 55, at p. 174.
103 Smith and Akagawa, supra note 94, at p. 3.
104 As noted in Kurin, supra note 94, at p. 66.
105 Blake, 'UNESCO's 2003 Convention', supra note 23, at pp. 45–6.

economic and cultural forces may be one of the threats to distinctive ICH held at the local level, communities and groups are to be empowered and capacitated to maintain ICH as the source of their own identities.[106]

Nonetheless, there is evidence that the nature of community participation was a matter of great controversy during the Convention's negotiation by the Intergovernmental Committee. Certainly both experts and state parties were divided between those inclined to give practitioner communities responsibilities and rights they could exercise and those who continued to prioritise state control and favoured only weak exhortations to encourage states to engage communities.[107] Although the ultimate priority given to the involvement of communities and civil society is evident, the appropriate mechanisms to achieve this without state initiative are still unclear. Indeed, the principle of community participation was difficult to implement even in the negotiations themselves. In more than ten governmental and non-governmental meetings, only two appear to have benefited from anything that might remotely be called the 'active participation' of 'representatives of communities and practitioners'.[108] Considerable work remains to be done to engage indigenous peoples and their representatives in UNESCO ICH decision-making processes; Henrietta Marrie suggests numerous procedural possibilities for so doing.[109] At the very least, we might expect that the UN Permanent Forum on Indigenous Issues will be more prominently represented in the implementation and operationalisation of UNESCO Conventions going forward, but a more formal intersessional process of consultation with indigenous groups on indigenous issues would be preferable from a rights-based perspective.

3.4 Convention on the Protection and Promotion of the Diversity of Cultural Expressions 2005

It might be argued that the Convention on the Protection and Promotion of the Diversity of Cultural Expressions (Diversity Convention)[110] does not concern itself with issues of cultural heritage and thus is not within our remit. Nonetheless, as the most recent international legal instrument to attend to issues of cultural protection and as the ultimate legal expression of UNESCO's 2001 Declaration on Cultural Diversity, it expresses values and commitments that are likely to influence approaches to cultural heritage issues. Certainly the preservation and safeguarding of diversity has been a core value in cultural heritage protections generally and ICH especially, because indigenous peoples are regarded as members of distinct societies whose distinction is manifested culturally. Moreover, as the first international instrument to express cultural rights principles in relationship to trade, the Diversity Convention speaks perhaps most squarely to this volume's themes. Nonetheless, we give it short shrift here for several reasons.

---

[106] Ibid., at p. 47.

[107] Aikawa-Faure, supra note 92, at p. 28.

[108] Ibid., at p. 39.

[109] Marrie, supra note 55.

[110] UNESCO, Convention on the Protection and Promotion of the Diversity of Cultural Expressions, 2440 UNTS 311 (adopted on 20 October 2005, entered into force 18 March 2007).

The Diversity Convention has two guiding rationales that are not always complementary. The first, grounded in human rights, promotes cultural development and intercultural dialogue, whereas the second is premised on the desire to protect state autonomy with respect to the governance of the products of creative industries from production through distribution and consumption.[111] The Convention acknowledges 'that cultural goods and services have dual nature and constitute on the one hand, commodities that can be traded and are, on the other hand, "vehicles of identity, values and meaning"'.[112] But the assertion that, therefore, 'the relationship between the two is somehow natural'[113] begs the question of when cultural goods and services become tradeable commodities and under what circumstances commodified exchange supports cultural identity and when it undermines it. The Convention does little to provide any guidance and largely focuses on the diversity of media as means to convey a diversity of expression. Sovereign parties are encouraged to undertake measures with respect to cultural policy that may include support for civil society initiatives and promotional and preservation initiatives, but since the Convention does not require that states even recognise diversity within their territories, and there are no monitoring bodies, measurement of the impact of the Convention is difficult.

As a recent treaty there is understandably little commentary on the Diversity Convention's operation. However, even as a text, critics find it lacking in clarity, particularly as it confuses the larger issue of cultural diversity with the narrower question of diversity in cultural expressions and largely focuses on expressions that circulate primarily as market goods.[114] Although there are references in the Preamble to the cultures of minorities and indigenous peoples, manifested in their freedom to create, disseminate and distribute their traditional cultural expressions so as to benefit from them for their own development, the Diversity Convention puts overarching emphasis upon state sovereignty. It provides no rights to minorities, to communities or to individuals, although civil society is acknowledged to play a fundamental role in creating, producing, disseminating and distributing diverse forms of cultural expression.[115] It contains few if any enforceable state obligations and the lack of any effective dispute settlement mechanism or the capacity to develop

---

[111] Nina Obuljen, 'From Our Creative Diversity to the Convention on Cultural Diversity: Introduction to the Debate', in Nina Obuljen and Joost Smiers (eds), *UNESCO's Convention on the Protection and Promotion of the Diversity of Cultural Expression: Making it Work*, Zagreb: Institute for International Relations, 2006, pp. 17–38, at pp. 17–20.

[112] Mira Burri-Nenova, 'Trade and Culture: Making the WTO Legal Framework Conducive to Cultural Considerations' (2008) *Manchester Journal of International Economic Law*, 5 (3), pp. 2–38. See also Christoph B. Graber, 'The New UNESCO Convention on Cultural Diversity: A Counterbalance to the WTO?' (2006) *Journal of International Economic Law*, 9 (3), pp. 553–74, at pp. 566–7.

[113] Burri-Nenova, at supra note 112, at p. 4.

[114] Karen Donders, 'The History of the UNESCO Convention on the Protection and Promotion of the Diversity of Cultural Expression', in Hildegard Schneider and Peter van den Bossche (eds), *Protection of Cultural Diversity from a European and International Perspective,* Antwerp and Oxford: Intersentia, 2008, pp. 1–30.

[115] Hélène Ruiz Fabri, 'Reflections on Possible Future Legal Implications of the Convention', in Nina Obuljen and Joost Smiers (eds), *UNESCO's Convention on the Protection and Promotion of the Diversity of Cultural Expression: Making it Work,* Zagreb: Institute for International Relations, 2006, pp. 71–88, at p. 81.

authoritative interpretations of the Convention's key provisions renders it of little legal consequence.[116]

Nonetheless, civil society initiatives pursuant to the Convention such as those of the International Network for Cultural Diversity (INCD) emphasise a wider range of diversity and indicate a desire to assist indigenous peoples in protecting, promoting and disseminating their distinctive cultural expressions. As director Garry Neil asserts:

> A key priority for the INCD in its organising activities is to continue to work to ensure that the concerns of traditionally marginalised communities are fully integrated into the global movement ... While the Convention does not provide a formal role for civil society groups to raise concerns about forms of cultural expressions that are 'at risk of extinction, under serious threat, or in urgent need of safeguarding,' this will be on INCD's agenda in the coming years. There are several priorities for building the movement. The first is to respond to the needs of the indigenous communities to create a forum, initially in the Americas, in which representatives from these communities can work together to address the particular challenges which globalisation presents to their arts and culture, including their languages. Preliminary work has been undertaken with a range of representatives from Indigenous Peoples in a number of countries.[117]

However, the momentum of this civil society network appears to have been slowed since the ratification of the Convention and there is insufficient evidence available to us to ascertain what if any impact this activity has had upon trade in intangible ICH. Due to the extent of the uncertainties that surround the international legitimacy and legality of this Convention's provisions and the fact that any such uncertainties would be resolved by state action without provision for indigenous involvement, we will not cover it in any further detail here.

4. CONSIDERING INTANGIBLE CULTURAL HERITAGE AND INTERNATIONAL TRADE

A reading of both UNESCO documents and critical research on cultural heritage more generally clearly indicates that heritage is now expected to 'pay its keep'. As a central component of sustainable development agendas, new means are being found to ensure that ICH delivers economic benefits to communities. As Blake notes, as a topic of international policy, cultural heritage indexes combined concerns with identity and development. During the UN World Decade for Cultural Development (1987–97), UNESCO officially noted the need to highlight the function of the intangible cultural heritage for the

[116] Christoph B. Graber, 'Substantive Rights and Obligations under the UNESCO Convention on Cultural Diversity', in Hildegard Schneider and Peter van den Bossche (eds), *Protection of Cultural Diversity from a European and International Perspective,* Antwerp and Oxford: Intersentia, 2008, pp. 141–62.

[117] Garry Neil, 'After the Convention: What's Next for INCD and the Cultural Diversity Movement?', in Nina Obuljen and Joost Smiers (eds), *UNESCO's Convention on the Protection and Promotion of the Diversity of Cultural Expression: Making it Work,* Zagreb: Institute for International Relations, 2006, pp. 255–66; and in Thomas MacPhail, *Global Communication and Technologies: Theories, Stakeholders and Trends*, 3rd edn, London: Wiley-Blackwell Publishers, 2010, at p. 22.

community as a living culture of the people, and asserted that it 'should be regarded as one of the major assets of a multidimensional type of development'.[118] Thus we have the strange policy phenomenon of states being asked to 'apply' 'bottom-up approaches' that are community-driven.[119]

Tourism and associated industries in souvenirs, the development of new place-based marketing for traditional foodstuffs and services, and capitalising upon local handicrafts are popular means of ensuring revenues from heritage industries.[120] As sociologist Antonio Arantes notes, UNESCO activities have encouraged emphasis upon 'traditional know-how and forms of expression … as effective cornerstones for the implementation and promotion of humanitarian as well as social and economic development programs in the poorer regions of the globe' and 'it is becoming part of the common sense among policy makers that the protection and enhancement of heritage can contribute to social and economic development.'[121]

Once distinctive cultural heritage is identified with specific social groups as a target of preservation or safeguarding efforts, it tends to become a resource for the production of consumer goods and services that circulate in wider economic circuits that may impose upon local communities demands that are in conflict with or put pressures upon local social organisation. Crafts production, for instance, when oriented to a tourist market, tends to demand increased volumes, standardisation and adaptation to tastes and values that are not necessarily the community's own. New demands tend to be brokered by outside agents and there is always a danger of local communities losing control of the process and having their work processes transformed in ways that are alienating and break down community social bonds. The desire to maximise returns has inevitably led to questions of collective intellectual property,[122] an issue that continues to vex WIPO and is elsewhere addressed in this book.

If we return to the management of cultural landscapes as world heritage, we witness a growing interest in finding ways to use these protected sites to support communities. In addition to employment in site management, tourism is recognised as adding value to the economic activities that have given rise to the distinctive cultural landscape,[123] particularly rural and associative cultural landscapes. Tourism is understood as potentially having a low impact on the cultural landscape, but helping to assist communities seeking transition to a more complex and diversified economic base, particularly when they are remote from metropolitan areas or in regions where more urban migration is undesirable.

---

[118] UNESCO, 1990, at para. 209, cited in Noriko Aikawa-Faure, 'The Conceptual Development of UNESCO's Programme on Intangible Cultural Heritage', in Janet E. Blake (ed.), *Safeguarding Intangible Heritage: Challenges and Approaches*, Builth Wells, UK: Institute of Art & Law, 2007, pp. 43–72.

[119] Blake, 'UNESCO's 2003 Convention', supra note 23, at p. 49.

[120] Colin Long and Sophia Labadi, 'Introduction', in Sophia Labadi and Colin Long (eds), *Heritage and Globalisation,* London and New York: Routledge, 2010, pp. 1–16.

[121] Antonio Arantes, 'Diversity, Heritage and Cultural Politics' (2007) *Theory Culture Society,* 24, pp. 290–96, at p. 294.

[122] Ibid.

[123] Jane Lennon, 'Values as the Basis for Management of World Heritage Cultural Landscapes', in UNESCO, *Cultural Landscapes: The Challenges of Conservation, World Heritage Papers No. 7,* Paris: World Heritage Centre, 2003, pp. 120–26, at p. 123.

Seeking means to ensure that tourism benefits are reinvested in local communities, promoting local products that reflect local values and seeking new governance structures for provision of transport, accommodation and touring that provide income and build capacity are all areas of ongoing research. As Lennon notes, 'generating income in ways that do not conflict with heritage conservation and are culturally sensitive is a management challenge.'[124]

Where the associative values that make cultural landscapes 'outstanding' are derived from the social life of resident communities, issues of sustainability become especially significant, which is one of the reasons why communities are now recognised as central agents in the process of maintaining heritage and finding ways to capitalise upon it. As the new Operational Directive under the ICHC stresses:

> Commercial activities that can emerge from certain forms of intangible cultural heritage and trade in cultural goods and services related to intangible cultural heritage can raise awareness about the importance of such heritage and generate income for its practitioners. They can contribute to improving the living standards of the communities that bear and practice the heritage, enhance the local economy, and contribute to social cohesion. These activities and trade should not, however, threaten the viability of the intangible cultural heritage, and all appropriate measures should be taken to ensure that the communities concerned are their primary beneficiaries. Particular attention should be given to the way such activities might affect the nature and viability of the intangible cultural heritage, in particular the intangible cultural heritage manifested in the domains of rituals, social practices or knowledge about nature and the universe.[125]

For example, farming communities may be encouraged to designate traditional foods that might be marketed without negatively affecting agricultural practice. Communities may need to find ways for traditional custodians to transmit landscape values to youth while providing viable employment for them in activities, such as cultural mapping, while using such maps to design activities for visitors. Sustainable development of ICH may also involve deciding how and if tourists will be welcome at festival and ritual events and what souvenirs they should take home with them. Although marketing is encouraged to increase revenues, promotional materials now focus more on the values of ICH for the communities themselves rather than educational or entertainment value for visitors.[126]

Janet Blake explains in great detail how communities are empowered under the ICHC (and its Operational Directives), and why their own free, prior and informed consent is necessary for identification, nomination, inscription and for the preparation, recognition and implementation of any safeguarding programmes.[127] Since the community is the essential social context for maintaining the vitality and viability of ICH, the economic,

---

[124] Ibid.

[125] 'Operational Directives for the Implementation of the Convention For the Safeguarding of the Intangible Cultural Heritage', Annex to UNESCO, General Assembly of the States Parties to the Convention for the Safeguarding of the Intangible Cultural Heritage, 'Resolutions', Third Session (UNESCO Doc. ITH/10/3.GA/CONF.201/Resolutions Rev, 2010), Article 116.

[126] Ibid., Article 120.

[127] Blake, 'UNESCO's 2003 Convention', supra note 23, at pp. 48–52.

social and cultural rights of communities in heritage management (and in some circumstances, groups and individuals) must assume priority. The new national policies envisioned under the ICHC are designed to give local communities far more power in determining what will be regarded as heritage, undermining state authority to designate official culture for a monolithic public, democratising the process of managing heritage and providing better benefits to local communities in the process of giving them political voice.[128] Trade policy proposals must pay heed to these priorities, promoting trade in intangible heritage goods only where this further reinforces culture as a source of identity and furthers community sustainable development. Issues of representation, misrepresentation and sustainability of economic practices to enhance community security need to be given emphasis. Rethinking unfair competition laws to meet community values in maintaining the integrity of indigenous identity, projecting community values through heritage goods that bear marks indicating conditions of origin, securing marketing assistance and building community capacities for communicating indigenous values in markets are all pressing needs.

We might also consider whether a single solution to managing indigenous cultural heritage in a global trade regime is desirable, given the very different attitudes of states with respect to the recognition of indigenous peoples within their territories. Many indigenous peoples live within states that refuse to recognise them as such. Other groups have arbitrarily been declared 'extinct' by states that are not likely to negotiate on their behalf. Moreover, in some countries with colonial legacies there are many different layers of indigenous governance in place representing different moments in histories of decolonisation. Indigenous political representatives with whom states wish to negotiate are not necessarily those whom communities recognise as legitimate.[129] Moreover, we need to recognise that indigenous identities and governance structures are evolving; not all indigenous peoples are in the same position in terms of the level and scale of their political organisation. Histories of cultural dispossession by the modern state have made it extremely difficult for indigenous peoples to fully reassemble and assert their customary laws; claims to control ICH are in fact integral to their struggle to reassert political autonomy.[130]

There is plenty of evidence to suggest that indigenous peoples, particularly those in Australia, Canada and New Zealand, have been independently engaged in this process over the past two decades. Hence a great deal of the local institutional work to enable indigenous peoples to connect to national heritage bodies and to seek UNESCO benefits may already have been done. Whether they will choose to do so, however, is another question. As Amanda Kearney suggests, indigenous peoples have their own impetus for

---

128 To support the vision of community involvement with respect to managing intangible cultural heritage embodied here, Blake (ibid., at pp. 56–7) points to the Mataatua Declaration (1993) on the Intellectual and Cultural Property Rights of Indigenous Peoples, which indicated that indigenous communities should define their own intellectual and cultural property, define the principles under which it is recorded, establish educational, research and training centres, develop and maintain customary practices for its protection, preservation and revitalisation, while creating local and representative bodies for this purpose.

129 See Kathy Bowrey, 'International Trade in Indigenous Cultural Heritage: An Australian Perspective', in this volume.

130 See Rebecca Tsosie, 'International Trade in Indigenous Cultural Heritage: An Argument for Indigenous Governance of Cultural Property', in this volume.

developing autonomous, localised projects that reflect and reinforce indigenous knowledge systems and governance principles so as to document these in furtherance of their self-determination:

> internationally, Indigenous people are lobbying for the right to determine what constitutes their ICH, to administer the mechanisms for safeguarding, developing and promoting ICH and to control any research methodologies and investigations that purport to protect this heritage.[131]

The Yanyuwa, indigenous peoples in northern Australia, for example, engage in documentation of their intangible cultural heritage – 'expressions, knowledges, and intimacies associated with spiritually powerful places across their homelands'.[132] Such material is governed by customary law and mediated through community heritage management programmes that involve scholars, film-makers and lawyers in collaborative research projects with host communities that deploy this documentation to further indigenous land claims.[133]

Proponents of enhanced roles for communities point to precisely such activities as models for what Convention activities in Member States might and should aspire to. Politically, however, this may be rather unrealistic. Where indigenous peoples have some political power and many outstanding legal complaints, the states in whose jurisdictions they are resident are unlikely to want to use an international instrument and the scrutiny it brings to bear to support activities that might further indigenous rights claims. On the other hand, the new normative obligations upon states that the ICHC imposes may provide new leverage and opportunities for indigenous peoples resident in state jurisdictions where relations are not so tense. Whether states will be prepared to assume a secondary and supportive role in relation to communities in new partnerships involving ICH is uncertain.

As anthropologist Regina Bendix suggests, the process of 'heritagisation' involves the strategic invocation of tradition and authenticity, the projection of identity and the cultivation of symbolic capital, the contestation of heritage values and the symbolic work that goes into their marketing.[134] Inevitably, the intangibility of that which is ennobled as ICH will require new mechanisms to make it tangible in some way in order to ensure profit from this new status.[135] Although tourists may be entreated to come and imbibe pure values, they are likely to desire and to demand a more tangible takeaway, by way of photographs, videos, CDs or souvenirs. Once the goods and experiences they consume are marked for marketing purposes, new forms of rivalry and competition may ensue. A community that successfully develops and builds its ICH into marketable goods will inevitably face competitors as well as counterfeiters.

---

[131] Amanda Kearney, 'Intangible Cultural Heritage: Global Awareness and Local Interest', in Laurajane Smith and Natsuko Akagawa (eds), *Intangible Heritage,* New York and London: Routledge, 2009, pp. 209–26, at p. 218.

[132] Ibid., at p. 219.

[133] Ibid.

[134] Regina Bendix, 'Heritage Between Economy and Politics: An Assessment from the Perspective of Cultural Anthropology', in Laurajane Smith and Natsuko Akagawa (eds), *Intangible Heritage,* New York and London: Routledge, 2009, pp. 253–69, at p. 256.

[135] Ibid., at p. 263.

As communities seek to maintain profits from heritage goods against competition, they may well consider forms of intellectual property as a means to do so.[136] This is not an area over which UNESCO has any jurisdiction. WIPO will be the international body responsible, either for developing new forms of intellectual property, or new guidelines for its governance with respect to community and indigenous intangible cultural heritage. This has already been a prolonged process that has produced much in the way of principle, but little in the way of state requirements or implemented legislation.[137] Nonetheless, we would argue that certain kinds of intellectual property lend themselves to the goals of safeguarding ICH better than others.

Marks indicating conditions of origin, such as certification and collective marks as well as geographical indications, appear to be especially suitable for the marketing of goods based upon traditional knowledge and ICH.[138] Because they can be collectively held and managed, mark places of origin and the reputation of particular localities may be used to reflect local cultural values and are in significant ways inalienable, they are amenable for use to advance the community development and empowerment envisioned by UNESCO and desired by indigenous peoples. For instance, we can imagine that in cultural landscapes protected as World Heritage sites as well as those recognised as such under national law, resident communities rightly seek employment opportunities and economic benefits; they must decide whether or not to encourage tourism and under what conditions. If they do so and local cultural values do not otherwise discourage commercial use, indexical features such as petroglyphs or rock art significant to the community and characteristic of the site might be used to mark goods coming from this place of origin.

The use of a legally protected mark – a collective or certification mark or even a geographical indication – might provide communities with means to educate consumers, protect them against unauthentic goods and protect themselves against the production and distribution of counterfeit goods that do not embody community values in their creation. This is one means by which indicia, iconic for a particular cultural landscape, might become the intellectual property of resident communities without resorting to inappropriate forms of privatisation or commodification. There is a growing emphasis upon the use of such marks to designate community heritage values. For example, Chiara Bortolotto shows how the Board of the Chamber of Commerce of Matera, a town in Southern Italy possessing inhabitable caves carved into limestone, encouraged use of a denomination of origin to promote and market traditional products based on traditional knowledge and

---

136 For example see Markus Tauschek, 'Cultural Property as Strategy: The Carnival of Binche, the Creation of Cultural Heritage and Cultural Property' (2009) *Ethnologia Europaea,* 39 (2), pp. 67–80.

137 See Girsberger and Müller, supra note 6.

138 Rosemary J. Coombe and Nicole Aylwin, 'Bordering Diversity and Desire: Using Intellectual Property to Mark Place-Based Products' (2011) *Environment and Planning A: Society and Space New Borders of Consumption*, 43 (9), pp. 2027–42; and Nicole Aylwin and Rosemary J. Coombe, 'Marks Indicating Conditions of Origin in Rights-based and Sustainable Development', in Per Zumbansen and Ruth Buchanan (eds), *Human Rights, Development and Restorative Justice: An Osgoode Reader*, Oxford: Hart Publishing (forthcoming).

traditional values associated with the site.[139] The community marked the interrelationship between the natural and cultural dimensions of their territorially based intangible cultural heritage using a collective mark that indicated the local origin and guaranteed the authenticity of products from the region.[140]

Such a strategy might well accord with and help to project indigenous values in a trade context while supporting arts and craftsmanship and protecting customary intellectual properties. To the extent that this strategy might also be integrated in the development of indigenous cultural tourism, further benefits are possible. Finally, this tactic has the benefit of being in compliance with the TRIPS Agreement,[141] avoiding the kinds of conflict of interest allegations that emerged with respect to the UNESCO Cultural Diversity Convention of 2005 and limited the perceived capacities of that instrument to achieve its mandate of internationally protecting cultural goods against trade-based pressures.[142] Indeed, we would go so far as to suggest that marks indicating conditions of origin are rare among legal vehicles that might ensure that cultural goods and services retain their capacities to act as instruments of identity, projecting local meanings and values while being traded in commodity markets.

Other trade issues will inevitably emerge as indigenous communities become more involved in managing cultural heritage sites. What recourse do communities have against the state should the state seek to license others to manufacture goods bearing such indicia without their permission? To what extent do UNESCO principles of community safeguarding ICH give indigenous peoples any greater power than they would have if such materials were treated as being in the public domain? In what circumstances could or would UNESCO support community collective properties? If an indigenous community chooses *not* to commercialise indicia of their cultural landscapes, what recourse would they have against those who seek to capitalise upon the site's notoriety by marketing goods bearing these signs as souvenirs? Ironically, they might find themselves in a position of having to seek trade mark, collective mark or certification mark protection to *prevent* unauthorised commercial usages of such symbolism. Some jurisdictions have allowed

---

139 Chiara Bortolotto, 'Globalising Intangible Cultural Heritage? Between International Arenas and Local Appropriations', in Sophia Lavbadi and Colin Long (eds), *Heritage and Globalisation*, London and New York: Routledge, 2010, pp. 97–114, at pp. 108–9.

140 Ibid., at p. 110.

141 WTO, Agreement on Trade Related Aspects of Intellectual Property Rights (TRIPS), Marrakesh Agreement Establishing the World Trade Organization, Annex 1C, 1869 UNTS 299; 33 ILM 1197 (adopted on 15 April 1994, entered into force 1 January 1995).

142 See Mira Burri-Nenova, 'Trade and Culture in International Law: Paths to (Re)conciliation' (2010) *Journal of World Trade*, 44 (1), pp. 49–80, at p. 49; Anke Dahrendorf 'Free Trade Meets Cultural Diversity: The Legal Relationship Between WTO Rules and the UNESCO Convention on the Protection of the Diversity of Cultural Expressions', in Hildegard Schneider and Peter van der Bossche (eds), *Protection of Cultural Diversity from a European and International Perspective*, Antwerp and Oxford: Intersentia, 2008, pp. 31–84; Shin-Yi Peng, 'International Trade in "Cultural Products": UNESCO's Commitment to Promoting Cultural Diversity and its Relations with the WTO' (2008) *International Trade and Business Law Review*, 11, pp. 218–35; and Jan Wouters and Bart De Meester, 'Cultural Diversity and the WTO: David versus Goliath?', in Hildegard Schneider and Peter van der Bossche (eds), *Protection of Cultural Diversity from a European and International Perspective*, Antwerp and Oxford: Intersentia, 2008, pp. 85–140.

indigenous peoples to act as guardians of such symbols pursuant to legislation giving rights to public authorities to hold exclusive rights to the use of symbols in the public interest,[143] but such legislation is contentious and not widely available. Could UNESCO assume a proactive stance here, using its considerable powers as an international public authority to protect indigenous communities from unfair and misleading competition that would siphon profits away from community safeguarding efforts?

Such questions raise the issue of property in a new way. Although the understanding of cultural heritage *as* property is one that has been undermined, it is nonetheless the case that properties, intellectual or otherwise, may embody ICH.[144] Although the WHC clearly indicates that recognition of a site as world heritage is 'without prejudice to property rights as provided in national legislation',[145] this would not make such sites national property in situations where property rights are contested or under negotiation, as they are with respect to many of the territories and resources held or claimed by the world's indigenous peoples. With respect to ICH, property issues promise to be particularly problematic. As Kearney argues, if acknowledging cultural rights to be specific to particular groups and communities is the key theme of the ICHC, state parties maintain ultimate control over the processes involved and are not called upon to formally recognise indigenous rights to ownership and control over their ICH.[146] No indigenous rights independent of those of states are acknowledged, which ultimately positions indigenous peoples as mere stakeholders with respect to the ICH that is acknowledged to provide them with a primary source of identity.

Although the WHC stressed the concept of 'the shared heritage' of humanity through its central focus on the concept of the 'universal value' of heritage, it was routinely criticised for legitimising a particular western – if not Western European – perception of heritage both in policy and in practice.[147] As we have shown, the World Heritage List was exposed as being not only Eurocentric in its vision and its composition, but as dominated by monumental and aesthetic valuations.[148] The ICHC is posited as a counterpoint to the

---

[143] For example, indigenous communities in Canada have registered images from petroglyphs found in their ancestral territories as marks held by them as a public authority so as to prevent their reproduction by others in commercial contexts they found objectionable. See George P. Nicholas and Kelly P. Bannister, 'Intellectual Property Rights and Indigenous Cultural Heritage in Archaeology', in Mary Riley (ed.), *Indigenous Intellectual Property Rights: Legal Obstacles and Innovative Solutions*, Walnut Creek, CA: AltaMira Press, pp. 309–40, at p. 327.

[144] Manlio Frigo, 'Cultural Property v. Cultural Heritage: A "Battle of Concepts" in International law?', in Laurajane Smith and Natsuko Akagawa (eds), *Intangible Heritage*, New York and London: Routledge, 2009, pp. 45–73.

[145] Convention Concerning The Protection of the World Cultural and Natural Heritage, Article 6.1.

[146] Kearney, supra note 131, at p. 209.

[147] See Smith and Akagawa, supra note 94, at p. 1; and Forrest, supra note 14, citing numerous scholars.

[148] Lourdes Arizpe with Alonso Guiomar, 'Culture, Trade and Globalization' *UN Development Programme, New York*, Human Development Report Working Papers (2000), at p. 36; Henry Cleere, 'The Uneasy Bedfellows: Universality and Cultural Heritage', in Robert Layton, Peter G. Stone and Julian Thomas (eds), *Destruction and Conservation of Cultural Property*, London: Routledge, 2001, pp. 82–104; and Kenji Yoshida, 'The Museum and the Intangible Cultural Heritage' (2004) *Museum International*, 56 (1–2), pp. 108–12, at p. 109.

WHC, and represents an honest attempt to acknowledge and privilege non-western manifestations and practices of heritage. Proponents stressed its greater relevance to Asian, African and South American countries and to indigenous heritage practices.[149] Arguably, ICHC embodies some fundamental contradictions; while it was deemed advisable to make reference to ICH as 'a universal heritage of humanity' in the Preamble as a justification for international activity, the term is not used in the definition itself, so as to safeguard the specific value that this heritage has for the community while underlining the need for its international protection.[150]

As we have seen, however, indigenous peoples themselves remain unconvinced that an international treaty produced without their input reflects their values, and to the extent that local cultural values are determinative in evaluating the significance of ICH, and such significance is the criteria for international recognition, UNESCO may find itself at an impasse with respect to indigenous intangible cultural heritage. This impasse may only be overcome if indigenous peoples are politically recognised as the primary actors with whom UNESCO must negotiate to incorporate intangible ICH into the intangible cultural heritage internationally recognised as in need of safeguarding, which seems unlikely except in those rare instances where indigenous peoples have considerable power vis-à-vis state governments (as, for example, they increasingly do in South America). Whether or not indigenous peoples wish to have their ICH so acknowledged is another discrete and distinct question, the answer to which will lie in the particular circumstances in which any given indigenous people or community finds itself in relationship to the state in which they are resident, their need for NGO and UNESCO assistance, and the political value of the international publicity that recognition of their ICH might afford.

State-based systems of assistance for trade in indigenous heritage goods pose particular dilemmas because of the likelihood that they will be based upon historical forms of governance over indigenous peoples and perpetuate state-based identifications of indigenous peoples and their cultures that have been experienced as colonial forms of discipline and power. For example, New Zealand attempted to create a system whereby the designation of 'traditional Māori weaver' could be applied for, to certify a craftsperson's goods and to prevent imitations of non-Māori origin from circulating as Māori goods.[151] In conversations with indigenous students, Coombe was told that the endeavour was resisted by Māori who were not willing to have themselves designated either as Māori or as traditional by a state government body that they themselves did not control. Indigenous peoples routinely reject state projects that identify them, ascertain their traditions, decide what is authentic, customary or traditional to them, and otherwise recognise them according to criteria which are not their own. Any state-based system should avoid violating the human rights principle of indigenous self-identification.[152]

---

[149] Smith and Akagawa, supra note 94; and Arizpe, supra note 52.

[150] Blake, 'UNESCO's 2003 Convention', supra note 23, at p. 12.

[151] For a longer discussion of the state's designation of this initiative as a failure and its abandonment by the New Zealand government, see Haidy Geismar, *Treasured Possessions: Property Relations and Indigenous Rights in the Face of the Free Market*, Durham: Duke University Press (forthcoming).

[152] The principle of self-identification can be gleaned from combining many rights held in the UN International Covenant on Civil and Political Rights, 999 UNTS 171 and 1057 UNTS 407; 6

We must also consider the possibility that states party to the ICHC have interests in safeguarding ICH that are less exalted than serving the interests of humankind and that indigenous resistance to the incorporation of their ICH into such regimes of recognition is less a particular rejection of state involvement in a regime of benign cosmopolitanism, and rather a resistance to the state's desire to incorporate them into new regimes of neoliberal market governmentality. Anthropologist Philip Scher reminds us that new forms of state discipline and surveillance accompany a renewed global emphasis upon heritage and cultural patrimony and that the desire to capitalise upon these values under 'neoliberal nationalism' is accompanied by new forms of cultural privatisation.[153] The recent emphasis upon inventorising ICH, reifying it, assigning appropriate caretakers for it and investing in 'capacity-building' to develop local expertise arguably constitutes a new regime of power which poses both promise and peril for the local communities and indigenous peoples deemed to bear the distinctive culture that these new regimes seek to value.[154] To the extent that those who hold ICH are recognised as such because new markets in informational capital seek to locate those who can contractually negotiate with respect to its use, indigenous peoples have reason to be wary that the esteem in which their culture is suddenly held reflects the fact that it is being targeted in new regimes of capital accumulation that do not necessarily accord with their own values and aspirations.

Similarly, we need to remain wary of responsibilities being vested in 'communities' who are not provided with resources with which to meet these new demands, considering that 'communities' are often constituted as such by states, who have particular ways of making communities visible and legible that may not necessarily accord with local values or social histories of identification and belonging. The devolution of responsibilities to lower levels of governance may entail greater democratisation, but it is also a way of extending neoliberal systems of government that encumber local peoples without necessarily empowering them[155] and may subject them to new forms of moral opprobrium and blame[156] for situations not of their own making. Conflicts over the appropriate scales for managing both cultural properties and cultural commons are endemic under new conditions of informational capital.[157] We have little sense of whether UNESCO has any independent means or inclination to intervene on behalf of communities if a state party refuses to fully respect the principles of community participation and involvement in

---

ILM 368 (adopted on 16 December 1966, entered into force 23 March 1976), Articles 18–22 and 27. See also UNDRIP, Article 33.

[153] Philip Scher, 'UNESCO Conventions and Culture as a Resource' (2010) *Journal of Folklore Research*, 47 (1–2), pp. 197–202.

[154] Coombe, 'Possessing Culture', supra note 55.

[155] Mary Coffee, 'From Nation to Community: Museums and the Reconfiguration of Mexican Society Under Neoliberalism', in Jack Z. Bratich, Jeremy Parker and Cameron McCarthy (eds), *Foucault, Cultural Studies and Governmentality*, Albany, NY: Suny University Press, 2003, pp. 207–42.

[156] Kathryn Lafrenz Samuels, 'Material Heritage and Poverty Reduction', in Sophia Labadi and Colin Long (eds), *Heritage and Globalisation*, London and New York: Routledge, 2010, pp. 202–18.

[157] Lorraine V. Aragon and James Leach, 'Arts and Owners: Intellectual Property Law and the Politics of Scale in Indonesian Arts' (2008) *American Ethnologist,* 35 (4), pp. 607–31; and Coombe, 'Cultural Agencies', supra note 55.

safeguarding activities, or does so in ways that indigenous communities find inappropriate. The ICHC may nonetheless achieve greater legitimacy amongst indigenous communities if the concepts and norms of property it validates are those recognised in indigenous customary law;[158] as will any trade-based measures.

5. CONCLUSION

International intangible cultural heritage protection has evolved over the last 60 years in a fashion that has brought it progressively more in line with human rights principles and indigenous interests in self-determination. Indeed, indigenous struggles to control cultural heritage to facilitate community development have helped to shape the direction of international law in this field. Although a history of preoccupation with issues of property, economic valuations, commercial considerations and the hegemony of market exchange is arguably rejected by recent policy developments pertaining to intangible cultural heritage, the desire to harness intangible cultural heritage for the purposes of community sustainable development are likely to ensure that issues of trade will be reconsidered.

While rejecting state-based regimes as politically inappropriate, we have suggested that protection against misrepresentation coupled with the creative use of intellectual property vehicles such as pre-emptive trade marks, geographical indications and marks indicating conditions of origin more generally are potential means through which indigenous peoples may seek to benefit from intangible cultural heritage in trade contexts. Ultimately, however, indigenous peoples are unlikely to accept principles and practices of international intangible cultural heritage law until they are recognised as political agents capable of representing their own interests in UNESCO policymaking fora. Only then will we be able to begin the difficult work of recognising the viability of indigenous customary law as a necessary and possibly superior juridical resource for addressing issues pertaining to trade in intangible cultural heritage.

---

158 Kearney, supra note 131.

12. International trade in indigenous cultural heritage: comments from UNESCO in light of its international standard-setting instruments in the field of culture

Francesco Bandarin*

1. INTRODUCTION

UNESCO is well known internationally for its work in the field of cultural heritage. Indeed, as the UN organisation with a specific mandate for culture, it has elaborated a significant body of conventions in this field, which constitute the cornerstones of international heritage law. While each convention has a specific history, focus and goals, all of them are driven by UNESCO's ethical mandate to promote culture in its diversity, through international cooperation and dialogue, based upon respect for shared values, human rights and the dignity of all cultures.[1]

The UNESCO General Conference reiterated this mandate in 2001 with the adoption of the UNESCO Universal Declaration on Cultural Diversity,[2] which contains specific references to the relationship between cultural diversity and human rights. It points to human rights as guarantees for cultural diversity, affirming that the defence of cultural diversity implies 'a commitment to human rights and fundamental freedoms, in particular the rights of persons belonging to minorities and those of indigenous peoples'.[3] It continues to say that '[n]o one may invoke cultural diversity to infringe upon human rights guaranteed by international law, nor to limit their scope'.[4] Thus, from 2001 onwards, indigenous peoples were recognised in UNESCO's standard-setting work and their

* Drafted with Susanne Schnuttgen and Sandrine Amiel, UNESCO, Cultural Policies Section, Cecile Duvelle and Frank Proschan, UNESCO, Secretariat of the Convention for the Safeguarding of the Intangible Cultural Heritage (2003); Mechtild Rossler, UNESCO, Secretariat of the Convention Concerning the Protection of the World Cultural and Natural Heritage (1972); and Laurence Mayer-Robitaille, UNESCO, Secretariat of the Convention on the Protection and Promotion of the Diversity of Cultural Expressions (2005).

1 See 'UNESCO's Constitution', in *UNESCO Basic Texts*, Paris: UNESCO, 2010, at pp. 5–19.

2 UNESCO, Universal Declaration on Cultural Diversity, 41 ILM 57 (adopted on 2 November 2001).

3 Ibid., Article 4.

4 Ibid.

cultures considered as part of the world's cultural diversity; the defence of this diversity, according to the UNESCO Declaration, is an 'ethical imperative'.[5]

The 2001 UNESCO Declaration reflects a strong commitment to cultural rights as an integral part of human rights. It says that 'the flourishing of creative diversity requires the full implementation of cultural rights', noting that 'all persons have the right to participate in the cultural life of their choice and conduct their own cultural practices, subject to respect for human rights and fundamental freedoms' (Article 5).[6] Thus, as Rosemary Coombe and Joe Turcotte observe in their contribution to this volume, UNESCO is the primary UN body responsible for preparing and interpreting international normative principles and instruments with regard to cultural rights.[7] While the UNESCO conventions are not human rights instruments as such, they have an important role to play, as instruments of international law, in creating the necessary conditions for the realisation of the right of everyone to take part in cultural life, fostering the availability, accessibility, enjoyment and benefits of cultural heritage and expressions, including those of indigenous peoples.

The UNESCO 2001 Declaration and the subsequent UNESCO conventions in the field of culture have articulated in their texts the links between culture and sustainable development. The understanding of development is broad, comprising all aspects of material, intellectual, emotional and physical well-being.[8] UNESCO's engagements in sustainable development are therefore not driven by economic or trade considerations, but by a holistic concern for the rights and well-being of communities who wish to transmit to future generations their cultural heritage or promote their cultural expressions. This holistic understanding resonates with the recent deliberations of the UN Permanent Forum on Indigenous Issues (UNPFII) that advocates development *with* culture and identity.[9] This holistic vision of sustainable development has to be kept in mind when discussing issues of trade in indigenous peoples' heritage.

---

[5] Ibid.

[6] See Article 5 of the UNESCO Universal Declaration on Cultural Diversity, 2001, which continues:

> All persons have therefore the right to express themselves and to create and disseminate their work in the language of their choice, and particularly in their mother tongue; all persons are entitled to quality education and training that fully respect their cultural identity; and all persons have the right to participate in the cultural life of their choice and conduct their own cultural practices, subject to respect for human rights and fundamental freedoms.

[7] Rosemary J. Coombe with Joseph F. Turcotte, 'Indigenous Cultural Heritage in Development and Trade: Perspectives from the Dynamics of Cultural Heritage Law and Policy', in this volume.

[8] 'Cultural diversity widens the range of options open to everyone; it is one of the roots of development, understood not simply in terms of economic growth, but also as a means to achieve a more satisfactory intellectual, emotional, moral and spiritual existence'; UNESCO Universal Declaration on Cultural Diversity, Article 3.

[9] This theme was at the centre of the 9th Session of the UN Permanent Forum on Indigenous Issues in 2010. For further information on this notion, see also Inter-Agency Support Group on Indigenous Peoples' Issues (IASG), 'Indigenous Peoples: Development with Culture and Identity in Light of the UN Declaration on the Rights of Indigenous Peoples. A Reflection Paper of the Inter-Agency Support Group on Indigenous Peoples' Issues', (UN Doc. E/C.19/2010/17, 2010), available online at http://www.un.org/esa/socdev/unpfii/en/session_ninth.html (all online sources were accessed 8 September 2011) .

Another characteristic of the UNESCO conventions is important for the debate in this volume. As instruments of international law, they are underpinned by an intergovernmental logic in which States are the primary and sovereign actors. This fact may at times, as Coombe and Turcotte point out, entail a number of challenges from the perspective of indigenous peoples and their aspiration for cultural self-determination, in particular in countries where there is a high political sensitivity regarding the issue. From an international perspective, however, it is clear that the international community has made a strong statement in favour of indigenous peoples' rights when adopting the UN Declaration on the Rights of Indigenous Peoples (UNDRIP) in 2007.[10]

A key question for UNESCO in the context of this volume is the following: how, in light of UNDRIP and within the intergovernmental reality in which UNESCO operates, can the implementation of its standard-setting instruments foster respect for and recognition of indigenous peoples' heritage values and identity, support their heritage safeguarding efforts and thus positively affect the rights and well-being of indigenous communities? In other words, how can the implementation of UNESCO's conventions help advance indigenous peoples' claim to 'maintain, control, protect and develop their cultural heritage' as stipulated in Article 31 of UNDRIP?

The focus and scope of the present volume suggests consideration of this question in light of debates around international trade and sustainable development. Thus, a second question to ask is how the UNESCO conventions in the field of culture articulate culture and trade. What do these normative instruments have to say about the relationship between trade and the safeguarding and promotion of cultural heritage and how might this affect indigenous peoples' cultural heritage within international trade?

In order to address these questions, three of the conventions that UNESCO developed in the field of culture will be considered, as they are of particular relevance to the topic of this volume: the 1972 Convention Concerning the Protection of the World Cultural and Natural Heritage,[11] the 2003 Convention for the Safeguarding of the Intangible Cultural Heritage[12] and the 2005 Convention on the Protection and Promotion of the Diversity of Cultural Expressions.[13] Section 2 will explore these normative instruments through the lens of indigenous peoples' rights, as they are enunciated in UNDRIP. Section 3 will discuss how the different conventions relate to issues of trade. Reference will be made to the various questions raised about UNESCO's work in the chapters of contributing authors to this volume in order to present some conclusive remarks and ways forward.

---

[10] UNDRIP includes a call to the United Nations and specialised agencies that they 'shall promote respect for and full application of the provisions of this Declaration and follow up the effectiveness of this Declaration'; UN, Declaration on the Rights of Indigenous Peoples (UNDRIP), GA Res 61/295 (UN Doc. A/61/L.67 and Add.1) (adopted on 13 September 2007). UN, Declaration on Principles of International Law concerning Friendly Relations and Cooperation Among States, Res. 2625 (XXV) (adopted on 24 October 1970), Article 42.

[11] UNESCO, Convention Concerning the Protection of the World Cultural and Natural Heritage, 1037 UNTS 151 (adopted on 16 November 1972, entered into force 17 December 1975).

[12] UNESCO, Convention for the Safeguarding of the Intangible Cultural Heritage, 2368 UNTS 1 (adopted on 17 October 2003, entered into force 20 April 2006) [hereinafter 'Intangible Heritage Convention'].

[13] UNESCO, Convention on the Protection and Promotion of the Diversity of Cultural Expressions, 2440 UNTS 311 (adopted on 20 October 2005, entered into force 18 March 2007).

2. INDIGENOUS PEOPLES IN THE UNESCO CONVENTIONS IN THE FIELD OF CULTURE

The present section explores how indigenous peoples and their heritage are recognised in the UNESCO conventions and how the latter provide opportunities for engagement of indigenous peoples in heritage protection and safeguarding.[14] It highlights in particular how these normative instruments may foster moral and political recognition of indigenous peoples as custodians of heritage, even if the instruments were not designed specifically for indigenous peoples.

2.1 Indigenous Peoples and the 1972 Convention Concerning the Protection of the World Cultural and Natural Heritage

Established long before the adoption of UNDRIP, the 1972 Convention Concerning the Protection of the World Cultural and Natural Heritage (World Heritage Convention) is the most widely known heritage convention. At the time of its conception, no specific attention was paid to indigenous peoples and hence no explicit reference is made in the text of the Convention. The implications of this standard-setting instrument for indigenous peoples are nevertheless far-reaching. Indeed, a number of World Heritage Sites bear significance for indigenous communities or are places of their living cultures, including for example Machu Picchu (Peru), Taos Pueblo (USA), Tongariro National Park (New Zealand), Uluru-Kata Tjuta National Park (Australia), Tsodilo (Botswana) and the Ifugao Rice Terraces (Philippines), among others.[15]

It is important to understand that the 1972 World Heritage Convention is framed around the concept of 'outstanding universal value'. While it is not clearly defined in the text of this legal instrument, its meaning was elaborated in more detail over time and is reflected in the Operational Guidelines (OGs).[16] The OGs can be modified to accommodate developments, including changes in the evolving concept of heritage value or significance. And indeed, in 1992, a new category of sites was introduced to the World Heritage Convention: the category of 'cultural landscapes'. This was a significant innovation, as it demonstrated the shift from monumental heritage to a more complex interaction between people and their environment.[17] As Coombe and Turcotte rightly mention in this volume, the introduction of the cultural landscape category is particularly relevant from an

---

[14] The distinction between protection and safeguarding, as reflected especially in the 2003 Convention for the Safeguarding of the Intangible Cultural Heritage, will be further explained below.

[15] The World Heritage List includes 936 properties forming part of the cultural and natural heritage which the World Heritage Committee considers as having outstanding universal value. It can be consulted at: http://whc.unesco.org/en/list.

[16] UNESCO, 'Operational Guidelines for the Implementation of the World Heritage Convention', (UNESCO Doc. WHC 08/01, 2008), at paras 77–95 [hereinafter UNESCO, 'OGs for WHC'].

[17] See Nora Mitchell, Mechtild Rössler and Pierre M. Tricaud, 'World Heritage Cultural Landscapes. A Handbook for Conservation and Management', *Paris, UNESCO World Heritage Centre*, World Heritage Papers No. 26 (2009).

indigenous peoples' perspective as it resonates with their cultural heritage values, which consider tangible and intangible heritage as indivisible and part of a larger whole.

2.1.1 Community participation

The emphasis on the interaction between people and their environment underlying the cultural landscape category recognises the strong agency of communities in identifying, managing and transmitting such heritage. A number of examples exist where indigenous peoples' participation in the identification and management of these types of sites became prominent. Coombe and Turcotte refer in more detail to research on the Uluru-Kata Tjuta National Park that was inscribed on the World Heritage List[18] in two stages, initially for its outstanding universal value under natural heritage criteria in 1987 and then for its cultural values in 1994 as a living cultural landscape. The change resulted in stronger participation of indigenous peoples in the management of the site. The case of Tongariro National Park (New Zealand) is another emblematic example where indigenous peoples' stewardship over the site increasingly became a guiding principle of its management. When Tongariro National Park was first inscribed on the UNESCO World Heritage List in 1990, it was solely on the basis of its natural and geological values, without regard for its sacred significance to the Māori. However, upon the demand of the Māori people, the site was re-nominated for its value as an 'associative cultural landscape' in 1993, which paved the way for the recognition of the sacred values cherished by the Māori.[19]

The year 2005 saw another landmark for advancing more participatory approaches to World Heritage conservation. The OGs were revised to recognise local communities 'as partners' in the site conservation and protection, which strengthens community involvement in nomination, monitoring and reporting.[20] Two years later another change was introduced. The World Heritage Committee, under the chairpersonship of Chief Tumu Te Heuheu, the paramount Chief of the Māori tribe Ngāti Tūwharetoa, introduced in 2007 the 'C' for 'community' as a fifth strategic objective in the implementation of the World Heritage Convention, in addition to credibility, conservation, capacity-building and communication that had been adopted in 2002. The fifth 'C' calls upon State Parties 'to enhance the role of communities in the implementation of the World Heritage Convention'. State Parties committed themselves to integrate them in their policies in accordance with Article 5 of the Convention.

The recognition of the role of communities as stewards of properties in the overall intergovernmental World Heritage system represented a significant change from the perspective of indigenous peoples. It meant that claims of indigenous communities for participation found support in the provisions of the Convention and its OGs. It furthermore gave legitimacy to the elaboration of new management approaches, including traditional management, introduced in 1992 for cultural landscapes and cultural sites and in 1998 for natural properties. The World Heritage Centre also worked closely with UNESCO's Science Sector, which produced guidelines for protected area managers on sacred natural

---

18 See supra note 15.

19 The case has notably been documented in Robert Wild and Christoph McLeod, *Sacred Natural Sites: Guidelines for Protected Area Managers,* Gland: International Union for Conservation of Nature, World Commission on Protected Areas, 2008, at p. 29.

20 See UNESCO, 'OGs for WHC', supra note 16, at paras 39–40.

sites.[21] These guidelines refer to Article 31 of UNDRIP to recommend, for instance, that 'any government support and recognition to sacred natural sites should be negotiated by all parties and be made in full consultation and with the free, prior and informed consent of custodians'.[22] But sacred sites are not the only instance where good-practice examples of community participation in World Heritage management developed. A number of other important cases have been documented, such as the Laponian area, where the Saami people are now actively engaged in a new coordinated management structure,[23] or the Main Andean Road/Qhapaq Ñan,[24] which established agreements with traditional authorities and collaboration of communities in the identification, registration and conceptualisation of the roads and related sites.

2.1.2 Recognising customary restrictions on access

As the role of communities became increasingly recognised in the management of World Heritage Sites, customary restrictions on access also received further consideration. A number of sites, including sacred sites, are therefore only accessible to certain groups: Mount Athos (Greece) is reserved to men; the Kii Mountains (Japan) have divided areas for men and women; and Uluru Kata Tjuta (Australia) can be completely closed for tourists if rituals of the Aboriginal community take place at the site. This approach has triggered debates, however, on why certain sites that are supposedly for the benefit of the whole of humanity cannot be visited by all. In this regard it is interesting to note that the UN Independent Expert in the field of cultural rights recommended in her recent Report to the Human Rights Council (March 2011) that varying degrees of access and enjoyment to cultural heritage may be recognised, 'taking into consideration the diverse interests of individuals and communities according to their relationship with specific cultural heritages'. Consequently, says the report, 'the general public may not enjoy the same rights as local communities'.[25] Respect for customary restrictions on access also finds support in several articles of UNDRIP, which grants indigenous peoples 'the right to maintain, protect, and have access *in privacy* to their religious and cultural sites'.[26]

---

[21] Wild and McLeod, supra note 19. See also UNESCO, Proceedings of the International Symposium (Tokyo, 30 May – 2 June 2005), *Conserving Cultural and Biological Diversity: The Role of Sacred Natural Sites and Cultural Landscapes*, Paris: UNESCO, 2006, available online at http://unesdoc.unesco.org/images/0014/001478/147863E.pdf?bcsi_scan_EC783A0C3C997A81=0&bcsi_scan_filename=147863E.pdf.

[22] Wild and McLeod, supra note 19, at p. 33.

[23] See statutory documentation on sites and nomination projects including management plans of existing sites as well as the Periodic Report from Sweden on implementing the World Heritage Convention; for the sites in Europe, the data sheets summarising extensive documentation, available at http://whc.unesco.org/en/list/774.

[24] See details about the Main Andean Road at http://whc.unesco.org/en/qhapaqnan/ detailing the work.

[25] UN, General Assembly, Human Rights Council, 'Report of the Independent Expert in the Field of Cultural Rights, Farida Shaheed', (UN HRC Doc. A.HRC/17/38, 2011), at paras 59 and 76.

[26] UNDRIP, Article 12 (emphasis added).

2.1.3 Indigenous peoples' participation in the 1972 World Heritage Convention Statutory Meetings

Decisions about the interpretation and implementation of the World Heritage Convention are taken by its statutory body, which is the 21-member intergovernmental World Heritage Committee. It meets on a yearly basis to, among other things, examine the state of conservation of World Heritage properties and inscribe new sites on the World Heritage List. The World Heritage Committee can revise the OGs and monitors how State Parties implement its decisions. From the perspective of indigenous peoples, it is important to note that the World Heritage Committee may at any time invite public or private organisations or individuals to participate in its meetings for consultation on particular problems.[27] It may furthermore invite representatives of other relevant intergovernmental bodies.[28]

In light of the above, it is worth noting that a member of the UNPFII participated as an observer in the recent sessions of the World Heritage Committee (Brazil 2010, Paris 2011) and made statements. The representative brought to the attention of the Committee a number of concerns from indigenous communities living in specific World Heritage properties, and shared recommendations addressed to the World Heritage Committee in the report of the 9th and 10th sessions of the UNPFII (May 2010 and 2011), notably regarding the state of conservation of properties and potential future revisions of the OGs with regard to nominations and site assessments to ensure they comply with international norms and standards of free, prior and informed consent.[29]

2.2 Indigenous Peoples in the 2003 Convention for the Safeguarding of the Intangible Cultural Heritage

The adoption of the Convention for the Safeguarding of the Intangible Cultural Heritage (Intangible Heritage Convention) in 2003 can be considered the most groundbreaking development in the field of international standard-setting for cultural-heritage protection in recent years, as it reflects most clearly the changing cultural-heritage paradigm of the late twentieth and early twenty-first centuries. What has been called, after long and thorough debates at the international level, 'intangible cultural heritage' (ICH) are the practices, representations, expressions, knowledge and skills that provide orientation to people's lives and give them a sense of belonging. The Convention recognises that heritage is alive and has continued social significance for those who practise it today. Many indigenous communities consider their contemporary livelihood practices as part of their cultural heritage and thus understand well this notion of 'living heritage' promoted by the Intangible Heritage Convention.

Indeed, the main goal of the Convention is to *safeguard* ICH, thus ensuring its continued practice and transmission from one generation to the next. The Convention is not about

---

27 World Heritage Convention, Article 10.2.

28 UNESCO, 'OGs for WHC', supra note 16, at para. 43.

29 UNPFII, 'Report on the Ninth Session of the United Nations Permanent Forum on Indigenous Issues (19–30 April 2010)', (UN Doc. E/2010/43-E/C.19/2010/15, 2010), at para. 131; UNPFII, 'Report on the Tenth Session of the UN Permanent Forum on Indigenous Issues (16–27 May 2011)', (UN Doc. E/2011/43-E/C.19/2011/14, 2011), at paras 40–42.

preservation in a narrow sense of documenting for a museum. Article 2.3 of the Convention explains that 'safeguarding' means 'ensuring the viability of the intangible cultural heritage';[30] this can only be done by the communities and groups themselves, who are its owners and stewards. This goal resonates with indigenous peoples' rights and aspirations to transmit to future generations their distinct customs and cultural practices.[31]

The definition of ICH as the 'practices, representations, expressions, knowledge, skills … that communities, groups and, in some cases, individuals recognize as part of their cultural heritage' (Article 2) is relevant to indigenous peoples' claim to determine what is, for them, their own intangible heritage.[32] No external expert, no political decision-maker, no international jury may decide for them, just the practitioners, bearers, those who enact and recognise a specific heritage as their own. This fundamental principle lies at the very centre of the Convention and has considerable implications for how it is to be carried out.

The definition in Article 2 goes on: ICH is 'transmitted from generation to generation, [it] is constantly recreated by communities and groups in response to their environment, their interaction with nature and their history, and provides them with a sense of identity and continuity'. This is precisely the experience of many indigenous communities. ICH is therefore not necessarily beautiful, original or exceptional. The framers of the Intangible Heritage Convention rejected any notion of 'outstanding universal value' or any hierarchies among different expressions of heritage. Each expression of intangible heritage is precious to those who practise it, providing them the very essence of their belonging to their community. Each element or expression has the highest value for its practising community. This is why the Convention is promoting genuine respect for cultural diversity and human creativity among different communities, including indigenous communities.

As an instrument of law the Intangible Heritage Convention imposes obligations on its State Parties, while also citing and incorporating 'existing international human rights instruments' (Article 2.1). These latter are, as noted by Coombe and Turcotte, fundamental in framing most, if not all, principles of indigenous cultural heritage protection. The Convention makes clear that for its purposes, only ICH that is consistent with internationally accepted human rights instruments and with the principle of mutual respect can fall within the scope of the Convention. The Convention, or the goal of safeguarding intangible heritage, cannot therefore be instrumentalised to contravene universal human rights. If international instruments addressing the rights of indigenous peoples – the most significant of these being UNDRIP – have fundamentally altered the international

[30] The Convention has four stated objectives in its first Article to: (i) safeguard intangible cultural heritage; (ii) ensure respect for the intangible cultural heritage of the communities, groups and individuals concerned; (iii) raise awareness at the local, national and international levels of the importance of the intangible cultural heritage, and of ensuring mutual appreciation thereof; and (iv) provide for international cooperation and assistance.

[31] See UNDRIP, which speaks about the right of indigenous peoples to 'manifest, practise, develop and teach their spiritual and religious traditions, customs and ceremonies' (Article 12); and the right to 'revitalize, use, develop and transmit to future generations their histories, languages, oral traditions, philosophies, writing systems and literatures' (Article 13).

[32] Coombe and Turcotte, supra note 7, quoting Amanda Kearney, 'Intangible Cultural Heritage: Global Awareness and Local Interest', in Laurajane Smith and Natsuko Akagawa (eds), *Intangible Heritage,* New York and London: Routledge, 2009, pp. 209–26, at p. 218.

consensus on the scope and meaning of cultural rights, this applies equally to the 2003 Intangible Heritage Convention: since 2007, it can only be read in the context of UNDRIP.

2.2.1 Community participation

The safeguarding approach of the Intangible Heritage Convention emphasises community involvement and consent and recognises 'communities, in particular indigenous communities, groups and, in some cases, individuals' as the primary agents in the 'production, safeguarding, maintenance and recreation of the intangible cultural heritage' (Preamble). However, elsewhere in the text of the Convention, indigenous peoples are not identified separately; they are fully encompassed within all references in the Convention and its Operational Directives (ODs)[33] to 'communities, groups and, in some cases, individuals'. The Convention thus asserts no rights unique to indigenous communities, while affording them the same rights vis-à-vis their ICH as any other communities – as those who 'recognize [certain phenomena] as part of their cultural heritage' (Article 2.1) and as those who 'create, maintain and transmit such heritage' (Article 15). As such, they are to be involved actively in its management (Article 15).

The relation of States to ICH is carefully distinguished from that of communities. A State Party has the obligation to 'take the necessary measures to ensure the safeguarding of the intangible cultural heritage *present in its territory*' (Article 11, emphasis added). The Convention carefully distinguishes that ICH is 'present' in the territory of States, but is the *possession* of the communities who are its creators, maintainers and transmitters. If certain national heritage laws assert that ICH is the property of the nation, or of the State, this finds no support in the Convention at the international level. The only instance of a possessive pronoun ('its' or 'their') with reference to ICH occurs in the Convention's definition (Article 2.1) and refers to communities and not to States. This contradicts Coombe and Turcotte's assertions that the Intangible Heritage Convention acknowledges no indigenous rights independent of those of States and positions indigenous peoples as mere 'stakeholders' with respect to their ICH. As regards the level of indigenous peoples' political agency in the Convention, Coombe and Turcotte furthermore seem to overlook that the Convention itself, along with its ODs, repeatedly emphasise that State activities can only be undertaken with the active involvement[34] or participation[35] of those communities and with their free, prior and informed consent.[36] The latter requirement is compulsory for inscription of ICH elements on the List of Intangible Cultural Heritage in Need of Urgent Safeguarding and the Representative List of the Intangible Cultural Heritage of Humanity as well as for the inclusion of programmes, projects or activities on the Register of Best Practices.

With regard to access rights, the Intangible Heritage Convention also takes into consideration customary practices, calling upon State Parties to 'ensur[e] access to the

---

[33] See 'Operational Directives for the Implementation of the Convention for the Safeguarding of the Intangible Cultural Heritage', in UNESCO, *Basic Texts of the 2003 Convention for the Safeguarding of the Intangible Cultural Heritage,* Paris: UNESCO, 2011.

[34] Intangible Heritage Convention, Article 15; and its ODs 12, 23, 109 and 160.

[35] Intangible Heritage Convention, Article 11; and its ODs 1, 2, 7, 12, 79–82, 88, 101, 109, 157 and 162.

[36] Intangible Heritage Convention; ODs 1, 2, 7 and 101.

intangible cultural heritage while respecting customary practices governing access to specific aspects of such heritage' (Article 13).

2.2.2 Opportunities for the engagement of indigenous peoples in the implementation of the Intangible Heritage Convention

Concretely, the Intangible Heritage Convention offers several ways for indigenous peoples to engage in its implementation, both at the national and international levels, either as a 'community' practising a certain form of intangible heritage that is to be safeguarded under the Convention or as a non-governmental organisation.

First, indigenous peoples may propose safeguarding projects to the governments of their countries that could be submitted for consideration under one or more of the following mechanisms: nominations to the Urgent Safeguarding List or the Representative List (Articles 17 and 16); proposals for the Register of Best Practices (Article 18); and International Assistance requests (Article 23). Such a 'community-driven' approach is in line with the spirit of the Convention. A number of examples concerning indigenous peoples' heritage already exist for each mechanism. Elements of intangible heritage inscribed on the Lists concerning indigenous peoples include the Andean cosmovision of the Kallawaya (Bolivia); the polyphonic singing of the Aka Pygmies of Central Africa (Central African Republic); the cultural space of the gongs (Viet Nam); and the Olonkho, Yakut heroic epos (Russian Federation). A recent example of financial assistance that concerns indigenous peoples comes from Kenya, which was granted assistance for the safeguarding of the traditions and practices associated with the Kayas in the sacred forests of the Mijikenda.[37]

Indigenous peoples might also consider engaging in the inventorying of intangible heritage, in line with Articles 11 and 12 of the Convention. According to these provisions, State Parties have to take the necessary measures at the national level to identify and safeguard the ICH present in their territory with the full participation of the communities, groups and relevant non-governmental organisations. The elaboration of one or more inventories that are to be regularly updated is an obligation laid out in the Convention. Indigenous peoples have been rightly concerned about the risks and opportunities of inventorying, so it should be emphasised that community participation is mandatory for inventorying under the Convention.

In the ODs, the Intergovernmental Committee for the Safeguarding of the Intangible Cultural Heritage encourages State Parties to establish cooperation among communities, groups and individuals who create, maintain and transmit ICH, as well as experts, centres of expertise and research institutes. More concretely, it encourages the creation of consultative bodies or a coordination mechanism to facilitate the participation of communities. Indigenous peoples can explore possibilities to engage in and/or network with these consultative bodies or coordination mechanisms at the national level (recalling Article 11 (b) of the Convention and the spirit of Article 15 of the Convention).

[37] See UNESCO, Intergovernmental Committee for the Safeguarding of the Intangible Cultural Heritage, 'Evaluation of International Assistance Requests of USD 25,000 or More', (UNESCO Doc. ITH/09/4.COM/CONF.209/11, 2009), available at www.unesco.org/culture/ich/doc/.../ITH-09–4.COM-CONF.209–11-EN.doc.

With regard to the participation of relevant non-governmental organisations at the international level, Article 9 of the Convention stipulates that the Committee shall propose to the General Assembly the accreditation of non-governmental organisations with recognised competence in the field of the ICH to act in an advisory capacity to the Committee. In 2010, the General Assembly of the State Parties to the Intangible Heritage Convention approved the accreditation of almost a hundred NGOs, a number of which are indigenous or indigenous-focused, such as the Center for Peace Building and Poverty Reduction among Indigenous African Peoples (Nigeria), the Centro de Trabalho Indigenista (Brazil), the Global Development for Pygmee Minorities (GLODEPM) (DRC), the Rural Women Environmental Protection Association (RWEPA) (Cameroun) and the Young Mizo Association (India).[38] Indigenous peoples' organisations that satisfy the criteria for accreditation are welcome to request accreditation as an advisory NGO. Accreditation automatically confers upon them an observer status in the meetings of the Intergovernmental Committee.

More generally indigenous peoples' organisations, both at the national and international levels, might wish to share their experiences and needs in safeguarding their intangible heritage so that they can inform the implementation of the Convention.

Coombe and Turcotte ask if UNESCO has any independent powers to intervene on behalf of communities to ensure that State Parties comply with the principles of community participation and involvement enshrined in the Convention.[39] Here one has to distinguish between the roles of the Intergovernmental Committee for the Safeguarding of the Intangible Cultural Heritage and the General Assembly of States Parties to the Intangible Heritage Convention, on the one hand, and the UNESCO Secretariat, on the other. In common parlance, 'UNESCO' is often understood as the Secretariat, but it is also the 193 Member States of the Organization or – by extension – the 134 State Parties to the Convention. The latter, through the General Assembly or the Committee, have the responsibility to ensure that other State Parties comply with their obligations and can therefore intervene on behalf of communities. States are accountable to one another in keeping the commitments made in the framework of a convention, and other States may address shortcomings in meeting such obligations, if they wish to do so. As regards inscriptions of elements on the List of Intangible Cultural Heritage in Need of Urgent Safeguarding or the Representative List of the Intangible Cultural Heritage of Humanity, for example, it is the State Parties as members of the Convention's Committee that are responsible for ascertaining that a nomination has enjoyed the free, prior and informed consent of its community or that the safeguarding plan reflects the aspirations of that community. Furthermore, it is worth noting that observers can take the floor during the meetings of the governing bodies, which could potentially offer accredited indigenous organisations an important way of expressing appreciation or concern regarding the fulfilment of State Parties' obligations. So far, there have been few cases where observers have used this provision.

---

[38] For further information on all the accredited NGOs, please visit UNESCO, 'Non-Governmental Organizations Accredited to Provide Advisory Services to the Committee', available at http://www.unesco.org/culture/ich/index.php?lg=en&pg=00331.

[39] Coombe and Turcotte, supra note 7.

In its capacity as the Secretariat of the Intangible Heritage Convention, the UNESCO Secretariat is not empowered to intervene in the decisions among States that are taken by the General Assembly and Committee, and it has no enforcement power or policing role. Rather, it has the responsibility to raise awareness and facilitate communication as well as strengthen capacities of state and non-state actors to ensure that the principles and commitments of the conventions are well understood on the ground and the required knowledge and competencies reinforced to translate them into concrete policy and programme options.

2.3 Indigenous Peoples in the 2005 Convention on the Protection and Promotion of the Diversity of Cultural Expressions

The 2005 Convention on the Protection and Promotion of the Diversity of Cultural Expressions (Convention on the Diversity of Cultural Expressions) deals specifically with contemporary cultural expressions as they are disseminated across the world. Its Preamble recognises the importance of traditional knowledge and, in particular, the knowledge systems of indigenous peoples as a source of intangible and material wealth and the positive contribution of traditional knowledge to sustainable development. The Convention Preamble also takes into account the importance of the vitality of indigenous peoples' cultures, as manifested in their freedom to create, disseminate and distribute their traditional cultural expressions.

Indeed, the Convention received the attention of the UNPFII not only through participation as an observer in some of the intergovernmental meetings elaborating the Convention, but also in the Programme of Action for the Second International Decade for the World's Indigenous People (2005–14).[40] The Programme encourages all relevant actors 'to work towards the adoption and ratification by States of the draft convention … to ensure the right of indigenous peoples to create and disseminate in a fair environment their cultural goods and services, and their traditional expressions, so that they might benefit from them in the future' (paragraph 14).

Therefore, a number of provisions of the Convention on the Diversity of Cultural Expressions deserve attention for the purpose of this chapter.

2.3.1 Considering needs and risks specific to different social groups

The Convention contains recurring references to indigenous peoples, not only in the Preamble as mentioned above but also in its operative text. It affirms the principle of the equal dignity of and respect for all cultures, including the cultures of persons belonging to minorities and indigenous peoples (Article 2.3). More concretely, the Convention calls on State Parties to introduce measures to promote cultural expressions that pay 'due attention to the special circumstances and needs of various social groups, including persons belonging to minorities and indigenous peoples'. The purpose of such measures is to encourage individuals and social groups to create, produce, distribute and have access to

---

[40] Programme of Action for the Second International Decade for the World's Indigenous People (2005–14), (UN Doc. A/60/270), available online at http://daccess-dds-ny.un.org/doc/UNDOC/GEN/N05/464/96/PDF/N0546496.pdf?OpenElement.

their own cultural expressions (Article 7.1.a). Indeed, the OGs[41] on Article 7 approved by the Conference of Parties in 2009 encourage States to foster the full participation and engagement of indigenous peoples in cultural policies and measures to promote the diversity of cultural expressions (see paragraph 1.3).

Moreover, State Parties have the right to take all appropriate measures to protect and preserve cultural expressions in situations where cultural expressions on its territory are at risk of extinction, under serious threat or otherwise in need of urgent safeguarding (Article 8). This is an interesting provision from the perspective of indigenous peoples, since many of their cultural expressions are at risk.

2.3.2 Opportunities for indigenous peoples' participation

The emphasis on civil society participation is a significant feature of the 2005 Convention on the Diversity of Cultural Expressions. Indeed, non-governmental organisations actively participated in the process of its elaboration and the opportunities for participation also apply to indigenous peoples' organisations. State Parties are called upon to strengthen partnerships with civil society, non-governmental organisations and the private sector in pursuit of the objectives of the Convention (Articles 11, 12.c, 12.d and 15). The Intergovernmental Committee may also invite at any time public or private organisations or individuals to participate in its meetings for consultation on specific issues (Article 23.7).

2.3.3 Supporting projects and activities for indigenous peoples' cultural expressions

The International Fund for Cultural Diversity (IFCD) is a specific financing mechanism of the Convention on the Diversity of Cultural Expressions of interest also to indigenous peoples (Article 18). The purpose of the Fund is to promote sustainable development and poverty reduction in developing countries that are parties to the Convention. It does this through support for projects and activities that aim to foster the emergence of a dynamic cultural sector. The guidelines on the use of the resources of the IFCD specifically list representatives of vulnerable groups and other social groups identified in the Convention (paragraph 9.1.6) that are beneficiaries for funding. Among the projects selected in 2010, a number had a focus on indigenous peoples' cultural expressions. For instance, the Fundación del Nuevo Cine Latinoamericano (FNCL) is carrying out within this framework a regional study with a multinational group of experts to gather and systematise information on audiovisual production in six Latin American countries, with a particular focus on the expressions produced by indigenous peoples about their own lives. The Instituto de Relaciones Internacionales e Investigaciones para La Paz (IRIPAZ) intends to support indigenous cultural industries in Guatemala by building the skills of a group of young Mayan, Garifuna and Xinca in becoming audiovisual creators and cultural entrepreneurs.

---

[41] The Operational Guidelines regarding a number of Articles for the implementation of the Convention on the Diversity of Cultural Expressions already exist and can be found on the UNESCO website, available at http://www.unesco.org/new/en/culture/themes/cultural-diversity/cultural-expressions/the-convention/operational-guidelines/#topPage.

2.4 Summary

In sum, a variety of opportunities for protecting and promoting indigenous peoples' cultural heritage and contemporary cultural expressions exist in the UNESCO body of standard-setting instruments pertaining to cultural heritage, whether in the texts of the conventions themselves or in their respective OGs and ODs. The Intangible Heritage Convention is arguably the furthest-reaching in proposing new ways of State and community collaboration in safeguarding heritage, recognising the right of communities, including indigenous communities, to act as agents in the identification and safeguarding process. The Convention on the Diversity of Cultural Expressions also offers some promising avenues for the protection and promotion of the diversity of indigenous peoples' cultural expressions that will need to be further explored as the implementation of the Convention gains maturity. As for the 1972 World Heritage Convention, it is giving increasing consideration to the notion of community participation, even if this had not initially been a central aspect in framing this Convention.

Just as the provisions of the conventions vary with regard to opportunities for indigenous peoples' engagement, so do the ways in which the UNESCO conventions discussed above consider the relations between culture and trade. This is indeed another key parameter to consider when exploring possible opportunities offered by international heritage law to protect and promote indigenous peoples' heritage in a context of open market policies and free trade.

3. CULTURE AND TRADE IN THE UNESCO CULTURE CONVENTIONS

Since the 1990s the international community has increasingly referred to the cultural consequences – both positive and negative – of globalisation, marked by economic integration and the unification of markets. The need to address the challenges for cultural diversity in the new era was one important consideration that inspired in particular the 2001 Universal Declaration on Cultural Diversity, but also the subsequent 2003 Intangible Heritage Convention and 2005 Convention on the Diversity of Cultural Expressions. These recent legal instruments are indeed explicit about the importance of cultural heritage and cultural expressions for sustainable development, as mentioned at the beginning of this chapter. The Convention on the Diversity of Cultural Expressions puts culture and development at its core. Its guiding principles firmly state that culture is one of the mainsprings contributing to sustainable development. They also recognise that the cultural aspects of development are as important as its economic components. Sustainable development is also a central concern of the Intangible Heritage Convention, which considers the importance of the ICH as 'a mainspring of cultural diversity and a guarantee of sustainable development' (Preamble and Article 2). Furthermore, the notion of sustainable development is also increasingly influencing the implementation of the 1972 World Heritage Convention, as will be discussed further below.

At the same time, as Fiona Macmillan eloquently explains in her contribution to this volume, cultural heritage and trade are governed by different international regimes.[42] The UNESCO conventions fall into the domain of public international law and not international economic law. As such their elaboration has been primarily driven by the concern to protect and promote cultural diversity for mutual understanding and human well-being within a larger human rights framework. Even when the conventions touch upon the relationship between culture and trade, they do so from a cultural perspective. International trade law, as part of international economic law, has a different focus. While the primary objective of trade law is to create the conditions for free global flows of capital, goods and people, international heritage law is concerned with the transmission of cultural and natural heritage to future generations. Indeed, the UNESCO conventions recognise these different regimes, adhering to the principle of non-interference with existing international instruments.

In light of the above, the present section will explore how culture and trade are articulated in each of the three conventions. It has to be emphasised that the Convention on the Diversity of Cultural Expressions is the only one focusing explicitly on the relationship between culture and trade and shall thus be considered first.

3.1 Culture and Trade in the 2005 Convention on the Diversity of Cultural Expressions

The connections between trade and culture were at the centre of the debates that led to the elaboration of the 2005 Convention on the Diversity of Cultural Expressions. Indeed, the Convention recognises that 'cultural activities, goods and services have both an economic and a cultural nature'. It is for this reason that, according to the Convention, they cannot be treated as 'solely having commercial value' or, in other words, be regarded as identical with other objects of trade negotiations.

The Convention's primary objective is to strengthen the five inseparable links of the same chain; namely, creation, production, distribution/dissemination, access and enjoyment of cultural expressions conveyed by cultural activities, goods and services – particularly in developing countries. It is guided by the principle of equitable access, which applies in two ways: access to a rich and diverse range of cultural expressions, and access for all cultures to adequate means of expression and diffusion. At a time when, on the supply side, there has never been such a large number of works on offer, the Convention aims to ensure that they are enjoyed by as many people as possible and that the choice available to individuals is not limited to a small number of works, whether they be of local or international origin. It seeks to champion a cultural wealth that draws its capacity for interaction, renewal and transmission from both its internal and worldwide sources.[43]

In this way, the Convention puts cultural development on a level with economic growth as essential conditions of human development. Protecting and promoting the diversity of cultural expressions becomes part of international solidarity, working through development

---

[42] Fiona Macmillan, 'Finding Space in the Margins? Recognising the Rights of Indigenous Peoples in the WTO', in this volume.

[43] UNESCO, *10 Keys to the Convention on the Protection and Promotion of the Diversity of Cultural Expressions*, Paris: UNESCO, 2006, at pp. 4–5.

cooperation and aimed at doing away with imbalances between those countries that have the means to produce, distribute and broadcast their cultural expressions and those that lack such means.[44]

One key question, in particular in the context of this volume, is the extent to which this standard-setting instrument can have an impact on the trade regimes of its parties. The Convention on the Diversity of Cultural Expressions concerns the diversity of cultural expressions and is aimed at protecting and promoting this diversity, in particular through cultural policies and measures and through the strengthening of international cooperation. Some consider that such policies and measures – aimed, for example, at encouraging domestic artists and local productions – may have an impact on the trade regimes of State Parties.[45]

However, Article 20 is clear on this point: nothing in the Convention shall be interpreted as modifying the rights and obligations of the State Parties under any other treaties to which they are parties. This provision applies to all treaties, whether they are already in force or in preparation. Thus, the Convention does not call into question the independence or the autonomy of international trade law. In this connection, it is important to note that the term 'protection', employed in the context of the 2005 Convention on the Diversity of Cultural Expressions, refers to 'the adoption of measures aimed at the preservation, safeguarding and enhancement of the diversity of cultural expressions'. The Convention does not aspire to control or even restrict, but rather to promote and protect the diversity of cultural expressions. The definition of protection thus seeks to ensure that the action taken and the means used by State Parties – whose sovereign rights are of course recognised – will aim to preserve, safeguard and enhance the diversity of cultural expressions and not to limit the flows on such grounds as protectionism or cultural isolationism.[46]

At the same time, Article 20 also stipulates that the State Parties must perform in good faith their obligations under the Convention as well as those under all other treaties they have signed, without subordinating the said Convention to the other treaties. To this end, the Convention calls on the State Parties to foster mutual supportiveness between the Convention and other treaties.[47] It also calls on them to take into account the relevant provisions of the Convention when interpreting or applying the other treaties to which they are parties or when entering into other international obligations. All fields of international legislation – trade obviously included – that are likely to interact with the implementation of the Convention are envisaged in a spirit of complementarities and mutual supportiveness; while all international treaties have different objectives, these objectives can be pursued in a compatible and complementary manner.[48]

---

44 Katérina Stenou/UNESCO, *UNESCO and the Question of Cultural Diversity: Review and Strategies, 1946–2007: A Study Based on a Selection of Official Documents*, Paris: UNESCO, 2007, at p. 134.

45 UNESCO, *30 Frequently Asked Questions Regarding the Convention on the Protection and Promotion of the Diversity of Cultural Expressions*, Paris: UNESCO, 2006, at p. 12.

46 Stenou/UNESCO, supra note 44, at p. 135.

47 Regarding these issues see also Christoph B. Graber, 'The New UNESCO Convention on Cultural Diversity: A Counterbalance to the WTO?' (2006) *Journal of International Economic Law*, 9 (3), pp. 553–74, at pp. 566–7.

48 UNESCO, supra note 43, at p. 8.

Finally, in the interests of concerted action and coordination between international legal instruments, the State Parties also undertake to promote the objectives and principles of the Convention in other international fora and to consult each other to that end (Article 21). This is another way of acknowledging the interactions liable to arise between the Convention and other international treaties, and State Parties are responsible for building such 'bridges' between the different international negotiation fora.[49]

Christoph B. Graber[50] refers to Article 16 of the Convention on the Diversity of Cultural Expressions that creates an obligation for developed countries to accord preferential treatment to artists and other cultural professionals and practitioners, as well as cultural goods and services from developing countries. He suggests, in particular, including concerns of indigenous peoples in the implementation of this provision. As noted in the OGs for the implementation of Article 16, preferential treatment as it is used in the context of this Article is wider than the narrow trade meaning. It is to be understood as having both a cultural and a trade component. Measures in implementing Article 16 might for instance include the development and implementation of 'specific agreements bringing together trade and cultural dimensions which concern notably cultural goods and services, and/or artists and other cultural professionals and practitioners (e.g. Florence Agreement and its Nairobi Protocol)'.[51] To effectively implement preferential treatment under Article 16, State Parties are invited to adopt consistent policies and approaches in the trade and cultural spheres. Parties are furthermore invited to seek close coordination between the national authorities responsible for culture and trade as well as other public authorities concerned, in developed and developing countries alike. It is also worth noting that civil society (which includes indigenous peoples' organisations) is encouraged to play an active role with respect to the implementation of Article 16 as detailed in the OGs of the 2005 Convention on the Diversity of Cultural Expressions.[52]

Therefore the suggestion to include concerns of indigenous peoples in the implementation of Article 16 is fully in the spirit of the active role assigned to civil society in terms

---

[49] UNESCO, supra note 45, at p. 11.

[50] Christoph B. Graber, 'Institutionalization of Creativity in Traditional Societies and in International Trade Law', in Shubha Ghosh and Robin P. Malloy (eds), *Creativity, Law and Entrepreneurship*, Cheltenham, UK and Northampton, MA: Edward Elgar, 2011, pp. 234–63, at pp. 247–8 and 253.

[51] UNESCO, 'Operational Guidelines of the 2005 Convention on the Protection and Promotion of the Diversity of Cultural Expressions', Article 16, Preferential Treatment for Developing Countries, Approved by the Conference of Parties at its 2nd session (June 2009), at para. 3.5 [hereinafter UNESCO, 'OGs for Convention on the Diversity of Cultural Expressions'].

[52] These provisions include:

> Contributing to needs assessment and provide information, advice and innovative ideas regarding elaboration, improvement and efficient application of preferential treatment frameworks and schemes; Providing, upon request by the competent authorities, consultative information on visa requests of artists and other cultural professionals and practitioners from developing countries; Providing feedback to the Parties and in its capacity as observer, to the organs of the Convention, concerning difficulties and challenges in the implementation of Article 16, notably in the field; Engaging and play an innovative and proactive role in the field of research on the implementation and the monitoring process of Article 16 at the national level.

UNESCO, 'OGs for Convention on the Diversity of Cultural Expressions', at para. 5.

of innovative advice and research. Given the scope of Article 16, however, this could only concern indigenous peoples from developing countries.

3.2 Culture, Trade and the Intangible Heritage Convention

While the Intangible Cultural Heritage Convention is not specifically concerned with international trade, it does stipulate that safeguarding contributes to sustainable development and community well-being. Indeed, as safeguarding of the ICH may be intimately linked with issues of subsistence and income generation, some references on how commercial activities related to intangible heritage shall be conducted can be found in the ODs of the Convention.[53] These acknowledge the potential of such activities for improving the living standards of the communities and stipulate that all appropriate measures should be taken to ensure that the communities concerned are their primary beneficiaries. Another important condition is that these commercial activities should not threaten the viability of the ICH. For this reason, particular attention should be paid to avoiding commercial misappropriation, ensuring that tourism activities are managed in an ethical and sustainable way, finding a proper balance between the interests of the commercial party, the public administration and the cultural practitioners.

The plan for the 'safeguarding of the traditions and practices associated with the sacred forest Kayas of the Mijikenda', which recently received financial support under the Convention's international assistance mechanism (Article 23), illustrates how the careful balance between cultural and economic well-being described in the ODs can be maintained in practice in heritage safeguarding efforts. The safeguarding strategy highlights rural-to-urban migration as a main threat to the continued transmission of this intangible heritage. The safeguarding measures proposed thus include income-generating schemes such as bee-keeping as well as tourism activities for the communities settled near the Kayas, to reinforce their economic viability as part of the safeguarding scheme. It has to be noted that when economic activities are carried out to support heritage safeguarding, the issue of ensuring that commercial use does not distort the meaning and purpose of the ICH for the community remains a continuous concern. So does the issue of equitable benefit-sharing. The examiners' reports assessing the international assistance request therefore recommend, for instance, that income distribution, management and use be discussed within these communities in training workshops, together with the mitigation of possible adverse effects of promoting the rituals as tourist events.[54]

Coombe and Turcotte question the extent to which UNESCO's principles of community safeguarding of the ICH give indigenous peoples any greater power than they would have if such materials were treated as being in the public domain, also asking if UNESCO could take a proactive stance in order to protect indigenous communities from unfair competition.[55]

In answering this question, it is important to recall that UNESCO – whether one is referring to its States or its Secretariat – cannot undertake such measures, since it is the

53 Supra note 33, ODs 116 and 117.

54 UNESCO, Intergovernmental Committee for the Safeguarding of the Intangible Cultural Heritage, supra note 37, Annex 1, at p. 9.

55 Coombe and Turcotte, supra note 7.

prerogative of each State Party to take such measures as it may wish to offer legal protections at the national level, including intellectual property protections, to the cultural expressions of the communities on its territory. A number of countries, in their domestic laws, already afford exclusive rights to certain communities (including indigenous communities) to label goods as produced by those communities, beginning with the Indian Arts and Crafts Act of 1935 in the United States.[56] That law – substantially revised and expanded in 1990 – made it a crime to 'offer for sale any goods … as Indian products or Indian products of a particular Indian tribe or group, resident within the United States … , when such person knows such goods are not Indian products or are not Indian products of the particular Indian tribe or group'.[57] Such protections do not, as yet, extend to the international level.

For its part, the Intangible Heritage Convention states clearly that its provisions may not be interpreted as affecting the rights and obligations of State Parties deriving from any international instrument related to intellectual property rights (Article 3). The legal protection of specific manifestations through intellectual property rights at the international level falls within the field of competence of the World Intellectual Property Organization (WIPO), whose Intergovernmental Committee on Intellectual Property and Genetic Resources, Traditional Knowledge and Folklore (IGC) continues its efforts to develop an international legal instrument (or instruments) to provide protection to such intellectual property. The ODs of the Intangible Heritage Convention do, however, recommend that State Parties shall endeavour to ensure, in particular through the application of intellectual property rights, that the rights of the communities, groups and individuals that create, bear and transmit their ICH are duly protected when raising awareness about their heritage or engaging in commercial activities (paragraph 104).

It is important to highlight, as authors of other chapters in this volume have done, that applying intellectual property rights with the current legal provisions in place might not be satisfactory or appropriate when dealing with ICH. Intellectual property rights have historically been based on the notions of a work having a fixed form and a clearly definable creator. However, ICH is characterised by its evolving and shared nature; because it evolves through continuous recreation by the communities and groups that bear and practise it, protecting a specific manifestation such as the performance of a dance, the recorded interpretation of a song or a particular handicraft pattern or technique may lead to freezing this ICH and hinder its evolution within its community. Moreover, as communities are the ones who create, maintain and transmit ICH, it is difficult – as the WIPO IGC has shown – to agree on an internationally acceptable framework for determining the collective owner of such heritage and ensuring that they benefit from its exploitation.[58]

---

[56] See Carole Goldberg, 'A United States Perspective on the Protection of Indigenous Cultural Heritage', in this volume.

[57] Indian Arts and Crafts Act of 1935, 25 U.S.C. § 305; Pub. L. 74–355.

[58] 'Questions and Answers about Intangible Cultural Heritage', at p. 8, in: UNESCO, 'Kit of the Convention for the Safeguarding of the Intangible Cultural Heritage', 2009.

3.3 Culture, Trade and the 1972 World Heritage Convention

The World Heritage Convention reflects awareness that economic pressures can put heritage at risk, noting already in its Preamble that cultural and natural heritage is 'increasingly threatened with destruction not only by the traditional causes of decay, but also by changing social and economic conditions which aggravate the situation'.

As the international community has embraced the concept of sustainable development, the contribution of World Heritage in this area has gained increasing attention in recent years.[59] The notion of sustainability entered the OGs for the implementation of the Convention in 1992. At its 26th Session (Budapest, 2002), the World Heritage Committee emphasised the need to 'ensure an appropriate and equitable balance between conservation, sustainability and development, so that World Heritage properties can be protected through appropriate activities contributing to the social and economic development and the quality of life of our communities'. More recently, the Committee requested the World Heritage Centre in 2010 to pursue the study of the revision of the OGs, to integrate sustainable development, and to further consider these matters within the framework of the reflection on the future of the Convention; a new paragraph on this subject was added to the OGs in June 2011.

Indeed, the protection of cultural and natural heritage can play a significant role in fostering strong communities and supporting the physical and spiritual well-being of its individuals, if carried out with adequate community involvement. At the same time, unsustainable development is perhaps the most significant threat to heritage conservation, both in developing and developed countries. In this sense, it can be argued that sustainable development is development that takes also into account the need to protect and promote cultural heritage.[60] This twofold analysis of the relations between heritage and sustainable development can inform thinking on international trade in indigenous peoples' cultural heritage.

The issue of local communities as beneficiaries of commercial activities deriving from World Heritage falls under the paragraphs of the OGs 'Partners in the protection of World Heritage' (paragraphs 39 and 40). A number of good-practice examples have been documented that illustrate how World Heritage conservation and community-based sustainable development are mutually supportive. The Reserve of Sian Ka'an (Yucatàn Peninsula, Mexico) is one case where a successful system of community organisation, supported by appropriate capacity-building efforts, has allowed continued economic benefits to the local communities while ensuring the sustainable use of natural resources in both tourism and fishing.[61]

---

[59] UNESCO, Report to the World Heritage Committee, 'World Heritage Convention and Sustainable Development', (UNESCO Doc. WHC-10/34.COM/5D, 2010), at pp. 2–3.

[60] Ibid, at p. 4.

[61] Francisco Ursúa Guerrero, 'Nature Tourism in Sian Ka'an. An Example of Community Work' (2010) *World Heritage*, 58, pp. 28–33.

3.4 Summary

Looking at the three conventions it is clear that the 2005 Convention on the Diversity of Cultural Expressions is most explicit about the relations between trade and cultural expressions, including the expressions of indigenous peoples, and includes many interesting possibilities for indigenous communities' engagement in this regard. However, the 2003 Intangible Heritage Convention and the 1972 World Heritage Convention also include provisions that acknowledge and foster the economic value of heritage safeguarding and protection, while emphasising that commercial activities should not have adverse effects on the protection/safeguarding of the cultural and natural heritage element or site in question. Indigenous communities who choose to engage with the implementation processes of these conventions, as detailed in the first part of this chapter, thus find a number of provisions that support them in their efforts to be recognised as the agents of their heritage protection and safeguarding.

4. CONCLUDING REMARKS AND WAYS FORWARD

The present chapter set out to present the possibilities to protect and promote indigenous peoples' heritage under three of the UNESCO conventions on heritage and the diversity of cultural expressions, considering in particular the context of international trade. It explained why any analysis of how these conventions relate to indigenous peoples' heritage protection and safeguarding has to take into account the fact that UNESCO instruments adhere to the principles of state sovereignty and non-interference with other international instruments. It also showed the importance of considering the specific historical context that determined the objectives, scope and implementation mechanisms of each convention in addressing questions of indigenous peoples' heritage and international trade. The chapter highlighted the entry points for the protection and promotion of indigenous peoples' cultural heritage in the conventions and as they developed in light of lessons learned from the practice of heritage protection and safeguarding. A growing recognition of indigenous peoples' stewardship in maintaining and transmitting their cultural heritage, commitment to community participation, respect for benefit-sharing and community well-being – all critical for the promotion of the rights of indigenous peoples – could be observed, notably in the later UNESCO standard-setting instruments and in the various updates of the ODs and guidelines that orient the implementation of the respective conventions. From the perspective of indigenous peoples, the broadening of the heritage paradigm from the protection of tangible heritage for the benefit of humanity at large to a dynamic approach that recognises the critical role of communities at all stages of identifying, maintaining and safeguarding heritage, both tangible and intangible, has been significant.

The chapter highlighted the new opportunities for tripartite partnerships and reciprocal engagement between States, communities and civil society that emerged in the provisions of the UNESCO conventions over the years, and discussed what these mean in terms of stronger indigenous peoples' agency in heritage matters. The chapter illustrated how the recent provisions can strengthen and expand indigenous peoples' agency in all processes of heritage protection and safeguarding. The opportunities for engagement include possibilities to inform the elaboration and revision processes of cultural policies and the identification and implementation of adequate heritage protection and safeguarding strategies. Indeed, as the Convention on the Diversity of Cultural Expressions underlines, strong national cultural policies are considered to reinforce and sustain processes of international cooperation in the field of culture and could thus also inform and provide ethical reference points for international trade negotiations. The coming years will reveal the extent to which connections can be drawn between the implementation of the UNESCO conventions and State Parties' positions or legal decisions concerning international trade negotiations, as the conventions are more firmly grounded at the national level. Thus the participation of indigenous peoples' organisations and communities in cultural policy and heritage safeguarding processes is crucial to ensure that their concerns are amply reflected.

Much remains to be done in terms of raising awareness and strengthening capacities to ensure that all concerned parties understand the latest developments in the field of international heritage law and can fully realise its potential for reinforced partnership. In this regard, it is worth noting that within the framework of the 2003 Intangible Heritage Convention, UNESCO – with generous support from a number of State Parties – has launched a global capacity-building strategy to reinforce the abilities of state actors, communities and civil society organisations to implement this normative instrument, which, as discussed above, bears great potential to reinforce communities' participation in safeguarding their ICH.

It is furthermore important to note that UNDRIP will continue to provide a critical reference document for UNESCO when implementing its programmes and supporting the State Parties in implementing the conventions. To further reinforce this commitment, the Director-General of UNESCO, Irina Bokova, has decided to initiate a process to elaborate a policy on engaging with indigenous peoples. This process was officially launched in 2011 at UNESCO Headquarters in close collaboration with indigenous peoples and experts. The policy will span the breadth of UNESCO's mandate and its development will be pursued throughout 2012 with inputs from all regions. The principle of free, prior and informed consent, as outlined in UNDRIP and discussed in this chapter, will have major importance in UNESCO's policy development process with respect to indigenous peoples. In particular, as the current OGs of the World Heritage Convention do not explicitly make reference to the free, prior and informed consent of indigenous communities, continuing efforts will be made in order to respond to this challenge.[62]

It is also noteworthy that the 40th anniversary of the 1972 World Heritage Convention is to be celebrated in 2012, under a theme which is of direct relevance to the issues discussed in this volume: 'World Heritage and sustainable development – the role of local communities'. Anniversary events will provide an excellent opportunity for indigenous peoples to engage with UNESCO, the World Heritage Committee and its Secretariat, in order to address concerns that have been raised within the framework of the UNPFII and to work towards constructive solutions to the challenges that UNDRIP brings to the international community as a whole.

---

[62] See UNESCO, 'Free Prior and Informed Consent', Statement at the Tenth Session of the UNPFII, supra note 29, available at http://www.docip.org/gsdl/collect/cendocdo/index/assoc/HASHbefc/9a7a182d.dir/PF11douglas071.pdf#search='Douglas NAKASHIMA'.

UNESCO will continue to follow the important debate on international trade in indigenous peoples' cultural heritage with interest, informed by the new insights shared through the project of this volume. While recent developments in international heritage law have been presented and analysed, only the future will provide the necessary evidence of how they might affect the complex interrelations between indigenous peoples' cultural heritage protection and promotion and the processes of international trade.

PART III

Country reports (United States, Canada, Australia, New Zealand)

13. A United States perspective on the protection of indigenous cultural heritage

Carole E. Goldberg

1. INTRODUCTION

There is no way to place a precise value on the knowledge and cultural heritage of indigenous peoples of the United States. There are, however, a few data points that suggest how enormous that value could be. In 1997, the United States Department of Commerce indicated that Indian arts and crafts were generating US$1.2 billion in gross revenue.[1] In 2003, a professor at the University of Hawaii proposed licensing the Hawaiian genome as the intellectual property of the Hawaiian people, pointing out that the great population loss that occurred among Native Hawaiians in the nineteenth century made them an unusually homogenous group, and therefore valuable for scientific research. A pharmaceutical company had paid US$200 million for rights to the Icelandic genome, which underwent a similar demographic experience.[2] The temptations to appropriate and commercialise that knowledge are undeniable.

Money is not the only measure of value for indigenous heritage, however. Many indigenous groups resist commercialisation, preferring that at least some of their traditional knowledge and heritage remain secret, or at least reserved for internal cultural uses. Knowledge that is sacred or connected to the spirit realm typically must remain forbidden to outsiders; and many ceremonies, songs, stories and designs require protection because they become less meaningful and powerful within the culture if they are commodified or widely circulated.[3]

Even where indigenous groups view certain knowledge, such as folkloric works and plant remedies, as appropriate for commercialisation, they seek to be the ones who benefit

---

[1] Julie Hollowell, 'Intellectual Property Protection and the Market for Alaska Native Arts and Crafts', in Mary Riley (ed.), *Indigenous Intellectual Property Rights: Legal Obstacles and Innovative Solutions*, Walnut Creek, CA: AltaMira Press, 2004, pp. 55–98, at p. 57.

[2] Cherryl Ernst, 'Licensing Hawaiian Genes for Medical Research' (2003) *Malamalama*, 2, at p. 16.

[3] See Angela R. Riley, '"Straight Stealing": Towards an Indigenous System of Cultural Property Protection' (2005) *Washington Law Review*, 80, pp. 69–164, at pp. 76–82.

from that knowledge. Too often, domestic and international law have denied them that opportunity to control and benefit from the knowledge and heritage that they have developed.[4]

Given these conflicts over commercialisation, misappropriation and control, how receptive is the United States to the protection of cultural knowledge and heritage of indigenous Americans under domestic law? Would the current United States legal regime for protection of indigenous heritage be appropriate under an international arrangement that conditioned preferential rules for indigenous cultural goods on respect for cultural self-determination, such as explored in Christoph B. Graber's chapter in this volume?[5]

The answer to both questions is 'somewhat'. The United States has not attempted any comprehensive characterisation of, let alone response to, the problems of misappropriation of Native American traditional knowledge and heritage. It has, however, made some episodic and ad hoc responses to particular threats to indigenous knowledge and cultural heritage. Furthermore, because the United States recognises more than 550 native nations as possessing some inherent and delegated powers of self-government, the door is opened for those native nations to establish protections of their own for traditional knowledge and heritage. An important caveat, however, is that for many purposes, United States law insists on a relatively narrow definition of which groups 'count' as indigenous, at least when compared with many definitions provided under international law.

What this legal regime bodes for United States participation in a procedural solution to interfacing global law and local traditions, as Graber proposed in his chapter, is unclear; but there are some promising possibilities. Several specific or more limited modes of United States relations with indigenous Americans could serve as broader models for United States participation in an international regime governing trade in indigenous knowledge and goods, especially a regime that emphasises procedural solutions.

This chapter assumes the value of protection for indigenous knowledge and cultural heritage, and focuses on the potential for United States law to mesh effectively with a procedurally oriented international regime that could afford such protection. Section 2 of this chapter analyses domestic United States law, including federal Indian law that addresses tribal sovereignty, law specifically directed at traditional knowledge and heritage, and more general laws dealing with intellectual property and cultural expression. Special attention is paid to the amount of control, if any, that these laws allow to indigenous peoples themselves. The focus shifts in section 3 to native nations' own laws, to discern the protection for indigenous knowledge and culture afforded under those legal systems and the limits that the United States places on such legal initiatives. Finally, in section 4, this chapter considers the possibilities and challenges of fitting current United

---

4 For a discussion of these two types of indigenous interests in controlling knowledge and cultural heritage, see Christine Haight Farley, 'Protecting Folklore of Indigenous Peoples: Is Intellectual Property the Answer?' (1997) *Connecticut Law Review*, 30, pp. 1–57, at pp. 13–15.

5 Christoph B. Graber, 'Stimulating Trade and Development of Indigenous Cultural Heritage by Means of International Law: Issues of Legitimacy and Method', in this volume. See also Christoph B. Graber, 'Institutionalization of Creativity in Traditional Societies and in International Trade Law', in Shubha Ghosh and Robin P. Malloy (eds), *Creativity, Law and Entrepreneurship*, Cheltenham, UK and Northampton, MA: Edward Elgar, 2011, pp. 234–63 [hereinafter Graber, 'Institutionalization of Creativity'].

States law and policy into an international regime of protection that adopts a procedural approach, focused on the participation of indigenous peoples in decisions about trade in traditional cultural knowledge.

2. DOMESTIC UNITED STATES LAW AND PROTECTION OF INDIGENOUS CULTURE

Domestic United States law offers no comprehensive or principled approach to the protection of indigenous cultural heritage, as defined very broadly to include both tangible and intangible aspects of collective life.[6] Rather, it provides some narrowly targeted protections through federal and, far less often, state law; and it creates conditions for consultation with native nations regarding the effects of a wide array of federal policies. Furthermore, the United States recognises powers of indigenous self-government under specified conditions, unleashing the potential for protections carried out by the native nations themselves. Some general background on the relationship between the United States and the indigenous peoples of North America is necessary to any understanding of the state of United States law.

2.1 Background on United States – Indigenous Relations

When Europeans invaded North America in the sixteenth century, hundreds of different linguistic and cultural groups occupied what is now the United States, comprising an estimated 5 million people.[7] Although disease, dispossession, massacres and war greatly diminished those numbers, Europeans still needed native allies in their struggles for survival and for political and economic domination. In the case of the English, who eventually gained ascendance in North America, the quest for allies led to a practice of treaty-making.[8] These treaties sought land cessions, trade preferences and military alliances, and purported to guarantee the native peoples territories protected from European incursion. Although these early guarantees never really held back the tide,[9] they established a policy of government-to-government relations through treaties that the

---

[6] For the definition of 'cultural heritage' see Christoph Antons, 'Intellectual Property Rights in Indigenous Cultural Heritage: Basic Concepts and Continuing Controversies', in this volume; and Martin Girsberger and Benny Müller, 'International Trade in Indigenous Cultural Heritage: An IP Practitioners' Perspective', in this volume.

[7] The population estimate is from Russell Thornton, 'Population History of Native North Americans', in Michael R. Haines and Richard H. Steckel (eds), *A Population History of North America*, Cambridge: Cambridge University Press, 2000, pp. 9–50, at p. 13. For an introduction to the diversity of native cultures, see Duane Champagne, *Native America: Portrait of the Peoples*, Detroit: Visible Ink Press, 1994.

[8] See Alden T. Vaughan (ed.), *Early American Indian Documents: Treaties and Laws, 1607–1789*, Newark, NJ: LexisNexis, 2004.

[9] See, for example, Daniel K. Richter, *Facing East from Indian Country: A Native History of Early America*, Cambridge, MA: Harvard University Press, 2001, at p. 108 (describing the experience of the Pamunkeys and their allies in Virginia following treaties made in 1667 and 1670).

Americans maintained after the Revolutionary War.[10] In the United States Constitution of 1787, native nations are not constituent parties, as the 13 original colonies were. Neither are they minority groups, as ethnic, racial and religious groups may be. Rather, the Constitution refers to most native peoples as outside the body politic of the United States, and gives Congress power only to 'regulate commerce … with the Indian tribes'.[11]

Congress officially ended treaty-making with Indians in 1871, after ratifying approximately 370 treaties;[12] but the federal government continued to make agreements with native nations that were memorialised in legislation, perpetuating the recognition of native nations as governments.[13] Congress and the President also continued to protect and set aside tracts of land for Indians, outside the treaty process.[14] Congress granted United States citizenship to Indians for the first time in 1924, regardless of their desire or consent, while continuing to recognise tribal citizenship and attendant rights.[15] And contemporary presidents, including both Presidents George W. Bush and Barack Obama, have affirmed the government-to-government relationship between native nations and the United States.[16]

This distinctive history of United States–indigenous political relations has had important ramifications for domestic United States law. Most significantly, it led to early United States Supreme Court decisions recognising *both* that native nations were forcibly incorporated into the United States *and* that native nations retain inherent powers of self-government that pre-date the formation of the American nation state.[17] Managing the

---

[10] Some indigenous groups in the United States, notably Pueblos in the Southwest and tribes in California and Alaska, do not have ratified treaties. In the case of California tribes, treaties were made but not ratified. In the case of the Pueblos, land titles had already been established under Spanish and later Mexican law.

[11] See United States Constitution, Article I, s. 2, cl. 3 (excluding 'Indians not taxed' from apportionment for purposes of representation and taxation); and Article I, s. 8, cl. 3 (Indian commerce clause).

[12] Vine Deloria Jr and Raymond J. DeMallie, *Documents of American Indian Diplomacy: Treaties, Agreements, and Conventions, 1775–1979,* vol. I, Norman, OK: University of Oklahoma Press, 1999, at p. 181.

[13] See Nell Jessup Newton et al., *Cohen's Handbook of Federal Indian Law*, Newark, NJ: LexisNexis, 2005 Edition, at pp. 74–5.

[14] The non-treaty reservations were established by federal statute and executive order. As of 2005, there were 314 reservations and other restricted and trust lands in the United States, located in 31 states, mostly in the West. These lands comprise nearly 100 million acres, 56 million in the continental United States and 44 million in Alaska. David E. Wilkins, *American Indian Politics and the American Political System*, 2nd edn, Lanham, MD: Rowman & Littlefield, 2007, at p. 35. The size of reservations varies enormously, from a few acres to the 24,078-square-mile Navajo Reservation, which is as large as the state of West Virginia.

[15] Indian Citizenship Act of 1924, 43 Statutes at Large 253.

[16] President George W. Bush, 'Memorandum for the Heads of Executive Departments and Agencies: Government-to-Government Relationship with Tribal Governments' (23 September 2004), available at http://www.epa.gov/tp/pdf/president-bush-2004.pdf (all online sources were accessed 9 May 2012); President Barack Obama, 'Memorandum for the Heads of Executive Departments and Agencies: Tribal Consultation' (5 November 2009), available at http://www.whitehouse.gov/the-press-office/memorandum-tribal-consultation-signed-president.

[17] See *Johnson v McIntosh* (1823) 21 US 543 (asserting United States authority over and title to indigenous lands); *Cherokee Nation v Georgia* (1831) 30 US 1 (articulating the status of native

tension between these two principles has been the task of federal Indian law, which includes both federal common law articulated by the courts and federal legislative and executive measures.[18] For example, federal Indian law has insisted on ultimate United States title to indigenous lands, while recognising that native nations have possessory rights that remain unless properly extinguished by the federal government.[19] It has also affirmed a broad federal 'plenary power' to abrogate treaties and to legislate regarding the internal as well as external relations of tribes, but has established rules of statutory and treaty interpretation that impede the exercise of that power.[20] A vaguely defined notion of federal 'trust responsibility' to the tribes informs executive and administrative action, including obligations of consultation with native nations over federal policies, but does not constrain Congress in its legislative role.[21]

Native nations have understood the body of federal Indian law as one arena – an imperfect one – for asserting their autonomy, articulating their vision of intergovernmental relations, and protecting their cultural distinctiveness.[22] Although they have been dispossessed of nearly 98 per cent of their ancestral lands and resources and subjected to sustained policies of forced assimilation, many native nations are deploying their sovereignty and protected land bases to sustain and revitalise their cultures and economies, taking some measure of control over the response to global forces for change.[23] Today, despite often severe fiscal challenges, many native nations in the United States operate

---

nations as 'domestic dependent nations' and articulating a federal trust responsibility towards tribes); and *Worcester v Georgia* (1832) 31 US 515 (affirming inherent tribal authority).

18 See generally Newton et al., supra note 13.

19 See *Johnson v McIntosh*, supra note 17.

20 *United States v Kagama* (1886) 118 US 375; and *Minnesota v Mille Lacs Band of Chippewa Indian* (1999) 526 US 172. See Philip P. Frickey, 'Marshalling Past and Present: Colonialism, Constitutionalism, and Interpretation in Federal Indian Law' (1993) *Harvard Law Review*, 107, pp. 381–440.

21 See Newton et al., supra note 13, at pp. 418–42; Mary C. Wood, 'Indian Land and the Promise of Native Sovereignty: The Trust Doctrine Revisited' (1994) *Utah Law Review*, pp. 1471–1569; Gabriel S. Galanda, 'The Federal Indian Consultation Right: A Frontline Defense Against Tribal Sovereignty Incursion' (2010) *Federal Indian Lawyer*, available at http://fedbar.org/Image-Library/Sections-and-Divisions/Indian/Federal-Indian-Consultation-Right.pdf. According to political scientist David Wilkins (supra note 14, at p. 49):

> Tribal nations tend to think of 'trust' as entailing four interrelated components: that the federal government ... was pledged to protect tribal property and sovereignty and would not move for or against tribes without first securing tribal consent; that the United States would act with the utmost integrity in its legal and political commitments to Indian peoples as outlined in treaties or governmental policies (e.g. provide health care, educational support, housing assistance); that the United States would act in a moral manner regarding tribal rights ... ; and that the United States would continue to support any additional duties and responsibilities in its self-assumed role as the Indians' 'protectors'.

22 See generally Carole Goldberg, Kevin K. Washburn and Philip P. Frickey, *Indian Law Stories*, Minneapolis: Foundation Press, 2010.

23 See Charles Wilkinson, *Blood Struggle: The Rise of Modern Indian Nations*, New York: W.W. Norton & Company, 2005; and The Harvard Project on American Indian Economic Development, *The State of the Native Nations: Conditions Under U.S. Policies of Self-Determination*, Oxford: Oxford University Press, 2008 [hereinafter Harvard Project].

complex governments, including civil and criminal justice systems, agencies to regulate the environment and natural resources, and social services for child protection and elder assistance.[24]

2.2 Who Counts as 'Indigenous' under United States Indian Law

As already noted, United States law recognises the inherent governing authority of native nations, subject to federal law limitations. That law also permits Congress to delegate additional powers to indigenous governments.[25] Treaties acknowledge distinctive rights of native nations; and in exercising its trust responsibility, Congress has conferred some distinctive benefits on native nations as well as on individual American Indian people, mainly those who belong to those native nations.[26] Significantly, the United States Supreme Court has concluded that such provisions do not violate constitutional requirements of equal treatment because they are based on tribal government status, not on race.[27]

This United States regime for recognising and privileging indigenous rights requires some sort of mechanism to establish which groups 'count' as native nations or tribes, because those nations and their members or citizens are the primary beneficiaries of such rights. Although a rapidly declining number of federal laws benefit native persons based on their indigenous ancestry alone, under most current laws, only native nations and their members will be able to benefit from and enforce indigenous rights.[28]

The mechanism in place under federal Indian law that gives official status to native nations is known as federal recognition or acknowledgment. As of 2011, there were 565 federally recognised native nations or Indian tribes. In 1994, Congress passed the Federally Recognised Tribes List Act, requiring the United States Department of the Interior to maintain an official list of federally recognised tribes, and to publish it regularly.[29] As a result, it is easy to see which groups are and are not entitled to the benefits of federal recognition.

Historically, ascertaining federal recognition was not as simple as consulting a list. For the country's first 200 years, federal recognition was measured by treaty relations or agreements, federal legislative designations and executive orders setting aside federal lands for the benefit of groups of Indians.[30] The United States Supreme Court furnished a general definition of 'Indian tribes' to aid the other branches of government when legislation referred to such groups in general terms.[31] Nonetheless, until the late twentieth century there was no centralised, formal process for registering or affirming federal recognition.

---

24 Wilkins, supra note 14, at pp. 138–62.

25 Newton et al., supra note 13, at pp. 204–48.

26 See *Morton v Mancari* (1974) 417 US 535, at p. 552 (discussing many of these special legal provisions).

27 Ibid.

28 See Newton et al., supra note 13, at pp. 177–81.

29 25 U.S.C. §§ 479a, 479a-1.

30 Newton et al., supra note 13, at p. 143.

31 *Montoya v United States* (1901) 180 US 261, at p. 266 (defining an 'Indian tribe' as 'a body of Indians of the same or a similar race, united in a community under one leadership or government, and inhabiting a particular though sometimes ill-defined territory … ').

Beginning in the 1970s, as federal policy embraced tribal self-determination and an array of new services to tribes, the benefits of federal recognition multiplied. Indigenous groups that had been overlooked or bypassed in the days of ad hoc recognition practice registered their complaints with the American Indian Policy Review Commission, which Congress had established in 1975. The rise of indigenous protests and demonstrations in the 1960s and 1970s, manifest at such places as Alcatraz Island in San Francisco, had made these groups more willing to assert their indigenous identity and to claim indigenous rights. What the protesting groups wanted was a way to demonstrate their entitlement to federal acknowledgment.[32] Their grievances were real. As the leading treatise on federal Indian law has observed, tribes lacking federal recognition 'suffer from lack of federal respect for their sovereignty and land bases, lack of protection from state jurisdiction, lack of access to repatriation rights and other forms of cultural protection under federal law, and denial of most benefits available to tribes that enjoy a government-to-government relationship with the United States'.[33] They may also be denied highly valued affirmation of their indigenous identity. While there are some states that provide their own recognition to tribes, state recognition typically confers far fewer protections and benefits than federal recognition.[34]

Responding to recommendations from the Commission, the Department of the Interior acted in 1978 to set up an administrative process for proving federal recognition. These regulations adopted a largely socio-anthropological approach, insisting that tribes demonstrate, among other things, existence as 'a distinct community' from historical times to the present, maintenance of political influence over the membership from historical times until the present and a membership that consists of individuals descended from a historical Indian tribe.[35] They must also be identified as an Indian group by outsiders, such as academics, local newspapers and community organisations. Significantly, if there are any gaps over time in proof of the maintenance of political influence, social cohesion or external identification, federal recognition will be denied. So, for example, if there was a period of time when members of a native group hid their existence from authorities and avoided gathering as a group because they would be discriminated against, subjugated or even massacred by hostile forces, that failure to engage in organised activity would count against federal recognition.

The Office of Federal Acknowledgment (OFA) within the Department of Interior, which administers the recognition process, has been attacked by indigenous groups for inconsistent and politically influenced application of the criteria,[36] placing excessively heavy burdens of proof on petitioning tribes, privileging documentary over oral historical

---

32 See American Indian Policy Review Commission, 'Final Report: Nonrecognized Tribes', 1977, ch.11, at pp. 457 and 477–82.

33 Newton et al., supra note 13, at p. 139.

34 Ibid., at pp. 168–71.

35 25 C.F.R. § 83.7.

36 See, for example, Hon. Ann Denson Tucker, Chairwoman, Muscogee Nation of Florida, 'Prepared Statement', *Process of Federal Recognition of Indian Tribes*, Hearing Before the Committee on Indian Affairs, United States Senate, 110th Cong., 1st Sess. (19 September 2007), S. Hearing, 110–189, at p. 27, available online at http://www.indian.senate.gov/public/_files/September192007.pdf.

evidence and placing inordinate emphasis on 'blood quantum' to the exclusion of other indicators of social cohesion.[37] Indigenous groups have also complained that the process is far too slow and costly, requiring hundreds of thousands of dollars and decades to navigate. Since 1978, over 300 tribes have filed notices of intent and petitions for federal recognition. OFA has granted 17 of these petitions,[38] and denied 32 others.[39] Congressional hearings have resulted in pressure on OFA to expedite its review of petitions, and an increase in staffing and the number of cases resolved; but a backlog remains.[40] Finally, OFA has flatly precluded consideration of federal recognition for Native Hawaiians, claiming that Congress envisioned a different legal relationship with Native Hawaiians when it admitted Hawaii first to territorial status and later to statehood in 1959.[41]

The deficiencies of the OFA process might not be so troubling if there were other routes for native groups to take to federal recognition. In fact, in 1994, Congress affirmed the existence of two alternatives – federal legislation and court rulings.[42] However, the OFA process has come to eclipse other means of achieving federal recognition, members of Congress and federal judges viewing it as an opportunity or excuse to dodge controversy. Congress has recognised only two tribes since 1995, and in both cases the action is best described as restoration of federal recognition following earlier termination.[43] Courts have

---

37 Mark D. Myers, 'Federal Recognition of Indian Tribes in the United States' (2001) *Stanford Law and Policy Review*, 12, pp. 271–86, at pp. 280–84. Although the regulations were liberalised somewhat in 1994, the underlying concerns of non-federally recognised tribes remained. For broader discussion of the challenges confronting non-federally recognised tribes, see Mark E. Miller, *Forgotten Tribes: Unrecognized Indians and the Federal Acknowledgment Process*, Lincoln, NB: University of Nebraska Press, 2004.

38 The two most recently recognised tribes are the Shinnecock Indian Nation in New York (2010) and the Mashpee Wampanoag Tribe in Massachusetts (2007).

39 Office of Federal Acknowledgement, 'Status Summary of Acknowledgement Cases' (as of 29 April 2011), available at http://www.bia.gov/cs/groups/xofa/documents/text/idc013624.pdf.

40 Ibid.; and Government Accounting Office, 'Indian Issues: Timeliness of the Tribal Recognition Process Has Improved, but It Will Take Years to Clear the Existing Backlog of Petitions', GAO-05–347T (10 February 2005), available at http://www.gao.gov/products/GAO-05–347T.

41 25 C.F.R. § 83.3(a). See *Kahawaiolaa v Norton* (2002) 222 F Supp 2d 1213 (D Haw); affirmed (2004) 386 F 3d 1271 (9th Cir); (upholding the different treatment of Native Hawaiians in response to a challenge under the Fifth Amendment's equal protection guarantee). Legislation to achieve federal recognition of Native Hawaiians (usually referred to as 'the Akaka bill' after its sponsor, Hawaii Senator Daniel Akaka) has been introduced into the United States Congress over the past decade, but has not garnered sufficient support to be passed. See Gene Park, 'Akaka Bill Headed Nowhere', *Honolulu Star Advertiser* (15 December 2010); and Malia Zimmerman, 'Inouye Not Planning to "Jam Through" Akaka Bill Via an Appropriations Measure, Spokesperson Says', *Hawaii Reporter* (2 December 2010).

42 Pub. L. 103–454, 103rd Cong. (11 November 1994), § 103: 'Indian tribes presently may be recognized by Act of Congress; by the administrative procedures set forth in part 83 of the Code of Federal Regulations … ; or by a decision of a United States court … '.

43 See Senate Report 111–116, 111th Cong. (10 January 2010) (remarks of Senator Dorgan). Senator Dorgan points out that Congress has recognised, restored or otherwise changed the status of 28 tribal groups since the federal acknowledgment process was created in 1978.

often deferred to OFA's administrative process in cases requiring a determination of whether a group is an Indian tribe for purposes of interpreting a federal statute.[44]

One can compare the difficult hurdles facing any indigenous group seeking federal recognition in the United States today with the expansive definitions of 'indigenous' in some international documents, where formal legal status as indigenous is not required, and the failure of other international instruments to define the term at all. For example, the ILO Convention No. 169[45] defines indigenous or tribal peoples as including groups who are simply 'regarded' as indigenous because they descend from populations that inhabited the geographic region before colonisation or establishment of current state boundaries, and 'who irrespective of their legal status, retain some or all of their own social, economic, cultural and political institutions'. In contrast, the 2007 United Nations (UN) General Assembly Declaration on the Rights of Indigenous Peoples (UNDRIP)[46] does not supply a definition at all, and that omission was deliberate.[47] A background paper prepared by the UN Secretariat when UNDRIP was under development instead points to the unofficial but widely accepted definition, put forward by José Martinez Cobo, former Special Rapporteur on Indigenous Issues:

> Indigenous communities, peoples and nations are those which, having a historical continuity with pre-invasion and pre-colonial societies that developed on their territories, consider themselves distinct from other sectors of the societies now prevailing on those territories, or parts of them. They form at present non-dominant sectors of society and are determined to preserve, develop and transmit to future generations their ancestral territories, and their ethnic identity, as the basis of their continued existence as peoples, in accordance with their own cultural patterns, social institutions and legal system.
>
> This historical continuity may consist of the continuation, for an extended period reaching into the present of one or more of the following factors:
>
> (a) Occupation of ancestral lands, or at least of part of them;
> (b) Common ancestry with the original occupants of these lands;
> (c) Culture in general, or in specific manifestations (such as religion, living under a tribal system, membership of an Indigenous community, dress, means of livelihood, lifestyle, etc.);
> (d) Language (whether used as the only language, as mother-tongue, as the habitual means of communication at home or in the family, or as the main, preferred, habitual, general or normal language);
> (e) Residence on certain parts of the country, or in certain regions of the world;
> (f) Other relevant factors.[48]

---

44 See, for example, *Western Shoshone Business Council v Babbitt* (1993) 1 F 3d 1052 (10th Cir); *Golden Hill Paugussett Tribe v Weicker* (1994) 39 F 3d 51, 58059 (2d Cir).

45 ILO Convention No. 169 Concerning Indigenous and Tribal Peoples in Independent Countries, 1659 UNTS 383 (adopted on 27 June 1989, entered into force 5 September 1991).

46 UN, Declaration on the Rights of Indigenous Peoples (UNDRIP), GA Res. 61/295 (UN Doc. A/61/L.67 and Add.1) (adopted on 13 September 2007).

47 UN, Permanent Forum on Indigenous Issues, 'The Concept of Indigenous Peoples', Background paper, Workshop on Data Collection and Disaggregation for Indigenous Peoples (19–21 January 2004).

48 Ibid., at p. 2.

Both of these definitions extend beyond the limiting confines of allowable recognition under United States law. The ILO definition states only that the groups must be 'regarded' as indigenous, without prescribing who or what entity must regard them as such and over what period of time. Thus formal legal status as indigenous is not required. For example, in the United States, some non-federally recognised tribes are nonetheless recognised by the states in which they are located,[49] and would presumably qualify as 'indigenous' under the ILO Convention No. 169. Furthermore, the ILO definition does not require documented continuity over time in social and political organisation, only that the group retains '*some or all* of their own social, economic, cultural and political institutions' (emphasis added).

The definition advanced by former Special Rapporteur Cobo is even more encompassing, placing far more emphasis on self-identification than United States law. For example, under the Cobo definition it is sufficient that groups 'consider themselves' distinct from the dominant nation state and that they be 'determined' to sustain their territories and identities in accordance with their own values and priorities. 'Historical continuity' with pre-contact societies is required, but that continuity can be demonstrated through a variety of means, including 'common ancestry'. There are no rigorous requirements to document political influence, external identification and social cohesion on a continuous basis, as there are under the OFA regulations.

United States policymakers are aware of these disparities in the understanding of who counts as indigenous peoples and are concerned. In October 2010, the United States Department of State conducted consultations with native nations and non-governmental organisations regarding possible endorsement by the United States of UNDRIP. Those who attended were asked to respond to several questions, including one that asked: 'U.S. law treats federally recognised tribes differently from other indigenous groups in the United States. Is this practice consistent with UNDRIP?'[50]

In sum, if an international trade regime is established for the protection and dissemination of indigenous heritage, any provisions empowering indigenous groups to control transactions relating to that knowledge and heritage must contend with likely differences between the definition of 'tribes' under United States law and the broader international definitions of indigeneity. United States law does sometimes display flexibility when it comes to participation by indigenous groups in protection of historic sites and cultural heritage, setting aside requirements of federal recognition.[51] This flexibility does not extend to self-determination or law-making authority, but it does sometimes put indigenous groups in the position of negotiating over cultural heritage protections. A survey of United States law bearing on indigenous heritage follows, with an emphasis on the extent, if any, of indigenous groups' control over decisions regarding access to their knowledge and heritage. Laws addressing both tangible items and intangible knowledge will be

---

[49] See text at supra note 34.

[50] See Kirsten Matoy Carlson, 'United States Reviewing Its Policy on the UN Declaration on the Rights of Indigenous Peoples', special feature article in conjunction with the Fall 2010 issue of the *Federal Indian Lawyer*, available at http://fedbar.org/Image-Library/Sections-and-Divisions/Indian/US-Reviewing-Its-Policy-on-UN-Declaration-on-the-Rights-of-Indigenous-Peoples.aspx. On 16 December 2010, President Barack Obama announced his support for UNDRIP. The United States had been one of four countries voting against UNDRIP in 2007. Ibid.

[51] See infra section 2.3.

included. Laws focused exclusively on protecting the integrity of sacred or culturally significant sites are not included, as they do not implicate trade or other commercial transactions.

2.3 United States Law Directed at Protecting Indigenous Cultural Knowledge and Heritage

The United States has no comprehensive or consistent policy regarding protection of indigenous knowledge and cultural heritage. Federal law embodies episodic and partial interventions, with limited benefit for indigenous groups. The extent to which indigenous groups actually control access to their knowledge and heritage varies considerably from law to law.

2.3.1 Repatriation under the Native American Graves Protection and Repatriation Act (NAGPRA)

The Native American Graves Protection and Repatriation Act (NAGPRA)[52] is a federal statute that enables federally recognised tribes and Native Hawaiian organisations[53] to reclaim human remains, associated and unassociated funerary objects, sacred objects and objects of cultural patrimony from museums and other institutions that receive federal funds. The terms 'sacred objects' and 'objects of cultural patrimony' have very specific definitions, which are discussed in further detail in section 2.3.3, below.[54] Limitations on the obligation to repatriate arise in cases involving ongoing scientific study of major public benefit and where the institution can show a right of possession or competing claims.[55] Since it applies to human remains and tangible property only, NAGPRA protects only the objects associated with sacred ceremonies and stories, not the ceremonies or stories themselves. To take advantage of repatriation under NAGPRA, tribes or Native Hawaiian organisations must show that they are 'culturally affiliated' with the human remains or objects in question, which means they must demonstrate a relationship of 'shared group identity', through linguistic, folkloric, oral historic, geographic or biological evidence, among forms of proof.[56] The burden of proof is on the claiming tribes or organisations, with the standard being 'a preponderance of the evidence'. Significantly, although folkloric and oral historic evidence are treated as probative, the relative weight to be assigned to different forms of evidence is not specified. Therefore, indigenous perspectives are admitted as legitimate for purposes of demonstrating 'cultural affiliation', but they

---

[52] The Native American Graves Protection and Repatriation Act of 1990 (NAGPRA), 25 U.S.C. §§ 3001–3013, 18 U.S.C. § 1170.

[53] 'Native Hawaiian organizations' are defined as organisations that serve and represent the interests of Native Hawaiians, provide services to Native Hawaiians, and have expertise in Native Hawaiian affairs; NAGPRA, 25 U.S.C. § 3001(11).

[54] 'Sacred objects' are objects in current use by ceremonial practitioners. 'Objects of cultural patrimony' are those 'having ongoing historical, traditional, or cultural importance central to the Native American group or culture itself', and therefore considered inalienable by any member of the group or culture.

[55] Newton et al., supra note 13, at pp. 1239–40.

[56] NAGPRA, 25 U.S.C. §§ 3001(2) and 3005(a)(4).

are not dispositive. And at least in the first instance, NAGPRA hands the task of evaluating the various forms of evidence to the museums and other holding institutions themselves. In practice, many museums and universities have resisted claims for repatriation of very old human remains and objects, arguing that cultural affiliation cannot be demonstrated over so long a span of time.[57] NAGPRA does allow for lawsuits to enforce repatriation rights; but courts have not been particularly receptive to repatriation claims for very old human remains, one federal court stating that 9,000-year-old human remains could not even be properly labelled 'Native American'.[58]

NAGPRA directs museums and other institutions to consult with tribes and Native Hawaiian organisations regarding the cultural affiliation of their Native American holdings and to file inventories of those holdings, noting cultural affiliation where appropriate.[59] Where the institution does not find cultural affiliation with a federally recognised tribe or Native Hawaiian organisation, the human remains or objects are to be designated 'culturally unidentifiable'.[60] Although NAGPRA does not specify what is to be done with such items, it established a process for determining their proper disposition. In May 2010, the Secretary of the Interior issued rules requiring the repatriation of culturally unidentifiable human remains according to prescribed priorities, and encouraging, though not requiring, repatriation of the associated funerary objects.[61] First in priority is the tribe or Native Hawaiian organisation 'from whose tribal land, at the time of the excavation or removal, the human remains were removed'. Next in priority is any tribe 'recognized as aboriginal to the area from which the human remains were removed'.[62] In the absence of a claim from a tribe or organisation with the top priorities, the institution is permitted, but not required, to transfer control to another federally recognised tribe or, with a recommendation from the Secretary of the Interior, to transfer them to a non-federally recognised tribe, or to reinter them.

With promulgation of the regulations on culturally unidentifiable human remains, the degree of indigenous control over tangible cultural heritage has increased greatly under NAGPRA. Indeed, the balance of power between museums and indigenous groups has undergone a tectonic shift; and the museums are likely to challenge the regulations in court as exceeding the scope of allowable administrative action under NAGPRA.[63] Assuming the regulations stand, the extent of indigenous control can be summarised as follows:

---

[57] For the resistance of anthropologists to NAGPRA, see Allison M. Dussias, 'Kennewick Man, Kinship, and the "Dying Race": The Ninth Cicuit's Assimilationist Assault on the Native American Graves Protection and Reparation Act' (2005) *Nebraska Law Review,* 84, pp. 55–161, at pp. 107–17; and Nina Swidler et al. (eds), *Native Americans and Archaelologists: Stepping Stones to Common Ground*, Walnut Creek, CA: AltaMira Press, 1997.

[58] See, for example, *Bonnichsen v United States* (2004) 367 F 3d 864 (9th Cir).

[59] NAGPRA, 25 U.S.C. § 3003.

[60] NAGPRA, 25 U.S.C. § 3006(c)(5).

[61] NAGPRA Final Rule of 2010, 43 C.F.R. § 10.11.

[62] Aboriginal occupation may be recognised by a final judgment of the Indian Claims Commission or the United States Court of Claims, or a treaty, Act of Congress, or Executive Order.

[63] See Letter from Ford W. Bell, President, American Association of Museums, to Sherry Hutt, Manager, National NAGPRA Program, 13 May 2010 (stating that the regulations '[exceed] the regulatory authority granted to the Department of the Interior in the original NAGPRA law'), available at http://www.friendsofpast.org/nagpra/2010NAGPRA/AAM.pdf.

- Federally recognised tribes and Native Hawaiian organisations can insist upon repatriation of all human remains found within their tribal and ancestral territories, unless those items are 'culturally affiliated' with (and must be repatriated to) another federally recognised tribe.
- Federally recognised tribes and Native Hawaiian organisations are not entitled to repatriation of associated or unassociated funerary objects, sacred objects or objects of cultural patrimony unless they can prove 'cultural affiliation', although return of associated funerary objects is encouraged to the tribe from whose ancestral territory they were removed.
- Non-federally recognised tribes may be the recipients of Native American human remains, but only if the museum holding them agrees that there is no federally recognised tribe that wants them, and the Secretary of the Interior so recommends.

This summary demonstrates that NAGPRA has many positive features. It does empower federally recognised indigenous tribes in their repatriation claims directed at federally supported museums and other non-indigenous holders of cultural heritage; and it establishes a participatory process for determining the tribes' entitlement to repatriation. Moreover, NAGPRA goes beyond the standard federal Indian law definition of 'federal recognition' by treating Native Hawaiian organisations the same as federally recognised tribes for purposes of repatriation. But it interposes a requirement of 'cultural affiliation' for repatriation of every type of cultural object other than human remains; and at least initially, museums get to determine whether that requirement has been satisfied, using criteria of relevant evidence and a standard of proof that put indigenous groups at a distinct disadvantage. Furthermore, non-federally recognised indigenous groups, other than Native Hawaiians, have no entitlements to repatriation under NAGPRA, although they may receive human remains under very limited conditions.

An important final caveat is that none of NAGPRA's repatriation requirements applies to museums and other institutions that receive no federal funds. Thus private collectors and museums operated entirely on private or state funds are under no obligations at all under federal law to return human remains or cultural objects.

2.3.2 Protection against excavation and removal of cultural resources under NAGPRA and the Archeological Resources Protection Act (ARPA)

Federal law also protects against removal of Native American human remains and cultural items that are located on or embedded within federal lands and tribal lands. Under the earliest of these laws, the Archeological Resources Protection Act (ARPA),[64] anyone seeking to excavate or remove archaeological resources (defined as 'any material remains of past human life or activities which are of archaeological interest') from federal or Indian lands must secure a permit. If the excavation is from Indian lands, the tribe with jurisdiction over that land and the Indian landowner must consent.[65] The term 'Indian lands' is limited to lands held in trust by the United States for the benefit of tribes or individual Indians,[66] so ARPA's requirements do not apply if the excavation takes place on

---

[64] Archeological Resources Protection Act of 1979 (ARPA), 16 U.S.C. § 470aa–470mm.

[65] ARPA, 16 U.S.C. § 470cc(g)(2); and 43 C.F.R. § 7.8(a)(5).

[66] ARPA, 16 U.S.C. § 470bb(4).

fee (private property) land, either Indian or non-Indian, within the boundaries of a reservation. Thus, ARPA authorises indigenous control over excavation only if the excavation occurs on Indian trust lands. Yet tribal and individual Indian trust lands represent only a small fraction of the ancestral territory of indigenous peoples in the United States.[67] Hence, ARPA's reach is quite limited.

In addition to dealing with repatriation, NAGPRA establishes rules for excavation and removal of Native American human remains and cultural items that are still in the ground.[68] Like ARPA, NAGPRA applies only to federal and tribal lands. Also like ARPA, NAGPRA insists upon tribal consent if the excavation is slated for tribal lands. But NAGPRA affords indigenous peoples far more control over the human remains and cultural items excavated or removed from the designated lands. First, NAGPRA has a much more capacious definition of 'tribal lands', including all lands within any reservation boundary, whether that land is owned by Indians or non-Indians, in trust or in fee. The definition also encompasses non-reservation lands set aside for Native Hawaiians.[69] Second, NAGPRA sets out requirements for consultation with the appropriate[70] Indian tribes or Native Hawaiian organisations before excavation can take place, including consultation with traditional religious leaders.[71] That consultation must conclude with a 'written plan of action' that addresses, among other things, which tribe or Native Hawaiian organisation has the right to custody of any human remains or cultural items that might be removed. Custody of human remains and associated funerary objects must go to lineal descendants, if they are known. For human remains and associated funerary objects where there are no known lineal descendants, and for all unassociated funerary objects, sacred objects and objects of cultural patrimony,[72] custody must go to the tribe or Native Hawaiian organisation with the closest cultural affiliation or with ancestral ties to the land.

NAGPRA also provides protection against inadvertent discoveries of Native American human remains or cultural objects on federal or tribal lands.[73] If such items are discovered in the course of construction, mining or other activity, the activity must cease, the discovered items must be protected and the appropriate federal land manager or tribe must be notified. At that point, the tribal consultation process must go forward as if the excavation had been intentional.

Taken together the two federal statutes, ARPA and NAGPRA, grant considerable control to federally recognised tribes and Native Hawaiians over excavation and removal of indigenous human remains and cultural objects, so long as those items are located on federal or tribal lands. Non-federally recognised tribes have no standing under these laws,

---

67 See discussion at supra note 23. Even within reservations set aside for tribal occupancy, federal policies of allotment forced tribal trust lands into individual ownership as private property, and produced a large-scale transfer of property from Indians to non-Indians. See generally Judith V. Royster, 'The Legacy of Allotment' (1995) *Arizona State Law Journal*, 27, pp. 1–78.

68 NAGPRA, 25 U.S.C. §§ 3002; 43 C.F.R. § 10.5.

69 NAGPRA, 25 U.S.C. § 3001(15).

70 Regulations elaborate on the word 'appropriate', specifying notice to Indian tribes likely to be culturally affiliated with any human remains or cultural items that may be excavated and any tribe whose ancestral territory is involved in the planned excavation; 43 C.F.R. § 10.3(c).

71 43 C.F.R. § 10.5(b)(3).

72 For definitions of these terms, see supra note 54.

73 NAGPRA, 25 U.S.C. § 3002(d).

however. Furthermore, private land – meaning most of the territory of the United States – is outside the scope of their protections. Some states, such as California, have adopted laws that empower indigenous people, including non-federally recognised groups, to monitor construction activities on private land and to direct the respectful reburial or other appropriate treatment of indigenous human remains and associated objects when they are found.[74] That is not, however, a uniform practice across the United States.

2.3.3 Protection against trafficking in Native American cultural heritage under NAGPRA

Another source of protection for Native American cultural heritage is the provision in NAGPRA establishing criminal penalties for selling, purchasing, using for profit or transporting for sale or profit Native American human remains and cultural items in violation of the statute.[75] Unlike other parts of the law, this section is not limited to institutions receiving federal funds or to tribal and federal lands. It applies to anyone who knowingly traffics in Native American human remains or objects without a proper right of possession. A right of possession will most often be lacking in cases of 'objects of cultural patrimony', as defined under NAGPRA to mean items central to the culture, that the tribe views as inalienable by any individual member of the tribe.[76] Thus, for example, if a dealer purchases a Zuni war god or Navajo medicine bundles from an individual tribal member, the criminal penalties could be invoked.[77] As with other parts of NAGPRA, this protection is limited to tangible objects and protects only federally recognised tribes and Native Hawaiian organisations. Furthermore, the trafficking must be 'knowing', which means that defendants will not be convicted unless they have some notice or underlying knowledge about the cultural items involved. Thus, professional dealers or experts in the field are most likely to be targeted for prosecution.[78]

2.3.4 Protection for Indian arts and crafts

In 1935, Congress established the Indian Arts and Crafts Board to ensure the authenticity and expand the market for Indian-made goods.[79] The Board was authorised to create 'trademarks of genuineness and quality for Indian products' that could be registered with the United States Patent and Trademark Office, free of charge.[80] Civil and criminal penalties were established for counterfeiting the Board's marks and for misrepresenting works of art as created by Indian artists.[81] Although the Act's clearest application has been to tangible, artistic production, at least one commentator has suggested that its protection

---

74 See, for example, Cal. Pub. Resources Code § 5097.98.

75 18 U.S.C. § 1170.

76 See supra note 54.

77 See, for example, *United States v Tidwell* (1999) 191 F 3d 976 (9th Cir); and *United States v Corrow* (1997) 119 F 3d 796 (10th Cir).

78 Ibid. (upholding the criminal provisions against contentions that they are unconstitutionally vague).

79 Arts and Crafts Act, 25 U.S.C. § 305. For the history of the Act, see Leonard D. DuBoff, '500 Years After Columbus: Protecting Native American Culture' (1992) *Cardozo Arts & Entertainment Law Review*, 11, pp. 43–58, at pp. 56–7.

80 Arts and Crafts Act, 25 U.S.C. § 305a.

81 18 U.S.C. §§ 1158 and 1159.

for 'Indian products' could extend as well to traditional seeds, cultural ideas and expressions, and property other than just the usual works of art and crafts.[82]

Although the Indian Arts and Crafts Act promised protection for indigenous artists against counterfeiters and fake Indian goods, it was barely enforced. Over its first 55 years, not a single prosecution was brought,[83] despite evidence that imported imitations of Indian arts and crafts were siphoning off as much as 20 per cent of the market for genuine handicrafts produced domestically.[84] Congress amended the law in 1990, expanding the Board's authority to assist tribes and individual Indian artists in securing registration of their trade marks, giving tribes the power to determine who may be considered 'Indian' for purposes of using the Board's certification marks and increasing penalties for violating the Act. Since that time, the Board has become more active, both in enforcing the law and in mounting public information campaigns directed at consumers, sellers of goods and native artists themselves.[85]

The Indian Arts and Crafts Act is a truth-in-labelling law, not a means of controlling the appropriation of indigenous knowledge and cultural heritage. Any seller that avoids misstatements of authenticity is safely outside the grasp of the law. Nonetheless, enforcement efforts, public outreach and greater public awareness of genuineness and fraud in the marketing of 'Indian' art can work to the benefit of indigenous artisans. The Chair of the Indian Arts and Crafts Board observed in 2000:

> The [Board's] own review of promotional materials distributed by Indian arts and crafts markets, festivals, fairs, juried competitions, and pow wows indicates that a growing number of these marketing events require official tribal enrollment documentation or Indian artisan certification from participants that are selling their work as Indian or as the product of a particular Indian tribe. The number of events specifying Indian Arts and Crafts Act compliance in their entry requirements continues to grow. Thus, these IACB outreach efforts are helping the market to become self-policing.[86]

---

82 See Richard A. Guest, 'Intellectual Property Rights and Native American Tribes' (1996) *American Indian Law Review*, 20, pp. 111–39, at p. 136. For a contrasting view, see Nancy Kremers, 'Speaking with a Forked Tongue in the Global Debate on Traditional Knowledge and Genetic Resources: Are U.S. Intellectual Property Law and Policy Really Aimed at Meaningful Protection for Native American Cultures?' (2004) *Fordham Intellectual Property, Media, & Entertainment Law Journal*, 15, pp. 1–146, at p. 95 (stating that the Indian Arts and Crafts Act 'does not address TKGRF material that is neither art nor craft').

83 DuBoff, supra note 79, at p. 57.

84 H.R. Rep. No. 101–400, 101st Cong., pt. 2, p. 5 (1990).

85 Statement of Faith Roessel, Chairperson of the Indian Arts and Crafts Board, Before the Senate Committee on Indian Affairs, Oversight Hearing on Indian Arts and Crafts (17 May 2000), available at http://www.doi.gov/iacb/pdf/iacbtestimony. See Roberto Iraola, 'The Civil and Criminal Penalty Provisions of the Indian Arts and Crafts Act of 1990' (2005) *Cumberland Law Review*, 36, pp. 293–319; *Native Am. Arts, Inc., v Waldron, Corp.* (2005) 399 F 3d 871 (7th Cir); (rejecting a challenge to enforcement of the Act on First Amendment grounds).

86 Statement of Faith Roessel, supra note 85, at p. 3.

Nonetheless, the flood of fake Indian goods seems, if anything, to have grown in strength.[87] In one notorious case, a non-indigenous entrepreneur began manufacturing fake Indian jewellery in a town in the Philippines that he arranged to get renamed 'Zuni'. His aim was to label the goods 'Made in Zuni', leading buyers to believe they came from Zuni Pueblo.[88]

At the time of the 1990 amendments to the Indian Arts and Crafts Act, the provision for federal assistance to tribes in registering trade marks was considered one of the Act's most promising features. Under the terms of the Act, the Board has the power to create trade marks for Indian products, either in the name of the Board itself, or for individual Indians or Indian tribes or Indian arts and crafts organisations.[89] The Board can also establish standards and regulations for use of government-owned trade marks in the Indian arts and crafts area, including setting licensing fees for trade mark use.[90] It can also register these government-owned trade marks with the United States Patent and Trademark Office, free of charge, and, since the 1990 amendments, assign them and their associated goodwill to individual Indians or Indian tribes, also free of charge.[91] This free trade mark programme for qualifying Indians has never been implemented, however,[92] because it runs into legal obstacles under the general federal trade mark law, the Lanham Act.[93] As one commentator has noted:

> Ironically, only the Board's own certification mark meets the statutory requirements [under the Lanham Act]. Today, [only] an Indian producer who has independently paid for and registered its own trademark can get permission to use the Board's mark in conjunction with the producer's own mark, thus certifying that the producer's goods meet the Board's standards.[94]

There is thus no way for qualifying Indian individuals and entities to obtain free trade marks of their own and use them independent of the United States government's name, standards-setting and control. Because of the Lanham Act, the Indian Arts and Crafts Board can establish its own certification mark, incorporating its own standards for authenticity, but not a mark that references a particular tribe or artist. A Navajo artist, for

---

87 See William J. Hapiuk, 'Of Kitsch and Kachinas: A Critical Analysis of the Indian Arts and Crafts Act of 1990' (2001) *Stanford Law Review*, 53, pp. 1009–75, at pp. 1042–3. For an assessment of the Act and its actual operation and impact, see Kremers, supra note 82. In 2010, Congress passed amendments to the Indian Arts and Crafts Act designed to strengthen enforcement efforts. Act of 20 July 2010, Pub. L. 111–211, Title I.

88 James Brooke, 'Sales of Indian Crafts Rise and So Do Fakes', *New York Times* (2 August 1997), p. A6.

89 Indian Arts and Crafts Act, 25 U.S.C. § 305a(g)(1).

90 Indian Arts and Crafts Act, 25 U.S.C. § 305a(g)(2).

91 Indian Arts and Crafts Act, 25 U.S.C. § 305a(g)(3).

92 Kremers, supra note 82, at p. 76.

93 Ibid. Under established trade mark law, an applicant for registration of a trade mark must itself use that mark in commerce or in good faith intend to so use it. Thus, if the United States attempts to register a trade mark for an Indian tribe or individual Indian, the mark is considered void. In 2000, the chair of the Indian Arts and Crafts Board testified before Congress, advocating a change in the law to eliminate this obstacle. Statement of Faith Roessel, supra note 85. The change was not made.

94 Kremers, supra note 82, at p. 76.

example, can use the Board's United States government mark for general affirmation that the work is Indian-made; but that Navajo artist cannot receive a federally created trade mark specifically identifying the work as authentically Navajo.

The most controversial feature of the Indian Arts and Crafts Act has been its definition of 'Indian' for the purpose of determining who may market their work with an 'Indian' label. According to the regulations promulgated by the Indian Arts and Crafts Board, an 'Indian product' is 'any art or craft product made by an Indian', either in a traditional or a non-traditional medium or style.[95] Under the statute, an 'Indian' is either 'a member of an Indian tribe' (either federally recognised or state recognised) or someone who 'is certified as an Indian artisan by an Indian tribe'.[96] Only the governing body of a federally recognised or state-recognised tribe can provide the necessary certification that a non-member is 'of Indian lineage of one or more members of such Tribe'.[97] Some states, notably Alaska, have created their own laws and programmes to certify the authenticity of native handicrafts, using criteria different from the Indian Arts and Crafts Act. For example, eligibility to use the 'Silver Hand' mark signifying an authentic Native Alaskan handicraft is reserved for individuals who reside in Alaska and have at least one-quarter Eskimo, Aleut or Indian ancestry, documented by a Bureau of Indian Affairs certificate or certification by a tribe or Alaska Native Corporation.[98]

By stressing tribal membership and giving control over certification to tribal governments, the Indian Arts and Crafts Act excludes some indigenous individuals who do not qualify for tribal membership, as well as indigenous groups lacking federal or state recognition. These exclusions, and the privileged role of tribes, have engendered controversy both within and outside Indian country. Some have argued that the classification is racially discriminatory and that it improperly curtails the liberty and market participation of individuals with legitimate Indian identities.[99] An alternative view is that the Act avoids racial distinctions and instead tells 'those who find it advantageous to sell their products by representing that the products are made by an "Indian" [that they] must look to sovereign tribes rather than the federal government for validation of that representation'.[100]

2.3.5 The United States Patent and Trademark Office database of Native American Tribal Insignia

Since 2000, the United States Patent and Trademark Office has maintained a database of Native American Tribal Insignia, defined as 'the flag or coat of arms or other emblem or device of any federally or state-recognised Native American tribe, as adopted by tribal

---

[95] Regulations Implementing Indian Arts and Crafts Act of 1990, 25 C.F.R. § 309.2(d).

[96] Indian Arts and Crafts Act, 25 U.S.C. § 305e(d)(1).

[97] Regulations Implementing Indian Arts and Crafts Act of 1990, 25 C.F.R. § 309.25(a).

[98] Kremers, supra note 82, at p. 83. For a detailed account of Alaska's 'Silver Hand' programme, see Hollowell, supra note 1.

[99] For a critique of these exclusions, see Gail K. Sheffield, *The Arbitrary Indian: The Indian Arts & Crafts Act of 1990*, Norman, OK: University of Oklahoma Press, 1997; and Hapiuk, supra note 87. For a contrasting view, see John P. LaVelle, 'The General Allotment Act "Eligibility" Hoax' (1999) *Wicazo Sa Review*, 14, pp. 251–302, at pp. 274–5. Artists who do not receive such certification may describe themselves as being of indigenous or tribal descent, so long as they do not describe their products as Indian-made; 25 C.F.R. § 309.24(b)(2).

[100] Newton et al., supra note 13, at p. 1266.

resolution and notified to the US Patent and Trademark Office'.[101] Federal trade mark examiners use the database as a reference tool, enabling them to deny trade mark applications that falsely suggest a connection with a Native American tribe that has its official insignia on file.[102] There is reason to suspect that the database was inspired by a desire to demonstrate pro forma compliance with international trade mark treaty obligations, rather than to provide robust protection for traditional indigenous knowledge.[103] As of late 2010, only 25 official tribal insignia are included on the tribal database. This low rate of tribal usage should not be surprising, as the database is more useful to trade mark examiners than to the tribes themselves. A more useful protection of insignias would require tribes to also register them as trade marks, which is a costly process.[104]

To the extent the database of Native American Tribal Insignia protects indigenous heritage, it does so by empowering federally recognised and state-recognised tribes to request that they be listed in the database. Significantly, the indigenous groups authorised to participate in this database include some, but far from all, federally recognised tribes. State recognition is most common for non-federally recognised tribes on the eastern seaboard of the United States, where the original 13 colonies often made their own treaties with native groups. As one moves further west, state recognition is far less common.

2.4 General United States Intellectual Property Law and Its Application to Indigenous Knowledge and Cultural Heritage

It is hardly news that United States intellectual property law, like most western intellectual property law, makes for a poor fit with traditional indigenous cultural expressions and knowledge.[105] Although the variety of indigenous groups, cultures and knowledge is great, clashes with intellectual property law generally fall into two broad categories.

First, as noted at the outset of this chapter, many indigenous groups resist commercialisation, seeking to keep their traditional knowledge and heritage secret, restricted to internal use or under tight, exclusive and perpetual control. By contrast, intellectual property law provides protection for limited periods of time only, so that knowledge will eventually enter into broader use and spark innovation and creativity.

Second, where indigenous groups deem trade or wider access as appropriate, those groups want to be the ones who benefit from their traditional knowledge and cultural heritage. Yet intellectual property law resists protecting such knowledge because it does not view protection as consistent with the primary rationale for creation of intellectual property rights – reward for individual creativity and invention. If that rationale is not satisfied, western property law prefers that information be treated as part of the public

---

[101] J. Thomas McCarthy, *McCarthy on Trademarks and Unfair Competition*, 4th edn, Minneapolis: Thompson West, 2002, s. 25: 67.1, at pp. 25–152–25–153 quoting United States Patent and Trademark Office, 'Report on the Official Insignia of Native American Tribes' (30 September 1999), at p. 24.

[102] Kremers, supra note 82, at p. 87.

[103] Ibid., at pp. 87–91.

[104] Ibid., at pp. 92–3.

[105] For a general discussion of this problem, see Jill K. Kelley, 'Owning the Sun: Can Native Culture be Protected Through Current Intellectual Property Law?' (2007) *Journal of High Technology Law*, 7, pp. 180–202.

domain. Since much traditional knowledge is developed collectively over time rather than advanced as individual creation, western intellectual property law deems it unnecessary to confer property rights.[106]

Specific intellectual property regimes place other obstacles in the way of indigenous groups benefiting from their traditional knowledge. For example, copyright law requires that the knowledge be put into a fixed form that traditional knowledge often lacks, because traditional knowledge is typically oral rather than written.[107] Under patent law, commercial control of traditional knowledge may be denied to indigenous groups because they cannot satisfy requirements that the inventions be 'novel' (that is, not already known by others) or recently developed.[108]

Current trade mark law does allow tribes to register their names, albeit only in connection with the goods and services they sell or contemplate selling.[109] When that is done, others can be prevented from making misleading representations about the nature and source of their products. In addition, the database of Native American Tribal Insignias, discussed above, does afford some protection against third parties who wish to exploit those insignias.[110] However, trade mark law has been inadequate to the task of protecting against disparaging and offensive use of Native American images and symbols as mascots. The Lanham Act states that a mark must be refused registration if it 'consists of or comprises immoral, deceptive, or scandalous matter; or matter which may disparage or falsely suggest a connection with persons, living or dead, institutions, beliefs, or national symbols, or bring them into contempt, or disrepute…'.[111] Yet Native American groups have encountered numerous hurdles in their attempt to invalidate marks they consider racist and degrading, such as the names and logos for the Cleveland Indians baseball team and the Washington Redskins football team.[112]

---

[106] See Brigitte Vézina, 'Are They In or Are They Out? Traditional Cultural Expressions and the Public Domain: Implications for Trade', in this volume. Consistent with this conception of intellectual property rights, the United States has resisted international law efforts to require disclosure of the sources of genetic materials and plant-based products obtained from indigenous peoples, as well as disclosure of any informed consent and benefit-sharing. See United States responses to the International Association for the Protection of Intellectual Property (AIPPI) in July 2006 and April 2010 to its Questionnaire on the Requirement of Indicating the Source and/or Country of Origin of Genetic Resources and Traditional Knowledge in Patent Applications, available at https://www.aippi.org/download/commitees/166/QS166usa06.pdf and https://www.aippi.org/download/commitees/94/QS94usa.pdf.

[107] See Riley, supra note 3, at pp. 79–81; Kremers, supra note 82, at pp. 23–6.

[108] See 35 U.S.C. §§ 102, 103; Paul Kuruk, 'Goading a Reluctant Dinosaur: Mutual Recognition Agreements as a Policy Response to the Misappropriation of Foreign Traditional Knowledge in the United States' (2007) *Pepperdine Law Review*, 34, pp. 629–713, at pp. 652–4.

[109] See Guest, supra note 82, at p. 129. When the Mohegan Tribe tried to assert control over the use of its name by another group, a state court turned it down. *The Mohegan Tribe of Indians of Connecticut v The Mohegan Tribe and Nation, Inc.* (2001) 769 A.2d 34, (Conn).

[110] See supra section 2.3.5.

[111] 15 U.S.C. §1052(a).

[112] Hurdles have included statutes of limitations and concerns that banning mascots may violate First Amendment protections for freedom of speech. See, for example, Mark S. Nagel and Daniel A. Rascher, 'Washington "Redskins" – Disparaging Term or Valuable Tradition? Legal and Economic

In sum, United States intellectual property law is insufficient to prevent the appropriation and commodification of indigenous culture.[113] Angela Riley offers the following illustrative example: '[I]f a sacred Indian dance or ceremony is secretly videotaped and mass-produced for sale on the Internet, there are no legal ramifications under copyright law because the work is thought to be in the public domain and therefore lacks those characteristics required for copyright protection.'[114] For a real-life example, one need only recall the 2004 Grammy Awards ceremony, when the group Outkast sampled Native American chants and appropriated their sacred symbols without consent or acknowledgment.[115]

Thus most legal scholars assume that United States intellectual property law would have to be modified substantially in order to provide protection for indigenous knowledge and cultural heritage.[116] Some have suggested ways in which existing intellectual property law could be better utilised to secure that protection. For example, indigenous groups might make more extensive use of certification and collective marks under trade mark law.[117] Nonetheless, the broad consensus is that a major transformation of established intellectual property law would be needed to accommodate indigenous heritage. Certainly that law does not afford special standing to indigenous groups – however defined – to claim intellectual property rights. At most, trade mark law allows them to prevent deceptive labelling of goods with tribal insignias.

Issues Concerning *Harjo v. Pro-Football, Inc.*' (2007) *Fordham Intellectual Property, Media, & Entertainment Law Journal*, 17, pp. 789–802.

113 See generally Keith Aoki, 'Weeds, Seeds & Deeds: Recent Skirmishes in the Seed Wars' (2003) *Cardozo Journal of International and Comparative Law*, 11, pp. 247–331; Susan Scafidi, 'Intellectual Property and Cultural Products' (2001) *Boston University Law Review*, 81, pp. 793–842; and Rebecca Tsosie, 'Reclaiming Native Stories: An Essay on Cultural Appropriation and Cultural Rights' (2002) *Arizona State Law Journal*, 34, pp. 299–358. In many European countries and Canada, creators of copyrighted works are understood to have 'moral rights' grounded in respect for their individual creative powers. These rights include rights to maintain the integrity of the work and to prevent wrongful attribution. While the recognition of moral rights might be useful for indigenous groups seeking to protect the dignity and identification of their knowledge and heritage, United States intellectual property law has not developed a comparable common law doctrine. The Visual Artists Rights Act of 1990, 17 U.S.C. § 106A, affords such protection only to paintings, drawings, prints, sculptures and still photographic images produced for exhibition, thereby excluding much of indigenous cultural heritage. Furthermore, a few states have enacted statutes premised on moral rights, but also mainly for visual artists. For Canada see Catherine Bell, 'Ownership and Trade of Aboriginal Cultural Heritage in Canada', in this volume. For the international level see Vézina, supra note 106.

114 Riley, supra note 3, at p. 80.

115 Ibid., at pp. 70–72.

116 See, for example, Angela R. Riley, 'Recovering Collectivity: Group Rights to Intellectual Property in Indigenous Communities' (2000) *Cardozo Arts & Entertainment Law Journal*, 18, pp. 175–225; Kelley, supra note 105; and Kremers, supra note 82.

117 See, for example, *Johnson v McIntosh*, supra note 17; and *United States v Kagama*, supra note 20; and Christoph B. Graber and Jessica C. Lai, 'Indigenous Cultural Heritage and Fairtrade – Voluntary Certification Standards in the Light of WIPO and WTO Law and Policymaking' (2011) *Prometheus*, 29 (3), pp. 287–308; and Rosemary J. Coombe with Joseph F. Turcotte, 'Indigenous Cultural Heritage in Development and Trade: Perspectives from the Dynamics of Cultural Heritage Law and Policy', in this volume.

Whether the United States could ever fashion an intellectual property law that accommodates indigenous knowledge and cultural heritage is uncertain. As one commentator has observed:

> Indigenous peoples do not view their heritage as property at all – that is something which has an owner and is used for the purpose of extracting economic benefits – but in terms of community and individual responsibility. Possessing a song, story, or medicinal knowledge carries with it certain responsibilities to show respect to and maintain a reciprocal relationship with the human beings, animals, plants and places which the song, story or medicine is connected. For indigenous peoples, heritage is a bundle of relationships rather than a bundle of economic rights.[118]

In other words, the mismatch between indigenous culture and United States intellectual property law may be too great to bridge, especially considering the large array of indigenous cultures. An alternative possibility is that indigenous peoples could develop their own, distinctive legal regimes to protect their knowledge and heritages, which is the subject of section 3 of this chapter.

3. NATIVE NATIONS' LEGAL PROTECTIONS FOR INDIGENOUS KNOWLEDGE AND CULTURAL HERITAGE

Compared with many other settler nations around the world, the United States acknowledges an unusual degree of self-governing authority in the indigenous groups it officially recognises as Indian tribes or nations. Federal Indian law supports the view that native nations retain inherent self-governing powers, especially as they apply to tribal members and internal affairs. Powers over outsiders are another matter, the Supreme Court having ruled that some of those inherent tribal powers have been lost, or 'divested'. At the same time, the Court has affirmed Congress's power both to curtail inherent tribal powers and to augment them with federally delegated power.

Native nations, meanwhile, have been utilising their powers to manage the pace of development of their economies, natural resources and cultures, forging agreements with states, counties, municipalities and federal authorities where needed to achieve more effective governance. The government structures that have been established to exercise these powers, including tribal constitutions, written laws, bureaucracies and court systems, are as much creatures of United States policy as they are indigenous creations. At various times the United States has promoted specific forms of tribal governance in order to advance assimilationist policy goals. Since the 1970s, however, native nations in the United States have increasingly found ways to adapt and institutionalise their governmental systems, making them better able to reflect indigenous ways of decision-making and community goals.[119]

---

[118] Thomas J. Krumenacher, 'Protection for Indigenous Peoples and Their Traditional Knowledge: Would a Registry System Reduce the Misappropriation of Traditional Knowledge?' (2004) *Marquette Intellectual Property Law Review*, 8, pp. 143–59, at pp. 150–51.

[119] See generally Eric D. Lemont (ed.), *American Indian Constitutional Reform and the Rebuilding of Native Nations,* Austin, TX: University of Texas Press, 2006; Duane Champagne,

As appropriation and misuse of their traditional knowledge and cultural heritage has become a subject of greater concern, native nations in the United States have sought ways to use their legal authority and justice systems to regain some measure of control. They have begun enacting laws and devising ways to enforce them. In that context, issues about the scope of their authority – such as where and over whom that authority may be exercised – have become more pressing. Where outsiders are involved, these issues have typically found their way into the United States legal system, usually to the detriment of native nations. Looking beyond jurisdictional doctrines, however, native nations have also considered other strategies, such as intergovernmental cooperation, that might achieve their objectives.

3.1 Native Nations' Authority under United States Law to Control Indigenous Knowledge and Cultural Heritage

Within reservations and other federally protected territories, native nations in the United States are recognised as exercising both inherent and federally delegated authority. Furthermore, unless Congress decrees otherwise, the power of states within those territories is substantially curtailed.[120] The federal government claims the power to restrict native nations' authority, however;[121] and it has done so, both through United States Supreme Court decisions and acts of Congress, with implications for tribes' ability to control their traditional knowledge and cultural heritage. Furthermore, the powers discussed below are limited to federally recognised tribes, excluding hundreds of groups that identify as indigenous.[122]

3.1.1 Inherent and delegated powers of native nations

Inherent tribal powers pre-date the formation of the United States, and emanate not from the federal government, but from indigenous sources, which may be understood as the Creator or the native polity. In recognising the distinctly indigenous origins of these powers, the United States Supreme Court has held that they are not subject to limitation under the United States Bill of Rights, which applies only to exercises of federal power.[123] These inherent powers may extend to Indians or non-Indians, subject to limitations discussed in section 3.1.2. They may also extend to activities that occur outside tribal territory, depending on the extent of the native nation's connection to and interest in the activities in question.[124]

'American Indian Values and the Institutionalization of IRA Governments', in Jennie Joe (ed.), *American Indian Policy and Cultural Values: Conflict and Accommodation*, Los Angeles: UCLA American Indian Studies Center, 1997, pp. 25–34; Wilkinson, supra note 23; and Harvard Project, supra note 23, at pp. 17–36.

120 Newton et al., supra note 13, at pp. 499–513.

121 See, for example, *Johnson v McIntosh* (1823) 21 US 543; and *United States v Kagama* (1886) 118 US 375.

122 See supra section 2.2.

123 See *Talton v Mayes* (1896) 163 US 376 (holding that the Fifth Amendment requirement of indictment by a grand jury does not apply to a tribal criminal proceeding).

124 See Newton et al., supra note 13, at pp. 513–14.

The extent of inherent tribal power is evident in the conflict that arose in 1984 when certain members of a clan of the Chilkat Indian Village in Alaska sold an exquisitely beautiful set of four carved wooden posts and partition, known as a rain screen, to a non-native art dealer. The rain screen had been created around 1830 when a structure was built for houses of the Ganexteidi Clan, and the screen tells stories of the entire clan.[125] Because art dealers had been attempting to get their hands on the screen for many decades, the Chilkat Indian Village adopted an ordinance in 1976 that prohibited removal of 'artifacts, clan crests, or other traditional Indian art work owned or held by members of the Chilkat Indian Village [or kept within the Village's property] without first requesting and obtaining permission to do so from the Chilkat Indian Village Council'.[126]

Chilkat Indian Village sued the art dealer in federal court, claiming that removal of the screen violated federal as well as tribal law. While rejecting the federal law claims, federal courts found a basis for tribal authority in the fact that the non-native dealer had made the purchase agreement with clan members within tribal territory, and the dispute involved property of great communal or national interest to the Chilkat Indian Village. As a result, the federal courts upheld the authority of the tribal court to adjudicate the dispute under Chilkat law.[127] Eventually, the tribal court ordered return of the rain screen and imposed a judgment for damages on the art dealer. After analysing the motives of the clan members who purported to sell the screen, and determining that they had all accepted responsibility, expressed regret and embraced the need for the screen to return to the village, the tribal court declined to hold them liable for payment of damages.

Augmenting these inherent tribal powers, Congress may delegate powers to tribes. These delegations are permissible under the United States Constitution through the provision authorising Congress to regulate Indian commerce, a provision whose central function 'is to provide Congress with plenary power to legislate in the field of Indian Affairs'.[128] For example, in 1990 amendments to the Clean Air Act, Congress has authorised tribes to regulate reservation air quality in accordance with minimum federal standards. This delegated authority encompasses parts of reservations that might be viewed as outside tribal jurisdiction because those lands are owned by non-Indians as private property.[129] Another type of federal delegation can be seen in the federal statutory scheme for regulating sale and possession of alcohol in Indian country. Specifically, Congress has made it a federal offence for anyone, Indian or non-Indian, to engage in liquor trafficking in violation of tribal law. In effect, Congress has delegated to native nations the power to criminalise certain conduct.[130]

---

125 See *Chilkat Indian Village, IRA v Johnson* (1993) 20 Indian Law Report 6127 (Chilkat Tr Ct).

126 Quoted in *Chilkat Indian Village v Johnson* (1989) 870 F 2d 1469, at p. 1471 (9th Cir).

127 See *Chilkat Indian Village, IRA v Johnson,* supra note 125; and Kelsey Collier-Wise, 'Identity Theft: A Search for Legal Protections of Intangible Indigenous Cultural Property' (2010) *Great Plains Natural Resources Journal*, 13, pp. 85–101, at pp. 92–3.

128 *Cotton Petroleum Corp. v New Mexico* (1989) 490 US 163, at p. 192. See Newton et al., supra note 13, at pp. 246–8.

129 See *Ariz. Pub. Serv. Co. v EPA* (2000) 211 F 3d 1280 (DC Cir); and Newton et al., supra note 13, at pp. 239–40 and 792–3.

130 See *United States v Mazurie* (1975) 419 US 544; and Newton et al., supra note 13, at p. 891.

Although Congress has not created a comparable regulatory regime for indigenous knowledge and cultural heritage, one could view parts of NAGPRA as a type of federal delegation. Specifically, the provisions protecting against trafficking in objects of cultural patrimony leave it to the tribes to determine when individual tribal members lack the legal right to alienate certain property.[131]

3.1.2 Federal limitations on tribal authority

Although a comprehensive account of federal limitations on tribal authority is beyond the scope of this chapter, it is possible to identify the three limitations most relevant to native nations' control over their knowledge and cultural heritage:

1. Under the Indian Civil Rights Act of 1968,[132] inherent tribal authority is subjected to some, but not all, of the provisions of the United States Bill of Rights. Among the protections that are extended are the right of free expression and the right to due process.[133] The only remedy outside tribal court for violation of the Indian Civil Rights Act, however, is a federal writ of habeas corpus. Thus, rights extended under the Indian Civil Rights Act may be raised in federal court only to challenge a tribal criminal conviction or some other tribal proceeding that results in a curtailment of individual liberty.[134] For example, a tribal member convicted in tribal court for disclosure of tribal secrets might be able to challenge that conviction in a federal court, claiming that the tribal prosecution violated her freedom of speech. However, if the tribe merely imposed a civil monetary penalty for the disclosure, the tribal member's exclusive remedy would be in tribal court. Federally delegated tribal authority is fully subject to the provisions of the United States Bill of Rights.[135]
2. The United States Supreme Court has held that native nations lack inherent criminal jurisdiction over non-Indians.[136] According to the Court, the tribes were 'implicitly divested' of this jurisdiction when they were (forcibly) incorporated into the United States. Thus native nations may not prosecute non-Indians for misappropriation of their knowledge or cultural heritage.
3. The Supreme Court has also limited inherent tribal powers to regulate and adjudicate civil matters involving non-Indians that arise on non-Indian fee lands.[137] Exceptions arise for situations where the non-Indians have engaged in consensual relations with the tribe or a tribal member, and where tribal control is necessary to protect the health, welfare and political integrity of the tribe.[138] Thus, if the transaction litigated in the Chilkat Indian Village case, discussed in section 3.1.1, had occurred on non-Indian-owned fee land, the non-Indian dealer would have been subject to

---

131 See *United States v Corrow* (1997), supra note 77; see supra section 2.3.3.

132 25 U.S.C. §§ 1301–1303.

133 25 U.S.C. § 1302(1) and (8).

134 *Santa Clara Pueblo v Martinez* (1978) 436 US 49.

135 See Newton et al., supra note 13, at p. 238.

136 *Oliphant v Suquamish Indian Tribe* (1978) 435 US 191.

137 See, for example, *Montana v United States* (1981) 450 US 544 (limits on regulatory authority); and *Strate v A-1 Contractors* (1997) 520 US 438 (limits on adjudicative authority).

138 Newton et al., supra note 13, at pp. 229–37.

jurisdiction because of the contractual relationship with the tribal member sellers and likely also because of the centrality of the rain screen to the Village's culture and well-being.

A vivid illustration of the limits on native nations' authority over their cultural resources is the dispute that arose over the use of the name 'Crazy Horse' on an alcoholic product known as malt liquor. Crazy Horse, or Tasunke Witko, was a nineteenth-century Lakota warrior and leader who is legendary for his firm opposition to alcohol and for his refusal to surrender to the United States. The executor of the Crazy Horse estate brought suit in Rosebud Sioux Tribal Court against Hornell Brewing Company, producer of Crazy Horse Malt Liquor, on a variety of tribal and federal claims, including violation of Lakota law regarding the ownership of names. Within Lakota tradition, as for many indigenous peoples, names carry a special significance and essence. As one Indian law casebook has noted, 'even without the defamatory connection to a non-Indian alcoholic beverage, it would have been inappropriate to use the name of this great leader without the family's permission.'[139] The connection to alcohol made the matter worse, however, because it legitimised drinking for tribal youth. Congress had tried to ban the use of the Crazy Horse name on any 'distilled spirit, wine or malt beverage product' but a federal court struck down the law as a violation of free speech.[140]

The Rosebud Sioux tribal court initially dismissed the lawsuit for lack of jurisdiction, noting that the defendants were not located or otherwise doing business on the reservation, and did not actually sell the Crazy Horse Malt Liquor on the reservation, though they did sell other products there. The Rosebud Sioux Supreme Court reversed, reasoning that the label on the beer specifically targeted tribal territory when it referenced the Black Hills and Crazy Horse, and that the sale of other products established a sufficient connection with the reservation. Furthermore, it found that the defendant's failure to seek permission from the Crazy Horse estate and the extreme harm caused by use of the Crazy Horse name to endorse alcohol use by Lakota youth warranted civil authority over a non-Indian, even if the activity occurred off-reservation on fee land.[141] Refusing to proceed with the tribal court process, the brewing company filed suit in federal court, seeking an injunction against the tribal proceeding on the ground that the tribal court had no jurisdiction. A federal appellate court agreed, holding that the tribal court suit could not go forward because Hornell Brewing Company did not sell the Crazy Horse Malt Liquor on the reservation, and the sale of other products was insufficient to confer jurisdiction.[142] Thus, so long as a culturally significant name is misappropriated outside the tribal territory, a tribal court may have no power to halt the harmful activity.

Interestingly, that was not the end of the dispute. Despite this favourable ruling, the brewing company defendant (by now under the name of Stroh Brewing Company) chose

---

[139] Robert N. Clinton et al., *American Indian Law: Native Nations and the Federal System*, 5th edn, Newark, NJ: LexisNexis, 2007, at p. 1182.

[140] *Hornell Brewing Co. v Brady* (1993) 819 F Supp 1227 (EDNY).

[141] The proceedings in the Rosebud Sioux courts are described in Joseph William Singer, 'Publicity Rights and the Conflict of Laws: Tribal Court Jurisdiction in the Crazy Horse Case' (1996) *South Dakota Law Review*, 41, pp. 1–44.

[142] *Hornell Brewing Co. v Rosebud Sioux Tribal Court* (1998) 133 F 3d 1087 (8th Cir).

to settle with the Estate of Crazy Horse and the Rosebud Sioux Tribe.[143] The settlement agreement provided for 'a public apology and acknowledgment of the Estate's right to protect the name of Crazy Horse, and for delivery of culturally appropriate damages – seven race horses and thirty-two Pendleton blankets, braids of tobacco and sweet grass'.[144] According to a press release issued by the Estate, the settlement was 'a historic victory in the battle to protect the name of Crazy Horse and the cultural property of all tribes', because it recognises the important role of tribal customary law and 'sends a strong message that people cannot just take Indian Cultural Property and use it without permission'.[145] Given the voluntary nature of the settlement following a court victory for the brewing company, the message seems considerably weaker than the press release indicates.

In sum, even for federally recognised tribes, federal law places considerable constraints on the protection of cultural knowledge and heritage. It is impossible to mandate tribal protections if external courts will not recognise and enforce them under many circumstances. Congress has the power to remove or lift these constraints either by delegating power to the tribes or by acknowledging (and thereby reactivating) inherent powers that the Supreme Court has found 'implicitly divested'.[146] But in the absence of support from Congress, native nations must contend with limitations embodied in the Indian Civil Rights Act, as well as federal courts' refusal to acknowledge their jurisdiction over those who misappropriate their cultural property on and off the reservation.

3.2 Native Nations' Legal Initiatives to Control Cultural Knowledge and Heritage

In this volume, Rebecca Tsosie proposes that tribal laws are effective means of protecting indigenous cultural heritage, notwithstanding the constraints that federal law may impose.[147] Like Tsosie, Riley has argued forcefully for the development of tribal laws that protect cultural heritage, notwithstanding the constraints that federal law may impose.[148] Such laws, she contends, will reinforce tribal sovereignty, draw attention to alternative indigenous values and the harms caused by misappropriation, and influence results in the dominant legal system. Furthermore, top-down attempts at protection, relying on western, market-based assumptions, cannot capture the value of cultural resources within indigenous societies grounded in gift-giving and exchange rather than markets.[149] As Riley

---

143 See Sarah La Voi, 'Cultural Heritage Tug of War: Balancing Preservation Interests and Commercial Rights' (2003) *Depaul Law Review*, 53, pp. 875–928, at p. 886.

144 Press Release, Estate of T'sunke Witko, 'One Brewing Company Settles Lawsuit with the Family of Crazy Horse and Rosebud Sioux Tribe', quoted in ibid.

145 Ibid.

146 See *United States v Lara* (2004) 541 US 193; Newton et al., supra note 13, at pp. 237–48. Congress's choice likely has implications for the applicability of the Bill of Rights and the operation of the double jeopardy clause.

147 See Rebecca Tsosie, 'International Trade in Indigenous Cultural Heritage: An Argument for Indigenous Governance of Cultural Property', in this volume.

148 See Riley, supra note 3.

149 See also Duane Champagne, 'Indigenous Self-Government, Cultural Heritage and International Trade: A Sociological Perspective', in this volume.

points out, '[t]hrough tribal law, indigenous governance of cultural property and traditional knowledge will correlate specifically to the works tribes seek to protect, allow for forms of punishment consistent with the community's values, and properly incentivize behavior that is good for the community at large.'[150]

Based on a 2002 survey of 193 publicly available tribal codes of native nations within the continental United States, Riley found 62 tribes with codes that address protection of cultural property in some way, including 27 that govern sacred sites and proper treatment of the dead. There were no laws seeking to protect intangible resources such as stories, dances or folklore; but a few focused on protecting plants, roots and other elements essential to traditional medicines or ceremonies.[151] Riley's expansive definition of cultural resource protection led her to include tribal laws promoting cultural activities, such as language revitalisation, as well as laws restricting or regulating access to cultural knowledge and heritage. But it is evident that most of the laws in the latter category focus on protecting sacred or culturally significant sites (such as burial sites) and tangible objects, including rock paintings, tribal weapons and memorials to the dead.[152] This emphasis is not surprising, given the greater likelihood that tribal authority will be upheld when the object of regulation is located or found within the tribe's territory. Significantly, Riley discerns a movement toward creation of tribal cultural preservation departments, which may provide the platform for development of additional laws and protections.

Evidence of new directions for tribal cultural resources laws can be found in a recent study of tribal initiatives to control genetic material and indigenous knowledge.[153] The authors highlight a law passed in 2004 by the Little Traverse Bay Band of Odawa Indians, which prohibits the patenting of organisms – one of the first tribal laws ever to do so. Under this tribal law, 'no person may patent or claim any exclusive property interest in the makeup of any organism' within areas under tribal jurisdiction. The Preamble to the Act finds that 'the patenting of organisms threatens the Tribe's health, welfare and economic security' because it 'threatens the loss of biodiversity by limiting access to genetic variants through enforcement of proprietary rights and encouraging the spread of a single variant of an organism in place of other natural variations'.

Although United States law is not entirely receptive to tribal legal initiatives, native nations are forging ahead with measures to protect their knowledge and cultural heritages. As the Harvard Project on American Indian Economic Development observes, '... Native nations ... are investing in the restoration of language, the protection of objects of cultural patrimony, the revitalization of ceremonial cycles and Native arts, and the defense of indigenous values and cultural practices.'[154] Some are establishing tribal museums, projects that will likely heighten tribal interest in retaining and regaining control of tribal cultural knowledge and heritage.[155] The legal protections for tribal cultures can come in

---

150 See Riley, supra note 3, at p. 90.

151 Ibid., at pp. 100–101.

152 Ibid., at pp. 107–8.

153 Debra Harry and L'a Malia Kanehe, 'Asserting Tribal Sovereignty Over Cultural Property: Moving Towards Protection of Genetic Material and Indigenous Knowledge' (2006) *Seattle Journal for Social Justice*, 5, pp. 27–55, at p. 41.

154 Harvard Project, supra note 23, at p. 277.

155 Ibid., at pp. 293–4.

the form of codes or through tribal courts elaborating on existing customary law. For example, under Kiowa customary law, certain tipi designs might be given as a gift and handed down hereditarily; but the individual who accomplished the war deeds comprising much of the design retained control of the right to reproduce those deeds.[156] These kinds of requirements, distinct from western intellectual property rules, are the strongest arguments for developing tribal cultural resources laws. The challenge for native nations is to assert these requirements within the framework of federal Indian law and its constraints on tribal powers.

4. THE PROSPECTS FOR A PROCEDURAL SOLUTION THAT RESPECTS INDIGENOUS CONTROL

Graber has advocated studying a procedural approach to interfacing global law and local traditions. Under this approach, preferential treatment under international trade law would turn on a WTO Member State's establishment of procedures to distinguish traditional cultural expressions that can be traded from those that cannot. Further, those procedures would have to involve the appropriate indigenous community or communities in the decision-making. Finally, a special commission, including some indigenous members, would be established within the WTO to formally adopt the decision, after supplying notice to potential third-party claimants and resolving any disputes as to the community's ownership.[157]

As section 2 of this chapter explains, the United States has already instituted several ad hoc legal regimes – NAGPRA and the Indian Arts and Crafts Act – that recognise indigenous control over traditional cultural expressions. These federal laws do not identify the class of indigenous groups as broadly as the most widely used international definition would. Nonetheless, they empower many indigenous groups to determine important matters, such as whether cultural items qualify as 'objects of cultural patrimony' and whether persons of indigenous descent should be allowed to identify their artistic productions as 'Indian made'. In the case of NAGPRA, there is also a process for addressing conflicting claims to human remains and cultural items. First, museums must circulate findings of cultural affiliation through published inventories, giving third parties an opportunity to contest those findings.[158] Second, if there are multiple claims for repatriation and the museum 'cannot clearly determine which requesting party is the most appropriate claimant',[159] the museum may retain the item until the requesting parties reach an agreement about its disposition or the dispute is resolved. A federal agency, the

[156] Candace S. Greene and Thomas D. Drescher, 'The Tipi with Battle Pictures: The Kiowa Tradition of Intangible Property Rights' (1994) *The Trademark Reporter*, 84, pp. 418–33.

[157] See Graber, 'Institutionalization of Creativity', supra note 5.

[158] NAGPRA, 25 U.S.C. § 3003.

[159] NAGPRA, 25 U.S.C. § 3005(e).

NAGPRA Review Committee, has been established to facilitate the resolution of such disputes. Alternatively, the disputes may be taken to court.[160]

Beyond these ad hoc measures, there are broad doctrines of federal Indian law that respect the authority of federally recognised tribes to make their own laws protecting traditional knowledge and cultural heritage. This tribal lawmaking authority is subject to some significant limitations under federal law, as explained in section 3.1.2. Given these constraints, tribal law is far more effective in controlling activities of tribal members and other Indians; it is far more effective in dealing with tangible rather than intangible property; and it is far more effective in controlling activities that actually take place within tribal territory, especially on tribal or Indian-held land. Yet modern technology has made it feasible for indigenous knowledge and cultural expressions to be appropriated and widely circulated at a far distance from indigenous territory, leaving native nations at a considerable disadvantage in asserting control. Of course, even this more limited indigenous control is confined to federally recognised tribes, excluding numerous indigenous groups that might be considered entitled to control under some international procedural regime.

Congress enjoys broad power over Indian affairs. Federal laws singling out Indians for special treatment do not run afoul of constitutional bans on racial discrimination if those laws are directed at native nations with which the United States maintains government-to-government relations.[161] So Congress, if it wished, could enact laws broadening the power of federally recognised tribes[162] to control trade in indigenous knowledge regardless of who is seeking to appropriate it, regardless of whether the knowledge is in tangible or intangible form, and regardless of where the activities take place.

Models exist for such legislation. The example of federal environmental statutes, such as the Clean Air Act, has already been discussed.[163] Another interesting case in point is the Indian Child Welfare Act of 1978,[164] which Congress enacted to stem the high rates of placement of Indian children in non-Indian homes. One provision of the Act directs the transfer of involuntary child welfare proceedings involving Indian children from state court to tribal court, even though the parents and children are living outside tribal territory.[165] Tribal interests in the well-being and retention of Indian children have been sufficient to sustain the provision against claims that it exceeds the scope of congressional power.[166] Similarly, tribal interests in protecting knowledge that is integral to indigenous culture and heritage could adequately support federal legislation acknowledging tribal control over trade in such knowledge. Congress could frame its legislation either as an acknowledgment of inherent tribal power or as a delegation of federal power, the choice

---

160 NAGPRA, 25 U.S.C. §§ 3005(e) and 3006(c)(4). In federal courts and most state courts, interpleader procedures enable a stakeholder to deposit contested property with the court, and let the competing claimants litigate who is entitled to it.

161 See text at supra note 26.

162 Federal equal protection doctrine would make it more difficult for Congress to afford these same powers to non-federally recognised tribes, because the courts would likely find that the legislation discriminates on the basis of race or ethnicity.

163 See text at supra note 129.

164 25 U.S.C. § 1901–1963.

165 5 U.S.C. § 1911(b). The transfer may be refused if either parent objects, the tribe does not want to receive the case or there is 'good cause' not to transfer.

166 See Newton et al., supra note 13, at pp. 848–9.

having potential implications for the types of individual rights protections that might be triggered.[167] And if Congress were concerned about overreaching by native nations, it could set minimum standards for exercising control over knowledge and cultural heritage, as it creates minimum environmental quality standards under the Clean Air Act and other environmental measures.

Following these models from existing federal legislation would not solve the problem of the mismatch between United States and broader international definitions of 'indigenous peoples'. That issue would remain. Nonetheless, legislation of this type would go some distance toward fulfilling the conditions presented in Graber's proposal, namely that the United States establish procedures for authorising trade in traditional cultural expressions that involve the appropriate indigenous community or communities.

Whether Congress would choose to enact such legislation is another matter entirely. In 2003, a United States representative stated at a meeting of the World Intellectual Property Organization (WIPO) that the United States 'is not of the view that special intellectual property protection is needed for traditional knowledge'.[168] Of course, since that time, leadership in the United States has undergone a dramatic change. In September 2007, the United States was one of four countries voting against UNDRIP. On 16 December 2010, President Barack Obama announced that the United States had changed its position and now supports UNDRIP. Notably, the detailed statement he issued in support of his decision stated:

> As President Obama has recognized, the indigenous peoples of North America have 'invaluable cultural knowledge and rich traditions, which continue to thrive in Native American Communities across the country.' The many facets of Native American cultures – including their religions, languages, traditions and arts – need to be protected, as reflected in multiple provisions in the Declaration.[169]

However, while the statement references measures to strengthen the Indian Arts and Crafts Act, to foster repatriation under NAGPRA and to protect sacred sites, it is silent as to initiatives that would promote broader native nations' control over indigenous knowledge and cultural resources. A more ambitious federal legislative agenda is required to achieve that end.

---

[167] See text at supra note 146.

[168] Eliana Torelly de Carvalho, 'Protection of Traditional Biodiversity-Related Knowledge: Analysis of Proposals for the Adoption of a Sui Generis System' (2003) *Missouri Environmental Law & Policy Review*, 11, pp. 38–69, at p. 59 (citing World Intellectual Property Organization, Survey on Existing Forms of Intellectual Property Protection for Traditional Knowledge).

[169] See 'Announcement of U.S. Support for the United Nations Declaration on the Rights of Indigenous Peoples: Initiatives to Promote the Government-to-Government Relationship & Improve the Lives of Indigenous Peoples', available at http://usun.state.gov/documents/organization/153239.pdf.

14. Ownership and trade of aboriginal cultural heritage in Canada

Catherine Bell*

1. INTRODUCTION

Ownership[1] and trade of indigenous cultural heritage in Canada is shaped by many legal influences, including Canadian common law, legislation, indigenous legal orders, constitutional law and international law. Nevertheless, it continues to be regulated in national law primarily through federal, territorial and provincial property legislation. Subject to a few notable exceptions, much of this legislation was enacted before recognition and protection of 'existing aboriginal and treaty rights of the aboriginal peoples of Canada' in section 35 (s. 35) of the Constitution Act 1982.[2] Canadian legal scholars and the 1996 Royal Commission on Aboriginal Peoples (RCAP) argue that this section and principles for its interpretation support the existence of constitutional aboriginal political, property and jurisdictional rights over cultural heritage 'integral' to 'the life and welfare of a particular Aboriginal people, its culture and identity'.[3] Aboriginal peoples have also increased control over some forms of their cultural heritage through negotiation of modern

* The author gratefully acknowledges the research assistance of Michael Solowan and Andrew Paterson.

1 I use the word 'ownership' here with some discomfort as a meta-theme running through all collaborative research and dialogues with indigenous peoples is that the concept of ownership is sometimes insufficient, incomprehensible and inadequate to describe the relationships of belonging and responsibility to tangible and intangible heritage considered integral to their distinctive cultural identities. For further discussion see case studies in Catherine Bell and Val Napoleon (eds), *First Nations Cultural Heritage and Law: Case Studies, Voices and Perspectives*, Vancouver: University of British Columbia Press, 2008 [hereinafter Bell and Napoleon]; and Brian Noble, 'Owning as Belonging/Owning as Property: The Crisis of Power and Respect in First Nations Heritage Transactions in Canada', in Bell and Napoleon, ibid., pp. 456–88.

2 Schedule B to the Canada Act 1982 (UK), c. 11 (Constitution Act 1982).

3 Royal Commission on Aboriginal Peoples (RCAP), *Report of the Royal Commission on Aboriginal Peoples: Restructuring the Relationship*, vol. II, Ottawa: Supply and Services Canada, 1996, at p. 167 [hereinafter RCAP Report, vol. II], uses the word 'vital'. However, *R v Sappier; R v Gray* (2006) 1 CNLR 368 Bastarache J (SCC) [hereinafter *R v Sappier*] decided post-RCAP provides for a less stringent test. The concept of 'integral to distinctive culture' developed in *R v Van der Peet* (1996) 2 SCR 507, at para. 45 Lamer J (SCC) [hereinafter *Van der Peet*] is properly understood as follows: 'identifying those practices, customs and traditions that are integral to distinctive aboriginal cultures will serve to identify the crucial elements of the distinctive aboriginal societies that occupied North America prior to the arrival of Europeans.'

treaties (post-1973) and land claim agreements (northern Canada), control over access to reserve and settlement land, and changes to institutional and government departmental policies and ethical codes of conduct.[4] There have also been some amendments to legislation increasing First Nation and Inuit control, particularly in northern Canada, and throughout Canada in the context of archaeological sites, ancestral remains and ethnographic objects found in or on aboriginal settlement and public lands. However, most heritage legislation continues to be influenced by private property rationale. Combined with increasing national and international indigenous demand, commercial and scientific interest in indigenous knowledge and cultural expressions and attention to human rights norms, these developments have created a complex legal and political landscape in Canada.

Drawing in part from research conducted in collaboration and dialogue with Inuit, Métis and First Nations, this chapter provides an overview of Canadian law and policy affecting aboriginal ownership and control of cultural heritage in Canada. The intent is not to provide an exhaustive review of aboriginal peoples' encounters with national law, but sufficient context to reflect critically on the extent Canadian law recognises the right of aboriginal peoples 'to freely determine their ... cultural development' and exercise 'autonomy or self-government'[5] in matters relating to cultural heritage.[6] Legal jurisdictions governing relations between aboriginal peoples and Canadian governments, the distinctiveness of aboriginal peoples' history and cultures, and evolving law on aboriginal constitutional rights make this – and the more specific question 'Who, according to National law, has the right to determine what aboriginal heritage can be the object of commercial trade?' – complex and difficult to answer.

I begin by exploring how various approaches to defining aboriginal peoples, self-government and forms of indigenous cultural heritage affect rights recognition, the degree of control aboriginal peoples may enjoy and the forms responses to their concerns may

---

[4] In 1973, the Supreme Court of Canada (SCC) affirmed in *Calder v The Attorney General of B.C.* (1970) 13 DLR (3d) 64 Davey J (BCCA), affirmed (1973) 4 CNLR 120 Pigeon J (SCC) [hereinafter *Calder*] the existence of an inherent common law right to aboriginal title. Aboriginal title is recognised in 11 numbered and other treaties between the British Crown and aboriginal nations signed during the nineteenth and part of the twentieth centuries. See infra note 23. Land claims settlements and treaties concluded after 1973 are commonly referred to as 'modern treaties'.

[5] Articles 3 and 4 of UN, Declaration on the Rights of Indigenous Peoples (UNDRIP), GA Res. 61/295 (UN Doc. A/61/L.67 and Add.1) (adopted on 13 September 2007). Article 3 reads as follows: 'Indigenous peoples have the right to self-determination. By virtue of that right they freely determine their political status and freely pursue their economic, social and cultural development.' Article 4 reads as follows: 'Indigenous peoples, in exercising their right to self-determination, have the right to autonomy or self-government in matters relating to their internal and local affairs, as well as ways and means for financing their autonomous function.'

[6] This question is at the heart of the procedural approach proposed by Christoph B. Graber for reconciling national, international and indigenous laws concerning trade in cultural heritage, Christoph B. Graber, 'Stimulating Trade and Development of Indigenous Cultural Heritage by Means of International Law: Issues of Legitimacy and Method', in this volume. See also Christoph B. Graber, 'Institutionalization of Creativity in Traditional Societies and in International Trade Law', in Shubha Ghosh and Robin P. Malloy (eds), *Creativity, Law and Entrepreneurship*, Cheltenham, UK and Northampton, MA: Edward Elgar, 2011, pp. 234–63 [hereinafter Graber, 'Creativity'].

take. Given the focus of this book on commercial aspects of trade, Canadian laws regulating intellectual property (IP) and export of 'cultural property' are emphasised.[7] A review of this legislation demonstrates:

1. Canadian responses have been predominantly policy and programme based.
2. Canadian legislation does not look to indigenous laws or practices to determine the sacred, communal or other nature of indigenous cultural heritage or forms that may be commercialised.
3. To the extent Canadian law and policy does recognise indigenous autonomy or self-government over matters of cultural heritage, it does not assume equality of rights among, or apply equally to, all aboriginal peoples of Canada.

2. ABORIGINAL PEOPLES AND ABORIGINAL RIGHTS

The aboriginal peoples of Canada consist of numerous 'organic political and cultural entities that stem historically from the original peoples of North America' and that exist within diverse historical, geographic, socioeconomic and legal environments within Canada.[8] Comprising approximately 1.17 million people and 3.8 per cent of the Canadian population, their aboriginal and treaty rights have been 'recognised and affirmed' in s. 35 of the Constitution Act 1982, which defines them for the purpose of this section, as the Inuit, Indian and Métis peoples.[9] Constitutional recognition protects, from unjustified Canadian governmental interference, treaty and inherent aboriginal rights[10] – inherent in that they originate in the socio-political organisation and substantial connection of aboriginal nations to ancestral lands prior to European colonisation, not Crown recognition (for example the right of aboriginal title).[11] Aboriginal rights continued in force after the assertion of European sovereignty and became part of the common law of Canada unless incompatible with Crown sovereignty, surrendered through the treaty process[12] or terminated by clear and plain federal legislation prior to their elevation to constitutional

---

[7] Definition under the Cultural Property Export and Import Act (CPEIA), RSC 1985, c. C-51 discussed in further detail infra section 3.5.

[8] RCAP Report, vol. II , supra note 3, at p. 107.

[9] Statistics Canada, '2006 Census Release Topics. Aboriginal Peoples' (2008), available at http://www12.statcan.ca/census-recensement/2006/rt-td/ap-pa-eng.cfm (all online sources were accessed 14 September 2011).

[10] See *R v Sparrow* (1990) 3 CNLR 160, at para. 71 Dickson and La Forest JJ (SCC) [hereinafter *Sparrow*]. For application of this doctrine to treaties see *R v Badger* (1996) 1 SCR 771.

[11] *Calder,* supra note 4, was the first decision to support this. See also *Delgamuukw v British Columbia* (1998) 1 CNLR 14 Lamer J (SCC) [hereinafter *Delgamuukw*].

[12] It is beyond the scope of this chapter to get into treaty rights analysis. However, it is important to note that the notion of surrendering aboriginal rights to be replaced by treaty rights is contested by Treaty Nations (see infra sections 2.1 and 2.2) who understand treaties as jurisdictional arrangements and affirmation of indigenous rights. For further discussion of application to heritage context see Catherine Bell, 'Restructuring the Relationship: Domestic Repatriation and Law Reform' [hereinafter Bell, 'Restructuring'], in Catherine Bell and Robert Paterson (eds), *Protection of First Nation Cultural Heritage: Laws, Policy and Reform*, Vancouver: University of British Columbia Press, 2008, pp. 15–77, at p. 31 [hereinafter Bell and Paterson].

status (that is, legislation that intentionally, but not necessarily through express language, extinguished aboriginal rights).[13] Constitutional aboriginal rights are not immune from government interference but the Crown must establish a 'compelling and substantial legislative objective' and implement that objective in compliance with its fiduciary obligation.[14]

A fundamental purpose of s. 35 is to 'provide cultural continuity and security' for aboriginal societies within Canada.[15] This purpose, combined with judicial trends in interpretation of s. 35, supports recognition of a general aboriginal right to cultural integrity. Brian Slattery (a leading Canadian scholar in British colonial history and Canadian constitutional law) defines this right as 'the right of aboriginal people to maintain and develop the central and significant elements of their ancestral culture'.[16] Also included in s. 35 aboriginal rights are more specific lifestyle rights that are grounded in activities, customs and traditions that were historically important features of aboriginal societies, and that continue to persist in the present day as integral elements of their distinctive cultures (for example ceremonial practice, sustenance hunting). Viewed in the abstract, these rights have some uniformity in scope across all aboriginal peoples. However, they vary in existence, form and exercise in accordance with historic practices, institutions, encounters with Europeans and legal history of specific aboriginal groups. Slattery gives the following example: 'the generic right of cultural integrity harbours an intermediate generic right to religion, which in turn shelters a range of specific religious rights vested in particular aboriginal groups.'[17]

Because of original occupancy and jurisdictions over their territories, the act of treaty-making and treaty relationships and continuity as distinctive peoples, RCAP, academics and some judges suggest that aboriginal peoples are properly understood in Canadian constitutional law as nations within Canada – a concept similar to that of 'domestic dependant nationhood' enjoyed by Native Americans in the United States.[18] This concept of nationhood forms the legal and political foundations for historical and

---

[13] The justification test is first stated in *Sparrow,* supra note 10, as a 'valid' legislative objective and is elaborated in *R v Gladstone* (1994) 4 CNLR 65, at para. 72 Lamer CJ (SCC).

[14] *Mitchell v Minister of National Revenue* (2001) 3 CNLR 122, at para. 10 McLachlin J (SCC) [hereinafter *Mitchell*] quoting Brian Slattery, 'Understanding Aboriginal Rights' (1987) *Canadian Bar Review,* 66, pp. 727–83, at p. 727. Canadian jurisprudence has not elaborated on what is 'incompatible with Crown sovereignty' but it has been interpreted in federal self-government policy, see infra section 2.2, to include international trade, despite the recognition in *Mitchell* that cross-border trade may in some instances continue as an aboriginal or treaty right

[15] *R v Sappier,* supra note 3, at para. 22.

[16] Brian Slattery, 'The Generative Structure of Aboriginal Rights' (2007) *Supreme Court Law Review*, 38 (2), pp. 595–628, at p. 600 [hereinafter Slattery, 'Generative Structure'].

[17] Ibid., at pp. 607–8.

[18] See, for example, *Worcester v Georgia* (1832) 31 US (6 Pet) 515, at para. 519 Marshall J (USSC) [hereinafter *Worcester*], one of the foundational cases for historical and ongoing recognition of Native American internal rights to self-government and in Canada see, for example, *R v Sioui* (1990) 1 SCR 1025 Lamer J (SCC) [hereinafter *Sioui*]. See on the American law Carole Goldberg, 'A United States Perspective on the Protection of Indigenous Cultural Heritage', in this volume. However, unlike rights protected in s. 35 of the Constitution Act 1982, such Native American jurisdiction continues to be subject to acts of state recognition and unilateral alteration or termination.

ongoing recognition of Native American inherent and internal rights to self-government in matters relating to their people and territory. In Canada the source, content and meaningful contemporary exercise of this right is a more recent subject of litigation and negotiation. In both countries, this concept of aboriginal nationhood exists in tension with many other competing legal identities brought on by a complicated history of treaty-making and outside naming, including through recognition or denial of indigenous legal and political identity in national legislation and policy.

2.1 Indian, Inuit and Métis Peoples

> The human rights situation of the Aboriginal people of Canada results not only from the different geographical settings and their socio-cultural variety, but also from the different approaches of public policy and the complex set of laws and jurisdictions governing relations between the State and the various categories of Aboriginal populations.[19]

Inuit territory within Canada is in the Arctic (north of 60th parallel) and sub-Arctic regions. Inuit share a common language (Inuktitut). However, this language has six different dialects and there are smaller, distinctive cultural and regional group identities among them.[20] Most Canadian Inuit are beneficiaries of contemporary land-claim and self-government agreements negotiated with northern aboriginal peoples. Subject to a few exceptions, Inuit and First Nations in the Yukon, Nunavut and the Northwest Territories (NWT) enjoy significantly more administrative powers and legislative autonomy over their cultural heritage than Indians (First Nations) within provincial boundaries. Typically these agreements set aside settlement land and address land and resource management, including through Inuit or First Nation representation, administrative boards and tribunals that make decisions affecting cultural landscapes, items recovered from, in or on the land, and heritage sites. More control has also been negotiated through complementing self-government agreements.

'Indians' live throughout Canada and speak more than 53 different languages.[21] Many are descendants of the 614 'Indian bands' (First Nations) recognised by, and subject to, the Indian Act.[22] Among these descendants are various legal categories of 'Indians' that arose from a history of treaty-making in some parts of Canada and national federal regulation of reserve lands throughout Canada. About half of federally recognised Indian bands are Treaty Indians whose ancestors entered into pre- and post-Confederation treaties, some of which are considered by Canadian courts and governments as extinguishing aboriginal

---

19 UN, Economic and Social Council, Commission on Human Rights, 'Indigenous Issues. Human Rights and Indigenous Issues. Report of the Special Rapporteur on the Situation of Human Rights and Fundamental Freedoms of Indigenous People. Rodolfo Stavenhagen. Addendum. Mission to Canada', (UN Doc. E/CN.4/2005/88/Add.3, 2004), at p. 7 [hereinafter UN Report, Stavenhagen].

20 David W. Elliott, *Law and Aboriginal Peoples*, 5th edn, Concord, Ontario: Captus Press, 2005, at p. 20.

21 Ibid., at p. 14.

22 RSC 1985, c. I-5. 'First Nation' is now the form of self-identification adopted by most Indian bands.

land and resource rights and replacing them with treaty rights.[23] However, treaties do not cover all of Canada. In much of Canada, aboriginal peoples were dispossessed of their traditional territories without treaty negotiation. A consequence is that some First Nations are in a stronger position than others to negotiate legislative, administrative and *de facto* control over their tangible cultural heritage located on or in their traditional territory as part of modern comprehensive treaty or land-claim negotiation. As elaborated later in this chapter, these processes assume a wide range of aboriginal rights and interests which are open for negotiation, including jurisdiction over some forms of cultural heritage within traditional territories; ownership, access to and control over archaeological and ethnographic objects; and repatriation.

First Nations (whether Treaty or non-Treaty) in turn enjoy significantly more access to negotiation and control over their cultural heritage than the Métis. Métis have historically been defined in Canadian legislation and policy by reference to their mixed aboriginal and European ancestry and exclusion from federal programmes and Indian legislation.[24] Exclusion of people with ancestral connection to scrip recipients under the Manitoba Act 1870 and Dominion Land Act from eligibility for federal Indian status has also resulted in this characteristic being associated with Métis legal identity.[25] However, for the purpose of s. 35, the Supreme Court of Canada (SCC) rejects these racial and process-based approaches to legal identity. The 'constitutionally significant feature of the Métis' in comparison with Inuit and First Nations 'is their special status as peoples that emerged between first contact and the effective imposition of European control'.[26] Ancestry is only one aspect of contemporary Métis constitutional identity and ancestral links can be established by 'birth, adoption or other means', such as community acceptance and statute.[27]

There are many other legal categories of aboriginal peoples generated by amendments to federal Indian legislation and policy. Reserve lands set aside pursuant to treaty, or designated unilaterally in the absence of negotiation of aboriginal rights, are governed by the aforementioned federal Indian Act. So too are the creation and recognition of band councils, acquisition and loss of 'Indian status' to receive benefits under the Indian Act,

---

23 Also referred to as land cession treaties, they were entered with First Nations as settlement moved west. They include the Robinson Huron Treaties (Lakes Huron and Superior area) and the 11 numbered treaties covering most of northwest Ontario, Saskatchewan, Manitoba, Alberta and a small area in the Northwest Territories. The numbered treaties refer to surrender of land in exchange for specific rights. However, Canadian courts recognise that not all oral terms or aboriginal terms are written in the treaties, giving rise to contemporary interpretation issues.

24 This includes the larger Métis Nation that emerged in the Red River area of what is now southern Manitoba and, under the leadership of Louis Riel, developed a distinctive Métis national identity, resisted the unilateral imposition of colonial settlement and government, asserted a political nation-to-nation relationship with Canada, and negotiated Métis political, land and language rights in the Manitoba Act 1870, RSC 1985, App. II, No. 8.

25 Manitoba Act, ibid., and SC 1879, c. 32. Scrip was a certificate issued to individual Métis redeemable for land or money. However, fraud and other problems with the scrip distribution system resulted in many Métis people being left impoverished and landless.

26 *R v Powley* (2001) 2 CNLR 291 (Ont CA), affirmed (2003) SCC 43, at para. 17 McLachlin J (SCC).

27 Ibid., at para. 32. See also *R v Lizotte* (2010) 1 CNLR 326 Hougestol J (Alta Prov Ct).

band council powers, reserve land management, trade in certain forms of cultural property, and many other aspects of 'status Indian' life. Both Treaty and non-Treaty Indians can be status Indians and recognised as 'Indian bands' for the purpose of federal Indian legislation, living on reserve lands, and access to self-government negotiation processes aimed at increasing band council control over reserve lands, which may include heritage objects and sites.

Prior to eligibility reforms in 1985 (known as Bill C31),[28] there were many ways to lose Indian Act status. These reforms sought to eliminate provisions of the Indian Act contrary to protections from discrimination based on gender and to address other status provisions that excluded certain classes of people who involuntarily lost Indian status through other means (for example post-secondary education, becoming a member of the clergy, and until 1961 status Indians had to give up status to vote). It was assumed that those who lost Indian status and were no longer entitled to live on reserves, or who were excluded from eligibility, would assimilate and become 'enfranchised' within the broader Canadian citizenry. As a result, some people who for a generation or two lived among, and were accepted by, Métis communities are now eligible to apply for Indian status and programmes (for example health and education benefits) not available to other Métis people. Added to this confusion are other constitutional instruments, court cases and federal and provincial laws and policies that define aboriginal peoples, First Nations, Métis and Indians for some specific form of rights recognition or ameliorative purpose.

It is beyond the scope of this chapter to go into all of the legal and constitutional definitions of aboriginal people in Canada. The point is that these definitions create barriers to rights recognition. Of particular note is the exclusion of Métis from land claim, modern treaty and self-government negotiation processes that assume the existence of a contemporary land base, like a reserve. An exception are Alberta's settlement Métis, who negotiated a land base and self-government with the province of Alberta in exchange for a stay of litigation for alleged provincial misappropriation of trust funds that were to be set aside for the benefit of Métis colonies established under provincial social welfare legislation.[29]

2.2 Self-determination, Self-government and Cultural Heritage

> Our position is that aboriginal rights, aboriginal title to land, water and sea ice flow from aboriginal rights; and all rights to practice our customs and traditions, to retain and develop our languages and cultures, and the rights to self-government, all these things flow from the fact that we have aboriginal rights … . In our view, aboriginal rights can also be seen as human rights, because these are the things we need to continue to survive as distinct peoples of Canada.[30]
>
> (John Amagoalik speaking for Inuit Committee on National Issues at First Ministers' Conference in 1983).

---

[28] An Act to Amend the Indian Act, SC 1985 c. 27.

[29] See, for example, Catherine Bell and Harold Robinson, 'Government on Alberta's Métis Settlements: Foundations and Future Directions', in Yale D. Belanger (ed.), *Aboriginal Self-Government in Canada*, 3rd edn, Saskatoon: Purich Publishing, 2008, pp. 260–86.

[30] RCAP, *Partners in Confederation: Aboriginal Peoples, Self-Government, and the Constitution*, Ottawa: Supply and Services, 1993, at p. 9 [hereinafter RCAP, 'Partners'].

Aboriginal self-determination is not generally asserted, or understood, in Canadian legal or political discourse as a right to political secession from Canada. It envisions 'internal' parallel jurisdictions within the constitutional arrangements and larger nation state of Canada. As a contemporary constitutional and political right, RCAP suggests self-determination in Canada is the 'right of an aboriginal nation to choose how it will be governed – whether, for example, it should adopt separate governmental institutions or join in public governments that embrace aboriginal and non-aboriginal people alike'.[31] Both the idea of autonomy over internal affairs and a potential outcome of the exercise of the right of self-determination is the right to 'self-government'.[32]

The SCC has not defined the contemporary right to self-determination or self-government. However, where band council governments established under the Indian Act have enacted their own band membership codes, Canadian courts have held such jurisdiction cannot be exercised in a manner that unjustifiably interferes with individual human rights protections against discrimination based on race, religion, gender or other analogous ground protected in the Canadian Charter of Rights and Freedoms (the Charter).[33] Further, the SCC has assumed in its reasoning that the right of self-government exists. There have also been decisions that affirm the survival of indigenous laws as part of Canadian common law and recognise s. 35 rights protection for indigenous laws founded on historical 'elements of the practices, customs and traditions of aboriginal peoples'.[34] In giving content to the right of self-government Chief Justice Lamer (as he then was) has also suggested that the SCC will be influenced by RCAP's self-government analysis in relation to 'territory, citizenship, jurisdiction, internal government organization ... '.[35]

The historical foundation of this approach is the existence of indigenous legal and political order at the time of European contact[36] and the treaty process which recognises First Nation rights to land and autonomy over their internal affairs with minimal intervention.[37] Because of the communal nature of aboriginal title, aboriginal self-government also necessarily includes the right to make decisions about the land (and archaeological, ethnographic or other objects in or on it) over which aboriginal title is established.[38] This understanding of self-government can be contrasted to approaches that require proof of specific pre-contact governmental activities and treat self-government as an empty vessel of yet to be proven activities, traditions and practices.[39] However, the SCC

---

31 RCAP Report, vol. II, supra note 3, at p. 175.

32 Ibid.

33 Canadian Charter of Rights and Freedoms, Part I of the Constitution Act 1982, c. 11 (UK). See, for example, *Sawridge Band v Canada (Minister of Indian Affairs & Northern Development)* (2009) 4 CNLR 340 Ryer J (FCA); *McIvor v Canada (Registrar of Indian & Northern Affairs)* (2009) 2 CNLR 236 Groberman J (BCCA); *Corbiere v Canada (Minister of Indian & Northern Affairs)* (1999) 3 CNLR 19 McLachlin and Bastarache JJ (SCC).

34 *Delgamuukw*, supra note 11, at para. 148; *Mitchell*, supra note 14.

35 *Delgamuukw*, supra note 11, at para. 171.

36 In the case of Métis this may be effective European control, the date at which European colonisation has an actual, rather than theoretical, impact on the life and land of Métis people.

37 *Sioui*, supra note 18, at para. 74.

38 Kent McNeil, 'Aboriginal Rights in Canada: From Title to Land to Territorial Sovereignty' (1988) *Tulsa Journal of Comparative and International Law*, 5, pp. 253–98, at p. 253.

39 *R v Pamajewon* (1996) 4 CNLR 164 (SCC).

has stated that its earlier reference to historical activities in determining the content of aboriginal rights to self-government was simply to make the point that parties must avoid asserting constitutional rights in excessively general terms (for example self-government) – not to equate constitutional jurisdictions with specific historical governmental activities.[40] Where the line is currently drawn is a matter of federal policy and negotiation.

Recognising the likelihood of some form of aboriginal constitutional right to self-government and to avoid litigation, in 1995 the federal government released its inherent right to self-government policy to guide negotiations about self-government.[41] The policy acknowledges the 'inherent right of self-government' as a s. 35 aboriginal constitutional right and assumes that 'Aboriginal peoples of Canada have the right to govern themselves in relation to matters that are internal to their communities, integral to their unique cultures, identities, traditions, languages and institutions, and with respect to their special relationship to their land and their resources.'[42] However, there is significant disagreement and diverse legal opinion on whether inherent rights need to be implemented through legislation, treaty or some other formal process before recognition and enforcement. So too is there disagreement on the form and content of self-government that has survived the assertion of sovereignty, division of constitutional jurisdictions between federal and provincial governments, the Indian Act and numerous other processes of colonisation. Further, although federal policy purports to recognise an inherent right of self-government, it predetermines areas that are 'internal' and 'integral' to aboriginal culture, thereby excluding certain areas from negotiation. Jurisdiction over trade, export, import and intellectual property law are among the jurisdictions excluded.

Federal policy on self-government of aboriginal groups mainly emanates from federal interpretation of SCC decisions and selective adoption of RCAP suggestions. It allows for comprehensive negotiation over a range of predetermined jurisdictions as well as in single or multiple spheres of jurisdiction (for example child welfare). In many instances provincial participation is required because of the numerous ways in which provincial services and laws of general application impact aboriginal life. Laws of general application are those that extend uniformly throughout the province and are not directed in object or purpose at a particular aboriginal group.[43] For example, all provinces have laws concerning the protection, excavation and destruction of archaeological resources. Therefore negotiations concerning some forms of cultural heritage are in part dependent on provincial willingness to negotiate – a willingness that varies considerably across the country, as do federal interpretations of the policy with changes from liberal to conservative governments.

---

40 *Delgamuukw*, supra note 11, at para. 170.

41 Aboriginal Affairs and Northern Development Canada (AANDC), 'The Government of Canada's Approach to Implementation of the Inherent Right and the Negotiation of Aboriginal Self-Government', available at http://www.ainc-inac.gc.ca/al/ldc/ccl/pubs/sg/sg-eng.asp#PartI [hereinafter AANDC, 'Inherent Right'].

42 Ibid.

43 *Kruger v R* (1977) 9 CNLR 624 Dickson J (SCC).

Although it is possible that Canadian governments will negotiate some forms of 'self-government' with aboriginal groups without a land base (that is, service delivery and administrative powers), Canadian negotiation policy largely assumes existence of a land base and membership in a recognised Indian band, thereby excluding most Métis and other non-status aboriginal groups who do not have a collective land base (for example groups whose ancestral bands lost status through allegedly flawed and fraudulently administered voluntary enfranchisement provisions of the Indian Act). The rights of aboriginal groups to exercise jurisdiction is similarly limited by membership and territory. South of the 60th parallel, it is predominantly restricted to reserve land (a very small portion of traditional territories of aboriginal nations) with limited administrative or concurrent jurisdiction in specified spheres over designated lands.

There are a number of areas that federal policy considers 'beyond matters that are integral to Aboriginal culture or those strictly internal to an Aboriginal group' and therefore not negotiable.[44] Subject matters in this group include divorce, labour, environment and a range of other areas but exclude trade, export, import and intellectual property, which are considered under current policy to be matters relating to sovereignty, external relations or other matters of national interest. '[A]boriginal groups' may negotiate 'some measure of aboriginal jurisdiction or authority' in these areas.[45] This includes a range of subject matters that currently impact protection and control over aboriginal cultural heritage. An example is environmental regulation and assessment. Indigenous knowledge is often included in research concerning the impact of resource and development projects that affect aboriginal peoples. Information shared includes locations of archaeological, ceremonial or other important sites, movement of wildlife herds, and location and properties of plants and natural resources.

In the north, aboriginal peoples have been able to negotiate significant control over tangible cultural heritage through self-government and comprehensive land claims processes. In some areas they are assuming the same jurisdictions of provincial governments, but this continues to exclude trade, export and intellectual property, which fall under federal jurisdiction. An example is Chapter 13 Yukon First Nations Land Claim Agreement (1993), which covers a wide range of heritage matters. Yukon First Nations (YFN) own and have responsibility for managing heritage resources on their settlement lands, while Canadian governments (Yukon and Canada) have responsibility for managing heritage resources on other lands in the Yukon Territory.[46] However, YFN ownership of moveable heritage resources also extends to all ethnographic heritage resources found on non-settlement public land and within their traditional territory. The Chapter also provides for protection of First Nations' burial sites, information-sharing on heritage resources between the Governments of Canada, the Yukon Territory and YFN, a permitting system

---

44 AANDC, 'Inherent Right', supra note 41.

45 Ibid.

46 AANDC, 'Umbrella Final Agreement between the Government of Canada, the Council for Yukon Indians and the Government of Yukon', c. 13, available at http://www.eco.gov.yk.ca/pdf/umbrellafinalagreement.pdf. Chapter 1 of the Agreement defines 'Heritage Resources' as including 'Moveable Heritage Resources, Heritage Sites and Documentary Heritage Resources'.

for research at heritage sites, and consultation with First Nations regarding sites related to their history and culture wherever situated. The Yukon Heritage Resources Board and the Yukon Geographic Place Names Board have also been created and each of the YFN has its own heritage department. Wherever found, heritage resources related to the culture and history of Yukon Indian People are to be managed consistent with YFN values and culture and in consultation with them, and all ethnographic objects discovered through excavation in the territory belong to the communities of origin. Significant control has also been obtained through the negotiation of public governments, such as Nunavut, in which Inuit are the significant majority, including the transfer of jurisdiction over all forms of tangible cultural heritage previously enjoyed by the territorial government and the ability to displace existing territorial legislation.[47]

The federal self-government policy is one of several possible interpretations of Canadian jurisprudence. For example, Slattery and RCAP argue that s. 35 recognises a Canadian constitutional order in which aboriginal, federal and provincial governments exercise authority within distinct but overlapping spheres of general legislative jurisdiction.[48] Adopting this approach, the following 'partial' list of core jurisdictional areas has been generated by RCAP:

> [I]t seems likely that an aboriginal nation with exclusive territory would be entitled as a matter of its core jurisdiction to draw up a constitution, set up basic governmental institutions, establish courts, lay down citizenship criteria and procedures, run its own schools, maintain its own health and social services, deal with family matters, regulate many economic activities, foster and protect language, culture and identity, regulate use of its lands, waters and resources, levy taxes, deal with aspects of criminal law and procedure, and generally maintain peace and security within their territory. *In particular, the regulation of many substantive aboriginal and treaty rights protected under s. 35(1) would probably fall within the core of aboriginal jurisdiction.*[49]

As I have argued in previous publications, certain forms of cultural heritage or indigenous laws concerning ownership, transfer and commercial use of moveable property may receive s. 35(1) rights recognition and therefore fall within aboriginal jurisdiction.[50] A possible outcome could be a blend of Canadian and aboriginal laws to resolve disputes concerning legitimacy of trade and title. For example, a common principle of western property law is that you cannot transfer more rights to property than you have yourself. This principle can be combined with local indigenous law to determine legitimacy of transfer of title, or original rights acquisition. We see this approach taken in the United States, where tribal law is used to determine the individual or communal nature of tangible 'cultural patrimony' (for example a ceremonial mask) and whether, at the time of its separation from the community, it could be owned or alienated by an individual member of

---

47 'Agreement Between the Inuit of Nunavut Settlement Area and Her Majesty the Queen in Right of Canada', Article 33, available online at www.gov.nu.ca/hr/site/doc/nlca.pdf.

48 Slattery, 'Generative Structure', supra note 16, at pp. 602–4. For an elaboration of this theory see RCAP, 'Partners', supra note 30.

49 RCAP Report, vol. II, supra note 3, at p. 219 (emphasis added).

50 See, for example, Bell, 'Restructuring', supra note 12, at pp. 25–7.

a Native American tribe.[51] However, in the United States this approach is not extended to intangible cultural heritage such as designs or songs.[52]

Before leaving considerations of self-determination, self-government and indigenous legal orders, it is important to consider treaty rights. First Nations whose ancestors entered into treaties with the Crown assert that their inherent right to self-government is evidenced in the original treaty relationship between them and the British Crown. Areas of jurisdiction not expressly surrendered, or delegated to foreign governments within their traditional territories, continue. Although these treaties speak to areas integral to survival and cultural integrity of the people signing them (for example land, lifestyle, education), they do not address in express terms ceremonial places, tangible culture or intangible cultural heritage. Not surprisingly, again the SCC has not ruled on the form or content of treaty rights of self-government with regard to such 'Treaty Nations'. However, the construction of British colonial treaties in the United States supports the conclusion that upon entering treaties with the British Crown, Indian Nations do not cease to be self-governing. Instead, powers of government both internal and external to Native American territory are presumed to remain unless they have been expressly surrendered or overruled by congressional enactments or reasonable state regulation.[53]

For these and other reasons the federal government is prepared to negotiate some stand-alone forms of self-government with Treaty Nations over certain jurisdictional sectors. In both Canada and the United States, this characterisation of treaties has not been interpreted as requiring aboriginal consent to terminate self-government or other treaty rights. However, the SCC has indicated that if there is an aboriginal or treaty right to trade property across international borders, it may be incompatible with Crown sovereignty and thus not protected as a s. 35 constitutional right.[54]

2.3 Cultural Property, Traditional Knowledge and Cultural Heritage

> I am connected to the land, to my land, to my territory, our territory. The properties that we have such as the totem poles, the crests, the blankets, the rattles, the aprons, the everything is connected to me and that's how I relate myself to the land. That is what you have to keep in mind is that everything about property relates me back to the land. That's why it's really important that we maintain such properties or obtain our property, such as rings around your neck, because it

---

[51] See, for example, *Journeycake v Cherokee Indian Nation* (1893) 24 Ct Cl 281, affirmed (1894) 155 US 196, at para. 302 Brewer J (USSC) (available on WL Can) explaining the concept of aboriginal communal property; and *Seneca Nation of Indians v Hammond* (1874) 3 Thompson and Cook 347 (NYSC) where the court concludes that those who purchased bark contrary to the laws of the Seneca Nation did not acquire title and could not confer title to the defendants. See also Native American Graves Protection and Repatriation Act (NAGPRA), 25 U.S.C. §§ 3001–3013 (West Supp 1001) section 2(3)D.

[52] See Goldberg, supra note 18.

[53] *Worcester*, supra note 18. See also Goldberg, supra note 18.

[54] *Mitchell*, supra note 14.

> signifies everything about us, right down to social order, spirituality, the emotional aspect and the physical.[55]
>
> (Victoria Russell, member of the Gitxsan House of Luuxhon)

When responding to aboriginal concerns with regard to cultural (and intellectual) property one has to consider the following challenge: conventional approaches to understanding property rights make it difficult to reconcile indigenous and western legal orders. For example, among Gitxsan and Tsimshian peoples there is no equivalent concept for the word 'intellect', which assumes separation of mental powers, body and emotion. Their language reflects the understanding that the heart is the seat of both feeling and thinking.[56] There is also no separation of certain forms of property, such as clan crest images, from self. The relationship to these images is not so much 'I own this' as 'I am this', or perhaps more accurately, 'we are this'.[57] Of concern to the Gitxsan is the inability to control the use of crest images intimately linked to their family histories and which constitutionally define each house group with other groups and link them to their territories. As lawyer Richard Overstall explains, trying to address this within the confines of cultural property and IP law can undermine the protection sought if abstracted out of local context:

> The concept of 'cultural property' obscures Gitxsan law; that is, through the implicit assumption that part of an indigenous legal culture can be carved out and separated from the rest of that culture. While this may be a valid approach to Canadian legal analysis – for example, looking at the obligations of museums to return certain artifacts or remains – it obscures the significance of objects, images, words, and inventions under indigenous law. Besides being possessions in their own right, many of the objects, and particularly the images, words, and music they contain, have a critical constitutional role in indigenous law.[58]

Nevertheless, aboriginal peoples of Canada have sometimes found it necessary to utilise property concepts to assert cultural rights and respect for indigenous laws and ways. An example is Blackfoot participation in the development and enactment of Alberta's First Nations Sacred Ceremonial Objects Repatriation Act (Alberta's Repatriation Act).[59] The Act provides a process for the Glenbow Alberta Institute (Glenbow) and Royal Alberta Museum to return 'sacred ceremonial objects' to First Nations in Alberta, 'the title to which is vested in the Crown under Canadian law'.[60] The Blackfoot do not recognise Canadian law concerning transfer of legal title and ownership of their ceremonial items. Further, they do not view ceremonial items, such as medicine bundles, as 'objects'. However, despite an agreement reached with the Glenbow, Alberta was of the opinion that provincial legislation was necessary to create a clear and transparent process and to

---

55 Quoted in Richard Overstall, 'The Law is Opened: The Constitutional Role of Tangible and Intangible Property in Gitanyow', in Bell and Napoleon, supra note 1, pp. 92–113, at p. 108.

56 Susan Marsden, 'Northwest Coast Adawx Study', in Bell and Napoleon, supra note 1, pp. 114–49, at p. 114.

57 Ibid.

58 Overstall, supra note 55, at p. 93.

59 RSA 2000, c. F-14.

60 See Catherine Bell, Graham Statt and the Mookakin Cultural Society, 'Protection: Reflections on the Kainai Experience', in Bell and Napoleon, supra note 1, pp. 203–57, at p. 238.

address potential issues of liability arising from large-scale repatriations of items that, by provincial legislation, were held for the benefit of the people of Alberta. Blackfoot laws could not be respected without provincial laws being changed and for that to occur, Blackfoot concepts had to be articulated in ways that had meaning in Canadian law. As a consequence of this legislation 251 ceremonial items have been transferred to the Blackfoot and put back into use. However, elders who participated continue to remain uncomfortable with reliance on Canadian legal language and process.[61]

Other significant 'conceptual and linguistic' hurdles in the realm of cultural property, cultural heritage, trade and IP law include categories of 'art' and 'artefact', archaeological and ethnographic, animate and inanimate, tangible and intangible and many other familiar dichotomies used to organise thought and characterise property rights in national and international law. Further, there may be divisions within indigenous understandings that do not correspond to western legal divisions. For example, like Native Americans, the aboriginal peoples of Canada also distinguish between 'art' that is integrated and essential to their legal and social orders, and cultural products which are intentionally put into the commercial market in a manner that does not violate indigenous law, dignity or human rights.[62]

In the area of intangible cultural property, Canadian common law has not defined 'traditional knowledge', 'traditional ecological knowledge', 'traditional cultural expressions' or 'indigenous knowledge', although the terms are invoked in legal and political discourse and given content in international law. To the limited extent that they are referred to by judges or legislation in Canada, they are still not defined.[63] When adopted in Canadian and aboriginal governments and agency, institutional, national and international reports and policies, they refer generally to an amalgam of historical and contemporary influences. They include knowledge, values, beliefs, customs, practices and traditions intimately connected to a people's land and culture, arising from intergenerational experience and passed down from generation to generation. For example, from 2002–05 the Department of Canadian Heritage held national gatherings on indigenous knowledge with participants from First Nation, Métis and Inuit communities. The purpose of these sessions was to open 'respectful dialogue' on indigenous knowledge protection, preservation and celebration and to 'develop practical strategies for working together in areas where the mandate, expertise and experience' of the Department 'coincide with the aspirations of aboriginal peoples'.[64] The final report from these dialogues explains indigenous or traditional knowledge in this way:

> Indigenous Knowledge is more about understanding one's role and responsibility in the world than about classifying information. It is a form of consciousness intimately related to the ecological order, a response of a people to their responsibility to participate in maintaining that order. Although recorded and passed on by such means as art, song, myth, story and ceremony,

---

61 Bell, 'Restructuring', supra note 12, at p. 41.

62 See also Rebecca Tsosie, 'International Trade in Indigenous Cultural Heritage: An Argument for Indigenous Governance of Cultural Property', in this volume.

63 See, for example, Yukon Environmental and Socio-economic Assessment Act (YESAA), SC 2003, c. 7, s. 121(a); and Canadian Environment Assessment Act, SC 1992, c. 37, s. 16.1.

64 Department of Canadian Heritage, 'National Gatherings on Indigenous Knowledge. Traditions. Final Report' (2005), available at http://www.pch.gc.ca/pc-ch/org/sectr/cp-ch/aa/trd-eng.pdf.

> Indigenous Knowledge is not cultural knowledge as such. The Mi'kmaq language, for example, has no single concept or word that captures what most Canadians would refer to as 'culture'. To the Mi'kmaq, aspects might be captured by *telilnuisink*, maintaining contact with tradition, or by *telilnuo'lti'k*, maintaining consciousness, or by *tlinuita'sim*, maintaining the Mi'kmaq language.[65]

Although there are similarities among indigenous knowledge systems, they are context-specific and local – that is, traditional knowledge is associated with a particular society and territory.[66] It may consist of information known generally, or practised commonly or selectively within an aboriginal community. Within its broad definition are intangible cultural expressions which national and international law regulate through IP law as the product of creative human thought. As Greg Young-Ing (Opsakwayak Cree Nation and Chair of the Indigenous Peoples Caucus of the Creator's Rights Alliance) explains, the concept of traditional knowledge:

> … encompasses a broad range of Indigenous knowledge ranging from: ancient stories, songs and dances; traditional architecture and agricultural; biodiversity related and medicinal, herbal and plant knowledge; ancient motifs, crests and other artistic designs; various artistic mediums, styles, forms and techniques; spiritual and religious institutions and their symbols; and various other forms of Indigenous knowledge.[67]

'Cultural heritage' is in essence the melding of the tangible and intangible expressions of human knowledge and creativity.

In Canadian law, it is tangible cultural property that receives the greatest attention in provincial heritage conservation and federal export laws. Inherent in these legal regimes is the balancing of resource development, free trade and other economic interests of industrialised nations with the various rationales for protecting and increasing aboriginal control over their cultural heritage. In balance for aboriginal peoples is preservation of cultural identity as part of a broader movement of self-determination and decolonisation that acknowledges the inextricable link between cultural heritage and the maintenance, strengthening, transmission and renewal of identity, knowledge, laws and practices. Fundamentally, then, for many aboriginal peoples the issue is not one of competing property rights, but respect for human dignity and human rights.

Within this context certain tangible culture or information may become so integrally related to group identity as to take on communal, sacred or other characteristics that may not have applied at the time the traditional knowledge or cultural object was initially separated from the community. An example is the repatriation of the Cranmer potlatch collection seized, and in some instances extorted, from the *Kwakwaka'wakw.* Interrupting continuity of aboriginal legal orders, cultural practices, transmission of indigenous knowledge and other dimensions of indigenous society were discriminatory Canadian

---

[65] Ibid., at p. 5.

[66] Robert Howell and Roch Ripley, 'The Interconnection of Intellectual Property and Cultural Property', in Bell and Paterson, supra note 12, pp. 223–77, at p. 223.

[67] Greg Young-Ing, 'Indigenous Knowledge and Intellectual Property Rights in Context', in Government of Canada, Department of Canadian Heritage (ed.), *Discussion Papers for Traditions: National Gatherings on Indigenous Knowledge*, Ottawa: Undated, at p. 47, as cited in Department of Canadian Heritage, supra note 64, at p. 4, note 3.

laws and policies designed to facilitate the 'civilisation' of Indians. These included provisions in the Indian Act that outlawed significant religious and cultural practices, such as the West Coastal Nations' Potlatch Ceremonies and Blackfoot Sundance Ceremonies. Even though they have skilled carvers in the community that can carve physical replicas of material sought, return of these items confiscated is seen as vital to the spiritual health and self-esteem of communities recovering from terrible injustices perpetrated upon them.[68]

Return of ceremonial material, such as Blackfoot medicine bundles, may also be necessary because of the intangibles associated with them. Held by individuals for the benefit of the tribe, bundles form the major basis of traditional intangible property in Blackfoot Nations of the Canadian plains. They consist of numerous items and associated songs, dances and information used in the performance of spiritual ceremonies and necessary for transmission of specialised knowledge, healing powers, rights and responsibilities to individuals within a society. When bundles are removed and unavailable for use, religious societies charged with keeping the knowledge and performing the songs, dances and stories associated with them may be unable to perform complete ceremonies and train new members in specific areas.[69]

More specific rationales for increased access to and control over cultural heritage vary. However, aboriginal peoples do not seek to make all cultural heritage inaccessible or prevent commercial use where appropriate from the perspective of indigenous law. They largely 'want to ensure their knowledge is used appropriately and their identity portrayed authentically. They also want fair remuneration when their intellectual and cultural property is turned into commercial use.'[70] Where public access is not appropriate, concerns relate to protection of what was (and is or has become) sensitive cultural information (for example confidential, sacred, ceremonial or other forms of knowledge intended to be transmitted in certain ways or only to certain people); respect for indigenous jurisdictions, laws, processes or protocols considered fundamental to continuity of cultural identity or legal, social or spiritual orders; controlling information considered vital to restore spirit, human dignity and/or well-being; and preventing uses that are inappropriate or illegal within indigenous contexts.

3. REGULATION OF ABORIGINAL CULTURAL HERITAGE

Legislative jurisdiction to enact laws over cultural heritage is divided in the Constitution Act 1867 between the federal and provincial governments, although significant powers over land and tangible cultural heritage have been delegated by the federal to northern territorial governments.[71] However, there is no general jurisdiction assigned to 'culture'

---

68 Catherine Bell, Heather Raven and Heather McCuaig, 'Recovering from Colonization: Perspectives of Community Members on Protection and Repatriation of Kwakwaka'wakw Cultural Heritage', in Bell and Napoleon, supra note 1, pp. 33–91.

69 Bell, Statt and Mookakin Cultural Society, supra note 60.

70 RCAP, *Report of the Royal Commission on Aboriginal Peoples: Gathering Strength,* vol. III, Ottawa: Supply and Services Canada, 1996, at p. 596 [hereinafter RCAP Report, vol. III].

71 Territorial governments in northern Canada exercise powers similar to provinces that are delegated to them by the federal government.

per se. As a consequence of this jurisdictional arrangement, each of these levels of government have passed laws that directly or indirectly affect ownership and trade of aboriginal cultural heritage. The extent to which such legislation limits or terminates asserted inherent aboriginal or treaty rights to exercise control over cultural heritage through self-government, aboriginal title or other potential s. 35 aboriginal constitutional rights is a question not yet addressed by Canadian courts and is a matter of academic and political debate.

The federal government has jurisdiction over federal lands, Indians and lands reserved for the Indians, shipping, navigation, intellectual property and the regulation of trade and commerce. The general rule is that only the federal government can pass legislation directed at First Nations, Inuit, reserve lands, aboriginal rights or other matters that fall under core section 91(24) federal jurisdiction over 'Indians and lands reserved for the Indians'.[72] Pursuant to this jurisdiction the federal government has enacted various laws that directly and indirectly affect aboriginal cultural heritage. As a matter of policy, the federal government also asserts ownership and control over archaeological property on federal Crown land. However, with the exception of limited protection offered under the Indian Act, there is no federal legislation specifically targeted at aboriginal art, moveable cultural property or intangible cultural heritage.

Provinces have jurisdiction over provincial Crown lands and property and civil rights within their provincial boundaries. Pursuant to this jurisdiction, provinces can enact laws of general application (for example heritage conservation laws uniformly applicable throughout the province) that have sections directed at 'Indians', or that disproportionately impact aboriginal property. For example, despite the fact that 90 per cent of the heritage resources affected by the British Columbia (BC) Heritage Conservation Act (HCA)[73] are aboriginal in nature, the SCC has held in *Kitkatla* that this is valid provincial legislation because of the general jurisdiction provinces have over lands, moveable property and resources.[74] However, if an aboriginal right to a heritage site is established, such legislation would be unconstitutional.[75] There are very few examples of provincial statutes aimed at First Nation or Métis moveable heritage, land or self-government. The validity of such legislation is debatable and uncertainty over which level of government has jurisdiction over aboriginal cultural heritage within a province (not located on or under federal or

---

72 Constitution Act 1867 (UK), 30 & 31 Vict, c. 3, reprinted in RSC 1985, App. II, No. 5, s. 91(24).

73 RSBC 1996, c. 187.

74 *Kitkatla Band v British Columbia (Minister of Small Business, Tourism and Culture)* (2002) 2 CNLR 143, at paras 65–73 Le Bel J (SCC) [hereinafter *Kitkatla*].

75 There has been limited litigation in Canada directly on this point. However, obiter comments by the SCC in *Kitkatla*, ibid., suggest that cultural heritage may in some cases 'be a key part of the collective identity of people' and that 'some component of cultural heritage' might go to the core of identity in such a way as to affect application of provincial law. In *Mohawk Band v Glenbow-Alberta Institute* (1988) 3 CNLR 70 Shannon J (Alta QB), it was recognised that the Mohawk claim to aboriginal rights to enforcement of traditional laws concerning use and display of a False Face Mask raised a serious legal issue to be tried. However, in this case the plaintiffs did not demonstrate irreparable harm would be suffered if the mask was not returned before trial, a condition that must be met in any injunction application. The matter was ultimately settled out of court.

reserve land within the province) continues to complicate any attempts at legislative reform in areas such as repatriation and trade within and between provinces.

As the focus of this chapter is indigenous cultural heritage and international trade, I am not considering all federal, territorial and provincial laws or policies that implicate aboriginal cultural heritage in detail. Rather, I discuss areas of federal and provincial law that have the most significant impact.

3.1 Heritage Conservation Law

> We follow what we call our *snu'uy'ulh* – teachings that tells us not to do these things to other people, people's human remains, their ancestors that have gone before us. Their ancestors, the non-First Nations ancestors, have what they call their *snu'uy'ulh*. It's written in law, Canadian law and British Columbia law. They call it the Heritage [Conservation Act], for one example. The Cemeteries Act, for another example … tells them that they have rules that they have to follow with regard to those things, and I think that, that our *snu'uy'ulh*, our rules should be respected as much as any other rules that are set by governments of Canada and B.C.[76]
>
> (George Harris, Elder, Chemainus First Nation)

All provinces have enacted heritage conservation laws that control excavations affecting historical resources through a permit system, provide for the reporting, designation and protection of historical resources, and vest ownership of archaeological and other historical resources and sites discovered in or on provincial public (and in some instances private) lands in the provincial Crown. In Ontario and Prince Edward Island, there is also special cemeteries legislation that requires permits and minimum disturbance to aboriginal burial grounds, but this legislation offers no greater protection than offered to archaeological sites elsewhere. In the absence of a land claim or modern treaty agreement to the contrary, provincial museums and universities are the primary repositories for items and remains acquired through statutory vesting of title. Statutory vesting under provincial law will not extinguish aboriginal constitutional rights to archaeological material if such rights can be established. However, continued application of provincial laws may be justified if a province proves a valid legislative objective.

What is largely missing in most provincial legislation is express legislative recognition of rights and interests of aboriginal people to own and participate in the management of their archaeological and ethnographic heritage. However, some form of notification or consultation with descendant communities, or First Nations on whose traditional territories (outside of the reserve) artefacts or remains are discovered, is now often done as a matter of government policy. Provincial museums and many universities accept an ethical obligation to return ancestral remains for interment. Such consultation by governments is now a constitutional legal obligation, as well, where their actions may impact on existing

---

[76] Eric McLay et al., 'A'lhut tu tet sul'mweentst (Respecting the Ancestors): Understanding Hul'qumi'num Heritage Laws and Concerns for Protection of Archaeological Heritage', in Bell and Napoleon, supra note 1, pp. 150–202, at pp. 178–9.

or potential aboriginal or treaty rights.[77] Although most legislation does not speak to ownership of remains, ownership of all forms of archaeological or ethnographic heritage recovered from the land continues to be a contested issue.

Unlike other provincial laws, the HCA mentioned before has undergone amendments that speak directly to some First Nation heritage management concerns. As part of the process the government sought input from BC First Nations and produced a Draft HCA.[78] The draft vested ownership of ancestral remains in BC First Nations and provided that any remains in the possession of the Crown were held in trust for them. It also attempted to deal with the removal of archaeological objects from BC. However, in so doing it 'managed to both offend certain Aboriginal groups (by a provision deeming pre-1858 found objects to be the property of the Crown) and to risk the possibility of being unconstitutional, in that this law could be challenged for straying into federal jurisdiction (because of provisions dealing with the international movement of heritage objects)'.[79] For this reason many provisions in the proposed law were dropped. As Robert K. Paterson (a Canadian expert on Canadian and International Cultural Property Law) argues, the resulting HCA does nevertheless create the possibility for the province to designate and protect 'heritage objects'. Section 4 of the HCA also enables the province to enter formal agreements (for example modern treaties) with a First Nation concerning 'the conservation and protection of heritage sites and heritage objects that represent the cultural heritage of the aboriginal people who are represented by that first nation'. Additionally, BC's legislation explicitly recognises aboriginal title in section 8, which states that nothing in this Act takes away from existing aboriginal or treaty rights.

In 1990, the federal government also proposed amended legislation with respect to items recovered from federal public lands (for example national parks). The draft federal law would have vested ownership in the federal Crown, provided for consultation procedures with cultural and religious groups, and allowed for the conclusion of agreements with aboriginal peoples. However, the draft legislation was not pursued. As only the federal government can terminate aboriginal rights, if a common-law aboriginal right to ownership and control of aboriginal cultural property existed prior to 1982, it has not been extinguished by federal legislation and receives constitutional protection.

3.2 Limitation of Actions and Access to Information Law

> They say, '[O]h well, it's too late' or '[A]fter fifty years it's now a museum piece.' They put a time limit – fifty years – and, and you know, our time is forever.[80]
>
> (Rosse Modeste, Elder, Cowichan Tribes)

---

[77] *Haida Nation v British Columbia (Minister of Forests)* (2004) 3 SCR 511 McLachlin J (SCC) [hereinafter *Haida Nation*]; *Mikisew Cree First Nation v Canada (Minister of Canadian Heritage)* (2005) 1 CNLR 78 Binnie J (SCC).

[78] See *Heritage Legislation: A Draft Bill*, Victoria: BC Ministry of Tourism and Ministry Responsible for Culture, 1992.

[79] Catherine Bell and Robert Paterson, 'Aboriginal Rights to Repatriation of Cultural Property', in Ardith Walkem and Halie Bruce (eds), *Box of Treasures or Empty Box: Twenty Years of Section 35*, Penticton: Theytus Books, 2003, pp. 104–54, at p. 104.

[80] McLay et al., supra note 76, at p. 180.

Limitation periods that prevent legal actions from being brought before Canadian courts to recover moveable cultural property also affect aboriginal peoples' rights to cultural heritage in the control of private persons or other custodians. Provincial and parallel federal legislation on limitation periods is of particular concern as they operate to unjustly vest title in current possessors even where there is no dispute as to the cultural significance of an item to a claimant aboriginal people, or its removal from the community, or use, being contrary to indigenous laws.

> In addressing limitations legislation, a significant hurdle for First Nations is a juridical concept of fairness in which protection of innocent good faith purchasers for value is a fundamental component. The primary purposes of limitation periods are to encourage prompt settlement of disputes, create certainty necessary for the operation of markets in a private property system, and protect reasonable expectations of good faith purchasers. They are also intended to address evidentiary problems that can occur as time passes ... [81]

Whether limitation periods apply to s. 35 aboriginal property claims varies from province to province, creating differential access to justice by aboriginal peoples. For example, in Saskatchewan, s. 35 rights are expressly exempted from provincial limitations law, but not in most other provinces.[82] Alberta does not apply limitation periods to items in public collections that fall within the legal criteria established for repatriation of sacred ceremonial items under its First Nations Sacred Ceremonial Objects Repatriation Act.[83] Some major museums that have aboriginal collections also do not rely on these technical legal arguments in negotiations for return of sacred, ceremonial or other significant cultural items. The resulting situation is a complicated patchwork in which technical arguments concerning ownership may or may not be used depending on the location and form of property being claimed.[84]

Interfering with the ability of aboriginal peoples to control and ensure appropriate use of traditional knowledge is provincial access to information and privacy legislation applicable to public bodies, which include universities, government agencies and departments, tribunals, municipal governments and many other public institutions that are repositories of aboriginal information. This legislation, which largely mirrors the Canada Access to Information Act (CAIA), applies to some, but not all, public museums and archives.[85] For example, section 68 of the CAIA provides that it does not apply to published materials, materials available for purchase, library or museum materials, or: 'material placed in the Library and Archives of Canada, the National Gallery of Canada, the Canadian Museum of Civilization, the Canadian Museum of Nature, the National Museum of Science and Technology or the Canadian Museum for Human Rights by or on behalf of persons or organisations other than government institutions.' Such legislation operates on the assumption of maximum public accessibility, but typically exempts from disclosure confidential information that could be harmful to intergovernmental relations, including relations with aboriginal governments. In light of these types of exemptions, aboriginal

---

81 Bell, 'Restructuring', supra note 12, at p. 33.

82 See, for example, Limitation Act, SS 2004, L-16.1, s. 3(2).

83 RSA 2000, c. F-14.

84 For arguments against application see Bell, 'Restructuring', supra note 12, at pp. 34–5.

85 RSC 1985, c. A-1.

governments are increasingly asking researchers to enter into agreements that provide for confidentiality of some or all data and information gathered from research conducted on reserve or settlement land and, in some instances, greater benefits and control over not only raw data, but intellectual and other products of research. Other areas of concern to aboriginal people include protecting information from uses that are offensive or that are in violation of laws that continue to be integral to their societies.[86]

Control over disclosure, access and use of recorded information, in whatever form it is held (for example book, tapes, computer programme, notes, maps, pictures) currently lies with the institution or public body that owns the record. However, this control may be restricted by conditions imposed by original donors, negotiated agreements, institutional policy or legislation. In a few provinces and territories there are other potential avenues for restricting access to aboriginal information, such as where disclosure could reasonably be expected to damage or interfere with the conservation of 'sites having an anthropological or heritage value or aboriginal cultural significance'.[87] In others, it is more difficult to fall under the exception for confidential intergovernmental relations as there is a need to prove potential harm from disclosure or that such protections are limited to aboriginal governments listed in the legislation. For example, under section 13 of the CAIA, information obtained in confidence from aboriginal governments (which are recognised under federal self-government, land claim and modern treaty agreements or legislation) is protected from disclosure without consent, unless such information was first made public. The only examples of access to information and privacy legislation containing express exceptions relating to traditional knowledge are found in territorial legislation concerning proceedings of administrative tribunals.[88]

3.3 Canadian Intellectual Property Law

> A good example of this is use of the word 'Nipika'. That's our word for, like, [the] Creator. And there's companies that use that word … [To] me it's no different than if we were to call the casino that we just opened up say, say, the 'Holy Mary Jesus Christ Casino' or something like that.[89]
>
> (Troy Hunter, Ktunaxa Kinbasket tribal council)

It is difficult to speak of traditional knowledge, intangible heritage, indigenous intellectual property and other aspects of indigenous cultural heritage in the abstract, as priorities and

---

86 For example, this theme arises in the case studies in Bell and Napoleon, supra note 1, and in testimony before the RCAP (RCAP Report, vol. III, supra note 70), and Canadian government consultations, infra note 100.

87 Access to Information and Protection of Privacy Act, SNWT 1994, c. 20, s. 19; Access to Information and Protection of Privacy Act (Nunavut), SNWT 1994, c. 20, s. 16; and Access to Information and Protection of Privacy Act, RSY 2002, c. 1, s. 20.

88 For example, enabling legislation for the Yukon Environmental and Socio-economic Assessment Board allows the Board to refuse to disclose 'traditional knowledge that is determined to be confidential under the applicable rules and that is provided in confidence to them for the purposes of this Act'; YESAA, supra note 63, s. 121(a).

89 Catherine Bell and Heather McCuaig, 'Protection and Repatriation of Ktunaxa/Kinbasket Cultural Resources: Perspectives of Community Members', in Bell and Napoleon, supra note 1, pp. 312–64, at p. 328.

understandings are community- and context-specific. Nevertheless, some common themes emerge in much of the work done on indigenous knowledge and IP reform. These are:

1. Intellectual property in the form of traditional knowledge often cannot be separated from tangible manifestations of that knowledge.
2. There is a perceived need for protection from, and control over what is referred to in western political discourse as 'cultural appropriation'.
3. Intellectual property law may be of some assistance where the values inherent in it are consistent with rationales for seeking protection and transferability of rights, which are reconcilable with indigenous legal orders or perspectives on appropriate commercial use.
4. Solutions founded in reforms to IP law alone are an inadequate response to indigenous concerns.

Despite the work that Canada has done to learn more about the interface of traditional knowledge and IP law, any progress made has been with a view to reconciling indigenous interests in a way that upholds existing IP values. Not surprisingly, then, the current IP regime is the same as that found in many other western industrialised nations.[90] Although, in 2003, a Canadian policy review identified aboriginal traditional knowledge as one of the 'long term' issues to be considered in future reviews of copyright legislation, the only significant amendments since 1982 have been in response to international trade and technological development to create more opportunities to commercialise intangible property.

There have been many writings on the limits of IP for protecting indigenous traditional knowledge. There remains a role for intellectual property law or law reform where concepts of property and transferability of rights are reconcilable with aboriginal legal orders and contemporary perspectives on commercial use. A well-known example in Canada is the defensive use of the Trade-Marks Act[91] by the Nanaimo First Nation to protect petroglyph images from use in advertising for, and on merchandise promoting, a music festival. Unlike New Zealand,[92] Canada's trade mark legislation does not prohibit use of marks likely to offend Canada's aboriginal peoples or provide a mechanism to determine this. However the Nanaimo Band council (Snuneymuxw First Nation) was able to invoke an obscure provision that allows for trade marks of 'official marks'.[93] Official

---

[90] The respective governing statutes are: Copyright Act, RSC 1985, c. C-42; Patent Act, RSC 1985, c. P-4; Trade-Marks Act, RSC 1985, c. T-13; Industrial Design Act, RSC 1985, c. I-9; Plant Breeders' Rights Act, SC 1990, c. 20; and the Integrated Circuit Topography Act, SC 1990, c. 37.

[91] Trade-Marks Act, ibid. See for further discussion Simon Brascoupé, *A Community Guide to Protecting Indigenous Knowledge*, Ottawa: Indian and Northern Affairs Canada, Research and Analysis Directorate, 2001; and Catherine Bell et al., 'First Nations Cultural Heritage: A Selected Survey of Issues and Initiatives', in Bell and Napoleon, supra note 1, pp. 367–414, at pp. 395–6.

[92] Trade-Marks Act 2002 (NZ), 2002/49. See Susy Frankel, 'A New Zealand Perspective on the Protection of Mātauranga Māori (Traditional Knowledge)', in this volume.

[93] Trade-Marks Act, supra note 90, s. 9(1)(n)(iii). To be recognised as a public authority the Snuneymuxw had to satisfy a two-part test: (1) a significant degree of control must be exercised by the appropriate government over the activities of the body; and (2) the activities of the body must benefit the public. See Canadian Intellectual Property Office (CIPO), 'Section on Public Authority

mark designation can be obtained by a 'public authority'. Unlike regular trade marks, which must be renewed, official mark protection is indefinite, subject only to withdrawal of the mark or a court decision. The Registrar of Trademarks declared that the band council met the test of a public authority and that the disputed petroglyph images were 'official marks' of the band council government. Trade mark status is maintained by using the images on the council letterhead, business cards, and so on. As a consequence, the Dancing Man Music Festival kept its name, but stopped using the popular images for promotion. The local museum stopped selling items with protected images on them, but also subsequently applied for a grant to make cement copies of the originals with permission of the Snuneymuxw First Nation.

There may also be a role for IP reform with respect to traditional knowledge and cultural expressions which, according to IP law, are now in the public domain but under indigenous law are not intended for external access.[94] As Young-Ing argues, 'the present reality is that TK is, or will be, in the Public Domain and that the IPR system overrides customary law.'[95] This means that, until the situation changes, protective mechanisms should be explored. One way he (and others) suggest greater protection may be accomplished is the recognition of moral rights of authors, artists and composers. Such rights, found in section 28.2(1) of the Copyright Act[96] were included to protect against 'distortion, mutilation of, or otherwise modified' in relation to the said work which would be 'to the prejudice of the honour or reputation of the author'. Such provisions hold promise where the objective is to 'ensure that their knowledge is used appropriately and their identity portrayed authentically'.[97] An example of the application of this provision is by the Ontario High Court in upholding that a sculptor's moral rights had been infringed when, in celebration of Christmas, red ribbons were tied around the necks of Canada geese that he had sculpted for public display at Eaton Centre in Toronto.[98]

However helpful, manipulations to existing IP law do nothing to address concerns about enforcement and respect for indigenous control over decisions about what should or should not be treated as commercial or capable of individual transfer or ownership under indigenous law, or 'fair remuneration when their intellectual and cultural property is turned into commercial use'.[99] For example, there are no special laws addressing entitlement to revenues from use of aboriginal knowledge or cultural expressions.

To date the federal response to aboriginal peoples' concerns has been to identify protection mechanisms available through means other than law reform and to create information tool kits to help aboriginal artists and communities take advantage of existing laws and enter contractual relations with researchers. Canada has also hosted World

---

Status Under Sub-Paragraph 9(i)(n)(iii)' (2002) *Trade-Marks Journal*, 49 (2501), pp. 249–50, at p. 249, available at http://www.ic.gc.ca/cipo/tradejournal.nsf/curEd/7DD1C6DCE89E23B385256D71005BCE9A/$File/2oct2002.pdf.

94 See on this Brigitte Vézina, 'Are They In or Are They Out? Traditional Cultural Expressions and the Public Domain: Implications for Trade', in this volume.

95 Young-Ing, supra note 67, at p. 61.

96 See supra note 90.

97 RCAP Report, vol. III, supra note 70, at p. 596.

98 *Snow v The Eaton Centre Ltd* (1982) 70 CPR 105 O'brien J (Ont H Ct J).

99 RCAP Report, vol. III, supra note 70, at p. 596.

Intellectual Property Organization (WIPO) workshops on IP and traditional knowledge, supported and participated in conferences concerning indigenous traditional knowledge and IP protection, hosted workshops in communities to discuss the benefits and limits of existing IP law, and commissioned research in these areas.[100]

3.4 Tangible Cultural Property and the Indian Act

> What I'm saying is that the laws are already there. Those items should never have been sold. But you have to appreciate the circumstances in and around the sale of those [communal property]; some of them were taken, some were exploited, our people were starving around that [time], some of them converted to Christianity, and it wasn't the owners, it was their children, their grandchildren, that took those out … . It was not to hawk to get a bottle of wine. Each story is different on how they left, even some very sad ones.[101]
>
> (Narcisse Blood, Blood Tribe Elder and President of the Mookakin Foundation)

As elaborated earlier in this chapter, section 91 of the Indian Act applies to status Indians and reserve lands. In the absence of written consent of the Minister, 'no person may … acquire title to any of the following property situated on a reserve, namely, (a) an Indian grave house; (b) a carved grave pole; (c) a totem pole; (d) a carved house post; or (e) a rock embellished with paintings or carvings.' Furthermore, no person may 'remove, take away, mutilate, disfigure, deface or destroy' any of the above. Objects 'manufactured for sale by Indians' are exempt from these provisions. Intentional violation of these laws by Indian agents, and mistakes of abandonment arising from lack of understanding of aboriginal lifestyles, resulted in carved poles being wrongfully severed and removed from Indian land. Perhaps the most famous example is the Haisla Spirit Pole repatriated from the Swedish Museum of Ethnology.[102] In 1927 the Indian agent at Bella Coola wrote to the Department of Indian Affairs seeking permission to let Olof Hansson, Swedish Consul for BC, take the Haisla Pole as the village was empty, which the agent mistakenly thought meant it was abandoned. Sixty-one years after the pole was taken, a photograph in an anthropology text alerted the community to its location. In 1991, the Haisla sent a delegation to Sweden to request the pole's return. As a condition of return a replica pole was provided. The pole was finally returned on 15 March 2006.[103]

Band councils also have limited jurisdiction, delegated from the federal government pursuant to sections 81 and 85.1 of the Indian Act, to enact by-laws, analogous to those of a municipality, concerning use of and life on reserve lands. These delegations were not made in recognition of an inherent aboriginal constitutional right to self-government, and the extent to which allocation of local governmental powers under the Indian Act to band councils modifies or terminates this right is uncertain in Canadian law. However, they do contain some avenues for regulating cultural heritage on reserve land. For example,

---

[100] See, for example, Brascoupé, supra note 91; and Brian Thom and Don Bain, 'Aboriginal Intangible Property in Canada: An Ethnographic Review', Industry Canada (2004), available at http://www.ic.gc.ca/eic/site/ippd-dppi.nsf/eng/ip01200.html; and Department of Canadian Heritage, supra note 64.

[101] Bell, Statt and Mookakin Cultural Society, supra note 60, at p. 231.

[102] Bell et al., supra note 91, at pp. 380–81.

[103] Ibid., at p. 381.

by-law powers relating to commercial activities on the reserve and control of access to reserve land have been used to control trafficking in cultural items on reserve lands.[104] In 1997 the Kamloops Indian Band enacted a heritage conservation by-law applicable to their reserve lands. The by-law established the Cultural Resources Management Department, which assumes responsibility for heritage protection and the excavation permit system, and liaises with other governments on heritage management issues.[105] A few First Nations have also increased their management and control of reserve lands and resources through the First Nations Land Management Act (FNLMA).[106] The FNLMA grants First Nations the power to manage their lands and resources, enact laws respecting their lands, and create summary conviction offences. Unlike by-laws, laws enacted by band councils managing lands under a negotiated Land Code or agreement with the federal government do not require ministerial approval.

3.5 Cultural Property Export and Import

> Well one of the problems with the Export Review Board is, of course, the prohibitive costs of … stopping the export. We'd have to come up with some monies to pay for the pieces, so that was one problem. And the other problem, of course, is a, is – what seems to happen when a piece is to be exported is the price skyrockets. An example is the piece from Bella Coola, where I think a collector bought it for a few thousand dollars and it cost the Bella Coola people I think near a quarter million dollars to get it back. That was a, that was a real tragedy there, but they did manage to get it back. But for the most part, lately we've been getting some very good cooperation from the museums in repatriation not only of actual physical property but also for the written materials and recorded materials.[107]
>
> (Bill Cranmer, Chief of 'Namgis Nation and President of the U'mista Cultural Society)

The Bella Coola (Nuxalk) Echo Mask referred to in the above quote was purchased for CN$35,000 from a poor elder, who was the keeper of the mask.[108] In the late 1980s, after several visits to the community, an art dealer aware of its commercial value persuaded her to sell it. Approximately 140 years old, Echo is capable of transforming into multiple identities and carries with it a web of rights and responsibilities, including societal status, spirit powers, names, songs, legends and dances. Under the laws of the Nuxalk Nation, the mask and the prerogatives associated with it may only be transferred at a potlatch under the witness of the community. The mask 'belongs to the family which has the custody of it', but is held for the benefit of families, religious societies and the people as a whole. The

---

[104] See, for example, Bella Coola Band, By-law No. 5–6 (30 January 1954).

[105] For discussion of this and other examples see Bell et al., supra note 91, at pp. 390–93.

[106] SC 1999, c. 24.

[107] Bell, Raven and McCuaig, supra note 68, at p. 83.

[108] Information for this account is taken largely from judicial pleadings and affidavits. It was first published by the author in, and is excerpted from, Catherine Bell and Robert Paterson, 'International Movement of First Nations Cultural Heritage in Canadian Law', in Bell and Paterson, supra note 12, pp. 78–109. For more detailed discussion see also Janet Kramer, *Switchbacks: Art, Ownership, and Nuxalk National Identity*, Vancouver: University of British Columbia Press, 2006, at pp. ix–xiii and 87–96.

keeper of the mask must care for it and bring it out to be danced for the potlatch. The mask cannot be sold by an individual and is to stay in the community for use in potlatches.

In 1995, the dealer applied for an export permit under the Cultural Property Export and Import Act (CPEIA)[109] to sell the mask outside of Canada for US$250,000. Notified about the pending sale by Simon Fraser University, the Nuxalk Nation met with the Royal British Columbia Museum (RBCM) and other supporters to develop a strategy to bring the Echo Mask back home. After the dealer refused to meet, litigation was commenced seeking a declaration that Echo could not be sold, traded or given away to a non-member, an injunction preventing the sale and export of the mask, and for the mask's return. After a year of negotiations, the matter was settled out of court. The dealer agreed to sell the Echo Mask back to the Nuxalk for CN$200,000, insisting throughout that he had legitimate title to it.

In Canada, export of cultural property is regulated by the CPEIA. The Act regulates the import and export of a wide range of moveable cultural property. It seeks to balance the ability to freely sell and trade in privately owned property, with the desire to keep cultural objects of national importance within Canada, through a system of export permits, tax benefits that encourage donations to Canadian institutions and public authorities, grants and loans. Section 4 establishes the Canadian Cultural Property Export Control List (the Control List)[110] and describes a wide range of tangible cultural heritage that may be included on that List in broad categories similar to those roughly based on the categories that comprise the definition of the term 'cultural property' in Article 1 of the 1970 UNESCO Convention on the Means of Prohibiting and Preventing the Illicit Import, Export and Transfer of Ownership of Cultural Property.[111] To be included on the Control List, property must be at least 50 years old and made by someone no longer living. Currently the Control List includes, among other things, archaeological material (aboriginal and non-aboriginal) of any value and non-archaeological Canadian aboriginal objects of a fair market value in Canada of more than CD$3,000.[112]

---

[109] Supra note 7.

[110] CRC 1978, c. 448.

[111] UNESCO, Convention on the Means of Prohibiting and Preventing the Illicit Import, Export and Transfer of Ownership of Cultural Property, 823 UNTS 231 (adopted on 14 November 1970, entered into force 24 April 1972).

[112] Section 4 outlines the range of items that can be on the Control List. Section 4(2) provides: Subject to subsection (3), the Governor in Council may include in the Control List, regardless of their places of origin, any objects or classes of objects hereinafter described in this subsection, the export of which the Governor in Council deems it necessary to control in order to preserve the national heritage in Canada: (a) objects of any value that are of archaeological, prehistorical, historical, artistic or scientific interest and that have been recovered from the soil of Canada, the territorial sea of Canada or the inland or other internal waters of Canada; (b) objects that were made by, or objects referred to in paragraph (d) that relate to, the aboriginal peoples of Canada and that have a fair market value in Canada of more than five hundred dollars; (c) objects of decorative art, hereinafter described in this paragraph, that were made in the territory that is now Canada and are more than one hundred years old: (i) glassware, ceramics, textiles, woodenware and works in base metals that have a fair market value in Canada of more than five hundred dollars, and (ii) furniture, sculptured works in wood, works in precious metals and other objects of decorative art that have a fair market value in Canada of more than two thousand dollars; (d) books, records, documents, photographic positives and negatives, sound recordings, and collections of any of those objects that

Under the cultural property export permit system, items on the Control List must be referred to expert examiners, chosen by the government, to make a determination of whether the object is of 'outstanding significance by reason of its close association with Canadian history or national life, its aesthetic qualities, or its value in the study of arts or sciences' and 'is of such a degree of national importance that its loss to Canada would significantly diminish the national heritage'.[113] Objects meeting these criteria are to be denied export permits. However, the exporter may appeal to the Canadian Cultural Property Export Review Board (the Review Board), which has the ability to delay an export for a maximum of six months. The purpose of this delay is to allow the Moveable Cultural Property Division (the Division) of the Department of Canadian Heritage (the Department) to notify Canadian institutions and public authorities (mostly museums and art galleries) so that they have an opportunity to purchase the item and prevent export.

Although the Act provides for grants and loans to buy back significant heritage, few aboriginal nations have institutions capable of meeting the criteria for both notice of exports and funding. The CPEIA itself places no conditions on funding, but as a matter of policy up to one half of the purchase price to be paid by the organisation applying for the grant is required. In the case of the Echo Mask, the Nuxalk Nation had to raise 30 per cent of the purchase price, a portion of which was ultimately donated by the art dealer himself.[114] Conditions on grants are those that anticipate museum-like facilities. At the time of writing, the mask was still on display in a secure and environmentally controlled case at a bank in the town of Bella Coola, since there was no location on the reserve that met the funding criteria. It is now governed by externally imposed preservation regulations as a museum object and is held by the elected band council on behalf of the Nuxalk. The intention is to move the mask to the reserve if and when funding for adequate facilities is obtained and such facilities are completed.

Although this story demonstrates how partnerships between First Nations, museums and academic and government departments can operate successfully to fulfil the objectives of the CPEIA, there is another very troubling side. Aboriginal peoples in Canada find themselves in the situation of buying back cultural property that may be considered sacred, acquired in violation of First Nation law (even those well known and followed for generations) in the community, and items 'found' or wrongfully removed from their traditional territories outside the border of reserve or settlement land. Although many dealers utilise the CPEIA in an ethical way, it is still possible to manipulate and inflate prices and items that are spiritually, historically or culturally important to Canadian First Nations and they disappear into private collections. First Nations and their allies must often negotiate directly with dealers. Funding for grants is limited and Canadian heritage budgets have also been significantly reduced. Needless to say, no matter how important the

---

have a fair market value in Canada of more than five hundred dollars; (e) drawings, engravings, original prints and water-colours that have a fair market value in Canada of more than one thousand dollars; and (f) any other objects that have a fair market value in Canada of more than three thousand dollars.

113 CPEIA, s. 11(1).

114 Kramer, supra note 108, at p. xii.

material is, many Canadian aboriginal peoples live below the poverty line and fundamentals such as water, housing, education and health may have to take first priority in band council budgets when such huge amounts of money are at issue.[115]

Attempts have been made in the administration of the CPEIA to address some of these concerns. For example, a First Nations artist is now on the Review Board.[116] However, drafted prior to constitutional recognition of aboriginal rights, the Act does not anticipate or incorporate unique rights or interests of aboriginal peoples. For example, there is no obligation to notify band councils, First Nation Cultural Education Centres, or other organisations from communities of origin or First Nation communities nearest to or occupying lands in which items were originally discovered.[117] Aboriginal people still rely on the goodwill of those who are entitled to notification and not all view this as an ethical obligation. There is no mechanism to investigate or challenge the legitimacy of the applicant's title based on indigenous law or other grounds, leaving the only options available (to aboriginal people fortunate enough to learn of a pending export) to either litigate or negotiate collaborations and the purchase of items. There is no requirement that aboriginal people act as examiners (although if they are staff members at a museum they could be expert examiners) or have a role in determining what should go on the Control List. 'The secrecy that surrounds private art dealing and collecting'[118] makes it hard for aboriginal people to recover items, let alone impact a system of export control in which there are few direct mechanisms to ensure that they will be 'heard in assessing the cultural importance of objects to be exported' or able 'to bid on important items with federal assistance'.[119]

There is nothing in domestic or international law that would prevent increased aboriginal participation in the export regime. For example, Nafziger, Paterson and Renteln argue that although resort to the World Trade Organization (WTO) to resolve issues concerning validity of cultural property is unlikely, greater restrictions on commercial trade in cultural property would not necessarily violate Canada's international obligations.

---

[115] See, for example, Parliament of Canada, Social Affairs Division, Chantal Collin and Hilary Jensen, 'A Statistical Profile of Poverty' (2009), available at http://www.parl.gc.ca/Content/LOP/ResearchPublications/prb0917-e.htm; and UN Report, Stavenhagen, supra note 19.

[116] Department of Canadian Heritage, 'Members of the Review Board' (2010), available at http://www.pch.gc.ca/pgm/bcm-mcp/cebc-cperb/cntct/membr-eng.cfm.

[117] Unless they fall within the definition of a category A institution. This designation is granted by the Minister of Canadian Heritage for an indefinite period of time to institutions and public authorities that fall within legal definitions given in the CPEIA and receive repeat gifts of cultural objects, are established primarily for the purpose of exhibiting, collecting and preserving tangible cultural heritage, are accessible to the public and meet certain legal, curatorial and environmental standards to effectively display and store (largely museums, galleries and universities). See Department of Canadian Heritage, Moveable Cultural Property Division, 'Cultural Property Export and Import Act: Designation of Institutions and Public Authorities. Information and Procedures', Ottawa (revised June 2000), at pp. 6–12, available at http://www.pch.gc.ca/pgm/bcm-mcp/publctn/desgntn/dsgntn-eng.pdf.

[118] Robert K. Paterson, 'Claiming Possession of the Material Cultural Property of Indigenous People' (2001) *Connecticut Journal of International Law,* 16 (2), pp. 283–97, at p. 289.

[119] Rebecca Clements, 'Misconceptions of Culture: Native Peoples and Cultural Property Under Canadian Law' (1991) *University of Toronto Faculty of Law Review,* 49, pp. 1–26, at p. 18. Unless, of course, they qualify as a designated institution, see supra note 117.

Rather section XX(f) of GATT 1994 appears to enable prohibitions that 'allow measures that are "imposed for the protection of national treasures of artistic, historic or archaeological value"'.[120] However, Canada has not taken any meaningful steps to increase aboriginal participation. The Canadian government did recommend some export prohibitions be placed on archaeological material in its 1990 proposal for federal archaeological protection legislation, but this legislation was never enacted.[121]

4. APPLICATION OF ABORIGINAL CONSTITUTIONAL RIGHTS

To illustrate the complexities of ownership analysis, I consider s. 35 aboriginal constitutional rights and its potential application to the CPEIA as an example. There are a number of different ways the constitutional question can be framed. One way is to ask whether or not a particular aboriginal nation had laws restricting trade of certain material to cross borders.[122] Another is to ask if an aboriginal people had, and continue to have, laws in the community concerning ownership and use of particular forms of property. In either case, it remains relevant whether rights to enact laws, or particular laws, were terminated by treaty or other means, and whether the exercise of these laws continues to be integral to their distinctive aboriginal societies.

The continued application of the CPEIA could be challenged as an unjustified interference with s. 35 aboriginal and treaty rights. The argument raised in the Nuxalk litigation is that s. 35 of the Constitution Act 1982 recognises and protects First Nation customary law (that forms part of title or was and continues to be integral to a distinctive culture) and as such their laws on legality of the disposition of cultural material must be taken into consideration in assessing the right to export First Nation cultural objects. Rights to tangible culture may also arise if an object is part of an activity, custom, practice or tradition that was historical and continues to be integral to the distinctive cultural identity of a First Nation, and (a) the object has pre-contact origins, or (b) the object is not pre-contact in origin but is central to an activity, custom, tradition or practice, which is pre-contact in origin.[123] Thus the Nuxalk statement of claim asserts that Echo and the mask, songs, stories, hereditary titles and other privileges associated with the Echo Mask are integral to the distinctive culture of the Nuxalk Nation.

---

[120] James A.R. Nafziger, Robert K. Paterson and Alison Dundes Renteln, *Cultural Law: International, Comparative and Indigenous*, New York: Cambridge University Press, 2010, at p. 299. On the GATT Article XX exceptions see also John Scott and Federico Lenzerini, 'International Indigenous and Human Rights Law in the Context of Trade in Indigenous Cultural Heritage', in this volume; and Fiona Macmillan, 'Finding Space in the Margins? Recognising the Rights of Indigenous Peoples in the WTO', in this volume.

[121] See Communications Canada, 'Proposed Act Respecting the Protection of Archaeological Heritage in Canada', Ottawa (19 December 1990). For a discussion of the text of this Bill, which was never passed, see David V. Burley 'Historical Developments in Canadian Archaeology and the Quest for Federal Heritage Legislation' (1994) *Canadian Journal of Archaeology*, 18, pp. 77–98.

[122] *Mitchell*, supra note 14.

[123] This argument is derived from the reasoning in *Van der Peet*, supra note 3. See Bell, 'Restructuring', supra note 12, at p. 32.

The SCC has also made it clear that the honour of the Crown requires consultation with First Nations and Inuit on legislation, including legislation of general application to all citizens, when the Crown has 'knowledge, real or constructive' of existing or *potential* aboriginal rights that might be adversely affected; that is, rights which have not yet been formally recognised by agreement or by Canadian courts.[124] Even where claims to potential legal rights are weak, there is a duty to 'give notice, disclose information, and discuss any issues raised in response to the notice'.[125] Where a strong argument exists for recognition, steps may have to be taken to 'avoid irreparable harm' and minimise adverse effects until the rights claim is resolved.[126] It can be argued these criteria apply not only to initial actions, but continuing application of existing statutory laws and policies that impact on s. 35 aboriginal constitutional rights. As elaborated earlier in this chapter, there are also strong foundations for recognition of what Canadian courts have referred to as 'customary law' of aboriginal peoples.[127]

5. CONCLUSION

The above discussion demonstrates that the principle of indigenous self-determination in the form of autonomy to decide either what heritage is integral to their distinctive cultures, or which forms of heritage can be traded commercially, is not reflected in Canadian legislation. However, through ongoing discussions with aboriginal peoples, non-legislative negotiated responses are being developed in some areas. There are various federal, provincial and territorial programmes designed to foster and protect aboriginal cultural heritage. Key non-legislated initiatives include the preservation of aboriginal languages, financial support for aboriginal land-use studies and heritage-resource inventories, moveable cultural property repatriation grants and loans programme, the museum assistance programme, the Canada Council for Aboriginal Arts, and Parks Canada consultations on protection of aboriginal landscapes, co-management of parks, aboriginal use of parks and repatriation of artefacts. However, funding for these initiatives varies across the country, among aboriginal peoples and changes with the priorities of each elected federal or provincial government. The federal government, at the time of writing, has significantly slashed funding in all of these areas.

This approach to indigenous cultural heritage can be compared with the United States, where Native American and Hawaiian ownership and control of certain forms of cultural property and ancestral remains is considered a question of national and international human rights, and determination of legitimate acquisition and transfer of title, a matter of tribal or Hawaiian law. As James Nafziger explains:

---

124 *Haida Nation*, supra note 77, at para. 35. See also *Taku River Tlingit First Nation v British Columbia (Project Assessment Director)* (2005) 1 CNLR 366 McLachlin J (SCC).

125 *Haida Nation*, supra note 77, at para. 43.

126 Ibid., at para. 47.

127 See, for example, Norman Zlotkin, 'From Time Immemorial: The Recognition of Aboriginal Customary Law in Canada', in Bell and Paterson, supra note 12, pp. 343–60.

> Congress clearly intended the legislation [Native American Graves Protection Repatriation Act, NAGPRA] to repair past wrongs and ensure present and future rights. As such, it must be seen and interpreted against the backdrop of modern human rights legislation at both domestic and international levels. NAGPRA also conforms with a general theory for repatriation. Accordingly it can be fairly described as an instrument of decolonization, self-determination, and repatriation; as a vindication of Native American religious and other cultural freedoms; as a means of enhancing cultural revival and transmission of cultural knowledge among tribes and Native Hawaiian groups; as a contributor to self-identity and community solidarity; and as a means for restoring Native American control over pertinent culture.[128]

With the exception of Alberta's Repatriation Act, which also emphasises human rights, this has not been the approach in Canada. Not surprisingly, at the same time Alberta enacted the Alberta Personal Property Bill of Rights[129] to protect private ownership. Nevertheless, despite limited instances of law reform, land claim and modern treaty agreements, provincial departmental policies and many other collaborative arrangements reflect changing relationships between aboriginal peoples in Canada and Canadian governments concerning cultural heritage as a human right. However, national responses continue to be largely grounded on the assumption of ethical and political obligations, not legal human or s. 35 aboriginal rights obligations, leaving many aboriginal peoples of Canada, particularly those south of the 60th parallel, vulnerable and with no meaningful autonomy in matters relating to cultural heritage control.

Other authors in this volume address in greater detail how the international systems of IP, trade and human rights law support increased restrictions on trade in indigenous traditional knowledge and cultural expression. Here I only mention that Canada's conservative government was among four countries in 2007 that voted against the United Nations Declaration on the Rights of Indigenous Peoples (UNDRIP),[130] and only after much public criticism, finally endorsed UNDRIP on 12 November 2010.[131] The Canadian government initially voted against adoption for several reasons, including vague wording of some provisions giving rise to multiple interpretations and insufficient consideration and balance of the rights of other Canadians, states and third parties. For example, Canada was concerned that Article 4, which provides: 'Indigenous peoples, in exercising their right to self-determination, have the right to autonomy or self-government in matters relating to their internal and local affairs, as well as ways and means for financing their autonomous functions', does not reflect the need for processes that will achieve harmony with all levels of government. This, Canada believes, is currently being achieved by the self-government processes I have outlined above. Ultimately, Canada attached no qualifications to the adoption of UNDRIP but continues to emphasise it is not a legally binding document.[132]

---

128 James A.R. Nafziger, 'The Protection and Repatriation of Indigenous Cultural Heritage in the United States', in Bell and Paterson, supra note 12, pp. 110–52, at p. 118. On NAGPRA, see supra note 51.

129 RSA 2000, c. A-31.

130 See supra note 5.

131 AANDC, 'Canada's Statement of Support on UNDRIP' (2010), available at http: www.ainc-inac.gc.ca/ap/ia/dcl/stmt-eng.asp.

132 Ibid.

It is within this broader legal and political environment that Christoph B. Graber's proposal for interfacing global law and indigenous law can be considered from a Canadian perspective. Graber proposes that disputes concerning international trade in traditional knowledge and cultural expressions be resolved through a procedural approach that has preferential rules for spiritually or communally significant 'indigenous cultural goods (or services) originating in WTO members that respect the rights of the cultural self-determination and self-governance of their indigenous peoples'.[133] As part of this approach it is assumed that WTO members will look to indigenous communities of origin to distinguish what cultural expressions can be traded from others. Three key components are:

1. prima facie assumption of indigenous ownership where certain criteria are met;
2. indigenous laws and processes determining ownership and nature of, or whether a particular traditional cultural expression can be traded; and
3. formal confirmation by a special WTO commission that would notify and take into consideration rights and arguments of dissenting claimants.[134]

To identify communities that own disputed cultural expressions, Graber calls on Member States to agree to a presumption of ownership on prima facie proof of one or more factors set out by Erica-Irene Daes, including 'priority in time with regard to use and occupation of territory, aspects of language or cultural expressions which may show the cultural distinctiveness of the community, issues of self-identification as a distinct group and experiences of subjugation, marginalization, and dispossession', among others, 'as prima facie evidence of communal indigenous ownership'.[135]

As Graber points out, there are many advantages to procedural approaches. However, to be implemented they require support by current WTO members. I have argued both normative and legal rationale in this chapter, and in other writings, for Canada to adopt law and policy consistent with such a proposed procedural approach. Given the history of the Canadian response so far, it is unlikely that we will see national rights recognition or enforcement through law and constitutional reform beyond Canada's current policy stance without specific direction from the SCC. It is more likely that support would not come from industrialised countries and art market countries, such as Canada, but from WTO members who already benefit from some preferential treatment in WTO disputes as

---

[133] Graber, 'Creativity', supra note 6.

[134] Ibid., at pp. 251–2.

[135] There is precedent for such an approach in international policy and cultural property law. For example, policies and international agreements that call upon museums and other institutions to review their collections 'for any indication of unlawful appropriation' during the Nazi era, with a view to negotiating restitutions. Bell, 'Restructuring', supra note 12, at p. 59; and Robert K. Paterson, 'Resolving Material Culture Disputes: Human Rights, Property Rights and Crimes Against Humanity', in James A.R. Nafziger and Ann Nicgorski (eds), *Cultural Heritage Issues: The Legacy of Conquest, Colonization, and Commerce*, Leiden: Martinus Nijhoff Publishers, 2009, pp. 371–88, at p. 371. However, even in this context opinions vary on how to 'treat transfers of title that were necessitated by the prevailing conditions' and sales made under unreasonable pressures but legal under the laws at the time.

'developing nations' and whose national economic interests align with increased control over exploitation of traditional indigenous culture.

We also need to carefully examine what we mean by cultural self-determination, self-government, local custom and indigenous law. For example, in Canada, comments by the SCC on the aboriginal right of self-government and the existence and continuance of indigenous laws are open to many different interpretations. The current interpretation of the federal and provincial governments on self-government and autonomy over aspects of their cultural heritage 'integral to their distinctive cultures' is contested by aboriginal peoples of Canada as well as legal scholars.

Assuming these challenges can be overcome, the third component of the proposal is that the WTO provides a 'corrective to the community's decision' about the traditional cultural expression at issue.[136] There are certainly precedents of aboriginal peoples of Canada going before international bodies to confirm their legal and human rights where they have felt Canadian courts and governments are failing to do this. They are also actively involved in various non-governmental organisations and consultations concerning international norms. A recent example concerning aboriginal cultural heritage is the petition by the Hul'qumi'num Treaty Group (HTG) before the Inter-American Commission on Human Rights (ICHR). Having been in treaty negotiations for 14 years – a process which is often funded on the First Nation side by monies that will eventually be deducted from their final settlement – HTG filed a human rights complaint against Canada asserting that 'Hul'qumi'num human rights to property and culture are being violated and ignored', including through the 'failure of Canada to deal with the 1884 E & N Railway grant (which privatized the entire southeast quarter of Vancouver island) through the B.C. treaty negotiation process, and the massive urbanization happening in what is now with little to no First Nation involvement' in areas claimed by them 'as the core of these human rights violations'.[137] Many other First Nations have filed *amicus* briefs in support of HTG's claim. In finding that the BC modern treaty negotiation process 'is not an effective mechanism to protect the right [to property] alleged', the ICHR also critiqued the ability of the BC Heritage Conservation Act to protect ancestral lands and sacred sites, noting it could not be relied on 'to comprehensively and permanently protect all HTG ancestral lands' because 'their purpose is not to recognize HTG's property rights to those lands or the obligation of the State to provide restitution'.[138]

My point here is that most instances in which First Nations, Métis and Inuit peoples have participated in international policy and dispute resolution fora have been initiated by them. This is different from a process that anticipates disputes being brought on their behalf by nation states or that holds that decisions of indigenous peoples will be of no force without adoption by a special international commission. As Graber astutely points out, there are also many more questions that arise in terms of dispute resolution design and assumptions about the hierarchy of legal orders that need to be unpacked and explored. This includes questions about how such a commission would be composed. Other fundamental questions are 'Whose values are reflected when there is opposition within or

136 Graber, 'Creativity', supra note 6, at p. 252.
137 *Hul'qumi'num Treaty Group* (2009) Inter-Am Comm HR No. 105/09.
138 Ibid., at para. 43.

between groups?' and 'How do we design processes that accommodate preferences for directness and indirectness, for unrestricted speaking time and tight limits on participation' and many other culturally based dispute resolution norms?[139]

[139] Michelle LeBaron, 'Learning New Dances: Finding Effective Ways to Address Intercultural Disputes', in Catherine Bell and David Kahane (eds), *Inter-Cultural Dispute Resolution in Aboriginal Contexts: Canadian and International Perspectives*, Vancouver: University of British Columbia Press, 2004, pp. 11–27, at p. 20.

15. International trade in indigenous cultural heritage: an Australian perspective

Kathy Bowrey

1. INTRODUCTION

Protection of Aboriginal and Torres Strait Islander traditional cultural expressions (TCEs) and traditional knowledge (TK) is a very significant specialisation in Australia. There are forests of reports and academic literature commenting on the nature of the problems, analysing progress to date, feeding the international appetite for the subject and, most commonly, expressing a heartfelt aspiration to do better. This chapter provides an overview of these issues, whilst trying to bring to life the importance of appreciating law and rights in terms of the domestic political context.

It is not altogether clear whether or not Australia is a post-colonial state. Government oversight and governance of Indigenous peoples[1] remains, regardless of Indigenous withdrawal, reservations on terms of engagement and attempts at forms of self-determination. The potential for improving Indigenous rights in Australia differs depending upon the time, the players and the categories of law deployed. It is hard to pinpoint success or progress such that one would seek to promote such solutions internationally. However, what has developed is a home-grown appreciation of the complexity of the issues, the likely failure of imposing solutions from above and the benefits of supporting local Indigenous agency in wrestling greater control over the trade in indigenous cultural heritage.

2. DEFINING AUSTRALIA'S INDIGENOUS PEOPLES

The simple question 'Who are the Indigenous people of Australia?' brings to the fore a number of significant tensions and anxieties. For the 240 years post-invasion there has been ongoing resistance to the exercise of state sovereignty over Aboriginal and Torres Strait Islander peoples. This has taken the form of confrontation, civil disobedience, strategic use of the domestic legal order to advance Indigenous rights and appeals to the international community to recognise Indigenous sovereignty. Resistance includes a struggle against the power of the nation state to define Aboriginal being and identity. The

[1] The term 'Indigenous' is capitalised, as appropriate, to acknowledge the sovereignty of Australian Aboriginal and Torres Strait Islander peoples and distinguish them from the more generic descriptor that embraces all indigenous peoples.

power of the state to name and identify Indigenous peoples within its boundaries sits oddly with concepts of Indigenous self-determination. There remain fundamental concerns about the legitimacy of Australian rule over Indigenous peoples:

- At what point is Aboriginal sovereignty conceded or erased?
- Where does the right to map, name or identify Indigenous communities originate?
- Given a significant and violent history of dispossession, what peoples or communities count as Indigenous?
- Who is an Indigenous person?
- How does one cease to be an Aboriginal or Torres Strait Islander person?
- Can one claim or reclaim an Indigenous identity?
- What is the State's or the law's interest or need for identifying Indigenous communities or persons?
- What would be the indicia of post-colonial politics in a settler state?
- Is there any meaningful capacity for Aboriginal constructions of identity within the coloniser's law?

Much of what we know of Aboriginal and Torres Strait Islander Australia comes packaged alongside a disastrous and tragic history where identification of Aboriginality has largely been for purposes of colonial administration with the aim of dispossessing Indigenous people of land, resources and culture. More 'enlightened' policies are marred by paternalism that continues to undermine Indigenous agency in surviving colonisation. *Indigenous persons have been and continue to be identified and named in terms that undermine Indigenous knowledge systems.* Given this history, any definition of indigenous persons needs to be treated as inherently suspect.

2.1 The Problems of Political Representation

There has been a significant history of lack of formal recognition of the civil and political rights of Indigenous people in Australia. There have been many political associations of Indigenous people, including an independence movement, the Aboriginal Provisional Government.[2] There is no treaty. The Australian Constitution was amended in the 1967 referendum to include the race power (section 51(xxvi)), which allows the federal government to make laws with regard to Aboriginal people. However, depressingly, the judiciary have declined to affirm that this provision requires such laws to be of benefit to Indigenous persons.[3] There is no bill of rights guaranteeing freedom of religion for Indigenous persons.[4] In the lead up to the 2007 federal election, the Race Discrimination

---

[2] See www.apg.org.au/ (all online sources were accessed 6 June 2011).

[3] See *Kartinyeri v The Commonwealth* (1998) HCA 52 [hereinafter *Kartinyeri*]; and Larissa Behrendt, 'Indigenous Rights and the Australian Constitution – A Litmus Test for Democracy', available at https://digitalcollections.anu.edu.au/bitstream/1885/42068/2/Behrendt.pdf.

[4] *Kruger v Commonwealth* (1997) 190 CLR 1 (HCA).

Act 1975 (Cth) was suspended to permit the Northern Territory (NT) Intervention in breach of the International Covenant on Civil and Political Rights.[5]

There is a current dialogue about notation of the First Peoples in the preamble of the Australian Constitution; however, assuming this clause could be passed by referendum[6] it is not clear how such a reference could meaningfully impact on the interpretation of legal rights of Indigenous peoples.[7] There have been various schemes that seek to represent the political interests of Indigenous peoples, including the statutorily set-up Aboriginal and Torres Strait Islander Commission (ATSIC) 1990–2005. In conjunction with the Australian Human Rights Commission and through the work of the previous Aboriginal and Torres Strait Islander Social Justice Commissioner, Tom Calma, a National Congress of Australia's First Peoples was set up in 2009. Such groups provide a platform for dialogue with the state and create capacity to address the non-indigenous media. However, such representative organisations have relatively weak political legitimacy. Participation requires claimants to identify with democratic, liberal, inclusive and universalist jurisprudence.[8] The presumption of representatives to contribute to national dialogues on behalf of Aboriginal peoples can be problematic, even when the representative is taken to only be speaking for the particular community or regional groupings with which delegates personally identify (such as the Anangu, Koori, Murri, Noongar, Nunga or Torres Strait Islanders).

As Irene Watson has argued, the requirement of 'representativeness' of a people is itself colonial in framing, as '[t]he idea of speaking "for" is alien to my knowledge of the possibilities of an Aboriginal political representation. ... There has never been an Aboriginal dialogue that has given over to this concept that is of giving the Aboriginal voice a political representative quality.'[9]

There is an ongoing and important debate within Australia and internationally about the role of 'indigenous technicians' who participate and collaborate in national and international fora. There is little capacity for participation in Indigenous terms:

> The captured voice of the 'native informant' is accommodated and becomes characterised as being representative of 'their' people. This has been repeated throughout Australia's colonial history, and it continues today. Political models and structures are imposed by government and adopted by communities who are wanting to or are forced due to economic necessity to engage. However it is these practices which erode Aboriginal models of engagement…

---

5 UN, Committee on the Elimination of Racial Discrimination, 'Consideration of Reports Submitted by State Parties under Article 9 of the Convention: Report on Australia', Seventy-seventh Session (UN Doc. CERD/C/AUS/CO/15–17, 2010); and UN, International Covenant on Civil and Political Rights, 999 UNTS 171 and 1057 UNTS 407; 6 ILM 368 (adopted on 16 December 1966, entered into force 23 March 1976).

6 44 referendums have been held, of which only 8 have been carried.

7 Megan Davis and Zrinka Lemezina, 'Indigenous Australians and the Preamble: Towards a More Inclusive Constitution or Entrenching Marginalisation' (2010) *University of New South Wales Law Journal,* 33 (2), pp. 239–66.

8 Sharon Venne, *Our Elders Understand Our Rights: Evolving International Law Regarding Indigenous Peoples*, British Columbia: Theytus Books, 1998.

9 Irene Watson, 'Aboriginal Sovereignties: Past, Present and Future (Im)possibilities', in Suvendrini Perera (ed.), *Our Patch: Australian Sovereignties Post-2001,* Perth, Western Australia: Network Books, 2007, pp. 23–43, at p. 32.

> … the question of Aboriginal representation, functions within a colonial context; the idea of representation is a false one, whereas an Aboriginal context is something else, still waiting the time and space to emerge, for that impossible space to open up.[10]

Fragmentary attempts at reconciliation and inclusion have been made with varying degrees of Indigenous participation and support. It is difficult to assess the 'progress' or empowerment associated with these initiatives. Experience differs depending upon locality and historical circumstance, government ambition and shifting tides of racism and of reconciliation rising and falling in the community and mainstream media.

2.2 The Deployment of Anthropology[11]

In academic writing there is often recourse to anthropology to provide expert knowledge of indigenous persons. However, this disciplinary expertise has played, and continues to play, a significant part in the dispossession and colonial governance of Indigenous persons in Australia.

The emergence of anthropology as a specific form of scientific knowledge is inseparable from the history of colonialism and empire. How and through what means different indigenous people became the subjects and objects of anthropological study is complex.[12] Nevertheless, there was relative consistency in the frameworks that were developed to interpret the 'Ab-original' within the stages of human development. In part because of a strong German Enlightenment tradition focusing on the study of languages (Sanskrit, Hindi, Persian, Turkish, Chinese, Arabic in particular), the 'Orient' was seen to generally exhibit key elements that fitted it (and the vast peoples and territories therein) into an emergent concept of civilisation, and what that constituted.[13] Distinctions were established between categories of 'advancement' and between what were considered 'primitive' and illiterate, Oriental and literate peoples. Oriental languages were documented, classified and contextualised and placed in a position of supremacy to that of 'primitive' languages. In anthropological discourse, Aboriginal and Torres Strait Islander peoples were situated toward the 'least civilised' end of the spectrum.[14] This classification fed the fiction that 'they' were an ancient and dying race.

'Dying race' theory has a long history in Australia. From the late nineteenth century it was sometimes associated with sympathetic accounts that sought to highlight the ravages

---

[10] Ibid., at p. 33.

[11] This section draws upon Kathy Bowrey and Jane Anderson, 'The Politics of Global Information Sharing: Whose Cultural Agendas are Being Advanced?' (2009) *Social and Legal Studies*, 18 (4), pp. 1–26.

[12] Tim Fulford, Debbie Lee and Peter J. Kitson, *Literature, Science and Exploration in the Romantic Era: Bodies of Knowledge*, Cambridge, UK and Port Melbourne, Victoria: Cambridge University Press, 2004; and Kathleen Wilson (ed.), *A New Imperial History. Culture, Identity and Modernity in Britain and the Empire 1660–1840*, Cambridge, UK and Port Melbourne, Victoria: Cambridge University Press, 2004.

[13] Francis Mulhearn, *Culture/Metaculture*, London and New York: Routledge, 2000.

[14] For an overview of evolution and the science of man, see John Gascoigne, *Joseph Banks and the English Enlightenment: Useful Knowledge and Polite Culture*, Cambridge, UK and Port Melbourne, Victoria: Cambridge University Press, 1994, at pp. 145–9 and 168–83.

of colonialism,[15] but, as O'Connell and McGregor note, these were also 'based on essentialist notions of Aboriginality which failed to recognise its survival in the colonial context'.[16] The 'dying race' legacy continues to resonate today, leading to justifications for ongoing misappropriations of Aboriginal culture by non-indigenous artists and galleries in Australia and overseas.[17]

Anthropological 'knowledge' has led to Australian Aboriginal and Torres Strait Islander peoples being mapped against degrees of genetic purity. Given the prevalence of the view of Aborigines as a 'dying race', historically the main regulatory focus was on those with 'diluted' parentage. These subjects were presumed as more likely and able to be assimilated such that their Aboriginality could be erased. As Marcia Langton explains:

> The label 'Aboriginal' has become one of the most disputed terms in the Australian language. There are High Court decisions and opinions on the 'term' and its meaning. Legal scholar John McCorquodale tells us that in Australian law there have been sixty-seven definitions of Aboriginal people, mostly related to their status as wards of the state and to criteria for incarceration in the institutional reserves. These definitions reflect not only the Anglo-Australian legal and administrative obsession, even fixation, with Aboriginal people, but also the uncertainty, confusion and constant search for the appropriate characterisation: 'full blood', 'half caste', 'quadroon', 'octoroon', 'such and such an admixture of blood', 'a native of Australia', 'a native of an admixture of blood not less than half Aboriginal', and so on. ... The fixation on classification reflects the extraordinary intensification of colonial administration of Aboriginal affairs from 1788 to the present.[18]

Biological descent tests have a long history in Australia and these remain present in Australian law, despite being based on misunderstandings of genetic science.[19] This is discussed further below.

There are other anthropological approaches that are less based on biology, such as Durkheim's work that revolves around identifications of forms of cultural knowledge and associations.[20] Within this framework property rights and other legal, economic and social

---

15 Susan Sheridan, *Along The Faultlines: Sex, Race and Nation in Australian Women's Writing: 1880s–1930s*, St Leonards, Australia: Allen and Unwin, 1995, at pp. 121–34.

16 Russell McGregor, *Imagined Destinies: Aboriginal Australians and the Doomed Race Theory, 1880–1939,* Melbourne: Melbourne University Press, 1997; and Kylie O'Connell, '"A Dying Race": The History and Fiction of Elizabeth Durack' (2001) *Journal of Australian Studies*, 25 (67), pp. 44–54.

17 O'Connell, supra note 16; and Damien Carrick (Producer), 'Wading into the Wanjina Controversy', *The Law Report*, Radio National, Australian Broadcasting Commission (29 June 2010), available online at http://www.abc.net.au/rn/lawreport/stories/2010/2939168.htm.

18 Marcia Langton, 'Aboriginal Art and Film: The Politics of Representation', in Michelle Grossman (ed.), *Blacklines. Contemporary Critical Writing by Indigenous Australians*, Melbourne: Melbourne University Press, 2003, pp. 109–24. See also Michael Dodson, 'The End in the Beginning: Re(de)finding Aboriginality', *The Wentworth Lecture 1994*, *Australian Aboriginal Studies* (1994), at pp. 2–13.

19 Debra Harry, 'Indigenous Peoples and Gene Disputes' (2009) *Chicago-Kent Law Review*, 84 (1), pp. 147–90.

20 Christoph B. Graber, 'Institutionalization of Creativity in Traditional Societies and in International Trade Law', in Shubha Ghosh and Robin P. Malloy (eds), *Creativity, Law and Entrepreneurship*, Cheltenham, UK and Northampton, MA: Edward Elgar, 2011, pp. 234–63.

entitlements are mapped against 'traditional knowledge' lines. This approach is also problematic. It establishes hierarchies that privilege and reify tropes such as 'the traditional' and 'authentic' cultural expression. This empowers indigenous voices only to the extent that they can conform to the expert anthropological criterion of 'traditional knowledge'. This feeds into a legal logic that empowers the state to judge who is, and is not, entitled to recognition.

First and foremost, reliance on anthropological foundations for identification of aboriginality requires revelation and delivery-up of indigenous culture for 'expert' evaluation and documentation. This dynamic empowers the state and western-trained technicians to examine, scrutinise and judge the native in accordance with European modes of discovery and authentication. Adopted as a legal strategy in order to advance indigenous claims, this has led to mixed results. The reliance on white anthropological evidence was felt key to a strategy for recognition of copyright of Aboriginal artists in some case law.[21] However, in other cases – and, most tellingly, in cases concerning access to rivalrous resources – native title claims and attempts to prevent development on Aboriginal land, anthropological evidence of spiritual knowledge, totems, sacred and secret knowledge has proved far more disappointing in furthering Indigenous empowerment.[22] Judicial interpretations of traditional knowledge have frequently depoliticised the context of colonisation. The more the reality of invasion is apparent within the subject community, the more likely it is that they will be judged as assimilated, rather than as staying within traditional culture. So, for example, as one High Court judge opines, '... for myself I might have questioned whether the use of a motor boat powered by mined and processed liquid fuel, and a steel tomahawk, remained in accordance with a traditional law or custom, particularly one of alleged totemic significance.'[23] The need to fight, to engage and to try and survive in the contemporary world can become legal justification for the state denying one's Indigenous status and knowledge. Anthropological reference to 'traditional practice' can as readily be used against Indigenous claimants as empowering them.

The struggle for limited forms of land rights achieved in the late twentieth century,[24] the Royal Commission into Aboriginal Deaths in Custody (1987–91),[25] the inquiry by the

---

21 See Tony Davies, 'Aboriginal Cultural Property?' (1996) *Law in Context*, 14 (2), pp. 1–28; Colin Golvan, 'The Protection of At the Waterhole by John Bulun Bulun: Aboriginal Art and the Recognition of Private and Communal Rights', in Andrew Kenyon, Megan Richardson and Sam Ricketson (eds), *Landmarks in Australian Intellectual Property*, Port Melbourne, Victoria: Cambridge University Press, 2009, pp. 191–208.

22 *Kartinyeri*, supra note 3; and *Members of the Yorta Yorta Aboriginal Community v Victoria* (2002) HCA 58 [hereinafter *Yorta Yorta*]. See also Gary Edmond, 'Thick Decisions: Expertise, Advocacy and Reasonableness in the Federal Court of Australia' (2004) *Oceania*, 74, pp. 190–223.

23 Callinan J in *Yorta Yorta*, supra note 22, at p. 187, referring to *Yanner v Eaton* (1999) HCA 53.

24 For an overview see Reconciliation Australia, 'Aboriginal Land Rights Q&A', available at http://www.reconciliation.org.au/home/reconciliation-resources/facts–figures/q-a-factsheets/aboriginal-land-rights.

25 National Archives of Australia, 'Fact sheet 112 – Royal Commission into Aboriginal Deaths in Custody', available at http://www.naa.gov.au/about-us/publications/fact-sheets/fs112.aspx.

Human Rights and Equal Opportunity Commission into the 'Stolen Generations'[26] and by the Commonwealth into 'Stolen Wages',[27] has put the trauma caused by denial of Indigenous rights and heritage before mainstream Australia. The report acknowledged a violent history of battles over rights to land, food and water sources. Indigenous children were kidnapped and exploited as servants, paid in rations of food and clothing. Governments and missionaries removed children from their families to be employed by colonial settlers and inculcated with European values and work habits.[28] The *Bringing Them Home* report eventually led to an Apology to the Stolen Generations by then Prime Minister Kevin Rudd in 2008.[29] A growing awareness of this history has impacted on broader understanding of the politics surrounding classification of Aboriginality, which can now be more easily seen as inherently unstable and problematic.[30] However, legally, Indigenous persons remain identified with reference to biological and cultural markers, informed through the insights of western science, anthropology and history.

In a recent inquiry into human genetic information, the Australian Law Reform Commission (ALRC) questioned 'whether there is any proper role for genetic testing in determining Aboriginal identity, which is basically a social and cultural matter'.[31] The report noted the insight of the Royal Commission into Aboriginal Deaths in Custody Commissioner, wherein Elliott Johnston QC stated that:

> How 'Aboriginal' has been defined, and the qualities attributed to Aboriginal people, have varied over time and from place to place, in ways that can only be understood in terms of the local, national and international concerns of a European colony of settlement in the South Pacific. Declaring this or that individual person Aboriginal or not Aboriginal has been a political act, prompted often enough by administrative convenience or economic advantage, such as access to land or the control of cheap labour. Correspondingly, Aboriginal people have at times denied Aboriginal identity, as a strategy for evading official harassment or popular discrimination, and at other times claimed it as a means of improving their material or political circumstances.[32]

The reason that there has been little capacity for definition of Indigenous persons or communities in terms of Indigenous knowledge is primarily because the need to identify the subject class(es) has overwhelmingly been motivated by governance projects of the state.

---

26 Ronald Wilson (Commissioner), *Bringing them Home, Report of the National Inquiry into the Separation of Aboriginal and Torres Strait Islander Children from their Families*, Sydney: Human Rights and Equal Opportunity Commission, 1997, at ch. 2 ('National Overview').

27 Senate Legal and Constitutional Affairs Committee, *Unfinished Business: Indigenous Stolen Wages*, Canberra: Commonwealth of Australia, 2006, available online at http://www.aph.gov.au/Senate/committee/legcon_ctte/completed_inquiries/2004–07/stolen_wages/report/index.htm.

28 Ibid.

29 For the text, see 'Text of PM Rudd's "Sorry" Address', *The Age* (13 February 2008), available online at http://www.theage.com.au/articles/2008/02/12/1202760291188.html.

30 Anna Haebich, *Broken Circles: Fragmenting Indigenous Families 1800–2000*, Perth: Fremantle Arts Centre Press, 2000.

31 ALRC Report 96, *Essentially Yours: The Protection of Human Genetic Information in Australia*, Sydney: Australian Law Reform Commission, 2003, at para. 36.3.

32 Ibid., at para. 36.6.

There remains a long connection between Australian legislative requirements of racial identification of Indigenous peoples and genocide. The largest Indigenous populations in Australia have recently been targeted through the Northern Territory National Emergency Response (also referred to as 'The Intervention'). The catalyst for the Intervention was a Report of the Northern Territory Board of Inquiry into the Protection of Aboriginal Children from Sexual Abuse, titled *Ampe Akelyernemane Meke Mekarle: 'Little Children are Sacred'*.[33] Under the auspices of finding better ways to protect Aboriginal children from sexual abuse, the federal government established compulsory income management of 50 per cent of welfare payments, removed permit systems that allowed for local control over entry onto lands, compulsorily acquired Aboriginal lands, abolished community development schemes, removed capacity for teaching in community languages (by increasing time commitments to study in the English language) and initially required mandatory health checks of children (a requirement withdrawn with recognition that this was itself a form of child abuse).[34] The Intervention coincides with a backlash against the recognition of customary law.[35] These initiatives suggest that regulatory attention has shifted back to a project of assimilating those 'traditional' Aborigines who have survived in regional and remote communities, now justified as part of the Government's agenda of redressing Indigenous disadvantage and colonial dysfunction. Such policy shifts sit uncomfortably with concepts of self-determination and any definition of a post-colonial practice.

In Australia, it is very difficult to separate out a space in which Indigenous self-determination and assertion of identity can be meaningfully exercised. Nonetheless, the ALRC has commented that 'these matters (of defining Aboriginality) should be determined by Aboriginal and Torres Strait Islander people themselves, working through their own communities, institutions and consultation processes.'[36]

2.3 Legislative Definition of Aboriginality

The current Australian scheme for identification of Indigenous persons is in part an attempt to redress classification errors of the past. There remain various approaches

---

[33] Northern Territory Government, *Ampe Akelyernemane Meke Mekarle: 'Little Children are Sacred'*, Inquiry into the Protection of Aboriginal Children from Sexual Abuse, 2007, available online at www.inquirysaac.nt.gov.au/pdf/bipacsa_final_report.pdf.

[34] The substantive provisions of the Government's 'Emergency Response' are contained in the following legislation: Northern Territory National Emergency Response Act 2007 (Cth); Social Security and Other Legislation Amendment (Welfare Payment Reform) Act 2007 (Cth); Families, Community Services and Indigenous Affairs and Other Legislation Amendment (Northern Territory National Emergency Response and Other Measures) Act 2007 (Cth); Appropriation (Northern Territory National Emergency Response) Act (No. 1) 2007–2008 (2007) (Cth); and Appropriation (Northern Territory National Emergency Response) Act (No. 2) 2007–2008 (2007) (Cth). See further Social Justice Report, 'Part 3: The Measures Enacted in the NT Emergency Response and Human Rights Standards', Australian Human Rights Commission (2007), available online at http://www.hreoc.gov.au/social_justice/sj_report/sjreport07/chap3.html#part3.

[35] Irene Watson, 'In the Northern Territory Intervention: What is being Protected and What is being Saved?' (2009) *Cultural Studies Review*, 15 (2), pp. 45–60.

[36] ALRC Report 96, supra note 31, at para. 36.10.

dispersed amongst different legislative schemes; however, the preferred legal test adopted by the federal government is a three-part test: 'An Aboriginal or Torres Strait Islander is a person of Aboriginal or Torres Strait Islander descent who identifies as an Aboriginal or Torres Strait Islander and is accepted as such by the community in which he [or she] lives.'[37] In interpreting this provision in *Shaw v Wolf* concerning the meaning of an 'Aboriginal person' for the purposes of the ATSIC Act, Merkel J noted:

> It is unfortunate that the determination of a person's Aboriginal identity, a highly personal matter, has been left by a parliament that is not representative of Aboriginal people to be determined by a court which is also not representative of Aboriginal people. Whilst many would say that this is an inevitable incident of political and legal life in Australia, I do not accept that that must always be necessarily so. It is to be hoped that one day if questions such as those that have arisen in the present case are again required to be determined that that determination might be made by independently constituted bodies or tribunals which are representative of Aboriginal people.[38]

The ALRC report continues, 'The courts, in interpreting statutory definitions in federal legislation, have emphasised the importance of descent in establishing Aboriginal identity, but have recognised that self-identification and community recognition may be relevant to establishing descent, and hence Aboriginal identity, for the purposes of specific legislation.'[39]

It is widely accepted that descent alone is an insufficient indicator of Indigeneity. Some commentators advocate abandoning descent as an independent limb of the test altogether.[40] However, the concern that arises with abandoning the descent test is that surviving lineages and connections will be devalued and undermined. To simply rely on self-identification and some form of community acceptance could quite negatively impact on surviving Aboriginal knowledge systems and forms of authority and legitimacy that are historically grounded in kinship connections. There are already strong tensions within communities around these issues.

The open-endedness of the currently preferred test reflects the state's own ambivalence toward answering the question 'Who is an Australian Indigenous person?' It is hard to draw the conclusion that this reflects a post-colonial turn and recognition of a right to self-determination, when government policies and laws continue to target Aboriginal Australia in ways that are not able to be reconciled with a commitment to self-determination or post-colonial politics.

---

37 Commonwealth of Australia, Department of Aboriginal Affairs, 'Report on a Review of the Administration of the Working Definition of Aboriginal and Torres Strait Islanders', 1981; cited in John Gardiner-Garden, 'The Definition of Aboriginality', *Parliament of Australia*, Research Note 18, 2000–01 (2000), at p. 2.

38 Cited in ALRC Report 96, supra note 31, at para. 36.27.

39 Ibid., at para. 36.28.

40 For example, Loretta De Plevitz and Larry Croft, 'Aboriginality under the Microscope: The Biological Descent Test in Australian Law' (2003) *Queensland University of Technology Law and Justice Journal*, 3 (1), pp. 104–20, at p. 105.

3. INTELLECTUAL PROPERTY PROTECTION OF TRADITIONAL CULTURAL EXPRESSIONS AND CULTURAL PROPERTY

The terms TCE and TK, as used on the international level by the World Intellectual Property Organization (WIPO), are not generally found in Australian legislation and the issue is overwhelmingly considered in terms of copyright.

It has become conventional wisdom to assert that copyright offers inadequate protection to indigenous peoples. An ill fit with western categories of protection, and cultural bias, has frequently been noted in Australian case law, parliamentary proceedings, academic texts and articles and Australian government reports. It needs to be remembered, however, that in addition to various points of recognition in national laws there remains significant capacity to assert indigenous rights through the mainstream categories of intellectual property (IP) law. Though there are limitations in a common law system, this strategy has significant potential.

3.1 The Copyright Cases

There has only been a relatively small amount of litigation concerning rights claims of a small number of Australian Indigenous communities in the past 20 years. Three cases in particular have been very widely reported and discussed in Australian and international literature as representing 'the Australian experience'. These cases are commonly drawn on to demonstrate the problems of using a western private property model to protect archetypical indigenous communal or collective property claims.

3.1.1 The $10 note case

In *Yumbulul v Reserve Bank of Australia*[41] an artist, Terry Yumbulul, a Yolngu man from Elcho Island, entered into a licensing agreement allowing the reproduction of an image of a ceremonial object on a new ten dollar note to be printed by the Reserve Bank. The artist did not engage in appropriate community consultation over the proposed use. The court dismissed the action against the Reserve Bank and Aboriginal Artists Agency to set aside the copyright agreement (based on unconscionable conduct and misleading and deceptive conduct) because Mr Yumbulul had understood the general nature of the licence he was signing. However, the court explicitly noted the need to reconsider law reform in order to better accommodate appropriate recognition of communal interests in indigenous art and cultural objects.

3.1.2 The *Carpets* case

The *Carpets* case[42] involved the unauthorised reproduction of Aboriginal art on carpets made in Vietnam, at the direction of an Australian company. The carpets were based on designs appropriated from a portfolio of artworks published by the Australian National Gallery (ANG). The portfolio had been produced for educational purposes and was described as representative of the best Aboriginal artworks in the ANG collection. The

---

41 *Yumbulul v Reserve Bank of Australia* (1991) 21 IPR 481.

42 *Milpurrurru and Ors v Indofurn Pty Ltd* (1994) 30 IPR 209; 130 ALR 659.

Australian importer knew that the carpets were reproduced from artworks that were in copyright. Attempts to obtain a licence were ineffectual and no agreement was sought with any artist or agency prior to the making, importation and exhibition of the carpets. However, the carpets had swing tags attached that suggested, 'These unique wall hangings and rugs have been designed by Aboriginal artists from areas throughout Australia. These artists are paid royalties on every carpet sold ... proudly designed in Australia by Australian Aboriginals. made in vietnam.' Copyright infringement was established, as was an action under sections 52 and 53 of the Trade Practices Act 1975 (Cth), in relation to the swing tag's false suggestion as to the origin of the carpet designs and the payment of royalties to Australian Aboriginals. Infringement was found for examples that very closely resembled the original designs, as well as ones where designs had been significantly modified but copying was still apparent. A radical approach to damages was adopted by Von Doussa J, who recognised damages for 'cultural harm'. He also permitted the community to determine the distribution of damages to community members. Unfortunately, while there was an award of record damages against the defendant, the company went into receivership, leading to considerable difficulties in recovering payments to the artists.

Some commentators in the popular media hailed the case as the 'Mabo of copyright'.[43] In 1992 in the *Mabo* decision[44] the High Court set aside the previously long-accepted doctrine of *terra nullius* finding, for the first time, scope for recognition of customary law and native title in Australia where the state had not extinguished such rights. The decision is treated as a watermark case that reinvigorated a much larger political debate about the capacity for western law and the willingness of judges to redress past injustices toward Aboriginal and Torres Strait Islander peoples; however, the *Carpet* case did not make any finding on communal ownership of copyright or 'common law native title copyright' at all.

3.1.3 The *Bulun Bulun* case

A third well-known case, *Bulun Bulun v R&T Textiles*,[45] directly confronted the issue of communal ownership. It involved the painting, *Magpie Geese and Water Lilies at the Waterhole*, executed by artist John Bulun Bulun, which had been reproduced with permission in a reputable art book. This book then became a source for later unauthorised reproductions. The artist had successfully sued Flash Screenprinters for reproduction of the image on t-shirts nearly a decade earlier.[46] R&T Textiles had also reproduced the work without permission on fabric, and the fabric was being used by the Northern Territory's

---

43 Virginia Trioli, 'Record Damages for Illegal Aboriginal Images', *The Age* (14 December 1994). See also *Copyrites,* produced and directed by Cathy Eatock and Kim Mordaunt, Australian Film Finance Corporation/Marcom Projects, 1997.

44 *Mabo v The State of Queensland* [No. 2] [1992] HCA 23; (1992) 175 CLR 1 [hereinafter *Mabo*].

45 *Bulun Bulun v R&T Textiles Pty Ltd* (1998) 41 IPR 513 [hereinafter *Bulun Bulun*]. The decision is discussed in greater detail in Kathy Bowrey, 'The Outer Limits Of Copyright Law – Where Law Meets Philosophy and Culture' (2001) *Law and Critique*, 12 (1), pp. 1–24.

46 *Bulun Bulun v Nejlam Pty Ltd* (1989) Federal Court, unreported. This is discussed further at infra section 3.2.3.

Chief Minister's Department in uniforms, worn by protocol staff on special occasions.[47] The artist, with the support of his community, the Ganalbingu people, argued that the copyright in the work reproduced without his permission, which expressed ritual knowledge of the community, should be treated by the courts as communally owned. The court noted that the *Mabo* decision:

> shows that customary Indigenous law has a role to play within the Australian legal system. Indeed the conclusion that native title survived the Crown's acquisition of sovereignty was dependent upon the Court's acceptance of antecedent traditional laws and customs acknowledged and observed by the Indigenous inhabitants of the land claimed.[48]

Members of the applicant's clan were the traditional owners of relevant land under the Aboriginal Land Rights (Northern Territory) Act 1976 (Cth) but a determination of native title had not been made. Detailed evidence of the customary law and artistic practices of the Ganalbingu people was heard. The Attorney General for the Northern Territory appeared as *amicus curiae*, arguing that any determination of native title had to be made in accordance with the provisions of the Native Title Act[49] and, thus, the Federal Court had no jurisdiction to consider the issue. Accordingly, Von Doussa J directed argument away from the submission that the ownership of land and ownership of artistic works were coterminous and that IP rights were thus an incident of native title. Instead of considering possible linkage between native title and IP claims, he considered whether or not customary Aboriginal laws relating to ownership of artistic works survived the introduction of the common law in 1788. Mainstream jurisprudential arguments about copyright law as positive law[50] were highlighted. Collective claims were only able to be accommodated as works of joint authorship under the Copyright Act 1968 (Cth). In this case, community interests in the work were not found to be a kind of contribution that amounted to 'joint ownership'. While sympathetic to the need to protect communal interests, Von Doussa J found that it was for Parliament, rather than the courts, to make necessary amendments to the law to acknowledge communal ownership.

In recognition of the peculiar vulnerability of community interests in a system of copyright that only acknowledged individual interests, his honour found a fiduciary obligation on the author 'not to exploit the artistic work in a way that is contrary to the laws and custom of the Ganalbingu people, and, in the event of infringement by a third party, to take reasonable and appropriate action to retrain and remedy infringement of the copyright in the artistic work.'[51] It was found that as Mr Bulun Bulun had taken legal action against the infringer, he had not breached his equitable obligations to his community.

---

47 Terri Janke (for WIPO), *Minding Culture: Case-Studies on Intellectual Property and Traditional Cultural Expressions*, Geneva: WIPO, 2003, at p. 53.

48 *Bulun Bulun*, supra note 45.

49 This post-*Mabo* legislation prescribes conditions for recognition of 'native title' under the legal system, primarily providing native title holders with certain limited kinds of rights to land and water. It is not a form of Aboriginal title. See infra section 7.

50 Section 8 Copyright Act 1968 (Cth) says, 'Subject to section 8A, copyright does not subsist otherwise than by virtue of this Act'. Section 8A reserves the prerogative rights of the Crown in the nature of copyright.

51 *Bulun Bulun,* supra note 45, p. 531.

3.1.4 A common heritage

What has not been much commented on to date is that these three Australian copyright cases have a common cultural, legal and political heritage. All relate to claims by members of clans from the same region, Aboriginal people of Central and Eastern Arnhem Land.[52] The Yolngu have an interesting track record of engagement with the invaders, allowing circulation of some of their imagery and stories in order to advance important political claims, and strategically using Australian law to advocate for protection on Yolngu terms. The communities from this region have been leaders in pursuing land rights claims in Australia. Artworks have frequently been utilised to explain and evidence these claims,[53] underscoring the connection between land, law and culture.

In the 1950s, Terry Yumbulul's father Burramurra was the instigator of a survival strategy that led to clans putting aside divisions and adopting a united face towards the missionaries. This was symbolised in the production of an important cultural work, the Elcho Island Memorial. This transgressive work displayed together sacred imagery reflecting a number of individual clan histories. Many of the designs had traditionally been considered secret and not to be seen by women and children.[54] The artwork is said to have influenced the Yirrkala land rights petition a decade later.[55] In 1963, in response to a government decision to allow the development of a Bauxite mine on their lands, the Yolngu at Yirrkala sent a petition on bark to the Australian Parliament demanding that their rights be recognised. The demand for recognition of land rights led to *Milirrpum v Nabalco* (the *Gove Land Rights* case) which, as pre-*Mabo* law, affirmed the supremacy of private property rights and the extinguishment of communal ownership.[56]

The same judge, Von Doussa, who later served as Australian Human Rights Commissioner 2003–08, and is a strong supporter of indigenous rights, heard both the *Carpets* case and *Bulun Bulun*.

Common social, cultural and legal relations contributed to the creation of a narrative coherence to the Indigenous claims and to the legal response, which no doubt has assisted those who have sought to later analyse Australian Indigenous cultural claims. However, numerous other Indigenous claims, and some from different Indigenous communities, have been pursued using copyright and other avenues. To rely on reported litigation as the superior record of the way western law accommodates Indigenous claims distorts the

---

52 Some Yolngu stories are retold in the film, *Ten Canoes*, directed by Rolf De Heer and the People of Ramingining/Madman Entertainment Distributor, 2006. *Ten Canoes* won the *Un Certain Regard* Special Jury Prize at the 2006 Cannes Film Festival.

53 Joan G. Winter, *Native Title Business: Contemporary Indigenous Art: A National Travelling Exhibition*, Southport, Queensland: Keeaira Press, 2002; Kirsten Anker, 'The Truth in Painting: Cultural Artefacts as Proof of Native Title' (2005) *Law Text Culture*, 9 (1), pp. 91–124; and Chris Cunneen, 'Framing the Crimes of Colonialism: Critical Images of Aboriginal Art and Law', in Keith Haywood and Mike Presdee (eds), *Framing Crime. Cultural Criminology and the Image*, London: Routledge, 2011, pp. 115–37.

54 Ronald Berndt, *An Adjustment Movement in Arnhem Land*, Paris: Mouton, 1962; and Howard Morphy, *Aboriginal Art,* London: Phaidon Press, 1998, at pp. 240–41.

55 Will Owen, 'Conversations with Terry Yumbulul', *Aboriginal Art & Culture: An American Eye* (17 February 2008), available at http://homepage.mac.com/will_owen/iblog/C1403073609/E20080217084834/index.html.

56 *Milirrpum v Nabalco Pty Ltd* (1971) 17 FLR 141.

complexity of the legal landscape and ignores some of the available avenues for protection of Indigenous rights. These other examples should not be considered as less representative of the Australian legal experience.

3.2 Lesser Known Cases

3.2.1 The $1 note case

The earliest documented successful assertion of IP rights by Indigenous artists dates from the era of the 1967 referendum over race power. It was also brought by a Yolngu artist. Decimal currency was introduced in 1966 and the Reserve Bank used a bark painting design of a Gurrmirringu mortuary feast by David Malangi as part of the graphic design of the $1 note.[57] David Malangi Daymirringu (1927–99) was a member of the Manharrngu clan of the Dhuwa moiety. In accordance with Yolngu law, he inherited rights and responsibilities in relation to particular tracts of land, ancestral sites and ceremonies and painted works related to particular areas of responsibility. Schooled at the Milingimbi mission in Arnhem Land, he did not learn to read or write. As was common in some missions at the time, artwork he produced was collected by government officials or anthropologists and commercialised. Malangi produced significant commercial work in the 1960s and 1970s.

In relation to the painting reproduced on the dollar note, the Reserve Bank simply assumed that the artist associated with the artwork was 'anonymous' or long dead. Accordingly, no one was notified of the reproduction, nor was there initially any consideration of copyright implications. However, the failure to acknowledge the artist was commented on in newspaper reviews of the currency at the time. This media attention marks a shift in public attitudes toward respect for the rights of Indigenous Australians occurring in the 1960s. When the decimal currency was taken back to the Milingimbi mission, the artist and community became aware of the problem. The community and the mission superintendent appealed to the Director of Social Welfare in Darwin, asking him to approach the Reserve Bank seeking appropriate recognition for Malangi. The Bank's Governor, H.C. Coombs, took legal advice and subsequently paid for the use of the image. He presented the artist with a gift of a fishing tackle box, AUD1,000 and a specially struck medallion, which apparently especially pleased the artist. Djon Mundine notes:

> First ... Malangi's case, finally, publicly, fixed the idea of the Aboriginal painter as an individually recognised art practitioner. Second, the fact that a Commonwealth Government Agency, the Reserve Bank of Australia, had paid royalty fees to an Aboriginal artist opened the whole copyright issue and respect for such artists Australia wide.[58]

3.2.2 The Mountford case

Further advocacy followed from this development. A decade later, the Pitjantjatjara Council litigated to try to prevent publication of *Nomads of the Australian Desert* by Charles Mountford. Mountford was a significant collector of indigenous art, artefacts and

---

[57] This account is predominantly taken from David Malangi, *No Ordinary Place: The Art of David Malangi*, Susan Jenkins (ed.), Canberra: National Gallery of Australia, 2004.

[58] Djon Mundine, 'Some People are Stories', in Malangi, ibid., pp. 34–5.

stories as an amateur anthropologist and ethnographer. He made numerous field trips to indigenous communities from the 1920s to the 1950s. While he characterised himself primarily as a recorder of culture, he was also an early promoter of Aboriginal art. Mountford appreciated the international art world's interest in 'primitive' styles adopted by acclaimed non-indigenous Australian artists such as Margaret Preston, Tony Tuckson, James Gleeson and others.[59]

Nomads of the Australian Desert contained information about secret ceremonies, which led to an action for breach of confidential information. Mountford was well aware of the sensitivity of the information about Pitjantjatjara culture he sought to reveal. Muirhead J notes:

> The plaintiffs' concern probably goes basically to the fact that the revelation of the secrets to their women, children and uninitiated men may undermine the social and religious stability of their hard-pressed community. Despite Dr Mountford's prognosis that their life and beliefs 'are so quickly vanishing', there is still an urgent desire in these people to preserve those things, their lands and their identity, and the existence of the council itself illustrates these objectives.[60]

Essentially Justice Muirhead refuted Mountford's Social Darwinist presumption that Aboriginal people were a 'dying race' whose culture belonged to no one or to the world at large. The Pitjantjatjara applicants were entitled to protection for breach of confidence under ordinary principles, as individuals or as representatives of the Pitjantjatjara people affected by the breach of confidential information. As the author was not prepared to withdraw the book from sale, in order to prevent further disruption to social systems the injunction restrained publication within the jurisdiction of the court – the Northern Territory. The order to remedy the breach affirmed that the western law did have a role to play in preventing losses of culture, and that the courts would provide assistance where established legal rules permitted. Whilst this case was reported, related litigation is less well known.

The Pitjantjatjara Council was later successful in obtaining an injunction to restrain the owner and the auctioneer of a large collection of Mountford's slides from displaying or selling them. Interlocutory orders allowed representatives of the Pitjantjatjara Council to inspect the slides, of which approximately 100 dealt with secret or sacred material. Final orders were made declaring that the property in and ownership of these selected slides, photographs and negatives vested in the Pitjantjatjara Council for and on behalf of the Pitjantjatjara, Yankuntjatjara and Ngaanyatjara peoples.[61] This second case is very significant for recognising that the remedy for breach of confidence required orders affecting claims to both tangible and intangible property – slides as chattel property and copyright in

---

[59] Margo Neale, 'Charles Mountford and the "Bastard Barks"', in Lynne Seear and Julie Ewington (eds), *Brought to Light: Australian Art, 1850–1965: From the Queensland Art Gallery Collection*, Brisbane: Queensland Art Gallery, 1998, pp. 210–17, at p. 212.

[60] *Foster v Mountford and Rigby Ltd* (1976) 14 ALR 71, at p. 73.

[61] *Pitjantjatjara Council Inc and Peter Nganingu v John Lowe and Lyn Bender* – Injunction to prevent display and sale of photographic slides – slides from collection of late Dr C. Mountford – slides showing secret ceremonies, Vic Supreme Court, unreported, 1982, Ross Howie (1982) *Aboriginal Law Bulletin*, 30; (1982) *Aboriginal Law Bulletin*, 1 (4), at p. 10.

the photographs. Almost thirty years later this remains a relatively unexplored remedy in relation to repatriation of secret material held in museums and university collections which warrants further consideration.

3.2.3 The Flash t-shirts case

As is common amongst disenfranchised persons, it is often argued that there is a need for new laws to protect rights. As Wanduk Marika explains:

> Sometime ago, I happened to see a tea-towel with one of my paintings represented on it; this was one of the stories that my father had given me, and no-one else amongst my people would have painted it without my permission. But some unknown person copied my painting and had it reproduced in this way, without even first asking my permission. I was deeply upset and for some years was unable to paint.
>
> It was then that I realised that I and my fellow Aboriginal artists needed some form of protection. It is not that we object to people reproducing our work, but it is essential that we be consulted first, for only we know if a particular painting is of special sacred significance, to be seen only by certain members of a tribe, and only we can give permission for our works of art to be reproduced. It is hard to imagine the works of great Australian artists such as Sydney Nolan or Pro Hart being reproduced without their permission. We are only asking that we be granted the same recognition, that our works be respected and that we be acknowledged as the rightful owners of our own works of art.[62]

The Melbourne barrister Colin Golvan became engaged in working in this area after hearing on the radio the artist Lin Onus decrying the theft of John Bulun Bulun's intellectual property and suggesting there ought to be a law against it. With Northern Territory solicitor Martin Hardie, Golvan ran a test case against the t-shirt manufacturer, Flash Screenprinters, for reproducing art works, including John Bulun Bulun's *At the Waterhole* without permission.[63] As the *Gove Land Rights* case had affirmed the supremacy of private property rights,[64] it was anticipated that there could be objections to the ownership claims. In copyright, the criterion of originality was thought to be a particularly important obstacle to protection of 'traditional' works – the presumption also being that if copyright had ever existed, it had long since expired. To rebut the presumption of a lack of originality in the works, considerable anthropological evidence about the creative process was brought before the court. However, in practice 'originality' did not prove to be a huge conceptual difficulty, given the generosity of the Anglo-Australian legal concept and clear articulation of the facts about the contemporary production of Aboriginal art.[65] Nonetheless, the logistics of producing evidence from artists resident in remote communities and credentialing indigenous evidence along with that of white experts (in

---

62 As cited in Jane Anderson, 'The Making of Indigenous Knowledge in Intellectual Property Law in Australia' (2005) *International Journal of Cultural Property*, 12, pp. 347–73, at p. 354.

63 Colin Golvan, 'Aboriginal Art and Copyright: The Case for Johnny Bulun Bulun' (1989) *European Intellectual Property Review,* 10, pp. 346–53.

64 *Milirrpum v Nabalco Pty Ltd*, supra note 56.

65 See Brad Sherman, 'From the Non-original to the Ab-original: A History', in Brad Sherman and Alain Strowel (eds), *Of Authors and Origins: Essays on Copyright Law*, Oxford: Clarendon Press; New York: Oxford University Press, 1994, pp. 111–30; and Kathy Bowrey, 'Economic

anticipation of problems in accepting indigenous evidence) should not be underestimated.[66] While protection may not be awarded on the terms as would be available or appropriate under Indigenous law, it is important not to downplay the reflexivity of Australian law in accommodating the alien claims, where political goodwill to protect such productions exists.

3.2.4 The *Brandl/Mimi rock art* case

The *Brandl/Mimi rock art* case is another example where a presumed major legal obstacle – lack of identification of the Aboriginal author of ancient rock art of the Deaf Adder Creek region of Arnhem Land – was overcome.[67] A researcher, Eric Brandl, had been funded by the Australian Institute of Aboriginal Studies (now the Australian Institute of Aboriginal and Torres Strait Islander Studies, AIATSIS) to record the Mimi imagery in the 1960s and a book was later published.[68] Under the grant, with copyright in any recordings made vested in the Institute and under the AIATSIS Act 1989 (Cth), the Institute has the power as a body corporate to institute legal proceedings. A well-known Australian anthropologist, Vivien Johnson, identified the imagery being reproduced on t-shirts in markets. A copyright action was initiated on the basis of the researcher's original authorship of the drawings and photographs of the rock art. Johnson provided evidence of Brandl's original skill and labour as an artist and photographer, and pointed out differences between his images and the rock art. A trade practices claim related to the suggestion that the conduct of the company was 'misleading or deceptive' or 'likely to mislead and deceive' consumers to believe that the t-shirts were made with the consent of the Indigenous peoples, the Brandl Estate or the Institute. The case was settled and a public apology was published regretting any cultural or other harm caused to the Badmardi Clan, AIATSIS or Margaret Brandl of the Brandl Estate.

3.2.5 The Katoomba/Wanjina sculpture case

In 2010, at Katoomba in New South Wales, a non-indigenous person, Vesna Tenodi, established a 'Wanjina-themed' art gallery and sculpture garden, including an 8.5 tonne sandstone sculpture, *Wanjina Watchers in the Whispering Stone*. The Wanjina are very sacred imagery and symbols that belong to the several Aboriginal communities in the Kimberley, Western Australia (WA).[69] The sculpture was carved by Ben Osvath under the direction of Tenodi, who believes she is in personal communication with the Wanjina spirits who instructed her to produce this imagery. The Kimberley and local Blue

---

Rights, Culture Claims and a Culture of Piracy in the Indigenous Art Market: What Should We Expect From the Western Legal System?' (2009) *Australian Indigenous Law Review*, 13 (2), pp. 35–58.

[66] See Golvan, supra note 21.

[67] The full account can be found in 'Case Study 6. Unauthorised Reproduction of Indigenous Rock Art', in Janke (for WIPO), supra note 47, at pp. 98–117.

[68] Eric Joseph Brandl, *Australian Aboriginal Paintings in Western and Central Arnhem Land: Temporal Sequences and Elements of Style in Cadell River and Deaf Adder Creek Art*, Canberra: Australian Institute of Aboriginal Studies, 1973.

[69] The Wanjina are discussed by Christoph B. Graber, 'Aboriginal Self-Determination vs the Propertisation of Traditional Culture: The Case of Sacred Wanjina Sites' (2009) *Australian Indigenous Law Review*, 13 (2), pp. 18–34.

Mountains Indigenous and non-indigenous communities were grossly offended by the culturally inappropriate and unauthorised use of this imagery, which constitutes a major affront to Aboriginal law and beliefs. The Blue Mountains City Council subsequently ordered removal of the sculpture under local planning and development laws, noting the negative social impact and community distress being caused by public display of misappropriated Indigenous imagery. Tenodi's appeal on the order for removal of the sculpture from public display to the Land and Environment Court was unsuccessful.[70] After further delays and ongoing vandalism of the work, it was finally removed in November 2011.

It is highly likely that copyright and trade practices actions could be taken to protect the Wanjina imagery along the same lines as in the *Brandl/Mimi* case. The Wanjina is a very sacred image that is repainted each year by the Aboriginal owners to ensure the rain that fills the waterholes. The work is well known largely through the work of anthropologists, through display in museums and through Wanjina art produced in the Kimberley community and sold by the Mowanjum Art Store and Mowanjum Art Centre since the 1970s. There was also a commercial agreement regarding display of Wanjinas in the Sydney 2000 Olympics, credited to a Mowanjum elder who is also a commercial painter – Donny Woolagoodja. The non-indigenous owner and artist, Tenodi and Osvath, would have been familiar with the look of the Wanjina imagery through one of these appropriated sources. It is highly likely that *Wanjina Watchers in the Whispering Stone* is substantially similar to some of the earlier, existing representations produced by Indigenous persons.

For much of western history, the prevailing view has been that non-indigenous people are entitled to access and represent indigenous culture and that there is no need to consult or negotiate with indigenous people over the kinds of uses made. However, the entitlement of non-indigenous persons to own and represent Indigenous culture has been persistently challenged by Indigenous persons in Australia, and Indigenous applicants to the court are often successful. These actions are costly and time-consuming to pursue; however, it is not the case that domestic law is so limited that these avenues are futile. Domestically there appears to be an emerging community expectation of Indigenous involvement and consent to Indigenous-themed enterprises in Australia, as part of the political agenda of reconciliation and in line with more established community values of giving Indigenous people 'a fair go'. There is a broad recognition that Indigenous communities have established reputations related to cultural ownership of particular imagery, and that this may also involve some forms of trade. The local outrage in the Blue Mountains and more generally over Vesna Tenodi's business suggests a far more sophisticated reading of this trade by consumers than has been assumed. It suggests there is a much larger potential for development of notions of 'misuse' and 'misrepresentation' under competition and consumer law and passing off law to protect indigenous culture. These areas of law interrelate with the normative expectations of 'ordinary' consumers. Given that the attraction to trade in cultural products generally relates to presumed associations with real Indigenous people, trader silence on the fact of association with Indigenous people could

---

[70] *Tenodi v Blue Mountains City Council* [2011] NSWLEC 1183.

amount to a misleading representation of 'authenticity' and a misappropriation of established Indigenous reputation.[71] Iconographic Indigenous imagery could be protected alongside protection afforded to other forms of 'secondary branding'.

3.3 Trade Mark Law

As several other chapters in this volume note, law in other jurisdictions may consider whether registration of a trade mark may offend a significant section of the indigenous community.[72] There are no equivalent provisions under the Trade Marks Act 1995 (Cth). Whilst the need for equivalent legislation to the New Zealand and US provisions was recommended in *Our Culture: Our Future*[73] and this has been subsequently noted in policy circles in Australia, no reform has been initiated. Australian discourse has been overwhelmingly fixated on the category of copyright, with little development of the trade mark discourse.

There is a long-standing prohibition against registration of scandalous marks (section 42(a)); however, its possible application to prevent cultural offence has never been judicially considered in relation to Indigenous persons.[74] This issue brings to the fore a clash between redressing a racist heritage and freedom of speech.[75]

Compared with other jurisdictions, there has also been little domestic discussion of the value of geographical indications (GIs) as an alternative avenue for the protection for Indigenous peoples with legal title to their lands. Australians have predominantly written about the utility of GIs in other regions with little detailed address to the application to Indigenous rights in Australia. The most significant work on the subject is by Sherman and Wiseman.[76] They note that the attraction of GIs includes its use as a regime for protecting 'traditional' knowledge and practices, there being no limitation on the period of protection, the rights are not freely transferable, the system can accommodate group rights and

---

[71] Australian Passing Off law has quite a generous and flexible approach to protecting reputation and is developing means of protecting secondary branding. See, for example, *Telstra Corporation Ltd v Royal & Sun Alliance Insurance Australia Ltd* (2003) FCA 786.

[72] Susy Frankel, 'A New Zealand Perspective on the Protection of Mātauranga Māori (Traditional Knowledge)', in this volume; and Rebecca Tsosie, 'International Trade in Indigenous Cultural Heritage: An Argument for Indigenous Governance of Cultural Property', in this volume.

[73] Terri Janke, *Our Culture: Our Future*, Sydney: Michael Frankel and Co, 1998, at pp. 142–9 (ch. 12. 'Amendments to the Trade Marks Act').

[74] See, however, the documentary *Nigger Lovers*, directed by Rhonda Hagan; produced by Daryl Sparkes and Stephen Hagan, Australia, 2007. The film documents Stephen Hagan's fight for the sign in his local rugby league grandstand, the 'ES "Nigger" Brown Stand' to be taken down. ES stands for Edward Stanley Brown, a white man whose nickname was 'Nigger', because at that time a shoe polish existed called 'Nigger Brown' (now being sold as 'Dark Tan'). The sign was taken down in 2008.

[75] Rosemary Coombe, 'Embodied Trademarks: Mimesis and Alterity on American Commercial Frontiers' (1996) *Cultural Anthropology*, 11, pp. 202–24; Megan Richardson, 'Trade Marks and Language' (2004) *Sydney Law Review*, 26 (2), pp. 193–220; and Patricia Loughlan, 'Oh Yuck! The Registration of Scandalous Trade Marks' (2005) *Intellectual Property Forum*, 61, pp. 38–42.

[76] Brad Sherman and Leanne Wiseman, 'From Terroir to Pangkarra: Geographical Indications of Origin and Traditional Knowledge', in Dev Ganjee and Justin Hughes (eds), *Research Handbook on Geographical Indications Law and Policy*, Cheltenham, UK: Edward Elgar, 2012 (forthcoming).

GIs reinforce the centrality of 'place' or 'country' to Indigenous culture. Nonetheless, the authors anticipate significant evidential problems confronting Australian Indigenous claims, unless the GI system moves beyond scientific modes of proof of links between product and place, to recognising human, rather than natural, dimensions to geographical connection. The process of proving claims introduces serious obstacles to Indigenous claimants:

> Although the evidence used to prove connection to place (or the boundaries of a would-be geographic area) takes different forms depending on the geographical indication in question, it is united by the fact that it conforms to certain unstated and shared presumptions about the type of evidence that will and will not be taken into account when deciding doctrinal issues such as proving connection to place. While scientific evidence that the distinguishing characteristics of a named product is directly (and uniquely) shaped by the geographic location where it is grown or produced, or historical evidence about a product's longstanding association with a particular location are clearly relevant, this is in marked contrast to the evidence that might be given by an Indigenous community. For example, paintings, or at least certain types of paintings, are used by Indigenous communities in Australia as a way of communicating connection to country to non-Aboriginal people and to the courts. This occurs because paintings make a 'normative claim about the basis for entitlement and the manner in which it can be proved'.
>
> ... it is highly unlikely that custodians of traditional knowledge would be able to use the existing rules of evidence to prove connection to place in a way that would accord with Indigenous ideas about evidence and proof.[77]

The authors note the difficulty of national courts or agencies that register GIs in global metropolitan centres being able to accommodate the 'alien' forms of evidence and law that mark the Indigenous communities seeking protection. Hearings of evidence *in situ* and in Indigenous languages are common in Australian native title and copyright cases. Sherman and Wiseman wryly note the highly unlikely scenario of the European Court of Justice decamping to the deserts of Australia to hear evidence in the form of discussion of paintings in relation to misuse of an Australian GI that occurred in Europe.

Obstacles exist for Indigenous persons within and across all the existing categories of IP protection, thus there remains nascent community-level interest in investigating use of GIs for protection of Indigenous knowledge and identity. However, Australia is relatively ambivalent about GI protection altogether (especially beyond the case for wine and spirits). Indigenous GIs may be considered a special case, but this is an area Australia is likely to develop by following, rather than leading or actively engaging with, international developments.

---

[77] Ibid. (footnotes omitted).

4. COMPETITION AND CONSUMER PROTECTION OF TCEs AND TK

4.1 Australian Consumer Law

Though it has no specific Indigenous reference, competition and consumer law has potential for protecting TCEs and TK. Section 52 of the Trade Practices Act (TPA) 1974 (Cth) prohibited a corporation from engaging in misleading or deceptive conduct in trade or commerce. Competition law strongly overlaps with the common law action of passing off, which also provides certain traders with a degree of protection against other traders using trade marks (whether registered or unregistered) or similar indicia in a manner that would mislead consumers in various ways. Though there are some differences between the two causes of action, the prevailing approach in Australia is to treat passing off and deceptive and misleading trade practices actions as having a largely 'merged' operation.[78] Section 52 of the TPA was successfully utilised in conjunction with copyright in several of the cases mentioned above.

On 1 January 2010, the 1974 TPA was repealed and replaced by the Competition and Consumer Act 2011. Section 52, which formerly dealt with misleading and deceptive conduct, has been replaced by an equivalent provision in section 18 of the Australian Consumer Law (ACL) (contained in Schedule 2 of the Competition and Consumer Act 2011). While it is assumed that the principles developed under the old law remain applicable, the new law has a longer reach as it covers the conduct of 'persons' rather than only 'corporations', as was the case under the TPA. Section 18 of the ACL states that a person must not, in trade or commerce, engage in conduct that is misleading and deceptive or likely to mislead or deceive.

Competition law has, as yet, largely untapped potential for regulating appropriation of TCEs and TK by non-indigenous persons. Section 29 of the ACL prohibits making false or misleading representations in relation to a large number of matters with respect to goods or services, including in relation to history, place of origin and approval or affiliation. It is arguable that this action could cover broader forms of misrepresentation such as where the nature of an enterprise may suggest a connection with an Indigenous community because the nature and manner of the trade conducted 'looks' to general members of the public as Aboriginal, or may be taken as a reference to a particular clan, when in fact no such connection exists. There is a long history of fake Aboriginal art where non-indigenous persons have adopted Indigenous personas to manufacture an 'authentic' traditional reference and personally benefit from the misleading reference.[79] There has been a practice of hiding behind copyright law's perceived limitations to defend such activities, such as arguing that the appropriative works reference indigenous ideas and general iconography, but not precise expressions, although such 'defences' are relatively unexplored in case law. Competition and consumer law has more potential to restrain such

---

[78] Kathy Bowrey, Michael Handler and Dianne Nicol, *Australian IP. Commentary, Law and Practice*, Melbourne: Oxford University Press, 2010, chs 14 and 15.

[79] A number of examples are discussed in Kathy Bowrey, 'Indigenous Cultural and Intellectual Property', in Kathy Bowrey, Michael Handler and Dianne Nicol (eds), *Emerging Challenges in Intellectual Property,* Melbourne: Oxford University Press, 2011, pp. 46–67.

activities than copyright because it is far less interested in justifications for the expression or trade and more concerned about the effects of representations on consumers and other traders with established reputations.

The Australian Consumer and Competition Commission (ACCC) is an independent statutory authority financed by the Australian Government, and the principal regulator of competition and consumer law in Australia. There is some capacity for interested individuals to enforce the ACL,[80] and the ACCC can choose from a range of enforcement and compliance tools to suit the individual case and to achieve a range of broader public outcomes, which can go beyond just punishing wrongdoing. The ACCC has instituted proceedings against a souvenir manufacturer accused of falsely labelling products as authentic Aboriginal art under the TPA. However, such actions face similar difficulties to those in the copyright cases, with company structures and bankruptcy proceedings disappointing expectations of enforcement of significant penalties. Notwithstanding this problem, the ACCC still regularly initiates actions against traders who have falsely attributed Indigenous associations.[81]

It is possible that freedom of artistic expression and trade referencing Indigenous culture could be more effectively regulated under passing off and the ACL if the concept of reputation and misrepresentation were extended beyond the situation of making overt false claims of Aboriginality. *Where the primary product represents Indigenous culture, silence as to cultural association may be a form of unlawful free-riding.* A trade strategy has potential to ameliorate some of the presumed deficits of copyright law in protecting ideas, concepts and Indigenous imagery presumed to have fallen into the public domain. As such it is an idea worth further development.

4.2 Indigenous Australian Art Commercial Code of Conduct

Following many reports of unscrupulous practices and a recommendation of the *Indigenous Art Inquiry*,[82] the federal government has endorsed a voluntary code designed to improve ethical standards and remove unconscionable conduct from the Indigenous arts and craft sector: the *Indigenous Australian Art Commercial Code of Conduct.*[83] It is consistent with ACCC guidelines for voluntary codes. Dealers must submit to an application process in order to market themselves as compliant. The code includes provisions about:

---

[80] Thanks to Mark Bender for this point.

[81] See, for example, Australian Competition and Consumer Commission, 'ACCC Alleges Misleading and Deceptive Conduct by Indigenous Art Dealer', *News Release* (28 July 2008), available at http://www.accc.gov.au/content/index.phtml/itemId/837212/fromItemId/621575; and 'ACCC Institutes Against Seller of Aboriginal Art for Misleading Representations', *News Release* (17 June 2009), available at http://www.accc.gov.au/content/index.phtml/itemId/877295.

[82] Senate Standing Committee on Environment, Communications, Information Technology and the Arts, *Indigenous Art – Securing the Future Australia's Indigenous Visual Arts and Craft Sector*, Canberra: Commonwealth of Australia, 2007 [hereinafter *Indigenous Art Inquiry*].

[83] Available at http://www.Indigenousartcode.org/the_code.

- dealings with artists;
- agreements with artists (including minimum terms, cooling off, and payment to artists);
- dealings with artworks (including misleading or deceptive conduct, authenticity, respect for Indigenous cultural protocols and artists' rights, and care of artworks); and
- recordkeeping and reporting.

Indigenous Australian Art Commercial Code of Conduct certificates can be issued to art centres, dealers and galleries who are signatories to the code and meet the requisite standard of integrity. These certificates can be attached to works on future sales. There is also a *Charter of Principles for Publicly Funded Collecting Institutions* to complement the commercial code.

If the voluntary code does not appear to be working after two years of operation (lapsing November 2012), it could become a compulsory industry code applying to anyone selling Indigenous visual artworks, who would then require licensing or accreditation under that code.

5. OTHER AVENUES FOR PROTECTION

5.1 Performers' Rights: Folklore

In Australia, performers' rights were amended in accordance with provisions of the WIPO Performances and Phonograms Treaty (WPPT)[84] as part of the package of reforms associated with the passage of the Australia-US Free Trade Agreement.[85] The key provisions include giving performers co-ownership rights with the maker of a recording of a live performance. In accordance with the WPPT these provisions explicitly include the making of recordings of an expression of folklore.[86]

The WPPT was a post-Berne[87] adjustment of the public domain in the interest of a broader range of creators. Thus the reforms permit a retroactive adjustment of economic rights existing in recordings, with the potential for some Indigenous control over archival recordings made of Indigenous people by non-indigenous persons in the past to be enlivened.[88] Indigenous ownership is here practically realigned with the fact of actual

---

[84] WIPO Performances and Phonograms Treaty, 2186 UNTS 203; 36 ILM 76 (adopted on 20 December 1996, entered into force 20 May 2002).

[85] See Kim Weatherall, '"Pretend-y Rights." On the Insanely Complicated New Regime for Performers' Rights in Australia, and How Australian Performers Lost Out', in Fiona Macmillan and Kathy Bowrey (eds), *New Directions in Copyright Law*, vol. III, Cheltenham, UK: Edward Elgar, 2006, pp. 171–97.

[86] Copyright Act 1968 (Cth), ss 22 and 84.

[87] WIPO, Berne Convention for the Protection of Literary and Artistic Works (adopted on 9 September 1886), as revised at Paris (24 July 1971) and as amended on 28 September 1979.

[88] See Anthony Taubman, 'Nobility Of Interpretation: Equity, Retrospectivity, and Collectivity in Implementing New Norms for Performers' Rights' (2005) *Journal of Intellectual Property Law,* 12, pp. 351–425.

participation in live performances. This effectively sidesteps the problem of legislatively defining community interests and ownership with reference to more abstract notions of inclusion and exclusion. While the shared administration of rights can be complex, these provisions potentially offer a very useful avenue to assert Indigenous interests in relation to the historical record. There is little experience of their use to date.

5.2 Resale Royalty Scheme

There has been significant publicity about record sales prices for indigenous art in Australia and overseas while the original artists remain living in poverty.[89] Introduction of an artist's resale royalty scheme for the benefit of Australia's Indigenous artists was first proposed by ATSIC in 1997 and endorsed in the *Our Culture: Our Future* report (1998).[90] Whilst the scheme applies to all artists,[91] it was enacted primarily through advocacy from the Indigenous sector. Press releases invariably referenced the high prices paid for the works of deceased Indigenous artists who lived their lives in poverty.

The Resale Royalty Right for Visual Artists Act 2009 (Cth) entitles artists to a royalty of 5 per cent of the sale price each time their work is sold after the second resale, for works sold after 20 August 2009. The scheme is administered by the educational collecting society Copyright Agency Limited (CAL). It is controversial because of debates about the likely distribution of economic benefits, the administrative efficiency and cost of the scheme, the ability to document progressive sale of works, and incentives to move significant works overseas to avoid the obligation.[92] A relatively small number of high-profile Indigenous artists (or, more likely, their estates) are expected to eventually benefit from the scheme, with Terri Janke and Robynne Quiggin noting that generally Indigenous artists, even those at the high end of the market, are not financially well off and often have financial commitments to extended families.[93] The scheme remains problematic because, legally, royalties attach to individual artists. This, combined with high mortality rates, high rates of intestacy and probate laws that distribute benefits in a manner at odds with customary obligations,[94] sits uncomfortably amongst policy discussions about legal recognition of communal rights. The lack of retrospective application also means it will take a considerable time before any artist benefits. Anecdotally, some artists express the concern that there is stockpiling of their works by investors with a view to

---

89 Benjamin Genocchio, *Dollar Dreaming: Inside the Aboriginal Art World*, Prahran, Victoria: Hardie Grant Books, 2008, at pp. 99–116 (ch. 6. 'The Market and the Makers'); and Robynne Quiggin, 'The Resale Royalty and Indigenous Art: An Opportunity for the Recognition of Economic and Cultural Rights?', in Fiona MacMillan and Kathy Bowrey (eds), *New Directions in Copyright Law*, vol. III, Cheltenham, UK: Edward Elgar, 2006, pp. 229–40.

90 Janke, supra note 73.

91 As recommended by the *Report of the Contemporary Visual Arts and Craft Inquiry*, Canberra: Commonwealth of Australia, 2002.

92 *Indigenous Art Inquiry*, supra note 82, at ch. 12 ('The Resale Royalty Scheme'). This inquiry did not recommend introduction of the scheme because of the lack of benefit to most artists.

93 As quoted in *Indigenous Art Inquiry*, ibid., at p. 172.

94 Prue Vines, 'Consequences of Intestacy for Indigenous People in Australia: The Passing of Property and Burial Rights' (2004) *Australian Indigenous Law Reporter*, 8 (4), pp. 1–10.

inflated resale after their deaths. Whilst the scheme is welcome, it still fails to address the poor living conditions of many of Australia's most successful surviving Indigenous artists.

5.3 Indigenous Cultural Protocols

In addition to the avenues available under general law discussed above, there is also an important system of regulation through cultural protocols. There has been significant progress in defining culturally appropriate conduct in Indigenous protocols. These tend to operate at a local level and as such avoid some of the problems of representing 'the indigenous' in the abstract and affirmatively defining membership of the community.

One reading of indigenous protocols is that they exist as 'voluntary' agreements in place of formal legal recognition of community custom. They stem from the failure inherent in Anglo-Australian jurisprudence to respect indigenous law. Thus, protocols can be characterised as the only avenue left for affected communities to post their views. However, there are huge numbers of protocol documents in Australia.[95] Protocols are prescriptive – they prescribe particular types of behaviour. They also convey a mode of behaviour that institutions and individuals are presumed to follow. Protocols prescribe modes of conduct by emphasising or normalising particular forms of cultural engagement. While any single effect is not assured, over time protocols do have the capacity to influence change in ways that differ from stringent bureaucratic or legislative programmes.[96] Protocols are part and parcel of raising the profile of indigenous cultural agendas.[97]

Most forms of public arts and cultural funding and academic research in relation to indigenous subject matter expect consultation and some form of compliance with cultural protocols as part of obtaining ethics clearance and funding for projects. This gives protocols considerable reach, as non-compliance has potential for real impact on future career and funding opportunities.[98] It is also possible that protocols could inform fiduciary obligations enforceable by the courts, as discussed in relation to the *Bulun Bulun* case.

Cultural institutions are increasingly aware of and sensitive to indigenous concerns about material held within their collections. Management practices are slowly changing in terms of regulating access to collections.[99] However, this is primarily seen as an academic and scholarly concern, rather than as a trade issue.

---

[95] See Terri Janke and Robynne Quiggin, *Indigenous Cultural and Intellectual Property and Customary Law*, Background Paper 12, Perth, WA: Law Reform Commission of Western Australia, 2005, at p. 484.

[96] They can, of course, also be implemented as bureaucratic ritual. For example, one wonders about the convention in public ceremonies in many universities to formally acknowledge the traditional owners of lands when there has been so little progress in including indigenous people as students, fellow academics and indigenous views and issues in the compulsory curriculum.

[97] Jane Anderson, 'The Pragmatic Politics of Protocols', *Sharing the Cultural and Theoretical Space*, AIATSIS Biannual Conference Indigenous Studies (Canberra, Australia, 25 November 2004). See also Stephen Gray, 'Imagination, Fraud and the Cultural Protocols Debate: A Question of Free Speech or Pornography?' (2004) *Media and Arts Law Review,* 9 (1), pp. 23–37.

[98] See Kathy Bowrey, 'Alternative Intellectual Property: Indigenous Protocols, Copy Left and New Juridifications of Customary Practices' (2006) *Macquarie Law Journal*, 6, pp. 65–95.

[99] See Jane Anderson, 'Indigenous Knowledge, Intellectual Property, Libraries and Archives: Crises of Access, Control and Future Utility', in Martin Nakata and Marcia Langton (eds),

Even where the intention is to treat material with respect and return it to traditional owners, this can lead to absurd bureaucratic scenarios. For example, recently the Tiwi Community sought to reclaim a large collection of recordings of their songs, including some made by Charles Mountford, from a range of institutions including the Indigenous-managed body AIATSIS, as part of a project of cultural renewal. Some of the material had been classified as restricted for cultural reasons and AIATSIS would not provide digital copies of the material unless this was authorised by community elders. The age and ill-health of the remaining elders and lack of access to funds made it difficult to travel to Canberra to hear the material *in situ*. Recordings of the material would not be released so it could be heard in the community, subject to undertakings of confidentiality. Without digital copies being made available to them, elders resident in the Tiwi Islands could not determine authorisations and gain access to the recordings for their community at all. The power to deny access is a significant one and exists for good reason. However, the power only exists because of the colonial relations at play at the time of making these recordings. To rearticulate such relations, now expressed through well-meaning bureaucratic policies designed to enable culturally appropriate access, can cause significant frustration and anger.[100]

Such problems could also emerge to frustrate Indigenous owners in asserting their newly won performers' rights to folklore.

5.4 *Sui Generis* Law Proposals

There is no national Australian bill of rights and, as discussed above in relation to the NT Intervention, domestic laws can target Indigenous communities in violation of the International Covenant on Civil and Political Rights,[101] seemingly without much ramification.[102] This puts into question whether international law has more than symbolic reach in Australia. However, there remains a strong interest and level of Australian participation in international fora concerning indigenous issues and these discussions keep domestic discourse over the need for *sui generis* rights alive.

Australian Indigenous Knowledge and Libraries, vol. XXXVI (2), Deakin: Australian Academic & Research Libraries, 2005, pp. 83–94; and Emily Hudson, 'Cultural Institutions, Law and Indigenous Knowledge: A Legal Primer on the Management of Australian Indigenous Collections', *University of Melbourne*, Legal Studies Research Paper Series, Research Paper No. 201 (2006), available at http://papers.ssrn.com/sol3/papers.cfm?abstract_id=955977.

100 Nicole Steinke, 'Tiwi Songs', *Into the Music*, Radio National, Australian Broadcasting Corporation (11 December 2010), available at http://www.abc.net.au/rn/intothemusic/stories/2010/3038053.htm.

101 Supra note 5.

102 See Editors, 'Indigenous Australians and a National Charter of Human Rights: Issues for Consideration', *Indigenous Law Bulletin*, 7 (10), pp. 2–3; Larissa Behrendt, 'Power from the People: A Community-Based Approach to Indigenous Self-Determination' (2003) *The Flinders Journal of Law Reform*, 6 (2), pp. 135–50; and Larissa Behrendt, 'As Good as it Gets or as Good as it Could Be?: Benchmarking Human Rights in Australia' (2009) *Balayi*, 10, pp. 3–13.

A *sui generis* law for the protection of indigenous cultural and intellectual property (ICIP) was suggested in a government policy paper in 1997.[103] This is supported by the UNESCO Pacific Regional Office/WIPO initiative, the *Pacific Regional Framework for the Protection of Traditional Knowledge and Protection of Culture* (2002).[104] More recently *sui generis* law has been advocated by the National Association for the Visual Arts, the Arts Law Centre of Australia, the Australia Council and the Arts Law Centre of Queensland – all drawing on the work of Janke and Quiggin.[105] The possible content of such a *sui generis* law includes protection in relation to:

- communal ownership;
- artistic styles;
- intangible forms of expression;
- time limitations;
- the use of indigenous cultural materials without the appropriate consent of indigenous custodians;
- wilful destruction of cultural property;
- ecology and biodiversity; and
- misrepresentations as to the source of ICIP.

A major reason a *sui generis* approach is seen to be necessary concerns the collective nature of indigenous rights and the associated custodianship claims of community. These are expressed by Janke and Quiggin as:

> laws … based on positive obligations toward cultural knowledge and the need to ensure that the culture is maintained and protected so that it can be passed on to future generations. To ensure this, there is often an individual or group who is the custodian or caretaker of a particular item of heritage. The traditional custodian acts as a trustee, whose role it is to pass on the knowledge and ensure that its use conforms to the best interests of the community.[106]

---

103 Michael Davis, 'Indigenous Peoples and Intellectual Property Rights', *Department of the Parliamentary Library*, Research Paper No. 20 (1997), available at http://www.aph.gov.au/library/pubs/rp/1996–97/97rp20.htm.

104 Secretariat of the Pacific Community (SPC), Regional Framework for the Protection of Traditional Knowledge and Expressions of Culture, 2002; and SPC, *Guidelines for Developing National Legislation for the Protection of Traditional Knowledge and Expressions of Culture Based on the Pacific Model Law 2002*, Noumea, New Caledonia: SPC, 2006; both available online at http://www.wipo.int/tk/en/laws/folklore.html.

105 Janke and Quiggin, supra note 95. See National Association for the Visual Arts, 'Submission by the National Association for the Visual Arts (NAVA)' (24 November 2006), available online at http://www.aph.gov.au/SEnate/committee/ecita_ctte/completed_inquiries/2004–07/Indigenous_arts/submissions/sub27.pdf; Arts Law Centre of Australia, 'Submission to the Inquiry into Australia's Indigenous Visual Arts and Craft Sector' (27 November 2006), at pp. 11 and 14, available online at http://www.aph.gov.au/SEnate/committee/ecita_ctte/completed_inquiries/2004–07/Indigenous_arts/submissions/sub36.pdf; and Arts Law Centre of Queensland, 'Submission to the Inquiry into Australia's Indigenous Visual Arts and Craft Sector' (27 November 2006), at p. 3, available online at http://www.aph.gov.au/SEnate/committee/ecita_ctte/completed_inquiries/2004–07/Indigenous_arts/submissions/sub45.pdf.

106 Janke and Quiggin, supra note 95, at p. 456.

However, I would query how such a law would avoid the definitional issues that have challenged the development of communal moral rights legislation in Australia. Further, without clarification of how such laws would sit alongside or be harmonised with mainstream IP laws,[107] it is hard to evaluate what real impact such laws could have in practical application.

Indigenous persons have ended up living in a diverse range of political arrangements with different levels of political recognition at national level and widely varying degrees of self-governance, self-determination and community recognition. In 'settler' countries such as Australia, with high levels of dispossession, stolen generations, urban, regional and remote communities and differing views on the success of native title law, there are many obstacles to effectively consulting or defining the intended beneficiaries of *sui generis* schemes in practice. This political agenda of *sui generis* rights is of symbolic importance; however, as with the native title legislation, it is doubtful the legislative outcome would be anything like an Indigenous expression of Aboriginal law or sovereignty. Such initiatives address the priority of attending to the legitimacy claims of law founded in its inclusiveness and fairness, but it is not clear how they would have practical impact. Nonetheless, the push for *sui generis* rights remains politically important as it keeps in view the limitations of domestic law and conventional IP categories for protecting TK and TCEs, and indirectly this political pressure can impact and liberalise interpretation of domestic laws.

5.5 Failed Legislative Reforms

Judicial notice of the need for reform led to legislative attempts that sought to re-empower communities in negotiating use of Indigenous works. There have been two unsuccessful reforms – an authenticity label scheme and a communal moral rights scheme.

5.5.1 The authenticity label

Based on the assumption that consumers would prefer to purchase authentic Indigenous works rather than rip-offs, a national labelling system was developed permitting use of registered certification and service marks: a Label of Authenticity, a Collaboration Mark and an Indigenous Arts Retail Licence.[108] The marks were applied for by the National Indigenous Arts Advocacy Association (NIAAA), which had long lobbied for better protection of Indigenous art and publicised problems with the tourist trade. This scheme faltered for a number of reasons, including issues related to managing the diversity of 'authentic' expressions, the inappropriateness of a unitary national system for Indigenous Australia, problems in defining and evidencing the requisite Aboriginality, associated

---

[107] For a discussion on the importance of an interface between a *sui generis* system and IP law, see Frankel, supra note 72.

[108] For the history of the scheme, see Leanne Wiseman, 'The Protection of Indigenous Art and Culture in Australia: The Labels of Authenticity' (2001) *European Intellectual Property Review*, 23 (1), pp. 14–25; Stephen Gray, 'In Black and White or Beyond the Pale? The "Authenticity" Debate and Protection for Aboriginal Culture' (2001) *Australian Feminist Law Journal*, 15, pp. 105–21; and Janke (for WIPO), supra note 47, at pp. 135–58 ('Case Study 8. Indigenous Arts Certification Mark').

questions about who could administer 'quality control' and management issues related to the NIAAA.[109]

In the *Indigenous Art Inquiry*, it was noted that, '[i]t became apparent that the "one size fits all" approach did not factor in the individual needs and differing situations of Indigenous communities, and that the test for Aboriginality was too complex with over 75 per cent of applicants failing the requirements.'[110] It was also noted that Indigenous artists who, for whatever reason, did not use the mark would be perceived in the market as 'inauthentic'.

More generally, there is concern amongst artists about the framing and marketing of Aboriginal art in line with an artificial divide between traditional/urban artists.[111] The representation of Aboriginal identity in Australia and demands made on Indigenous subjects is a common theme explored in art.[112] This tension is exemplified in the award-winning artwork by Richard Bell that states: 'Aboriginal Art – it's a white thing.'[113]

5.5.2 Communal moral rights

When the Copyright Amendment (Moral Rights) Act 2000 (Cth) was enacted it determined that only individuals could exercise moral rights. At a late stage in discussions, the only Aboriginal member of Parliament, Senator Aden Ridgeway, proposed an amendment to include Indigenous communal rights, which eventually led to the Copyright Amendment (Indigenous Communal Moral Rights) Bill 2003 (Cth). The aim was to give 'Indigenous communities legal standing to safeguard the integrity of creative works embodying traditional community knowledge and wisdom'. Like the authenticity label scheme, this reform also faltered. There were similar problems relating to regulating notions of authenticity and 'traditional expression'. Communal moral rights were also dependent upon an underlying copyright work. There was an additional requirement for a voluntary agreement to be instigated between Indigenous communities and creators drawing upon Indigenous community knowledge.[114] This was a most peculiar requirement, given that the most common and egregious scenarios relate to circumstances where permission is not sought and the Indigenous community is unaware of the appropriation. The utility of communal moral rights that exist only when non-indigenous persons agree to consult and negotiate is clearly very limited. In such cases, where permission is first sought over a proposed use of Indigenous culture there may already be scope for

---

[109] For discussion of the demise of the scheme see Matthew Rimmer, 'Australian Icons: Authenticity Marks and Identity Politics' (2004) *Indigenous Law Journal*, 3, pp. 139–79 at p. 178; and Christoph B. Graber and Jessica C. Lai, 'Indigenous Cultural Heritage and Fairtrade – Voluntary Certification Standards in the Light of WIPO and WTO Law and Policymaking' (2011) *Prometheus*, 29 (3), pp. 287–308.

[110] *Indigenous Art Inquiry*, supra note 82, at pp. 122–3.

[111] See Kathy Bowrey, 'Law and its Confinement – Reflections on Trevor Nickoll's "Brush with the Lore"' (2011) *Griffith Law Review*, 20 (3), pp. 729–50.

[112] See Brenda Croft (ed.), *Culture Warriors: Australian Indigenous Art Trienniel*, Canberra: National Gallery of Australia, 2008.

[113] Richard Bell, 'Scientia e metaphysica (Bell's theorem)' (2003). The painting won the major Telstra National Aboriginal and Torres Strait Islander Art Award (NATSIAA).

[114] Jane Anderson, 'The Politics of Indigenous Knowledge: Australia's Proposed Communal Moral Rights Bill' (2004) *University of New South Wales Law Journal*, 27, pp. 565–605.

enforcement of the community interest under the notion of fiduciary duty as outlined in the *Bulun Bulun* case.

The Arts Law Centre of Australia has since recommended that:

> the WIPO [Intergovernmental Committee on Intellectual Property and Genetic Resources, Traditional Knowledge and Folklore] IGC act cautiously when considering the introduction of pre-conditions to protection which require the registration of traditional knowledge and cultural expressions or impose an onerous burden of proof on Indigenous communities. Such measures have the potential to reduce the protection of traditional knowledge and cultural expressions, rather than enhance it.[115]

Given the history and inherent tensions surrounding the state power to define Aboriginality, I am doubtful of the wisdom of pursuing programmes that require proactive registration of rights claims by Indigenous communities. This is a burden not generally borne by non-indigenous claimants.

In non-indigenous contexts, the widespread culture of piracy has encouraged development of much tougher legal obligations owed to owners, casting protection around a highly flexible and mobile legal definition of property. Similar reforms to stamp out 'piracy' in indigenous contexts are worth serious consideration.[116] Similar empowerment of indigenous persons would offer avenues for reconsidering new collective forms of cultural ownership and protection. International initiatives for protection of indigenous culture could support these efforts.

6. CULTURAL PROPERTY AND CULTURAL HERITAGE PROTECTION

There are a myriad of Commonwealth, state and territory laws that touch on Indigenous cultural heritage.[117] These include protection of moveable heritage and of sites. However, the potential of heritage laws needs to be considered against the broader context of the history of colonisation, empire and denial of property rights to indigenous people. Significant 'indigenes' accumulations held in collections overseas and in Australia were one consequence of the violence done to indigenous people in 'settler' communities. There remain significant problems in repatriating this material today.[118]

---

[115] Patricia Adjei, 'Indigenous and Local Communities' Concerns and Experiences in Protecting their Traditional Knowledge and Cultural Expressions', Presentation to WIPO, IGC (3 July 2007), available at http://www.artslaw.com.au/Indigenous/WIPOPresentation2007.asp.

[116] This is discussed in Bowrey, supra note 65.

[117] See generally, Janke, supra note 73, at pp. 77–87 (ch. 6. 'Protection under Cultural Heritage Laws').

[118] See Bowrey and Anderson, supra note 11; Tatiana Flessas, 'The Repatriation Debate and the Discourse of the Commons' (2007) *Social and Legal Studies*, 17 (3), pp. 387–405; and Catherine Bell and Robert K. Paterson, *Protection of First Nations Cultural Heritage: Laws, Policy and Reform*, Vancouver, Toronto: University of British Columbia Press, 2009.

6.1 Moveable Cultural Property

Legal characterisation of TK and TCE associated with moveable cultural property utilises a property paradigm. There is a culturally inappropriate separation into tangible/intangible, with heritage legislation primarily confined to regulating real and tangible property. This is then bisected into separate categories for moveable heritage and protection of archaeological sites. Underpinning this jurisprudence is a deeper philosophical divide into fact/value, where the empirics of the object is prioritised over 'opinion' as to its significance. As Leiboff notes, the law:

> assumes the veracity of the object as a physical presence as a *fact*, which can provide a trustworthy source of information about the object itself ... the legal enterprise is blind to the effect its rationalist and empiricist methodologies have on its decision-making about art or cultural forms, or cultural or artistic value or merit (to be called here a 'cultural object').[119]

'Facts' of an indigenous connection signify a potentially valuable artefact or chattel property, marking the object or site as potentially worthy of regulation. However, a cultural connection or significance has to be verified before it can be acted upon. This jurisprudential approach allows the state to, firstly, assert control over the objects and sites, and secondly, to seek expert advice and opinion to determine what cultural values or significance, if any, should be attached to them. This allows protection to accommodate a number of government priorities and agendas. The entire process alienates indigenous knowledge and experience where:

> Heritage includes all expressions of the relationship between the people, their land and the other living beings and spirits which share the land, and is the basis for maintaining social, economic and diplomatic relationships – through sharing – with other peoples. All of the aspects of heritage are interrelated and cannot be separated from the traditional territory of the people concerned. What tangible and intangible items constitute the heritage of a particular Indigenous people must be decided by the people themselves.[120]

The Protection of Moveable Cultural Heritage Act 1986 (Cth*)* has been described as:

> extraordinary in a number of respects, not least because of its complexity, being made up of a range of interlocking provisions based in and around a core set of provisions within the body of the legislation, and then supplemented by a generalised list of objects that are potentially capable of meeting the ultimate test of their significance to Australia.[121]

The List is divided into the two classes: Class A and Class B. Class A objects can never be permanently exported, but can be given a certificate of exemption for export in limited

---

[119] Marett Leiboff, 'Law's Empiricism of the Object: How Law Recreates Cultural Objects in its Own Image' (2007) *The Australian Feminist Law Journal*, 27, pp. 23–50, at pp. 23–4 (emphasis in original).

[120] Erica-Irene Daes (Special Rapporteur of the Sub-Commission on Prevention of Discrimination and Protection of Minorities, and Chairperson of the Working Group of Indigenous Populations), 'Study on the Protection of the Cultural and Intellectual Property of Indigenous Peoples', (UN Doc. E/CN.4/Sub.2/1993/28, 1993), at p. 39.

[121] Leiboff, supra note 119, at p. 33.

circumstances. This includes Indigenous objects such as bark and log coffins, human remains, rock art, carved trees, sacred and secret ritual objects. Class B objects can only be exported if a permit or certificate is granted: sections 8 (2)(a) and (b).

6.2 Heritage and Sacred Sites

Most Australian states and territories have heritage registers that list known Indigenous sites. These are to be consulted for consideration in planning approvals for development. Such lists are incomplete and there are many examples of poor practice in this area. A commonly heard view is that heritage legislation merely 'regularizes the obliteration of Aboriginal heritage. ... It is legislation by the non-indigenous community for the non-indigenous community that creates a superficial veneer of protection for Indigenous interests. The result is that the colonizing power can continue to do with Aboriginal places and materials exactly as it wants.'[122]

In *Kartinyeri*,[123] concerning a development on Hindmarsh Island, an exemption from heritage legislation was granted, thus obviating the need for consideration of Indigenous knowledge claims at all. The case involved opposition by the Ngarrindjeri women to a development application for a marina affecting Aboriginal heritage grounds and secret 'women's business'. An application for Ministerial protection was sought under the Aboriginal and Torres Strait Islander Heritage Protection Act 1984 (Cth) and referred for report. However, a declaration based on the report was then quashed and this was affirmed on appeal. Objections were then upheld over the appointment of Justice Jane Mathews to prepare a second report. In the interim the Hindmarsh Island Bridge Act 1997 (Cth) was crafted in order to prevent further application by the Ngarrindjeri women under section 10 of the Heritage Protection Act. The High Court found the partial repeal of the Heritage Protection Act, allowing the development to be assessed without reference to impact on women's secret business, to be valid.[124]

The weakness of heritage law is also shown by controversy over rock art in the Burrup Peninsula, WA. The Burrup Peninsula contains the world's largest outdoor rock engraving site, dating back to 30,000 years ago. In 1996, Justice Elizabeth Evatt presented a report into state and commonwealth Aboriginal heritage processes commissioned by the federal government and made several recommendations for reform of WA heritage legislation and processes to offer stronger protection. None were adopted by the state government.[125] The region remains a governmental focus for development in the Pilbara region and there is a plan to turn part of this site into a natural gas production and processing facility against the wishes of some of the site's Aboriginal custodians and the scientific community.

---

122 David Ritter, quoted in Robin Chapple, 'The Dampier Archipelago and the Burrup Peninsula: The Values of Indigenous Heritage', Parks And Protected Areas Forum (Fremantle, Western Australia, September 2007), available at www.dampierrockart.net/2007–09–24%20Burrup%20Heritage%20Paper.pdf. See also Graber, supra note 69.

123 *Kartinyeri*, supra note 3.

124 For an excellent summary see Editors, 'Kartinyeri v The Commonwealth – Case Summary' (1998) *Australian Indigenous Law Reporter*, 3 (2), at p. 180.

125 Cited in Chapple, supra note 122.

Under section 18 of the Aboriginal Heritage Act 1972 (WA), a developer may apply to the Minister for Aboriginal Affairs for permission to destroy any Aboriginal site. The Aboriginal Cultural Materials Committee (ACMC) provides ministerial advice:

> A 2004 parliamentary question in relation to s 18 applications established that the current Government had received and approved 208 applications to destroy Aboriginal sites since coming to power in 2001. Only three of these had been opposed by the ACMC, but each of these recommendations were subsequently overruled by the Minister.[126]

As Patricia Adjei notes:

> Whilst Australia has in place legislation to protect material of significance to Indigenous communities, from the experiences on the Burrup Peninsular it is clear that the existing framework is insufficient. In February 2007 *The Australian* newspaper reported that 'scraped and smashed rocks, with carvings visible on some surfaces' lay in piles several metres high following development work by the gas processing plant.
>
> The removal and destruction of the rock art on the Burrup Peninsular is occurring with approval under the cultural heritage laws. The resource company has successfully applied to the government authority to remove or destroy Aboriginal sites or objects. It is for these reasons that stronger protection of Aboriginal traditional knowledge and cultural expressions is required.[127]

Australian heritage laws serve as a reminder that the existence of legislation ostensibly for the benefit of Indigenous people should not be presumed to function to empower or protect the interests of Indigenous persons in practice. This is a depressing political reality that needs to be kept in mind in international fora. The politics brings into question the motivations for Australian participation in international policy-making. As Bluemel observes:

> ... most justifications for... participation are based upon an analysis of the benefits of participation for the governance system rather than also considering the impact of participation upon the groups. Justifications for group participation are typically borne from a functionalist perspective which concludes the international (and domestic) system needs group participation to enhance the system's legitimacy, but those justifications do little to show how particular group representation solves either systemic or group needs.[128]

This activity can provide a veneer of legitimacy to governance projects that further erode Indigenous rights.

7. NATIVE TITLE LAW

In recognising common law native title in *Mabo*, Brennan J stated:

---

126 Ibid.

127 Adjei, supra note 115.

128 Eric B. Bluemel, 'Separating Instrumental from Intrinsic Rights: Toward an Understanding of Indigenous Participation in International Rule-Making' (2005) *American Indian Law Review*, 30 (55), pp. 55–132, at p. 57.

> Native title has its origin in and is given its content by the traditional laws acknowledged by and the traditional customs observed by the Indigenous inhabitants of a territory. The nature and incidents of native title must be ascertained as a matter of fact with reference to those laws and customs.[129]

This suggests the legal concept of native title is much broader than traditional common law concepts of property. *Ward v WA and NT* regarded native title as '*sui generis*'.[130] Thus, case law suggests there is some scope for native title to encompass forms of Indigenous heritage. As David Bennett notes in relation to activities nominated under the Native Title Act 1993 (Cth):

> Traditional or customary hunting, fishing or gathering are specific processes ... [I]t is conducting these activities in accordance with traditional practices that separates them from other forms of the same activities. Or to put this another way, it is the intellectual property of a group in terms of their traditional knowledge which divides a native title right to hunt, fish or gather from other forms of the same activity.[131]

Two very carefully considered academic analyses suggest that there remains untapped capacity for native title to encompass Indigenous knowledge. Stephen Gray suggests there remains the potential for rights in art to nonetheless be viewed as a 'nature and incident' of native title and this could be considered by the Native Title Tribunal. However, he suggests it may be preferable for some Indigenous people to argue that traditional rights in art are separate from native title rights in land rather than a 'nature and incident' of such title.[132] Kristin Howden also argues there is capacity for protection here, but notes the 'worrying' reluctance of the Federal Court to recognise a right to protect traditional knowledge as within the scope of native title.[133] It is not clear how the Native Title Tribunal would assess any conflict between protection in accordance with Indigenous law as recognised as part of native title, and perceived rights to appropriate Indigenous knowledge under copyright and patent law. However, in line with the dicta of *Bulun Bulun*, it is probable that Australian copyright legislation extinguishes any native title rights where there are conflicts of laws.

It should be noted that as at May 2010, 129 determinations of native title (many of them by agreement) and 430 Indigenous land-use agreements had been registered with the National Native Title Tribunal. As shown by the *Yorta Yorta* decision,[134] native title is by no means an easily won entitlement for all dispossessed people. As Australians for Native Title and Reconciliation (ANTaR) notes:

---

[129] *Mabo*, supra note 44, at p. 58 Brennan J.

[130] *Ward v WA and NT* (1998) 159 ALR 483. See further Kristin Howden, 'Indigenous Traditional Knowledge and Native Title' (2001) *University of New South Wales Law Journal*, 2 (1), pp. 60–84, at pp. 67–70.

[131] Quoted in Howden, supra note 130, at p. 74.

[132] Stephen Gray, 'Peeking Into Pandora's Box. Common Law Recognition of Native Title to Aboriginal Art' (2000) *Griffith Law Review*, 9 (2), pp. 227–47.

[133] Howden, supra note 130. See also Graber, supra note 69, at pp. 23–5.

[134] *Yorta Yorta*, supra note 22.

> the potential of native title rights to deliver social, cultural, spiritual and economic benefits to Indigenous peoples has not been fulfilled. This is partly due to the litigious nature of the native title system, which involves long delays and high costs, and the limitations on the use of native title land.[135]

Given the current state of play it is difficult to assess the utility of a native title approach to protection of Indigenous knowledge. It remains a strategy worth trying, given the jurisprudential limitations of all western categories of law in respecting Indigenous law, but to date it does not suggest significant potential.

8. THE INDIGENOUS ART MARKET

It is impossible to estimate the overall revenue associated with the Indigenous art market. The *Indigenous Art Inquiry* noted:

> 2.1 The Indigenous visual arts and craft sector has been growing at a considerable rate for many years. It is now a dominant element of the arts in Australia, and is recognised as such internationally.
>
> 2.2 … The fact that Indigenous art is not only an industry but also an integral part of a culture makes it difficult to define what should be measured as the 'size' or the 'scale' of the sector. This is most relevant when considering the magnitude of the role of art centres.[136]

The Myer Report 2002 estimated the total Indigenous art and craft market was worth almost AUD200 million per annum.[137] The preferred statistics referred to by the Inquiry estimated the industry was worth AUD100–300 million.[138]

A 2006 analysis of Aboriginal and Torres Strait Islanders' participation in arts and culture revealed that:

> of the 282 000 Indigenous Australians aged over 14, 16.2 per cent said they had participated in arts or crafts activities in the last year. The levels were higher in remote areas (19.1 per cent) than non-remote (15.1 per cent). The disparity between remote and non-remote is much more striking when the question concerned whether people were paid for that activity. A total of 9.9 per cent of remote Indigenous Australians, or around 7 600 people, received payment for making art or craft. That percentage dropped to just 3.1 per cent for Indigenous people in non-remote areas, although this still represents around 6 400 people.[139]

Art production is, thus, a significant source of Indigenous employment.

---

[135] Kate Aubrey-Poiner and Jacqueline Phillips, *Are We There Yet? Ten Years on from the Decade of Reconciliation: A Reconciliation Progress Report*, New South Wales: Australians for Native Title and Reconciliation, 2010, at p. 15, available online at http://www.antar.org.au/are_we_there_yet.

[136] *Indigenous Art Inquiry*, supra note 82, at p. 5.

[137] Ibid., at p. 7.

[138] Ibid., at p. 9.

[139] Ibid., at p. 7.

8.1 Indigenous Art Companies

The development of the Indigenous art market needs to be more broadly understood as part of Australia's colonial heritage. Aboriginal art and craft has a long history as a distinctive regulatory object in Australia.[140] The development of Indigenous art enterprises are part of this heritage. Whilst today Indigenous art centres have a much larger role to play in developing the industry, it needs to be kept in mind that the centres work alongside commercial enterprises run by both reputable and non-reputable non-Indigenous traders.

Many Indigenous-owned and -operated art centres are related to past missions and located in remote regions. There are at least 110 art centres around the country.[141] These are associated with four peak bodies:

- ANKAAA, the Association of Northern, Kimberley and Arnhem Aboriginal Artists;
- Desart, the Association of Central Australian Art and Craft Centres;
- Ananguku Arts and Culture Aboriginal Corporation (known as Ku Arts) representing artists of the Anangu Pitjantjatjara Yankunytjatjara Lands in the far north-west of South Australia and has a membership of some 400 residents of the ten major communities and homelands in the region;
- UMI Arts was established in late 2005 to support artists and craftspeople from Mount Isa, across the Gulf of Carpentaria, Cape York and the Torres Strait.

Revenues primarily come from art sales. Centres have also received support from welfare, education and training schemes such as the Commonwealth Employment and Development Scheme. Centres are not simply organisations that facilitate cultural trade, and within communities there are potential overlaps and conflicts between the management roles of local art centres and that of land councils, local government and other community organisations. As the very successful 'Papunya Tula Artists Pty Ltd' notes, funds generated from art sales are utilised to provide important services to the community, including a renal dialysis unit, staff and vehicles associated with providing patient care, a community swimming pool, funeral costs, support for ceremonies, and school equipment and excursions. The artists' concern, however, was that:

> [t]he company's ability to provide this assistance and support is currently under threat, as the main artists are being targeted by private operators and the money being generated taken away from the community. ...
>
> Since the industry 'explosion' in recent years, the recognised artists, that is those with a high industry profile and whose work sells easily, have become targets for private operators intent on making quick cash and riding on the back of industry success.[142]

---

140 See generally Bowrey, supra note 65.

141 *Indigenous Arts Inquiry*, supra note 82, at pp. 28–9.

142 Papunya Tula Artists Pty Ltd, 'Submission to the Inquiry into the Indigenous Visual Arts Sector' (27 November 2006), at p. 2, available online at http://www.aph.gov.au/SEnate/committee/ecita_ctte/completed_inquiries/2004–07/Indigenous_arts/submissions/sub14.pdf.

Where available, market returns can be used by communities to provide basic health, education, transport and welfare services. As such, Indigenous art production *remains* part of the 'problematic flow of goods, money, and services between Aboriginal people and the state' identified by Fred Myers as originating in the 1970s.[143] To carve out this production as simply a segment of the regular 'culture trade' suppresses this heritage and the ongoing political significance of art centres.

Elders, and especially those that have achieved international recognition such that their works are sought after for investment, have been 'cherry-picked' by private dealers. Not all arrangements with private dealers are necessarily considered problematic – reputable private dealers have also contributed to building the industry. However, not all private dealers are reputable. The most exploitative arrangements noted in submissions to the *Indigenous Art Inquiry* occur where family crises caused by endemic poverty come to be 'managed' by a private art dealer.[144] Often this involves the dealer trespassing on land (where access to lands could be legally controlled) to approach artists, paying for food, servicing other debts or providing four-wheel drives necessary for travel in remote communities, in exchange for painting services using canvas and paint provided by the dealer. In the most extreme cases, artists are taken to a hotel on promise of free accommodation and a place to paint, and are then charged for the (segregated) accommodation where they can only service the debt by producing more works, which subsequently incurs more accommodation costs. That across the sector a common form of payment for significant paintings has come to be provision of four-wheel drive motor vehicles points to the peculiarities of the market incentives at play in Indigenous communities.

Arts and community centres are looked upon as a layer of governance for keeping in check predatory practices facing individuals inexperienced in managing market relations. Private individuals and small businesses working in the arts sector have difficulties pursuing access to justice.[145] With disproportionate levels of Indigenous disadvantage in Australia, the remoteness of many communities, and often also English literacy issues, Indigenous Australians are especially vulnerable to exploitation.

Centres provide a source of community financial management. Whilst governments have, to date, only provided funding for centre infrastructure mainly in remote communities in the Northern Territory, Western Australia and South Australia,[146] the *Indigenous Art Inquiry* recommended the provision of more support for the development of art

---

[143] Fred Myers, *Painting Culture. The Making of an Aboriginal High Art*, Durham, NC and London: Duke University Press, 2002.

[144] See, for example, Desart (Association of Central Australian Aboriginal Art and Craft Centres), 'Submission to Inquiry into Australia's Indigenous Visual Arts and Craft Sector' (27 November 2006), at pp. 34–8 (appendices 3–5), available online at http://www.aph.gov.au/SEnate/committee/ecita_ctte/completed_inquiries/2004–07/Indigenous_arts/submissions/sub49.pdf.

[145] David Throsby and Virginia Hollister, *Don't Give Up Your Day Job: An Economic Study of Professional Artists in Australia*, Sydney: Australia Council, 2003.

[146] Japingka Indigenous Fine Art Gallery, 'Submission to Senate Inquiry into Australia's Indigenous Visual Arts and Craft Sector' (27 November 2006), available online at http://www.aph.gov.au/SEnate/committee/ecita_ctte/completed_inquiries/2004–07/Indigenous_arts/submissions/sub21.pdf; and Jennifer Herd, 'Submission – Inquiry into Australia's Indigenous

centres because of their key role in communities in supplying canvas and paint, liaising with galleries and other buyers, and administering government education and training programmes for unemployed Indigenous people.[147] Painting is also recognised as providing people with a purpose and activity that assists in minimising petrol sniffing, alcohol consumption and other drug-taking, especially by youth. However, as one submission to the *Indigenous Art Inquiry* warns:

> Another reality check we must consider is that – even for successful operations such as Papunya Tula Artists ... it is virtually impossible for this successful centre to cater to all the artists' desires and needs, or at least satisfy the demands made upon them for money, canvas, advances, support, travel assistance and administrative and social support.[148]

The notion that the Government should provide or facilitate basic access to essential medical care, transport and education has been watered down with the neoliberal shift towards privatisation and user-pays models in urban and regional Australia. However, for remote Indigenous communities, it is precisely the lack of these services and support that creates particular vulnerability to the most predatory behaviour by unscrupulous dealers. Further, based on the submissions to the *Indigenous Art Inquiry*, the only realistic expectation for basic service delivery is accepted as coming in conjunction with some sort of 'self-determined' action, supported by government programmes at community level. It is thus very hard to separate the lack of means to redress the historical denial of basic entitlements to Indigenous citizens from the incentives to produce artworks for sale and the Indigenous cultural trade. This context in turn makes it difficult to separate expectations about art sales and calls for improved regulation of the sector from broader political, economic and social problems affecting communities and ongoing governance of Indigenous people.

As Myers notes, historically there have been three distinct but related roles or expectations carved out in relation to Indigenous artistic practice – 'art as enterprise', 'art as cultural and spiritual renewal' and 'art as Aboriginal identity'.[149] Translated into policy areas and laws, these generate different discourses and directions. However, in none of these approaches is delivery of basic services directly in focus as the primary responsibility of the Government. Rather, the presumption is that Indigenous 'communities', wherever they have ended up being located, are themselves responsible for seizing the initiative to develop their own resources and expertise through painting or whatever other

---

Visual Arts and Craft Sector' (27 November 2006), available online at http://www.aph.gov.au/SEnate/committee/ecita_ctte/completed_inquiries/2004–07/Indigenous_arts/submissions/sub47.pdf.

[147] *Indigenous Art Inquiry,* supra note 82, at p. xi (recommendations 4 and 6).

[148] Michael Eather (Fire-Works Gallery), 'Notes for Senate Inquiry' (May 2007), at p. 8, available online at http://www.aph.gov.au/SEnate/committee/ecita_ctte/completed_inquiries/2004–07/Indigenous_arts/submissions/sub88.pdf.

[149] Fred Myers, 'The Wizards of Oz: Nation, State and the Production of Aboriginal Fine Art', in Fred Myers (ed.), *The Empire of Things: Regimes of Value and Material Culture,* Oxford: James Curry, 2001, at p. 167.

virtues they possess to provide for themselves.[150] The Government's role is thus simply to assist with the exercise of community responsibility for 'resolving' problems of past and ongoing colonialism through developing successful art enterprises. In government policy and in relation to assignment of bureaucratic oversight, centres are treated primarily as arts organisations and/or Indigenous cultural organisations.

Government policy seeks to support cultural trade; however, arts organisations are treated as if they have arisen spontaneously in response to the 'art market', rather than as being essential to the development and maturation of this market in the first place, and as playing a part in the governance of Indigenous people in Australia. Any regulatory focus on the Indigenous art trade needs to understand the colonial heritage and support the public, political and economic significance of the role of Indigenous-owned and -managed art centres in Australia.

8.2 Who Decides Which Indigenous Heritage Can Be Traded?

I agree with the view of Christoph B. Graber that '[i]f we recognize the right of an Indigenous people to retain control over all aspects of its heritage, it seems self-evident to assign the competence to the heritage-owning Indigenous community.'[151] Yet, how this could be realised in an Australian context is unclear.

There is no formal Indigenous representation in trade negotiations. This has been criticised in Australia, where trade issues have been raised as part of the human rights discourse.[152] However, it also needs to be noted that generally there has also been little IP expertise involved in trade negotiations,[153] with Australian officials privately noting that this 'lack' also reflects US dominance of the international trade agenda. There have been numerous academic studies of the political manoeuvres, power and privilege of multinational actors – big media, big pharma – on the international IP stage.[154] At the same time as these actors have had privileged access to the corridor of power, NGO representatives of open source, third-party developers, human rights, education and development interests have all noted being excluded from participation in global trade fora.

---

150 For a discussion of the moralistic elements of this politics, see Watson, supra note 35; and Wendy Brown, 'Neoliberalism and the End of Liberal Democracy', in Wendy Brown (ed.), *Edgework: Critical Essays on Knowledge and Politics*, New Jersey and Oxfordshire: Princeton University Press, 2005, pp. 37–59, at pp. 42–4.

151 Graber, supra note 20, at p. 250.

152 Megan Davis, 'International Trade Rules and Indigenous Knowledge: A Basic Introduction' (2006) *Indigenous Law Bulletin*, 6 (20), pp. 10–12.

153 Kathy Bowrey, 'Can We Afford to Think about Copyright in a Global Marketplace?', in Fiona Macmillan (ed.), *New Directions in Copyright Law*, vol. I, Cheltenham, UK: Edward Elgar, 2005, pp. 51–69; and Kimberlee Weatherall, 'Of Copyright Bureaucracies and Incoherence: Stepping Back from Australia's Recent Copyright Reforms' (2007) *Melbourne University Law Review*, 31 (3), pp. 967–1016.

154 Peter Drahos, *The Global Governance of Knowledge*, Cambridge: Cambridge University Press, 2010; Susan Sell, *Private Power, Public Law: The Globalization of Intellectual Property Rights*, Cambridge: Cambridge University Press, 2003; and Michael Ryan, *Knowledge Diplomacy. Global Competition and the Politics of Intellectual Property*, Washington DC: Brookings Institution, 1998.

The Australian Government publicly expresses sensitivity towards the plight of Indigenous persons at the WTO, WIPO, UNESCO and UN human rights bodies. There is no open government opposition to the development of a trade agenda encompassing concerns about TK and TCEs. Exploitation of Indigenous communities is also a staple of media coverage, leading to continued pressure on the Government to respond.[155] Further, public speeches by the Minister for Innovation, Industry, Science and Research, Kim Carr, suggests a commitment to maintain an interest and presence in discussions:

> Last year, United Nations discussions on traditional knowledge came perilously close to collapse. The Government moved to ensure that Australia played a significant role in securing an extension to the mandate of the responsible UN IP Committee. With its renewed mandate, this Committee may well design a legal instrument that will give effective protection of traditional knowledge, traditional cultural expressions and genetic resources. Recommendations will be presented next September to the World Intellectual Property Organization's General Assembly in Geneva. The Australian Government takes these negotiations seriously, and given the complexity, and contestability, of the economic, legal and cultural issues involved, so it should. We want to ensure that Australia continues to play a significant role in shaping international discussions.[156]

There are already a number of Australian Indigenous persons participating in international discussions, but the problem of allowing for meaningful Indigenous representation, as discussed above, needs to be kept in mind. Simply including indigenous persons does not provide legitimacy in indigenous terms to this decision-making. What knowledge or expertise can the delegate represent? Sometimes the indigenous delegates involved do not have the requisite specialist knowledge, especially practical legal knowledge, and it is hard to discern the extent of community ties or consultations. *Though such persons may be earnest in their endeavours, there remains the question whether their inclusion is to serve the legitimacy needs of the state, more than to advance self-determination of indigenous peoples.* This is especially so when the indigenous delegate is endorsed by the state. As can be seen from recent submissions to the IGC, the problem for indigenous people is that the governments of Australia, Canada, New Zealand and the United States of America frequently work together in international fora.[157] This cooperation generally has had the effect of preserving the rights of the state and frustrating actions for self-determination.[158]

---

155 See most recently Damien Carrick, 'Biopiracy', *The Law Report*, Radio National, Australian Broadcasting Commission (14 December 2010), available online at http://www.abc.net.au/rn/lawreport/stories/2010/3091832.htm.

156 Kim Carr (Minister for Innovation, Industry, Science and Research), 'Launch Of Dream Shield Intellectual Property Resources For Indigenous Businesses', *Speech* (11 November 2010), available online at http://minister.innovation.gov.au/Carr/Pages/LAUNCHOFDREAMSHIELDINTELLECTUALPROPERTYRESOURCESFORINDIGENOUS BUSINESSES.aspx.

157 WIPO, IGC, 'Compilation of Comments on WIPO/GRTKF/IC/16/7 "Submission by Australia, Canada, New Zealand, Norway and the United States of America"' (WIPO Doc. WIPO/GRTKF/IC/17/INF/10, 2011).

158 Irene Watson and Sharon Venne, 'De-Colonisation and Aboriginal Peoples: Past and Future Strategies' (2007) *Australian Feminist Law Journal*, 26, pp. 111–12; and Sharon Venne, 'Extra Audio: The Law Report', on Carrick, supra note 155, available at http://www.abc.net.au/rn/lawreport/stories/2010/3092470.htm.

As noted by a statement of 16 organisations representing indigenous people in response to the 6–10 December 2010 IGC meeting:

> it is presumptuous to claim that Indigenous Peoples' rights and interests are protected at the community level and will be secured under domestic law once an international legal instrument is negotiated. States who come to these IGC and related meetings should be held accountable to their history and their current actions to protect Indigenous Peoples' traditional knowledge and their genetic resources.[159]

International initiatives for the inclusion of indigenous voices in the WTO, WIPO, the UN Permanent Forum on Indigenous Issues or UNESCO are welcome. These institutions have important agenda-setting roles. However, the proliferation of agendas and institutions also divides and diverts energies. Few experts have the capacity to be across the issues in all these discussions, let alone NGOs and grassroots indigenous organisations. The proliferation of institutions and proposals points to the extent of political crisis and a degree of international crisis management in this area. Even if a 'harmonisation' approach were eventually adopted in relation to this activity, the larger problem remains that of translating real (as opposed to symbolic) commitments agreed to into domestic law and changing local practice.[160]

Recently, Graber has suggested the need for clearer identification of TK and TCE that can be traded.[161] For reasons noted above, this initiative requires careful implementation to ensure that too strong a burden is not placed on indigenous owners. For this requirement to have significant bite, it would need to include knowledge and material hitherto assumed to be already in the public domain. This is obviously a major difficulty. For material that is not already considered in the public domain, it cannot be assumed that material has been obtained from indigenous peoples with consent.[162]

8.3 A National Indigenous Cultural Authority

There is an existing Australian proposal to facilitate authorised and licensed use of TCE and TK with consent of Indigenous people, through the establishment of a National Indigenous Cultural Authority (NICA).[163] This is conceived of as a rights promotion and management body, also providing administration for prior informed consent to the use of TCE and TK, overseeing use of a 'fair trade' inspired certification mark to promote

---

[159] See Kaitlin Mara, 'WIPO Members Move To Detailed Talks Toward Folklore Treaty', *Intellectual Property Watch* (11 December 2010), available at http://www.ip-watch.org/weblog/2010/12/11/wipo-members-move-into-detailed-talks-toward-folklore-treaty/.

[160] It should be noted that harmonisation of IP laws post-TRIPS has not lived up to expectations. Regional and domestic differences have proliferated, as sponsored by bilateral free trade agreements.

[161] Graber, supra note 20, at pp. 250–51.

[162] Debra Harry and Le'a Malia Kanehe, 'Asserting Tribal Sovereignty over Cultural Property: Moving Towards Protection of Genetic Material and Indigenous Knowledge' (2006) *Seattle Journal for Social Justice*, 5 (1), pp. 27–54, at p. 27.

[163] Terri Janke, *Beyond Guarding Ground: A Vision for a National Indigenous Cultural Authority*, Sydney: Terri Janke and Company Pty Ltd, 2009.

authorised uses, an informal register of rights owners, and providing standard licensing agreements.[164]

Attention needs to be paid to critical insights into Indigenous consent and existing benefit-sharing agreements.[165] As Jon Altman notes in relation to mining on Aboriginal land, '[i]n Australia, benefit-sharing agreements have proven to be poor instruments for the delivery of development, no matter who defines development – the State, mining companies or intended Indigenous beneficiaries. This is primarily due to the absence of a cogent policy framework to ensure the beneficial agreements generate positive outcomes.'[166] *It cannot be assumed that local Indigenous, wider community interest and state interests coincide.* A narrow focus on consent and projected economic outcomes can alienate deeper Indigenous concerns over the meaning of progress and development and a more holistic and profound respect for TK and TCE.

Janke's proposal for the NICA envisages rights management; however, there is potentially cause for conflict between Indigenous rights claimants and between Indigenous owners and owners as assigned under existing Australian laws. Indigenous alternative dispute resolution mechanisms are recommended as a preferable means of resolving such conflicts within communities.

Dispute mechanism processes are currently available to Indigenous persons in Australia including in native title, family law, criminal justice and through the Human Rights and Equal Opportunity Commission and State and Territory Equal Employment Opportunity, Human Rights and Anti-Discrimination Commissions.[167] The National Alternative Dispute Resolution Advisory Council recommended that the Australian Government evaluate a proposal for a national network of Indigenous dispute resolution practitioners, developed by the Indigenous Facilitation and Mediation Project at the AIATSIS. AIATSIS, through the work of Toni Bauman, has continued to develop this proposal.[168] However, there remains a significant skill shortage in this area. Nonetheless, Indigenous dispute resolution at the local level is preferable to WTO intervention and state governance of indigenous peoples.

The problem remains of identifying the potential of dispute resolution processes where there is a clash of laws. It is trite but true to acknowledge that it is very difficult to carve out a meaningful space for Indigenous law within a colonised space.

---

164 For an excellent analysis of fair trade marks see Margaret Chon, 'Marks of Rectitude' (2009) *Fordham Law Review*, 77, pp. 101–41. See also Graber and Lai, supra note 109.

165 See Rachel Wynberg, Doris Schroder and Roger Chennels (eds), *Indigenous Peoples, Consent and Benefit Sharing*, Dordrecht, Netherlands et al.: Springer, 2009.

166 Jon Altman, 'Benefit Sharing is No Solution to Development: Experiences from Mining on Aboriginal Land in Australia', in ibid., pp. 285–302, at p. 294.

167 National Alternative Dispute Resolution Advisory Council (NADRAC), 'Indigenous Dispute Resolution and Conflict Management' (2006) available online at http://www.nadrac.gov.au/publications/PublicationsByDate/Documents/Indigenous Dispute Resolution and Conflict Management.pdf.

168 See AIATSIS, 'Indigenous Decision Making and Dispute Management', available at http://www.aiatsis.gov.au/ntru/decisionmaking.html.

9. CONCLUSION

Whilst seeking to analyse a wide range of legal developments critically, I hope this chapter does not strike the reader as a one-note story. There is always room for creativity in framing demands on law and government for strengthening indigenous rights. There remains plenty of space for more thoughtful contributions, and the reality is that we will continue to see constant movement within and across the various categories of the law into the future.

Recourse to legislative reform is a common strategy for advancing the rights of minorities and disadvantaged peoples. Public law and human rights perspectives are frequently utilised as the models of empowerment; however, it is often presumed that a new law or new rights are needed, without fully and creatively exploring existing potential, especially within existing western paradigms. It needs to be remembered that corporate capital is extremely adept at such a strategy – developing ever more mobile and flexible understandings of property rights to advance their interests domestically, as well as fashioning new treaties.[169] Nonetheless, international initiatives can help frame and shift perceptions in domestic law, and reforms to include indigenous perspectives on trade discourse should be encouraged. It is the interface between international agendas and domestic law where much more research is needed to effect change and prevent ongoing misappropriation of TCEs and TK.

---

[169] The shift in power from WIPO to the WTO being one such obvious example, coupled with the recent emergence of indigenous agendas within the WTO.

16. A New Zealand perspective on the protection of mātauranga Māori (traditional knowledge)

Susy Frankel*

1. INTRODUCTION

In 1991 several Māori people began a journey by lodging a claim before the Waitangi Tribunal.[1] Six claimants brought the proceedings on behalf of their iwi (tribe) and as individual claimants. The claimants were Haana Murray of Ngāti Kurī, Hema Nui a Tawhaki Witana of Te Rarawa, Te Witi McMath of Ngāti Wai, Tama Poata of Ngāti Porou, Kataraina Rimene of Ngāti Kahungunu and John Hippolite of Ngāti Koata.[2] At the core of the claimants' reasons for bringing the claim was the view that successive New Zealand governments had failed to allow Māori to exercise te tino rangitiratanga[3] (literally chieftainship, but perhaps more accurately self-determination and control) over things Māori and, in particular, in regard to the body of knowledge and understanding; that is, mātauranga Māori (traditional knowledge, including Māori culture). The claim alleged that this failure had been a major cause of the loss of Māori culture. The claim became known by the claim number Wai 262. I refer in this chapter to the short title of the report on the claims, *Ko Aotearoa Tēnei*.[4]

The claim was wide in its scope and complex in its depth. It asked whether the Crown had honoured its obligations, under the Treaty of Waitangi, including the Crown's obligations in relation to Māori culture and mātauranga Māori, Māori peoples' relationship with the environment, Māori language and Māori medicinal practices. The claim

* The author was Consultant Counsel on intellectual property to the Waitangi Tribunal in the Wai 262 claim. The views expressed in this chapter are the perspective of the author and not necessarily that of the Tribunal. Thanks to Jessica C. Lai for her assistance in completing this chapter.

1 See discussion of the Waitangi Tribunal and its function below.

2 It is important to record the people who brought that claim. At the core of Māori culture lies that belief that who a person is and what they do is interconnected with their ancestors and their whakapapa (genealogy and connection between all people and the environment).

3 Te tino rangitiratanga is guaranteed to Māori under Article 2 of the Treaty of Waitangi, see discussion below.

4 Waitangi Tribunal, *Ko Aotearoa Tēnei: A Report into Claims Concerning New Zealand Law and Policy Affecting Māori Culture and Identity* (2011) Wai 262 [hereinafter *Ko Aotearoa Tēnei*]. Translated, Ko Aotearoa Tēnei means 'This is Aotearoa/New Zealand'. Aotearoa is the Māori name for New Zealand.

resulted in a report from the Waitangi Tribunal in 2011. In essence the report is about Māori culture and identity; New Zealand's laws, government policies and practices that affect that culture; and whether Māori are able to live and develop (both culturally and economically) as Māori.

The claim is unique and yet at the same time has resonance beyond New Zealand. All over the world, indigenous people seek greater control of their culture. The UN Declaration on the Rights of Indigenous Peoples is one reflection of this.[5] The claims of indigenous peoples in relation to intellectual property are global. There is much written about those claims which need not be repeated here;[6] suffice to say that the claims of indigenous peoples to their traditional knowledge and to its protection, both as a kind of intellectual property and from the incursion of existing intellectual property, have become acute. In part this has occurred because many indigenous peoples are in need of economic development in a world where trade, including trade in indigenous culture and trade that utilises indigenous culture, including traditional knowledge, is more globalised than ever before. The uniqueness of New Zealand is perhaps that the indigenous peoples are in a position to bring such a claim, both because they have rights to their land[7] and because the Waitangi Tribunal procedure provides a forum for such a claim.

There are two chapters of *Ko Aotearoa Tēnei*, which discuss intellectual property law and the protection of Māori culture. These are Chapters 1 and 2: 'Taonga Works and Intellectual Property' and 'Genetic and Biological Resources of Taonga Species'. Part 2 of the present chapter explains the Waitangi Tribunal process. Part 3 discusses each chapter of *Ko Aotearoa Tēnei* and their recommendations. Also discussed in Part 3 are the existing protections of Māori interests in the trade mark law of New Zealand. Part 4 discusses the interface of *sui generis* protection of mātauranga Māori and intellectual property law, using New Zealand's approach as an example. This chapter emphasises the importance of an effective interface between intellectual property and other methods of protecting

---

5 UN, Declaration on the Rights of Indigenous Peoples, GA Res. 61/295 (UN Doc. A/61/L.67 and Add.1) (adopted on 13 September 2007).

6 See other chapters in this volume. For example, Christoph Antons, 'Intellectual Property Rights in Indigenous Cultural Heritage: Basic Concepts and Continuing Controversies', in this volume; John Scott and Federico Lenzerini, 'International Indigenous and Human Rights Law in the Context of Trade in Indigenous Cultural Heritage', in this volume; Rebecca Tsosie, 'International Trade in Indigenous Cultural Heritage: An Argument for Indigenous Governance of Cultural Property', in this volume; and Karolina Kuprecht and Kurt Siehr, 'International Trade in Moveable Tangible Cultural Heritage of Indigenous Peoples: A European Perspective', in this volume.

7 In Peter Drahos and Susy Frankel, 'Introduction', in Peter Drahos and Susy Frankel (eds) *Indigenous Peoples' Innovation: Intellectual Property Pathways to Development*, Canberra: epress, at p. 12, we state:

> In the case of Aboriginal people in Australia the place-time nature of their system means that land rights justice is the primary necessary first step. Land rights justice, although not completely resolved, is considerably closer to having been achieved in New Zealand through the Waitangi Tribunal and Treaty Settlement Process. That is perhaps why Māori were able to bring the Wai 262 claim about the protection of their knowledge, culture and identity to the Waitangi Tribunal. This claim shows how progress on land rights justice opens the way to progress on the protection of indigenous knowledge and culture more broadly.

traditional knowledge and related cultural interests. The importance of the interface is to provide a way in which the two systems can work together and create a framework to resolve conflict, which will inevitably arise. Overall, this chapter gives a perspective on the New Zealand law of intellectual property and the protection of mātauranga Māori.

2. THE WAITANGI TRIBUNAL AND *KO AOTEAROA TĒNEI*

The Waitangi Tribunal is a tribunal of inquiry established by statute.[8] The Tribunal investigates claims made under the Treaty of Waitangi (Te Tiriti O Waitangi). The Treaty is a founding document of New Zealand.[9] In essence it sets out the agreement between Māori and the Crown over the governance of New Zealand and is consequently of constitutional significance. The Treaty of Waitangi is in both Māori and English and both versions are official versions, as they are not direct translations of each other.[10]

The second Article, *Ko te Tuarua*, is of direct relevance to intellectual property and is the Treaty basis for *Ko Aotearoa Tēnei*. The relevant Article in both languages and a literal translation (which is not official) is set out in Table 16.1.[11]

Table 16.1 The second Article of Ko te Tuarua

Ko te Tuarua	**Article the second**	**Literal translation***
Ko te Kuini o Ingarani ka wakarite ka wakaae ki nga Rangatira ki nga hapu – ki nga tangata katoa o Nu Tirani te tino rangatiratanga o ratou wenua o ratou kainga me o ratou taonga katoa	Her Majesty the Queen of England confirms and guarantees to the Chiefs and Tribes of New Zealand and to the respective families and individuals thereof the full exclusive and undisturbed possession of their Lands and Estates Forests Fisheries and other Preemption over such lands	The Queen of England acknowledges and guarantees to the Chiefs, the Tribes, and all the people of New Zealand, the entire supremacy of their lands, of their settlements, and of all their personal property

Note: * See the website of Te Puni Kōkiri (the Ministry of Māori Development): www.tpk.govt.nz (all online sources were accessed 3 November 2011).

---

8 Treaty of Waitangi Act 1975 (NZ), s. 5.

9 For the Treaty's history see Claudia Orange, *The Treaty of Waitangi*, Wellington: Bridget Williams Books, 1992. For a discussion of its legal status see Matthew S.R. Palmer, *The Treaty of Waitangi in New Zealand's Law and Constitution*, Wellington: Victoria University Press, 2008. For many years New Zealand courts doubted the legal importance of the Treaty of Waitangi; Prendergast CJ in *Wi Parata v Bishop of Wellington* (1877) 3 NZ Jur (NS) SC 72.

10 Treaty of Waitangi Act 1975, s. 2, which defines 'the Treaty' as including both the English and Māori version set out in schedule 1 of the Act.

11 This table is reproduced from Susy Frankel, *Intellectual Property in New Zealand*, 2nd edn, Wellington: Lexis Nexis, 2011. See Chapter 3 of that text for further discussion of the Treaty of Waitangi.

The scope of the Waitangi Tribunal's jurisdiction is important. It is not a court; rather it is a commission of inquiry that makes recommendations to government. Government then decides how to respond to the recommendations. There are other institutions involved in the Treaty of Waitangi process. A key one is the Office of Treaty Settlements, which negotiates settlement with Māori where a settlement, such as in land claims, is the appropriate remedy.

Another important feature of the Tribunal's jurisdiction is that it deals with issues that relate to the Treaty of Waitangi. It cannot make recommendations where there is not a connection to the Treaty.

In many ways *Ko Aotearoa Tēnei* is a unique claim in the Waitangi Tribunal process. One aspect of its uniqueness is that it is about future policy rather than settlement of past grievances. Also, it is the first claim made to the Waitangi Tribunal that involves the whole of government.

Another important feature of the Tribunal's role of inquiry and role of recommendation is that the report describes policy. It does not draft laws, nor is it appropriate for the Tribunal to be too specific about the details of laws that follow its recommendations.[12] The Wai 262 claimants also did not seek that specificity. Some of the Tribunal recommendations in *Ko Aotearoa Tēnei* are quite specific and others are broader. In both cases there are details for policy-makers and legislative drafters to grapple with when they implement any new policy and draft laws, should the government follow the Tribunal's recommendations. The aim of this chapter is not to draft such details, but to discuss the interface between existing intellectual property law and what the Tribunal recommends.

3. KO AOTEAROA TĒNEI

3.1 Taonga Works and Intellectual Property

The chapter about taonga (treasures) works in *Ko Aotearoa Tēnei* begins with scene-setting narratives and explanations of the nature and significance of taonga works to Māori and how the laws of New Zealand, in particular intellectual property law, have not provided Māori with the protection that they seek for taonga works. One such narrative is about the haka, known as 'Ka Mate Ka Mate', and how it is significant to one of the claimant iwi, Ngāti Toa.[13] The narrative describes the importance of the warrior, Te Rauparaha, who first created and performed this haka, and why the haka remains significant today to his descendants.[14] Ngāti Toa wish to control the commercial

[12] Although if a claimant were to ask that the Tribunal do so it arguably could, but any such drafting would still be recommendations to the government.

[13] *Ko Aotearoa Tēnei*, supra note 4, at pp. 40–41.

[14] This particular haka the All Blacks, New Zealand's national rugby team, use. See also Susy Frankel and Megan Richardson, 'Cultural Property and "the Public Domain": Case Studies from New Zealand and Australia', in Christoph Antons (ed.), *Traditional Knowledge, Traditional Cultural Expressions and Intellectual Property Law in the Asia-Pacific Region*, Alphen aan den Rijn, Netherlands: Kluwer Law International, 2009, pp. 275–292.

exploitation of the haka[15] and to ensure that, where it is performed, it is done in a culturally appropriate way.[16]

Not all of the claimants took the same approach and so *Ko Aotearoa Tēnei* records aspects of those differences and the common ground. Broadly, however, the claimants sought to own and control taonga works and related mātauranga Māori that is expressed in those works. They saw the control as necessary for specific purposes, including that Māori maintain and develop their relationship with taonga works. The relationship is one of guardianship over the taonga, thus making Māori kaitiaki (guardians) of their taonga and specific Māori kaitiaki of specific taonga. The kaitiaki relationship is one that relates to the past, present and future. As kaitiaki of taonga there is an ancestral relationship (whakapapa) and kaitiaki are both guardians of that heritage and of the taonga and mātauranga Māori for future generations.[17] As well as being able to be kaitiaki of their taonga, the claimants wished to be free to develop that relationship and, where the kaitiaki consider it appropriate, to economically exploit and benefit from that relationship.

The Tribunal explained that what makes a work a taonga work is the relationship between Māori and the work. The relevant Māori could be an individual, a whānau (family), an hapū (extended family group) or an iwi. In all cases, the relevant people are the kaitiaki of the taonga work and it is that relationship between the kaitiaki and the taonga work, that the Tribunal found Article 2 of the Treaty of Waitangi guarantees an appropriate degree of protection for. The consequence of the focus on the relationship is that there are works, which involve Māori elements, which may not be taonga works. The Tribunal described these works as taonga-derived works and concluded that such works have no kaitiaki and, therefore, protection of them is necessarily less. *Ko Aotearoa Tēnei* states:

> There is another, more amorphous category of works. These are works that have a Māori element to them, but that element is generalised or adapted, and is combined with other non-Māori influences. Works like these are inspired either by taonga works or by the mātauranga Māori underlying those works, but the connection to mātauranga Māori is far more tenuous than is the case for taonga works themselves. We call these taonga-derived works. We put them into a different category because they are so generic or derivative they have no whakapapa and no kōrero except at a generalised level. Most importantly, taonga-derived works have no kaitiaki. By this we mean there is nothing about the Māori element of the work that would lead one to conclude that the responsibilities of kaitiakitanga in respect of it belong to a particular community or kin group. In short, there is no natural connection with a kaitiaki community.[18]

The distinction between taonga-derived works and taonga works might also be seen as reflecting the reality that allowing non-Māori to use Māori culture is also a benefit for Māori, as such use contributes to the culture's survival. It is for that reason that the

---

[15] *Ko Aotearoa Tēnei*, supra note 4, at p. 41.

[16] See also Ngati Toa Rangatira Letter of Agreement from the Crown, available at http://nz01.terabyte.co.nz/ots/DocumentLibrary/NgatiToaofferletter.pdf, where it is stated, at paragraph 42, that '… the expectation of Ngāti Toa that the primary objective of this redress is to prevent the misappropriation and culturally inappropriate use or performance of the haka "Ka Mate".'

[17] *Ko Aotearoa Tēnei*, supra note 4, at pp. 38–43.

[18] Ibid., at pp. 84–5.

Tribunal also said it did not recommend mātauranga Māori be treated as owned by Māori. The Tribunal said that 'building a legal wall around mātauranga Māori would … choke it'.[19]

The Waitangi Tribunal was careful to recognise that there are competing interests that should be considered alongside the Māori interests in taonga works. These include the rights of existing intellectual property owners and the general public interest in the use of Māori culture in the arts. Some people with competing interests, including New Zealand artists and designers as well as other holders of intellectual property rights, gave third-party evidence at the hearings of the claim.[20] The current position is that those competing interests usually trump the Māori interest. *Ko Aotearoa Tēnei* recommends shifting that balance so that the Māori interests might, in appropriate circumstances, be the key interest that the law protects. The Tribunal also, in its recommendations, wanted to make sure that the recognition of other interests was balanced and did not result in marginalising the Māori interest or making it impossible for Māori to develop their culture. Therefore, the approach of the Tribunal was to recommend a regime that will shift the balance in the status quo, but will not make it impossible for all New Zealanders to use Māori culture. The recommendations are, however, that such uses take place within a new framework. Some will undoubtedly disagree with the Tribunal's recommended balancing approach, thinking that it gives too much recognition to Māori. On the other hand, others might have hoped for greater Māori control. One commentator about the report has expressed the view that something short of complete ownership is not enough.[21] Others will see *Ko Aotearoa Tēnei* as recommending a progressive way forward.

After discussing the different issues, including the nature of taonga, the Treaty of Waitangi, the existing laws (relating to copyright, trade marks and related rights) and international obligations, the kaitiaki relationship and balancing other interests, the chapter concludes with recommendations. With regard to taonga works and related mātauranga Māori, the Tribunal recommended that they should be legally protected. Part of the Tribunal's rationale was that Māori and New Zealand would benefit because, 'Taonga works are not just about Māori identity – they are about New Zealand identity, and a regime that delivers kaitiaki control of taonga works will also deliver New Zealand control of its unique identity'.[22]

The broad recommendations that the Tribunal made in order to achieve the protection of taonga works and mātauranga Māori are:

---

19 Ibid., at p. 92.

20 Ibid., at pp. 74–7.

21 See Moana Jackson commenting on video 'Moana Jackson Considers the Waitangi Tribunal Report for Wai 262 Claim and How Well it Meets the Wishes and Desires of the Original Claimants', Wai 262. Taonga. Kaitiaki, available at http://wai262.weebly.com/moana-jackson.html.

22 *Ko Aotearoa Tēnei*, supra note 4, at p. 91.

> 1. New standards of legal protection governing the use of taonga works, taonga-derived works, and mātauranga Māori …
>
> (a) A general objection mechanism to prohibit the derogatory or offensive public use of taonga works, taonga-derived works, or mātauranga Māori … [23]
> (b) A mechanism by which kaitiaki can prevent any commercial exploitation of taonga works or mātauranga Māori (but not taonga derived works) unless and until there has been consultation and, where found appropriate, kaitiaki consent … [24]
>
> 2. An expert commission to have wider functions in relation to taonga works, taonga-derived works, and mātauranga Māori.[25]

Ko Aotearoa Tēnei sets out how the proposed Commission should have adjudicative, facilitative and administrative functions. The adjudicative functions would involve hearing complaints about (a) and (b) above and deciding what steps must be taken to remedy the situation. This will also involve determining whether any particular work is a taonga work, or a taonga-derived work or otherwise, and who is kaitiaki of any taonga work.[26] This adjudicative function is not only for fully fledged disputes, but the Tribunal also recommended that the Commission has the power to give rulings where parties are uncertain if they should proceed or otherwise. The Tribunal suggested such a mechanism with the aim that it should ameliorate any chilling effect away from uses of Māori culture.

The facilitative function of the Commission includes producing guidelines and best-practice information for both kaitiaki and other users of Māori culture.

The recommended administrative function relates to maintaining a register of kaitiaki in respect of particular taonga works. The register is voluntary because kaitiaki must be free to keep their taonga and mātauranga Māori secret if they wish.

If the Commission finds that a work is a taonga work, the Tribunal recommends that kaitiaki must be involved in any decision about the taonga work's future, if any, commercial use. This involvement could entail a right to be consulted or to give consent. Depending on the nature of the relationship that the kaitiaki has with the taonga work or mātauranga Māori, the Commission should determine what is an appropriate level of kaitiaki control. This decision will be where the Commission balances the competing interests, discussed above.

These recommendations are for a *sui generis* law to protect Māori traditional knowledge (mātauranga Māori) and associated taonga works. The Tribunal said:

> This approach is not intended to create a new category of proprietary right, but is rather a way of recognising the relationship of kaitiaki with taonga works and some aspects of mātauranga Māori where it is proposed to exploit those things commercially. It is important to understand

---

[23] The Tribunal recommended that anybody should be entitled to object to the derogatory or offensive public use of taonga works, taonga-derived works, or mātauranga Māori.

[24] The Tribunal recommended that only kaitiaki should be entitled to object to any non-derogatory or non-offensive commercial use of taonga works or mātauranga Māori.

[25] The Tribunal recommended that the government establish a commission. The commission should have multi-disciplinary expertise (encompassing mātauranga Māori, IP law, commerce, science, and stewardship of taonga works and documents at both commissioner and secretariat levels).

[26] *Ko Aotearoa Tēnei*, supra note 4, at p. 99.

> that our recommendations do not represent a wholesale change to the current system of IP protection, particularly copyright and trade mark protection. Nor would they grant perpetual copyright to kaitiaki. These recommendations are sui generis in that they would operate outside the Copyright Act 1994, the Trade Marks Act 2002, the Designs Act 1953, the internet registration system, and any other relevant Acts which protect IP or related rights. They would have independent legal enforceability in their own right. However, as we noted above, this sui generis system must effectively interface with the IP system so that no irresolvable conflict arises between them. The commission should provide that point of interface.[27]

New Zealand's existing law affords Māori some protection. In particular, New Zealand has a system where Māori and others can object to the registration of offensive trade marks, discussed below. In this chapter, I characterise that protection as an aspect of the interface between intellectual property and *sui generis* protection. Such an objection-based procedure might also be described as a defensive mechanism or a defensive interest. It is true that such mechanisms are defensive against others obtaining rights and such a mechanism does not confer rights, in the sense of giving control, but that is precisely why an objection-based procedure is an important interface. If there are competing interests, the resolution of that competition could be that one interest is given rights and thus trumps the other interest. That is what currently occurs, for the most part, if an intellectual property rights owner asserts that right against a claim to protect or control mātauranga Māori. The intellectual property right prevails because there is no protection for mātauranga Māori. The function of the interface is to resolve conflicts, not to confer positive rights. This is discussed further below.

In New Zealand, the interface has proceeded in trade mark law even though there has not been any *sui generis* protection of taonga works and mātauranga Māori. The Wai 262 claimants recognised that the interface is not enough to protect their interests. *Ko Aotearoa Tēnei* recommends expanding the interface and protecting mātauranga Māori and taonga works.

Since 2002, New Zealand trade mark law has included a system where Māori can object to the registration of trade marks on the grounds that the trade mark applied for is culturally offensive or is likely to cause offence.[28] This is what the statute categorises as an absolute ground against registration of trade marks. The Commissioner can request advice from a committee about whether a Māori trade mark is offensive or otherwise.[29] Elsewhere, I have contrasted this system with the now-repealed provision that allowed the Commissioner of Trade Marks to refuse registration of trade marks on the basis of morality.[30] Similar morality provisions are also found in other countries. I have also

---

27 Ibid., at p. 92.

28 Trade Marks Act 2002 (NZ), s. 17(1).

29 Trade Marks Act 2002 (NZ), s. 178.

30 Susy Frankel, 'Third-Party Trade Marks as a Violation of Indigenous Cultural Property – A New Statutory Safeguard' (2005) *Journal of World Intellectual Property Law*, 8, pp. 83–98.

contrasted New Zealand's culturally offensive ground for objection to trade mark registration to the United States objection system and concluded that New Zealand's law is stronger and gives greater weight to indigenous peoples' interests.[31]

In *Ko Aotearoa Tēnei*, the Tribunal recommended that the proposed Commission take over the role of the Trade Marks Advisory Committee. It also concluded that the current role of the committee as advisory is not enough. It recommended that the Commission be the decision-maker. Although the current system is advisory, it is notable that the Commissioner has not rejected the committee's advice.[32] However, the law allows for the possibility that the Commissioner will reject the committee's advice. The Tribunal in recommending that the Māori interest be rebalanced sees the decision to follow the committee's advice as key to that rebalancing. Consequently, the Tribunal recommended that the committee be more than advisory and is a decision-maker in conjunction with the Commissioner of Trade Marks. The function of this committee is also key to making the intellectual property system interface with any *sui generis* protection.

3.2 Genetic and Biological Resources of Taonga Species

In the chapter with this title, in *Ko Aotearoa Tēnei*, the intellectual property aspects of genetic and biological resources[33] are discussed in conjunction with other issues of relevance to genetic and biological resources. Those issues include bioprospecting and biosecurity (primarily issues relating to genetic modification). *Ko Aotearoa Tēnei* links these fields because they are all part of the research process.[34] This makes for a lengthy consideration of the three strands separately as well as how they come together. As in the taonga works chapter, discussed above, this chapter begins with narratives. These tell of the importance of certain biological resources to Māori and of how Māori have used those resources as part of everyday life. The narratives also describe how Māori have made very little use of the patent system and plant variety rights and why those intellectual property systems are not designed for and cannot protect the relationship between Māori and biological and genetic resources. The Tribunal describes the relationship as follows:

> ... the elements that make [Māori culture] distinctive in the world can be traced to the relationships kaitiaki built up with the land, water, flora, and fauna of [New Zealand]. In this way, the mauri, or inner well-being of land and water spaces, and the whakapapa of flora and fauna do not just serve to articulate the human relationships with these things; they are the building blocks of an entire world view and of Māori identity itself. They play a similar role to the core definers

---

[31] Susy Frankel, 'Trade Marks, Traditional Knowledge and Cultural Intellectual Property', in Graeme B. Dinwoodie and Mark D. Janis (eds), *Trade Mark Law and Theory: A Handbook of Contemporary Research*, USA: Edward Elgar Press, 2007, pp. 433–63.

[32] See www.iponz.govt for the work of the committee.

[33] Rio Convention on Biological Diversity (CBD), 1760 UNTS 79; 31 ILM 818 (opened for signature 5 June 1992, entered into force 29 December 1993), Article 2 defines biological resources as including 'genetic resources, organisms or parts thereof, populations or any other biotic component of ecosystems with actual or potential use or value for humanity'. Genetic resources are defined as 'genetic material of actual or potential value', and genetic material is defined as 'any material of plant, animal, microbial or other origin containing functional units of heredity'.

[34] *Ko Aotearoa Tēnei*, supra note 4, at p. 115.

> of Western culture such as the arts, democracy, the rule of law, and so forth. But while the more human-centred Western culture tends to define itself by reference to its own thought and labour, Māori culture relies on pre-existing, pre-human definers – mountains, rivers, plants, animals, and so on. Māori culture seeks to reflect rather than dominate its surroundings. That is why the relationship between humans and taonga species is a definer of Māori culture itself. It is a preoccupation of the body of distinctive Māori knowledge that today we call mātauranga Māori.[35]

Analogous to the Tribunal's reasoning about taonga works, the Tribunal concludes that the Treaty of Waitangi requires a degree of protection of the relationship between Māori and biological and genetic resources. Where there is a kaitiaki relationship with a biological and genetic resource, the Tribunal describes such resources as taonga species. The Tribunal said:

> Whether a species is a taonga species can be tested. Taonga species have mātauranga Māori in relation to them. They have whakapapa able to be recited by tohunga (expert practitioners). Certain iwi or hapū will say that they are kaitiaki in respect of the species. Their tohunga will be able to say what events in the history of the community led to that kaitiaki status, and what obligations this creates for them. In essence, a taonga species will have kōrero tuku iho, or inherited learnings, the existence and credibility of which can be tested. When we use the term 'taonga species', we too are drawing on these multiple meanings.[36]

The Tribunal does not find that Māori own taonga species, but that where there is a kaitiaki relationship with a biological resource, that relationship is entitled to an appropriate degree of protection in accordance with Article 2 of the Treaty of Waitangi. The Tribunal also found that kaitiaki have rights, which are not exclusive ownership, in respect of the mātauranga Māori associated with taonga species of which they are the kaitiaki. The Tribunal said, '[Therefore] activities involving the commercial exploitation of mātauranga Māori must give proper recognition to the prior interests of kaitiaki; they are entitled to acknowledgement, and to have a reasonable degree of control over the use of mātauranga Māori'.[37]

What amounts to 'proper recognition' will depend on balancing the kaitiaki relationship against the interests of researchers and of applicants or owners of intellectual property rights, on a case-by-case basis. (In this context the relevant intellectual property rights are patent or plant variety rights.) Broadly, the Tribunal recommends decision-making mechanisms that treat the Māori interest as a key factor in the decision-making process. In relation to an application for a patent this would include consideration of the kaitiaki interest in the criteria for patentability (for example whether a patent is novel and involves an inventive step).[38] In order to achieve this, the Tribunal recommended:

---

35 Ibid.

36 Ibid., at pp. 114–15.

37 Ibid., at p. 210.

38 The criteria for when an invention is patentable include novelty and inventive step. Both are legal concepts of some depth and difference. They both, however, use the prior art as the key evidence in analysing whether there is novelty or inventive step in any particular case. The issue relevant to traditional knowledge is whether and how that knowledge forms part of the prior art. If it does, it might affect these criteria. However, even if some traditional knowledge is part of the prior

> the establishment of a Māori committee to advise the Commissioner of Patents about whether mātauranga Māori or taonga species have contributed in any way to the invention, and whether the proposed use is consistent with or contrary to tikanga Māori. This advice should be relevant to the requirements of patentability and (even if the patentability criteria are satisfied) whether there are kaitiaki interests at risk.[39]

Any consideration of whether kaitiaki interest would mean that an invention is not patentable, for reasons other than those relating to the patentability criteria, would need to be provided for as an exception to patentability. This is because of the Agreement on Trade-Related Aspects of Intellectual Property (TRIPS) requirements.[40] The relevant exception would be a morality or *ordre public* based exception.[41] Consequently, the Tribunal recommends such an exception. There is such an exception proposed in the Patents Bill.[42] Because the Bill was before Parliament at the time of the report, the Tribunal could not comment directly on the Patents Bill.[43]

That Bill also proposes the introduction of a Māori advisory committee to the Commissioner of Patents.[44] The Tribunal recommended that the committee should have powers greater than merely being advisory and that the Commissioner should be 'required to take formal advice from it, and work in partnership with a member of the Māori committee when making patent decisions that affect the kaitiaki relationship'.[45] The Tribunal also

---

art the use of the traditional knowledge may not necessarily affect the patentability criteria of novelty or inventive step.

[39] *Ko Aotearoa Tēnei*, supra note 4, at p. 212.

[40] WTO, Agreement on Trade Related Aspects of Intellectual Property Rights (TRIPS), Marrakesh Agreement Establishing the World Trade Organization, Annex 1C, 1869 UNTS 299; 33 ILM 1197 (adopted on 15 April 1994, entered into force 1 January 1995), Article 27, provides that patents must be available for inventions in all fields of technology provided they meet the criteria of novelty, inventive step and usefulness.

[41] TRIPS Agreement, Article 27.2 provides:

> Members may exclude from patentability inventions, the prevention within their territory of the commercial exploitation of which is necessary to protect *ordre public* or morality, including to protect human, animal or plant life or health or to avoid serious prejudice to the environment, provided that such exclusion is not made merely because the exploitation is prohibited by their law.

[42] Patents Bill (As Reported from the Commerce Committee) 2010 (NZ), cl. 14 provides:

> (1) An invention is not a patentable invention if the commercial exploitation of the invention, so far as claimed in a claim, is contrary to – (a) public order (which in this section has the same meaning as the term *ordre public* as used in Article 27.2 of the TRIPS Agreement); or (b) morality …
>
> (3) The Commissioner may, for the purpose of making a decision under this section, seek advice from the Māori advisory committee or any person that the Commissioner considers appropriate.

[43] Waitangi Tribunal Act 1975, s. 6 (6) provides: 'Nothing in this section shall confer any jurisdiction on the Tribunal in respect of any Bill that has been introduced into the House of Representatives unless the Bill has been referred to the Tribunal pursuant to section 8 of this Act.' The Patents Bill was not referred to the Tribunal. However, the Crown made submissions in relation to the Patents Bill policy and the draft Patents Bill (which was circulated before the Bill was introduced to parliament). The Tribunal could comment on the policy and the draft bill.

[44] Patents Bill (As Reported from the Commerce Committee) 2010 (NZ), cls 14(3) and 275.

[45] *Ko Aotearoa Tēnei*, supra note 4, at p. 212.

recommended that the committee should have an analogous function in relation to the plant variety rights system.[46]

A further Tribunal recommendation was that a register be established so that kaitiaki could notify their interest, but that notification would not be compulsory and kaitiaki could still object to patents if they had not registered their interest. This places a burden on kaitiaki. The Tribunal also recommended a burden on patent applicants to disclose 'whether any mātauranga Māori or taonga species have contributed to the research or invention in any way.'[47]

Disclosure of the origins of genetic resources in patent applications is an international issue.[48] Related issues include what the consequences of non-disclosure should be. The Tribunal recommended that the failure to disclose the use of taonga species and mātauranga Māori should result in substantive consequences for the patentee.[49] A disclosure obligation in the patent system is a mechanism to interface the patent system with the protection of traditional knowledge.

4. PROTECTING MĀTAURANGA MĀORI AND THE INTELLECTUAL PROPERTY INTERFACE

4.1 Taonga Works

Figure 16.1 shows the interface between *sui generis* protection and intellectual property protection.

Without the interface, the two areas will exist in silos and not be able to function in a way that is conducive to resolving conflict. If the law has *sui generis* protection of traditional knowledge, potential conflicts are between the protection of those *sui generis* rights and intellectual property rights. When domestic law does not provide for *sui generis* protection, any conflict is between unrecognised claims and recognised legal rights. For example, as reported in *Ko Aotearoa Tēnei*, Ross Scott gave evidence about how he had tried to register as a trade mark Tetaumatawhakatangihangakoauauotamateaurehaeaturi pukakapikimaungahoronukupokaiwhenuakitanatahu.[50] This is known as the longest place name in the world.[51] The protection Mr Scott sought was to enable the name to be used respectfully and by the descendants of the man who created the name; and that the kaitiaki control when the name could be used for commercial purposes. The name was not registrable as a trade mark because it was a place name. The name was registered, however, with a few changes so that it was not exactly the place name. Ross Scott told the

---

46 Ibid., at p. 206.

47 Ibid., at p. 212.

48 For a discussion of many issues relating to disclosure requirements see WIPO, Intergovernmental Committee on Intellectual Property and Genetic Resources, Traditional Knowledge and Folklore, 'WIPO Technical Study on Disclosure Requirements Concerning Genetic Resources and Traditional Knowledge', Third Intersessional Working Group, WIPO Publication No. 786 (WIPO Doc. WIPO/GRTKF/IWG/3/14, 2011).

49 *Ko Aotearoa Tēnei*, supra note 4, at p. 205.

50 Ibid., at pp. 38–9 and 65–6.

51 Ibid., at p. 38.

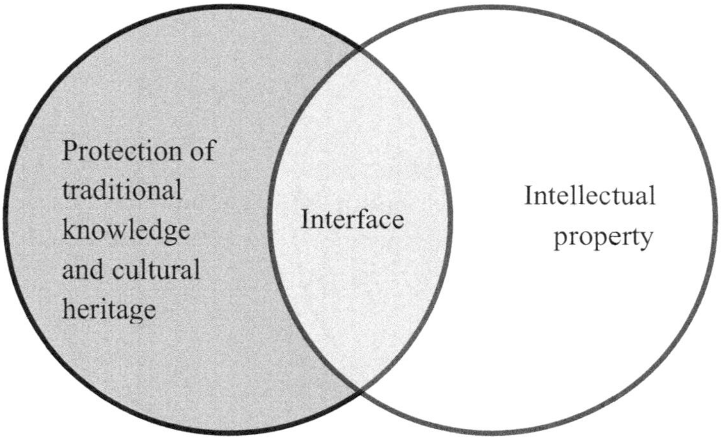

Figure 16.1 The interface

Tribunal that he was unhappy that he could not protect what his people consider is important about the name.[52]

Sui generis protection, in the form that the Tribunal has recommended, could protect the mātauranga Māori that is embodied in the name. An effective interface with trade mark law would require that this protection existed, even though trade mark protection for the name could not be granted.

Another, and perhaps more obvious, function of the interface would be the refusal of a third-party application to register the name or a variant on the name, which, but for the objection procedure, would otherwise be registrable.

Figure 16.2 shows the interface between *sui generis* protection and trade mark law.

The Tribunal's recommendations about the functions of the Commission are broader than trade mark law. The Tribunal's recommendations relate to taonga work and mātauranga Māori regardless of which, if any, particular intellectual property right may intersect with kaitiaki interest in taonga works and related mātauranga Māori. The recommended role of the Commission is, therefore, much broader than trade mark registration and would also involve issues relating to intellectual property rights that are not registered rights, which include copyright and what are sometimes called unregistered trade marks.[53]

Another example illustrates the interface of *sui generis* mātauranga Māori protection and intellectual property law in a different way. If a person uses a waiata (song) that a kaitiaki claims is a taonga work, to create a new song, *sui generis* protection of the taonga and the mātauranga Māori may apply. The *sui generis* interest that would be involved would be the laws created to reflect the Tribunal's recommendations that the kaitaki should, in appropriate circumstances, be able to object to offensive or derogatory

[52] Ibid., at pp. 65–6.

[53] An unregistered trade mark can give rise to an action in passing off. The report recommends that the commission look at all alleged offensive or commercial uses of taonga works, including those that would not give rise to an action in passing-off or an infringement of any intellectual property right.

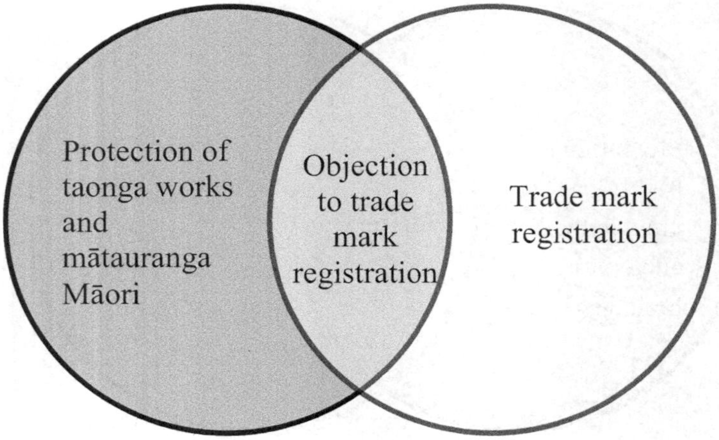

Figure 16.2 The interface and registered trade marks

treatment of the waiata and be consulted on any commercial use. Yet, even if the law provides for that *sui generis* protection, copyright law may vest an interest in any new work,[54] even though it was created using the waiata. The interface should function to resolve those potentially competing claims. In such an instance, the proposed Commission would need to determine the balance between those competing interests.

There are many taonga works that are analogous to copyright works and some aspects of those works copyright may protect. However, the protection of the kaitiaki relationship is not the same as that which copyright protects.[55] This is so even if copyright has the effect of limiting uses of the taonga work. Often, however, copyright will not prevent the mātauranga Māori being used. This is because the mātauranga Māori is analogous to the knowledge that the work conveys. Copyright, it is often said, does not protect the knowledge conveyed, or the ideas of the work. Rather it protects the expression.[56] Also, in many instances copyright relating to a taonga work will have expired.

As trade marks are registered intellectual property rights, the registration system provides an opportunity to provide an interface with any *sui generis* protection of taonga works and mātauranga Māori. As mentioned above, copyright does not present this registration opportunity for an interface.[57] Therefore, the proposed Commission's role would potentially operate in the same way, but also differently. Where the rights for

---

54 Copyright law creates a copyright in a work when an original work is created, Copyright Act 1994 (NZ), s. 14. For a discussion of New Zealand law, see Frankel, supra note 11.

55 Copyright gives the owner of the copyright a number of rights, including the prevention of reproduction. Copyright therefore allows others to use the knowledge or ideas conveyed in the work, but not to reproduce the expression of the work in which those ideas are conveyed.

56 This principle is enshrined in international copyright law. See TRIPS Agreement, Article 9.2.

57 The Berne Convention, incorporated into the TRIPS Agreement, prohibits formalities, particularly registration, for copyright to vest; WIPO, Berne Convention for the Protection of Literary and Artistic Works (adopted on 9 September 1886), as revised at Paris (24 July 1971) and as amended on 28 September 1979, Articles 1–21 incorporated into the TRIPS Agreement by Article 9.1.

protection of taonga works and mātauranga Māori overlap, with either trade marks or copyright, the Commission would be the institutional face of the interface. The Tribunal recommended that the Commission's role in relation to copyright will, like trade marks, relate to adjudication about offensive use and commercialisation. The Tribunal recommends the same facilitative and administrative functions for the use of taonga works and mātauranga Māori; these functions are not dependent on the category of intellectual property right, but on the claim of kaitiaki.

However, because copyright vests when a work is created, this may occur before a matter reaches the Commission. Therefore, when a kaitiaki claim activates the Commission's adjudicative role and there is a competing copyright interest, any conflict is more likely to arise when commercial exploitation or offensive use takes place, rather than at the stage of creation of the intellectual property right. In relation to taonga works that might be used as trade marks, it may be the application for registration which activates the Commission's role. Although it may also be that in trade-mark-related situations, commercial activity triggers any kaitiaki to invoke the Commission's adjudicative function, particularly in situations where an application for registration follows rather than precedes use.[58]

The Tribunal's recommendation that the Commission should also be able to give rulings before uses of taonga works take place and that the Commission should have a facilitative function, including providing guidelines and best practices, are recommendations with the goal of reducing the number of complaints after use has taken place.

4.2 Taonga Species

At the international level, the debate over the relationship between the use of biological and genetic resources and the use of traditional knowledge about those biological and genetic resources is well documented. The focus of the TRIPS Council discussion, which has not progressed, is a disclosure requirement of the origin of genetic resources in the patenting system.[59] A disclosure requirement is an example of an interface between the protection of traditional knowledge as a *sui generis* regime and the existing intellectual property regime of patents.

The Nagoya Protocol[60] of the Convention on Biological Diversity (CBD)[61] provides for more than disclosure. It also sets out a regime for prior informed consent and access and benefit-sharing.[62] These proposed regimes are in relation to the biological and genetic resources and also traditional knowledge 'associated with biological and genetic resources'. Without a mechanism for the interface, such as a disclosure mechanism, there

---

58 TRIPS Agreement, Article 15.1 allows for registration of trade marks to be available based on use that gives rise to distinctiveness.

59 For discussion of the proposals before the TRIPS Council, see Daniel Gervais, *The TRIPS Agreement: Drafting History and Analysis*, 3rd edn, London: Sweet & Maxwell, 2008, at paras 1.91–1.104.

60 Nagoya Protocol on Access to Genetic Resources and the Fair and Equitable Sharing of Benefits Arising from their Utilization to the Convention on Biological Diversity (UN Doc. UNEP/CBD/COP/DEC/X/1) (adopted on 29 October 2010).

61 CBD, supra note 33.

62 Nagoya Protocol, Articles 4.1bis, 5.1bis and 5bis.

is no effective way for the kind of protection that the Tribunal recommended to function alongside the patent regime. If the patent system can operate without any recognition of *sui generis* protection, the *sui generis* protection will fail because third-party patent interests will most likely trump it.

At the World Trade Organization, the United States has recommended that the relationship be dealt with as a matter of contract law.[63] The problem with reliance on contract law, or any other mechanism outside of the patent system, is that it removes the direct interface that disclosure offers and this arguably reduces the likelihood of competing interests being effectively resolved.

4.3 The Tribunal's Overall Approach

Overall, the Tribunal's recommendations if adopted would provide Māori with the ability, in the above described circumstances, to object to and in some instances effectively veto uses of taonga. The mechanisms are not property rights in taonga, but rather provide protection of the kaitiaki relationship through robust procedural mechanisms. 'Procedural' in this context is discussed by Christoph B. Graber, in this volume and elsewhere.[64] This procedural approach provides a way to interface, and in appropriate circumstances modify, existing intellectual property law. The Tribunal analyses this interface through the mechanism of balancing competing interest. Procedural regimes, as described by Graber, are not substantive in a way akin to property rights, but that does not mean that such regimes cannot be powerful. The Tribunal's approach is procedurally strong because not only does it recommend several direct interfaces with the intellectual property system, it also recommends strong *sui generis* protection of kaitiaki interests.

5. PROTECTING TAONGA WORKS AND THE INTERFACE WITH THE PUBLIC DOMAIN

One of the frequent objections to protecting traditional knowledge is the perceived threat to the public domain. Copyright provides a useful example to illustrate the issues, as it raises particular concerns over the protection of taonga works and related mātauranga Māori. Broadly, these concerns reflect the way in which copyright policy encourages the creation of new works that use known art and literature, including taonga works that are available to the public. If protected by copyright the knowledge and ideas conveyed in a work may be used by others and if the taonga work is not protected by copyright they are treated as available for all to use and in the so-called public domain. The haka, Ka Mate,

---

63 A summary of the different proposals from members of the WTO, 'Intellectual Property: Geographical Indications and Biodiversity', July 2008 Package: Briefing Notes, available at: www.wto.org/english/tratop_e/dda_e/meet08_brief05_e.htm.

64 Christoph B. Graber, 'Institutionalization of Creativity in Traditional Societies and in International Trade Law', in Shubha Ghosh and Robin P. Malloy (eds), *Creativity Law and Entrepreneurship*, Cheltenham, UK and Nothampton, MA: Edward Elgar, 2011, pp. 234–63, at pp. 251–2.

provides such an example.[65] *Ko Aotearoa Tēnei* states that whether the law treats something as if it is in the public domain, or otherwise is, to an extent, a matter of policy choice that governments make.

> That said, there is by no means any agreement amongst IP practitioners and scholars about the parameters of the public domain. In short, it is a hotly debated topic. The fact that IP law gives private rights over things in the public domain means that setting its boundaries is an ongoing balancing act between public and private interests. There are no principles that render the line immutable or unmovable, or that dictate that i[t] must be drawn here or there. For example, in 1981 the Flags, Emblems and Names Protection Act … ring-fenced from the public domain various cultural symbols perceived to be of national and international importance. Thus, balancing what is in the public domain with what is not – or, put another way, determining what should and should not be protected in law (including IP law) – is a policy choice. And it is a balance that must constantly be recalibrated as circumstances change. Just where to draw the line is a central issue in the Wai 262 claim. The claimants ask that it be redrawn in two respects. First they want to prevent those who are not kaitiaki from acquiring private rights in taonga works and in their associated mātauranga Māori. Secondly, they seek recognition of their own kaitiakitanga over these things and the right to object in any case of offensive treatment.[66]

The report acknowledges that international instruments require certain protections of copyright, but that does not prevent countries from protecting that which is appropriate in given domestic circumstances. Indeed, countries can provide greater protection than the minimum standards of international agreements.[67] Furthermore, there is enough flexibility in international agreements to allow the protection in accordance with those international commitments.

6. THE BUILDING BLOCKS OF TAONGA WORKS

The report also considers areas of Māori culture that are the building blocks of taonga works, although not on that basis. There is a chapter about Te Reo (Māori language), Rongoā (Māori medicinal practices) and where the Crown controls mātauranga Māori through its funding of Māori creative arts and culture, including museums. Each of these chapters considers issues that are not directly intellectual property issues, but relate to those issues.

Without Te Reo functioning as a widely used language among Māori, the ability to create, for example, waiata (songs) and other Māori works of art and literature is minimised. For this reason and others, the Tribunal emphasised the importance of the partnership between the Crown and Māori to develop a Māori language strategy and Māori-medium education programmes.[68] Also, there are recommendations about Crown

---

[65] There are many other examples throughout *Ko Aotearoa Tēnei*.

[66] *Ko Aotearoa Tēnei*, supra note 4, at p. 63.

[67] See TRIPS Agreement, Article 1.1; and Berne Convention, Article 19. See also Susy Frankel, 'Attempts to Protect Indigenous Culture through Free Trade Agreements', in this volume.

[68] *Ko Aotearoa Tēnei*, supra note 4, at pp. 477–88.

funding and support of mātauranga Māori and how Crown entities deal with tangible artefacts of Māori cultural heritage.[69]

Many Māori uses of flora and fauna are for medicinal purposes and, without Māori having the ability to use resources for such purposes, the mātauranga Māori is likely to be lost or compromised. Another possibility is that Māori medicinal practices will only develop as part of European culture, rather than developed by kaitiaki. The Tribunal recommended that the Crown provide more support for rongoā, including working to ensure the survival of the needed plants and access to them.[70]

Ko Aotearoa Tēnei also discusses the Māori relationship with the environment and with the Department of Conservation. From the perspective of the creation and development of Māori culture, access to and control over natural resources may provide the building blocks for creating development opportunities. If, for example, flax is required to make a medicine or a creative product, then access to that taonga species is vital.[71]

7. CONCLUDING THOUGHTS

In order for any system of traditional knowledge protection at domestic law to be effective, it must interface with the intellectual property system. Unless there is an effective linkage between the systems, there is no method to resolve conflict. Thus, if a country has a law, for example, that requires that a researcher obtain consent for uses of the traditional knowledge, then unless there is some relevant connection to copyright, trade mark or patent law, that *sui generis* traditional knowledge law may be ineffective. If the law requires consent to use the knowledge before it is incorporated into an art work, for example, and the art work created is a copyright work in its own right, then without an intersection between the systems at domestic law it might not be clear which right prevails. In this chapter I do not seek to answer which rights should prevail in any particular instance. Such a question needs detailed consideration at domestic level and in the particular circumstances of any given case.

It is also likely that if a *sui generis* system is enacted in New Zealand, the interface between intellectual property and that system is one that will continue to develop. Indeed, this is part of the function of the Commission that the Waitangi Tribunal has recommended be established. This continuing cycle of development is illustrated in Figure 16.3.

---

69 The Tribunal recommended more shared decision-making, for example, within the Ministry of Culture and Heritage, and in museums such as Te Papa; *Ko Aotearoa Tēnei*, supra note 4, at pp. 584–5. The Tribunal also recommended that Crown archives and libraries that hold mātauranga Māori in documents, images or footage should allow for relevant kaitiaki to object to commercial use of such, without consultation or their consent; *Ko Aotearoa Tēnei*, supra note 4, at p. 586.

70 *Ko Aotearoa Tēnei*, supra note 4, at p. 657.

71 The report recommended an increase in Māori control or involvement in decision-making in environmental and conservation management; *Ko Aotearoa Tēnei*, supra note 4, at pp. 285–6 and 372–3.

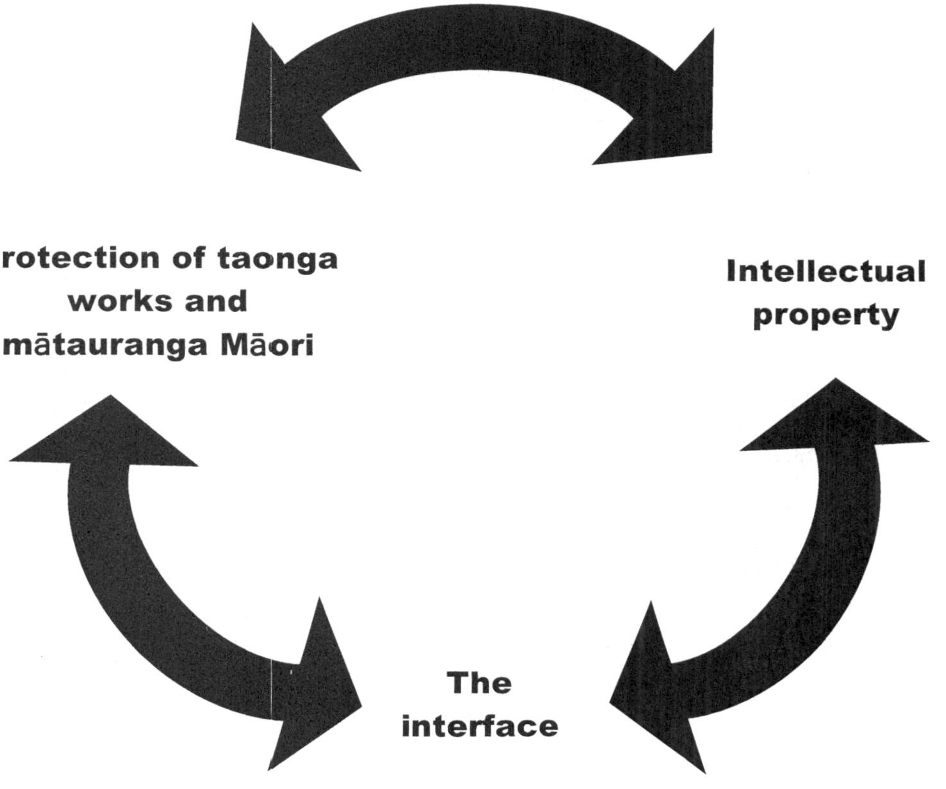

Figure 16.3 Protection as a cycle

Finally, any domestic system only affects protection in that jurisdiction. In this chapter, I have not traversed the international protection issues. The development of an effective relationship between different national intellectual property laws and *sui generis* traditional knowledge protection also requires recognition of an effective interface at international level. Such an interface has begun to develop through a series of interactions between the different regimes. Any continuing development, leading to agreement, is likely to arise through acquired knowledge and changes in behaviour that arise from such interaction, as illustrated in Figure 16.4.

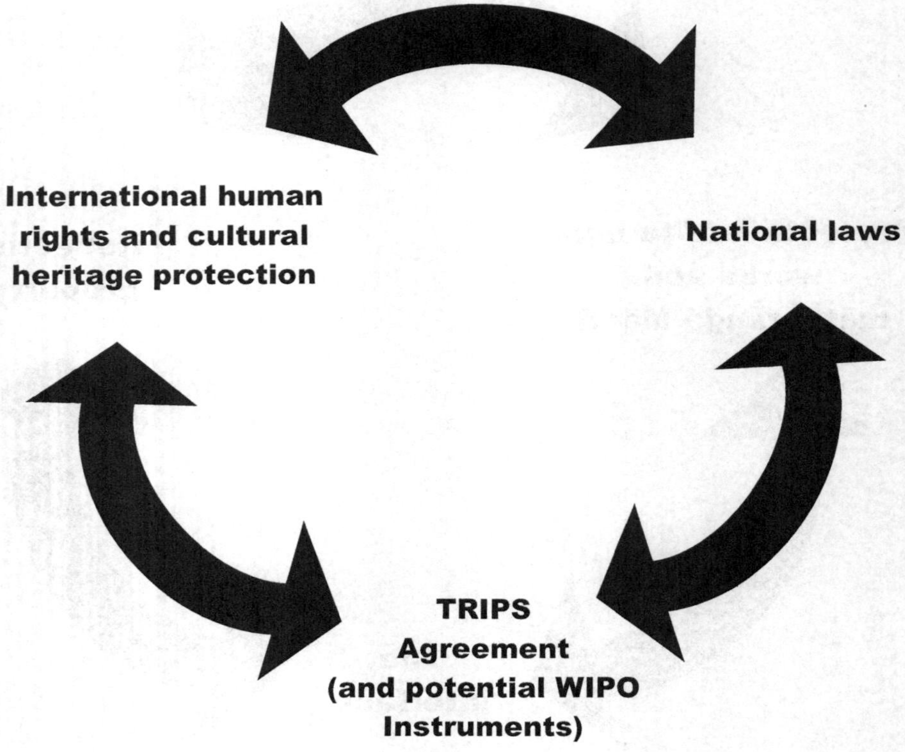

Figure 16.4 The relationship between national and international protection

Table 16.2 Glossary

Haka	Māori posture dance, often but not exclusively with vocal accompaniment, performed for a variety of reasons including as a welcome or as a challenge.
Hapū	A sub-division of iwi (clans within an iwi). Membership is determined by genealogical descent and a hapū is made up of a number of whānau.
Iwi	These are Māori tribes, consisting of several related hapū (clans or descent groups).
Kaitiaki	A person or several people who have the mana (authority) to be a trustee, minder, guard, custodian, guardian or keeper over something that is taonga.
Kaitiakitanga	Māori stewardship or guardianship over their people, lands, villages and treasures.
Kōrero	Narrative, story, discussion or conversation.
Kōrero tuku iho	Inherited learnings.
Mātauranga Māori	Māori knowledge; traditional knowledge of cultural practice; the body of knowledge originating from Māori ancestors, including the Māori worldview and perspectives, Māori creativity and cultural practices.
Mauri	The life force.
Rongoā	Māori medicinal practices.
Taonga	Treasures or highly prized possessions or holdings.
Te reo Māori	The Māori language.
Te tino rangatiratanga	Sovereignty, chieftainship, self-determination.
Tohunga	Priests; experts in Māori medicine and spirituality.
Waiata	Song or chant.
Whakapapa	Whakapapa represents more than lineage and genealogy, but also connects Māori existence to the atua (gods), creation and all life and represents the inheritance Māori receive from descent. It encompasses the view of existence itself and the relationship between this and the natural world.
Whānau	This means extended family and includes anyone connected by blood, no matter how distantly connected.

PART IV

Conclusions

17. The trade and development of indigenous cultural heritage: completing the picture and a possible way forward

Christoph B. Graber, Karolina Kuprecht and Jessica C. Lai

1. INTRODUCTION

The chapters collected in this volume are the fruit of a multi-year research project endeavouring to explore how trade and development of indigenous cultural heritage (ICH) could be stimulated by the means of international law. As noted in the Preface in this volume, these texts result from a three-day workshop that took place at the University of Lucerne in January 2011. After having been discussed during the three days, the authors worked over the chapters in continuous response to each other's comments and encouragements. This chapter aspires to put the major points of agreement and disagreement among participants of the workshop and authors of the present volume into perspective and to identify some prospective directions for further research.

An important achievement for the project is that a common understanding was reached on our initial assumption – that is, that national and international trade of indigenous cultural heritage (ICH) can be socioeconomically beneficial to indigenous peoples provided that it is indigenous peoples who have the choice of when and whether to commercialise or trade their ICH. In order for this to occur, it came through clearly that indigenous peoples need to better utilise the tools already available to them at the national level, whether in existing cultural and intellectual property or human rights norms, for example. At the same time it was also acknowledged that existing national legal regimes are not sufficient and often not appropriate. In developing means to better protect ICH, there needs to be 'deep listening' (a term used by indigenous peoples in Australia to describe true dialogue)[1] with indigenous peoples. Moreover, these discussions need to address the right questions in order to ascertain what it is that indigenous peoples really care about.

The development of strong national laws is inarguably important, but they require a mechanism at the international level to take into account the reality that we all live in a globalised world. In order to avoid shortcomings of an overly substantive and prescriptive top-down approach, which can be both ineffective and marginalising, the possibility of a

[1] See John Scott and Federico Lenzerini, 'International Indigenous and Human Rights Law in the Context of Trade in Indigenous Cultural Heritage', in this volume.

procedural approach to overcome problems of legitimacy and to coordinate between national and international levels of regulation – as proposed in the *reference paper*[2] – was discussed and well received. An intensively debated question was whether a procedural approach would require normative standards of 'fairness'. A difficulty identified by the participants of the workshop is that 'fairness' is culturally imbedded. For example, the western normative standard of 'democratic deliberation' – as most prominently articulated in Jürgen Habermas's discourse theory – is not always consistent with indigenous customary law and so it is not appropriate. After the workshop, the proposal for a procedural approach was reviewed and an improved version was included in Christoph B. Graber's contribution in this volume, 'Stimulating Trade and Development of Indigenous Cultural Heritage by Means of International Law: Issues of Legitimacy and Method'.

The project started with the assumption that there is potential in the WTO legal framework for promoting trade in ICH, provided there are some adjustments to the existing legal framework. One of the important outcomes of this project comes from learning that this aspiration is not realistic – partly because of structural deficiencies of the WTO itself and partly because of the bulkiness of indigenous issues in international trade law. Although participants/authors supported the idea of making WTO law more conducive to ICH trade and development, many raised doubts as to whether this would be politically (rather than legally) feasible, as WTO law-making is very cumbersome and has been stalled for the past ten years. Furthermore, it became apparent that, of all the different areas of international law examined, international trade law (specifically the WTO) comprises the least directly applicable laws towards indigenous issues and would probably be the least receptive in making adjustments for such. Rather than the multilateral forum, the most active and actualised movement for the regulation of international trade in ICH is currently taking place in bilateral free trade agreements (FTAs).[3] The problem of FTAs, however, is that structurally they will not contribute to the mainstreaming of indigenous rights standards in international trade relations. To be sure, recent cases of trade in ICH (we discuss the kava situation and the seal ban case in this chapter) demonstrate that, because of market dynamics, not even providing trade preferences to indigenous peoples for their cultural knowledge assets would necessarily contribute to increasing their share in international trade.

The identified shortcomings of WTO law and other top-down approaches to stimulate ICH trade and development were taken by several authors as a motive to suggest thinking about alternative approaches that may better respond to what indigenous peoples really seek. We feel that this may be a very promising avenue that has not yet been sufficiently researched. Hence, the last sections of this chapter will be dedicated to shedding some

---

[2] As mentioned in the Preface, a reference paper (published as Christoph B. Graber, 'Institutionalization of Creativity in Traditional Societies and in International Trade Law', in Shubha Ghosh and Robin P. Malloy (eds), *Creativity, Law and Entrepreneurship*, Cheltenham, UK and Northampton, MA: Edward Elgar, 2011, pp. 234–63) introduced one possible solution and identified a set of questions to be addressed by the individual participants of the workshop.

[3] Susy Frankel, 'Attempts to Protect Indigenous Culture through Free Trade Agreements', in this volume.

light on the potential of future research on voluntary standards supported by certification trade marks as a means to promote ICH trade and development.[4]

2. LESSONS TO TAKE FORWARD

2.1 The Role of National and International Laws

The discussions regarding indigenous rights pertaining to cultural heritage have a strong focus on the international level. It seems to be perceived that only global recognition can truly move indigenous interests forward. This is a reflection of the fact that most indigenous peoples have historically had difficulties in their states in gaining recognition, whether with their laws and customs or their rights relating to their land and cultural heritage. It has pushed indigenous peoples to aim higher, believing that international recognition will force their states to comply. The eventual recognition of indigenous rights, particularly in the two 1966 UN human rights covenants,[5] in ILO Convention No. 169[6] and in the UN Declaration on the Rights of Indigenous Peoples (UNDRIP),[7] is viewed as proof that such an international strategy pays off for indigenous peoples.

Notwithstanding this important development in the field of human rights, the authors of this volume doubt that equally positive results may be achieved where indigenous issues are at stake in international economic law.[8] Their feeling is that it would be unrealistic to perceive the emergence of effective international laws on ICH trade and development without there first being a social and legal institutionalisation of norms at the national level.[9] This is a lesson learned from intellectual property (IP) norms existent in modern

---

[4] Both the terms 'certification trade mark' and 'certification mark' can be found in the literature and are used synonymously throughout this chapter.

[5] UN, International Covenant on Economic, Social and Cultural Rights, 993 UNTS 3; 6 ILM 360 (adopted on 16 December 1966, entered into force 3 January 1976); and UN, International Covenant on Civil and Political Rights, 999 UNTS 171 and 1057 UNTS 407; 6 ILM 368 (adopted on 16 December 1966, entered into force 23 March 1976).

[6] ILO Convention No. 169 Concerning Indigenous and Tribal Peoples in Independent Countries, 1659 UNTS 383 (adopted on 27 June 1989, entered into force 5 September 1991).

[7] UN, Declaration on the Rights of Indigenous Peoples (UNDRIP), GA Res. 61/295 (UN Doc. A/61/L.67 and Add.1) (adopted on 13 September 2007). For a comprehensive analysis of the long development leading from the recognition of individual human rights of indigenous peoples in the two binding UN human rights covenants of 1966, the ICESCR and the ICCPR, to the recognition of collective indigenous rights in the non-binding UNDRIP of 2007, see Scott and Lenzerini, supra note 1.

[8] The term 'international economic law' is understood broadly to encompass also trade-related legal aspects of intellectual property, cultural property and tangible and intangible cultural heritage.

[9] Similar was the view of the New Zealand Government in 2002; see Ministry of Foreign Affairs and Trade, 'New Zealand and the World Trade Organisation. Intellectual Property. The Protection of Traditional Knowledge. Intervention by New Zealand at the TRIPS Council', (17–19 September 2002), available online at http://www.mfat.govt.nz/Trade-and-Economic-Relations/NZ-and-the-WTO/Strengthening-trade-rules/0-tripsintellprop-intervention.php (all online sources were accessed 19 November 2011).

international treaties, which were formed after the most powerful states of that time already had developed strong IP laws. The differences between the laws of those states were also not too vastly pronounced for the formulation of the international laws. This is in stark contrast to the field of indigenous issues, where there is a lot of difference, not only in indigenous laws and customs, but also in the historical background and in the recognition of indigenous cultural rights by the respective states.[10]

The development of national laws regarding ICH is at its infancy, whether tangible, intangible, moveable or immoveable. States themselves are internally trying to work out the best method to meet the interests of their indigenous peoples, taking into account the particular situation within their nations, including considering the balance of interests and the greater public. There is little consistency between the means by which different states have decided to approach the issues involved. Moreover, no state appears to have a comprehensive system in place. For instance, the United States has well-developed federal cultural property law with the Native American Graves Protection and Repatriation Act (NAGPRA) for old and tangible moveable Native American property. NAGPRA even contains a referral to tribal law, which is applicable when determining the individual or communal nature of tangible 'cultural patrimony' and its alienability. Yet, the United States has little to protect the IP interests of its indigenous communities.[11] On the other hand, New Zealand has an innovative means to prevent the registration of trade marks offensive to the Māori (and is developing a similar system for patents), but does not have anything equivalent to NAGPRA.[12]

However, in situations in which states will not develop the necessary laws, the impetus from the international level may be crucial, as was noted by Rosemary Coombe and Joe Turcotte in their contribution to this volume.[13] The failure of states to self-act could be for policy reasons (such as not wanting to recognise indigenous peoples or their rights) or could be an issue of resources; it could be too resource-intensive for small nations to develop the required policy. However, given the state of national laws regarding indigenous rights over their cultural heritage, the creation of binding international laws is still very challenging, even if only done so in a broad manner, as can be observed in the struggles of WIPO's activities.[14] This is not to deter discussion and debate at the international level, as it is important to remember that efforts at the international level, even if not resulting in a binding document, can at least politically influence national law and even give it a certain direction. But, because of the resource-intensive nature of

---

[10] UNDRIP recognises in recital 23 of its Preamble that 'the situation of indigenous peoples varies from region to region and from country to country and that the significance of national and regional particularities and various historical and cultural backgrounds should be taken into consideration'.

[11] Carole Goldberg, 'A United States Perspective on the Protection of Indigenous Cultural Heritage', in this volume.

[12] See Susy Frankel, 'A New Zealand Perspective on the Protection of Mātauranga Māori (Traditional Knowledge)', in this volume [hereinafter Frankel, 'A NZ Perspective'].

[13] Rosemary J. Coombe with Joseph F. Turcotte, 'Indigenous Cultural Heritage in Development and Trade: Perspectives from the Dynamics of Cultural Heritage Law and Policy', in this volume.

[14] Martin Girsberger and Benny Müller, 'International Trade in Indigenous Cultural Heritage: An IP Practitioners' Perspective', in this volume.

international negotiations, the international community and individual states need to work out how to best use their resources and may decide that it is preferable, at this stage, to do this predominantly at the national level.

In addition, it is questionable to what extent any international regulations should be substantive in nature (as discussed further below). There is a risk that overly prescriptive international laws prevent states from addressing issues particular to their nation or to particular communities within. It is clear from the chapters on the perspectives from the United States, Canada, Australia and New Zealand that, though there are similarities in the experiences and expectations of the indigenous peoples within, there are also important differences. Even internally within each of these four states, the indigenous communities are not homogenous, but have different languages, customary laws and knowledge systems.

As a consequence of the differing situations in every locality, states should be left to design the appropriate means to address local issues themselves. As stated by the New Zealand Waitangi Tribunal in the recently released (and long-awaited) Wai 262 Report,[15] governments are well advised to become active before the international community imposes mandatory rules:

> We are mindful of the risk that unless New Zealand formulates policies that are based in its own particular circumstances, standards for the protection of traditional knowledge that may not adequately protect the interests of all New Zealanders might be imposed from outside. Moreover, if New Zealand is at the forefront of creating relevant protections in domestic law, it can play a significant role in developing international standards that might benefit New Zealand interests internationally.[16]

If international laws are to be substantive, they can be formed from national models, as minimum standards. In stating this, it is vital that the development of international law in the field reflects the experiences and needs of all indigenous peoples and not just those from politically strong states. If this were to occur, the law developed could end up being analogous to the formation of international IP laws, which developing countries have struggled to implement.[17]

In developing laws and policies at the national level, the authors in this volume conclude that some common concepts and realities need to be taken into account. This includes respect for the indigenous peoples' very special relationship with their traditional lands. Land is the source of indigenous peoples' identity; it is the beginning and the end of everything in their spiritual life.[18] Moreover, the non-divide between tangible and intangible cultural heritage in indigenous worldviews must be acknowledged. Many cultural objects simultaneously contain images, words and music that have critical social, legal and

---

[15] *Waitangi Tribunal, Ko Aotearoa Tēnei: A Report into Claims Concerning New Zealand Law and Policy Affecting Māori Culture and Identity* (2011) Wai 262 [hereinafter *Ko Aotearoa Tēnei*]. This Report is discussed by Frankel, 'A NZ Perspective', supra note 12.

[16] *Ko Aotearoa Tēnei*, supra note 15, at p. 53.

[17] This is because IP laws do not benefit developing countries since they are not at a development level capable of gaining from the standards and, arguably, also do not have a culture that can be reflected in classical IP norms.

[18] Scott and Lenzerini, supra note 1.

even constitutional content to indigenous groups.[19] Tangible and intangible components of indigenous heritage often may not be separated and ought to be treated in an integrated and broad construction of indigenous rights to cultural heritage.[20] This point is related to the problem of defining the relevant subject matter. In addition, existing regimes need to be better utilised by indigenous peoples to protect their interests. This includes not only human rights, cultural property, cultural heritage or intellectual property laws, but also common law and consumer protection law. Thereby, common law jurisdictions may make use of common law's flexibility, encompassing fiduciary duties, trade secrets, privacy, confidence and passing off. Civil law is less flexible, but may reach similar results by analogies and interpretations of existing statutory law. In any case, to actualise the greater employment of existing mechanisms, there needs to be a better transfer of knowledge to indigenous peoples about how this can occur.

In addition, in countries with federalist governmental systems like those of the United States, which officially recognise indigenous nations that enjoy inherent and/or delegated powers of self-governance, tribal legal initiatives may complement the national policies. However, as the example of Canada shows, the acknowledgement of self-governance does not as such convey enforceable inherent rights. In Canada, the debate turns on the question of whether rights evolving from self-governance still require implementation through legislation, treaty or some other formal process before recognition and enforcement. For Rebecca Tsosie, indigenous self-determination is nevertheless the necessary starting place for achieving the requested recognition of the rights of indigenous peoples. At the same time, she places the responsibility upon indigenous peoples that enjoy such self-governmental rights to generate their own laws to govern their cultural heritage and trade with what is deemed capable of alienation. Without such an initial step from within, she holds that it is difficult to persuade the states to step in and protect what the indigenous peoples at stake think of as 'cultural heritage'. In any case, even where the issue of self-determination and self-governance is resolved and tribal cultural heritage law exists, the difficulty shifts to the question of what jurisdiction and conflict of law regulations are adequate and necessary to integrate tribal law into the existing national and international legal systems.

States also need to be open to modifying or re-interpreting existing legal norms to better take into account the interests of indigenous peoples. As Susy Frankel notes, the reason why the Māori Trade Marks Committee (which advises the Commissioner whether an application for registration is offensive) works is because it interfaces with an existing IP regime, rather than being a stand-alone *sui generis* mechanism.[21] An example of a possible re-interpretation of an existing norm was made by Brigitte Vézina, who noted that indigenous needs could be partially addressed through interpreting the IP public domain in

---

[19] Catherine Bell, 'Ownership and Trade of Aboriginal Cultural Heritage in Canada', in this volume.

[20] Rebecca Tsosie, 'International Trade in Indigenous Cultural Heritage: An Argument for Indigenous Governance of Cultural Property', in this volume.

[21] Frankel, 'A NZ Perspective', supra note 12.

conjunction with the customary laws of indigenous peoples.[22] In attempting to accommodate indigenous interests in their cultural heritage, policymakers and lawmakers are trying to 'merge' knowledge systems and worldviews which, as recalled above, are fundamentally different. Thus, interfaces that fill in the grey areas between indigenous and non-indigenous worldviews or push up against boundaries are important. Having separate *sui generis* systems in the black and the white, which do not interface, will only create further confusion and problems. NAGPRA is an example which might – at first sight – be identified as a *sui generis* system. It is a stand-alone legal act setting up a completely new law with regard to Native American cultural property. However, when looking at its legislative process as well as its legal details, it becomes apparent that the Act is rather a normative interface between indigenous and non-indigenous worldviews. To this end, procedural approaches are of great importance and consequently play an important role in NAGPRA.[23]

2.2 Respecting Cultural Diversity in Law- and Decision-making: A Bottom-up Approach

In the view of the authors of this volume, it is important that states include indigenous peoples in their law- and decision-making in order to design laws specifically addressing indigenous issues. In the same way that international laws must reflect the needs of particular nations, national laws must mirror the particular interests of their indigenous communities. History is replete with examples of laws that, though made with the best of intentions, have not met the interests of their targeted beneficiaries and/or have been culturally inappropriate, or even seen as imperialistic, due to the failure to overcome ill-informed presumptions. As examples, one could mention the views that western knowledge systems are 'better' than indigenous ones, rather than just being different, or that indigenous peoples are dying races, so the appropriation of their cultural heritage is for the benefit of mankind, by ensuring its survival.

Thus, there needs to be better communication with indigenous peoples in creating laws and policies that are directed at them or will strongly affect them. In doing this, states need to ensure that they ask the right questions and find out what exactly it is that indigenous peoples are trying to protect, what they expect and why. As stated by Coombe and Turcotte in this volume, '[t]he right of communities, minorities and indigenous peoples to participate in the process of determining how cultural heritage of significance to them will be protected is arguably the most important issue of cultural heritage law and policy today.'[24]

A bottom-up, rather than top-down, approach would better allow for indigenous communities to be the ones that decide what is or is not protected subject matter and who are the beneficiaries of any rights created. It would also allow indigenous peoples to decide what of their cultural heritage is or is not tradeable. In addition, a top-down approach

---

22 Brigitte Vézina, 'Are They In or Are They Out? Traditional Cultural Expressions and the Public Domain: Implications for Trade', in this volume.

23 Christoph B. Graber, 'Stimulating Trade and Development of Indigenous Cultural Heritage by Means of International Law: Issues of Legitimacy and Method', in this volume.

24 Coombe and Turcotte, supra note 13.

would not work considering the empirical reality of the existing cultural diversity among indigenous peoples.

Whether a bottom-up approach requires the recognition of self-governing authority of indigenous groups depends on the states' political and legal structures as well as the peculiarities of the indigenous population. In the United States, self-governance has opened the door for native nations to establish cultural heritage laws of their own. However, the effect of such protection ends where the jurisdiction of native nations is confined, just as national protection ends at the borders of national jurisdiction. A bottom-up approach in a national and international setting, thus, requires important work at the intersections of the different jurisdictions.

However, as indicated by the chapters herein on national perspectives, there is an important problem with getting indigenous peoples' involvement at the national and international level, especially appropriate and good representation. This is particularly noted by Kathy Bowrey in this volume.[25] Often representatives are expected to embody the interests of too great a number of communities. For example, one person of Aboriginal descent may be supposed to represent the concerns of all Australian indigenous peoples, when each community is different and they do not all recognise the 'leadership' role the individual has taken. Not only may the individual not be recognised as a 'leader', he or she may not be capable of taking the role of responsibility, not knowing, understanding or being able to reflect all the different customary laws and expectations of all the different communities. For example, an interesting dynamic in the United States is that some indigenous tribes would rather have their cultural items handled by non-indigenous people than by members of other tribes.[26] Moreover, these individuals are often expected to be capable of representing a range of interests, from human rights, land rights, cultural property, cultural heritage and intellectual property to international trade law and everything in between.

This overburdening of responsibilities is, of course, partly a result of states trying to simplify their processes by having a 'go to' representative, allowing them to show tokenistic inclusion of the 'indigenous perspective' in their policy- and decision-making. It is also a result of indigenous communities being small and fragile, particularly in Australia, and unable to expend resources and manpower in every field.[27] This is not to say that those individuals do not mean well and cannot forward the interests of indigenous peoples, but rather that such perfunctory consultation may result in the development of laws and policies that may look like progress from the outside, but which do not actually meet the needs of most of the local communities that are the targeted beneficiaries. Indeed, because outsiders (that is, the majority) may see the developments as progress, they may be more reluctant to later commit to more in-depth and encompassing processes or laws and policies. Thus, the simplification would appear to be a 'showy' short-term fix, which could create greater long-term problems. The use of a small number of representatives

---

[25] Kathy Bowrey, 'International Trade in Indigenous Cultural Heritage: An Australian Perspective', in this volume.

[26] Peter K. Yu, 'Cultural Relics, Intellectual Property, and Intangible Heritage' (2008) *Temple Law Review*, 81, pp. 433–506, at p. 490, citing Michael F. Brown, *Who Owns Native Culture?*, Cambridge, MA: Harvard University Press, 2003, at p. 32.

[27] The authors thank Peter Drahos for pointing this out to them.

further perpetuates the fallacy that indigenous peoples, at least within their states, are homogenous.

The failure to acknowledge the diverse range of indigenous perspectives within a state and across the globe is an inner barrier to advances in this area that needs to be acknowledged. There is still a lot of work to be done to raise the awareness that inclusion of indigenous peoples in law-making leads to more appropriate and ultimately more efficient laws. As Martin Girsberger and Benny Müller indicate in their chapter, a key factor in this process is funding, probably through the state.[28] As with all matters in the area of indigenous rights, things can only be done correctly with the full support of the state.

2.3 The Need for International Trade Law to be Consistent with Public International Law

There is general consensus among the authors of this volume that trade in ICH could positively affect indigenous peoples' social and economic development, provided that they have the power to decide whether and – if so – to what extent certain assets of their knowledge may be commercialised. In order to prevent a negative impact of such trade on indigenous peoples, it is indispensable that legal measures are available at the national and international level which effectively protect the tangible as well as the intangible expressions of indigenous culture.

With regard to the original idea to stimulate ICH trade and development by adjusting existing WTO law, several authors advised caution due to consistency problems in the relationship between the law of the WTO and public international law. Fiona Macmillan identified a systemic divide between the law of the WTO and public international law as something that would fundamentally inhibit an effective protection of indigenous knowledge assets in the WTO framework.[29] As she recalled, this divide is rooted in the emergence, after the Second World War, of two distinct legal orders at the international level, separating international trade law from public international law. If there is space in the WTO for the recognition of values generated in the public international law system with respect to ICH, it will crystallise in an evolutionary interpretation of WTO case law rather than in the politically unrealistic amendment of WTO agreements. In this line of thought, John Scott and Federico Lenzerini emphasised that international trade law must be operated in a way fully consistent with the basic principles of international law (including international customary law). Human rights and indigenous peoples' rights are perceived by them to represent supreme values that inform the entire framework of international law.

This view contrasts to a certain extent with the WTO Understanding on Rules and Procedures Governing the Settlement of Disputes (DSU).[30] According to Article 1 DSU,

---

28 Girsberger and Müller, supra note 14.

29 Fiona Macmillan, 'Finding Space in the Margins? Recognising the Rights of Indigenous Peoples in the WTO', in this volume.

30 WTO, Understanding on Rules and Procedures Governing the Settlement of Disputes (DSU), Marrakesh Agreement Establishing the World Trade Organization Annex 2, 1869 UNTS 401; 33 ILM 1226 (adopted on 15 April 1994, entered into force 1 January 1995).

the rules and procedures of the DSU apply to disputes between WTO members brought pursuant to the dispute settlement provisions of the 'covered agreements' listed in Appendix 1 DSU, including, *inter alia*, the GATT 1994,[31] the GATS[32] and the TRIPS Agreement.[33] Hence, WTO dispute settlement authorities have to decide disputes brought before them exclusively on the grounds of an interpretation of WTO law. To be sure, according to Article 3(2) DSU, and in conjunction with Article 31(3)(c) Vienna Convention on the Law of Treaties (VCLT),[34] they may take account of general principles of public international law together with the context of the provision of WTO law that they are interpreting. Indeed, in its landmark report *US – Shrimp*, the WTO Appellate Body did make extensive use of principles contained in several multilateral environmental agreements (including the UN Convention on the Law of the Sea, the Convention on Biological Diversity and the Convention on the Conservation of Migratory Species of Wild Animals (CITES)).[35]

Since WTO Panels and the Appellate Body have to make findings based on the interpretation of the 'covered agreements', the major problem in a potential dispute on ICH trade will be to find an 'exception' within the law of the WTO, enabling the dispute settlement authorities to link the interpretation of the WTO provisions at issue to provisions of public international law protecting indigenous rights. For Scott and Lenzerini, the only effectively available option would be the general exception of Article XX(b) GATT, allowing trade-restrictive measures that are 'necessary to protect human, animal or plant life or health'.[36] Whereas this exception may be useful in cases involving genetic resources, seeds, medicines, knowledge of the properties of fauna and flora, and so on, it cannot be invoked when cultural artefacts are at issue. In our view, Article XX(a) GATT, allowing for trade-restrictive measures that are 'necessary to protect public morals', could potentially be available as a defence in this context.[37] Our argument is supported by the

---

[31] WTO, General Agreement on Tariffs and Trade (GATT), Marrakesh Agreement Establishing the World Trade Organization, Annex 1A, 1867 UNTS 187; 33 ILM 1153 (adopted on 15 April 1994, entered into force 1 January 1995).

[32] WTO, General Agreement on Trade in Services (GATS), Marrakesh Agreement Establishing the World Trade Organization, Annex 1B, 1869 UNTS 183; 33 ILM 1167 (adopted on 15 April 1994, entered into force 1 January 1995).

[33] WTO, Agreement on Trade Related Aspects of Intellectual Property Rights (TRIPS), Marrakesh Agreement Establishing the World Trade Organization, Annex 1C, 1869 UNTS 299; 33 ILM 1197 (adopted on 15 April 1994, entered into force 1 January 1995).

[34] Vienna Convention on the Law of Treaties, 1155 UNTS 331; 8 ILM 679 (adopted on 23 May 1969, entered into force 27 January 1980).

[35] WTO, Appellate Body Report, *US – Import Prohibition of Certain Shrimp and Shrimp Products*, WTO Doc. WT/DS58/AB/R, adopted 12 October 1998, at para. 129. As Peter Van den Bossche (*The Law and Policy of the World Trade Organization: Text, Cases and Materials*, 2nd edn, Cambridge: Cambridge University Press, 2008, at p. 58) cautions, however, it is not clear whether WTO Members 'can base a claim before a WTO panel on the violation of rights and obligations set out in a non-WTO agreement'.

[36] Article XX(f) GATT provides for an exception for measures 'imposed for the protection of national treasures of artistic, historic or archaeological value'. This clause can be invoked to protect indigenous peoples' cultural heritage only 'whether and to the extent that such a heritage is also considered as heritage of the national state concerned'; Scott and Lenzerini, supra note 1.

[37] Macmillan, supra note 29.

WTO dispute *China – Trading Rights* involving a number of measures regarding publications and audiovisual media, including Chinese censorship of imported media products.[38] China argued that these measures were justified under Article XX(a) GATT since they served its efforts to fight pornographic and violent content and to protect 'Chinese culture and traditional values'.[39] Interestingly, neither the Panel nor the Appellate Body denied that the measures at issue were measures to protect public morals. Accordingly, it does not seem unfeasible that a country could also invoke Article XX(a) GATT to justify a measure protecting the rights of indigenous peoples in a context of ICH trade. On the other hand, since the argument was not discussed by the Panel or the Appellate Body directly, it is difficult to know what weight or significance it could receive in future cases.

Whereas the arguments discussed so far relate to difficulties of *defending* indigenous interests in a WTO framework, Graber's reference paper suggested studying the possibility of *actively* promoting trade and development through the means of WTO law and policy.[40] One concrete idea aired in the reference paper was to explore whether trade preferences – in particular the conditionality permitted by general systems of preferences (GSP) – could be used to stimulate a form of trade in ICH that respects the rights and development interests of indigenous peoples. Whereas preferential treatment exists for developing countries in the current WTO framework, it has been little discussed whether such rules could also be drafted for the benefit of indigenous peoples. Several authors in this volume have referred to this idea and commented upon it in the workshop and/or in their chapters. The general feeling is that – although the idea is welcome in principle – the current WTO legal structure would inhibit an implementation in favour of indigenous peoples. One problem is that GSP conditionality has mainly served major trading nations (including the United States and the European Union) to promote their national political or economic interests in a sometimes arbitrary way. GSP conditionality was used, for instance, to push developing countries to implement the TRIPS Agreement. A second shortcoming of GSP conditionality is the state-centralism of GSP programmes. Since beneficiaries of GSP programmes would be states rather than indigenous peoples, the effectiveness of the programme would depend on the status of indigenous peoples in domestic law. This may be problematic, because the interests of indigenous peoples and the governments of the territories where they live are often not identical.

2.4 The Devil in the Details: The Extent to which Key Terms Should be Defined

Whether or not key terms in the area of law should be defined was a stark point of divergence, even among indigenous experts. The main terms in contention were 'indigenous people' and the 'beneficiaries' that certain rights would be targeted at, the discussion over which arose repeatedly. Tsosie (of Native American descent) argued strongly for having set concrete definitions of terms, particularly those relating to the right-holders.

---

[38] WTO, Panel Report, *China – Measures Affecting Trading Rights and Distribution Services for Certain Publications and Audiovisual Entertainment Products*, WTO Doc. WT/DS363/R, adopted 12 August 2009.

[39] Ibid., at para. 7.753.

[40] Graber, 'Institutionalization of Creativity in Traditional Societies and in International Trade Law', supra note 2.

This was for legal certainty, as legally bestowed rights require that the beneficiaries thereof be identifiable, otherwise the law has no true effect. Furthermore, overly broad and ambiguous definitions of terms, such as 'intangible cultural heritage' and 'cultural expressions', would lead to an instrument's lack of effectiveness and create difficulties in associating it with enforceable property law. Tsosie pointed, in this regard, to the 2003 UNESCO Convention for the Safeguarding of the Intangible Cultural Heritage and the 2005 UNESCO Convention on the Protection and Promotion of the Diversity of Cultural Expressions.[41]

Others did not agree and the divergence of opinion observed was by no means related to having indigenous heritage or not. For example, Mick Dodson[42] and John Scott (both of Australian Aboriginal descent) did not like the idea of defining 'indigenous peoples', stating that they know who they are and do not need to be defined from above. Definition removes their ability to self-identify. The view of Dodson and Scott is a reflection of the fact that whether and to what extent terms such as 'indigenous peoples', 'beneficiaries', 'cultural heritage', 'cultural property', TK and TCE should be defined is closely tied into the issue of an overly top-down approach. In the experience of Australian (and many other) indigenous peoples, top-down government definitions of 'indigeneity', in particular, have been used to control rights and to assert authority over identity.[43] The ability to define one's own identity, as an individual and as a community, is an important part of autonomy and self-determination. The meaning of the other terms listed above are also viewed by some as only being capable of definition by their traditional owners for similar reasons. This is because, in many indigenous worldviews, cultural heritage (in its broadest sense) is an integral and inseparable part of identity, and related to the land of their ancestors.

Hesitations in having set definitions at the international level (including of 'indigenous people') were also raised because it would remove the flexibility of states to address specific local issues. As noted above, it is important that states are able to develop solutions specifically moulded for the particular interests of their local indigenous communities. Moreover, even if a broad definition is given – such as the very wide definition of the beneficiaries of the WIPO drafts – there is a risk that it removes the strength and meaning of the rights held within the documents.[44] Whereas, on the other hand, definitions that are too narrow risk inappropriate exclusion.

The balance is by no means simple, as the failure to define key terms can allow the flouting of the intention of certain laws. For example, the failure to define 'indigenous peoples' in an international treaty could result in states declaring that they have no

---

[41] Tsosie, supra note 20. UNESCO, Convention for the Safeguarding of the Intangible Cultural Heritage, 2368 UNTS 1 (adopted on 17 October 2003, entered into force 20 April 2006). UNESCO, Convention on the Protection and Promotion of the Diversity of Cultural Expressions, 2440 UNTS 311 (adopted on 20 October 2005, entered into force 18 March 2007).

[42] Michael Dodson participated in and contributed to the Workshop, 'International Trade in Indigenous Cultural Heritage' (University of Lucerne, Switzerland, 17–19 January 2011), hosted by the 'International Communications and Art Law Lucerne' research centre, which was the precipitant for this volume.

[43] See Bowrey, supra note 25.

[44] The problem of keeping the needs of indigenous peoples separate from non-indigenous but traditional peoples is indeed one (among others) major obstacle of reaching a solution in WIPO.

indigenous peoples and that the treaty has no application for them (as indicated by Christoph Antons).[45] As Scott and Lenzerini have noted, this has already happened in the case of Indonesia and India. The first considered the rights of indigenous peoples stipulated in UNDRIP as not applicable in Indonesia due to the political, social and anthropological reality in the country. Similarly, the latter declared that its entire population is 'indigenous', which strips UNDRIP of its purpose.[46] The same scenario is foreseeable if states do not draft their federal laws clearly, which could allow sub-federal states to contravene the objective of the state.

Overall, it seems that instruments, whether at the international or national level, cannot be overly prescriptive, or else the ability to address more local concerns could be inhibited and the ability of indigenous peoples or communities to exert self-identity and autonomy would be affected. At the same time, the instruments can lose their effect if they fail to clearly indicate their targeted beneficiaries. If either anyone and everyone or no one at all can fall within the boundaries of an instrument, it is of little practical value.

On the national level, there exist several approaches to deal with the question of defining indigenous peoples. The United States has ultimately chosen to establish a mechanism of federal recognition that gives official federal status to Native American tribes. The United States Department of the Interior maintains an official list of such federally recognised tribes. However, as the definition underlying recognition of Native American tribes is much narrower than international working definitions, the system may be challenged by such international law. Many indigenous groups that would qualify as indigenous peoples from an international perspective do not qualify for federal recognition in the United States.[47] In Canada, the question of who is indigenous is moulded by the great diversity of organisational and legal relations between indigenous communities (including Indian, Inuit and Métis peoples) and the federal as well as provincial governments.[48] International definitions may thus still have an important influence in any effort to define indigenous beneficiaries.

For the international level, we suggest interfacing broad, but clear, definitions with a procedural approach for application at a more local level. The definition of 'indigenous peoples' shall serve as an illustration, because it is the first and central problem of any indigenous rights debate, as noted by Graber in this volume.[49]

Scott and Lenzerini suggest working with a list of criteria with common characteristics or understandings that describe indigenous peoples instead of a formal definition. Thereby, the listed criteria should be treated with a sufficient degree of flexibility in their application, so that not all the criteria need to be met in all cases for a community to be recognised as indigenous. Rather the application of the criteria should vary according to

---

45 Christoph Antons, 'Intellectual Property Rights in Indigenous Cultural Heritage: Basic Concepts and Continuing Controversies', in this volume.

46 Scott and Lenzerini, supra note 1.

47 Goldberg, supra note 11.

48 Bell, supra note 19.

49 Graber, supra note 23.

the different situations and experiences of the communities concerned. This would allow including the tribal peoples of Asian and African regions under the term of indigenous peoples.[50]

Similar to this suggestion, we propose starting at the international level with the widely accepted statements made by José R. Martinez Cobo[51] and Erica-Irene Daes,[52] as cited and discussed by Graber and several other authors in this volume.[53] An international regulation would not need to implement such definitions, but would have to oblige the states to develop national definitions that conform with the general Martinez Cobo and Daes definitions. This would allow states to tailor the definition for the specific needs of the nation and even to particular localities within it (such as at the sub-federal level). It is suggested that there be national procedural approaches to allow communities to claim for recognition as being 'indigenous'. These procedures should be designed with the relevant stakeholders, so as not to end up being too burdensome or even too 'western'. Ideally, there would be a body sitting at the international level, able to assess whether the states indeed support the defining of indigenous peoples and whether such definitions are consistent with the Martinez Cobo and Daes statements. Moreover, this body should also be able to perform the concluding stage of each nation's procedural approach, acting as a final 'appellate body'. The presence of a body at the international level is important to ensure that countries do not flout the purposes of an international definition. Preferably, the body's definitions, processes and decisions would apply across all international instruments. For example, if the body is run through the UN, other treaties or agreements formed through the WIPO, WTO, CBD, and so on, should refer to the UN process. Otherwise, legal certainty and efficiency would be lost.

3. DEEPENING THE ANALYSIS AND IDENTIFYING PROSPECTIVE FUTURE DIRECTIONS OF RESEARCH

So far the discussion concerning the regulation of international trade in ICH has remained in the abstract. In this section we would like to deepen the analysis by discussing two interesting recent cases, the 'kava ban' case and the 'seal ban' case. Although the two case studies involve assets of indigenous knowledge that are cultural only in a broader sense, they serve well to show some of the challenges for ICH trade at the international level. The chapter then continues by discussing – as a possible way forward – whether voluntary standards administered through certification trade marks would potentially be an instrument working in favour of indigenous interests.

---

[50] Scott and Lenzerini, supra note 1.

[51] José R. Martinez Cobo (Special Rapporteur of the Sub-Commission on Prevention of Discrimination and Protection of Minorities), 'Study of the Problem of Discrimination Against Indigenous Populations. Conclusions, Proposals and Recommendations', (UN Doc. E/CN.4/Sub.2/1986/7/Add.4, 1987), at para. 379.

[52] Erica-Irene Daes (Chairperson-Rapporteur of the Working Group on Indigenous Populations), 'The Concept of "Indigenous Peoples"' (1997) *Australian Indigenous Law Reporter*, 2 (1), pp. 162–74, at para. 69.

[53] Graber, supra note 23.

3.1 Problems with the International Trade Arena: The Kava 'Ban'

The first case relates to the 'kava ban' situation which arose in the early twenty-first century. Kava is a traditional drink from Fiji and many other Pacific Island nations, drunk by the indigenous peoples, often as part of traditional and ceremonial rituals.[54] It is derived from water extracts of the root of the *Piper methysticum* plant, which has a relaxing effect. Customarily, the root is either pummelled in water, which is then drunk, or the root is dried into powder form and later mixed with water. It has been safely used in the Pacific for hundreds (possibly thousands) of years in this manner. More recently, European pharmaceutical companies have used either acetone or ethanol to extract the chemically active component from the plant roots and also other parts of the plant not traditionally used.[55] The extracts were then put into concentrated pill or capsule form. In 2000, Germany's Federal Institute for Drugs and Medical Devices connected cases of severe liver problems with kava consumption, which led to Germany and Switzerland banning all kava-containing products in 2002. Several other countries, including Austria, France, the Netherlands, Portugal, Ireland, the UK,[56] Australia[57] and Canada, followed suit in restricting access of kava products, stopping imports and executing product recalls (at least for a period of time).[58] Further, the relevant governmental departments of New Zealand and the United States released warnings and other countries had in place other market restrictions.

Unfortunately, the bans and other import and trade restrictions failed to distinguish products made – and to be used – in the traditional way from modern versions. The regulations on kava-containing products essentially destroyed the global kava market,[59] on which depended many small-island developing and least-developed countries in the Pacific (the latter included Samoa, the Solomon Islands and Vanuatu).[60] In 2003, the

---

54 Lamont Lindstrom, 'Kava Pirates in Vanuatu?' (2009) *International Journal of Cultural Property*, 16, pp. 291–308, at p. 292.

55 Kava is often cited as an example of biopiracy of traditional knowledge; see ibid.

56 UK, Foods Standards Agency, Kava-Kava in Food (England) Regulations 2002, made according to the Food Safety Act 1990 (UK); and WTO, Committee on Sanitary and Phytosanitary Measures, 'UK. Notification of Emergency Measures', (WTO Doc. G/SPS/N/GBR/3, 2002). See also Food Standards Agency in Northern Ireland, 'The Kava-Kava in Food Regulations (Northern Ireland)' (2005); WTO, Committee on Sanitary and Phytosanitary Measures, 'UK. Notification of Emergency Measures', (WTO Doc. G/SPS/N/GBR/4, 2005); The Medicines for Human Use (Kava-Kava) (Prohibition) Order 2002, Statutory Instrument 2002 No. 3170, according to the Medicines Act 1968 (UK); and WTO, Committee on Technical Barriers to Trade, 'UK. Notification', (WTO Doc. G/TBT/N/GBR/3, 2002).

57 Kava has had quite a history of being regulated in various ways in Australia, see Food Standards Australia New Zealand, 'Initial Assessment Report – Proposal P256 – Review of Kava (O10/2.6.3)' (9 October 2002), at pp. 18–20.

58 Joerg Gruenwald, Cordula Mueller and Juergen Skrabal (for Phytopharm Consulting), 'Kava Report 2003: An In-Depth Investigation in EU Member States Market Restrictions on Kava Products – Part I Situation Analysis', prepared for the Centre for the Development of Enterprise (CDE), 2003, at pp. 5–7.

59 Lindstrom, supra note 54, at pp. 302–3.

60 For discussions on the effects the kava bans and restrictions have had, see Tuisugaletaua A.S. Aveau (Minister of Agriculture, Forests, Fisheries and Meteorology, Samoa), 'Pacific Islands

International Kava Executive Council (IKEC) estimated a 'loss of revenue' of around US$200 million per year for Pacific Island producers.[61] The kava market has yet to recover.[62]

In 2007, the World Health Organization reviewed the liver toxicity of kava products, finding that the customary use could not be associated with liver disease. Following this, European countries, including Germany, finally removed their bans, in 2008, after threats of WTO dispute resolution action and a ten-day roundtable consultation between Pacific Island ambassadors and European Commission leaders.[63] A two-year plan was laid out to redevelop the kava trade in the EU, particularly in Germany.[64]

The mechanisms that different states used to regulate the kava trade in their territories fell under the disciplines of the WTO's Agreement on Sanitary and Phytosanitary Measures (SPS Agreement)[65] and/or the Agreement on Technical Barriers to Trade (TBT Agreement).[66] This depended on the way that kava products were defined, for example as dietary supplements or as food (SPS), or as medicinal products (TBT). It also depended on the nature of the measure utilised, for example labelling requirements (such as those used in New Zealand)[67] would come under the TBT Agreement. Whether the grounds for implementing the different regulations were compliant with the SPS or TBT Agreements

---

Perspective', *Small Island Developing States Panel*, UN, Food and Agriculture Organization (FAO) (UN Headquarters, New York, 6 October 2004); Pacific Network on Globalisation (PANG), 'Lift the Kava Ban Now – Provide an Economic Lifeline for the Pacific!' (2007) (PANG is a Pacific Islands regional fair-trade organisation based in Suva, Fiji); Biman C. Prasad, 'Impediments to Market Access for Exports and Environmental Requirements under the World Trade Organisation (WTO): The Case of Fisheries, Sugar and Garment Industries in Fiji', available online at http://www.ias.unu.edu/binaries2/Fiji_WTO.pdf; UN FAO, *WTO Agreement on Agriculture: The Implementation Experience – Developing Country Case Studies – Fiji*, Rome: UN, 2003; and Jane Kelsey, 'World Trade and Small Nations in the South Pacific Region' (2005) *Kansas Journal of Law and Public Policy*, 14, pp. 247–306.

61 'Europe Lifts Ban on Kava', *Fiji Times* (12 November 2008).

62 Lindstrom, supra note 54, at p. 294.

63 'Europe Lifts Ban on Kava', supra note 61.

64 IKEC, 'Lifting the German "Ban" on Kava Exports – Outcome and Strategies of IKEC-EU Consultations', *Press Release* (29 October 2008), available at http://www.acp-eu-trade.org/library/files/IKEC_EN_291008_IKEC_Lifting-the-German-ban-on-Kava-exports.pdf.

65 WTO, Agreement on Sanitary and Phytosanitary Measures (SPS Agreement), Marrakesh Agreement Establishing the World Trade Organization, Annex 1A, 1867 UNTS 493; 33 ILM 1125, 1153 (adopted on 15 April 1994, entered into force 1 January 1995).

66 WTO, Agreement on Technical Barriers to Trade (TBT Agreement), Marrakesh Agreement Establishing the World Trade Organization, Annex 1A, 1868 UNTS 120; 33 ILM 1125, 1145 (adopted on 15 April 1994, entered into force 1 January 1995).

67 New Zealand Food Safety Authority, 'Kava as a Dietary Supplement – Privileged Statement Issued under Delegated Authority from the Director-General of Agriculture and Forestry Pursuant to Section 37 of the Food Act 1981', (16 August 2002).

was never decided by a WTO decision-making body. However, the case for the kava-producing nations would have been strong, particularly with regard to the SPS Agreement.[68]

Despite how the issue was dealt with in the media, kava products were not strictly speaking absolutely 'banned' across the EU or other countries. Firstly, each EU nation legally dealt with the situation independently and differently;[69] there was no EU decision, directive, regulation or methodology. Thus, Germany's decision for an initial absolute ban was national and not made at EU Member State level. Secondly, most states did allow the import of some kava-related products into their territories, albeit with limitations and technical barriers. For example, in the UK, Australia and New Zealand, food containing kava was legally banned through food safety regulations.[70] However, in the UK and Australia, medicines containing kava (or kava extracts) that were licensed or regulated according to the relevant regulations/legislation could be imported, supplied and sold.[71] In New Zealand, kava products derived the traditional way (that is, from cold-water extraction for the purposes of drinking or the dried or fresh form of the root or root peelings) were allowed, but with strict labelling requirements for the packaging.[72] The laws and standards outlining these are still in force.

However, even the regulations that were not, legally speaking, absolute bans (that is, not import prohibitions), were effectively so. The rigid specifications that had (and have) to be met for certain kava-containing products to enter a territory were (and are) perceivably

---

[68] See, generally, Meredith Kolsky Lewis, 'Safety Standards and Indigenous Products: What Role for Traditional Knowledge?', in Meredith Kolsky Lewis and Susy Frankel (eds), *International Economic Law and National Autonomy*, Cambridge: Cambridge University Press, 2010, pp. 169–92.

[69] The Standing Committee on the Food Chain and Animal Health of the EU decided that there was no basis for taking any action on food containing kava; see EC, Standing Committee on the Food Chain and Animal Health, Section on General Food Law, 'Summary Record of Meeting' (13 June 2002), at para. 5.

[70] In the UK, Kava-Kava in Food (England) Regulations 2002, supra note 56. In Australia and New Zealand, *Australia New Zealand Food Standards Code Volume 2*, Standard 2.6.3, 2, as amended by Food Standards Australia New Zealand, 'Australia New Zealand Food Standards Code Amendment' (2009) *Gazette*, 72, at para. 9.

[71] In the UK, The Medicines for Human Use (Kava-Kava) (Prohibition) Order 2002, supra note 56. In Australia, Therapeutic Goods Regulations 1990 (Cth), made according to the Therapeutic Goods Act 1989 (Cth), updated on 29 October 2010; kava is regulated under Part 8, Schedule 4, Part 4, Division 2 (Plant material from which herbal substances may be derived for listable goods that are consistent with certain qualifications), Item 35.

[72] Under the latest version of the *Australia New Zealand Food Standards Code Volume 2*, Standard 2.6.3, 2, as amended by Food Standards Australia New Zealand, 'Australia New Zealand Food Standards Code Amendment' (2009) *Gazette*, 111, at para. 15. Though the standard applies to Australia as well, its application is subject to the Australia Customs (Prohibited Imports) Regulations (1956) (Cth) and certain state and territory restrictions on the supply of kava. Under the 1997 amendments, the importation of kava for commercial purposes required both a licence to import kava and a permit for each consignment of kava. Passengers arriving in Australia could import up to two kilograms of kava for personal use without a permit. However, as a result of kava abuse in Aboriginal areas, Australia banned the import of kava in its traditional powder form in June 2007.

impassable borders for low-income countries.[73] For example, though the absolute German ban set in 2002 was officially lifted in 2005, kava products were still restricted from entering into the country, as the ban on licences for the sale of kava products was only lifted on a 'case-by-case' basis.[74] For this, various conditions had to be met, such as scientific testing for the safety and efficacy of each product individually.[75] Fijian people perceived the onerous testing requirements as the equivalent of a continuation of the kava ban.[76] The fact that the restrictions were not globally (or even regionally) uniform increased the cost of export further.

The New Zealand standard appears to be the only regulation that took and takes into account and differentiates (though not by name) the particular traditional indigenous use of kava (allowing it, so long as labelled according to standard requirements). Thus, though there were legal ways for the Pacific Islands to continue to export at least some of their kava products, the fact that the laws and regulations were mostly not designed to account for traditional indigenous use, but rather set blanket requirements of scientific proof of safety, essentially destroyed the kava export market of the Pacific Islands.

That the trade of kava could be limited so quickly and without difficulty is due to the ease with which states are able to enact trade-restrictive measures under the auspices of the SPS and TBT Agreements. As mentioned above, it is doubtful whether the measures taken could have withstood scrutiny. However, there is no body that oversees such measures on their enactment. Rather, complaining states must take their grievances into the WTO dispute settlement process. However, this is: (1) costly, possibly restrictively so for developing countries; and (2) time-consuming, which could result in irreparable damage to producers' market share and possibly even an entire market. This is likely why the Pacific Islands sought a diplomatic solution and only threatened to take the dispute to the WTO. Thus, the answer to the problem may lie in making it harder for states to enact such broad and encompassing measures. The obstacles could be legal or political.

The kava situation led Meredith Kolsky Lewis to conclude that (particularly in taking SPS measures) states should have to assess the safety of traditional uses of indigenous products separately from newer adapted uses.[77] However, as the following example of the 'EU seal ban' demonstrates, even if a trade regulation separates products stemming from indigenous communities' traditional use from others, the effect on the market of the product at issue may still not meet indigenous communities' needs and interests.

---

[73] Fiji Government, 'ACP/EU Joint Meetings Has Agreed to Reverse Kava Ban', *Press Release* (23 February 2004), available online at http://www.fiji.gov.fj/cgi-bin/cms/exec/view.cgi/15/1995/printer.

[74] Mark Blumenthal, 'German Government Reconsiders Kava' (2005) *HerbalGram*, 67, pp. 21–2.

[75] Lindstrom, supra note 54, at p. 304.

[76] The Chairman of the Fiji Kava Council stated: 'These are just words really … the tests they want could take decades and would cost millions of dollars to carry out.' Wesley Morgan, 'Time to End Kava Trade Ban', *Fiji Times* (23 September 2007).

[77] Kolsky Lewis, supra note 68.

3.2 Separate Treatment of Indigenous Products in Trade Regulations: The European Seal Ban

The second case that gives insight into the problems of implementing indigenous interests into international trade regulations is the dispute about the European seal ban. As the example will illustrate, even if trade regulations differentiate between trade in indigenous and non-indigenous products (as was the request after the kava 'ban' dispute), they may still not meet indigenous peoples' interests.

The European seal ban is rooted in a powerful animal welfare movement that triggered public concern about the killing and skinning of seals. Since seals are mammals allegedly capable of experiencing pain, the killing and skinning was perceived immoral if pain, distress and other forms of suffering were not avoided.[78] The animal welfare movement forced several European states to react. They chose using regulatory trade bans with the goal of restricting activities linked to the production of seal products.[79] In order to harmonise such national activities and to eliminate obstacles to the functioning of the EU internal market, the EU became active as well. It adopted a European-wide Regulation known as the 'Seal Ban Regulation' on 16 September 2009.[80]

In contrast to the kava trade restrictions (apart from that of New Zealand), the EU tried to take into account that the ban might affect indigenous peoples' livelihoods. Seal hunting is an old tradition of Inuit populations in the northern hemisphere and is an important part of their livelihoods. As a consequence, the European ban explicitly excludes from the ban (and thus allows) trade in seal products resulting from hunts traditionally conducted by Inuit and other indigenous communities for contributing to their subsistence (Article 3[1]). In its Preamble, the Regulation legitimises the exception by referring to UNDRIP and states that the hunting of seals is 'an integral part of the culture and identity of the members of the Inuit society'.[81]

This indigenous product exemption in a European trade ban regulation is the result of a lesson learned by the EU from a prior trade dispute with indigenous peoples. In 1991, the EU adopted the 'Leghold Trap Regulation',[82] which, *inter alia*, prohibited the importation of products from wild animals caught by the means of leghold traps. Many aboriginal tribes commonly use such traps to capture wild animals sold for fur. Thus, indigenous

---

78 Commission of the European Communities, 'Proposal for a Regulation of the European Parliament and of the Council', COM(2008) 469 final, COD 2008/0160 (23 July 2008), at p. 2 (not published in the Official Journal of the European Union).

79 Ibid.

80 Regulation (EC) No. 1007/2009 of the European Parliament and of the Council of 16 September 2009 on trade in seal products, OJ 2009 L 286/36 [hereinafter Seal Ban Regulation].

81 Seal Ban Regulation, Preamble (14).

82 Council Regulation (EEC) No. 3254/91 of 4 November 1991 prohibiting the use of leghold traps in the Community and the introduction into the Community of pelts and manufactured goods of certain wild animal species originating in countries which catch them by means of leghold traps or trapping methods which do not meet international humane trapping standards, OJ 1991 L 308/1. Implemented by Commission Regulation (EC) No. 35/97 of 10 January 1997 laying down provisions on the certification of pelts and goods covered by Council Regulation (EEC) No. 3254/91, OJ 1997 L 8/2.

peoples, mainly from Canada, opposed the Regulation as they feared for their livelihoods.[83] As a result of this, the European Commission discussed an amendment to the Regulation that would have excluded fur pelts trapped by indigenous persons from the trade ban.[84] However, the dispute was ultimately not resolved this way, but through a multilateral Agreement on International Humane Trapping Standards (AIHTS) between the EU, Canada and Russia,[85] and between the EU and the United States.[86] The idea of exempting indigenous products from a trade ban, as originally intended for the Leghold Trap Regulation, was however later implemented in the Seal Ban Regulation. Article 3 of the Seal Ban Regulation, together with an 'Implementation Regulation' of the Commission, entered into force on 20 August 2010 (together the 'Seal Ban Regulations').[87]

Nevertheless and strikingly, the indigenous peoples themselves have challenged the Seal Ban Regulations (including the Implementation Regulations) despite the privileged treatment of their products. Private Inuit seal hunters, trappers and processors of seal products, together with companies that are active in the processing and marketing of seal products, and non-profit-making organisations and associations representing Inuit interests all residing or being established in Canada, Norway or Greenland (Denmark), filed claim. On 11 January 2010, they brought an action to the General Court of the EU against the European Parliament and Council seeking the annulment of the Seal Ban Regulation.[88]

The claimants alleged that the EU Regulations would bring to a halt the majority of exports of all seal products to the EU. The exception for Inuit products would be an 'empty box' as its implementation would be 'extremely costly, complex and time-consuming'. The prohibition on trade in seal products would 'likely result in the loss within the EU of infrastructure such as auction houses and tanneries, which are mostly held by "non-Inuit"

---

83 Peter Michaud, 'Caught in a Trap: The European Union Leghold Trap Debate' (1997) *Minnesota Journal of Global Trade*, 6, pp. 355–78, at pp. 362–4; Gillian Dale, 'The European Union's Steel Leghold Trap Ban: Animal Cruelty Legislation in Conflict with International Trade' (1996) *Colorado Journal of International Environmental Law and Policy*, 7, pp. 441–6; and Richard Maracle, 'A Case Study: Aboriginal Involvement in Achieving an Agreement with European Union to Address the European Union's Wild Fur Import Ban' (2002), available at http://www.fur.ca/files/Case%20study%20re%20aboriginal%20involvement%20in%20EU%20fur%20ban.pdf.

84 Ibid., at p. 377.

85 OJ 1998 L 42/43.

86 Council Decision 98/487/EC of 13 July 1998, OJ 1998 L 219/24, concerning the conclusion of an International Agreement in the form of an Agreed Minute between the European Community and the United States on humane trapping standards.

87 Commission Regulation (EU) No. 737/2010 of 10 August 2010 laying down detailed rules for the implementation of Regulation (EC) No. 1007/2009 of the European Parliament and of the Council on trade in seal products, OJ 2010 L 216/1, Article 12 (date of publication in the Official Journal plus 3 days) [hereinafter Implementation Regulation]. The Seal Ban Regulation itself entered into force nine months earlier on 20 November 2009. Seal Ban Regulation, Article 8(1) (date of publication in the Official Journal of the European Union plus 20 days).

88 General Court of the European Union, *Inuit Tapiriit Kanatami et al. v Parliament and Council*, 11 January 2010, Case T-18/10. A second action against the European Commission seeking annulment with additional plaintiffs from the United Kingdom, Canada and Turkey was filed on 9 November 2010; General Court of the European Union, *Inuit Tapiriit Kanatami et al. v Commission*, 9 November 2010, Case T-526/10.

commercial corporations serving the "non-Inuit" trade in those products, and, without that infrastructure, the Inuit simply cannot bring their sealskins to the European market'.[89] The claimants also held it to be 'extremely difficult to create a new and alternative market niche for Inuit seal products', and they argued that the Regulations 'did not take into consideration that the international market for sealskins is driven primarily by fashion trends rather than specific demand for Inuit products'.[90]

In parallel to the legal dispute at the EU level initiated by private indigenous claimants, the Governments of Canada and of the non-EU member Norway took joint action against the EU in the WTO. On 14 February 2011, Canada requested the establishment of two official WTO Dispute Settlement Panels, after consultations with the EU in the years 2007, 2009 and 2010 failed.[91] Canada was followed by Norway, which likewise requested the establishment of a WTO Dispute Settlement Panel on 15 March 2011.[92] In their requests, the governments most importantly raised the claim that the European Seal Ban Regulations discriminate 'like products' originating from different countries (the principle of most favoured nation)[93] and that the regime's measures result in less favourable treatment of seal products from outside the EU to products originating from the EU (the principle of national treatment).[94] Furthermore, they claimed that the measures result in a prohibition or restriction on the importation of seal products in violation of provisions relating to quantitative restrictions[95] and create an unnecessary obstacle to international trade without a legitimate objective.[96] Finally, the claimants intervened on the failure of the EU to prepare conformity assessment procedures in a way that grants non-discriminatory access

---

[89] Order of the President of the General Court, *Inuit Tapiriit Kanatami et al. v Parliament and Council*, 25 October 2010, Case T-18/10 R II, at para. 35.

[90] Ibid., at para. 34.

[91] WTO, Request for the Establishment of a Panel by Canada, 'European Communities – Certain Measures Prohibiting the Importation and Marketing of Seal Products', (WTO Doc. WT/DS400/4, 2011) [hereinafter 'Canada's First Request for a Panel']; and WTO, Request for the Establishment of a Panel by Canada, 'European Communities – Certain Measures Prohibiting the Importation and Marketing of Seal Products', (WTO Doc. WT/DS369/2, 2011) [hereinafter 'Canada's Second Request for a Panel']. The first request concerned the EU Seal Ban Regulation, and the second request concerned the national seal ban laws enacted in Belgium and the Netherlands. Two panels have been established – 25 March 2011 for Canada and 21 April 2011 for Norway.

[92] WTO, Request for the Establishment of a Panel by Norway, 'European Communities – Certain Measures Prohibiting the Importation and Marketing of Seal Products', (WTO Doc. WT/DS401/5, 2011) [hereinafter 'Norway's Request for a Panel']. Two panels have been established – 25 March 2011 for Canada and 21 April 2011 for Norway – but neither have been composed; see WTO, Dispute Settlement, 'Dispute DS369 European Communities – Certain Measures Prohibiting the Importation and Marketing of Seal Products' http://www.wto.org/english/tratop_e/dispu_e/cases_e/ds369_e.htm. As at 24 January 2012, there had been no forward movement of the dispute.

[93] GATT 1994, Article I:1; and TBT Agreement, Article 2.1.

[94] GATT 1994, Article III:4; and TBT Agreement, Article 2.1.

[95] GATT 1994, Article XI:1; and WTO, Agreement on Agriculture, Marrakesh Agreement Establishing the World Trade Organization, Annex 1A, 1867 UNTS 410 (adopted on 15 April 1994, entered into force 1 January 1995), Article 4.2.

[96] TBT Agreement, Article 2.2.

to suppliers from WTO Members.[97] Canada, in addition, challenged the national trade ban in Belgium and the Netherlands, claiming that the freedom of transit of products through countries was violated.[98]

In contrast to the proceedings before the General Court of the EU, which have had an explicit focus on the indigenous peoples' exception, on the WTO level, the dispute has turned into a multilateral affair between states. The banning, as such, and public morals and/or animal welfare concerns will be at stake, but it is unclear whether and how the WTO Panel will address the indigenous peoples' exception.[99] The EU may defend its position against the claims of the Canadian and Norwegian Governments by relying on Article XX of GATT 1994.[100] This is the GATT's 'general exceptions' rule justifying import bans, discrimination against imports and other deviations from the GATT's rules in specific circumstances. From the EU Commission's draft proposal for the Seal Ban Regulation, one can infer that the EU will likely invoke Article XX(a), the specific exception for trade regulations necessary to protect 'public morals'.[101] This proposal states:

> As to the import ban, it is in conformity with Article XX(a) of the General Agreement on Trade and Tariffs (GATT), under which the adoption or enforcement by any contracting party of measures necessary to protect public morals is allowed provided that such measures are not applied in a manner which would constitute a means of arbitrary or unjustifiable discrimination.[102]

In addition, the EU may refer to Article XX(b), stating an exception for measures protecting 'human, animal or plant life or health', or Article XX(g), stating an exception for measures protecting natural resources.[103] In parallel with Article XX of GATT 1994, the EU may also invoke the TBT Agreement, which allows members to restrict trade in order to accomplish a 'legitimate objective'.[104] It must be in this defensive line that the EU

---

[97] TBT Agreement, Article 5.1; as well as specifically Articles 5.2, 5.4, 5.6, 5.8, 6.1, 6.2, 7.1, 7.4, 7.5, 8.1, 8.2, 9.2 and 9.3. 'Canada's First Request for a Panel', supra note 91. WTO; and 'Norway's Request for a Panel', supra note 92.

[98] GATT 1994, Article V:2–4. 'Canada's Second Request for a Panel', supra note 91.

[99] It might be discussed in the realm of the 'necessity' test.

[100] Robert Galantucci, 'Compassionate Consumerism within the GATT Regime: Can Belgium's Ban on Seal Product Imports be Justified under Article XX?' (2009) *California Western School of Law*, 39, pp. 281–312, at pp. 287–311; and Maurizio Gambardella, 'The EU Ban on Seal Products: Some Customs and WTO Open Questions' (2010) *Global Trade and Customs Journal*, 5 (4), pp. 145–54, at pp. 149–53.

[101] See above, supra note 78 and accompanying text.

[102] Commission of the European Communities, supra note 78, at p. 8. See, for discussion of this defence, Courtney Pope, 'For the Sake of the Seals' (2009) *Asper Review of International Business and Trade Law*, 9, pp. 225–51, at pp. 245–8; Galantucci, supra note 100, at pp. 287–300; and Xinjie Luan and Julien Chaisse, 'Preliminary Comments on the WTO Seals Products Dispute: Traditional Hunting, Public Morals and Technical Barriers to Trade' (2011) *Colorado Journal of International Environmental Law*, 22, pp. 79–121, at pp. 109–11.

[103] Gambardella, supra note 100, at pp. 150–52; Pope, supra note 102, at pp. 242–5; and Galantucci, supra note 100, at pp. 303–11.

[104] TBT Agreement, Article 2.2; and Lesley Peterson, 'Talkin' 'bout a Humane Revolution: New Standards for Framing Practices and How They Could Change International Trade as We Know It' (2010) *Brooklyn Journal of International Law*, 36, pp. 265–98, at p. 285, footnote 155.

addresses the indigenous product's exception and its potential influence on the question of whether the Seal Ban Regulations conform to the GATT 1994 and the TBT Agreement. If the WTO Panel were to discuss the indigenous peoples' exemption, this would be quite a step in the discourse on indigenous peoples' rights. It would be the first time that a WTO body officially considers indigenous peoples' interests in the context of multilateral trade regulations.

The seal ban case allows for several conclusions. First, it shows that legal protection measures on behalf of indigenous peoples' traditional lives, as requested by UNDRIP, are toothless if they do not also sufficiently take into account indigenous peoples' trade interests. The arguments of the Inuit hunters in the EU seal ban proceedings reveal that the commercialising of their products is strongly connected with non-indigenous, conventional trade structures. Indigenous peoples rely on such structures, even if they are not commensurate to the local and social structures that define their harvesting, hunting and, thus, their culture, identity, tradition and heritage. *Prima facie*, one would expect that a trade-ban exemption on behalf of indigenous peoples' products would help to bridge this dilemma, as it disconnects trade competitors and opens a way for rebuilding new trade lines with sustainable indigenous products. However, insurmountable trade realities seem to counteract the good intentions of the EU legislator to protect indigenous peoples' traditional lives. As an earlier experience showed, a trade ban – despite the exemption on behalf of indigenous products – may even have a devastating effect for indigenous peoples. In 1983, by means of Directive No. 83/129EEC, the EU prohibited the import of seal pup skins into the EU. It excluded products resulting from traditional hunting by the Inuit people from such a ban.[105] As the claimants in the current EU seal ban dispute have put forward, the Directive led to a total collapse of the seal product market, including Inuit products, despite the exception on their behalf.[106] It was said that many Inuit lost their livelihoods as a consequence.[107]

As a second insight, the seal ban case shows how indigenous peoples' trade interests on an international level are intrinsically entwined with their state's interests in regulating or protecting international trade. Whether a trade regulation with preferential treatment of indigenous peoples' products effectively works depends to a large extent on the state's willingness to support the implementation of such a legal rule. That is why the Seal Ban Regulations introduce an implementation concept for the Inuit exemption that is supposed

---

Towards this, the recent Panel decision on United States tuna labelling requirements, which turned on Article 2.2 of the TBT Agreement, may be helpful; WTO, Panel Report, *United States – Measures Concerning the Importation, Marketing and Sale of Tuna and Tuna Products*, WTO Doc. WT/DS381/R, 15 September 2011, at paras 7.379–7.623 [hereinafter *US – Tuna*]. This case was appealed to the Appellate Body on 20 January 2012; see WTO, Dispute Settlement, 'Dispute DS381. United States – Measures Concerning the Importation, Marketing and Sale of Tuna and Tuna Products', available at http://www.wto.org/english/tratop_e/dispu_e/cases_e/ds381_e.htm.

[105] Article 3, Council Directive 83/129/EEC of 28 March 1983, OJ 1983 L 91/30, as amended by Council Directive 89/370/EEC of 8 June 1989, OJ 1989 L 163.

[106] Order of the President of the General Court, supra note 89, at para. 35. See also Michaud, supra note 83, at pp. 363–4.

[107] Michaud, supra note 83, at p. 363, footnote 64, citing a statement of Bill Erasmus, the Northwest Territories' Dene national chief and holder of the Assembly of First Nations' wild fur issue portfolio in 1994.

to facilitate trade in indigenous peoples' seal products. According to the President of the General Court of the EU, in Greenland such implementation measures are already well advanced and have helped to uphold the trade infrastructure for Inuit seal products.[108] However, in Greenland, the Inuit make up almost 90 per cent of the population and almost all of the seals are caught by Inuit.[109] In contrast, the indigenous peoples in Canada constitute a minority, making up only 3.8 per cent of the Canadian population.[110] It is obvious that the Canadian Government may not accept a trade ban that negatively affects the majority interests, which it would by prioritising implementation measures for preferential trade with minority products. That is why the indigenous claimants in the EU seal ban proceedings require that the EU and the Canadian Government conclude an umbrella agreement, as otherwise the Seal Ban Regulations would leave the Inuit to persuade the Government to make the necessary investments.[111] In a trade ban dispute, the focus of the governments with indigenous minorities rather lies on the question of how to use indigenous peoples' interests and movements to serve the majority interests, as the leghold trap case shows. In this dispute, the Canadian Government financially supported the indigenous peoples' activities and movements to fight against the ban on behalf of the whole Canadian wild fur trading branch.[112] The support by the Canadian Government to fight the ban was more attractive to indigenous peoples than the offer of the EU to except their products from the ban.[113] This cooperation between the indigenous peoples and their governments is now mirrored in the seal ban case, in which indigenous peoples are fighting even a ban with an explicit exemption for their products.

This leads to the third conclusion that may be drawn from the seal ban case. A unilateral trade regulation of a state, or a trade bloc such as the EU, can raise awareness for minority interests of indigenous peoples, but cannot impose an effective preferential trade system upon other states. A bilateral or multilateral agreement will be needed, of which the home states of indigenous peoples are Member States and as such bound to implement the international law, in order to truly advance minority interests of indigenous peoples in international trade. This becomes obvious from the AIHTS, which was the solution in the leghold trap ban dispute. Another example of such a multilateral agreement advancing indigenous minority interests is the International Convention for the Regulation of Whaling of 2 December 1946 (ICRW).[114] This Convention limits and for certain species even prohibits the hunting of whales. Since its inception, the Convention has differentiated between commercial and aboriginal subsistence whaling and allows – within a defined framework – the hunting of whales by indigenous peoples, whereas it completely prohibits any other whaling methods.[115] The Convention itself provides thus direct legitimacy to

---

[108] Order of the President of the General Court, supra note 89, at paras 83–9.

[109] Ibid., at paras 83–9.

[110] Bell, supra note 19.

[111] Order of the President of the General Court, supra note 89, at para. 36.

[112] Maracle, supra note 83, at pp. 11–12.

[113] Ibid., at p. 11.

[114] 161 UNTS 72 (adopted on 2 December 1946, entered into force 10 November 1948).

[115] Stephen M. Hankins, 'Comment: The United States' Abuse of the Aboriginal Whaling Exception: A Contradiction in United States Policy and a Dangerous Precedent for the Whale' (1990) *UC Davis Law Review*, 24, pp. 489–530, at pp. 507–8. Under the current Schedule to the

Member States to support their indigenous peoples' interests, even though potentially not in line with the trade interests of the majority. The Government of the United States thus had no domestic problems in defending their Alaska Inuit when the International Whaling Committee voiced its concern with regard to the demise of the bowhead whales stocks.[116]

3.3 Voluntary Standards and Certification Trade Marks: An Alternative Approach with Political Clout

The above examples illustrate that classic trade regulations do not appear to be capable of helping indigenous peoples to participate more actively in international trade. Either states completely fail to take into consideration indigenous products or their customary usage (as in the kava example), or they do so, but the measures taken nevertheless remain without any positive effect on indigenous peoples' trade efforts (as in the seal example). As alluded to in both situations, this can largely be due to the difficulties that must be overcome in order to take advantage of the relaxing of restrictions or of a specific exclusion, as benefiting from these requires taking on a great and possibly insurmountable administrative and financial burden. These difficulties often relate to the inefficiency of several separate producers (as with the kava and seal situations) having to deal with many different rules (at least in the kava situation).

In such trade disputes, even bestowing trade privileges on indigenous peoples over their cultural heritage would not be of any benefit to the particular issues at hand.

Given these observed issues, we suggest taking into account market forces and thinking on a scale of increased economic efficiency, all the while allowing for a bottom-up approach, due to the identified problems with top-down paternalism.[117] In saying this, we acknowledge that consumerism is often not desired by indigenous peoples. However, when market participation is desired, the entering of markets should be as simple and streamlined as possible, rather than having means that are technically available, but practically inaccessible. This efficiency could be achieved through international standardisation, used in conjunction with internationally registered certification trade marks, developed in a bottom-up manner. As has been concluded by Peter Drahos, it is crucial that 'producers should unite around a few or ... one highly visible certification mark.'[118]

Certification marks can be registered for a set of standards. The owner of the registered mark undertakes the responsibility to monitor and certify the standards and license out the mark.[119] The mark can then be used by the consumer to indicate that those standards have

---

International Convention for the Regulation of Whaling of 1946, as amended by the International Whaling Commission at the 62nd Annual Meeting in June 2010, aboriginal subsistence whaling is nevertheless subject to catch limits (para. 13).

116 Ibid., at p. 516.

117 Graber, supra note 23.

118 Peter Drahos, 'A Networked Responsive Regulatory Approach to Protecting Traditional Knowledge', in Daniel Gervais (ed.), *Strategies to Optimize Economic Development in a TRIPS Plus Era,* Oxford: Oxford University Press, 2007, pp. 379–410, at p. 397.

119 Collective marks are registered and protected under Article 7bis of the Paris Convention for the Protection of Industrial Property (incorporated into the TRIPS Agreement, Article 2.1). Though the Paris Convention only mentions collective marks, this is generally taken to include certification marks.

been achieved. Certification marks are particularly suitable for indigenous interests because they can be used in a bottom-up fashion, with indigenous peoples themselves setting the standards. Standards could be, for example, related to the material used or the method of production. There is generally no limitation on who can apply for certification per se, though one of the standards could stipulate this, for example requiring indigenous descent. Certification marks are further attractive because they have a low cost of registration, can be used to ensure correct attribution of identity of the producer and can potentially exist for an unlimited duration.[120] They are often registered for geographical indications (GIs), but their use is not limited to this. Finally, a certification system does not prevent an indigenous community from developing its own trade mark and brand identity at the same time as it takes advantage of the certification standard.[121]

An example of a successful certification mark scheme is the FLO Fairtrade label,[122] which is known for its social standards, such as minimum prices for products and equal distribution of profits among all producers. This system (and indeed, in theory, any voluntary certification system) does not limit the rights of other traders per se,[123] only affecting producers of non-labelled products indirectly.[124] Rather, it is a marketing tool to promote the standards. An important lesson to be learned from the Fairtrade label is that it owes much of its success to good marketing and consumer education.[125] Consumers need to be made aware of what the mark represents; otherwise there is little purpose in setting up such a system. Thus, though the use of such a system for indigenous interests could potentially be bottom-up in nature, the marketing required to allow for the system to succeed may mean that substantial financial assistance from the state is needed,[126] at least

---

[120] Daphne Zografos, *Intellectual Property and Traditional Cultural Expressions*, Cheltenham, UK: Edward Elgar, 2010, at ch. 4.

[121] With thanks to Peter Drahos who pointed this out to the authors.

[122] The Mark is now the most widely recognised social and development label in the world; see FLO, 'About the Mark', available at www.fairtrade.net.

[123] Jasper Stein, 'The Legal Status of Eco-Labels and Product and Process Methods in the World Trade Organization' (2009) *American Journal of Economics and Business Administration*, 1 (4), pp. 285–95, at pp. 285 and 292.

[124] There are some that argue that though conforming to and applying for a certification mark may be 'voluntary', the actual market effect makes it *de facto* mandatory, as non-compliance can mean a producer loses its market share; Cora Dankers, 'Environmental and Social Standards, Certification and Labelling for Cash Crops', UN FAO, 2003, at p. 76, citing a submission made by Switzerland to the Committee on Trade and Environment; WTO, Committee on Trade and Environment, 'Marking and Labelling Requirements', (WTO Docs WT/CTE/W/192 and G/TBT/W/162, 2001). See also Kommerskollegium National Board of Trade, Global Trade Division, Sweden, 'Eco-Labelling and the WTO: Issues for Further Analysis and Clarification', Report No. 119–007–2002 (2002), at p. 5.

[125] See, for example, Stein, supra note 123, at p. 285, who notes that it is not the label itself that inherently affects consumers, but rather the information marketing that takes place about what the label represents.

[126] Drahos has noted that superficial assistance assisted in the failure of the Australian Authenticity Marks; see Peter Drahos, 'Towards an International Framework for the Protection of Traditional Group Knowledge and Practice', UNCTAD-Commonwealth Secretariat Workshop on Elements of National *Sui Generis* Systems for the Preservation, Protection and Promotion of

initially. The coordination between intra- and inter-state indigenous communities would be perceivably difficult without government support.

In the context of the kava situation discussed above, a certification standard and its associated mark could have been used by indigenous communities to differentiate their products from other 'modern' producers. The standards involved would not have necessarily required information on the producer per se, such as being of indigenous descent, though there is no reason why this could not be a standard. Necessary standards would have been related to the method of production of the kava product, requiring a traditional method. With respect to the seal ban case, standards would be related to 'indigeneity' (as required by the exception to the ban) and possibly to a traditional method of capturing and killing the seals.

Interestingly, in the Seal Ban Regulations (specifically the Implementation Regulation),[127] the European Union requires a certification system to implement the exemption of indigenous products from the ban. It stipulates that a document of certification needs to accompany the indigenous seal products that are to be placed on the European market. This certification needs to confirm three standards in addition to the requirement that the hunt is performed by Inuit or other indigenous communities, namely: the hunt needs to be conducted in a tradition of seal hunting; the products resulting from the hunt must be at least partly used within the community; and the hunt must contribute to the subsistence of the community.[128] The certifications need to be issued by recognised bodies which are included in a specific list of entities.[129] This certification system would exclude non-indigenous producers and would thereby enable the certification system to establish a real advantage for indigenous products. In combination with a certification mark, the certification might even be turned into an effective marketing label, effective and protected beyond the European market. However, the system as such emerges from a top-down approach and the certification is mandatory. It, thus, fundamentally differs from the proposed certification trade mark system and it is questionable whether it is going to work. Though the European Union requires the certification, it does not provide any funding for the realisation of the system. Indigenous producers will have to find the necessary means within their own state. Furthermore, the Seal Ban Regulations did not allow for sufficient time for indigenous producers to develop the certification system as a market instrument before the total ban of seal products became effective. The Implementation Regulation only entered into force several months after the ban was imposed.[130] It is thus no surprise that the claimants in the European seal ban dispute equally attacked the Implementation Regulation, after the President of the General Court dismissed two requests for interim measures for suspension of the operation of the Seal Ban Regulation.[131] Finally, the question of whether the non-voluntary certification system in the Seal Ban Regulations

---

Traditional Knowledge, Innovations and Practices and Options for an International Framework (Geneva, 4–6 February 2004), at p. 33.

[127] Implementation Regulation, supra note 87.

[128] Ibid., Article 3.

[129] Ibid., Article 6.

[130] Ibid.

[131] Order of the President of the General Court, supra note 89, at para. 112. *Inuit Tapiriit Kanatami et al. v Parliament and Council*, supra note 88.

satisfies the requirements of the TBT or SPS Agreements would warrant a whole chapter in and of itself.[132]

With regard to the kava case, the attempt of the Pacific Island Vanuatu to achieve some kind of voluntary certification label system for kava also deserves mention. The Vanuatu Kava Act 2002 (which has not entered into force) would require that producers label their products with the variety of the kava, the place of origin, which organs the kava was extracted from and the term 'Original Vanuatu Kava'.[133] The Act would also regulate the method of cultivation and production and which varieties could be sold in Vanuatu and exported.[134] The hope is that this would help to distinguish the different and 'noble' varieties of kava. Lamont Lindstrom concluded that the kava market should attempt to imitate that of wine, champagne and other products that depend on GIs on a more global level.[135] However, Lindstrom's solution is limited in that he perceives the protection of individual varieties of kava through GIs, rather than through a single or a few marks. This would be inefficient for both producers and consumers. Unlike with wines and spirits, the kava market is not so developed that something as specific as the plant variety from which a kava product is extracted can be a natural distinction for consumers, without great investment in marketing. Thus, producers would have to waste a lot of resources each individually marketing (and marking) their variety. As for consumers, they would have to spend time educating themselves about the meaning of each variety name or mark – time which they may not have or may not be willing to spend. The lower the number of marks, the more economically efficient it would be to market and educate consumers about them.

Indeed, if products were better and more efficiently marked to designate source and consumers were better educated about the market at issue and the full indication behind certain marks, all-out bans may not be required, as market forces could diminish the market share of unmarked products. In other words, it would be politically difficult for states to justify trade restrictions on the market products. For example, had the Inuit seal traders set up such a mark earlier and it had been properly marketed, perhaps the market could have sifted out the unwanted trade by itself, meaning that the EU would not have felt the need to put in place the ban. With respect to the kava situation, perhaps it would not have been so easy to indiscriminately close borders to all kava products had there already been a strong certification system and mark in place for traditionally made products. It is possible that nations may have been more willing to differentiate the products that were certified from those that were not.

Certification marks are also favourable in that they are part of existing intellectual property systems. As noted by Antons in his contribution in this volume, 'such "branding"

---

[132] The conformity of a government-set, non-voluntary labelling system with the TBT Agreement was recently decided by a WTO Panel (*US – Tuna,* supra note 104). The US Tuna case also related to environmental protection and the results will likely be instructive towards the analysis of the compliance of the seal ban case with the TBT Agreement. As noted above (supra note 104), the dispute has been appealed to the Appellate Body.

[133] Kava Act 2002 (Vanuatu), ss 4 and 7. Only the first two requirements are required for kava products for local markets, whereas all four are required for exported products.

[134] Kava Act 2002 (Vanuatu), ss 2, 3 and 6.

[135] Lindstrom, supra note 54, at pp. 304–5.

of their TCEs can prove a very useful and simple manner of using the IP system'.[136] Furthermore, public domain arguments (as discussed by Vézina)[137] do not usually apply to trade marks. This is because infringement is limited to the use of exact or similar marks in trade, meaning that such systems do not raise controversy and do not require considerable balance against the rights of others. Their existence is simpler to economically justify (for example lowering consumer search costs), compared with copyright and patent law, which are predominantly based on an incitement/reward system and require consideration about what will ultimately better benefit the public domain and general public.

Finally, as Graber and Lai have discussed elsewhere, it does not appear that such a voluntary certification mark system would be contrary to WTO law or policy, even if government-supported.[138] Indeed, WTO Member States are encouraged to adopt international standards when they enact regulations under the Agreements on SPS[139] and TBT,[140] where they exist. Kolsky Lewis has noted that increasing harmonisation of SPS measures through more standardisation would improve the ability of developing countries to export, so long as the standards are not too stringent.[141]

Ultimately, using voluntary certification systems in the ICH context is not about limiting the rights of others to trade, but rather about promoting the trade of indigenous peoples. A similar finding was made by Coombe and Turcotte, who, in their contribution to this volume, concluded that 'the creative use of intellectual property vehicles such as

---

136 Antons, supra note 45.

137 Vézina, supra note 22.

138 Christoph B. Graber and Jessica C. Lai, 'Indigenous Cultural Heritage and Fairtrade – Voluntary Certification Standards in the Light of WIPO and WTO Law and Policymaking' (2011) *Prometheus*, 29 (3), pp. 287–308.

139 SPS Agreement, Article 3. Under the SPS Agreement, measures that 'conform to international standards, guidelines or recommendations' are presumed to be consistent with GATT 1994. Higher standards can be adopted, if there is 'scientific justification'. The definition of 'international standards, guidelines and recommendations' is set out under Annex A, para. 3: for food safety are those developed by the Codex Alimentarius Commission; for animal health and zoonoses, the International Office of Epizootics; for plant health, the Secretariat of the International Plant Protection Convention; and for matters not covered by the above organisations, 'appropriate standards, guidelines and recommendations promulgated by other relevant international organizations open for membership to all Members, as identified by the Committee'.

140 TBT Agreement, Articles 2.4–2.6. Members shall use 'international standards' for their TBTs, if they exist or their completion is imminent, unless they would not be an effective or appropriate means to fulfil the legitimate objectives pursued (Article 2.4). When a regulation is in accordance with an international standard, it shall be presumed to not create an unnecessary obstacle to trade (Article 2.5). 'International standard' is undefined in the TBT Agreement. In the recent *US – Tuna* case, the Panel stated that an 'international standard' is (1) a standard; (2) adopted by an international standardising body; and (3) made available to the public (supra note 104, at para. 7.664). Though 'international standardizing body' is also undefined, the Agreement defines 'International body or system' as a '[b]ody or system whose membership is open to the relevant bodies of at least all Members' (Annex 1, para. 4). It further states that '[g]eneral terms for standardization and procedures for assessment of conformity shall normally have the meaning given to them by definitions adopted within the United Nations system and by international standardizing bodies taking into account their context and in the light of the object and purpose of this Agreement' (Article 1.1).

141 Kolsky Lewis, supra note 68, at pp. 183–4.

pre-emptive trade marks, geographical indications and marks indicating conditions of origin more generally are potential means through which indigenous peoples may seek to benefit from intangible cultural heritage in trade contexts.'[142] Vézina likewise stated that, when TCE-holding communities want to trade, they need assistance in supporting and building their business capacity and skills, particularly for trade on the global scale.[143] Along with this,

> use of the current IP system, such as trade marks and GIs, could be encouraged in order to sustain a traditional skill base. In that respect, promotion of a balanced use of IP tools within indigenous peoples and traditional communities could form an integral part of a comprehensive approach to the protection of TCEs. This could also permit the use of licensing mechanisms to ensure that whenever TCEs are being used in trade, benefits accruing from such exploitation are shared with their holders.[144]

In summary, the voluntary certification mark system could be used as an integral part of a bottom-up mechanism, employed by indigenous peoples to promote the trade of their goods or services. The market force of such promotion, if financially supported and executed correctly, should not be underestimated. Therefore, we suggest the following:

Firstly, indigenous peoples need to be made aware that certification trade marks are a very valuable and already existing tool that they can use to their benefit. Secondly, indigenous peoples should come together and create one or a few (possibly related) certification trade marks, to be used and operated on the global scale. They should form an international organisation, analogous to the FLO. The certification trade marks must be created with as much input from indigenous peoples as logistically and financially possible.

Two of the standards to be met for the certification trade marks would have to be for 'indigeneity' and for a 'cultural product'. We suggest that this is done according to the procedural proposal made earlier in this chapter – in other words, a general and broader definition at the international level, but allowing for more specific definitions at the local level. This would have to be monitored by the international organisation or its national counterparts as the certifier. How this would look for the definition of 'indigeneity' was discussed above. As to 'cultural product', we suggest that this must be something (whether a good or service) that is somehow related to, or a development of, an aspect of an indigenous community's traditional culture. For example, seal hunting is a traditional activity of the Inuit, such that the trade of seal furs is a natural modern-day extension of this. The kava trade can be analysed similarly. Comparatively, casinos on Native Indian reserves in the United States cannot be perceived this way.

Once set up, the marks must be well marketed to educate consumers as to what they represent. The complexity of organising the communities together to create the marks and the cost of the initial set-up and marketing would be perceivably high. This means that governmental involvement and support may be required. However, it is suggested that this

---

142 Coombe and Turcotte, supra note 13.

143 Vézina, supra note 22.

144 Ibid (footnotes omitted).

be as non-intrusive as possible and that the system eventually becomes completely indigenous-run.

4. SUMMARY

1. National and international trade in indigenous cultural heritage (ICH) can be socioeconomically beneficial to indigenous peoples, provided that it is indigenous peoples who have the choice of when and whether to commercialise or trade their ICH.
2. Participation of indigenous peoples in law- and policy-making on ICH trade and development is crucial and constitutes a precondition for any legitimate decisions taken in this regard (preference for bottom-up over top-down approaches).
3. Methodologically, a procedural approach is recommended as a means to acknowledge indigenous epistemological sovereignty and, in line with the principle of subsidiarity, decentralised structures of decision-making would be preferred over centralised ones.
4. In contrast to the current trend, opting for national solutions in law and policy-making on ICH trade and development generally seems to be more promising than going for international negotiations.
5. In developing laws and policies at the national level, some common concepts must be present, including indigenous peoples' very special relationship with their traditional lands and the non-divide between tangible and intangible assets of indigenous knowledge.
6. Rules providing procedural interfaces between indigenous custom and modern law as well as between the local/national and the international levels are very important.
7. For a number of reasons, the WTO does not seem to be the forum of choice for stimulating trade and development of ICH. First, consistency problems in the relationship between WTO law and public international law may inhibit an effective protection of indigenous knowledge assets in the WTO framework. Second, and more concretely, trade preferences afforded by GSP programmes do not seem to be useful in indigenous contexts, mainly because of their state-centralism.
8. The kava ban and the seal ban case studies illustrate definitively that international trade regulations in general and WTO law in particular are not sufficiently responsive to indigenous interests. Either states fail completely to take into consideration indigenous products or their customary usage (kava case), or, when they do so, fail to confer realistic positive effects on indigenous peoples' trade efforts (seal case).
9. Voluntary certification standards and certification trade marks seem to pave an interesting alternative avenue that deserves to be studied in more detail.
10. Certification marks are particularly suitable for indigenous interests because they can be used in a bottom-up fashion, with indigenous peoples themselves setting the standards.

Index